The Real Professor Higgins

Walter de Gruyter

1749
250
1999

Berlin · New York

The Real Professor Higgins

The Life and Career of Daniel Jones

by
Beverley Collins
Inger M. Mees

W
DE
G
Mouton de Gruyter
Berlin · New York   1999

Mouton de Gruyter (formerly Mouton, The Hague)
is a Division of Walter de Gruyter & Co., Berlin.

♾ Printed on acid-free paper which falls within the guidelines of the
ANSI to ensure permanence and durability.

Library of Congress Cataloging-in-Publication-Data

Collins, Beverley.
    The real Professor Higgins : the life and career of Daniel
Jones / by Beverley Collins, Inger M. Mees.
        p.   cm.
    Includes bibliographical references and index.
    ISBN 3-11-015124-3 (acid-free paper)
        1. Jones, Daniel, 1881−1967.   2. Linguists−Great
Britain−Biography.   3. Phonetics−Study and teaching−
Great Britain.   I. Mees, Inger.   II. Title.
P85.J648C65   1998
410′.92−dc21   98-37959
[B]   CIP

Die Deutsche Bibliothek − Cataloging-in-Publication-Data

Collins, Beverley:
The real Professor Higgins : the life and career of Daniel Jones /
by Beverley Collins ; Inger M. Mees. − Berlin ; New York :
Mouton de Gruyter, 1999
    ISBN 3-11-015124-3

Printing: Druckhaus Berlin-Mitte GmbH, Berlin.
Binding: Lüderitz & Bauer, Berlin.
Cover Design: Christopher Schneider, Berlin.
Printed in Germany.

In memory of

Antonie Cohen
(1922–1996)

whose book in part is this.

Contents

Foreword

I am delighted to have been invited to add a few words by way of introduction. I have to confess that when I started to read the manuscript I found it so absorbing that for the next two days I shamefully neglected several of my professional duties.

I have put my own thoughts on Jones and the close connection with Shaw's Professor Higgins into print some time ago (see p. 103). I suppose I must be one of the last phoneticians who can claim to have been personally trained by Daniel Jones, even if in my case the training lasted only an hour or two. I had been introduced to phonetics in 1959–60 by J.L.M. Trim at Cambridge University, where I was reading classics. I knew at once that phonetics was the subject I wanted to pursue after getting my first degree. Trim, himself trained by Jones shortly before he retired, recommended me to his former colleagues at University College London, and I duly enrolled for the then two-year London MA in General Linguistics and Phonetics. As I completed this course in 1962, Dennis Fry, Head of the UCL Department of Phonetics, offered me the post of Assistant Lecturer. I accepted with alacrity. It was just after this that I first met Jones, now well into retirement, when he visited UCL for the annual Assembly of Faculties. In the course of our brief conversation, Jones invited me to visit him at home in Gerrards Cross.

One afternoon, therefore, I duly journeyed out to Marsham Way. I found him sitting at a desk in his study, a wizened arthritic old man surrounded by electric fires. "Ah, Wells," he said, "good of you to come. Now sit down here, will you, and read to me from this." It was a passage of Hindi in phonetic transcription: Jones was putting me through my paces. But Trim, Fry, Gimson and O'Connor had trained me well: I was able to produce satisfactory monophthongal [e:] and [o:], to control aspiration at will, to distinguish retroflex stops from dental, to articulate a retroflex flap and a nasalised [i]. With some relief I realised that I had passed the test. We moved on to an animated discussion about EPD.

It was a pleasure, a few years later, to have Beverley Collins in one of my classes and later to have taught Inger Mees on the UCL vacation course and to be able to ordain them, as it were, into the apostolic succession of practical phonetics deriving from Daniel Jones.

J.C. Wells
Department of Phonetics and Linguistics
University College London

List of illustrations

Photographic illustrations

This illustration (provided by Dr L. van Buuren) shows Sweet shortly before his death. It was taken in the summer of 1911 when Sweet was spending his holidays with his pupil and friend A.O. Belfour in Carlingford in Ireland, by "one of a bunch of unknown girls they happened to meet". According to Belfour, "Sweet was in excellent spirits"—cf. Bernard Shaw's comments below. The photograph was given to Dr and Mrs van Buuren by Belfour when they visited him in his home in Larne, Northern Ireland, on 10 August 1964, together with a letter from Shaw to Belfour, dated 17 October 1941, an extract from which is quoted below:

> "The photograph of Sweet is extremely interesting. In it he is Sweet as I remember him 60 years ago. But when I saw him in Oxford last he was utterly metamorphosed. He was not recognisably the same man. He was wizened, ugly, as if he had been stewed for half a century in injurious and implacable resentments. And now you send me a later picture in which he is his old much more prepossessing self again. That seems a miracle; but at all events it is a very pleasant one; and I thank you very warmly for

sending me the evidence of it.... Some of Sweet's pupils and disciples, with whom he was very popular, should write his life and letters. He must have written dozens of topical papers, mostly, I expect, unprintably libellous lampoons on victims now dead, but very readable. Do you know anyone with the necessary leisure and literary skill?"

row (from l. to r) Lilias Armstrong, Simon Boyanus, Ida Ward, A.N. Tucker, Beatrice Honikman, Dennis Fry.

45. An informal group taken at the 1938 Ghent Phonetics Congress. L. to r.: E.M. Stéphan, Beatrice Honikman, Daniel Jones, Elizabeth Uldall (née Anderson), Ida Ward.
46. Jones with son and daughter on Helvellyn in the Lake District (1939)

between pages 358 and 359
47. Bomb damage to UCL (1941)
48. Jones feeding his hens
49. With a group of English and Scandinavian colleagues outside Skovriderkroen (an inn at Charlottenlund, Denmark). Identifiable from l. to r (1) ? (2) ? (3) Eli Fischer-Jørgensen (4) ? (5) ? (6) Daniel Jones (7) ? (8) Louis Hjelmslev (9) ? (10) C.A. Bodelsen (11) ? (12) ? (13) Knud Schibsbye (14) ? (15) Paul Christophersen (16) J.D. O'Connor.
50. J.R. Firth, David Abercrombie and Jones (l. to r.)

between pages 388 and 389
51. Paul Passy in his latter years
52. Jones speaking in the presence of the French ambassador at Linguaphone headquarters in London in 1956. The ceremonial dinner marked the unveiling of a plaque to Paul Passy. At the far left is the Provost of University College, Sir B. Ifor Evans.
53. Jones at home (1953)
54. With David Abercrombie at Jones's honorary degree ceremony at Edinburgh University (1958)

between pages 422 and 423
55. Dennis Ward
56. A.C. Gimson, who on Jones's retirement took over many of his roles
57. J.C. Wells, present Head of the UCL Phonetics Department
58. Jones in 1964 (three years before his death) still immersed in his academic work
59. With Professor Masao Onishi of Tokyo (1964)
60. One of the last photos of Jones, taken at the age of 84

We are grateful to the following persons and organisations for providing us with the photographic material and, where appropriate, granting permission for publication: Dr L. van Buuren (19); Dr Paul Christophersen (49); National Portrait Gallery (20); Professor Masao Onishi (58, 59); Elizabeth Uldall (24, 38, 41, 43, 44, 45); University College London (7, 18, 22, 23, 25, 29, 36, 47, 56); Professor Dennis Ward (55, 60); Professor J.C. Wells (5, 57). The remaining photographs were supplied by Michelle Stanbury or taken by ourselves.

Line illustrations

List of Abbreviations

Jones's work
The following books and articles are referred to in the text in abbreviated form as shown below. Jones's shorter works are indicated by "Jones" with date and distinguishing letter, as listed in the Daniel Jones *Chronological Bibliography*.

Chindau	*The pronunciation and orthography of the Chindau language* (1911)
EPD	*An English pronouncing dictionary* (1917)
HMTP	"The history and meaning of the term 'phoneme'" (1957)
Outline	*An outline of English phonetics* (1918a)
Phonetic dictionary	*A phonetic dictionary of the English language* (1913)
Phoneme	*The phoneme: Its nature and use* (1950)
Phonetic readings	*Phonetic readings in English* (1912b)
Phonetic transcriptions	*Phonetic transcriptions of English prose* (1907)
Sinhalese reader	*A colloquial Sinhalese reader* (1919)

Other publications
BDPS	*A biographical dictionary of the phonetic sciences*, Bronstein *et al.* (1977)
DNB	*Dictionary of national biography*
JIPA	*Journal of the International Phonetic Association*
MPh	*Le Maître phonétique*
NS	*Die neueren Sprachen*
TPhS	*Transactions of the Philological Society*
ZPh	*Zeitschrift für Phonetik*

Miscellaneous
IPA	International Phonetic Association
SSS	Simplified Spelling Society
UCL	University College London

Preface

Daniel Jones was the first professor of phonetics at a British university, and the man now generally considered to be the pre-eminent British scholar in the field of phonetics this century. Jones was at the centre of phonetics and linguistics for over sixty years; his numerous publications—notably *The Pronunciation of English, An Outline of English phonetics*, the *English pronouncing dictionary* and *The Phoneme: Its nature and use*—and his role as the founder of linguistics as an academic discipline in Britain have rendered his place in the history of the subject secure. This is the first full-scale biography of the man who was—to quote the introduction to the current edition of the *EPD*—the "greatest of British phoneticians".

Was Jones actually the real Henry Higgins of *Pygmalion* fame? He was certainly the outstanding phonetician of the era and quite possibly the man George Bernard Shaw had at the back of his mind when he wrote his famous play. The evidence is examined in Chapter 4.

In producing this book, our researches have involved journeys to many parts of the United Kingdom, and the establishment of contacts in several other countries, including France, the Netherlands, Denmark, Germany and the USA. At the outset of this project, we were fortunate in having the help and backing of Jones's surviving relatives and friends, and the cooperation of his colleagues and former pupils at the Department of Phonetics and Linguistics at University College London—the department which he had himself initiated in 1907. We were allowed full access to unpublished papers and lecture notes, and to a wealth of (luckily preserved) correspondence. Above all, we felt ourselves privileged to have the chance to interview 35 individuals, who, with very few exceptions, also granted permission for their words to be recorded on tape. This provided us in total with over 40 hours of audio documentation from those who were closest to Jones in his lifetime, including some of the most prominent figures in twentieth-century British linguistics. This spoken material enabled us to gain insights which the printed word would certainly not have revealed.

Early on, we decided not to confine ourselves merely to a treatment of Jones's linguistic career. Other facets of his life are also addressed: his connections with distinguished personalities in the academic world—notably Henry Sweet, Paul Passy, Harold Palmer and J.R. Firth—and with people from other walks of life, for example, Bernard Shaw and Robert Bridges. Jones's work for the International Phonetic Association, spelling reform and the BBC is also treated in detail. We have tried to shed light on some hitherto neglected areas of Jones's life—for instance, his unorthodox religious views—and have not excluded personal relationships and conflicts which we think may have influenced the path his career followed and the evolution of his linguistic ideas.

Throughout the book, we have endeavoured to introduce not only some general flavour of the times in which Jones lived but also to indicate the background of contemporary linguistic thought. To provide the reader with more information on the development of phonetics and linguistics in Britain and elsewhere leading up to Jones's era, a short historiographical appendix has been included.

We have assumed that most people reading this work will have some knowledge of phonetics and linguistics and that explanation of basic terms and concepts would be superfluous. It should be noted that modern bracketing conventions have been applied in those sections where Jones was (explicitly or implicitly) utilising the phoneme concept. Direct quotations from Jones follow his own practice.

Acknowledgements

Having received more help than we had any right to expect from a multitude of people, we feel no need to apologise for the length of this section. It is now a pleasure to record our thanks.

Our most obvious debt is to the late Professor Antonie Cohen, formerly head of the Phonetics Institute of the University of Utrecht. He gave unstinting help, incisive advice and stimulation over a period of many years, continuing, long after the appearance of the original project, regularly to offer wise counsel right up to the time of his death in 1996. Our dedication of this book to his memory can merely be a small token of our gratitude and regard.

Professor Noel Osselton (formerly of the University of Leiden and the University of Newcastle upon Tyne) supervised the work at the outset and, through his historiographical expertise, gave guidance in its planning and organisation. In more recent years, the late Professor Herman Wekker (University of Groningen) helped us in an editorial role.

It would not, of course, have been possible even to start writing this biography without the help of members of Daniel Jones's family and his personal friends. The main debt of gratitude is to his daughter, Michelle Stanbury, who not only granted us access to all Jones's original papers, lecture notes, letters and many family photographs, but also patiently allowed herself to be interviewed on a number of occasions. Her own interest in the life and work of her father was a valuable stimulus at all times. Our special thanks also go to other family members, especially Meryl Phillips, P.M. Platts, Sylvia Montgomery and Colonel Henry Dannatt, for sharing their memories of Jones; they gave us the chance to talk to the late Gisèle Dannatt and Renée Upcott, DJ's sisters-in-law, whose memories went all the way back to the time when Jones first met Paul Passy in Bourg-la-Reine in 1904. Deborah Monnington, Jean Overton Fuller and Dr C.T. Maitland provided several interesting insights into Jones's personality and later career, whilst Joanna de Mowbray passed on material on family pedigrees. Other assistance on aspects of Jones's education, career and life came from the BBC Written Archives, Caversham; Linguaphone; the Lawn Tennis Museum, Wimbledon; the Theosophical Society; Barbara Smoker and the Shaw Society; Ludgrove School; Radley College; University College School; and King's College, Cambridge.

Among our Danish colleagues, Dr Arne Juul (of Copenhagen), who was aware of the project almost from its inception, gave us much useful encouragement and advice; in particular, we are grateful to him for reading the entire manuscript several times; we envy him his painstaking meticulousness in detecting inconsistencies. Anna Halager and Anne Fabricius worked unstintingly as our research assistants (financed in part by grants provided by the Department of English of the Copenhagen Business School); countless errors, stylistic imperfections and numerous misquotations were tracked down and eradicated as a result of their efforts. Finally, our thanks go to Professor Eli Fischer-Jørgensen (University of Copenhagen), whose memoirs provided welcome assistance on several matters.

Professor Colin Ewen (University of Leiden), Dr Robert Druce (formerly of the University of Leiden), Dr Cees Dekker (University of Leiden) and Dr Simon Varey (formerly of the University of Utrecht and now at the University of California) all read through the manuscript at various stages and gave much useful comment. Thanks also go to Professor Keith Busby (University of Oklahoma) and Francine Melka-Teichroew (University of Utrecht) for checking the French quotations; we should point out that no attempt has been made to alter the phrasing of the original transcriptions. Dr G. Dimmendaal and Dr Ben Groen (both of the University of Leiden) advised on aspects of African languages and Russian, respectively.

Discussions were held with Dr Luuk van Buuren and G. Meinsma (both of the University of Amsterdam), and the late Mary Schafer Webb; all of these passed on correspondence, papers or photographs relating to Jones. We are grateful to Dr Arthur van Essen (University of Groningen), Vincent Phillips (formerly of the National Museum of Wales) and the late Dr Bill Lee for interesting insights gained on Jones and his circle. We have a special debt to Jack Windsor Lewis (University of Leeds) for many hours of lively, thought-provoking debate; the idea for the title of this book is only one of the many contributions he has made.

At the Department of Phonetics and Linguistics of University College London, we received notable help from the late Professor A.C. Gimson. He, with the generosity typical of him, fostered the project at an early stage, providing access to all the resources available in the form of departmental and college archives, and introducing several important contacts for further research. His successor, Professor J.C. Wells, has been just as supportive, and in addition arranged for one of the authors to be financed to compile and edit the Daniel Jones Papers, which have now been deposited in the University College Library as an aid to future researchers. He has also been kind enough to write the foreword to this volume.

Pat McKee, Judith Crompton and Molly Bennett allowed us to use the UCL departmental office and provided help in scores of ways. Professor Adrian Fourcin enabled us to listen to recordings of the Cardinal Vowels from the departmental sound archives. Great assistance came from Rosamund Cummings and her staff at the UCL General Record Office, and from Gill Furlong of the UCL Library manuscripts collection.

At London University, and elsewhere, we had invaluable interviews with present and past members of staff who had worked with Jones. In particular, we wish to mention Professor Jack Carnochan, Beatrice Honikman, Dr J.T. Pring, Professor R.H. Robins, J.L.M. Trim and Professor W. Jassem (University of Poznań). Paul Christophersen not only provided us with one of our photographs but also sent an extract from his unpublished memoirs. Others, now deceased, who helped us were Marguerite Chapallaz, Hyacinth Davies, Professor Dennis Fry, Professor Eugénie Henderson, Johanna Talma-Schilthuis, Olive Tooley and Eileen Whitley.

At Edinburgh University, Elizabeth Uldall went out of her way to assist in many matters, but especially those relating to Jones's contacts with her late husband, H.J. Uldall. The late Professor David Abercrombie, in the course of several hours of interviews, came up with a hoard of interesting personal memories of DJ, in addition to the loan of correspondence. Professor Dennis Ward also passed on letters from Jones, and

Dr Michael MacMahon (University of Glasgow) contributed crucial information on Henry Sweet and Laura Soames. Professor Alan Cruttenden (University of Manchester) sent us his unpublished thesis on intonation. Elizabeth Ewert (of the Taylorian Institute) provided us with details on Jones's period of time at Oxford.

Graham Pointon (head of the BBC Pronunciation Unit), the late John Snagge and his wife, Joan Wilson, all gave considerable help in tracing the course of Jones's work in broadcasting. Sinclair Eustace, Christopher Upward and the late Sir James Pitman passed on information about Jones's work for the Simplified Spelling Society; we are especially grateful to Stanley Gibbs and Chris Jolly for allowing us to borrow the Society's records. We wish to thank the International Phonetic Association, especially its Secretary, John Esling, for permission to reproduce a mass of material. From the USA, Professor Arthur Bronstein (City University of New York), Professor Edward Mammen and Johanna Blidner Glass produced information about William Tilly; helpful letters on other matters were received from Professor Kenneth Pike and Antony Oldknow.

Funding for this project has come from the Department of English, Copenhagen Business School, without whose generous help it would have been quite impossible to complete the work. Additional support in the form of sabbatical leave has been received from the University of Leiden. We wish to thank all our colleagues in both universities for their cooperation over the years. We also wish to express our gratitude to the staff of Mouton de Gruyter, our publishers, including Heide Addicks, Annette Hemmati, Katja Huder, Dorothée Ohlmeier and, especially, Chief Editor Dr Anke Beck.

In matters such as word processing and printing, we are indebted to Colin Ewen, whose help at the outset was absolutely indispensable. The responsibility for the final camera-ready proofs has lain with Dr Peter Kahrel (of Lancaster), who has used his combination of computer skill and linguistic expertise to solve problems which for anybody else would have been quite insurmountable. Assistance also came from Simon Cook, Rias van den Doel, Jan Willem van den Doel, Martijn van Hulzen, Dr Rob McDonnell, Dr James Pankhurst and Tom Reece.

In our immediate family circles, we were aided in various ways by Erik Gilijamse, Karen Gilijamse, Madeleine Collins-Llewellyn, Philip Collins and Rachel Collins. Mogens Baumann Larsen (formerly of the University of Aalborg) read the entire manuscript, providing much welcome encouragement as well as useful criticism. The late Birthe Mees transferred a major portion of the initial typescript to computer disk, whilst Sandra Collins-Fyfe not only gave moral support but also many hours of help in producing the bibliographies and the index, in addition to reading and criticising the entire manuscript.

We mention elsewhere that Daniel Jones was fond of quoting a Tswana proverb, which, roughly translated, states: "Alone I am not a human being; I become one only with the help of others". As far as we are concerned, its truth has been proved over and over again.

Beverley Collins
Inger Mees

Utrecht and Copenhagen, 27 December 1997

Chapter 1

In the days of his youth (1881–1903)

1.1. Birth

Norfolk Crescent, where on September 12, 1881, Daniel Jones was born, is located in a leafy district of central London, formerly designated "Hyde Park". The park itself lies a few hundred yards to the south, and about a quarter of a mile to the east is Marble Arch. In the 1880s, the street consisted of a curving terrace of large, elegant, early Victorian houses, similar to those still lining many London streets north of the Thames. Although Daniel Jones's birthplace (number 12) and the adjacent houses have since been pulled down and replaced, the crescent formation and the street name have been retained. The area remains today, as it was in the Victorian age, an oasis of calm, secluded privilege—even though situated just a minute's walk away from the clamour of the busy Edgeware Road linking London to the North of England.

Jones was always proud of his London birth and ancestry, mentioning such matters in the introduction to later editions of his *English pronouncing dictionary* (Jones 1917a, henceforth *EPD*): "Readers may like to know that my father and mother were both Londoners, and that I have lived all my life in or near London" (*EPD*[11] [1956]: xv n.) Both sides of Jones's lineage could claim long established London roots, and family trees, drawn up by Daniel Jones and his relations, indicate that Jones's ancestors had settled in the capital well before the end of the seventeenth century (see Figure 1.1). Nevertheless, because of his typically Welsh name, many people (including George Bernard Shaw, see Section 4.9) appear to have thought that his origins were in Wales. Confusion over this may be why Jones wished to make clear that he was not only English but in no sense a provincial.[1]

The Census returns of April 1882 reveal that in the year of Jones's birth there were nine people living in the house. Baby Daniel Jones had been given exactly the same name as his father and, in fact, the family trees show that he was now the fourth member of his family to bear this name. Daniel Jones Senior (known as "Dan" to friends and the family circle) was forty-seven years old. His first wife, Jessie (née Hickson), had died tragically young, and he had recently remarried. Dan Jones's second wife was Viola Carte, a woman fourteen years younger than himself. There were two sons from his first marriage: Arthur Daniel, seven years old, and Wilfred Henry, who was six. A maiden aunt, Fanny Hale, was also living with the family.

The Joneses retained in service a cook, a housemaid, a nurse and a footman. In the context of the late Victorian period, such a complement of domestic servants would not have been regarded as at all excessive for the needs of a man of Dan Jones's social standing. Yet, four full-time domestic staff living in, together with a large house with a prestigious address close to Hyde Park, certainly give an indication of the status and wealth Dan Jones enjoyed. He was, in fact, one of London's most successful barristers.

1.2. Family background

Dan Jones had been a brilliant student in his youth, reading mathematics at Cambridge and eventually gaining a first class honours degree (so becoming a Wrangler in Cambridge parlance). He turned from mathematics to law, going on to make his career at the Bar, where he was noteworthy not only as an excellent advocate but even more for length of service. In fact, he continued in chambers until two years before his death in 1915, reluctantly retiring at the age of seventy-nine.

But any claim he might have to fame today would be for his services to lawn tennis, then in its infancy. He was one of the founder members of the Wimbledon All England Club, and managed to outlive all the others.[2] On his death, it was reported that Dan Jones "had never missed a championship meeting there [Wimbledon] since the championship was instituted",[3] appearing even in his eighties in "striped flannels and his Indian pith helmet".[4] His obituaries pay tribute to his fanatical enthusiasm for tennis and his part in drawing up the laws of the modern game. His brother, Henry Jones, was also fascinated by games and wrote world-famous columns on whist for *The Times* and the *Field*, under the nom-de-plume of "Cavendish"; to this day, he is recognised as the greatest authority there has ever been on whist.[5]

It is curious that Daniel Jones Junior, coming from this kind of background, is remembered in later life as having no interest in games—although, as will be seen, he did fairly well at sport when he was in prep school. The only game he is known to have enjoyed as an adult was chess but he gave up playing in his thirties, claiming to be no longer able to stand the excitement.[6] See Section 9.7.

In the 1880s, both of the Jones brothers, Dan and Henry, were to play major roles in transforming lawn tennis from a domestic pastime to a major sport. Dan Jones, then President of the Hyde Park Club as well as a member of the All England Lawn Tennis Club, was largely responsible for bringing the two organisations together, thus forming the present-day Lawn Tennis Association, and for establishing its headquarters at Wimbledon.[7]

As stated in a tennis handbook of the time (Wilberforce 1890: 7):

Much as Mr. Jones has done for the game in years past, it may be doubted whether any service he has yet rendered it can be looked upon as so entirely beneficial to all parties concerned as this, his successful reconciliation of what at the time appeared to be divergent interests.

Dan Jones had been noted as a "skilled musician with a penchant for glee-singing",[8] but the Cartes were truly distinguished in the field of music. Of his mother's family,

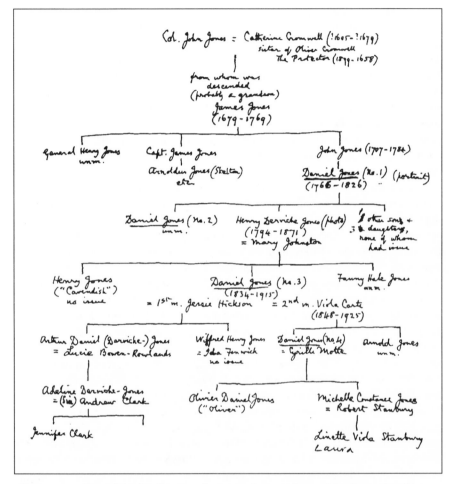

Figure 1.1. One of the family trees drawn up by members of the Jones family. This example, claiming descent from the sister of Oliver Cromwell, is in Daniel Jones's own handwriting.

Jones himself wrote:

> Carte was my mother's maiden name. Her brother was Richard D'Oyly Carte, the founder of the Gilbert & Sullivan combination, builder of the Savoy Theatre, etc.
>
> My mother's father, Richard Carte, was a fine musician—the best flute player of his day—[and] used to travel about giving lectures on music with flute illustrations. Many of the fingerings & keys on modern flutes were of his invention. He eventually made flutes with Rudall, founding the firm of Rudall, Carte & Co., in Berners St.[9]

When Daniel Jones was granted an honorary LL.D. by Edinburgh University in 1958, it was stated in the public address: "It may be that the son of the sister of Richard D'Oyly Carte had in him the sense of sound which animated his uncle, and demanded an outlet."[10] To this influence may perhaps be traced the love of music that Jones retained all his life and which he handed on to his daughter, Michelle Stanbury, who eventually became a professional violinist. She remembers her father (who insisted on her practising the piano before breakfast) listening to her play whilst he was shaving, and banging on the floor with a stick if she played a false note, or was lazy in her interpretation of a passage. Daniel Jones, in fact, not only possessed an amazing talent for the auditory analysis of speech sound, but also had a particularly acute musical ear. This enthusiasm for music was known to all his colleagues and relations; he was especially devoted to Bach, and had an encyclopaedic knowledge of the composer and his music. Jones was also known for his ability to distinguish the pitch of any note—a gift which he was later to utilise in the writing of one of his early books, *Intonation curves* (Jones 1909a); see also Section 3.3. (Contrary to what many of his friends and colleagues believed, Jones's faculty was not in fact "perfect pitch" of the "absolute" type, but very finely trained and developed "relative pitch".)[11]

Once tennis had become established at Wimbledon, the Jones family soon followed, moving out of central London in 1890. Wimbledon then still had something of a village atmosphere, but it was a village rapidly developing into a London suburb. Dan Jones acquired a newly built villa in Copse Hill, one of the most affluent roads in the area, with views over open fields to Wimbledon Common. The house was known as St John's Cottage—a peculiarly inappropriate name, it might be thought, given the size and opulence of the place. It was actually a huge red-brick construction, built in ornate late-Victorian style, with steeply pitched roofs and featuring a tall "smoker's tower" surmounted by a weather vane. There was also a vast surrounding garden—which offered plenty of room for laying out a tennis court. The house still stands (though the name St John's Cottage is long forgotten, and the property has now been subdivided into 7 and 7A Copse Hill). Despite the fact that semi-detached houses built opposite have robbed the house of its open aspect, it is easy to imagine how St John's Cottage would have provided young Daniel with an enviably prosperous background to his teenage years.

Arnold, Daniel's only full brother, was born in 1883. Although it was often remarked how different the two boys were in character, Daniel and Arnold had a close relationship, which was maintained in adult life—a bond which was broken only by Arnold's early death at the age of forty-four (see Sections 6.6 and 10.4).

1.3. Ludgrove Preparatory School

Daniel Jones was a sickly child, and doctors predicted several times during his youth that he would be lucky to survive. Nothing is known of Daniel Jones's early schooling up to the age of eleven—neither apparently did he talk to his friends or his family about this period of his life. It is probable that he was taught at home by a tutor, a practice which was quite common in the Victorian era. He certainly started school rather late; the delay being perhaps the result of his history of poor health since birth.

The first records that exist of Daniel Jones's school career are at the preparatory school to which he was sent as a boarder, as was more or less obligatory for any upper middle-class youngster of the period. In Jones's case, the choice fell on Ludgrove, a school which had been recently established in New Barnet—now part of north London but then a small Hertfordshire country town.[12] Ludgrove is today regarded as one of Britain's top prep schools—indeed patronised by royalty—but at that time it was a tiny concern, and had actually been founded only in 1892. When Jones arrived there in the summer of 1893, the school numbered a mere seventeen boys, and there were just forty-five by the time he left in the summer of 1895. Such a small school would have been able to provide a sheltered and caring atmosphere for its pupils—which may have been why the Jones family selected it, since Daniel had been considered so frail from his early childhood. They must have been quite satisfied with the schooling he received, for in the year that Daniel left, his brother Arnold was sent to follow him at Ludgrove.

There was a strong emphasis on sport at the school (the headmaster and founder of Ludgrove was a former Association Football amateur international) and Daniel Jones performed creditably. In 1894, he played in the school cricket XI, and in both of the two winter terms that he was at Ludgrove he reached the finals of the racquets competition—which would have pleased his father. Academically, Daniel was also doing well. His early talent for mathematics was beginning to develop, and it was already obvious that he had inherited his maternal family's musical gifts. He enjoyed the French classes given by H.P. Hansell, who in 1902 was appointed private tutor to the Prince of Wales. Hansell, in fact, later became a member of the International Phonetic Association for a while. When attempting to set up his "Phonetics Institute" (see Section 9.3), Jones wrote a letter to his old schoolmaster, mentioning how useful French had been to him in his life, and asking him to persuade the Prince of Wales to support the scheme.[13] Jones must have believed that Hansell had influence in high places—even though no royal response seems to have materialised.

Jones won two school prizes in 1895, reflecting two facets of his early talents—a Division Prize for mathematics and the Cecil Sharp Music Prize. He was entered for a scholarship to Radley College (worth the considerable sum of £80) but was deprived of success by a piece of bad luck. The school magazine for this year contains the information that "D. Jones was very unfortunate in developing measles three weeks before his Radley Scholarship Examination." He failed to win the award, but it was noted that "he did very creditably and would have been nearer the goal had there been more mathematical work set for him." His future academic career is nicely prophesied in these words: "with perseverance [he] ought to get on very well indeed".[14]

1.4. Radley College

Despite his lack of success in the examinations for a scholarship, Jones's father decided in any case to send him to Radley—no doubt because Daniel had performed well, and perhaps because the boy had set his heart on going to the school. In the Autumn term of 1895, Daniel Jones, now a lad just turned fourteen, took the train to Abingdon in Buckinghamshire to start his public school career. Radley College (nowadays regarded as an excellent place of education) was in the 1890s very much the archetype of a minor Victorian public school. It was similar to several others which had been established in the mid-nineteenth century in order to satisfy the demands of the new upper middle class—successful businessmen, or professional people like Daniel Jones's father—for a traditional education similar to that given to the aristocracy at great public schools such as Eton, Harrow, Rugby and Winchester.

When Daniel Jones arrived there in 1895, Radley was still a rather small school, with only about 160 boys. The school historian Boyd (1948: 246–248) admits that the accommodation was primitive. Although the school had been built around a beautiful Georgian house, Radley Hall, set in fine grounds, the buildings were now quite inadequate for the school population. Dormitories had been hastily converted by partitioning larger rooms and were hopelessly overcrowded. Rats (it was claimed) were by no means an uncommon sight, and heating was often non-existent. The previous winter, three boys had died in an influenza epidemic; in one classroom, on a remarkably cold day, the ink had remained frozen in the inkwells till noon. According to Boyd (1948: 240):

> Life generally was still hard and uncomfortable, and there was much suffering from cold and chilblains in the bitter winters of that time. Early school, starting with prayers in School at 7 and lasting till 8, went on all the year round.

Other aspects of school life were just as harsh. Corporal punishment was a ritualistic aspect of the regime, with four officially recognised categories—ranging from vicious birchings and canings administered by the masters, through to the everyday punishments for minor offences inflicted on the youngsters by prefects wielding a fives bat. Of these last, Boyd (1948: 244), with unconscious irony, writes: "Such beatings…were not severe, the strokes varying from one to four; the victims accepted them as all in the day's work."

The school also emphasised organised religion. The Warden (as the headmaster of Radley is known) and several of his staff had been ordained, and two chapel services were held every day. Sunday involved "full Mattins, with sermon, and Evensong, in addition to Holy Communion.... There was an hour's Divinity lesson in the afternoon between roll and Chapel" (Boyd 1948: 242). Games and athletics also dominated school life—cricket and rowing being especially venerated. Other sports were catered for, however, even the novelty game of lawn tennis. By the time Daniel Jones en-

1. Daniel Jones as a baby

2. At about 9 years of age

Daniel Jones sen^r + jun^r

3. With his father; the annotation is in Jones's own hand

4. Daniel with his mother

5. St John's Cottage, Wimbledon (taken in 1997)

rolled, Radley had three tennis courts—which may have been one reason why his father took a fancy to the school in the first place.

Since establishments like Radley had been in existence for such a comparatively short time, every effort was made to create as much sense of tradition as possible. School "customs" were invented and invested with almost religious significance—which meant that life in the school was full of meaningless rules, both official and unofficial. Boys were encouraged, in fact obliged, to use a special type of slang, much of it borrowed from Eton or other major public schools—Boyd (1948: 445-449) provides a list of over a hundred "Radley words" of this sort. Although there was no official school uniform, Daniel, as a "new bug" (first-year boy), was expected to wear an Eton collar, whilst on Sundays—like every Radleian, down even to the youngest— he would have been obliged to don a bowler hat (Boyd 1948: 215).

Bullying was rampant—though Radley was not exceptional, since it was the plague of all English boarding schools—and a blind eye was generally turned to fighting between boys. The school was not renowned at this time for the academic performance of its pupils; Warden H.L. Thompson, who retired during the time Jones was at the school, had said sanguinely on his arrival in 1888: "The standard of scholarship is not high, but I dare say it may be raised a bit in time" (Boyd 1948: 226). In his history of the school, Boyd (1948: 237) sums up the intake of students at the time in these words: "It did not attract genius, and rarely first-rate ability"; and whilst some members of the staff were excellently qualified men, the pupils were on the whole inclined to denigrate any form of intellectual leaning. Special scorn was reserved for boys (nicknamed "drips" in the Radley school slang) who revealed themselves to be overkeen on academic work; these were "subjected to every discouragement" (Boyd 1948: 238).

Young Daniel Jones was unlikely to have flourished in such an atmosphere. He was already noted as weak and prone to illness, so the harsh living conditions would have exacerbated his poor health. To his schoolmates, he must have appeared to be an obvious "drip", and as such would have been the victim of constant taunting, bullying and general persecution. Whatever happened to him at Radley, no record of his experiences has remained, but it is doubtless significant that he was to leave Radley College after only two years. All that survives of his time there are the cursory entries in Radley's school registers. There is no mention of him in the school magazine, the *Radleian*, in the years between his arrival in 1895 and his departure in 1897—nor indeed any other note of his existence until his obituary notice seventy years later.[15]

1.5. University College School

Why exactly Jones left Radley is unclear. There appears to have been no question of scandal or disgrace. It is therefore likely that it was the result of an accumulation of misery over two years of enduring the dreadful living quarters, the petty sadism of prefects' punishments and constant chivying from his schoolfellows. It could be that the low academic standard of the school—particularly the lack of interest in mathematics—finally made itself clear to his father. For whatever reason, Dan Jones decided to remove his son from Radley in the summer of 1897, and give him a quite different type of education. In the choice of the alternative, it would seem that Daniel Jones's mother's views ultimately prevailed. The Cartes had something of a tradition as free-thinkers, and Viola's brothers had both been educated at University College School, a famous London boys' school which was noted both for its religious tolerance and a liberal attitude to education.[16]

So in the autumn of that year, Daniel Jones began his education anew at University College School, where he was to stay until 1900. The school was at that time still housed in Gower Street, in Bloomsbury, actually in the same buildings as University College itself—so this was, in a sense, Jones's first contact with what was to be his future place of work. The school occupied four floors of one wing of the college, with classrooms leading off from internal corridors, and even used the university Botanical Theatre in lieu of a school hall. University College School remained in this cramped accommodation until 1907, which happened, coincidentally, also to be the year in which Jones started lecturing at University College (Usher—Black-Hawkins—Carrick 1981: 57).

The journey to Gower Street from Wimbledon was long and tedious, involving firstly a long walk to Wimbledon railway station from Copse Hill. Jones quarrelled with his father over this, later claiming that his father forced him to walk huge distances every day (presumably by refusing him the money for cab or horse omnibus fares) and that this accounted for the dislike of walking which he had in adult life.[17] On getting into Wimbledon, he would have boarded a District Railway train which ran via Earls Court. The last portion of the journey was on the "Underground" section —then still operated by steam trains, choking their passengers with sulphurous fumes, and bitterly cold in winter. The train followed the route of the present-day Circle Line, and Jones got off each day at Gower Street Station (known today as Euston Square). H.C. Barnard (1970: 93), who co-incidentally happened to enter University College School in the same year as Jones, has described the hordes of pupils arriving by train every morning from all over London and jostling with an "army of business and professional men (most of them wearing frock-coats and top hats)". The noisy throng of boys (Daniel Jones amongst them) would surge out of the station, and rush the few hundred yards down Gower Street to the school. It was perhaps this early acquaintance with the railways which accounts for Jones's expertise in later life at finding his way around railway routes and timetables; and perhaps explains his odd predilection for entertaining any academic guests, no matter how illustrious, by taking them to lunch at the railway buffet at Marylebone Station.[18]

University College School was about as different from Radley as can be imagined. Though fee-paying, it was non-boarding, and it was not at the time generally regarded as a public school; indeed, the school strove to distance itself from that type of education. However, to refer to it as a "London secondary school" as Jones was wont to do (see below), gives quite the wrong impression. It had been founded in 1830 to supply the new University of London with potential students and was run in accordance with Benthamite principles of education. It had a broader-based curriculum than most schools, with less concentration on the classics. Science, mathematics and modern languages had important places in the timetable. The school was proud of its progressive approach to education, one example of this being that pupils were put in sets (in present-day terminology) according to their differing abilities in each subject. Apart from this, what made University College School almost unique in British education of this period was the lack of any form of compulsory religious training together with a prohibition on any kind of corporal punishment—summed up in a phrase sometimes applied to the school by its detractors: "No rod—no God". Discipline was enforced by an elaborate system of punishment books, and detailed records were maintained of each pupil's conduct and progress through the school (Usher—Black-Hawkins—Carrick 1981: *passim*, Barnard 1970: 85–91).

There were about 325 boys in University College School when Jones began. The roll had been falling for many years, in part because of the difficulties of running a school in central London (Usher—Black-Hawkins—Carrick 1981: 38–39), but also perhaps because progressive ideas were less in fashion than they had been earlier in Victoria's reign. The headmaster, H.W. Eve, who had been at the school for twenty years, was due to retire. In 1898, University College School welcomed a new, vigorous, young headmaster, John Lewis Paton, a progressive educationist with a brilliant academic record, only thirty-five years old, and an enthusiast for physical fitness. He was determined to revitalise the school, and derived some of his ideas from the time that he had spent at school himself in Germany; he may have been one of the people who drew Jones towards the idea of going to the Continent (Usher—Black-Hawkins—Carrick 1981: 53–56; Barnard 1970: 106–114). Paton was interested in languages and later, like Jones, joined the Simplified Spelling Society (see Section 3.6). In 1903, Paton was appointed High Master of Manchester Grammar School, and was another former teacher whom Jones contacted at the end of the First World War when attempting to obtain support for a proposed Phonetics Institute (see Section 9.3).

The University College School staff numbered about 21—also far fewer than some years previously. In the words of Jones's contemporary Barnard (1970: 101), they were "for the most part good scholars... they possessed personality and character... they were educators and not simply teachers". There is no doubt that in general the teaching at University College School would have been greatly superior to what Jones had experienced at Radley, and that academically far more would have been expected of the pupils. There was an atmosphere which fostered the pursuit of excellence and no-one needed to fear being thought a "drip". Jones spent much of his time reading classics, which he evidently found boring, but which was to ensure him a place at Cambridge. He afterwards wrote in a short magazine article entitled "In the days of my youth" (Jones 1926e: 394): "I read classics chiefly and I disliked them." He would one day, however, come to approve of the new pronunciation of Latin that he had to learn at University College School—different from the traditional method still retained at Ludgrove and Radley. University College School, in keeping with its progressive image, had introduced the "reformed" system of Latin pronunciation with "continental" vowel qualities as early as 1860 (Barnard 1970: 89); most English schools retained the practice of pronouncing Latin as if it were English, and many held out against the new system till the nineteen twenties. There was later to be lively correspondence in *Le Maître phonétique* on this topic (see Section 3.5). Daniel Jones was to become University College School's most brilliant pupil at mathematics, fulfilling the early promise shown at Ludgrove, and his talents were recognised when he won the school's Cook Prize in this subject.

Barnard (1970: 97-105) has drawn sympathetic brief character sketches of many of the masters who were in the school at the time. Undoubtedly, Jones would have found modern languages the most interesting of his lessons, and University College School had a tradition of French being taught by native speakers (Usher—Black-Hawkins—Carrick 1981: 37). According to Barnard (1970: 100–101), these particular teachers provided the boys with much entertainment because of their amusingly incompetent English pronunciation. German was a strong subject in the school, taught by "two vigorous and up-to-date young masters" (Barnard 1970: 98). One of these was E.R. Edwards (see Section 2.5 for biographical detail), later to be Jones's immediate predecessor as a lecturer in phonetics at University College, and who at this time was engaged on writing his doctoral thesis under Professor Paul Passy at the Ecole des Hautes Etudes at the Sorbonne. How much contact Edwards had with Daniel Jones at University College School is not certain, though it is clear that the two met (Jones 1926e: 394), and Edwards was later to play a crucial role in supporting Jones when he applied for his first part-time post at University College in 1907. It seems likely that someone on the University College School staff (probably Edwards) stimulated Daniel Jones's interest in modern languages about this time; it is known that whilst at University College School, in 1898, Jones took a short course at a London language school and on leaving school made his first visit to France (see Section 1.6).

Nevertheless, Jones emerged with a poor opinion of his formal education. Indeed, he later wrote: "I have no recollections of school life that are worth chronicling" (Jones 1926e: 394). Even so, Jones realised that in one respect his education was unusual: "I am one of the very exceptional persons who have had experience of life first in a public school and then in a London secondary school." It is significant that in later editions of the *EPD*, he added a footnote mentioning his educational background (*EPD*[11] [1956]: xv n.). Jones always regarded public school education as being the most formative influence on the development of the British English prestige accent, Received Pronunciation, or RP. He even referred to this type of speech as "Public School Pronunciation" (or "PSP") in the first editions of his pronouncing dictionary (*EPD*[1] [1917a]: viii) (see also Section 7.2). One might conclude that he was grateful for his brief public school career at Radley if only because it provided him with appropriate social credentials for passing judgements on RP and standards of pronunciation.

Yet University College School would have had a far greater influence on the young Daniel Jones. The atmosphere of intellectual endeavour and curiosity, the encouragement of self-discipline, the emphasis on tolerance and internationalism and the importance of moral values which were not based on formal religion: all these were reflected in Jones's adult personality. The seeds of such opinions may have been there from the start—but it is difficult not to believe that Jones was encouraged to develop his particular view of the world at least in part by J.L. Paton and the staff at University College School.

1.6. Cambridge and after

Daniel Jones left school with the award of a place at King's College, Cambridge, and he went up to begin reading for the Mathematics Tripos in October 1900. With the Cook Prize behind him, he seemed to have every prospect of repeating his father's spectacular performance. Yet, three years on, Jones obtained his degree with disappointing results, writing later of his student career: "Cordially as I disliked classics, I hated mathematics more" and he finally "came out bottom of the Second Class in the Mathematical Tripos" (Jones 1926e: 394).

Jones led an extremely subdued life at Cambridge, leaving little behind him apart from the bare records of his enrolment and his graduation, and spoke sparingly of his time at university even to his close relatives. Apart from mentioning that he considered that "the other fellows were a bit silly",[19] he seems to have exposed few recollections, happy or otherwise, of his student days. Many years later, he did, however, express his disappointment with many aspects of the university teaching he experienced in his youth. Jones claimed that "tutorial work was alone useful" to him and that he "never learned anything from formal lectures".[20] He frankly revealed some of his difficulties in coping with his mathematics lecture course.

> If I concentrated sufficiently so as to understand what the lecturers said, I never had time to write proper notes, and therefore soon forgot what had been taught. I also tried the plan of writing down as much as I could without understanding it, hoping to learn the subject matter later from my notes. But that plan did not succeed either.[21]

Despite the fact that his degree was lacking in distinction, Daniel Jones's Cambridge BA was the only widely recognised academic qualification that he was ever to obtain—apart from his Bar examinations. Like most Oxbridge graduates, he later took the opportunity of converting it, without the need of any form of further examination, to an MA. In later life, Jones claimed that he was not interested in people's paper qualifications, and was certainly prepared even to engage staff who had no conventional qualifications whatsoever, providing they indicated that they had potential talent in practical phonetics.[22] However, it is possible that Jones felt the lack of conventional academic success more deeply than he was prepared to admit, since it is striking that he always cited his honorary degrees on the title pages of his books, even after his reputation was secure world-wide.

On coming down from Cambridge in 1903, Jones enrolled at Lincoln's Inn to begin the long process of preparing for his Bar examinations—once again, shadowing his father's career, and probably under paternal pressure to do so. However, by this time, as A.C. Gimson (1968: 2) has said: "Neither mathematics nor law held any real interest for him. Already he had become fascinated by languages."

As early as 1898, whilst still a schoolboy, Jones had taken a course in conversational French at the Gouin School of Languages in London (Gimson 1968: 2). It was an institution which employed occasionally curious, but, for the period, very progressive methods of language teaching, in the spirit of the "Reform Movement" (see A.4). Gouin's ideas and schools are discussed further in Gouin (1892) and Howatt (1984: 314 *et passim*). The school's methods were a favourable early influence on Jones, and he enjoyed the lessons so much that he was inspired to start on a number of other European languages—Italian, Portuguese and Spanish. Between school and university, in the summer of 1900, he also spent a month in France, staying with a family in Argenteuil, where he made the pleasant discovery, as he would later say with typical understatement, that he had "some aptitude for getting the pronunciation of French right" (Gimson 1968: 2). The visit was the beginning of a life-long attachment to France, things French and (above all) the French language. Like Henry Sweet, Jones eventually came to be convinced that no English phonetician could be regarded as reasonably equipped unless he attained a considerable degree of proficiency in spoken French (Abercrombie 1980: 5).

Whilst he was up at Cambridge, therefore, Jones again took the opportunity in his vacations to go to France and also to Germany, being "anxious to learn to speak both languages" (Jones 1926e: 394). He decided to spend his first Christmas as a university student (December 1900 to January 1901) in Germany. On the recommendation of a college friend, he had booked in for a month's course at a famous language institute at the University of Marburg, run by an Australian by the name of Tilly.[23]

These few weeks Jones (1926e: 394) was later to regard a turning-point in his life: "It was there I had my first introduction to phonetics."

1.7. William Tilly

William Tilly (1860-1935) was originally called Tilley, but changed his name to fit in with German spelling (Jones 1935e: 62 n.).[24] He was born of missionary parents in Sydney and had experienced a curious academic career—though he attended numerous university courses, he appears to have gained few qualifications. After attending theological college and following classes at Sydney University, he went on to learn Pitman's shorthand (known then as "phonography", see A.3) at a "Mechanics' Institute" in Melbourne, obtaining a certificate in 1877. He became a schoolteacher, and eventually a headmaster.

Tilly was fascinated by foreign languages and in 1890 went to Germany, realising that this was the country which led the world in language study at the time. Tilly attended classes in a variety of linguistic subjects at Giessen and Marburg, and in 1893, with the support of Professor Wilhelm Viëtor (see A.4), he was appointed to a lectureship at Marburg University. He then founded his language school, *Institut Tilly*, dedicated to teaching German and other modern languages by what were at that time

INSTITUT TILLY

Ringstrasse 40

BERLIN-LICHTERFELDE-WEST.

(Telephone: Amt Lichterfelde, No. 125.)

BOARD AND TUITION IN GERMANY

IN THE FAMILY OF A

UNIVERSITY LECTURER

(SPECIALIST IN MODERN LANGUAGES)

Instruction in **German** alone, or in conjunction with
French, Italian, Spanish, &c.

The undersigned, late lecturer in the University of Marburg, receives as resident students (as for the past twenty-on years) gentlemen who come to Germany to study German and other languages — either to acquire a rapid and practical, or a more scientific knowledge of them.

a) *Junior Students* (not under 17 years of age), who having left the English Public Schools, intend proceeding to the University or entering business.

b) *Senior Students* Public School Masters (particularly those who wish to study the Phonetic Method of teaching Modern Languages), Professors, Medical Men, Clergymen, University Students of Graduates, Candidates for Indian Civil Service, Student Interpreterships, Military and Naval Officers preparing for grade of Interpreter, &c.

The number of boarders is limited, so that full individual attention is assured.

Junior students are accepted on the understanding that they are to conduct themselves as *students* and not as school-boys, to have proper regard to the customs of the country and in particular to avoid all noisy conduct and *all playing* in house and garden.

Lady students may also be accepted.

Non-resident students cannot be received.

Gross-Lichterfelde-West with its dry clear air, is situated in the healthy district to the south-west of Berlin beyond the line of the suburbs, on high sandy soil, with extensive woods and lakes close at hand. There are facilities for all kinds of out-door sports (bicycling, tennis, swimming, rowing, sailing, &c., in winter extensive provision for skating). At the same time Berlin, with its exceptional educational advantages, its art-collections museums, concerts etc., can be reached in a few minutes by train (monthly ticket 6 s.), Potsdam in half-an-hour.

Instruction in German. Those who come to the continent to learn German, generally go the wrong way to work for want of experience and guidance, thus wasting both time and money. They either go to the one extreme and attempt to "pick up" the language merely by hearing and speaking — they may by this means in course of time succeed in understanding a little and in being understood in their "pidgin" German with some difficulty, but this cannot be called learning the language. Or they set to work with Grammar and Dictionary as at home this makes the work very slow and uninteresting. At the same time they continue the use of their own language.

Our arrangements are designed to avoid both these dangers, to render the acquirement of the language (first speaking, then reading) as rapid as possible; and at the same time to ensure accuracy in pronunciation and grammar. The instruction is conducted on the latest scientific principles.

Students *pledge* themselves *to avoid the use of their own language* (not to *speak, read, hear* or, correspondence excepted, *write* English, *under all circumstances* (*outside* as well as inside the house) and during the whole period of their stay — except in communication with me and that for the first few days only. The observance of this rule is insisted on in the case of all students *absolutely*. No English books are to be brought to the house [or, if brought, are to be handed to me on arrival] and no English newspapers sent to students. German

Figure 1.2. Extracts from one of Tilly's brochures dating from after he had moved from Marburg to Berlin (cont. p. 14).

Certificates can be obtained from me entitling students under 19 years to travel 1st Class with 2nd Class ticket on the steamer Queenboro-Flushing or Harwich-Hook of Holland.

If possible, *arrive not later than 9 p. m.* See that registered luggage is examined by the customs' officers at German *border* station. Students can be met at the Berlin station; new students requested to tie a handkerchief round right arm for recognition, the messenger from the Institute does the same.

Terms (strictly in advance): For each month of four weeks, reckoned from date of entrance, Twelv Guineas (£ 12. 12. 0 = 258 Marks German = 62 Dollars); for a term of six *calendar* months sixty-five Guineas (which can be paid in two instalments, 36 Guineas on entry and the remaining 29 Guineas at the expiration of three *calendar* months), third quarter 33 Guineas, fourth quarter 32 Guineas; under no circumstances liable to reduction, no allowance made for short absences. The most convenient method of payment is by an ordinary crossed cheque payable in London (to "W. Tilly"). *Notice of removal to be given a month in advance.* These terms include board and lodging (no extras except washing) and the following tuition:

Courses not marked optional are obligatory for all and no exemption can be granted from these till students have reached the fourth group; Conversation-walk on Saturday and Wednesday optional. Courses marked A are given by myself; B by phonetically trained members of my family; C by the Professor of French (a native of France); D by the Professor of Italian (a native of Italy); E by the Professor of Spanish (a native of Spain) F by German assistants. When not otherwise indicated, all lessons are given in German. For a period of ten days at Christmas and Easter only the lessons *"German"* (A or B) three each day 8— 0.45, and *"Conversatio"*) are given and during the Whitsuntide week only *"German"* (A or B, one each day 8—8.45) and *"Conversation"*; these lessons are then optional. A course in French C cannot be taken till the student shows by Examination that he has mastered French A; the same applies to Italian and Spanish. Once a month an excursion for the study of works of art in Berlin or Potsdam takes the place of the regular lessons and lectures. Beyond the singing which forms part of the regular language instruction (see Time Table), no musical practice can be allowed in the house; piano and violin practice can be had outside. At 8.40 simple gymnastic (and breathing) exercises are taken, these are obligatory for juniors, optional for seniors.

Our arrangements are not suitable for those who think they can learn modern languages without work who only come "to take a holiday and pick up a little German at the same time", who regard correct pronunciation as unimportant and consequently "do not need phonetics"; who only wish to gain a superficial knowledge, what they call "medical German" or "natural-science German", an article of no practical value. *Regular and thorough work* is required of all, seniors as well as juniors.

W. Tilly.

Figure 1.2. (cont.)

completely revolutionary methods. These followed a radical interpretation of the views put forward by members of the "Reform Movement" (see Howatt 1984:169–191), similar to what would today be termed an "immersion technique". He joined the International Phonetic Association in 1892 and remained a member all his life, ultimately being elected to the Council of the IPA. The fame of Institut Tilly and of its founder spread, attracting a large body of pupils who came from all over the world to study at Tilly's school.

Althaus (1911: 6), referring to Tilly's school as one of the "two homes of phonetics" (the other being Motte's establishment at Bourg-la-Reine, see Section 2.2), described it in these terms:

> Mr. Tilly's programme spells thoroughness, and personal corroboration of the fact is at hand on every side. Even pupils who have not been able to spend more than one or two holiday periods with Mr. Tilly bear his mark upon them, and testify to the soundness of his methods....

Its popularity was such that Tilly eventually decided to give up university lecturing in order to concentrate on his private school. In 1902, he transferred his institute to Berlin (see Figure 1.2), where he continued to teach until 1914 when, on the outbreak of war, he was interned as alien. Once he was released, Tilly, now devastated by his experiences in wartime Germany, seized the chance to emigrate to America, where he was soon appointed Professor of Phonetics at Columbia University, a post he retained until retirement.

Tilly's approach is described in a short anonymous item in the diary column of a London newspaper, written on his death in 1935.

> His success was founded upon two principles. He was Cromwellian in the thoroughness of his discipline. He exacted from his pupils a pledge that during their stay in his institute they would neither speak nor read a word of their own language. If the pledge was broken, the culprit left the same day.... All were treated alike. I have vivid memories of Otto Jespersen, then the world's greatest philologist, doing copy-book exercises so that he might write the Gothic script correctly.
>
> Harold Temperley, the famous historian, was another professor who was taken to task for not rounding his lips properly during the unison chorus of practice in sounds. It was here, too, that Daniel Jones, now Professor of Phonetics at London University, served his apprenticeship.[25]

Edward W. Mammen (Professor Emeritus, City University of New York), a former student of Tilly's, provided this description of the language teaching pioneer as he was in 1927, shortly before his retirement at the age of sixty-seven:

> Tilly was a portly, courtly and Teutonic-looking gentleman, white hair *en brosse*, always immaculately outfitted in what might have been the uniform of a success-ful German Herr Professor.... a dark or black formal-looking jacket, a touch of stiff white cuffs showing, gray or possibly pin-striped trousers, bow-tie, and a lightcolored vest tightly stretched over his well-developed "corporation". His lectures were not long—a pleasant blend of formal and informal. He spoke of Henry Sweet, and Wilhelm Viëtor, and the founding of IPA.... After this lecture or talk, he led us in drill on some foreign sounds, the class repeating after him exercises involving Sanskrit, perhaps....
>
> There was great stress, moreover, on how to record small changes by means of modifiers.... Tilly used ... a very "narrow" transcription, and indeed a cum-bersome one. It was far different from the "broad" system use[d] by Daniel Jones.[26]

1.8. Jones at Institut Tilly

Having completed the long journey by rail and steamer to Marburg, Daniel Jones was ready to begin his course. Like every other student there, he had signed a pledge to speak no word of English during his stay, and declared his willingness to submit to

Tilly's methods *in toto*. One account, originally written in 1910, indicates just how rigidly disciplined these could be:

> ...daily phonetic drill routine, when every morning "on the stroke of eight," the students, "including heads of schools, lecturers, medical men, military and naval officers, journalists and undergraduates," met together, all provided with hand-mirrors, and, at the word of command, turned towards the light and enunciated sounds, the while [sic] they studied the movements of their organs of speech.[27]

Not perhaps surprisingly, Jones's initial impressions were somewhat unfavourable (Jones 1926e: 394):

> I remember very well that, the first day I was there, Tilly started giving one of the lessons and wrote a lot of German words in phonetics on the blackboard. I had not the slightest idea what it was all about, and I said to myself: "I really can't be bothered with that sort of stuff; there's nothing in it for me." So little do we know what the future holds in store!

In line with the general approach of its founder, Institut Tilly demanded full payment in advance and gave no refunds whatsoever. So to avoid wasting his fees, Jones decided nevertheless to stay for the full duration of the month-long course. He found himself, as the days went by, disliking the phonetic approach to language study less, no doubt realising that for him phonetic symbols had a more practical application than the mathematical abstractions he was beginning to abhor. It would have been uncharacteristic of Daniel Jones to be immediately won over to any new way of thought, even phonetics, without careful consideration. He has said himself (Jones 1926e: 394) that it was a question of recognising the utility of the subject rather than any sudden enthusiasm for a new science: "During that first month, too, I began to see the use of phonetics, but mine was no dramatic conversion to its value. It was a gradual process."

As a teacher, and as a personality, Tilly made a lasting impression on Jones, as can be seen from this extract from the latter's obituary of his very first phonetics instructor (Jones 1935e: 62):

> Tilly was an exceedingly fine teacher. His greatest work was done in his institute in Germany, where he had full scope for exercising his remarkable gifts, and where he had complete charge of his students. The greater number of his pupils consisted of young men who had just completed a "public school" education in England. Many of them had never learnt what work really meant. Tilly ruled them with a rod of iron, and *taught them how to work*; they often didn't like his methods at first, but in the long run most of them came to have unbounded admiration for him.

This last comment appears in fact to reflect Jones's own experience at Tilly's hands, since, by the end of the month, he was determined to return: "I got to have such an immense admiration for his teaching that I went to him on two subsequent occasions to learn German and phonetics" (Jones 1926e: 394).

In his essay "The London School of Phonetics" (Jones 1948f [1973]: 180, 186 n.), Jones refers to Tilly as "that great linguist and teacher" and "this great man". And he later claimed, somewhat extravagantly, in correspondence with Tilly's biographer (Johanna Blidner Glass) that Tilly "was...the finest language teacher (English, German and French) who ever lived".[28] Jones also put on record the fact that it was Tilly who led him to meet a second even more profound influence on his career:

> I am one of those who owe a particular debt of gratitude to Tilly. In fact without him I should probably never have found my profession as a phonetician.... From Tilly I heard of Paul Passy the famous professor of phonetics in Paris.[29]

Chapter 2

An aptitude for phonetics (1904–07)

2.1. A timely illness

From the time he came down from Cambridge, after having enrolled at Lincoln's Inn, Daniel Jones did his best to interest himself in the law books that he was compelled to read for the Bar examinations. He found it hard going, soon discovering that law interested him no more than had classics or mathematics. Possibly it was only the risk of parental displeasure which kept him at the task.

In the winter of 1904–05, Jones suffered a period of "serious illness" (Jones 1926e: 394). After his childhood illnesses, he continued to be plagued by poor health throughout his life and eventually became preoccupied with disease and medicine to a degree bordering on hypochondria. This was the first recorded instance of numerous health breakdowns. The complaint was diagnosed as pneumonia and, as a consequence, he was warned by his doctor that a winter spent in England might be injurious to his health; at this time, long before any legislation to restrict air pollution, the reputation of London for being fog-bound much of the year was completely justified. Jones decided to spend the next six months in France, taking the opportunity to improve his knowledge of French through a course of study at the University of Paris. Of course, it could also have been that the idea of a long stay near Paris—indulging his hobby of learning languages and developing his new-found interest in phonetics—attracted the youthful Daniel Jones more than the unwelcome prospect of spending long months in his father's chambers in Carey Street, attempting to settle down to a career in law for which he had no inclination.

So Jones, helped by his timely illness, seems to have managed to persuade his father into letting him spend a prolonged period of time in France in exchange for a promise to complete his Bar examinations as soon as possible on his return.[1]

2.2. The Motte family

Jones travelled across to France in the autumn of 1905 and made his way to Paris. Once there, using William Tilly's recommendation, and possibly also that of his former schoolmaster E.R. Edwards, he gained an introduction to Paul Passy, the famous professor at the Sorbonne, who was "Directeur Adjoint" at the Ecole des Hautes Etudes.

Jones called to see the phonetician at his home in Bourg-la-Reine—today part of the sprawl of metropolitan Paris but then a small town a few kilometres outside the city.

anɔ̃:s

Famille française à la campagne près de Paris, Bourg-la-Reine, prend pensionnaires désireux d'étudier le Français, le dessin et la peinture. Leçons de Français et de phonétique si on les désire. Installation très comfortable, grand parc, atelier de peinture, billard, piano et harmonium. Communications faciles avec Paris, par chemin de fer ou tram électrique; 25 minutes de la Sorbonne. — S'adresser à H. M., au bureau du journal.

Le Gérant: P. Passy.

Figure 2.1. One of Henri Motte's advertisements in *Le Maître phonétique* (1906, p. 76).

Having decided to begin a course of study under Passy, Jones asked him if he knew of a family living near Paris who would accept him as a lodger. Passy suggested that Jones should contact his sister-in-law, Mme Constance Motte, who lived in the big house, called "Pin Ginko", which backed on to his own. Passy (1930–32: 76) later wrote in his autobiography:

> Mon beau-frère Henri Motte était…notre voisin à Bourg-la-Reine. Son métier de peintre ne lui rapportait pas, tant s'en faut, de quoi nourrir sa nombreuse famille (neuf enfants). Comme il avait une très grande habitation et un vaste parc, il s'est mis à prendre des pensionnaires: ma belle-sœur…a dirigé ainsi pendant plusieurs années, avec une énergie extraordinaire, une maisonnée qui comprenait parfois 20 ou 25 personnes.

Passy may well have drawn the young Englishman's attention to one of the advertisements which Henri Motte placed regularly in *Le Maître phonétique* (Figure 2.1). Jones (1926e: 394) accepted the professor's suggestion with enthusiasm, and immediately got in touch with Constance Motte.

> This appealed to me as an ideal place to live in, for one member of the family was, herself, a first-rate teacher of phonetics, and there were nine children, so that I was certain to get plenty of conversation in French.

The "first-rate teacher of phonetics" was Sophie Lund, a young Danish woman who lived with the Mottes, effectively as a member of the family. She acted as a governess to the children and was called "Marraine" by them, and indeed eventually by everybody. The boys were afterwards sent to school, but the Motte girls were kept at home and were taught everything from Sophie Lund. In addition, she gave classes in phonetics (eventually assisted by the Motte daughters) to the "pensionnaires". Althaus (1911: 6–7) describes Motte's establishment in these terms:

At Bourg-la-Reine one is, of course, at the fountain-head of phonetic teaching; for though M. Passy no longer teaches, but confines himself to examining, the instruction is in the hands of a pupil of his, of sixteen years' standing, Mlle S. Lund, than whom no abler or more sympathetically enthusiastic professor could be found.... Serious preparation in the practice of sounds, in reading aloud, and learning of poetry by heart, is required. Transcriptions are done, and daily dictations in French or in *langue inconnue* are given.... Mlle Lund is now assisted by two nieces of M. Passy, who are also diplômées.

Outside the area of phonetics, Sophie Lund may have had another significant influence on the young Daniel Jones. She later became a dedicated theosophist and it could well have been she who at this time first stimulated Jones to take an interest in this form of religion (see Section 10.8).

It was not only in their ideas on education that the Motte family was unusual. Daniel Jones used subsequently to recall that "all the Motte children looked alike, even the boys had long hair"[2]—something which would have seemed very odd at the time. Their appearance was indicative of the relaxed eccentricity—a mixture of the aristocratic and the intellectual—which permeated the household. Mme Constance Motte (née Ivatts) was of English stock, but had lived in France all her life. Nevertheless, she was in the habit of addressing her daughters in English and also spoke German to the succession of Swiss maids who made up the domestic staff.[3] Her husband, Henri, was thoroughly French, apparently speaking scarcely any English. He was a well-known artist, and his paintings, historical and military pieces on a grand scale, had enjoyed enormous popularity in the nineteenth century. But with the coming of impressionism, and the consequent changing patterns of taste, he was eventually scarcely able to sell a single canvas. Motte's money had been invested in his huge house, which he called "Pin Ginko" after a strikingly beautiful tree which grew in the garden. But he now found it difficult to keep up the lifestyle that such a grand piece of property demanded. Hence, he had resorted to taking in "pensionnaires" as a way of making ends meet.[4] (Passy 1930–32: 68–70 provides further details of the Motte-Ivatts families.)

The atmosphere of faded glory which pervaded Pin Ginko perhaps appealed to Daniel Jones as a refreshing contrast to the rigidity of his own upbringing in Victorian England. He enjoyed his stay with the Motte family immensely and returned on several occasions to spend the vacation periods at their house. One young member of the family, Cyrille, attracted his special interest: "Some years later I carried off one of these daughters as my wife" (Jones 1926e: 394). His marriage to Cyrille would set a trend for the rest of the family; three of the Motte daughters (Cyrille, Gisèle and Renée) married Englishmen, whilst another (Odette) married an American.

Nevertheless, whilst Jones would have counted himself lucky to be able to live in such congenial surroundings and company, what he probably would have valued most highly at this time were his contacts with Passy himself.

2.3. Paul Passy

Paul Passy (1859–1940) was born into a family background of privilege combined with distinguished academic achievement. His father, Frédéric Passy, was an eminent economist and the very first winner of the Nobel Peace Prize. He brought up his family in a progressive atmosphere of culture, where language learning was of supreme importance. Although he learnt four languages at home, Passy never actually attended school. Perhaps for that reason he (like Jones and Sweet) initially found university dull—failing his *Licence* three times (Jones 1941c: 31). His academic record soon improved once he was able to concentrate on language study in the traditional training of philology. At the age of nineteen, in order to avoid military service, he started working as a teacher of English and German. By his early twenties, he had firmly centred his interest on phonetics, and he went on to gain his doctorate with a phonetic discussion of sound change: *Etudes sur les changements phonétiques* (Passy 1891). He was shortly afterwards appointed to a specially created chair of phonetics at the Ecole des Hautes Etudes and became its Assistant Director in 1897, always being noted as a dedicated and inspiring teacher. In 1913, Passy was dismissed on political grounds, but after the war he returned, finally retiring in 1926.

Very early in his career, Passy took a step which in itself would have been enough to make him one of the most significant influences on the history of phonetics. In 1886, so as to start a pressure group for improving language teaching methodology, he founded a society for teachers of English, under the name of the "fonètic tîtcerz' asóciécon" with himself as President. He was helped in his work by his brother, Jean Passy (1866–98), who was appointed Secretary of the Association. Jean also showed himself in his brief life to be a promising and innovative phonetician, one of his most significant contributions being the invention of the technique of teaching ear-training through the medium of dictation of meaningless sequences of sounds (J. Passy 1894a, 1894b). Jones later, in the first edition of his *Outline of Phonetics* (p. 187), coined the term "nonsense words" to refer to such recognition exercises, and they were widely employed by him and his colleagues (and still form a part of training in the British tradition to this day). Its organ, *Dhi Fonètik Tîtcer*, began to appear in the same year (Figure 2.2), and Passy's society soon attracted the greatest names in the field: Sweet, Viëtor and Jespersen all joined early on.

The success of the society, and its obvious international appeal, prompted changes in its structure. In 1889, the name was changed to "Association Phonétique des Professeurs de Langues Vivantes" so as to appeal to modern language teachers in general—rather than just English specialists. The journal was now renamed *Le Maître phonétique* and, though it continued to be printed in transcription, the alphabet was changed to one which Passy had devised himself, based largely on Sweet's Broad Romic. This transcription system eventually evolved into the "International Phonetic Alphabet". It was not till 1897 that the organisation adopted the name "Association Phonétique Internationale" ("International Phonetic Association" or IPA). By this time, Passy had taken over from his brother Jean (who was dying of tuberculosis) as

Secretary. Thanks largely to Paul Passy, and làter to Daniel Jones, after he joined in 1905, the Association was to have enormous influence on the history of phonetics up to the outbreak of war in 1914. For most people interested in language at this time, the IPA effectively embodied the subject; its lasting legacy is the creation of the IPA

DHI

FONÈTIK TÎTCER

Dhi organ ov dhi fonètik tîtcerz' asóciécon

èdited bai PAUL PASSY

NEUILLY-SUR-SEINE (NIR PARIS) FRANS

7. Novèmber 1886. (500 kopiz)

Djenral niuz iz ràdher skærs dhis mœnth, dhó dhi stedi inkris ov aur mèmbercip mœst enkœredj œs. Dhi negóciéconz ar not yet ended abàut traiiɴ dhi fonètik method in sœm œdher pœblik skûlz besàidz dhi Ecole Normale, az dher ar financal and œdher points tu setl ; bœt dhi prinsipl iz adopted, and dhi ekspèriment wil sûn bi traid in dhi haier klàsez ov sœm ov dhi pràimeri skûlz. Aur sister-sosàieti, dhi Skandinévian *Quousque Tandem,* iz gróiɴ at a rét dhat sìmz laikli sûn tu liv œs behàind. Wi ar sori tu sé dhis iz nó grét wœnder, aur Nordhern frendz biiɴ far ahèd ov œs in dhi mater ov fonètiks and ov laɴgwedj-tìtciɴ in djenral.

Ai 'l pé yû aut !

A hen trod on a dœk's fut. Ci didnt min tu dû it, and it didnt hœrt mœtc, bœt dhi dœk sed, " ai 'l pé yû aut ! " Só ci flû at dhi hen, bœt az ci did só, her wiɴ strœk a kok, hû stud klós bai.

" Ai 'l pé yû aut, " kraid hi, and hi flû at dhi dœk ; bœt az hi did só, hiz klò tór dhi fœr ov a kat, hû woz djœst dhen in dhi yard. " Ai 'l pé yû aut, " kraid ci, and ci flû at dhi kok. Bœt az ci did só, her tél strak dhi ài ov a cip, hû woz nir. " Ai 'l pé yû aut, " kraid hi, and hi ran at dhi kat ; bœt az hi did só, hiz fut koht dhi fut ov a dog, hû lé in dhi sœn. " Ai 'l pé yû aut, " kraid hi, and hi ran at dhi cip. Bœt az hi did só, hiz leg tœtct an óld kau hû stud bai dhi gét. " Ai 'l pé yû

aut, " kraid ci, and ci ran at dhi dog. Bœt az ci did só, her horn grézd dhi skin ov a hors, hû woz bai a tri . " Ai 'l pé yû aut, " kraid hi, and hi ran at dhi kau.

Dhær woz a sìn ! Dhi hors flû at dhi kau, and dhi kau at dhi dog, and dhi dog at dhi cip, and dhi cip at dhi kat, and dhi kat at dhi kok, and dhi kok at dhi dœk, and dhi dœk at dhi hen. Hwot a noiz dhé méd, tu bi cur !

" Hwot's ôl dhis ? " sed a man, hû tuk kær ov dhem. " Ai wónt hav dhis noiz. " Só hi tuk a grét stik. " Yû mé sté hir, " hi sed tu dhi hen. Bœt hi dróv dhi kok tu hiz rûst, dhi dœk tu her pond, dhi kat tu her harth, dhi cip tu hiz fóld, dhi dog tu hiz kenel, dhi kau tu her fìld, and dhi hors tu hiz stòl. " Ai 'l pé yû ôl aut, " sed hi.

Getiɴ œp (1).

It 's àfter siks — kwait taim tu get œp. Kœm — djœmp aut and get yursèlvz woct az sûn az yû kan. Dónt forgèt tu brœc yur hær. Dhær 'z dhi fœrst bel riɴiɴ for brekfast, bi kwik and get daun in taim !

Hi dhat wud thraiv mœst raiz at faiv ; hi dhat haz thrivn mé lai til sevn.

Erli tu bed and erli tu raiz méks a man helthi, and welthi, and waiz.

(1) Aur " beginerz' plsex " dhis taim, ôl eksèpt dhi fœrst, ar tékn from Vietor and Dœrr'z fortbkœmiɴ Iɴglic rider, hwitc promisez tu bi a fœrst-rét buk. Dhi fœrst iz from Prof. Beljame'z *First Reader.*

Figure 2.2. Passy's journal *Dhi Fonètik Tîtcer*, the forerunner of *Le Maître phonétique.*

alphabet and its wide acceptance by linguists up to the present day. MacMahon (1986: 37) emphasises the significance of Passy's contribution:

> We all owe him a great debt of gratitude, for it was his unswerving belief in pho-
> netics, which at times had almost a religious fervour to it, coupled with his prodi-
> gious energy and enthusiasm, that really laid the firm foundations for our present-
> day IPA.

For more detailed accounts of the early history of the IPA, see Jones (1935d; 1941c: 34–35). For a detailed history of the development of the IPA alphabet, see Albright (1953, 1958) and MacMahon (1986).

Apart from his significance in setting up and organising the IPA, Passy is also note-worthy for his many publications and the framework of phonetic description which he set up within them. Following upon his thesis, he produced a significant early work, *Les Sons du français* (Passy 1887), which went into numerous editions; Passy asked Daniel Jones and D.L. Savory to translate it into English and it appeared as *The sounds of the French language*, Daniel Jones's first book-length publication (see Section 2.6). With H. Michaelis, Passy produced the *Dictionnaire phonétique de la langue française* (Michaelis—Passy 1897), which was the first attempt at a pronouncing dictionary of any European language using IPA symbolisation. It provided the model—including the inconvenient scheme of listing words under their phonetic representations—for the *Phonetic dictionary of the English language* (Michaelis—Jones 1913a; see Section 5.3). Another notable, though modest, book, is Passy's (1906) excursion into comparative phonetics, *Petite phonétique comparée*. Passy produced a huge number of publications of one kind and another—apart from theoretical phonetic textbooks, he also compiled a large number of phonetic readers; in addition, he wrote several works of a religious or political nature, and even a two-part autobiography, *Souvenirs d'un socialiste chrétien* (Passy 1930–32). In total, over fifty books and pamphlets by Passy are listed in a bibliography which appeared on his death.[5]

Passy remained Secretary of the IPA until 1927, when he was succeeded in the post by Jones. In his later life, after his retirement from academic work, Passy became more and more involved with the ideas of Christian Socialism. He set up a co-opera-tive agricultural commune near Fontette, an isolated area of Aube, for working-class men (many of whom were the long-term unemployed). He called the project Liéfra—a name derived from the slogan of the French Revolution, *liberté, égalité, fraternité*. There he attempted to live out his ideal of a rustic—almost primitive—lifestyle, combining fundamental Christianity and socialism with language teaching and learning. His commitment to his new role was complete; David Abercrombie and Marguerite Chapallaz, who both stayed at Liéfra in the 1930s, were witnesses to the spartan conditions that he imposed on himself and others.[6] It was there, surrounded by his followers, that he died in 1940.

Passy's contribution is not only to be measured in the breadth of his publications, but also for his ability to refine and simplify the complexity of phonetic and phonological information so as to produce an easily learnt framework which can be widely utilised. Clarity of exposition shines through his work; he honed down elaborate and over-involved theory to what he considered to be the essentials. It was a technique which is well exemplified by Passy's description of the French vowels, which he produced from the complexities of the Bell-Sweet tradition, and which was in turn to form the basis of Daniel Jones's own Cardinal Vowel system (see Section 7.3). Passy was determined to eschew academic complication and looked for practical applications when considering theories, striving to present his ideas in clear, lucid prose. In so doing, he provided an important element necessary for the popularisation of phonetics which took place in the first quarter of the twentieth century. All these facets of Passy's view of phonetics were admired by Daniel Jones and emulated in the latter's own work. Less happily, it must be admitted that Jones also took over Passy's somewhat narrow view of language study, with the tendency to exclude anything which was not connected with pronunciation training—as opposed to the broader linguistic viewpoint of, for instance, Sweet and Jespersen.

Throughout Jones's *œuvre*, it is possible to find statements and ideas which can be traced to Passy. Daniel Jones also saw in Passy someone to whom he could look as a mentor, and a model of industry and application to teaching and research—as is clear from Jones's tribute to Passy (Jones 1941c). The parallels of their dedication to a work ethic—albeit derived in one case from Christian Socialist beliefs, and in the other from humanitarian and theosophical principles—united them more closely than most true co-religionists. Their close relationship was even more firmly bonded once Jones married into Passy's family (see Sections 4.2 and 4.3).

In summary, it may be said that, after Sweet, Passy was the most stimulating force in the development of articulatory phonetics around the turn of the century; indeed, his unique contribution has yet to be fully acknowledged. Furthermore, there is no doubt that as far as Daniel Jones's early phonetic career was concerned, no-one matched the influence of Paul Passy.[7]

2.4. Passy's classes and the IPA examination

Elna Simonsen (1939: 20) has written of Passy's charisma as a teacher:

> Qu'est ce qui faisait de Paul Passy un professeur unique? Je me rappelle encore très nettement ce premier mardi du mois de novembre 1894 où j'entrai—un peu avant l'heure—pour la première fois dans la salle de conférences de l'Ecole des Hautes Etudes. Paul Passy se trouvait déja au pied de la chaire, les bras ballants, presque gêné, si simple que j'en étais toute impressionnée. Son regard limpide faisait le tour des élèves—il y en avait de tous les pays—puis il commença son "Introduction générale à la phonétique historique". Sa voix était claire, distincte, son sujet l'entraînait; plaidant chaleureusement pour ce qu'il savait juste et voulait faire comprendre, aimé à tout ce monde, il captivait de plus en plus ses auditeurs.

What was the content of Passy's classes at the Ecole des Hautes Etudes? Information about this comes, indirectly, from Jones himself, who supplied the details to L.H. Althaus (1911) for a supplement to *Le Maître phonétique* giving details of the availability of courses in phonetics for modern language teachers.

Passy taught three courses: an elementary treatment of the phonetics of the chief European languages, a more advanced course on the phonetics of Old French, and a class "for students wishing to do original work in various branches of phonetics". From what Jones says, it would seem that Passy favoured advanced teaching methods for his time, with an emphasis on a heuristic approach. The class in Old French which Jones attended in 1906 involved students collecting for themselves the philological materials and "M. Passy applying his expert knowledge to deducing facts of pronunciation from these materials".

Every member of the class for research students was ". . . expected to read at least one paper on a phonetic subject. These papers are discussed by the other members of the class, and finally Passy sums up the various points and gives his own opinion of the paper and criticisms of it". The report goes on to say: "The subjects treated in the class for original workers are various, the most usual being the descriptive phonetics of less well-known languages and dialects." Jones also mentioned that there was an opportunity for English students "whose pronunciation differs from the standard to read papers describing their own pronunciation or the pronunciation of some dialect with which they are familiar". In return, they would have "the inestimable advantage of having their observations checked by M. Passy and discussed by the class" (Althaus 1911: 17).

To round off his stay in France, Daniel Jones attempted the examinations of the Association Phonétique Internationale in the phonetics of French. Passy conducted the examination on June 9.[8] Jones's scores were remarkable (Figure 2.3); he received fifty-six marks out of a possible total of sixty, the highest ever obtained by a non-native French speaker (Gimson 1968: 2–3). The full results were as follows:

Phonetic dictation of French	10
Dictation of an unknown language	10
Transcription	10
Phonetic reading	8
Orthographic reading	8
Theory questions	10

Passy added the following prophetic note to the certificate:

J'ai suivi depuis plusieurs mois les travaux de M. Jones, soit à l'Ecole des Hautes Etudes où il a été mon auditeur régulier, soit au cours de nombreux entretiens. J'ai été très frappé de ses aptitudes soit scientifique[s] soit pédagogiques, ainsi que de son ardeur au travail. Je le crois destiné à tenir une belle place, dans la science comme dans l'enseignement pratique.

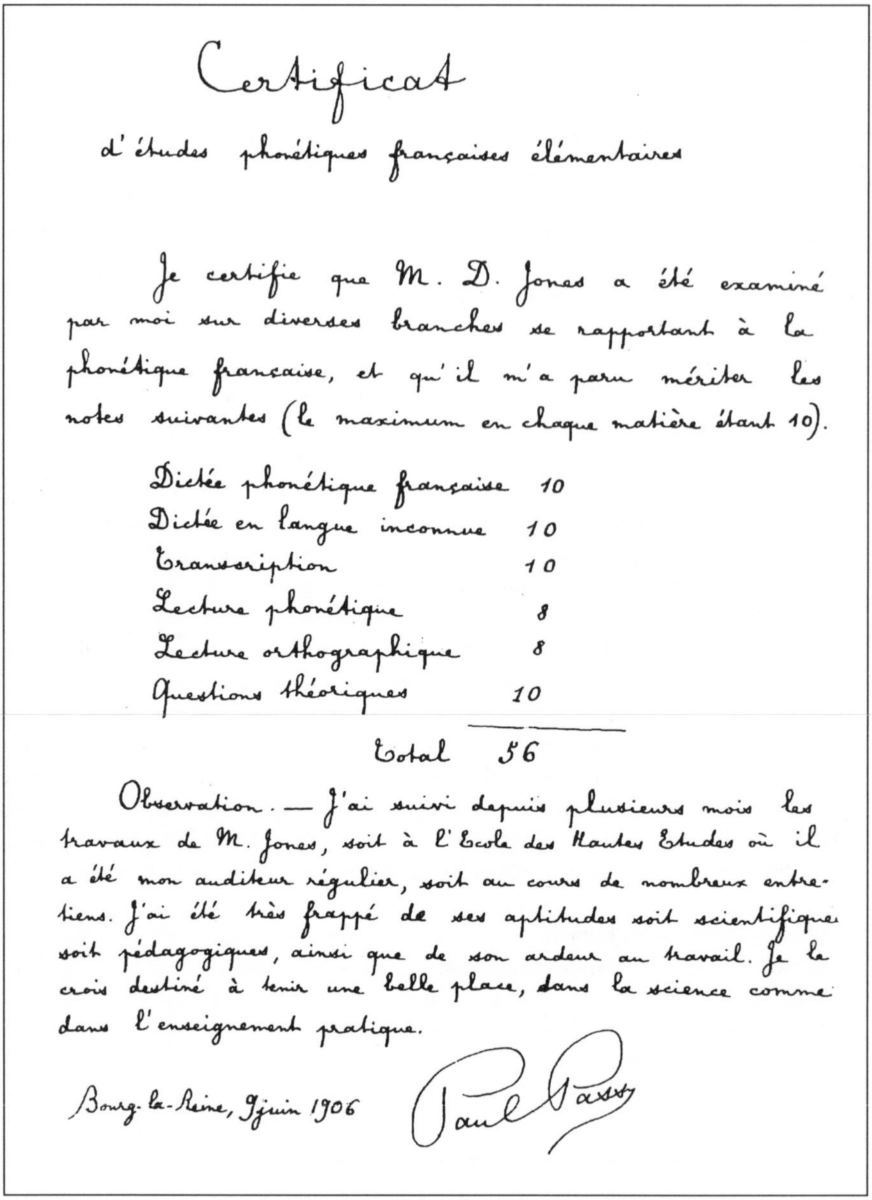

Certificat

d'études phonétiques françaises élémentaires

Je certifie que M. D. Jones a été examiné par moi sur diverses branches se rapportant à la phonétique française, et qu'il m'a paru mériter les notes suivantes (le maximum en chaque matière étant 10).

Dictée phonétique française	10
Dictée en langue inconnue	10
Transcription	10
Lecture phonétique	8
Lecture orthographique	8
Questions théoriques	10
Total	56

Observation. — J'ai suivi depuis plusieurs mois les travaux de M. Jones, soit à l'École des Hautes Études où il a été mon auditeur régulier, soit au cours de nombreux entretiens. J'ai été très frappé de ses aptitudes soit scientifiques soit pédagogiques, ainsi que de son ardeur au travail. Je le crois destiné à tenir une belle place, dans la science comme dans l'enseignement pratique.

Bourg-la-Reine, 9 juin 1906   Paul Passy

Figure 2.3. Jones's IPA certificate awarded to him by Paul Passy.

This spectacular performance had obviously convinced Passy of Jones's potential, and he advised him to think of a future career in the phonetic world. Daniel Jones stated modestly: "Professor Passy seemed to think that I had some aptitude for phonetics, and recommended me to take it up" (Jones 1926e: 394). Jones later used to recall that he had answered: "How can I possibly do that? There are no posts in the subject." "Just try", had been Passy's response (Gimson 1968: 3). But where, in Britain, or Europe, or even further afield, could Jones begin trying? In fact, the answer lay almost on his doorstep. By chance, it turned out that the institution which was to provide Daniel Jones with this first opportunity in the academic world would be one with close connections to his last school—situated in the very building where he had spent the final and happier portion of his teenage years. He was to return to Gower Street and try for a post at University College London. And against all the odds, he would obtain it.

2.5. Phonetics at University College

Phonetics had first been taught at University College London more than forty years before Daniel Jones was to go there seeking employment. In fact, the subject appeared in various guises in the syllabus for several years during the mid-nineteenth century and was then, it seems, forgotten about. The first mention of what were, in effect, phonetics classes occurs in the session 1864–65, when a lecturer named Charles Furtado gave a course covering the following subject areas:

Rhetorical Delivery.
Examination of the systems of John Walker, Steel [sic], Sheridan, &c.
Formation and development of the voice, pitch, articulation, emphasis, inflection, gesture.[9]

No indication exists of how this course—typical of the elocution teaching of the period—went down with his students. It was in any event successful enough for Furtado to be asked to teach his classes again for one more year, after which he handed over to a more eminent successor, namely Alexander Melville Bell (see A.3). In 1865, Bell had moved from his post in Edinburgh and taken up an appointment in University College. It was while he was lecturer in elocution there that he published *Visible speech* (A. Melville Bell 1867). During the 1866–67 session, for two evenings a week, Bell taught classes which, it was stated:

…will embrace a systematic development of the Principles of Elocution, in the three departments of, I. Pronunciation; II. Expression; III. Action; with a large amount of practical training in each.[10]

By 1869, Bell was providing a full course containing a strong phonetic element, including lectures on topics such as: "The Relation of Tones to Language", "Principles of Emphasis", "The Organic Mechanism of Speech", "Characteristics of English Pronunciation", ending, tantalisingly, with a "Review of Vices of Speech".[11] In 1870, Bell emigrated to Canada and thence to America, taking with him his son, Alexander Graham Bell, who had also been following courses at University College and indeed assisting his father in his teaching (Bruce 1973).

In the sessions 1870–71 and 1871–72, a course was announced in "Short-Hand and Phonetics" which was to be given by a certain M.C. Soutter, M.R.C.S.[12] However, even though this is the first UCL course actually to have "phonetics" in its title, it is clear that the main aim was to teach the writing of Pitman's system of shorthand, which was based on phonetic principles (see A.3). After this date, there is no further trace of phonetics at University College for three decades, until E.R. Edwards was given an appointment to lecture on the phonetics of French.

As noted in Section 1.5, Ernest R. Edwards (1871–1948) was one of Jones's language teachers at University College. Edwards spent his childhood in Japan (returning to England at the age of eleven) and spoke Japanese fluently. He had obtained his doctorate from the Sorbonne with a thesis on the phonetics of Japanese (Edwards 1903), prepared under Passy's supervision. This work was considered at the time to have a remarkably advanced approach, being a synchronic description of the phonetics and phonology of the colloquial language (as opposed to the historical treatments favoured at this period). Jones claimed that through its publication Edwards had "created quite a stir in the phonetic world" (Jones 1948c). Edwards went on to become an important member of the International Phonetic Association, being elected to the Council in 1906, and presiding at the General Meeting in 1935.

Edwards was appointed to teach phonetics at UCL in 1903, giving two evening classes per week ("General Phonetics" and "Applied Phonetics") for two sessions.[13] In 1905 he was appointed an Inspector of Schools and from that powerful position "was able to do an immense amount in the way of encouraging the use of phonetics and the direct method [of language teaching]" (Jones 1948c). Edwards acted as a noteworthy stimulus to the use of applied phonetics in the English school system; he also played a vital part in the establishment of phonetics as a university discipline by reintroducing the subject to University College and, even more significantly, recommending Daniel Jones as his successor to carry on his work.

Edwards's entry to the inspectorate meant giving up his evening classes. In the following year, another member of the college staff, R.A. Williams—a Reader in the German Department—gave lectures on General Phonetics with special reference to English and German. Williams was, in fact, the first person in UCL to give a course specifically on the phonetics of English.[14] But in 1907, Williams was to leave UCL to take up a chair at Dublin (Jones 1948f [1973]: 181). So it proved fortuitous that when Jones was faced with the dilemma of just how to "do something in the way of making phonetics a profession" (Jones 1926e: 394), a need for a teacher of the subject arose in University College.

It was his former schoolmaster, E.R. Edwards, remembering him from University

College School days, who put Jones's name forward. "Dr. Edwards knew me and recommended the authorities of the college to get me to give a course of lectures" (Jones 1926e: 394).

It is also certain that Passy was instrumental in Jones's appointment; Passy had undoubtedly discussed his promising new young British student with his former protégé. Jones says: "... mainly as the result of a letter of recommendation from my teacher, Professor Paul Passy, it fell to me to revive the courses previously conducted by Dr Edwards, and I gave my first lecture at University College (on phonetics as applied to French) in January 1907" (Jones 1948f [1973]: 180).

Daniel Jones gave just one lecture per week in the spring term of that session. The course was attended by eighteen students (all of whom were teachers in London schools) and proved a success, indicated by the fact that the students themselves asked for a continuation in the form of a practical course in the following Summer term (Gimson 1968: 3). This was approved by the College authorities and duly given by Jones, who had meanwhile discovered (1926e: 394) that:

...lecturing was a very much more difficult task than I had ever imagined it could be. In preparing my lectures I left nothing to chance or the inspiration of the moment, for I realized my shortcomings in the art of extempore speaking. I wrote out every word I was going to deliver. If I had not done that I am sure I could never have carried the lectures through.

In fact, in this respect, his teaching methods showed little change over the years. Notes for lectures to be given in the final years of his career display the same meticulous, almost anxious, care in their preparation, and frequently have any jokes or apparently impromptu asides written out in full.

It was fortunate that Jones was still living at home at this period since he appears to have been very short of money. "When I took stock of the financial result of those lectures, I came to the conclusion that the prospect of making a living by teaching phonetics was very remote" (Jones 1926e: 394). Possibly it was a period of unrest at home, as Daniel Jones Senior realised gradually that his son was determined not to succeed him in his barrister's chambers, but was apparently set on the foolhardy idea of eking out a living by teaching an obscure new science on a part-time basis. To keep his promises to his father, Jones, on his return from France, had taken his law examinations at Lincoln's Inn, and was called to the Bar on January 28, 1907. On hearing that he had passed, Daniel Jones proceeded to heap all his law books into a pile—and then set fire to the lot.[15]

To compensate for any inadequacy he may have felt as a potential lawyer, Jones could consider himself very much a success in his new job at University College. The lectures on phonetics had gone down well, and Passy was able to insert this brief note in the "Famille phonétique" section of *Le Maître phonétique*: "D. Jones a fait à University College, London, une série de conférences de phonétique qui paraissent avoir été très appréciées."[16]

In the Autumn term of 1907–08, the College asked Jones to continue his lectures in the French Department and, in addition, take other classes over from Williams (Jones 1948f [1973]: 180).[17] Jones (1948f [1973]: 180–181) says of this period:

> The time was propitious. The principles of phonetics had been preached in England by Henry Sweet, of Oxford, during the preceding thirty years, and were being popularized among school teachers by Walter Ripman. Many English school teachers were also being trained in phonetics by Professor Wilhelm Viëtor, of the University of Marburg, by Paul Passy at the Ecole des Hautes Etudes, Paris, and above all by that great linguist and teacher William Tilly in his Language Institute at Marburg and (subsequently) Berlin. The result was that from the first the phonetics courses at University College were well attended—mostly by language teachers.

Jones was characteristically modest in his assessment of the reasons for the success of his classes. He appears to have planned his material with great care and delivered his lectures competently. Nonetheless, there was truth in what he said: public interest in phonetics in Britain was far greater than ever before.

This is reflected in the membership figures for the International Phonetic Association (IPA). In 1892, the United Kingdom membership was only 21, compared with 150 in Germany and 105 in Sweden. By 1898 there were still only 59 British members; Germany had 284 and France 99, and Austria-Hungary, Denmark and Finland were all ahead of Britain. The figures for 1908 show that a very different pattern had emerged. United Kingdom membership was now 292—more members than any other country; Germany had 247 and France 107. The phonetic centre of gravity had moved to Britain—and it is also noteworthy that membership in the United States was now 70 (almost double the figure four years earlier) and that other English-speaking countries, namely Australia, New Zealand and Canada, also had sizable membership totals (IPA 1908: 3–29).

Another indication of the increasing interest in phonetics in the English-speaking world was that, even though *Le Maître phonétique* continued to use French as its official language, more and more of the contents were being published in English. In addition, people abroad were beginning to realise the importance the English language would have in the twentieth century, and to appreciate that applied phonetics provided an excellent way of learning the correct pronunciation of English.

Jones later wrote: "Phonetics began to 'catch on' and a demand soon arose for courses on the phonetics of English for foreign students..." (Jones 1948f [1973]: 181).

In the autumn of 1907, *Le Maître phonétique* carried this announcement, giving a good idea of Jones's activities at University College in that year:

Courses of lectures on phonetics at the University of London.
The following is a list of the courses of lectures on phonetics to be delivered at University College, London during the coming session by Mr Daniel Jones:

1. **French phonetics**
    a. Elementary course: first term, Mondays at 5.30, beginning October 7th.
    b. Advanced course (including Old French and the development of the language): second term, Mondays at 5.30, beginning January 20th.
2. **English phonetics**
    a. Course intended primarily for English students (with special reference to elocution): first term, Thursdays at 5.30, beginning October 3rd.
    b. Course *for foreign students*: second and third terms, Thursdays at 5.30, beginning January 16th.
3. **General phonetics** (speech sounds in general and the modes of representing them): third term, Mondays at 5.30, beginning May 4th.

The special attention of our readers is called to the course of *English phonetics for foreign students* (2b above), which is to begin next January and will be continued until about the middle of June, with a few weeks' break at Easter. This course is a new institution, and it is hoped it may be found of use to the numerous foreigners who come to London to learn English, and who have had hitherto very limited opportunities of studying systematically the correct pronunciation of the language. Particulars of this course or any of the others may be obtained on application to the Secretary, University College, London.[18]

The announcement provides some clue of how Jones at this time viewed the teaching of his subject. The mention of "special reference to elocution" in the English Phonetics course shows that at this point Jones had quite different ideas from those he put forward later in his life: "I take the view that people should be allowed to speak as they like. And if the public wants a standardized pronunciation, I have no doubt that some appropriate standard will evolve itself. If there are any who think otherwise, it must be left to them to undertake the invidious task of deciding what is to be approved and what is to be condemned" (*EPD*[10] [1949] : x). See also Section 3.4 for Jones's early prescriptive attitude to "correct" speech.

It is also noticeable that the advanced course in French includes historical work and the development of the language. Jones was not at all enthusiastic about the conventional historical study of language, and probably he also realised that he lacked any appropriate training in this area of linguistics. By the end of the nineteenth century, philological research, including the development of linguistic sound changes, had already established itself as a powerful academic discipline, and in Germany was being carried out with a degree of efficiency, thoroughness and precision which was turning it almost into an industry (see A.4). English philology was dominated by Henry Sweet (Section 2.9), who combined a vast record of published philological work with a wide knowledge of living languages and a genius for phonetic analysis. Jones could not possibly have competed in the study of historical sound change, nor did he ever attempt to do so. We must assume that the reason he included historical material was that this would have been considered crucially important in language departments at this time. A set of notes on the historical phonology of French survives, but Jones seems to have made little use of the information in his publications, or in his research.[19] Jones has indicated elsewhere that he saw a practical role for phonetics in enlivening the procedures of historical phonology;[20] and he had a genuine enthusiasm for attempting to reconstruct the pronunciation of Chaucerian and Elizabethan English. His interest in this may have been sparked off in part by the historical work that he was compelled to do as part of his preparation for these early lectures.

The "course for foreign students" obviously represented matters much closer to his true interests. It is apparent that this was the first time that Jones was able to try out in practice the ideas that he was developing for teaching English pronunciation to foreign learners through applied articulatory phonetics—ideas that were eventually to be incorporated into *An outline of English phonetics* (Jones 1918a, henceforth *Outline*), which, although it did not appear till many years later, was in large part written during Jones's first years as a lecturer at UCL (see Section 8.2).

2.6. Joining the IPA and early publications

Jones joined the International Phonetic Association in 1905; his name appears among the new members for December of that year, with his address given as: 21 Grande rue, Bour-la-Reine [sic], Seine.[21] (It is possible to detect Passy's influence even in Jones's adoption of the reformed spelling, corresponding to that advocated by Passy at this time.)

An entry, in the same issue, notes that his contribution had been received in September.[22] He had joined as a "membre actif à vie", paying ninety francs—a fairly large sum of money at the time. Jones never acted hastily and was always cautious over even small items of expenditure. So this payment for life membership of the IPA at this point—coming so shortly after obtaining his excellent results from Passy—can be seen to mark Jones's personal commitment both to the science of phonetics and to the Association itself.

But even more significant was another event which was shortly to follow. In August 1906, startling news came from Switzerland: Richard Lloyd, a Vice-President of the IPA and a member of the Council (see Section A.3), had met a tragic death by drowning whilst swimming in the Rhone near Geneva.[23] This left an unexpected vacancy to be filled on the Council and arrangements had to be set in motion for an election to be held. Daniel Jones would have needed little persuading to have his name put forward. The rules, which allowed a replacement to be elected by the Council members themselves, rather than by a full vote of the membership, would work in his favour.[24] He was known to at least four of the council already (Paul Passy, E.R. Edwards, Sophie Lund and William Tilley); Passy undoubtedly drummed up support amongst the others. Jones beat two rival candidates and was declared the winner. Just a year after joining the Association, he would begin in January 1907 as a member of the IPA Council.[25]

By now Jones had also begun to publish, in a minor way at first, with some notes and brief articles in *Le Maître phonétique*. In 1906, his first piece appeared in *Le Maître phonétique* for February-March; this is also Jones's first known publication of any kind. Headed "En Angleterre", it is a report of the Modern Language Association conference held at University College London in December 1905 (Jones 1906a). It is written in French and in phonetic transcription; the latter being required for all material appearing in *Le Maître phonétique*. Its content is of little interest today. In the following (April) issue the first piece on a phonetic topic appeared in the *Correspondance* section. A mere eighteen lines in length, it is a speculative attempt to explain the origin of the Danish *stød* (Jones 1906b). A review of two books containing collections of transcriptions of elementary French followed in November 1906 (Jones 1906c). The author of these books was Douglas Savory, who was at the time working with Jones on the translation of Paul Passy's *Sons du français* (see below). In the same issue, Jones published, in the section called "Here and There", a report of an address given to St Andrews University on the subject of spelling reform (Jones 1906d). A third contribution in this November issue is a *spécimen* of Scottish English taking the form of a "well-known Scotch poem by Burns" transcribed by Jones with the help of an informant (1906e). The following number, December 1906, also includes a brief contribution from Jones, which was simply a collection of three extracts from magazines, plus a quotation from Walter Skeat, all dealing with spelling reform (1906f).

Jones's first year of writing in *Le Maître phonétique* can only be called undistinguished, and perhaps understandably none of these pieces is mentioned in the one bibliography of Jones's work available till now (Abercrombie et al. 1964: xi-xix). However, nondescript as they are, these contributions mark the start of an era when Jones's name was hardly ever absent from the pages of *Le Maître phonétique*. Throughout his life he remained loyal to the journal, providing a steady flow of articles and comment, and choosing comparatively rarely to publish work elsewhere.

Daniel Jones had some reason to be thankful that he did not have a full-time post at this time, since teaching in the evenings left his days free for his remarkable publishing activity. He produced three books in 1907, and was undoubtedly also working hard on the two further works which were to appear in 1909.

His first book to come out was a slight work entitled *100 Poésies enfantines* (Jones 1907a). It was produced by the German firm of B.G. Teubner in Leipzig and this began an important relationship with these publishers for Jones; they were afterwards to publish *Intonation curves* (Jones 1909a) and the *Outline*—the latter in several editions. *100 Poésies enfantines* is a book which shows clearly the influence of Paul Passy. As the title suggests, it is simply a collection of French children's rhymes and proverbs transcribed phonetically, and illustrated by line drawings (Figure 2.4). It is written in the sort of simple language that Passy would have admired and, in being directed to children, fitted in with another belief of Passy's, namely that it was of the utmost importance for children to be taught by methods which involved the use of phonetic techniques (Jones 1941c: 37). It seems likely that the book was Passy's idea, since his love of children was well known, whereas we have the evidence of members of the Motte family that Daniel Jones was not interested in talking to young children at this time.[26]

(pa:ʒ ˈkɛ̃:z.) 15

37
(nymero trɑ̃tˈsɛt).

ʒə sɥiz ə̃ pti garˈsɔ̃
də bɔn fiˈgy:r,
ki ɛ:m bjɛ̃ le bɔ̃:ˈbɔ̃
e le kɔ̃:fiˈty:r.
si vu vule m ɑ̃ dɔˈne,
ʒə səre bjɛ̃ le mɑ̃:ˈʒə,
la bɔn avɑ̃:ˈty:r,
o ˈge!
la bɔn avɑ̃:ˈty:r.

ʒə səre ˈsa:ʒ e bjɛ̃ ˈbɔ̃,
pur plɛ:r a ma ˈmɛ:r;
ʒə səre bjɛ̃ ma ləˈsɔ̃,
pur plɛ:r a mɔ̃ ˈpɛ:r.
ʒə və ˈbjɛ̃ le kɔ̃:tɑ̃:ˈte,
e s il ˈvəl m ɑ̃:braˈse,
la bɔn avɑ̃:ˈty:r,
o ˈge!
la bɔn avɑ̃:ˈty:r.

ˈlɔrskə le pti garˈsɔ̃
sɔ̃ ˈʒɑ̃:ti e ˈsa:ʒ,
ɔ̃ lər ˈdɔn de bɔ̃:ˈbɔ̃,
də bɛlz iˈma:ʒ;
mɛ kɑ̃t il sə fɔ̃ grɔ̃:ˈde,
s ɛ lə ˈfwɛ k il fo dɔˈne,
la trist avɑ̃:ˈty:r,
o ˈge!
la trist avɑ̃:ˈty:r.

makˈsim. la vɛrˈty tru:v tuʒu:r sa rekɔ̃:ˈpɑ̃:s.

Figure 2.4. A page from Jones's first published book, *100 Poésies enfantines* (1907a).

Jones's second work to appear, though only a translation of the work of another author, was a far more weighty contribution to phonetics. It was an English version of the sixth edition of *Les Sons du français* (Passy 1887 [1906⁶]) on which Jones had worked together with his friend, Douglas L. Savory, later Professor Sir Douglas L. Savory (1878–1969). Savory was a lecturer in French at Goldsmiths' College, London, where part of his work involved classes in phonetics to teachers of French employed by the LCC (London County Council). Jones, too, was later to teach similar courses. Savory was again to collaborate with Jones on holiday courses (see Section 2.10). In 1909, when still in his early thirties, Savory was awarded a chair (something which may have fuelled Jones with similar ambitions) and went to Ireland to become Professor of French at Queen's University Belfast. He held this post until 1940 when he was elected Unionist MP for Queen's University. When the university seats were abolished in 1950, Savory became MP for the constituency of South Antrim (1950–55). In 1952, in recognition of his distinguished role in many aspects of education and Anglo-French relations, he received a knighthood. From 1940 onwards, he was one of Jones's most highly placed contacts and an ally in such matters as furthering phonetics and spelling reform.[27] Passy indicates in an introductory preface (p. i) that Savory was the instigator of the project and that Jones played a lesser role in producing the work. Be that as it may, *The sounds of the French language* (Savory—Jones 1907c) provided the young Daniel Jones with his best opportunity so far to make his name known. Passy's book (some editions of which he produced in a simplified orthography) had already proved very successful, and 1906 saw the sixth edition appear.

STAIL 'EI

prönʌnsi'eiʃən 'sju:təbl fö rɪ'saitiŋ ɔː 'riːdiŋ in
'pʌblik

I ('wʌn).   ðə 'baibl ('ɔːθöraizd 'vəːʃən)

1 ('wʌn).   ðə 'wʌn 'hʌndrəd ænd 'twenti 'fəːst 'sɑːm

ai wil 'lift ʌp main 'aiz ʌntu ðə 'hilz, fröm 'ʍens 'kʌmɪθ
mai 'help.
    mai 'help 'kʌmɪθ fröm ðo 'lɔːd, ʍitʃ 'meid 'hevən ænd
'əːθ.
    'hiː wil nɔt 'sʌfə ðai 'fut tu bi 'muːvd ; 'hiː ðæt 'kiːpɪθ
ði: wil nɔt 'slʌmbə.
    bɪ'hould, 'hiː ðæt 'kiːpɪθ 'izreiəl ʃël naiðə 'slʌmbə nɔː
'sliːp.

Figure 2.5. Style A from *Phonetic transcriptions of English prose* (p. 2).

STAIL 'BI:

prənʌnsi'eiʃn 'juːzd in 'keːəful kɔnvə'seiʃn ɔː
'riːdiŋ ə'laud in 'praivɪt[1]

V ('faiv).   'bəːk

br'saidz 'ðouz 'θiŋz witʃ di'rektli sə'dʒest ði: aidiə əv
'deindʒə, ənd 'ðouz witʃ prədjuːs ə 'similər ɪ'fekt frəm ə
mɪ'kænikl 'kɔːz, ai nou əv 'nʌθiŋ sə'blaim witʃ iz nɔt
'sʌm mɔdifi'keiʃn əv 'pauə. ənd 'ðis 'brɑːntʃ raizɪz, əz
'næt((ə)rəli əz ði: 'ʌðə 'tuː 'brɑːntʃɪz, frɔm 'terə, ðə 'kɔ-
mən 'stɔk əv 'evriθiŋ ðət iz sə'blaim. ði: aidiə əv
'pauə, ət 'fɔːst 'vjuː, 'siːmz əv ðə 'klɑːs ɔv ðouz in'difrənt
wʌnz witʃ mei 'iːkwəli brlɔŋ tə 'pein ɔː tə 'pleʒə. bət

Figure 2.6. Style B from *Phonetic transcriptions of English prose* (p. 12).

Passy says modestly in his preface to the translation (Savory—Jones 1907c: iii): "the book contains no new theories, no important discoveries, hardly anything that is not generally known and received" and adds (Savory—Jones 1907c: iv) "the present edition is not a mere translation. ...this may be considered, to all intents and purposes, as a seventh edition of my work".

Passy attributes the success of *Les Sons du français* to its being "a popular work on scientific lines" (Savory—Jones 1907c: iii), which is an accurate description. The English version reads with surprising freshness today—as indeed does Passy's French text. The description of vowels seems an obvious precursor of Cardinal Vowel theory (Savory—Jones 1907c: 57). It includes the categories: "Closed—Half-closed—Half-open—Open" for tongue height (in the original: "Fermées—Mifermées—Miouvertes—Ouvertes", Passy (1887 [1899[5]]: 80) with Front and Back ("d'avant, d'arrière") and the arrangement of the "normal" vowels in a symmetrical form (see Section 7.3). For Jones, the importance of this translation was twofold. Firstly, he was now in part responsible for the best description of spoken French available in the English language; and secondly, we may see in it much of the approach which Jones was shortly to use in his own work *The pronunciation of English* (see Section 3.4).

2.7.   *Phonetic transcriptions of English prose*

The third book that Jones published in 1907 was *Phonetic transcriptions of English prose* (Jones 1907b). This, like the *Sounds of the French language*, was published by the prestigious Clarendon Press of Oxford University—and it was an honour in

STAIL ꞌSI:

prənʌnsiꞌeiʃn ꞌjuːzd in ꞌræpid kɔnvəꞌseiʃn

XV (ꞌfifꞌtiːn).   ꞌbòzwəl¹

ət ꞌsʌpə, ꞌlèldɪ məꞌklaꞌuꞌd mənʃn̩d dòktə kəꞌdʌgənz ꞌbùk ɔ̀n ðə ꞌgaùt. — ꞌdgɔ̀nsn̩. ꞌɪt s ə ꞌgùd bùk ɪn ꞌdʒənɹəɫ, bət ə ꞌfuːhʃ wʌn ɪn pəꞌtikjələz. ɪt s ꞌgùd ɪn ꞌdʒənɹəɫ, əz ɹèkəmɛ̀ndɪŋ ꞌtèmpɹɔns ənd ꞌèksɔsnꞌɪ·z, ən ꞌtʃʃəfꞌɪnɪs. ɪn ꞌðæt ɹɪspèkt ɪt s ꞌðúnlɪ dòktə ꞌtʃɛ̀ɪnz bùk ꞌtɔ̀ùld ɪn ə ꞌnjuː ꞌwèꞌiꞌ; ən ðèə̀ ʃəd ꞌkʌm ꞌaùt ꞌsʌtʃ ə ꞌbùk ꞌəvɹɪ ꞌθə̀ꞌtɪ ꞌjə̀ːz, ꞌdɹèst ɪn ðə ꞌmòꞌùꞌd əv ðə ꞌtaìmz. ɪt s ꞌfuːhʃ, ɪn mèntèɪnɪŋ ðət ðə ꞌgaùt s ꞌnɔ̀t hɪꞌɹèdɪtɹɪ, ən ðət ꞌwʌn ꞌfɪt əv ɪt, wèn ꞌgɔ̀n, ɪz laìk ðə ꞌfiːvə wèn gɔ̀n.ꞌ—ꞌlèldɪ məꞌklaꞌuꞌd əbdʒèktɪd ðət ɔ̀ɪ ꞌɔꞌθɔ ꞌdʌznt ꞌpɹæktɪs wɔ̀t (h)iꞌ ꞌtiꞌtʃɪz. — ꞌdgɔ̀nsn̩. ꞌaɪ ꞌkaꞌnt ꞌhɔ̀lp ꞌðæt, mædəm. ꞌðæt dʌznt

Figure 2.7. Style C from *Phonetic transcriptions of English prose* (p. 28).

itself for a new writer to have two books coming out from Oxford in one year.

The transcriptions are arranged in three "styles" (see Figures 2.5, 2.6 and 2.7)—Style A "suitable for recitation or reading in public", Style B "used in careful conversation or reading aloud in private", and Style C "used in rapid conversation" (Jones 1907b: v). The differences between the styles form one of the more interesting facets of the book. Style A is a completely artificial type of English, lacking weak forms and, to an extent, vowel gradation. Style B is much more in keeping with what is expected from transcription today—even though it would be regarded as a particularly careful type of speech.

The "rapid" Style C, however, strikes the present-day reader as being almost as careful a form of pronunciation as B, and certainly not one which bears any relation to what we now consider to be rapid speech. Possibly Jones was just being ultra-cautious—and given the hostile reaction to his writing which was to come from such figures as Robert Bridges and Lascelles Abercrombie (see Section 4.11) such caution was understandable, if somewhat timid. However, another fault in the book is that Jones complicates unnecessarily the transcription systems.

The treatment of vowels for the formal Style A is illustrated by Jones with the vowel triangle shown in Figure 2.8. This is the first published example of a diagram of this sort from Jones himself (as opposed to Passy, as in the *Sounds of the French language*) and is an interesting forerunner of his later vowel quadrilaterals (see Section 7.3). The centralised vowels required for the formal transcription (Style A) are indicated by a diaresis.

Jones appeared at this time to be going through a stage when he felt that the tran-

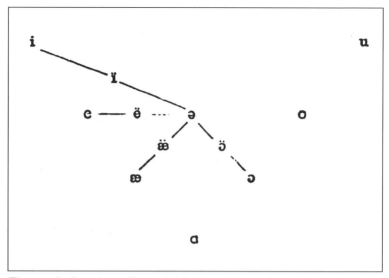

Figure 2.8. Jones's earliest published vowel diagram showing treatment of vowel gradation in "style A" (*Phonetic transcriptions of English prose*, p. vi).

scription of English as used in *Le Maître phonétique* by most IPA members was inadequate for expressing all the nuances of pronunciation he wished to see rendered. In particular, he wanted to have a means of distinguishing the quality of the vowels. Ideas on these lines are expressed in his reply to Sweet (Jones 1907e) discussed below (Section 2.10). The introduction of extra symbols is criticised by Savory (1908: 49) in his review of the book, which appeared in *Le Maître phonétique*.

> He maintains that this sound ɪ occurs in *language* and in *basket* as distinguished from the ì in *Cambridge* and in *rabbit*. In our own pronunciation the last vowels in these four words are absolutely identical.

Savory (1908: 48) also disapproves of the use of [ʍ] in Style A:

> He admits that it is purely artificial. Then why encourage the fads of elocutionists and attempt to revive a pronunciation which has disappeared from Standard English?

Furthermore, he criticises Jones's avoidance of weak forms and especially the replacement of [ə] by the semi-peripheral vowels:

> In style A a few symbols have been introduced to which certain values are given differing from those of the mf. In order to indicate a series of vowels intermediate

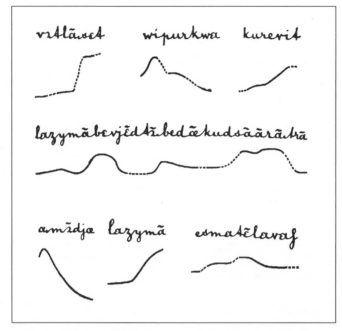

Figure 2.9. Intonation curves from *Sounds of the French language* (p. 116).

between **i** and **ə**, **e** and **ə**, **æ** and **ə** , **ɔ** and **ə**, the symbols **ï**, **ë**, **ǣ** and **ö** have been used. It is no doubt true that these vowels are sometimes heard, but in the great majority of instances where they are given in these transcriptions we should ourselves simply use **ə** even when reading aloud in public. Take for example the following sentence which the author transcribes as follows: —"ðə ˈlöːd ʃæl prɪˈzəːv ðai ˈgouiŋ ˈaut ænd ðai ˈkʌmiŋ ˈin frəm ˈðis ˈtaim ˈfɔːθ, ænd ˈiːvən fər ˈevə ˈmɔː." We have little doubt that most clergymen when reading this passage in church would say simply ʃəl, ənd, frəm, etc.

But Savory congratulates Jones on achieving "a satisfactory compromise between absolute accuracy of transcription and the obvious necessity of making it easily legible", and applauds the idea of introducing one example of a narrower transcription for each style. He also approves of Jones's indication in these narrower transcriptions of a differentiation between clear and dark-l. He describes Jones prophetically as "the rising hope of the English phonetic school, and a worthy follower in the footsteps of Ellis and Sweet" (Savory 1908: 48).

One feature of Jones's book that Savory also picks out for special mention is the treatment of intonation. This had been presaged to a certain extent by the intonation patterns shown in Savory—Jones (1907c: 116–117), which Passy states were made

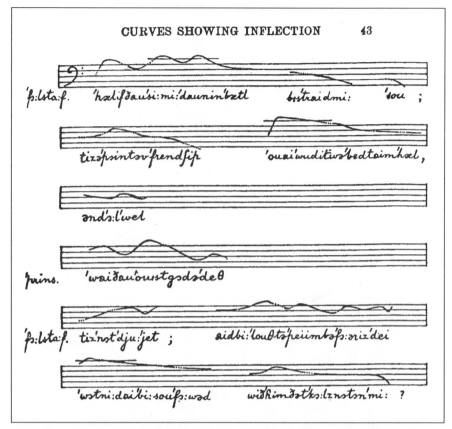

Figure 2.10. Intonation curves from *Phonetic transcriptions of English prose* (p. 43).

by "the author assisted by Miss S. Lund and Mr D. Jones" (Savory—Jones 1907c: 115). However, these earlier texts, although showing intonation by a wavy line (see Figure 2.9), made no claim to having used the objective technique of the "Curves showing Intonation" in Jones (1907b: 43–44); see Figure 2.10. The method by which he achieved the representation of the wave form of intonation is described in detail (Jones 1907b: 41):

> The pronunciation is taken from a gramophone record (No. G.C.1316 in the Gramophone Co.'s catalogue for January, 1907) made by Mr. Beerbohm Tree, the well-known actor. By lifting the needle in the middle of a voiced sound the approximate note sounded can generally be heard and the absolute pitch determined. By this means the absolute pitch of the voice in all the principal vowels and voiced consonants in the piece has been ascertained, and recorded on an ordinary

bass clef. In some cases it was found necessary to take two or even three observations of pitch in different parts of the same sound.

It is not clear whether this ingenious system was hit upon by Jones, or if he merely modified an idea of Passy's. However, it is certain that Jones developed the method successfully and took it further than Passy had done. Thanks to his gift of relative pitch, Jones was able to refine the approach into a fairly efficient means of determining intonation patterns and this was to be utilised again, and more ambitiously, for *Intonation curves* (see Section 3.3).

2.8. *Le Maître phonétique* 1907

From 1907 onwards, Jones became increasingly involved with the IPA, and with the writing and editing of *Le Maître phonétique*. In so doing he moved even closer to his mentor, Paul Passy, and this relationship was further enhanced by Jones's frequent trips to France to stay with the Motte family (see Section 4.1).

Jones's initial membership of the IPA in 1905 was followed by a period as Passy's assistant on the journal. In 1907, this was recognised in the January issue, which stated that: "notre collègue D. Jones a été adjoint à P. Passy comme rédacteur du mf. Il s'occupera spécialement de la partie anglaise et de ce qui concerne les pays de langue anglaise".[28]

Jones's own contributions to *Le Maître phonétique*, after an unimpressive start, became increasingly significant, and even by 1907 his work was much more important—in both quality and quantity—than that of any other single writer. In that year, Jones produced a total of seven articles for the journal. Several of these were short news items—for example, a report on second language teaching by a committee drawn from the Modern Language Association and two other bodies (1907g), and a short piece called "Phonetics in Scotland" (1907h). Jones also put forward a scheme for a "Diploma for Proficiency in Phonetics" to be awarded by the IPA (1907j). The article followed a suggestion of Passy's (1907d) in the previous number, and except in detail Jones's proposals were similar. One innovation that Jones proposed was that a significant proportion of the marks awarded during the examination should be allotted to the candidate on the basis of the performance in the language in which the examination was conducted—this to be other than a mother tongue. Once again we can see here the concern of Jones for the practicalities of language learning (1907j: 92):

> It may frequently happen that an Englishman knows the phonetics of French thoroughly, can pronounce all the sounds, and can read French aloud slowly with a good pronunciation, and yet in ordinary speaking falls back into many of the usual English faults.... The study of phonetics loses much of its value if its principles are not consistently put into practice, and I think that a correct pronunciation of

the ordinary spoken language ought to have considerable weight in an examination of the kind proposed.

The proposals for the certificate, with Jones's modification, but awarding fewer
marks to the pronunciation component than he had suggested, were accepted by the
IPA in 1908 and form the basis of the Certificate awarded by the Association at the
present day.[29]

2.9. Henry Sweet

In Britain, at this time the major force in phonetics was undoubtedly Henry Sweet
(1845–1912), who was not only an influence on Jones through his writing, but also
known to Jones in person. With one exception—namely Passy—Sweet was the greatest single inspiration on Jones's view of phonetics.

Sweet was of Scottish ancestry, though only on his mother's side. Like Jones, he
was the son of a London barrister, and was born and raised in the capital. Though he
spent his youth in business, when he was nineteen, he went to Heidelberg University
for a short time. There he first encountered the systematic and scholarly approach
which the Germans were developing towards language study (see A.4). Initially,
Sweet appears to have been attracted to the German style of linguistics, though later
his enthusiasm waned and he became positively opposed to it. It was in this early stage
of his life that Wrenn ([1966]: 514) believes that Sweet must have discovered the
work of Melville Bell, which "first showed him the thrilling scientific possibilities of
the accurate recording of the facts of spoken language". Sweet was proud of the fact
that he "studied practically under Mr. Bell himself" and that he had discussed "doubtful points" with both Bell and Ellis (Sweet 1877: ix).

Sweet's whole life was stormy, and erratic, and probably no academic can ever have
had such a strange undergraduate career. He was relatively old, twenty-four, when he
went up to Oxford and entered Balliol. Even in his freshman year he managed to publish a seminal article in the *Transactions of the Philological Society* (Sweet 1869).
During 1873, the year in which he came down from Oxford, he began writing his
impressive series of phonetic/phonological descriptions of a number of European
languages. Amazingly, he left Oxford with the ignominy of a fourth class degree—the
"beginning of that series of academic disappointments and rebuffs which…had their
effect on Sweet's later work" (Wrenn [1966]: 516).

Yet within a few years he had produced several philological publications of primary
significance, and then wrote *A handbook of phonetics* (Sweet 1877)—his first and,
many would contend, his best, work on the subject. Today the *Handbook* still
reads with a freshness and lucidity uncommon in a publication more than a century
old. The phonetic description is a marked advance on Bell, both in terms of accuracy
and in the efficiency of its organisation, as Kelly and Local (1984: 8) have demonstrated:

A glance at the contents page of, say, *Visible speech* and the *Handbook* of ten years later (covering much the same ground), throws these differences into relief. Bell's "Contents" includes "Voiced Consonants" as an entry, but not voiceless ones, includes "Shut Consonants" but no "Open Consonants" or anything that might be construed as the converse of "Shut". And there is no systematic listing of laryngeal or air-stream mechanism activities. Sweet's contents page is much more systematic and consistent than this, presenting a ground-plan for presentation and discussion that many later textbooks have taken as a model. Sweet also places phonetics firmly within the academic study of language and languages, and attempts the difficult task of codifying...all then known about phonetics.

Such codification is, though, much more than a simple *mise au point*, including a lot of improvement and innovation. Improvement takes place on the basis of use and experiment, both in the matter of the design of the symbols and in the details of phonetic analysis.

Kelly and Local go on to show how "Sweet also adds to theory, filling out gaps", giving as an example his treatment of lip-posture, where he introduces "outer rounding" to provide an opposition to Bell's earlier "inner rounding". Sweet also brings in the concepts of "over-rounding" as against "under-rounding", deriving these last from work he had undertaken on Swedish (Sweet 1879).

Wrenn's ([1966]: 517) judgement, borrowed from C.T. Onions, that the book "taught phonetics to Europe and made England the birthplace of the modern science" is perhaps chauvinistic, but also contains some truth.[30] Instrumental phonetics had made considerable advances in Germany and France (see A.4 and A.5); but the presentation of articulatory phonetics in Sweet's (1877) *Handbook*, by virtue of a combination of novel phonetic insights and the clarity of the exposition of the material Sweet had derived from Bell, provided a methodological framework of description which had previously been lacking. The book also won its author a measure of fame in continental Europe (particularly in Germany) of a kind which had not come the way of Ellis, Pitman, Melville Bell, or any previous British linguist. Indeed, it can fairly be said that Henry Sweet awakened the minds of many people—in Britain, continental Europe and elsewhere—to the very existence of phonetics.

Sweet devised two alphabets which he termed "Romic" (see Figure 2.11) because the letters are merely those of the normal Roman alphabet, albeit capitalised, italicised, turned or raised; he derived the scheme largely from the work of Ellis (see A.3). Kelly and Local (1984: 8) claim that Sweet's "final achievement" was "to produce, out of Bell's diffuse and unwieldy alphabet, a device which allows the linguistic phonetician to make truly impressionistic records"; but they ignore the fact that Sweet's work was based largely on Ellis, and that Sweet returned to a Bell-type organic alphabet in later work (for Jones's views, see below).

The transcription in the *Handbook* is vitally important in one other respect. Through it, Sweet actually identifies the kernel of the phoneme concept (although he does not employ the term itself). Referring to the broad version of Romic transcription, Sweet (1877: 103) says that "in treating of a single language, it is necessary to have an alphabet which indicates only those broader distinctions of sound which actually correspond to distinctions of meaning in language". Sweet's part in the discovery of the phoneme principle appears to have gone unrecognised for many years, and it was thanks largely to Jones's (1957a) *History and meaning of the term "phoneme"* that Sweet's importance in early phoneme theorising was recognised by modern linguists (to cite but one, S. Anderson 1985: 172–173).

---

1. *In Narrow Romic.*

1. kɛmɛ·pʌt ·wɛns \

2. : dhise¹zdhʌ ·thæhɪɪd .tehɪhɪmeh·ɪhv ª hæhɪdʌve¹zre¹ tæhɪɪn \

3. – hɪj ᵇ dɛznts·ɪɪjmtʌ (·)fiɪjle¹tʌ (·)tɔɪl \ ᶜ

4. hɪɪʌrʌn ᵈ dhæɪʌrʌn ·evɪre¹wh·æɪʌ \

5. – dheɪh ·keɪɪhm bækdhʌ ᵉ seɪɪhm deɪɪh \

6. – dhʌ mænɪɯh·æddhʌ ·hætɪʌnɪhz hedɪ \

7. kɔkɪne¹z sɛmɪt·ehɪhɪmz ·feɪɪhltʌdɪhs tiɑɪgwe¹shbʌ twiɪjndhʌ ·¹hæɪɪrʌndheʌ hedɪzʌndhe¹ ·¹æɪɪʌwɪj brɪɪjdh \

8. – dhʌ ·boɪhɪ aɪs(k)te¹z faɪɪdhʌre¹fɪj wɯdntr·aɪdhʌ goo¹ʌl·ɪtl faɪɪdhʌ \

9. – behɪh ·ɔɪl miɪjnz sedɪe¹zpʌ paɪɪ \ – ehɪhm ·kwehɪht rede¹ \

2. *The same in English Broad Romic.*

1. kəmə·pət ·wəns \

2. : dhisezdhə ·thəəd taima·iv həədəvezre təən \

3. – hiy dəznts·iymtə fiyletə taol \

4. hiiərən dhaerən ·evrewhaeə \

5. – dhei keim bækdhə seim dei \

6. – dhə mænuh·æddhə ·hætənez hed \

7. koknez səmt·aimz ·feiltədes tiqgweshbə twiyndhə ·¹haerəndheʌ hedzəndhe ·¹aeəwiy briydh \

8. – dhə boi aas(k)tez faadhərefiy wudntr·aadhə gouə litl faadhə \

9. – bai ·aol miynz sedezpə paa \ – aim ·kwait rede \

Figure 2.11. Narrow Romic and Broad Romic as shown in Sweet's (1877) *Handbook of phonetics* (pp. 113, 114).

Sweet firmly believed that any study of a language demanded a thorough *practical* knowledge of its grammatical structure and, especially, of its phonetics and phonology. In the phrase he frequently employed, and with which he opens the *Handbook*, Sweet (1877: v) termed phonetics (by which he meant *articulatory* phonetics) "the indispensable foundation of all study of language—whether that study be purely theoretical, or practical". Sweet thought, furthermore, that a competent phonetician should have heard from the lips of a native speaker all the sounds he attempted to describe, and indeed should be able to imitate these sounds to the satisfaction of a native listener. This reverence for practical abilities of observation and imitation was part of Sweet's phonetic philosophy which he was to hand on to Daniel Jones.

Sweet is also widely regarded as being peculiarly brilliant at the practical phonetic skills. However, these should not perhaps be overestimated, and there is something of a tendency to regard Sweet as a genius whose talents knew no bounds. In fact, some of his phonetic statements about individual languages can appear questionable—as will be seen, for instance, from a close examination of his work on Dutch.[31]

For over fifteen years, Sweet allowed his handbook to remain as his only long work on phonetics, while he got on with other projects. However, the phonetics section of the *Elementarbuch des gesprochenen Englisch* (Sweet 1885a), a short textbook aimed at German students of English, contained some advances on the *Handbook*. The *Elementarbuch* focussed on the pronunciation of English rather than dealing with a wider theory of phonetics (MacMahon 1991: 16). In it, for example, Sweet introduced his economical but effective system of indicating a simple model of intonation by using angled marks before the stressed syllables—a method of showing pitch which was afterwards incorporated into the IPA alphabet. Sweet's intonation marking can also be seen as the ancestor of the systems used in the British school of intonation analysis by Palmer (1922) and his later successors such as Kingdon (1958a) and O'Connor and Arnold (1961). The *Elementarbuch* with its emphasis on the importance of the colloquial language, and its large number of transcribed passages of conversational English, was in advance of its time as a language textbook.

Later, at the turn of the century, Sweet was to follow it up with an elaboration of his views on language teaching, first promulgated in a paper to the Philological Society (Sweet 1885b) and later published in book form. The book, containing a large section on applied articulatory phonetics and pronunciation training, was entitled *The practical study of languages* (Sweet 1899). Jones (1912i: 98) regarded it highly—a judgement in part confirmed by Oxford University Press's decision to reprint the original text virtually unchanged as part of an applied linguistics series in 1962. Sweet's main emphasis throughout is the necessity to concentrate on the modern form of the colloquial language with an overt use of phonetics for pronunciation. In fact, though much of the book is now dated, Sweet's pungent attacks on the language teaching practices of his era, and his suggested alternatives, make stimulating—and often entertaining—reading even today.

His second manual, *A primer of phonetics* (Sweet 1890a) was largely an updating of the *Handbook*; yet it also incorporated many changes, partly as a result of Sweet's

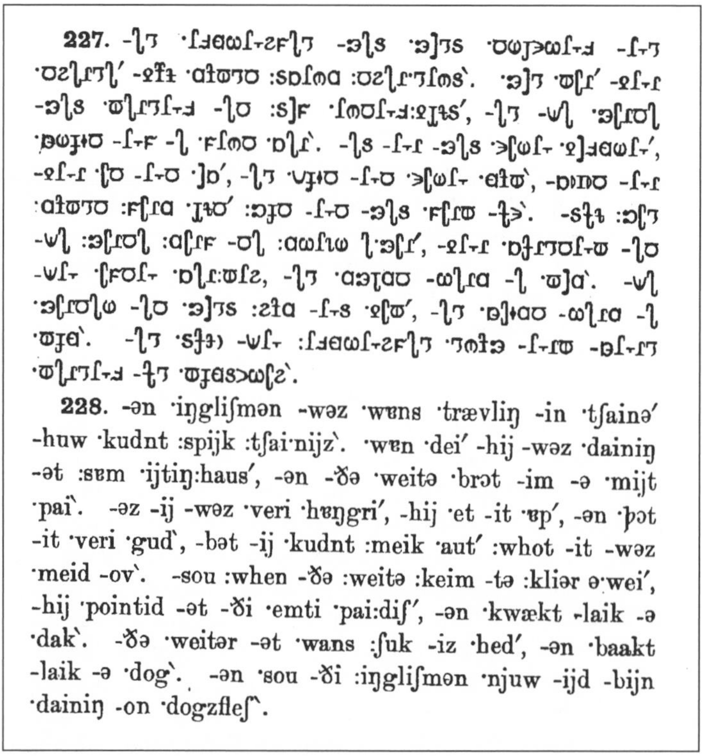

227. -ᒪ ·ꝑᗡᗯᒪᶘᴈꜰᒪ -ᴈᒪꜱ ·ᴈ]ꜱ ·ᴐᗯᶲᗯᒪᶘ -ᒪᶘ ·ᴐᴢᒪᒥᒪ' -ᴈ�??↓ ·ᴀᶒᗯᴈᴐ :ꜱᴐᒪᗯᴀ :ᴐᴢᒪᒥᴈᒪᗯꜱ' ·ᴈ]ᒪ ·ᗯᒪ' -ᴈᒪᶘ -ᴈᒪꜱ ·ᗯᒪᒥᴈᒪᶘ -ᒪᴐ :ꜱ]ꜰ ·ᒪᗯᴐᒪᶘᴈᴢᒪꜱ' -ᒪᒪ -ᗯᒪ ·ᴈᒪᴀᒪ ·ᴃᗯᶘᴀᴐ -ᒪᶘꜰ -ᒪ ·ꜰᒪᗯᴐ ·ᴐᒪᒥ' -ᒪꜱ -ᒪᶘᒥ -ᴈᒪꜱ ·ᴈᒑᗯᒪᶘ ·ᴈ]ᴈᴀᗯᒪᶘ' -ᴈᒪᶘᒥ ·ᒑᴀ -ᒪᶘᴀ ·ᒑᴀ' -ᒪᒪ ·ᴠᒑᴀᴀ -ᒪᶘᴀ ·ᴈᒑᗯᒪᶘ ·ᴀᶒᗯ' -ᴀᴐᴀᴀᴐ -ᒪᶘᒪ :ᴀᶒᗯᴐ :ꜰᒪᴀᴀ ·ᒑᴀᴀᴐ' :ᴀᒑᴐ -ᒪᴀ -ᴈᒪꜱ ꜰᒪᗯᗯ -ᶘᴈ〉 -ꜱᴀᶘ↓ :ᴀᒪᒪ -ᗯᒪ :ᴈᒑᴀᴐᒪ :ᴀᒑꜰꜰ -ᴐᒪ :ᴀᗯᶒᒪᗯ ᒪᴈᒑᒪꜰ' -ᴈᒪᶘᶘ ·ᴐᒑᒥᒪᴐᒪᴀᴐ -ᒪᴐ -ᗯᒪᶘ ·ᒑꜰᴐᒪᶘ ·ᴐᒑ:ᗯᒪᴢ -ᒪᒪ ·ᴀᴈᒑᴀᴀ -ᗯᒪᒑᴀ -ᒪ ·ᗯᒑᴐ' -ᗯᒪ ·ᴈᒑᴐᒪᗯ -ᒪᴐ ·ᴈ]ᴈꜱ :ᴈᶒᴀ -ᒪᶘꜱ ·ᴈᴐᴀ' -ᒪᒪ ·ᴃᒪᴀᴀᴐ -ᗯᒪᴐᴀ -ᒪ ·ᴀᒑᴀ' -ᒪᒪ ·ꜱᶘᴈᴀ -ᗯᒪᶘ :ᒪᗡᴀᴐᒪᶘᴈꜰᒪᒪ ᵔᴀᶒᒑᴀ -ᒪᶘᗯ -ᴈᒪᶘᒪᒪ ·ᗯᒪᒥᴈᒪᶘᴈ -ᶘᒪᒪ ·ᗯᒑᴀꜱᵡᗯᒪᴢ'.

228. -ən ·iŋglifmən -wəz ·wɐns ·trævliŋ -in ·tʃainə'
-huw ·kudnt :spijk :tʃai·nijz'. ·wɐn ·dei' -hij -wəz ·dainiŋ
-ət :sɐm ·ijtiŋ:haus', -ən -ðə ·weitə ·brɔt -im -ə ·mijt
·pai'. -əz -ij -wəz ·veri ·hɐŋgri', -hij ·et -it ·ɐp', -ən ·pɔt
-it ·veri ·gud', -bət -ij ·kudnt :meik ·aut' :whot -it -wəz
·meid -ov'. -sou :when -ðə :weitə :keim -tə :kliər ə·wei',
-hij ·pointid -ət -ði ·emti ·pai:dif', -ən ·kwækt -laik -ə
·dak'. -ðə ·weitər -ət ·wans :fuk -iz ·hed', -ən ·baakt
-laik -ə ·dog'. -ən ·sou -ði :iŋglifmən ·njuw -ijd -bijn
·dainiŋ -on ·dogzfleʃ'.

Figure 2.12. The Organic Alphabet and Broad Romic as shown in
Sweet's (1890a) *Primer of Phonetics* (p. 82).

reading of German phonetic work—which he regarded as "indigestible" (Sweet
1890a: v) but could ill afford to ignore. Throughout his career, Sweet had ambivalent
feelings towards the German linguists, despising their predilection for what he called
"'paper phonetics'—getting up phonetics by reading the statements of others and
attempting to harmonise their conflicting views". Nevertheless, he acknowledged the
value of the sheer scale of late nineteenth-century German linguistics, and the industry
of German scholars—compared with what Sweet saw as the general apathy towards
language study in his own country.

The *Primer* is written largely around the "Organic Alphabet" (see Figure 2.12)
which Sweet had derived from Bell's Visible Speech. Jones (1912i: 98) has pointed
out that this acted as a deterrent to his readers, because of the obvious difficulty of
coping with the alphabet as a transcription system. On the other hand, Jones saw
Sweet's "Broad Romic" (see Figure 2.12) as a major achievement in the development
of phonetics (see Section 4.8).

Sweet produced one more elementary handbook, *The sounds of English* (1908),
which returned to the more simplified approach of the *Handbook*, contained no organic alphabet transcription, and concentrated on the English sound system. It proved

successful, but was soon overshadowed by Jones's (1909b) own less accurate but more easily understood *Pronunciation of English*. A final significant contribution was the article "Phonetics" in the *Encyclopaedia Britannica* (Sweet 1911), regarded today as a classic summary of the views of the time. In addition, Sweet wrote more advanced works, such as his *History of English sounds from the earliest period* (1874) and his *New English grammar* (1892b; 1898), which contained sizable sections on phonetics and phonology.

Sweet was (together with Viëtor and Passy) an early and active member of the Phonetic Teachers' Association, which later developed into the International Phonetic Association (see Section 2.3); eventually Sweet became its Honorary President. It is noteworthy that it was Broad Romic which formed the basis of the IPA alphabet. Sweet used *Le Maître phonétique* from 1900 onwards as his mouthpiece in a series of short articles on a variety of phonetic topics.

One further link between Sweet and the earlier British tradition is to be seen in the system of "Current Shorthand", which he invented. Sweet had hoped that this would be taken up by the general public and make him rich. Bernard Shaw (1916: 101–102) points out in his "Preface" to Pygmalion that whilst Sweet's system is probably the most efficient shorthand ever invented for English, Pitman nevertheless completely dominated the market. A critique of Sweet's shorthand is to be found in MacMahon (1981).

Although Sweet was regarded by Jones as a "slow worker" (see Section 4.8), few can ever have equalled him in terms of sheer quantity of academic output (even though, like many other academics, he was not averse to using the same, or slightly altered, material in two or more publications). Sweet realised quite well that he was Britain's—indeed the world's—leading linguist, and not just in one but many specialist areas. To quote Henderson (Sweet [1971]: ix), he was: "a brilliant phonetician, a highly distinguished comparative and historical linguist, a perspicacious grammarian, an eminent Anglicist, the inventor of an excellent system of shorthand, and a passionate advocate of spelling reform; and his work in any one of these fields was enriched through his knowledge of the others." See MacMahon (1991) for an assessment of Sweet's overall contribution to the development of phonetics.

Sweet's lack of recognition by British university authorities contrasted starkly with the glitter of his reputation abroad. Many would agree with Henderson's judgement that "as an all-round linguist, Sweet has seldom been equalled and never surpassed"; yet, ironically, because he could find no university post, this truly exceptional linguistic scholar was forced for many years to exist on what he could earn as a freelance author and private teacher. But this undoubtedly forced him to concentrate on writing. Indeed, it is interesting to speculate how different Sweet's publication record might have looked if his 1885 attempt to obtain the Merton College Chair of English had been successful and he had subsequently been forced to cope with the workload of teaching and administration this would have entailed. After another unsuccessful bid for a chair in 1901, Oxford offered a kind of consolation prize in the form of a readership—which, with reluctance, Sweet accepted.

The lack of any proper recognition of his talents was probably the most telling factor in Sweet's embittered isolation, which developed virtually into a form of persecution mania in the years before his death in 1912.

2.10. Jones's first encounters with Sweet

It was at this point, in the last decade of Sweet's life, when he was generally regarded as quite unapproachable, that the young Jones encountered Henry Sweet in person for the first time. He has described the circumstances thus:

> I first met him at a Vacation Course in Edinburgh about 1907, shortly after I had made up my mind (on the advice of Passy) to make my career in phonetics.[32]

The course was organised by John Kirkpatrick, "a very capable man...extremely keen on promoting modern methods of language teaching, including the use of phonetics", who had invited Viëtor, Passy and Sweet "in order that his course should be as up-to-date as possible".[33] It was apparently rumoured that Kirkpatrick was so keen to have this distinguished trio on his courses that he paid them out of his own pocket. Passy probably suggested Jones for the course, since he had also taught on it two years earlier when he, too, had been impressed by Kirkpatrick's efficiency. Passy (1905: 109) had sat in on Sweet's lectures, which had allowed him to renew their personal contact:

> Les conférences de phonétique anglaise...était faites par Sweet lui-même; j'espère en avoir bien profité, ainsi que des conversations assez prolongées que j'ai eues avec ce maître de la science.

Passy also notes here that Sweet's readings from Chaucer and Shakespeare in reconstructed pronunciation of the periods were particularly interesting.

Jones went to Edinburgh (together with Douglas Savory) "in the capacity of a junior teacher, conducting practical classes for some of the students.... Of course we junior teachers all attended the lectures of the great phoneticians." Jones, like Passy, clearly enjoyed the course—notwithstanding the fact that he later, in the Paris Lecture (see Section 4.6), recorded his surprise that so many foreigners went to Scotland to learn standard English. Later, Jones and Savory were to give the main lectures on English and French themselves. His experience of the Edinburgh vacation courses must have been a factor in inducing Jones to start his own highly successful vacation courses in London (see Sections 10.3 and 14.4).[34]

Unlike Passy, Jones was quite unimpressed with Sweet's lectures:

> He was not at all a good lecturer to an audience consisting largely of beginners. I verily believe that Savory & I were the only two people in that audience of some 200 who really understood everything he said.... He was very short-sighted. His lecture notes were written (in the "Current Shorthand" which he invented) on tiny

6. At the end of his schooldays

7. William Tilly

8. Paul Passy's house at Bourg-la-Reine

9. Henri Motte in old age

10. Paul Passy (1901)

11. Pin Ginko as it was when Jones first arrived in France

bits of paper which he had to hold close to his eyes. (In the last year or two of his life he became nearly if not completely blind.)[35]

Despite their initial disappointment with the reality of a man who was a legend in his own time, Jones and Savory both nevertheless later made arrangements to have private lessons from the great phonetician. These were to show Sweet in a far better light and would provide a valuable point of contact between the two men. See also Section 4.8.

Jones makes no mention of Sweet's giving readings in Chaucerian and Shakespearean English, and so it cannot be established that Sweet was a stimulus to Jones in extending his own research into these areas; however, like Sweet, Jones went on to develop an ability to recite Chaucer and Shakespeare in the original pronunciation (see Section 3.2).

Daniel Jones's article "Simplified phonetic spelling" (Jones 1907e) is a polite rejoinder to two pieces which Sweet (1906a; 1906b) had published in *Le Maître phonétique*. Sweet had advocated a modification of the IPA alphabet in order "to face the problem of popularising phonetic spelling not among enthusiasts, but among the lazy and prejudiced majority" (Sweet 1906b: 127). Sweet was in favour of simplifying the system and removing certain letter shapes which were, in his view, unpleasant, such as the "unmeaning and unwritable ʌ" and the "ugly and unwritable ø". Many of his points, such as the lack of a symbol for an open central vowel and the excessive influence of French on the scheme of the IPA alphabet, are reasonable—even if overstated in immoderate terms. His main concern was to provide systems of transcription for languages, in particular for English, which would conform to what would today be termed phonemic principles, and which excluded superfluous information of a phonetic nature. To this end, Sweet distinguished between alphabets of a "practical" and "scientific" type, saying that he was only concerning himself with the former (Sweet 1906b: 125).

Jones, bravely for a young phonetician at the start of his career, chose to engage in argument with the irascible IPA President. Sweet had a point, Jones (1907e: 37) conceded, if simplified systems of spelling for individual languages were considered, but that was not the purpose of the IPA alphabet, which was intended as an international system.

> It would certainly be an excellent thing in many ways for each language to have its separate phonetic alphabet, but is it not the principal aim of the a.f. ["association phonétique", i.e. the IPA] rather to devise an alphabet which can be used without modification for any language?

Jones says that he feels that the transcription of English used in *Le Maître phonétique* "had been simplified more than was desirable", and that in particular he felt the need of a pair of symbols for "lax ì, ù" (i.e. ɪ and ʊ). He goes on (p. 38):

> The use of **i, u** to denote lax ì, ù in English has another disadvantage; it often

reduces the symbols **ː, j, w** merely to the position of diacritics. Thus we write the English words "beat" and "bid" as **biːt** or **bijt** and **bid** respectively, while in reality the vowels in the two words are of about equal length, and the vowel in "beat" is so short that there is hardly time for it to be diphthongised by those who would diphthongise the vowel in **hij**. I think it is a recognised principle that in general we ought not to use diacritics except on occasions where special nicety is required. If the shades of sound are sufficiently distinct to be noted at all in a practical international alphabet, separate symbols ought to be provided.

In all, Jones provided a well thought-out mild rebuff to Sweet, and undoubtedly in so doing pleased Passy, who had written a rather more strongly worded response to Sweet in the same issue (Passy 1907b). It is interesting, however, to see Jones writing in these terms, since his later views on transcription of English is similar in many ways to the opinions Sweet expresses here (see Section 14.9).

2.11. "Implosives and clicks" and the Organic Alphabet

In this productive year, Jones wrote two articles of more theoretical content. "French b, d, g" (Jones 1907k) considers the voicing of stop consonants in French as opposed to English, but provides little in the way of novelty. Jones's main concern was to show that the difference was not one of "voiced on-glide" in French as opposed to "breathed on-glide" in English but the precise point at which voicing began. However, as Jones himself had to admit, "there is nothing new in all this" (p. 95).

"Implosive sounds and clicks" (Jones 1907m) is of greater interest, with Jones exploring territory which was inadequately charted at this time—namely sounds produced on non-pulmonic airstreams. Sounds of this type are mentioned by A. Melville Bell (1867: 62) and discussed cursorily by Sweet (1877: 54–55, 78); Sweet mentions that he has derived his information partly from Merkel (1866: 149).

Jones introduces his subject in characteristically practical style (p. 111).

The subject of the so-called implosive sounds and clicks forms an interesting branch of phonetic science, which, owing no doubt to the fact that these sounds do not form an integral part of the most important languages, does not seem to have been dealt with at any length in the textbooks on phonetics. Practising the various possible implosive sounds and clicks, however, is a most valuable exercise for obtaining control over various parts of the organs of speech...

Jones surveys the various articulatory possibilities, firstly classifying pulmonic sounds as "normal" or "inverse"—presumably meaning by the latter term what are nowadays called implosives. Jones may have misunderstood the part played by the larynx in the formation of these sounds, but, more likely, was confused by the terminology current at the time (Abercrombie, personal communication). The remaining sounds are categorised thus: "When compression and suction are produced by organs other than the lungs, the sounds producible are called *implosive sounds* and *clicks* respectively" (p. 111). The categorisation is muddled since it would appear from his description that by "implosive" Jones means what would nowadays be termed an ejective, i.e. a sound produced on a glottalic egressive air-stream mechanism (Catford 1968: 312–318). The inappropriate term appears to have been derived from Sweet, see above.

Jones goes on (p. 112):

> In the production of this implosive p, the lips are closed, the glottis is closed and the soft palate is raised to its fullest extent, so that the air which is enclosed in the mouth, pharynx and upper part of the larynx cannot escape. The larynx is then slightly raised. This compresses the air enclosed in the mouth etc., and on opening the lips, the glottis remaining closed and the soft palate raised, this air escapes with an explosive sound resembling a p. If on the other hand the larynx be lowered, the air in the cavity is slightly rarefied, and on opening the lips air must enter the mouth from outside, thus producing the corresponding click.

By "click", Jones here intends a voiceless implosive. But Jones's terminology confuses his description; he cannot be blamed, of course, for not conforming with modern usage but nevertheless it is illogical that a so-called implosive should result in "an explosive sound".

The article continues to discuss what would today be termed velaric ingressive and egressive air-stream mechanisms—clicks and "reverse clicks". Whilst Jones accurately describes the mechanisms of these sound types, and also mentions the lateral click of Xhosa (termed at this date "Kaffir"), the article leaves the impression of a confusing mixture of phonetic fact and much speculation. It must be remembered, of course, that Jones at this time had little reliable previous work to build on and furthermore had no instrumental resources, or for that matter, informants who spoke languages containing the sounds he is attempting to describe. The article has to be judged as an early attempt to describe what has always been a problematical area in phonetics. It was not until the studies of Doke (1926) and Beach (1938) that reliable data on click languages were obtained. Later, the work of Catford (1939, 1947, 1964, 1968) and Pike (1943) was to bring the classification of air-stream mechanisms and phonation types together into a reasonable model. It is noteworthy that three of the scholars involved, i.e. all except Pike, were pupils of Daniel Jones.

The article is also an early sign of Jones's curiosity concerning sound types other than those found in European languages—thus pointing the way to his research work on African, Indian and Far Eastern languages which was to begin shortly. This research interest was perhaps aroused by work which Jones did in connection with another 1907 publication, "Alphabet phonétique organique" (Passy—Jones 1907d).

Though the organic alphabet was published as a supplement to the November-December issue of *Le Maître phonétique* (see Figures 2.13 and 2.14), it appears to have been distributed earlier with the May-June number, which also contained an

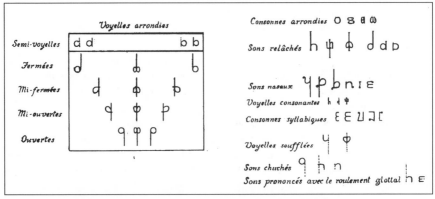

Figure 2.13. The Passy—Jones Organic Alphabet (Supplement to *Le Maître phonétique* 1907).

article by Passy (1907c) explaining how the alphabet had been produced. Apart from providing the background information to the particular publication, Passy indicates regard for the young Jones: "un vrai phonétiste (en tout cas futur)".

Passy had been interested at one time in Bell's organic alphabet, Visible Speech, and in the successor to this produced by Sweet (see Section 2.9 and A.3), and had been in correspondence with Sweet on the subject. Passy wished to design an alphabet which preserved as far as possible the shapes of the Roman letters, but redistributed their shapes on a more logical basis, taking account of articulatory features "à son semblable, signe semblable" (p. 56). Though he had developed the idea to some extent, Passy says "mon alphabet n'a jamais vu la lumière" (p. 56). Few people knew of its existence when Passy mentioned the alphabet "presque par hazard" to Jones in 1906 (p. 57). Jones's curiosity was aroused and Passy dug up his papers and the two men examined them together.

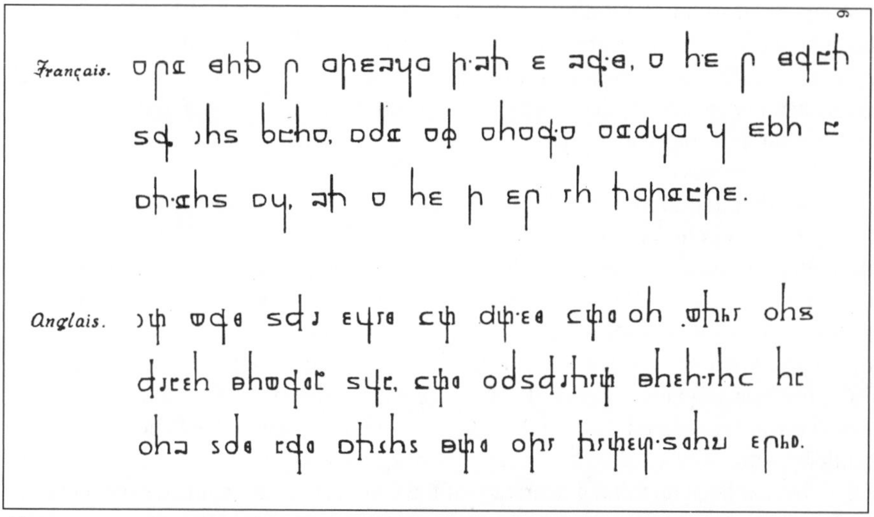

Figure 2.14. Samples of French and English in the Passy—Jones Organic Alphabet.

Most of the revision work was done by Jones (p. 57):

Il m'a signalé des défauts et des lacunes… bref, nous nous sommes mis ensemble à le réviser, ou plutôt Jones l'a révisé en se servant de quelques-unes de mes indications.

Jones seems to have been forced to abandon Passy's idea of forming an alphabet entirely on Roman letter shapes, but what emerged did retain far more of the feeling of familiar letter forms than either Bell's or Sweet's systems, and it would undoubtedly have been easier to write—which was Passy's main aim.

On its appearance as a supplement, Jones attempted to teach with the alphabet for a year, but realising the inherent limitations of such systems thereafter abandoned it for good. Abercrombie (1983: 5) wrote: "[The organic alphabet] was hardly ever heard of again. I never heard Jones talk about it." The alphabet, as it appeared in the supplement, is reproduced as Figure 2.13 together with samples of French and English written in its characters (Figure 2.14).

2.12. Provost Gregory Foster

The years immediately after Jones's appointment at University College were ones of furious activity. Jones was still living at his family home in Wimbledon and travelling into London each day—repeating the tedious journey, in fact, that he had complained about when he was a schoolboy at University College School, though presumably without the long walk that had been imposed on him by his father. He had to cope with his teaching—phonetics was in great demand and he had no shortage of students—and find time for his publishing activities. This aspect of his work grew steadily in importance; Jones has himself said: "Ever since 1907, and especially after my marriage in 1911, I devoted much time to the writing of books" (Jones 1926e: 398).

From the initial insecurity of 1907, Jones's position at University College gained strength. He was lucky in starting there at a time when University College was going through a period of expansion under its first Provost, T. Gregory Foster. Foster had taken charge of the College in 1904, as "Principal"; in 1906, Foster became the first person to have the new title of "Provost". His connection with the college dated from the 1880s when he enrolled as a student. All through his life he was connected with UCL in some way; his loyalty to the College and his determination for it to grow and develop were renowned. As a student, he had been President of the Union; for a short while he worked as a master at University College School, and before becoming Principal, he had been appointed Secretary of the College. He maintained excellent relations both with the staff and the students. His correspondence with Jones indicates that the two men had a warm regard for each other. Foster was to remain at UCL until 1929, by which time the Phonetics Department was well established. It has been said of him: "Gregory Foster was very largely responsible for founding the twentieth- as distinct from the nineteenth-century College" (Harte—North 1978: 131) and in no academic area was this more true than in phonetics. Foster was also an able organiser and decision maker who "endowed the College with an administrative machine capable of handling the larger problems spelt by an increase of income from £29,000 in 1902 to upwards of £188,000 in 1927".[36]

It was Daniel Jones's good fortune that Gregory Foster was a man who was not a mere cold-blooded administrator but someone who saw problems in human terms. It has been written of him that "the really striking thing about him was the way that he projected his essential humanity" and that this was returned in the "warm affection of successive generations of students" (D. Taylor 1968: 29). It needed a man of Foster's humanity, insight and intellectual security to appoint a young man with few qualifications to teach a subject which was in its infancy in Britain. Jones himself has said: "Fortunately the value of phonetics was recognized by that great and far-seeing administrator Dr (afterwards Sir) Gregory Foster, who was Provost of the College at that time, and through his encouragement and help assistance was gradually provided" (Jones 1948f [1973]: 181). Foster was to make it possible for Jones to found his Department and acquire the staff he needed; he was later to ensure that Jones achieved professorial status.

The climate in University College was favourable in other ways as well. Late in the nineties, the college had been subjected to a "treasury inspection", which had determined that "it was a place of learning of some considerable prestige and tradition" dedicated to maintaining high levels of achievement in academic work: "In no college has the advancement of knowledge for its own sake as the ideal of University work been more distinctly kept in view" (D. Taylor 1968: 33–34). Money began to flow in to University College in the early years of the century, from both government and private sources (Bennot 1929: 412–413). Furthermore, the College was expanding physically; in 1907, Daniel Jones's old school, University College School, moved out from its premises within the Gower Street building to a new site at Frognal in Hampstead, thus freeing a considerable amount of space for the university departments (Harte—North 1978: 132–133). Over three decades, Gower Street was to have its peace constantly shattered by the racket of construction teams cramming new buildings into what was rapidly turning into the most over-crowded corner of Bloomsbury, and the official early history of the College devotes several pages to the detail of the additions and alterations (Bennot 1929: 408–412). A more recent history of the College (Harte—North 1978: 144) summarises the main changes of the period:

> Between the 1890s and the 1920s, the expansion in the College's activities was matched by striking developments in the buildings…. First the Front Quadrangle was closed in by the new buildings added to the North and South Wings and fronting on to Gower Street—Engineering, Architecture and Statistics. Secondly, Physics, Chemistry, Physiology, Pharmacology and Anatomy began the process whereby the larger science departments moved out of the original building into more generous quarters on the periphery, leaving the main building for the most part to the Library, administration and Arts.

At University College, Jones seemed to have what was needed for a man of ambition wishing to start a new discipline in a university. He had an ample supply of students who were interested in the subject. There were funds available for expansion—if they could be tapped. Space would always be a problem, but the new science buildings held out at least a promise of vacated accommodation being available in the future. Perhaps most important of all, he had Gregory Foster, who had taken a liking to him and who was enthusiastic about the possibilities for what could be presented to the world as the new science of phonetics.

Of course, phonetics was not new. And it is also questionable whether it is correct to use the term "science" of British phonetics at this period. Even though, in Germany, France and the USA, phonetics was beginning to be regarded as more of a scientific discipline (see A.3, A.4 and A.5), this was not at all true of Britain. Phonetics was still considered as allied more closely to elocution and speech training, in the tradition of Sheridan, Walker and Bell (Sections A.2 and A.3). For example, in UCL phonetics was placed as a matter of course in the Faculty of Arts since it originally functioned mainly as a service section to the language departments, especially French, German and English. It is noticeable that although Jones refers to "phonetic science" in his scholarly writing (as in Jones 1907m, quoted above, Section 2.11), in his initial period at UCL, he tended to understate the scientific aspect of the subject—perhaps by inclination, but more probably at this stage because he saw that his future lay in teaching students who were primarily interested in the humanities. This can also be detected in the *Pronunciation of English*¹, where a definition of phonetics as a science is notably absent. By 1911, however, Jones had set up his first laboratory (Section 5.10), and by the time he was writing the *Outline* (largely completed by 1914, see Section 8.2), he defined phonetics clearly as "the science of pronunciation, the science which investigates the mode of formation of speech sounds and their distribution in connected speech" (*Outline*¹: 1 n.).

During the 1907–08 Session, Jones consolidated his position at University College. The minutes of the College Committee show that he was re-appointed, on a temporary basis, "to deliver courses of lectures on General Phonetic Theory and on English and French Phonetics during the Session 1908–09".[37] In 1908, his post was renewed again, this time "for a further period of three years from September 1st, 1909".[38] He now had the necessary security for planning and developing his professional life.

Chapter 3

Early years at University College London (1908–10)

3.1. Teaching at University College 1908–09

In the 1908–09 session, Jones again taught on the same two evenings of the week
—Monday and Thursday—as he had the previous session but now managed to fit
in as many as seven advertised courses. In the first two terms, he taught an elementary course on English phonetics aimed at foreign students; in the third term this
was replaced by a course on English for English native speakers. Jones's conviction
of the importance of ear-training and performance was already apparent. "Each
Lecture to be followed by a Practical Class in English Pronunciation" stated the
programme for foreign students. A practical class was also offered to the English
native speakers.[1]

Notably absent from the new programme is any mention of elocution. It is probable
that a combination of factors was involved in dropping this element from the course.
Jones's first doubts about the wisdom of elocutionary training were undoubtedly
developing and he also had to consider how much time he could allow for various
aspects of his course. In any case, elocution, allied as it is to drama training and public
speaking, might not be the sort of subject to attract an introvert personality like Daniel
Jones (but, as we shall see, he was in suitable circumstances prepared to go on the
stage himself). A further possible reason for dispensing with elocution was that another lecturer, Rev. W. Garwood, MA, was announced as giving classes in "Elocution
and Voice Production" and had, in fact, been doing so since 1906. Nevertheless, when
Garwood gave up these classes in 1909, Jones made no attempt to take them over into
his own advertised programme.[2] Since no lecture notes on English survive from this
period, it is a matter of conjecture how much elocutionary training Jones retained in
his courses.

Daniel Jones allowed his wider theoretical interests to be utilised in the "Course on
General Phonetic Theory, Organic Alphabets, etc. with illustrations from European
and other languages". The "organic alphabets" component would have been mainly
concerned with Passy's scheme, revised by Jones and published the previous year
(Section 2.11); this is the only indication of the alphabet ever being employed in any
way whatsoever.

French was catered for by a class in the second term with the title "Phonetics of
French (Elementary)" and this was also followed by a practical class in French pronunciation held in the third term. In the same term, Jones also began a "Course on the
development of the French Vowel System with special reference to the pronunciation
of Lafontaine and the Chanson de Roland". As a counterpart to this last, he also of-

fered "A Course on the Pronunciation of Early English, with special reference to the pronunciation of Chaucer and Shakespeare".[3]

3.2. Chaucer and Shakespeare

The last two courses mentioned show that Jones was beginning to have his own interpretation of one theoretical facet of his discipline. Whilst he recognised that phonetics should make a contribution to historical linguistics (or philology as it would then have been termed), it is characteristic that he should concentrate on the reconstruction of the pronunciation of a given period in a holistic manner—dealing with the complete sound system and attempting to bring this to life—rather than carrying on with the usual pattern of philological analysis by tracing back individual speech sounds through previous stages of a language. Jones's method of presentation probably found more favour with the students, and one indication of this success is the fact that after instituting these courses, Jones took a major part in an unusual type of entertainment.

This took the form of a public presentation at University College of "Scenes from Shakespeare in the original pronunciation". In the review under that heading in *Le Maître phonétique*, G. Noël-Armfield (1909b: 117), who was later to be the first assistant in Jones's Department, wrote:

> Saturday, 3 July, 1909, marks an epoch in the history of Elizabethan representations of Shakespeare. On that date people living in the twentieth century heard some of Shakespeare's work in the pronunciation which may be safely accepted as that used by the poet himself and his fellow actors.

Daniel Jones played the parts of Prospero in *The Tempest* and Sir Andrew Aguecheek in the extract from *Twelfth Night*. The review by Noël-Armfield (1909b: 118) emphasises Jones's part in the production:

> Our friend Mr D. Jones was, of course, responsible for the phonetic transcription, as well as for the actual pronunciation of the performers, and it is a testimony to the care and thoroughness with which he rehearsed his little company that we noticed very few deviations from the printed transcription.

Noël-Armfield also reported that the audience included, amongst others, E.R. Edwards (who had now become Vice-President of the IPA). But perhaps for Jones, the most significant person present was the Provost, Gregory Foster, who must have noted the enthusiasm of his junior member of staff and remembered the success of the evening whenever matters concerned with phonetics came up later for discussion in College committees.

Jones published a supplement to *Le Maître phonétique* (Jones 1909c) containing the phonetic transcription of the scenes (Figure 3.1) and also an article (Jones 1909i) outlining the methods of research, in which he paid due acknowledgement to the previous work of Ellis, Sweet and Viëtor (for further discussion, see Section 14.15).

The success of the Elizabethan evening inspired Daniel Jones to repeat the experiment at Wimbledon in December of the same year, with some slight alterations of cast, and the addition of more music (Jones himself singing madrigals). Encouraged by his success, Jones then devised a "Chaucerian entertainment" (see Figure 3.2), which was presented under the auspices of the Poetry Recital Society at the Boudoir Theatre in London in May 1910. According to the review in *Le Maître phonétique*, "the performance was given twice and in each case to a full and appreciative house. It was indeed a revelation of charm and beauty.... Never had we known till then the beauty of that language." Daniel Jones was singled out for praise, both for his reading of *The pardoner's tale*, and his "expert knowledge and thorough teaching" in training the performers. A total of seventeen persons took part, including Noël-Armfield as the Clerk. The audience "came away with an interest in the *Canterbury tales* unfelt before" and the performance ended "amid rounds of applause" (Heward 1910: 102).

Jones had obviously hit on an aspect of phonetics and linguistics which had a wide appeal. After the success of this sequence of performances, he returned to the idea

```
æntoni.]   frendz, roːmænz, kuntrimen, lend mi
                                 iur eːrz;
ij kum tu beri seːzær, not tu præiz him.
ðe iːvil ðæt men duː livz æfter ðem;
ðe gud iz oft intered wið ðæir boːnz;
so let it biː wi seːzær.   ðe noːb,l briutus
hæθ tould iu seːzær wæz æmbisi-us:
if it weːr soː, it wæz æ griːvus faːlt,
ænd griːvusli hæθ seːzær ænswerd it.
heːr, under leːv ov briutus ænd ðe rest—
for briutus iz æn onoræb,l mæn;
so ær ðæi aːl, aːl onoræb,l men—
kum ij tu speːk in seːzærz fiuneræl.
hi wæz mij frend, fæiθful ænd dʒust tu miː:
but briutus sæiz hi wæz æmbisi-us;
ænd briutus iz æn onoræb,l mæn.
hi hæθ brout mæni kæptivz hoːm tu ruːm,
hwuːz rænsomz did ðe dʒen(e)ræl koferz fil:
did ðis in seːzær siːm æmbisi-us?
```

Figure 3.1. Extracts from: (1) *Julius Caesar* in Viëtor's (1906a/b) reconstruction of Shakespeare's pronunciation (above) and, on p. 60, (2) *The Tempest* (Jones 1909c).

PROS.   seilɛns! ɔːn wørd mɔːr
        ʃal mæːk miː tʃeid ðiː if not hæːt ðiː. hwat!
        an advɔkat fɔr an impostɔr! huʃ!
        ðou θiŋkst ðɛːr iz nɔː mɔːr sutʃ ʃæːps ax hiː,
        haviŋ siːn but him and kaliban; fuːliʃ wɛnʃ,
        tu ð mɔːst ɔv mɛn ðis iz a kaliban
        and ðai tu him æːr andʒɛlz.
MIR.   mei afɛksionz
        æːr ðɛn mɔːst humbl; ei hæːv nɔː ambision
        tu siː a guːdlier man.
PROS.   kum ɔn; ɔbai.
        ðei nɛrvz æːr in ðair infansi again
        and hæːv nɔː vigɔr in ðɛm.
FER.   so: ðai æːr;
        mei spirits, az in a drɛim, æːr aːl bound up.
        mei fæːðɛrz lɔs, ðɛ wɛːknɛs hwitʃ ei fiːl,
        ðɛ wrak ɔv aːl mei frɛndz, nor ðis manz θrɛts,
        tu hwuːm ei am subdiud, æːr but leiçt tu miː,
        meiçt ei but θruːx mei prizon ɔːns a dai
        bihɔːld ðis maid. aːl kornɛrz ɛls ɔ ð ɛɪrθ
        lɛt libɛrtei mæːk ius ɔv; spæːs inux
        hæːv ei in sutʃ a prizn.

Figure 3.1   (cont.)

several times in the course of his life. For example, he was to suggest a Shakespearean evening to Foster as one way of popularising the idea of a Phonetics Institute for London University (Section 9.3). And he was at times prepared to recite some Chaucer or Shakespeare as a turn at public gatherings such as dinners or weddings.[4] His remarkable skills were noted when at the 1935 International Congress of Phonetic Sciences (see Section 11.10): "... Professor Jones recited for our entertainment one of the *Canterbury Tales* of Geoffrey Chaucer running up to over 350 lines...without looking at the book (Chatterji 1968 [1981]: 24).

The culmination of Jones's fascination with this aspect of phonetics was to come much towards the end of his career with his set of recordings for Linguaphone (Section 11.5) and his radio broadcast of Shakespeare (Section 12.9).

3.3. *Intonation curves*

Intonation curves (Jones 1909a) was completed in April, 1909 (*Intonation curves*: xi). Its contents are precisely summarised in the subtitle: "A collection of phonetic texts in which intonation is marked throughout by means of curved lines on a musical stave." The texts Jones chose were in three languages (English, French and German) and amongst the voices analysed were those of Sarah Bernhardt and, again, Herbert Beerbohm Tree. The material was on records easily available from the catalogue of the Gramophone Company; in addition, Jones used a passage of English conversation published by Langenscheidt of Berlin.

The interest of the book today perhaps lies chiefly in the method by which the mate-

---

THE TEMPEST, Act I, latter part of Scene 2

Dramatis Personae

Ferdinand	...	...	...	...	Mr B. MacDonald
Prospero	...	...	...	...	Mr D. Jones
Ariel	...	...	...	...	Miss E. Hocking
Miranda	...	...	...	...	Miss D. Wooldridge

TWELFTH NIGHT, Act I, Scene 3

Dramatis Personae

Sir Toby Belch	...	...	...	...	Mr B. MacDonald
Sir Andrew Aguecheek	...	...	...	...	Mr D. Jones
Maria	...	...	...	...	Miss D. Wooldridge

Stage under the direction of Mr Bernard MacDonald
Pronunciation under the direction of Mr Daniel Jones
At the Virginal Dr G. Coleman Young
Virginal by Domenicus of Venice, dated 1556, kindly lent by
Messrs W. E. Hill and Sons
Costumes by Frecknall

During the interval between the Scenes Dr Coleman Young will play on the Virginal

Variations on "O Mistris Myne"
Variations on "The Carman's Whistle" } by William Byrd (1538—1623)
(from "Queen Elizabeth's Virginal Book")

and Miss Hocking will sing
"Where the bee sucks" (setting of R. Johnson, 1612)

Figure 3.2. Programmes for Jones's (1) "Scenes from Shakespeare" (above) and (2) his "Chaucerian Entertainment" (cont. p. 62).

PROGRAMME

OF A

Chaucerian ✦ Entertainment

GIVEN UNDER THE AUSPICES OF THE

POETRY RECITAL SOCIETY

AT THE

BOUDOIR THEATRE,

WEDNESDAY, MAY 25th, 1910.

🍃 🍃 🍃 🍃 🍃

STAGE under the direction of **Mr. Bernard MacDonald.**

CHAUCERIAN PRONUNCIATION under the direction of **Mr. Daniel Jones.**

MUSIC under the direction of **Dr. G. Coleman Young.**

ORGAN kindly lent by **J. W. Walker & Sons.**

COSTUMES by **Fox.**

The THEATRE has been kindly lent for the occasion by **Mr. Vaughan Grey.**

THE POETRY RECITAL SOCIETY, CLUN HOUSE, SURREY STREET, W.C.

Figure 3.2   (cont.)

rial was analysed, which was the same as that used in the *Sounds of the French language* and *The pronunciation and orthography of the Chindau language* (1911a; see Section 3.9), namely the employment of a gramophone record player as an aid to the auditory judgement of pitch. This procedure allowed long sections of text to be subjected to intonation analysis with a reasonably high degree of accuracy.

In his introduction to *Intonation curves*, Jones (*Intonation curves*: iv) defends his method of analysis over the use of kymograph tracings.

> Accurate records of intonation have, it is true, been produced by means of tracings of voice vibrations, obtained by the use of a kymograph or otherwise.... Such curves are, however, inconveniently large and elaborate, and the phonetic symbols to which the various parts of the curves correspond have to be placed far apart and at irregular intervals, thus rendering the text difficult to read. Besides this the work of preparing curves by this method is so laborious, that no one has ever yet analysed texts of sufficient length to be of any practical value to language students.

What Jones is therefore in fact pleading is that analysis by ear—though using the mechanical aid of a gramophone recording—provides a convenient short cut over the more rigorously scientific methods of acoustic analysis then available. With hindsight and awareness of the deficiencies in the kymographic techniques of the time, it is not difficult to grant Jones his point. (Fischer-Jørgensen 1981: 64, provides an amusing account of just how primitive phonetic kymographic equipment was even in the 1930s.) It is interesting to compare Jones's views on the use of the kymograph in *Intonation curves* with his later obvious interest in kymographic work (as in the *Outline*[1]: 168–182, see Section 8.8).

Jones (*Intonation curves*: v) states that:

> In a complete analysis of pronunciation the following elements of speech must be represented: (i) the quality of the various sounds, (ii) the quantity of the sounds (length), (iii) their relative loudness, and (iv) the pitch of the voice in pronouncing them. All these essentials are represented in detail in the English, French and German texts here given. The quality of the sounds is shown by phonetic symbols, their length by the use of the marks : and ·, their loudness by the stress mark ′ and by the bar lines on the accompanying musical staves—these bar lines being placed at every point where there is a minimum of loudness (i.e. at the limits of the syllables)—and lastly the pitch of the voice by curves on musical staves.

Jones's claim for a "complete analysis", including prosodic features, appears today to be naïvely overconfident. But given the limitations of contemporary instrumentation, and approaches to intonation, it must be granted that *Intonation curves* was a notable achievement. It was the only analysis of a relatively large corpus of speech available at the time, and indeed for many years thereafter. A significant criticism of

Intonation curves would be that the recordings available to Jones were of types of speech far removed from genuine colloquial language. Jones, however, shows himself to be aware that the conversation passages may be "to some extent artificial" (*Intonation curves*: xi):

Figure 3.3. Examples of Jones's "intonation curves" (*Intonation curves*, p. 19).

In order that a talking record should be really good, the articulation of the speaker must be very clear, far clearer than it usually would be in conversation.... In judging of the pronunciation therefore due allowance must be made for the fact that the speakers were obliged more or less to "recite" the conversations.

In fact, it is the conversation passages which show the most convincing representation of intonation (see Figure 3.3). It is, for example, possible in the English conversation section (*Intonation curves*: 16–29) to discover patterns similar to those made familiar by later systems of analysis (see Section 14.12 for further discussion). On the other hand, the passages of English drama and poetry show intonation which appear to be far removed from that of natural speech, and which certainly would not have been of any use to the language learner—which was one of the declared aims of Jones in writing the work.

Intonation curves has been virtually forgotten, except by academics rooting around in the history of intonation study; the book is a curiosity—a museum piece. Yet, it deserves recognition as being the first full-scale attempt at utilising an instrumental approach to intonation for the analysis of anything other than brief utterances. One writer who has recognised the importance of *Intonation curves* is Cruttenden (1981: 25), though he errs in implying that Jones pioneered the technique in this work. That had already been achieved earlier in the *Sounds of the French language*; the importance of *Intonation curves* lies in the scale of the operation, which demonstrated clearly that it was quite possible to analyse fairly long texts using Jones's method.

3.4. *The pronunciation of English*

April 1909 is also the date given at the foot of the preface to the second book published by Jones in that year, *The pronunciation of English*. Jones had managed to interest another prestigious academic publisher—this time Cambridge University Press (Figure 3.4). Jones was engaged by them to act as the editor of a series to be known as the "Cambridge Primers of Pronunciation". Jones took the opportunity to publish this book as the first in the series, which was later also to include *The pronunciation of Russian* (see Section 10.5). *The Pronunciation of English* (1909b) was to prove to be the most influential and successful book that Jones had written so far, and it is ironical that he was later to despise its earliest editions, saying that "every copy should be burnt!"[5]

Certainly, it cannot be claimed that the first edition is an attractive book in terms of its appearance. David Abercrombie (1983: 6) has said of it:

...the first two editions of his *Pronunciation of English* (1909 and 1914) were typographically hideous: at that date I do not think he was able to impose his will on his publishers as he could later.

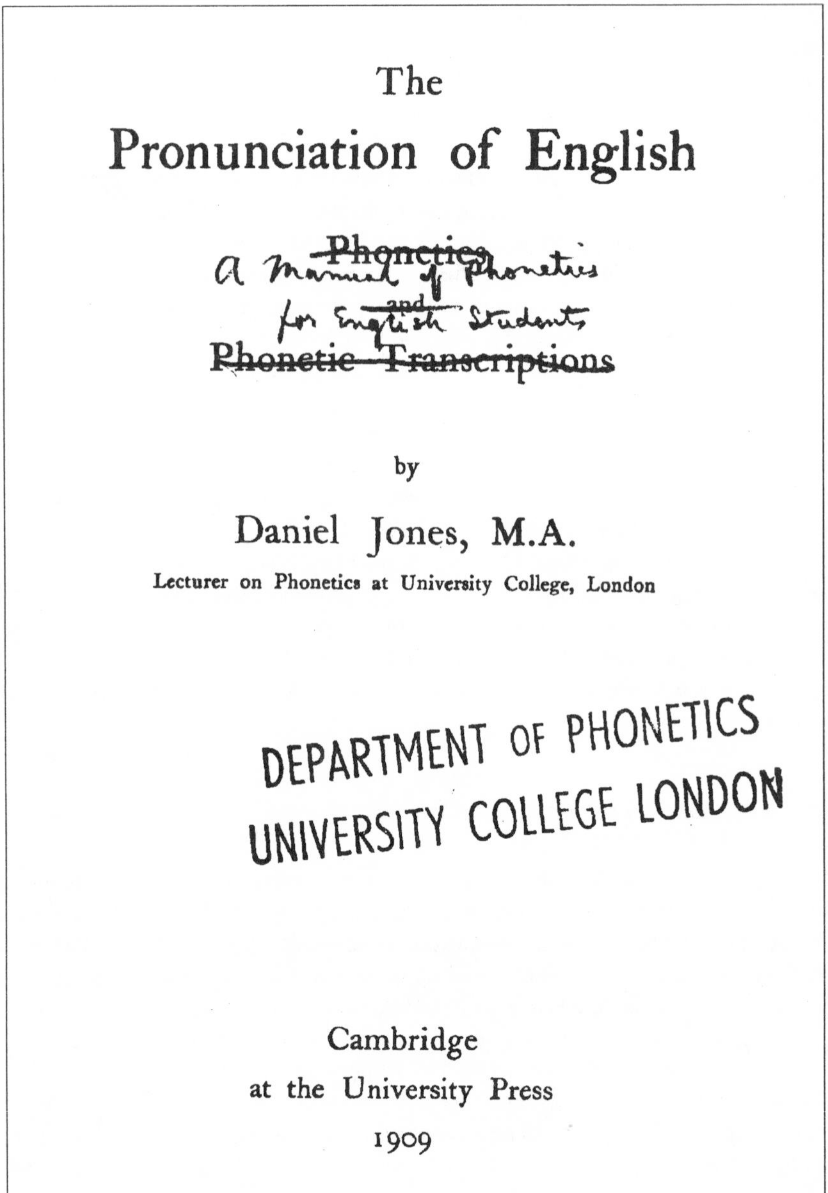

The

Pronunciation of English

a Manual of phonetics for English Students

~~Phonetics~~

~~Phonetic Transcriptions~~

by

Daniel Jones, M.A.

Lecturer on Phonetics at University College, London

DEPARTMENT OF PHONETICS
UNIVERSITY COLLEGE LONDON

Cambridge

at the University Press

1909

Figure 3.4. Title page of the first edition of the *Pronunciation of English* (the suggested alteration to the title, in Jones's own handwriting, was never actually adopted).

Jones's *Pronunciation of English*[1] is a modest work, exactly a hundred and fifty pages in length, and divided into two sections, the first dealing with "phonetics proper" and the second consisting of various phonetic transcriptions "selected from well-known English authors". However, "phonetics proper" is defined somewhat narrowly as "the analysis and classification of the elementary speech sounds of the English language". Jones goes on to claim that "Standard Southern English pronunciation is dealt with in detail and the principal varieties of pronunciation heard in London and elsewhere are described" (*Pronunciation of English*[1]: v). In fact, he covers this ground in a mere sixty-nine pages (for which he has been praised by Robert Burchfield, see Section 14.5) but such an economical treatment leaves no room for Jones to provide the detail that had been promised. It is possible that the compression of the first part of the book was forced upon Jones by the publisher—or that he wished to have space to devote to the transcribed passages. The brevity is perhaps the reason for the flimsiness of some of the description and analysis. It is noticeable that much of what is mentioned almost *en passant* in the *Pronunciation of English*[1] is developed at greater length in the *Outline*, and it will be demonstrated in the discussion of the latter book (see Chapter 8) that many of Jones's most perceptive ideas first appeared as tantalisingly brief snippets in the *Pronunciation of English*. Though Jones was right in believing that the *Pronunciation of English* was not up to the standard of his later work, it nevertheless shows considerable awareness of speech phenomena, albeit mixed with much dubious proscriptivism at times.

The remainder of the book contains not only a number of phonetic transcriptions—twenty-six in all—but also biographical details about the "particular speakers" and notes on their idiolectal variation, for Jones had not merely taken his own impression of English speech, but had obtained information on the speech habits of ten informants. Jones was advanced for this period inasmuch as he was not content merely to rely on introspective judgements of his own speech but also wanted to obtain data from a small sample of speakers. Among his informants were G. Noël-Armfield (who was later to be Jones's first assistant at University College) and E.R. Edwards, Jones's old schoolmaster who had helped him to get his appointment at UCL, and who was now an influential member of the School Inspectorate. Another was R. Bruce Lockhart, who later produced an account of the time he and Jones spent with the Motte family at Bourg-la-Reine (see Section 4.2).

In most cases, Jones had asked the speakers themselves to furnish him with a transcription, but Noël-Armfield was responsible for transcribing the speech of three informants. Two passages were taken, with permission, from published works—those of R.J. Lloyd (1899 [1908]) and G.E. Fuhrken (1907) (*Pronunciation of English*[1]: vi–vii). The extracts are mostly of "Standard Pronunciation" (see below) but Jones also has educated varieties of Scottish English (J. Sinclair and Bessie Robson, *Pronunciation of English*[1]: 123–125), Lloyd's "Northern English" (*Pronunciation of English*[1]: 115–117) and a type of West Country English (J.H. Fudge, *Pronunciation of English*[1]: 120–121). Another passage (*Pronunciation of English*[1]: 126–128) has dialogue "in one of the many forms of uneducated London pronunciation". Whilst

If you want to be able to cure looking i... , ... the ... is to be able to pronounce yourself.

viii   PREFACE   *Democracy*

of their own language. The fact that the Board of
Education has now introduced the subject into the
regular course of training of teachers for service in
public elementary schools is sufficient proof that its

/2   importance is now generally recognised.

*Elocutionists from ... t Oxford, talk with contempt of the
people who have not been 'Oxford accent'.*

                        WIMBLEDON,
                         April, 1909.
                                                              D. JONES.

*The semi-educated person who tries to speak elegantly, so does just
... light of nature (with out ... been properly taught) ... ...
In order to secure unity, persons ... to ... other
dialects are recomm... to consult with the of authorities
as to the best form of of script to adopt*

*The standard ... Scotch Standard. ...
Personal preference for ikspekt niglekt
VulgarPron. Pron. of vulgar person who try to speak elegantly*

*Every person thinks his own pron the best possible.
... considers himself a competent judge on
what is right or wrong in pron. His opinion gen.
turns out to be in favour of his own. People of
say I am sure no educated person pronoun ... that way.
Teach stressed syll. The unstr. will take
care of themselves.*

Figure 3.5   Jones's annotations on his personal copy of the *Pronunciation of English*[1] (cont. on p. 69).

Pronunciation of the future
Cockney Vowels
Precise pron. of unstressed syllables
(weak vowels, h in him etc)
Spelling pronunciations.
Question of best pron. inseparable from question of
social class. If you look at matter impartially you will find
that whenever a person objects to a pron. it is because that pron.
happens to be used by persons whom he considers his inferiors
Miss Stent's experience.

CONTENTS

untrained persons can't hear differences wh do exist, & think they hear diffs wh. don't exist

Figure 3.5. (cont.)

the transcriptions of these varieties do not appear to be at all reliable, it is nevertheless to Jones's credit that he recognised that a survey of different types of English
accent was needed in a book of this type, and he appears to have been the first to
attempt the task.

The transcriptions include some with intonation marking and these are a further
stage in the development of Jones's "intonation curves". In the *Pronunciation of
English*[1], Jones abandons the musical stave with five horizontal lines and instead
shows his intonation pattern between two widely separated lines—a form of presentation which seems much more familiar to the present-day reader. He also abandoned
the dotted line to indicate voiceless consonants, thus giving a simplified unbroken
curve. Furthermore, the patterns in the *Pronunciation of English*[1] were apparently not
produced from disc recordings but seem to be Jones's impressions of typical English
intonation. Later on, when a revised second edition was issued in 1914, Jones "corrected" portions of the curves and issued disc recordings (through Deutsche Grammophon-Gesellschaft in Berlin) of one passage in transcription and another in transcription plus intonation curves.[6] Attempting to follow the patterns drawn several years
earlier must have been a strain even for someone with Jones's talents for recognising
and reproducing pitches, and this could account for the need for some of these changes
from the 1909 edition (*Pronunciation of English*[2] [1914]: viii). In many ways, one can
regard the move away from the analysis of real speech—albeit speech produced in the
unnatural conditions of an early twentieth century recording studio—as being a step
backwards, and certainly some of the patterns in the *Pronunciation of English*[1] seem
less realistic than those found in *Intonation curves*.

The *Pronunciation of English*[1] was aimed at native speakers of English and is
severely normative in its approach to "Standard Pronunciation"; Jones was not as
yet using the term "RP" but for this book had coined the abbreviation "StP" (*Pronunciation of English*[1]: 1). The following passage indicates his views at the time
(*Pronunciation of English*[1]: vii):

> The present work is primarily designed for the use of English students and teach-
> ers, and more especially for students in training-colleges and teachers whose aim
> is to correct cockneyisms or other undesirable pronunciation in their scholars. At
> the same time it is hoped that the book may be found of use to lecturers, barris-
> ters, clergy, etc, in short to all who desire to read or speak in public. The dialectal
> peculiarities, indistinctness and artificialities which are unfortunately so common
> in the pronunciation of public speakers may be avoided by the application of the
> elementary principles of phonetics. It may be added that a study of the pronuncia-
> tion of the mother tongue is the indispensable foundation for the acquisition of the
> correct pronunciation of foreign languages.

The last sentence would still find support from many concerned with the application
of phonetics to the teaching of foreign languages. It is interesting to find Jones borrowing (surely not unconsciously?) the phrase "the indispensable foundation", which

	Labial		Dental	Palatal	Velar	Glottal
	Bi-labial	Labio-dental				
Plosive	pb		td		kg	ʔ
Nasal	m		n		ŋ	
Lateral			l		(l)	
Rolled			r			
Fricative	w	fv	θð, sz ʃʒ, ɹ	j	(w)	h

Figure 3.6. Consonant classification table (*Pronunciation of English*[1], p. 9).

was Henry Sweet's favourite expression for underlining the importance of phonetics in language study.

However, the remainder of the quotation above sounds quaint, almost embarrassing, to anyone who has absorbed the liberal attitudes towards language varieties that have been current in linguistics in the twentieth century. Here we have one of the clearest indications of Jones's proscriptive approach to pronunciation at this time, but throughout the *Pronunciation of English*[1] there are many echoes of this viewpoint (see Section 4.11 for further discussion). In his review of the *Pronunciation of English*[1], Passy (1909: 127) tellingly criticises Jones for not distinguishing properly between phonetic description and proscription:

> Je n'ai rien à dire contre le désir évident de l'auteur, de corriger les "mauvaises prononciations" (encore faudrait-il dire *pourquoi* on les trouve mauvaises, et distinguer entre les archaïsmes, les développements phonétiques naturels, et les déformations orthographiques); mais cette correction devrait être rigoureusement séparée de l'étude même des faits. D'abord montrez les choses comme elles sont; ensuite indiquez comment on voudrait qu'elles soient.

At the outset of his review, Passy warns: "Il faut un certain degré d'audace pour écrire, en anglais, un traité de phonétique anglaise, après les ouvrages si connus de Sweet!" (Passy 1909: 126) In fact, Sweet's last book, *The sounds of English*, had appeared only a year previously in 1908. But Passy goes on to say that he considers that Sweet's work was "trop strictement scientifique, professionellement linguistique" to have any chance of wide popular success. Despite his reservations, Passy concludes: "Jones a écrit un bon livre, et je le recommande à nos collègues."

A favourable review from Passy was not all that surprising since the close relationship between the two men was now so firmly cemented. Furthermore, Passy must have been aware that his own *Sons du français* had considerable influence on Jones's popular and deliberately simplified approach. The *Pronunciation of English*[1] was a success; it was reprinted in 1911 before going into the second edition in 1914 mentioned above. The book, for all its faults and its dated proscriptivism, was to establish Jones as a writer of significance in the world of phonetics, and provided the first challenge to Sweet as far as a phonetic description of English was concerned.

Perhaps the most significant aspect of the *Pronunciation of English*[1] from the point of view of Jones's personal development was that the book established certain clear indications of the path Jones was going to follow in the future. He chooses here to

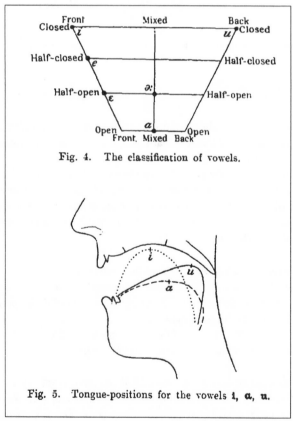

Fig. 4.   The classification of vowels.

Fig. 5.   Tongue-positions for the vowels **ɪ, ɑ, ʊ**.

Figure 3.7. Vowel quadrilateral and cross-section illustrating tongue postures for vowels [i ɑ u] (*Pronunciation of English*[1], p. 11). Cf. tables (*Pronunciation of English*[1], p. xiii) reproduced as Figure 8.4.

ignore the precision advocated by the German school (see A.4), and at the risk of appearing unscientific, opts for an uncomplicated, direct approach. His goal was to popularise phonetics, and to establish it as a valid discipline at levels below university level—i.e. in schools and with teachers in training. To achieve this aim, he adapts Passy's down-to-earth style (with concise sentences, and avoidance of elaborate scientific language) to English. By using simple models of vowel and consonant description, derived mainly from Passy, Jones successfully manages to avoid the sort of complexities in which Sweet allows himself to indulge even when ostensibly writing for an audience of non-experts, as in his *Sounds of English*. This is striking if one compares Jones's economical scheme of vowel description (*Pronunciation of English*[1]: 9–14) with Sweet's elaborate system of classification (Sweet 1908 [1929]: 24–39). Though Sweet has far more information, much of which is of interest even today, his approach is over-complex for most of his readers and for his declared purpose (p. 3). Yet, Jones's system is quite adequate for the task in hand and easy for inexperienced learners to grasp. The contrast comes out most sharply if one compares Jones's vowel diagrams (Figure 3.7) with Sweet's vowel tables, as illustrated in Figure 3.8. In his review of Sweet's book, Passy (1908: 69) comments unfavourably:

> Est-il bien utile, quand on décrit simplement l'anglais, de développer minutieusement la classification de Bell, avec les modifications introduites par l'auteur, et d'épouvanter le néophyte par un tableau de 72 voyelles, dont la plupart ne se rencontrent dans aucune langue connue?

It must be acknowledged, however, that certain parts of the *Pronunciation of English*[1] are grossly over-simplified, even if judged by the standards of an elementary textbook, as the following extract shows (*Pronunciation of English*[1]: 6):

> All sounds may be roughly divided into two classes, noises and musical sounds. Everyone knows with sufficient accuracy what is meant by this classification, and it is not necessary to attempt a rigorous definition.

Admittedly, Jones then directs his readers to Helmholtz (1863)—but this would hardly benefit his audience at this elementary level.

However, despite these lapses, the *Pronunciation of English*[1] must eventually be evaluated on its own terms as a book aimed at what was then a gap in the market, filling the need for a really simple introduction to phonetics for English-speaking readers. Its brevity and simplicity was probably the reason for its success in its day —and also the reason for much of the dissatisfaction that some of its content provokes in the modern reader. Nevertheless, the *Pronunciation of English*[1] was able to compete not only with Sweet's works but also with Ripman's useful, if limited, elementary textbook (1906) and reader (1908). Jones's *Pronunciation of English* has outlived them all and, in drastically revised form, remains in print to the present day.

A second edition of the *Pronunciation of English* came out in 1914. This is very much the same as the *Pronunciation of English*[1], although there are minor emendations, perhaps the only change of any note being that, in the description of vowels and in the accompanying diagrams (p. 11), "closed, half-closed" is now replaced by "close, half-close".[7] A fully rewritten edition of the book, *Pronunciation of English*[3],

1. ᴧ	7. ï	13. i	19. ɑ	25. ï	31. i
2. a	8. ë	14. e	20. a	26. ĕ	32. e
3. ʙ	9. ä	15. æ	21. ɒ	27. ä	33. œ
4. u	10. û	16. y	22. u	28. ü	34. y
5. o	11. ö	17. ə	23. o	29. ö	35. ə
6. ɔ	12. ö	18. œ	24. ɔ	30. ö	36. œ

37. ïc	43. ᴧɔ	49. ic	55. ïc	61. ɑɔ	67. ic
38. öc	44. aɔ	50. ec	56. ëc	62. aɔ	68. ec
39. äc	45. ʙɔ	51. æc	57. äc	63. ɒɔ	69. æc
40. üc	46. uɔ	52. yc	58. üc	64. uɔ	70. yc
41. öc	47. oɔ	53. əc	59. öc	65. oɔ	71. əc
42. öc	48. ɔɔ	54. œc	60. öc	66. ɔɔ	72. œc

Figure 3.8. Table of vowels devised by Sweet (1908: 38–39).

had to wait until 1950. A slightly revised version of this, *Pronunciation of English*[4], appeared in 1956 (see Sections 13.10 and 13.11).

3.5. Articles in 1908–09

In 1908, Jones produced fewer articles—probably because he was now busy completing work on the two important books which were to come out the following year. One contribution follows on from a piece by an IPA member, Evacustes Phipson (1908), who protested against the pronunciation traditionally employed for the classical languages in British schools.[8] Jones (1908e: 100) writes:

> Many readers of the m.f. will be amazed to find that any civilised nation should adopt such a barbarous pronunciation of Latin and Greek as that indicated above by Mr Phipson.

Jones then appends two samples of the "barbarous" pronunciation referred to, which, he says, "I was first taught at school". The pronunciation of Latin and Greek, as taught at Ludgrove and Radley could account in part for Jones's hatred of classical languages (Jones 1926e: 394) since it must have been frustrating to be forced to learn such obviously artificial forms of dead languages. And he would have been made aware of the advantages of the reformed pronunciation because University College taught in this way—then almost uniquely amongst British schools (see Section 1.5). Jones reports that a decision to change the teaching of Latin had been taken in 1906 by the Classical Association. Perhaps partly due to pressure from members of the IPA, most schools rapidly fell into line as far as Latin was concerned. The traditional pronunciation of Greek survived much longer (see Allen 1965: 102–110, and Allen [1987]: 140–149 for further discussion). The pronunciation of classical languages in various countries had become a major interest of *Le Maître phonétique*, and articles giving details of the teaching of pronunciation of Greek and Latin were submitted from several European countries.

Jones's only other contribution of any significance in this year was a reply to a "well-known advocate of spelling reform", one H. Drummond (by this time, the Simplified Spelling Society had been started, see Section 3.6). Drummond, whose letter is published only in extracts, appears to have had little phonetic expertise, and his criticisms of the IPA, the IPA alphabet, and *Le Maître phonétique* itself are easily dispatched by Jones. However, the reply entitled "The m.f. alphabet and spelling reform" (Jones 1908g) is of some interest in that it enables Jones to state views on transcription and spelling reform far more bluntly than he dared when writing to Sweet (see Jones 1907e). He goes over much the same ground, pointing out (Jones 1908g: 127) that the aims of spelling reformers, on the one hand, and phoneticians, on the other, are quite different:

The former seek to *make reading easier* by modifying the ordinary spelling in the direction of making it phonetic. The latter are concerned with the *science of pronunciation*, and the script used by them must be designed so as to facilitate this study; it must therefore be more complex and more difficult to learn, and must differ from the ordinary spelling to a much greater extent than the spelling of the spelling reformers.

The most important article Jones produced in 1909 was his study of the English of the Shakespearean period entitled "The pronunciation of early English" (Jones 1909i), which has already been referred to earlier in this chapter. For further discussion, see Sections 3.2. and 14.15.

Several other articles appeared under Jones's name in 1909. He attached a brief response to a piece by H. Molenaar, writing from Munich, who had devised a new international language called "Universal". Jones was enthusiastic about Molenaar's invention, and backed it against the most widely employed artificial language, which was, then as now, Esperanto. Jones states: "The superiority of "Universal" over Esperanto is obvious..." (Jones 1909e: 51). This appears to be the only case of Jones favouring any of the numerous artificial languages which were current in the early part of the twentieth century. Unlike Jespersen, who was fascinated by the idea of an artificial form of international communication, and who invented his own "Novial" system, Jones does not appear to have found the idea particularly attractive. This may be because he saw the obvious disadvantages of Esperanto, as he makes clear in this article, but could not see any rival to it in terms of the practicalities of acceptance by the world; or merely because there is really little of interest to a phonetician in an artificially constructed language; on the other hand, it offers far more to a grammarian, or an all-round linguist like Jespersen. See Large (1985) for a detailed discussion of the artificial language movement.

3.6. Foundation of the Simplified Spelling Society

However, another aspect of linguistic innovation claimed Jones's attention, and continued to fascinate him throughout his life. The Simplified Spelling Society (or SSS) was set up in 1908, and Jones introduced its ideas to IPA members by means of an article in *Le Maître phonétique* (Jones 1909g). Though he was not co-opted on to the committee until 1911, Jones appears to have been associated with the Society from an early stage, joining around 1910 (see 4.10). The article consists for the most part of extracts from the inaugural address of the SSS President—the etymologist Walter Skeat. Jones was not at this stage even an SSS member (though that is not made clear) but he expresses firm views on the concept of simplified spelling (Jones 1909g: 82):

The only practicable method of reforming our spelling is that advocated by the S.S.S., namely the gradual introduction of simplifications into the current orthography. And it must be borne in mind that only such simplifications are admissible as are in accordance with the pronunciation of all educated English-speaking people, or at any rate the majority of them.

Jones was concerned that the American Simplified Spelling Board had not always kept to this principle, and hoped that the SSS would not fall into the same trap; the differences between British and American usage in particular disturbed him. Jones was certainly prophetic in stating: "It can scarcely be expected that the British public will *rapidly* become convinced of the desirability of spelling reform." Nevertheless, spelling reform was to become a long-term interest in Jones's life, and this article is the first where his ideas are set out. See Sections 4.10 and 11.11 for further discussion.

3.7. Grenoble

Another minor article, "Phonetics at Grenoble" (Jones 1909j), provides some interesting indications of Jones's thinking at this time. It deals with "an important step in the progress of phonetic science…marked by the establishment of the new Phonetic Institute attached to the University of Grenoble." Jones was making his own beginnings with experimental phonetics (see below), and one can detect envy in his description of the Grenoble Institute (under the direction of T. Rosset), which contained (Jones 1909j: 143):

…a lecture theatre, a phonographic classroom, five other permanent classrooms (facilities being afforded for the use of several others, if necessary), a large laboratory fitted with phonetic apparatus, a professor's room, a photographic darkroom, etc.

He must have read the prospectus from which he says he derived this information with considerable jealousy, as he compared the accommodation and conditions with his own cramped premises at UCL, where his job was without tenure and where his one hope of teaching any experimental phonetics was to use lantern slide illustrations of the work of others—since no proper apparatus was available for his use (see Section 3.11). However, he also points out that the Grenoble complex had "grown up gradually from small beginnings"; and his description of the methods of raising the necessary finance piecemeal—"partly from state grants, partly from grants from the university, partly from students' fees and partly from the sale of a book"—must have set his own mind working to consider the possibilities for the future in London. It is possibly here that we can see the first seeds of Jones's grandiose scheme for a London Phonetics Institute, with himself at the head—a project doomed to failure and personal disappointment (see Section 9.3). The remainder of the article deals with Rosset's methods of teaching French pronunciation to foreign learners, and his form of phonetic transcription. Jones expresses approval for Rosset's enthusiasm for the use of the phonograph (although he points out that gramophone disc recordings are superior). The transcription system favoured by Rosset (derived from the work of Rousselot, see Section A.5) comes in for considerable—and predictable—criticism since it does not accord with IPA principles.

A later piece with the same title (Jones 1910a) consists of a letter from Rosset (pp. 41–42) and, within the same item, a response from Jones (pp. 42–44). Jones objects to Rosset's use of accents to indicate whether a vowel is "ouvert" or "fermé", showing that these terms could not be used to distinguish the open vowels [a] and [ɑ]. He rebuts Rosset's charge of inconsistency in the IPA's own use of accents, stating that diacritics can be used in order to show narrower shades of sound differentiation. In their discussion, the contemporary lack of the phoneme concept can be seen to hinder the argument, owing to the difficulty of a clear and concise definition of broad as against narrow transcription, and Jones has to admit that "the question how far it is desirable to represent minute differences of sound is no doubt a difficult one, and there is room for variety of opinion" (p. 44). Jones, finally, defends the IPA alphabet against Rosset's accusation that it is difficult to use as a practical method for teaching French as a foreign language, and points out that it has an excellent record of success over the period of the Association's history.

3.8. Discussions with Palmer

Jones returned to the recurrent problem of transcription himself in 1910 in reply to a long, chatty article by Harold Palmer—later to be one of Jones's first junior staff, and afterwards a major figure in his own right in the teaching of English as a foreign language. This is the first record of any contact between the two men although, in his obituary of Palmer, Jones said that they were corresponding "fairly frequently from 1907 onwards" (Jones 1950c: 4). Yet their approaches to the subject are already in line with their later development. Palmer's (1910) article, "The transcription of English vowels", introduced a form of transcription which indicated vowel qualities (distinctions of tenseness and laxness, in Palmer's terms) by means of grave and acute accents. He also introduced new ways of representing the diphthongs and free vowels and chose to employ ᴀ instead of the more common ʌ. Although Palmer provides a good case for his innovations, and indeed claims to be following Sweet's Broad Romic in many of his representations, the overall effect is confusing (the article is written in Palmer's transcription). Jones (1910g: 128–129) in his reply chooses not to criticise Palmer's transcription for the bewildering array of diacritics with which he deluges his reader, but instead concentrates on his usual theme of the need for unity in matters affecting transcription.

> The real point at issue is not so much the details of Mr Palmer's system as the more general question whether we are to use as far as possible *one* system for all branches of practical work.... The attitude of most members of the a.f. is that one system for all purposes is to be preferred, whenever practicable.... Is it worth

while diverging to so great an extent from this usual form of transcription in order to effect changes which can only be of use to one class of [French] students, and when the benefit derived by this class of students from the proposed changes is after all comparatively insignificant?

The intellectual stance of the two linguists here is typical of them both. Palmer is innovative, inquisitive and eager to test his ideas out on others; Jones is more cautious and pragmatic, and unwilling to upset the balance which has already been achieved. Yet, Palmer appears to have made an impression on Jones with his well-argued approach, and this exchange of views seems only to have added to their mutual respect.

3.9. *Chindau*

By far the most important article to be published by Jones in 1910 was "Uniform spelling for the African languages (with a short analysis of the Chindau language)" (Jones 1910k). The work was later republished in a modified form by London University, appearing the following year as *The pronunciation and orthography of the Chindau language* (Jones 1911a, henceforth *Chindau*). The article consists of an analysis of Ndau, a Bantu language of south east Africa;[9] together with a brief introduction mentioning the efforts of Dr W.L. Thompson, who was attempting to introduce a uniform scheme of alphabetisation for the languages of Africa—most of which still lacked any system of orthography. Thompson—an American physician, and a member of the IPA—was living as a missionary in Mount Selinda in Rhodesia (present-day Zimbabwe). Having already contributed to *Le Maître phonétique* on the matter (Thompson 1909), he took the opportunity during a visit to London in September 1910 of getting in touch with Daniel Jones at University College. With him he brought a native speaker of Ndau by the name of Simbini Nkomo. Thompson put to Jones the idea of making a phonological analysis of Ndau and Jones hurriedly set to work. Jones says (*Chindau*: 3):

> Dr. Thompson and Mr. Nkomo were in London for a few days only, and should any inaccuracies be detected, they must be attributed to the shortness of the time at our disposal.

He goes on confidently (*Chindau*: 3):

> I believe, however, that the work is substantially correct, and that the errors, if any, are insignificant.

On the segmental level Jones's analysis appears to have been competent, although the presentation in just over two pages in Jones (1910k), expanded to seven in *Chindau* itself, hardly allows a full exploration of the material. An obvious omission, however, is the lack of any analysis of the tonal system of Ndau, and it must be concluded that Jones did not seem to realise the significance of pitch levels in the language. Although he provides a sample of Ndau with "intonation ... recorded by means of an approximate musical notation", he says merely: "It may be of interest to mention that the intonation of the language is somewhat different from that which we are accustomed to in Europe" (*Chindau*: 12). Despite the mention of "the frequent use of level or very slightly rising intonation at the ends of sentences", terming this "a notable feature", there is no indication that Jones was aware of the linguistic implications of Ndau tones (*Chindau*: 13). The oversight is surprising, in view of Jones's interest in pitch and intonation, and his later pioneering work in the description of tone in Tswana, such as *A Sechuana reader* (Jones 1916a) and two more advanced analyses discussing grammatical tone features (Jones 1917c; 1928a). Tone phenomena in African languages had been described in previous work as early as the mid-nineteenth century (Lepsius 1863 [1981]: 275–281) and it is curious that Jones did not investigate pitch in Ndau more closely.

The work on Ndau lacks the thoroughness of his later pioneering research on exotic languages—on which Jones looked back with pride all his life (Gimson 1977: 151). Nevertheless, it marks an important stage in Jones's development, when he was beginning to be fascinated with the phonetic and phonological analysis of previously inadequately studied languages through informant work. Shortly before (in the previous issue of *Le Maître phonétique*) a brief "spécimen" of Latvian ("Lettish") was published; this had been prepared by a phonetician from Riga in collaboration with Jones (Paegle—Jones 1910i). The same issue had contained a similar piece on the Gheg dialect of Albanian, which Jones had prepared "from the dictation of Miss M.E. Durham" (Jones 1910j). However, the Ndau research (whilst it might appear today to be modest in scope) was Jones's first sustained attempt at analysing the full sound system of a hitherto undescribed language; furthermore, it may also have been his first contact with informants from a non-European country. Jones never lost his taste for informant work of this type, relying totally on his powers of recognition by ear and imitation, conscious (though he never stated it himself) that he could do this better than anyone else in the world.

Chindau is also notable for providing the model for the series of University of London readers which was to follow over a period of twenty years. The simple layout consisted of a short description of the sound system, written with a minimum of technical terminology; a consonant and vowel grid showing place and manner of articulation; and specimen phonetic texts with literal translations. Apart from the addition of vowel diagrams once the theory of Cardinal Vowels had been established, all the "London Readers" followed this scheme; so, though it does not bear the label, the Chindau pamphlet is really the prototype of one of the most influential series of pioneer descriptive linguistic publications.

Jones also completed a number of minor contributions to *Le Maître phonétique* over this period, including numerous reviews and many contributions to the "partie des élèves", short exercises for practice in reading phonetic transcription. His total contribution to the journal, especially if his position of Assistant Editor to Passy is taken into account, was indeed formidable. However, it was not only in the field of academic publication that Jones had established himself, but also within the structure of the IPA itself.

3.10. Elections in the IPA

Following his rapid election to the Council so shortly after taking out life-membership, and his almost equally rapid appointment as Assistant Editor of *Le Maître phonétique*, it was almost inevitable that with the backing of Paul Passy Daniel Jones was set to rise within the organisation of the IPA. In 1908, he was re-elected to the thirty-member Council (coming seventh in numbers of votes received, an indication of popularity which must have pleased him).[10] However, Jones failed miserably in the elections for the two vacancies for Vice President. Jespersen and Edwards were successful, whilst Jones received only two votes. However, in compensation he was elected on to the "comité exécutif"—a new five-member body which Passy had decided to set up to deal with urgent business, owing to the difficulty of contacting the widely dispersed members of the Council.[11] Since one of the five members elected was Paul Passy himself, and another was Sophie Lund, it would appear that Passy had managed to obtain an inner caucus with a strong Bourg-la-Reine bias, so it was likely that this was where the real power of the IPA organisation would lie from now on.

In 1908, a Belgian member of the Council, Professor E. Monseur of the University of Brussels, suggested that Jones should be made Assistant Secretary.[12] It seems probable that Monseur was acting in collaboration with Passy in making this suggestion, though there is no certain evidence; however, in the March-April issue the following year, this announcement appeared from Passy:

> Je pense que vous êtes satisfait de la collaboration de D. Jones au m.f, et désirez qu' elle soit continuée. Etes vous d'avis alors, comme le conseillait Monseur dès l'année dernière, de lui donner officiellement le titre de Secrétaire Adjoint de l'a.f.?[13]

The announcement of Jones's election to this post appeared in the very next issue; he was resoundingly returned with only one vote against, and three abstentions; a total of twenty-four Council members backed him. Jones's position in the IPA was now virtually impregnable; he remained in this post until 1928, when he was elected Secretary (see Section 10.9). But Jones was not only establishing himself within the IPA. Perhaps even more importantly for him at the time, he was continuing to build up his position at University College.

3.11. Teaching at University College 1909–10

The 1908–09 session had already seen a wide array of classes in phonetics on offer for Jones's students. In the academic year 1909–10, four new courses were introduced.[14] "The Development of the English Vowel System" seems to have been a conventional application of phonetics to the history of language. Two of the new courses, "The Theory of Alphabetic Representation of Languages" and "General Phonetic Theory (Classification of Vowels, etc.)", reflect Jones's increasingly analytical approach to phonetics which was now becoming apparent. The first course was possibly a means of salvaging some of the material on organic alphabets which he had previously taught and combining this with theories of sound-symbol relationships. No lecture notes survive from this period, but it is clear that Jones was preoccupied with problems of transcription—an area which throughout his life he was to regard as crucial (see Section 14.9). The subtitle of the "General Phonetic Theory" course indicates that Jones was already interested in the problematic topic of vowel description and was perhaps now moving towards developing a system for this, which would eventually emerge as the theory of Cardinal Vowels (see Section 7.3).

The most interesting development in the 1909–10 session, however, was the introduction of a course called "Experimental Phonetics". This was a modest beginning with classes given only in the third term on Saturday mornings for an hour each week. No indication is given of its content—possibly, like many university teachers, Jones first put a course into the Calendar and did not worry about planning its detail until he saw whether there were going to be any takers. The 1910–11 Calendar elaborates: "A course of eight lectures illustrated with apparatus and lantern slides", and also states that the class was to be given on Thursday evenings—a more attractive time, since most of Jones's classes were taught in the evening. The lantern slides were obviously an attempt to make up for the lack of a phonetics laboratory with proper apparatus— facilities which were not to arrive at University College for some time (see Section 5.10). We have already seen that Jones was envious of the resources of a continental university, Grenoble. No doubt he used the Grenoble prospectus and his information on the equipment available to phoneticians in Germany, France and America to squeeze money out of the authorities in London to provide funds for a proper phonetics laboratory at UCL.

In the 1910–11 session, a change of direction becomes noticeable, with Jones dropping the more theoretical courses and returning to safer areas like English for foreign students, and French for the English, plus some philologically biased classes on Old French and Chaucer.[15] Presumably, the response to the theoretical approaches was poorer than he might have hoped; perhaps the organic alphabet had acted as a deterrent to any but the most eager students. Phonetics now figures in the Report of the College Committee with a paragraph of its own for the first time:

> The efficiency of the Departments of Modern Languages is being extended and aided by the work done under the Lecturer in Phonetics. The Courses in Phonetics have been extended so as to provide a complete training in the theory and practice of Phonetics, for those who desire to utilize Phonetics for the purposes of teaching. There are, in addition, Courses in Phonetics for foreign students.[16]

Jones had also busied himself with another aspect of university teaching. From 1907 onwards, he had been giving public lectures—these being regarded in University College as a service to the general public which was of particular importance. Each year, a number of open lectures were given to function as a link between the world of scholarship and the interested layman. Jones seems to have been particularly enthusiastic about the idea, giving two public lectures in his first year, and continuing to do so in subsequent sessions. No other lecturer is shown as giving more than one of these public lectures per year, yet in the 1909–10 session Jones gave four lectures, covering a diverse range of topics. In 1910–11 he gave three, and for the first time included experimental phonetics as one of the topics. Jones seems to have seen the public lectures as an ideal opportunity to explain his unfamiliar new discipline to the population at large, and possibly pick up some potential students in the process—those who were interested enough to go to a public lecture might be tempted to enrol in an evening class.

He continued to give these public lectures, however, long after his Department was firmly established, and even into his retirement—the last being in 1957 (see Section 13.14). According to one of his pupils, J. Carnochan, Jones had a particular talent for explaining his subject to the non-specialist:

> He used to give lunch-hour lectures…about three a year…he was the sort of professor I admire very much because he could make his subject interesting to the layman—the person who'd come in out of the rain—all sorts of people would come in from Gower Street…there are lots of professors who can't talk about their subject to the layman…but he had the knack of being able to give a talk on his…recondite subject which would interest people who didn't know anything about it at all.[17]

In 1910, Jones's efforts saw an important return. The Professorial Board of UCL agreed to accept Jones's proposal for a Certificate Course in Phonetics and gave permission for the Certificate to be awarded in the following academic year.[18] Jones could therefore offer a paper qualification with the authority of London University behind it. Although the new IPA examinations were already firmly established and successful (the results were being regularly published in *Le Maître phonétique*), it was nevertheless a significant step for Jones to have an examination course where he had complete control of the syllabus and the standard. He was now able to state that a certificate would be awarded to: "Students attending a full Course in Phonetics and attaining a sufficient standard in the examinations connected therewith."[19]

By 1910, Daniel Jones had good reason to be satisfied with his life and his career. He already had a considerable number of publications to his credit—including five books. More books were soon to appear, and work had already started on the planned *Outline*.[20] He was a major force in the most important international association in his field, and Assistant Editor of its influential journal. He had made important contacts and had some powerful friends both in England and abroad. Whilst he was still on a temporary lectureship, with phonetics not yet recognised as a department in its own right, and though he was still working without any assistance, he realised that all this would rapidly change.

Early in the new academic year, in October 1910, the Professorial Board recommended that he should be granted the status of "Recognised Teacher of the University"; this was passed by the College Committee shortly afterwards.[21] The extra security in his professional career implied by this new status must have been all the more welcome to Jones since he was planning a major change in his life. He had decided to marry Cyrille Motte.

Chapter 4

Building up the Department (1911–14)

4.1. The links with Paul Passy

After his first long stay in France in 1905–06, Daniel Jones was careful not to lose contact with the Motte family. Each year he had returned to Bourg-la-Reine in order to spend some weeks recapturing the atmosphere of Pin Ginko, keeping up his colloquial French, and taking every opportunity to discuss developments in phonetics with Paul Passy, accompanying him most days to the Sorbonne.[1]

There had been much to discuss. Firstly, the translation of *Les Sons du français*, then their joint project of the "Alphabet Organique". And from 1907 onwards, there were the everyday problems of administration of the IPA, such as keeping its widely dispersed membership informed of events, and also ensuring that the Council members were able to take a full part in elections and decision making. There had been additionally all the editorial problems of bringing out a journal every two months. *Le Maître phonétique* was in so many respects an editor's nightmare. Not only did it attempt to combine the functions of a learned journal, a newsletter and a pupil's reader, but it was also written completely in phonetic transcription, the precise variety of which was decided by the contributor of each article. To complicate matters further, three languages—French, English and German—were in regular use, and some contributors chose to submit in Italian or Spanish. It is a tribute to the dedicated industry of Passy and Jones that the journal came out regularly on time and that typographical errors were remarkably rare.

But the stress was taking a toll. Paul Passy was always obsessed about his health, perhaps with reason, having lost two close relations through tuberculosis. He had felt it necessary to spend a period of time in Switzerland to recover from strain—and he gradually came to rely increasingly on his young English colleague, making the need for the two men to meet regularly even more important.[2]

4.2. Cyrille Motte

For Daniel Jones, there was another good reason to spend a considerable time each year at Bourg-la-Reine. During his first prolonged stay at Pin Ginko, he had been somewhat overwhelmed by the Motte daughters, but nevertheless had been attracted to one of them, Cyrille. She had then been only fourteen, but throughout her teens, he became more and more fascinated by her. In her early photographs, Cyrille Motte appears as a good-looking young girl. Henri Motte was from Lille in northern France, but Cyrille was the only one of his daughters to inherit his Flemish features of light brown hair and blue eyes.[3] Her quizzical smile reflects the lively humour and sharp wit that she was said to possess in her youth. It is not difficult to understand why Daniel Jones was captivated by her.

However, when recalling the courtship, after a lapse of almost eighty years, Cyrille's younger sisters still professed surprise that she had been interested in him. As young children they had found Jones tiresome company: "He was a bore. All he did was talk about phonetics!" was his sister-in-law Gisèle's blunt comment.[4] Cyrille's first impressions of Jones were also unfavourable since for some odd reason she disliked even the sound of his name. The very first time he wrote to the Motte family, she apparently looked at the signature and said: "Daniel Jones—quel nom horrible!" She was perhaps the only person he ever allowed to shorten his name to "Dan".[5] The relationship began with him as the butt of Cyrille's jokes. In her sister's words: "She teased him quite a lot to start with. He was a serious young man."[6]

But Cyrille herself soon became interested in phonetics and language teaching— inspired undoubtedly by the enthusiasm of "Marraine" (Sophie Lund) and the example of "Oncle Paul" (Passy). She shared this interest with her elder sister Irène. Robert Bruce Lockhart (1957: 56) has written in his autobiography:

> Of the five girls, Irène and Cyrille were in their late teens. They had been brought up in the French way, were completely natural, and gave most efficient aid to their mother in running the establishment. They even helped in teaching the English and Scottish visitors.

Daniel Jones also had regard for Cyrille's views on phonetic matters—especially on the pronunciation of French. He would later refer to her as being "always of the greatest assistance to him" and as being herself "a phonetician of no mean ability" (Jones 1926e: 398). For several years (1913–21) she was to be a part-time member of staff in his Department. In 1911 Cyrille began making contributions to the "partie des élèves" of *Le Maître phonétique*.[7] Shortly after she left France, her first publication appeared: a collection of phonetic transcriptions of French called simply *Lectures phonétiques* (Motte 1912).

Jones's visits to Bourg-la-Reine were now being made in winter, because the Motte family spent a long summer holiday each year at their country house on the coast of Brittany. Like many French upper-class families, they would move their whole household away from Paris for as much as two and a half months. The house, near Trégastel, in a beautiful but wind-swept area, was called by the Breton name of Pon-ar-Brun.[8] By 1910, Daniel Jones's prospects at London must have been considered good enough for him to contemplate marriage. Daniel Jones Senior had come over to meet Cyrille and the Motte family, and the parents on both sides had approved of the match.[9] Cyrille said nothing to her younger sisters for a long time: "She was funny— but we all knew."[10]

Bruce Lockhart (1957: 56) recalls this period:

12. The Motte children

13. The young Cyrille Motte

14. The wedding (1911)

15. Jones (hatless, centre background) and guests waiting for the bride

In April, 1911...I came back to Bourg-la-Reine...for a last visit. As the schools were then on holiday, the *pavillon* was full of English schoolmasters. Four of the girls were now grown up, and romance was in the scent of the rambler roses on the walls of the *pavillon*. Irène, the eldest, was already engaged.... Cyrille was engaged to Daniel Jones and was married to him in 1911.

The marriage would have been a particular joy to Passy, devoted as he was to his nephews and nieces, even though he apparently had little contact with Henri Motte himself. Passy and his wife were childless, although later they were to adopt two children.[11] He seems by this time to have regarded Daniel Jones almost as a surrogate son, referring to him in publications as "mon neveu".[12] Passy now arranged another significant step in Jones's career, namely his first lecture at the Sorbonne, delivered to the "Société pour la propagation des langues étrangères" on January 9, 1911. The topic was: "The pronunciation of English, past, present and future";[13] an article with the same title later appeared in the *Revue de l'Enseignement des Langues Vivantes* (Jones 1911u).

4.3. A wedding in Brittany

Plans went ahead for the wedding. It had been decided that Cyrille and Daniel would be married at Trégastel that August. Since both the Jones and Motte families were Protestant, there were no religious barriers, and the only problem was how to find an appropriate clergyman in fiercely Catholic Brittany. An ingenious solution was found: Daniel Jones Senior brought a Protestant minister over from England.[14] The May-June issue of *Le Maître phonétique* carried this notice in the "famille phonétique" section: "Nous avons le plaisir d'annoncer que notre rédacteur adjoint D. Jones doit prochainement épouser Mlle Cyrille Motte, nièce de notre secrétaire."[15]

On Wednesday, August 29, the weather—by the generally unpredictable standards of Northern Brittany—was fair, and luckily the strong winds, which so often blew around Pon-ar-Brun, had for once dropped. Photographs show that though the sky was overcast much of the time, now and again the sun broke through the clouds. In his richer days, Henri Motte had rebuilt an old coach house adjacent to Pon-ar-Brun and converted the ground floor into a large reception room and it was here that the ceremonies took place.[16] Afterwards, the whole company assembled in the open air for a photograph to be taken.

In fact, several photographs survive of the wedding, the greatest event in the Motte family for many years. In some, the formal morning dress of the guests contrasts oddly with the primitive structure of the old Breton village buildings in the background. The group photograph was taken in a field of roughly scythed grass away from the house, and in total nearly seventy people are present. Cyrille sits a little apart from Daniel Jones who looks fraught, and has his legs crossed. The guests appear exhausted by the tensions of the day, and there is hardly a smile to be seen. The parents give the impression of being fugitives from the previous century; the fathers both have white beards and their wives wear elaborate dresses and enormous flowered hats. The English parson has been placed at the end of a row of relations. Several women, presumably servants or villagers, are dressed in Breton folk costume. The four sisters —Irène, Gisèle, Odette and Renée—make a fine party of bridesmaids. Possibly language problems had played a part in exhausting the two families; Henri Motte spoke no English whatsoever, and, given what is known of the deficiencies of English schools in the nineteenth century, it is possible that the Jones family spoke very little intelligible French.[17]

4.4. Return to London

Daniel Jones returned to London to face the problems of setting up house with his young French wife. Though now thirty, he had only recently left his parents' home in Wimbledon, having lodged first of all at 1 Upper Westbourne Terrace, in the neighbourhood of Paddington Station. After his marriage, he moved to 74 Gloucester Place near Portman Square. This was a more prestigious address, close to the area behind Hyde Park where he had spent his early childhood, and it had the advantage of being only a few minutes' walk away from University College. Cyrille had to adjust rapidly to many changes in her life once she came to England. She was just twenty years old and had gone through a peculiarly sheltered and isolated upbringing within a close-knit family. Robert Bruce Lockhart (1957: 57) has written of the Mottes:

> It will be long before Western Europe sees again so large a family united in happiness; because it formed a community in which each member had his or her own special responsibility towards the others. Duties came before rights, and unselfishness before all thought of self.

Even allowing for Bruce Lockhart's tendency to hyperbole, there is some truth in the remarks. Since the children had never gone to school, and had hardly left the house except for their annual visit to Trégastel, Pin Ginko had been a very protected atmosphere in which to grow up. And though the house was run down, and the family finances were in a desperate condition, Cyrille had been accustomed all her life to having servants on hand, and parents to shelter her from everyday difficulties of life. Her eight brothers and sisters provided companionship, and an endless stream of young schoolmasters from abroad brought interest into their lives.

From this, Cyrille was suddenly plunged into an isolated existence in the heart of what was then the largest city in the world. She knew nobody in London and her social contacts consisted solely of Daniel Jones's friends and family. Jones had to teach on several evenings of the week, and much of the rest of his time was spent writing articles and books and editing *Le Maître phonétique*. She also had to deal with the problems of a foreign country and learning the language; although she eventually spoke English fluently, she was always happier in her mother tongue (she normally gave her classes entirely in French).[18] Cyrille also had to cope with the difficulties of housework for the first time, which, in that era, before most modern aids to housekeeping were available, would have been a formidable task for a young girl newly arrived from abroad (even though, like all British middle-class people at this time, the Joneses would have had domestic help, almost as a matter of course). In fact, running a house was something Cyrille never ever came to terms with; apart from cooking—at which she eventually became adept—she found it tiresome.[19]

4.5. Departmental status

Daniel Jones had come back to his post at University College to face a busy programme of teaching. To his previous classes, he had now added a *"Class for Advanced Students* desirous of doing original work in any branch of Phonetics." In this course, arranged for the summer term, "each Student attending this class will be expected to read at least one paper in the course of the Term. The papers will be discussed by the class."[20] This is the first indication that we have that Jones was now expecting some of his pupils to produce work of a high level which was comparable to that undertaken in the senior classes of established departments.

Jones's career prospects continued to improve in the first half of 1911 when he was reappointed for a further period of three years.[21] The college authorities then decided that Jones, together with other lecturers without permanent appointments, would be paid by a new system. Lecturers had previously been paid a salary consisting in part of a portion of their students' fees but this was now replaced by a fixed annual salary. Under this scheme Jones was to receive £200 per annum, and he could in one way be pleased with this outcome since it was the highest sum paid to any ordinary lecturer in the College; in fact, only one other lecturer received as much.[22] However, London University was a notoriously mean employer, and the salary, whilst adequate, would still not have been considered good in relation to other professions.

Daniel Jones had already been allocated his first assistant member of staff: G. Noël-Armfield, a member of the IPA, and also a contributor to *Le Maître phonétique*—as we have seen from his notice of Jones's reconstruction of Shakespeare (Noël-Armfield 1909b). He had also produced a short children's reader (Noël-Armfield 1909a), which Jones had criticised in a rather sharp review which complained about its many misprints (Jones 1910d: 82). Despite this minor brush, Jones obviously had a high opinion of Noël-Armfield's general competence, and was probably particularly impressed with the almost perfect French which his French mother had passed on to him.[23] Noël-Armfield had some teaching experience, and was the ideal person to start up the course on Spoken English that Jones planned for the 1912–13 Session. The appointment was announced in the College Committee minutes of 1911, and he began work in the autumn of 1912.[24] In the Report on the year, Jones says:

The number of classes held this session has been considerably greater than in any previous session. This increase is chiefly due to the creation of a special branch devoted to Spoken English (for foreign students) ...under the direction of Mr G. Noël-Armfield, the newly appointed Assistant to the Phonetics department.[25]

The course in Spoken English is interesting in the development of the Department in several respects. Firstly, Noël-Armfield's appointment marked the transition to departmental status, as opposed to Jones working as a solitary lecturer. Secondly, for the first time a course dealt with aspects of language other than phonetics. In addition, this was the first course to be conducted in a British university in what would today be termed English as a Foreign Language. It provided the foundation for the University of London to be, as Howatt (1984: 213–214) has put it, "the principal if not the sole centre of university-level activity in the field for the next half century".

4.6. The Paris Lecture

Jones returned to France in the Christmas vacation of 1911–12 (presumably the main purpose of the visit was to allow Cyrille to visit her family in Bourg-la-Reine), and delivered a lecture to the *Guilde Internationale* in Paris early in 1912 (henceforth the Paris Lecture).[26] The typed notes have survived and appear to be the earliest extant dated example of Jones's lecture preparation. The Paris Lecture, entitled "On the teaching of English pronunciation to French students", is a lively and informative introductory talk for phonetically inexperienced learners of English from a francophonic background. It is peppered with anecdotes and amusing examples and would seem to confirm Carnochan's view (see Section 3.11) that Jones had a talent for lecturing to audiences of laymen.

After an introduction in which he discusses the different types of learners' problem —intelligibility, lexical confusion and (potentially humorous) distracting pronunciation—Jones then introduces the principles of phonetics and its application to language learning. He proceeds to give examples of how it is possible to train French speakers to pronounce English correctly by combining elementary articulatory instruction with imitation of a native speaker. Jones's methods are simple—occasionally almost simplistic. For example, English [æ] is related to the bleating of a sheep: "A sheep says bæː and that is much the same sound as we make when we begin to say the word bad" (Paris Lecture, p. 8). Other instructions include unrounding of the lips using a mirror for [əː] as in *bird*, and employing a cork ("not less than 2 cm. in diameter") for obtaining the correct articulation for English [r]—using French [ə] as a starting point. Jones goes on to discuss the use of phonetic transcription, demonstrating that it can solve problems such as indicating the distribution of English /r/ and the incidence of vowels. Although this seems very familiar today, it must be remembered that Jones in this lecture was addressing a 1912 audience who probably had little or no knowledge of phonetics.

Jones attacks the systems of pseudo-phonetic transcription to be found in teaching manuals and phrasebooks, giving examples such as: *Dzé are cheuttinngue dzemm, Chî iz ouér-inngue braoune gleuvz* (for "they are shutting them", "she is wearing brown gloves") (p. 13).[27] He goes on to introduce the concept of vowel gradation in weakly stressed syllables, introducing [ə], and the use of weak forms (pp. 15–16). Jones then discusses the best variety of English to serve as a model for a foreign learner, coming down predictably in favour of "Southern British" (pp. 17–18).

> It must be pointed out emphatically that these [accent] differences exist and are of considerable importance. It doesn't do for a Frenchman who is going to mix chiefly with Southern English people to talk with an American accent, nor does it do for a Frenchman who is going to live in Scotland to talk Cockney.... It seems to me that foreigners go to Edinburgh by hundreds in order to learn English. Well, I have no objection to Scotch pronunciation, but I have sometimes thought it a little strange that people should go out of their way to go to Scotland when there are so many parts of England nearer at hand...although Scotch pronunciation is very nice in its way, I don't think we can say that it is really always the best for foreigners to learn. In London it sounds very funny when we hear a Scotch person talking, and it sounds still funnier when we hear a foreigner talking with a Scotch accent on the top [sic] of his foreign accent.

Jones reveals some interesting aspects of his own accent prejudices in this section of the Paris lecture. Undoubtedly, later he would have wished to retract much of what he says here and, in fact, a handwritten addition states: "On the other hand Southern pron[unciation] sounds just as ridiculous to a Scotchman." It must also be remembered that not only had Jones worked on Kirkpatrick's Edinburgh courses but from 1910 onwards had been partly responsible for their organisation (Section 2.10).

He presents his audience with a strong advocacy of phonetic transcription as a language teaching method, stating (p. 22):

> When you can pronounce the sounds by themselves and you know the phonetic symbols it is a good thing to practise all kinds of isolated syllables so as to become accustomed to the combinations of sounds commonly occurring in the language. The instruction in vocabulary, grammar and syntax should be given on the lines of the ordinary direct method, but I strongly advise the use of nothing but phonetic script at first. If time permits I would recommend working with phonetic script only *for at least one year*, and preferably *two*.... At the end of that time you will find that you have a remarkable command of the spoken language.

These extreme views on the use of transcription are also apparent in aspects of Jones's later works—for example, in the almost complete exclusion of conventional Russian orthography from the *Pronunciation of Russian* (Trofimov—Jones 1923a); see Section 10.5.

Jones appears to have given the Paris Lecture again on many occasions—a pencilled note refers to "this phonetics sect[n] of the work of this H.C." (i.e. "holiday course") so we may assume that these notes were the basis of some of his vacation course material. More curiously, given the French–English contrastive approach, the dates written on the title page imply that the Paris Lecture was used at several venues on the Scandinavian and Indian tours of 1912 and 1913 (see Section 4.7 below).

4.7. Tours of Scandinavia and India 1912–13

At the beginning of the summer term in 1912, Jones embarked on a lecture tour of Scandinavia and Germany. His programme was a full one, beginning in Sweden with a lecture in Gothenburg on April 12. Lectures were then given at Stockholm (April 15), Uppsala (April 22), Gefle (April 24). A short break followed before Jones spoke in Copenhagen (May 2) and ended his tour in Hamburg (May 10).[28] An announcement in *Le Maître phonétique* mentions that Jones spoke on the phonetics of English,[29] but it is uncertain what form his lectures took—one must assume that if Jones used the Paris Lecture (see Section 4.6) as a basic framework, as the dates on its title page imply, then he must have made considerable alterations, changing the material to fit the language backgrounds of his audiences.

It is known that he took his wife with him on this trip, since several photographs of them on their travels around have been preserved. On his return journey, Jones—quite by chance—met Harold Palmer for the first time. In writing Palmer's obituary, Jones (1950c: 4–5) took the opportunity to recall the incident.

> The meeting was an accidental one on board an Ostend-Dover boat. Seeing my name on a luggage label, he came up to me and we had a memorable talk on phonetics, and we struck up a friendship which it has been a privilege to me to enjoy ever since. This meeting confirmed the opinion I had already formed, namely that he possessed unusual talent for linguistic theory and pedagogy.

The Scandinavian venture seems to have been a success, and Jones developed a taste for foreign travel. Early in 1912 he applied to the College Committee for leave of absence to undertake a lecture tour of India during December and January. The College Committee minutes state that in his request for leave "Mr. Jones reported that he could provide a deputy to carry on the work in Phonetics during his absence".[30] The deputy is not named but it was probably Noël-Armfield, who is reported as having run the Department on his own in Jones's absence.[31]

In November 1912, Daniel Jones set out to begin the adventure of his Indian tour. On arrival, in the heat of Madras, he may have realised that he had set himself an exhausting schedule; in the course of his tour, he "gave altogether about 50 lectures and classes".[32] The invitation had come from the Universities of Bombay, Madras and the Punjab, and the lectures dealt with English pronunciation with practical demonstration classes; in addition, he gave some classes (in Madras) on "the application of phonetics to the study of early English" and (at Lahore) a lecture on "the use of phonetics to missionaries".[33]

Jones also went out with a brief from the Simplified Spelling Society, of which he was now an active member and on whose behalf he had already given several lectures in England. The Society's journal, the *Pioneer*, printed some of Jones's own reports on his reception. In December, when he lectured at Madras, he considered the city "far ahead of any other centre, both as regards phonetics and as regards S.S.". At Lahore (January 1913), his audience "numbered about three hundred, nearly all being Indians". In Bombay, Jones's next stop, the audience was "small, select—about sixty I should think, including many white people", but he was told that this was "a much larger audience than usually assembles at the Teachers' Association meetings...". Jones concluded that "the Indians are *very keen* on S.S. but most of the English people (with a few brilliant exceptions) still require convincing" and that he had "been able to pave the way for phonetics in the Punjab and Bombay" (Jones 1913q).

Jones made a favourable impression on the Indian educational world. A talk on spelling reform in the Senate House at Madras, for example, was well received: "The lecture was greatly appreciated and had an influence far beyond the immediate audience."[34] On the other hand, India was a telling experience for Jones; for the first time, he came into contact with a non-European civilisation based on quite different religious values from those which he had previously encountered. He found it absorbing, and it is here that he would have gained an early insight into Hinduism and Buddhism, laying the foundation for his interest in theosophy, which was to be such an important influence on his thought and action in his later years. He would have plenty going through his mind as his ship steamed back from India to the cold February fogs of London.

4.8. The death of Sweet

In the world of phonetics, other events of 1912 were largely overshadowed by the death of Henry Sweet, who had been for so long the generally acknowledged "elder statesman" of the science, indeed of language study generally. The May-June number of *Le Maître phonétique* carried the news within a funereal black border under the sombre heading: "L'a.f. en deuil" (see Figure 4.1).[35]

Towards the end of his life, Sweet suffered from the then incurable disease of pernicious anaemia, and his publications had become sparse. There is indeed evidence that he had been increasingly mentally unstable from about 1906 onwards, when his tendency to paranoia began to exhibit signs of more than mere eccentricity (MacMahon 1985). Nevertheless, he remained a figure of authority, and it must have seemed that phonetics (especially British phonetics) was virtually unthinkable without him. It was fitting that Jones—who would later assume a similarly dominant role—should write Sweet's obituary (Jones 1912i).

lə
mɛːtrə fɔnetik

ɔrgan
də l asɔsjɑːsjɔ̃ fɔnetik ɛːtɛrnasjɔnal

vɛ̃tsɛtjɛm ane. — 5–6. — mɛ-ʒɥɛ̃ 1912

sɔmɛːr

l **af** ɑ̃ dœːj.

kɔ̃trɑ̃ːdy. — H. Morf, *Zur sprachlichen Gliederung Frankreichs* (P. P.) — F. Heimann, *Lehrbuch der französischen Sprache* (P. P.) — R. Ekblom, *Rysk Grammatik.*

kɔrɛspɔ̃ːdɑ̃ːs. — swiːdiʃ vauəlz (Buergel Goodwin). — sʌm æbədiːnʃə vauəlz (J. L. Wilson).

divɛːr. — sa ə la. — fonetik ɑɹkaivz in ʃəkɑgo (E. B. Thorntun).

parti dez elɛːv. — frɑ̃ːsɛ : le ʹvjø, sɥit (Motte). — dɔytʃ : ʹduːdən-ʹhøːfərs ʹlɛːnçən (Horn). — itaɲaːno : l ortolaːno e il kattʃatoːre (Camilli).

parti administratiːv. — sirkylɛːr. — egzamɛ̃ d fɔnetik. — nuvo mɑ̃ːbr (1470—1502). — ʃɑ̃ːʒmɑ̃ d adrɛs. — sitɥɑːsjɔ̃ finɑ̃ːsjɛːr (+ frɑ̃ 364.25).

syplemɑ̃. — *Notes sur la Prononciation de la Langue Mandarine de Pékin*, par R. Ch. Guernier. — *Das begriffliche Lehrverfahren, insbesondere beim Lesenlehren*, von Hans Spieser.

l **af** ɑ̃ dœːj

nɔtrə prezidɑ̃ d ɔnœːr HENRY SWEET ɛ mɔːr lə 30 avril dɛrnje, aprɛz yn ase lɔ̃ːg maladi. nu dɔnrɔ̃ yn notis nekrolɔʒik dɑ̃ l prɔʃɛ̃ nymero dy **mf.**

Figure 4.1. The announcement of the death of Henry Sweet in *Le Maître phonétique.*

Jones's personal contact with Sweet dates from 1907 (see Section 2.10). However, much earlier, Jones had already come under the influence of Sweet's published work and it is known that Sweet was one of the names most frequently mentioned in his conversations with Paul Passy and Sophie Lund when they met at Bourg-la-Reine.[36] Like many others, Jones appears to have been somewhat in awe of Sweet, who was notorious for his devastating attacks on his fellow academics. Jones commented on Sweet's acid tongue in the obituary, referring diplomatically to his "quaint dry humour, which was often highly entertaining" (Jones 1912i: 99), but in a personal letter written only three years before his own death, Jones felt able to expand on this.

He had a keen dry humour, & often said very funny things. His sayings, however, generally had a little sting in them directed against someone far less capable than himself, who had (in his eyes) done something foolish or indiscreet. Traces of this attitude may be seen in some of his prefaces and even in some of his texts.[37]

After meeting Sweet at the 1907 vacation course, Jones and his colleague Savory had both asked to have private lessons from him (see Section 2.10). These revealed Sweet to be "an excellent private teacher for good students" despite his apparent failings as a lecturer.[38] Jones probably took advantage of Sweet's system of having pupils staying at his house for weekends, where they would be offered board and lodging in addition to intensive tuition in aspects of practical phonetics. It is not certain how long this pupil-teacher relationship continued, but it perhaps helped to ensure that Jones's name was put forward when a replacement for Sweet's teaching of phonetics at the Oxford Taylorian Institute had to be found on his death (see Section 5.9).

In his obituary, Jones praises Sweet for his great contributions to phonetics and other branches of linguistics, saying that his "lamented death…deprived the world of its foremost phonetician". The admiration for Sweet is obviously sincerely felt, and Jones places him in the line of "other distinguished phoneticians… Ellis, Bell and Storm" but rates him above any of these (Jones 1912i: 97). Jones (1912i: 98) has interesting comments on Sweet's development of various forms of transcription:

I think we shall not be far wrong if we attribute much of the success of Sweet's work to the excellent "broad Romic" system of phonetic transcription which he invented. His predecessors used phonetic systems which were admirable in their way, but were far too complicated for the needs of the average student. Sweet, though even greater as a phonetician, did not, in works intended for popular use, deter readers by using a script of a complexity proportional to his knowledge. Though a strong supporter of Bell's "Visible Speech" system, he made no extensive use of it in his elementary books. And we cannot help feeling that his *Primer of phonetics* (which must be regarded as an advanced book in spite of its title) would have done more for promoting the cause of phonetics if he had dispensed with the use in it of "Visible Speech".

This section clearly states Jones's views on transcription, which he did not subsequently change much. It confirms that by this time Jones had become very suspicious of any form of "organic alphabet" despite his earlier collaboration with Paul Passy (see Section 2.11). He goes on to say that the IPA owes a "special debt of gratitude to Sweet" since Broad Romic "forms the basis of the a.f. system", and claims that "without it the a.f. might never have existed".

Jones emphasises the importance of Henry Sweet's contribution to language teaching and, in particular, his insistence on the value of applied phonetics in this field. He says of the *Practical study of languages* (Sweet 1899) that it is "a book for all time". Of Sweet's more advanced works, Jones states them to be "masterpieces of erudition and models of conciseness", adding that "his style of writing was peculiarly concise and the amount of information packed into his volumes is amazing" (Jones 1912i: 98–99).

Jones's assessments of Sweet are of value as a contemporary judgement on a scholar who is now fully recognised as one of the greatest early pioneers of modern linguistics, and whose "modernity" is increasingly being stressed (Kelly—Local 1984). In addition, Jones has here acknowledged the important influence of Sweet's works—together with the inspiration of Tilly, and the direct guidance given by Passy. Furthermore, from Jones's comments on Sweet, one may deduce what form Jones thought his own contribution to phonetics should take—and it must be remembered that at this time he was engaged on writing several important works, among them the *Outline*[1]. He envied Sweet's compressed style and wished to emulate it. Jones saw clearly the disadvantages of organic alphabets and the virtues of the economical and elegant "Broad Romic" transcription in Sweet's own books, and ignored the former in favour of varieties similar to the latter in his own works. Daniel Jones realised that Sweet was right to emphasise the importance of the application of basic phonetic principles to foreign language teaching. And when he says of Sweet: "He was a hard though slow worker, but his slowness was compensated for by his extreme accuracy" (Jones, 1912i: 99), Jones must have realised that these words could be applied with equal justification to himself.

Jones's private views on Sweet—as revealed in the personal letter quoted above—confirm what he said in 1912, but he goes into further detail on Sweet's defects of personal character. The obituary says that Sweet "was not a man who sought for a wide circle of acquaintances, but he was kindness itself to the few who were privileged to be his friends, and he was always ready to help ungrudgingly all who asked his assistance" (Jones 1912i: 99). The 1964 letter states baldly: "I doubt if Sweet had any real friends…unfortunately he was of a rather difficult disposition, and was apt to alienate those who might have been friends by criticizing them".[39]

Jones goes on to say that Sweet "made no allowance for the fact that pioneers generally have to be followed by 'popularizers' of inferior intellect, or by 'followers' who do not really understand properly what the pioneer teaches". It is not clear whether Jones was modestly placing himself in either of these categories; more likely, he was thinking of the many books which employed portions of Sweet's work in modified and simplified form, and of the way in which Jones's own books were later similarly treated. The mellower side of Sweet's nature is confirmed: "He was always kind to me when I had lessons with him." He apparently criticised Jones's early work, but Jones admits: "Later on I found that he was right in the matter he criticised, & I had to do what I could to rectify my errors." Though it would now be impossible to distinguish those revisions which stem from Sweet's criticisms, the remark indicates clearly that Sweet remained an influence throughout Jones's career, and that their personal contact was crucial to its development.

An interesting sidelight on Henry Sweet, which is revealed in a postscript to the letter, is that Jones appeared to regard him as being in a sense a co-religionist:

> Sweet was not an irreligious man, though I don't think the conventional Christianity of the Church of England could have appealed to his eminently logical mind. He was, I believe, well versed in the theological writings of Swedenborg. Also in Theosophy (in the days before distortions of the original teachings began to creep in).
>
> He once said to me "Do your duty in this world so as to prepare yourself for the next"—a wonderful rule of life, which must be taken into account by anyone who attempts the difficult task of estimating his qualities as a man.[40]

It therefore seems probable that conversations with Sweet influenced Jones's views not only on phonetics, but also on the religious philosophy which was eventually to be such an important part of Jones's later life. (For Sweet's religious beliefs, see also Wrenn 1946 [1966]: 529, who pointed out that in his latter years Sweet "though he would not have accepted any religious 'label' ... was ... something like a follower of Swedenborg".)

The two men seem to have held each other in high regard, though from Jones's side a certain sense of intimidation is also detectable. However, on Sweet's death, one of Jones's first acts was to ask Sweet's widow for a photograph of the great man.

> After some delay she consented. I had it framed & hung up in the Dept. of Phonetics, University College, London, where it still is. It is a very good likeness.[41]

4.9. Bernard Shaw and *Pygmalion*

Sweet is perhaps best known in the popular mind as the supposed inspiration for the character of Henry Higgins in Bernard Shaw's *Pygmalion*.[42] This version of events has been generally accepted by literary scholars and also by phoneticians (see, for example, Fromkin 1985a: 1).

Shaw began *Pygmalion* in March 1912, when Sweet was in the terminal stages of pernicious anaemia, and completed writing the play in June of that year, by which time Sweet was dead.[43] *Pygmalion* was written by Shaw with the declared intention of bringing the science of phonetics to the notice of the layman since he was convinced that phonetics had an important contribution to make in providing equality of opportunity and removing social class differences. "But if the play makes the public aware that there are such people as phoneticians, and that they are among the most important people in England at present, it will serve its turn" (Shaw 1916: 102). Daniel Jones, writing in the collection of tributes to Shaw published to celebrate his ninetieth birthday, says (Jones 1946a: 158):

> So convinced did Shaw become of the valuable potentialities of the subject, that some twenty-eight years ago he conceived the idea of making the general public aware, by means of a play, of what phonetic science is and what can be done with it. Hence his *Pygmalion*, which he tells me is the most popular of his plays. One of the purposes of this comedy was to show up the somewhat disagreeable fact that under present conditions people's manner of speaking has much to do with their success or failure in life (in the material sense). A second was to call attention to phonetics as a means of enabling a dialectal speaker to change his accent. In *Pygmalion* phonetics is represented as providing a key to social advancement— a function which it may be hoped it will not be called upon to perform indefinitely.

To a large extent, Shaw can be said to have achieved his aim. There is little doubt that the success of *Pygmalion* was responsible for bringing the newly established science of phonetics to the attention of many people for the first time, or as Jones has put it: "countless numbers of the public who without the stimulus applied by Shaw might never have learnt anything of the value of phonetics, or might even never have known that such a science exists" (Jones 1946a: 160). Later on, in the fifties, *My fair lady*, the American musical based on *Pygmalion*, also with the phonetician Henry Higgins as the hero, had a far wider international impact, and for most people probably remains all that they have ever heard about the subject.

Yet Shaw knew little about the discipline whose cause he espoused with such enthusiasm. Though he had been interested in phonetics since the 1870s and had conversed with both Ellis and Sweet, also having considerable correspondence with the latter (Shaw 1916: 99–102), his knowledge of the content of phonetics was limited; most of his writings on language show a combination of a little half-understood information with many bigoted opinions on the social characteristics and aesthetics of various accents of English; Shaw (1965) provides a collection of his polemics on linguistic matters. The view of phonetics presented in *Pygmalion* is essentially that of the elocutionist working skilful transformations with "people troubled with accents that cut them off from all high employment" (Shaw 1916: 103). Even in Bell's day, this would have been a somewhat one-sided view of the science. By 1912, it was unfair to concentrate on a tiny area of a diverse subject and present it (even in a comedy) as virtually the total substance of the science.

Shaw states in his *Preface*: "Pygmalion Higgins is not a portrait of Sweet, to whom the adventure of Eliza Doolittle would have been impossible", though he also claims "there are touches of Sweet in the play" (Shaw 1916: 102). One may accept the limited truth of this statement, but it is very difficult to go along with Wrenn (1946 [1966]: 529), who regards "Shaw's *Pygmalion* as presenting in Professor Higgins a dramatic portrait of Sweet which is true in substance as well as showing many of his external qualities". In fact, the character of Henry Higgins is in most ways remote from Sweet's personality. However, this raises the question whether there is any element in the stage phonetician Higgins other than that supplied by Shaw's imagination, and in particular whether there is anything of Daniel Jones. Shaw (1916: 102) demurs: "Of the later generations of phoneticians I know little. Among them towers the Poet Laureate [Robert Bridges], to whom perhaps Higgins may owe his Miltonic sympathies, though here again I must disclaim all portraiture."

Three points emerge from this odd apology of Shaw's. Firstly, it underlines his ignorance of linguistic matters inasmuch as he considers Bridges to be a phonetician at all, let alone a leading figure in the field (see below, Section 4.11). Secondly, it is suspicious, and strangely unlike Shaw, to proclaim that he was out of touch with recent scholarship in an area when he had just written a play dealing with that very topic. Lastly, what Shaw claims is simply not true, since there can be no doubt that Shaw was indeed quite well acquainted with Daniel Jones.

One critic, Irving Wardle, has already noted the inconsistencies in the *Preface*, but has then jumped to the conclusion that Higgins represents Shaw himself: "The Shavian red herring, linking Higgins with the philologist Henry Sweet, has fooled nobody (least of all those acquainted with the laborious Sweet) into missing the uncommonly direct and critical selfportraiture in the role" (Wardle 1979: 161). But although elements of Shaw's own personality may be discernible in Higgins, and certainly Shaw used the character as a means of publicising Shavian prejudices on language, the true reason for the emphasis on Sweet in the *Preface* to *Pygmalion* is quite different.

The most likely explanation for this strange section of the *Preface* lies in the contemporary British law of libel.[44] Although it would be perfectly permissible for Professor Higgins to be based on Sweet (now safely dead and buried), there had to be no suspicion that Shaw's hero was in any way similar to the leading *living* British phonetician—who was obviously Daniel Jones and certainly not Robert Bridges. Jones was the only person in Britain in charge of a university phonetics department. At this time, with his readership in the offing (see Section 6.3), Jones would have felt particularly vulnerable to any hint of scandal or unfavourable publicity. Had there been any mention of a libel action, Shaw would undoubtedly have been made aware of Jones's legal connections. It is clear that Shaw met Jones before the play was completed, having sought him out in order to get advice on phonetic matters. This is presumably the reason why *Pygmalion*, although containing much amateurish exaggeration and prescriptive polemic about phonetics and pronunciation, nevertheless has some sections which ring true, such as the well-known passage on vowel discrimination (Shaw 1916: 118–119) where the precepts of Jonesian ear-training techniques can be detected.

Pickering: I rather fancied myself because I can pronounce twenty-four distinct
vowel sounds; but your hundred and thirty beat me.
Higgins: Oh, that comes with practice. You hear no difference at first; but you
keep on listening, and presently you find theyre all as different as A from B.

Furthermore, the description of the apparatus in Higgins's Wimpole Street laboratory
(Shaw 1916: 117) is detailed and quite authentic for the period:

In this corner stands a flat writing-table, on which are a phonograph, a laryngoscope, a row of tiny organ pipes with a bellows, a set of lamp chimneys for singing flames with burners attached to a gas plug in the wall by an indiarubber tube,
several tuning-forks of different sizes, a life-size image of half a human head,
shewing in section the vocal organs, and a box containing a supply of wax cylin-
ders for the phonograph.

This was much the sort of equipment which Jones, with his limited resources, would
have used at University College, before the laboratory proper was set up in 1913. The
"tiny organ pipes" mentioned are almost certainly the "sirène à ondes" vowel
synthesiser which Jones received as a gift from the University of Paris around this
time (see Section 5.10). The description would therefore have been based either on
information supplied by Jones or, more probably, from the visit made by Shaw to
Jones at UCL.[45]

However, apart from what can be deduced from the circumstantial evidence to be
found in the text of the play, we have another source which indicates the importance
of Jones in supplying information and advice on phonetic matters for *Pygmalion*, and
that is Jones himself. He confided to his friend (and former student) Jean Overton
Fuller—who later put the matter on record in a letter to the *Observer*—that Shaw had
visited him when writing *Pygmalion*, and that the surname of the hero had come about
in the following manner:

Shaw afterwards told him that it was whilst riding on the deck of a bus through
South London, wondering what name he should give him, that he saw over a shop
Jones and Higgins. As, because of the fiction, "he could not call me Jones, he
called me Higgins."[46]

According to Miss Fuller, Shaw offered to provide Jones in perpetuity with compli-
mentary tickets for productions of his plays. Shaw's generosity (Jones claimed) was
intended as a token of gratitude to Jones "for having accepted in good part the fiction
Shaw had woven around him after a visit to his department".[47]

This information would establish a clear connection between Jones and *Pygmalion*,
whilst not, of course, meaning that the character of Higgins is meant to represent
Daniel Jones. Indeed, apart from a boundless enthusiasm for phonetics, there are few
ways in which Jones bore much resemblance to Henry Higgins—no more than did

Henry Sweet. But further evidence to link Jones with *Pygmalion* comes from Molly Tompkins, an American actress friend of Shaw's in the early 1920s. Shaw helped her in various ways, one of which was to ask Jones to give her private elocution training with the apparent intention of camouflaging her southern American accent. Tompkins (1961: 23–24) writes:

> Then, as he had promised, Shaw arranged for me to take lessons from a Welsh professor of Phonetics at London University in order to get rid of what he called my "provincialisms". Twice a week I would go to him from the Academy. He was an old friend of Shaw's, one of the real persons from whom he had drawn the character of Higgins in *Pygmalion*, a slender dark-haired man in his forties, clean shaven, with a quiet manner. I was comfortable with him, and loved learning from him. He would make me read things aloud and correct my pronunciation. There wasn't much Shaw wanted him to do, but about *those* things he was very particular, especially the removal of the *coup de glotte* which most Americans have when they say bu*dd*er instead of bu*tt*er. He did not want me to learn Mayfair or Oxford English, but to be able to speak clearly and effectively on the stage.

Despite the fact that Jones obviously failed to bring across the concept of *coup de glotte*, the lessons were apparently in other respects a great success (Tompkins 1961: 56):

> With Mr. Jones my phonetics progressed so satisfactorily that when he invited three other professors to listen to me read, one of them thought I was Russian, another English but none guessed I was American. So I graduated from his course with honours.

Apart from her confusion on phonetic matters, Molly Tompkins's memory failed her on two points. Jones was, of course, neither Welsh nor clean-shaven (he has a moustache in photographs of the period). But Molly Tompkins may have been misled into thinking Jones was Welsh by Shaw himself, who was under that misapprehension when he wrote to her in December 1921 (Tompkins 1960: 11):

> You will have to acquire the English alphabet in Gower St: you still have very queer Rs from the cockney standpoint, and one or two other letters that will bear polishing. Dont pick up smart English, which is bad English: all you need to do is to drop certain provincialisms. However, your Welsh instructor will take care of that: University College is not Oxford, thank heaven![48]

Though evidence for the Jones-*Pygmalion* connection seems beyond doubt, yet the question remains—why did Jones remain so quiet about his part in helping Shaw with his play? It must be concluded that Jones asked Shaw to agree to a pact of public silence.

On meeting Shaw, Jones would have speedily discovered just how shaky his knowledge of phonetics really was, and that therefore the presentation of the subject in any play he wrote unaided was likely to be amateurish. It is typical of Jones's widely acknowledged academic generosity that he should have given his advice willingly, perhaps flattered that a famous literary figure should seek his help, or perhaps in trepidation of how phonetics might be portrayed if some of Shaw's notions were not corrected. It cannot, however, be imagined that Jones had any detailed foreknowledge of the plot of *Pygmalion*, or the character of Higgins. With his prospects of promotion, Jones would most definitely not have wished to be associated with a play like *Pygmalion*, not only because of the taboo language featured in it, which shocked post-Edwardian England, but essentially because the action centres around the relationship of a professor of phonetics with one of his young female pupils. In any case, he would not have approved of the way in which Shaw presented the science of phonetics on the stage.

Pygmalion opened in London on April 11, 1914, and Jones was shocked to discover what Shaw had put into the play—only actually on the first night, according to Jean Overton Fuller.[49] Jones was furious about how phonetics—and phoneticians—would appear in the eyes of the general public. Shaw must therefore have agreed not to disclose the fact that Jones had advised him and furthermore slanted the *Preface* (which appeared first in the 1916 edition) in such a way as to disclaim any connection with, or even knowledge of, Jones. Instead, Shaw took pains to emphasise his contacts with the deceased Sweet, and also drew in Bridges as a decoy. Even in his later years, Jones does not appear to have wished to be connected (at least, publicly) with the Higgins character, or the Eliza Doolittle story. Because both Shaw and Jones were men of their word, the silence remained (in public) unbroken.

Nevertheless, in the course of time, Jones's attitude to the play itself—as opposed to his connection with it—changed. Jones even arranged a special production of *Pygmalion* by students from the Royal Academy of Dramatic Art for the entertainment of his phonetician colleagues at the 1935 International Congress of Phonetic Sciences held at UCL (see Section 11.10). However, perhaps a tiny echo of Jones's original irritation is still apparent in this largely favourable reference to *Pygmalion* contained in notes for a public lecture which he gave towards the end of his career.

> He wrote [*Pygmalion*] with the express object of bringing the idea of Phonetics to the notice of people at large. He of course held up the subject to considerable ridicule in that play, and made absurd claims for it, but he certainly succeeded in his Shavian way in opening the eyes of a great many people to the nature and some of the possibilities of phonetic science.[50]

The question remains whether Higgins's personality can be considered in any sense to be based on Jones. In fact, the Higgins character, no matter what its sources may have been, in addition to serving as a mouthpiece for Shaw's prejudices on speech and the appropriate social role of phonetics, would appear to have taken on a vivid life of its own during the writing of the play. So what Shaw claims in his *Preface* is literally true: Higgins is not *directly* based on any phonetician of the time. Nevertheless, an eagerness to dissociate his hero from the person of Daniel Jones has certainly resulted in Shaw's successfully misleading most commentators (*pace* Wardle) into thinking that Sweet is the sole original of Higgins, whilst Jones's crucial role in the writing of the play has so far gone almost entirely unnoticed by Shavian critics.

The case argued above was stated in detail for the first time in Collins (1986), although the claim of Jones to be the original of Higgins is mentioned briefly by Amos (1985: 248–249). Cf. J.C. Wells's interview with Gemma Bodinetz which was published as programme notes to the National Theatre's production of *Pygmalion* (first performance, Olivier Theatre, 9 April 1992).

4.10. The Simplified Spelling Society

Bernard Shaw and Jones were to meet again when they worked together on the BBC Pronunciation Advisory Committee (see Section 10.11); and in Shaw's final years, Jones was to attempt unsuccessfully to make him change his will so as to benefit the Simplified Spelling Society's campaign for spelling reform (see Section 12.8).

The foundation of the Simplified Spelling Society (henceforth SSS) has been already referred to above (Section 3.6). The brief article in *Le Maître phonétique* (Jones 1909g) is firm evidence of Jones's interest in the spelling reform campaign from its earliest days. The SSS was started in 1908 as a counterpart to the American Simplified Spelling Board, and from the first meeting (held on 10 September 1908) the need for co-operation with the American organisation was stressed. Fruitful results of this Anglo-American emphasis came in the form of a cheque for a thousand pounds— a sizable sum of money at the time—from the American philanthropist Andrew Carnegie (J. Pitman 1964: 177). The SSS began life in prosperity, and soon attracted a remarkable array of British scholars to its membership, amongst them William Archer, F.J. Furnivall, Gilbert Murray, S.A. Napier and H.C. Wyld. Others followed, including Walter Ripman, who became Treasurer in 1910 on Furnivall's death.

When exactly Jones became a member is not recorded but he himself believed it to be 1910.[51] In any case, his name appears for the first time in the minutes for December 19 of that year when he was proposed as one of the representatives for a conference between the English and American spelling reform organisations (J. Pitman 1964: 178). The conference, held actually in the Council Room of University College in September 1911, did not bring the hoped for co-operation. Jones referred to it later in these words: "A most interesting set of meetings, at U.C.L.—delightful people: but beyond providing useful exchanges of ideas, it was a complete failure." The American delegation were not prepared to consider anything as radical as the SSS alphabet, whilst the British refused to go along with the American plans for "simplifications by degrees".[52]

In the same year, Jones was called in to provide expert criticism of the Society's pamphlet on spelling reform, which contained its new orthography for English (Rippmann—Archer 1910). Jones's value to the Society was recognised when in September 1911, together with his old schoolmaster, E.R. Edwards, he was proposed for membership of the committee (J. Pitman 1984: 178). So began a period of involvement with the running of the Society which did not end until his death, since even after he retired as Chairman in 1950, he retained the title of President (see Section 12.8).

When it became known that Jones was to travel to India, the SSS took steps to ensure that he would work on their behalf, and that he would be paid for his trouble. He was asked to "lecture in as many centres of India as possible at the fee fixed for lecturers in this country" and "to bring back a report on the movement in India".[53] The arrangement would obviously have been financially attractive to Jones, and his exhausting schedule of lectures (see Section 4.7) was fixed accordingly. It is not stated anywhere explicitly that Jones's tour was sponsored by the SSS, but it is clear that without the support of the Society (which at this time had large resources) Jones would very probably not have been able to visit India at all, since much of the finance and a major purpose of the trip was provided in this way.

By 1913, the Society was prospering. Its membership was increasing month by month and the Ripman-Archer orthography was now well established and being employed in its organ, the *Pioneer*—the journal in which Jones's report of his Indian tour appeared (Jones 1913q). Jones was proving a good propagandist for the SSS as well as being a stalwart committee member, and on October 9, 1913 he took the chair at a meeting for the first time.[54] Jones's commitment to the SSS was firm and though the IPA remained his first allegiance, he was to prove unstinting in his efforts to further spelling reform.

4.11. The battles with Bridges

The SSS was soon able to return Jones's loyalty. In the March number of the *Pioneer* an editorial appeared, under the title "Poëts, fonetics and unstrest silablz" (Anon. 1913), which defended Jones against attacks which had been made on him by Robert Bridges (the recently appointed Poet Laureate) and the literary critic Lascelles Abercrombie.[55] The article by Abercrombie which prompted the response in the *Pioneer* was "Phonetics and Poetry" (L. Abercrombie 1913) but in fact the disputes had begun very much earlier in 1910, when a long article by Robert Bridges appeared in *Essays and studies*, the new and prestigious annual compilation of the English Association.

Though Bridges had been put forward by Shaw (possibly with tongue in cheek) as Britain's leading living phonetician (Section 4.9), the reality was quite different. Bridges could scarcely be credited with having any phonetic expertise at all—though curiously, he is thought to merit a fairly long article in the *Biographical dictionary of the phonetic sciences* (Bronstein—Raphael—Stevens 1977). Bridges came from a

16. On holiday in Denmark (1912)   17. Arnold Jones

18. Jones in Madras in 1912.

19. Henry Sweet on holiday near Carlingford Lough

20. George Bernard Shaw (1914)

21. Robert Bridges, the poet laureate

family of landed gentry, and after being educated at Eton and Corpus Christi College, Oxford, later qualified in medicine. At thirty-seven, he gave up his practice and retired to devote himself to poetry and his other interests—which included music, printing and typography, and also an amateurish preoccupation with certain aspects of phonetics. He was a figure of considerable reputation in his lifetime—not only was he created Poet Laureate in 1913, but in 1929 he received the rare honour of being made a member of the Order of Merit. After his death, his reputation waned and he is now regarded as a minor poet.[56]

Bridges' involvement in phonetics centred around two matters—the study of prosody, and standards of pronunciation in English; and it was the latter aspect which brought his wrath down on Daniel Jones. Bridges believed sincerely that the pronunciation of English was gravely threatened by declining standards, and was therefore determined to fight to restore it to what he considered to be its proper state. In Bridges' view, this was to be determined by the orthography. His tract "On the present state of English pronunciation" (Bridges 1910) begins with the rhetorical questions: "Is English pronunciation at the present time on the road to ruin? and [sic] if so, can anything be done to save it?" (p. 42). This sets the tone for the remainder. He is particularly concerned with what he terms the "degradation of the unaccented vowels" (p. 42)—by which he means the use of /ə/ in unstressed syllables: "Do not əə, my beloved brethren, and had I been writing a sermon, I might have chosen those words for my text" (p. 43).

Bridges then begins to make slighting references to Jones's work (p. 43):

> To show how far this sound is ousting all the proper vowels, it will suffice to take a book that was issued three years ago by the University Press at Oxford—of which I learn that over 1000 copies are already in circulation—the *Phonetic Transcriptions of English Prose*, by Daniel Jones, and to examine what is there described as the "Pronunciation used in careful conversation, or in reading aloud in private", which is "the pronunciation recommended for the use of foreigners".

Bridges then quotes thirty-five words, taken from the first page of *Phonetic transcriptions of English prose*, which Jones has represented containing /ə/ in either weak forms or unstressed syllables, and continues (p. 45):

> Now please observe, most gracious reader, that this is not a dream nor a joke. It shows the actual present condition of things, as formulated by an expert, promulgated by the University of Oxford, and recommended *ter* foreigners. Foreigners are really being taught that the pronunciation of *to* (tŭ), which is hundreds of years old, is now changed to *ter* (tə), and that in our "careful conversation" we say *ter* and *inter* for *to* and *into*.

He later goes on to rail against "phonetic decay" (p. 48):

Degradation of speech has no limit but its own actual unintelligibility. Decay is always pushing in, because of the laziness of the speaker, who will take no more trouble than is necessary. Phonetic laws meanwhile only decide the manner of his corruptions.

Daniel Jones is criticised, not for any inaccuracy in representing the forms of spoken English that Bridges objects to—since Bridges has to admit that these are normal, even in the speech of his own social circle—but for condoning such forms and not wishing to change them in any way (p. 46).

The only question can be whether Mr. Jones exaggerates the actual prevalence of degradation. Some will acquit him of any exaggeration. Others I know very well will regard him as a half-witted faddist, beneath serious notice, who should be left to perish in his vain imaginings.

Such extreme language must have irritated Jones, even though he would have fully realised the stupidity of Bridges' position, for even Bridges himself acknowledged that anyone "may congratulate himself if he does not pronounce more than seventy per cent. of his words as Mr. Jones represents them" (p. 46). Nevertheless, the assaults would have caused Jones concern—if only because he was attempting to establish himself in the academic world, and to gain acceptance for phonetics as a recognised discipline in universities and colleges.

Curiously, Bridges was in favour of a type of spelling reform and even devised what he termed a "literary phonetic alphabet" (p. 53), with no fewer than fifty-eight symbols "taking for my basis...the half-uncial of the eighth century" (p. 52). He appended several transcriptions to his essay, including one portion alongside an extract taken from Jones's *Phonetic transcriptions of English prose* (see Figure 4.2). Jones chose not to commit himself to print on the matter throughout this whole affair, although it transpires that he did make his views known to Bridges in private (see below), and also in public at two meetings of the English Association, which he later described as: "...quite sensational affairs, remarkable in the history of this very sedate society for extremely lively discussions and the use of language a good deal more outspoken and emphatic than would appear from the official accounts given subsequently in our bulletins."[57]

In fact, Jones did not make any further public statement until nearly thirty years later, long after Robert Bridges was dead. In 1946, he gave a lecture to the English Association (henceforth, the English Association Lecture) asking his audience whether they "would like an old controversy...to be revived".[58] Quoting Wyld (1909: vii): "Everyone who writes about English pronunciation must expect to be abused", Jones describes his difficulties with "the type of person who doesn't like being told how people pronounce words". Referring to the beginning of his own professional career, he recalls:

I. Mr. Daniel Jones, p. 10.

bɪˈsaidz ˈðouz ˈθiŋz witʃ diˈrektli səˈdʒest ði: aidiə əv ˈdeindʒə, ənd ˈðouz witʃ prədjuːs ə ˈsimilər ɪˈfekt frəm ə mɪˈkænikl ˈkɔːz. ai nou əv ˈnʌθiŋ səˈblaim witʃ iz nɔt ˈsʌm mɔdifiˈkeiʃn əv ˈpauə. ənd ˈðis ˈbrɑːntʃ raiziz, əz ˈnætʃ(ə)rəli əz ði: ˈʌðə ˈtuː ˈbrɑːntʃiz, frəm ˈterə, ðə ˈkɔmən ˈstɔk əv ˈevriθiŋ ðət iz səˈblaim. ði: aidiə əv ˈpauə, ət ˈfəːst ˈvjuː, ˈsiːmz əv ðə ˈklɑːs əv ðouz inˈdifrənt wʌnz witʃ mei ˈiːkwəli biloŋ tə ˈpein ɔː tə ˈpleʒə. bət in riˈæliti. ði: əˈfekʃən əˈraiziŋ frəm ði: aidiə əv ˈvɑːst ˈpauə iz iksˈtriːmli rɪˈmout frəm ðæt ˈnjuːtrəl ˈkærəktə. fə ˈfəːst, wiː mʌst rɪˈmembə ðət ði: aidiə əv ˈpein, in its ˈhaiəst dɪˈgriː, iz ˈmʌtʃ ˈstrɔŋgə ðən ðə ˈhaiəst dɪgriː əv ˈpleʒə; ənd ðət it prɪzəːvz ðə ˈseim sjuːpiəriˈoriti θruː ˈɔːl ðə səˈbɔːdənit grəˈdeiʃnz. frəm ˈhens it iz, ðət wɛə ðə ˈtʃɑːnsiz fər ˈiːkwəl dɪˈgriːz əv ˈsʌfəriŋ ɔːr inˈdʒɔimənt ər in ˈeni ˈsɔːt ˈiːkwəl, ði: aidiə əv ðə ˈsʌfəriŋ məst ˈɔːlweiz bi ˈprevələnt.

II. The same, in my script.

Bɛsịɒs ᴄhoş ᴄhiŋş which ɒiʀɛᴄᴄly şᴠgɛsᴄ ᴄhɪ jɒᴄa¹ oꝼ ɒaŋʒɛʀ, anɒ ᴄhoş which pʀoɒụ̧ a similaʀ ɛꝼɛᴄᴄ ꝼʀom a mɛᴄanic·l ᴄᴠş, ị knɛw oꝼ nᴠᴄhiŋ şᴠblịm which iş noᴄ şᴠm moɒiꝼicaᴄịᴠn oꝼ pauʀ. ᴀnɒ ᴄhiş bʀanᴄh ʀịşɛş, aş naᴄᴠʀaly aş ᴄhɪ ᴠᴄheʀ ᴄω bʀanᴄheş, ꝼʀom ᴄɛʀoʀ, ᴄhɪ comᴠn şᴄoᴄk oꝼ ɛᴠɛʀyᴄhiŋ ᴄhaᴄ iş şᴠblịm. ᴄhɪ jɒᴄa oꝼ pauʀ, aᴄ ꝼɛʀşᴄ ᴠᴠ, şᴠmş oꝼ ᴄhɪ claş oꝼ ᴄhoş inɒiꝼɛʀɛnᴄ wᴠnş which mɛy ᴠᴄ̧ᴠaly bịloŋ ᴄᴠ pɛin oʀ ᴄᴠ plɛşᴠʀ. Bᴠᴄ in ʀɛaliᴄy, ᴄhɪ aꝼɛᴄᴄịᴠn aʀịşiŋ ꝼʀom ᴄhɪ jɒᴄa oꝼ vaşᴄ pauʀ iş ɛᴄᴛᴠmly ʀịmoᴄ ꝼʀom ᴄhaᴄ nᴠᴄᴛ·l caʀacᴄeʀ. Foʀ ꝼɛʀşᴄ, wɪ mᴠşᴄ ʀị-membɛʀ ᴄhaᴄ ᴄhɪ jɒᴄa oꝼ pɛin, in iᴄş hịhɛşᴄ ɒịgʀɛᴄ, iş mᴠᴄh şᴄʀoŋgɛʀ ᴄhan ᴄhɪ hịhɛşᴄ ɒịgʀɛᴄ oꝼ plɛşᴠʀ; anɒ ᴄhaᴄ iᴄ pʀịşɛʀᴠş ᴄhɪ şam şᴠpʀịoʀiᴄy ᴄhʀω ᴠl ᴄhɪ şᴠboʀɒinaᴄ gʀaɒaᴄịᴠnş. Fʀom hɛṇ iᴄ iş, ᴄhaᴄ whaˑʀ ᴄhɪ chançɛş ꝼoʀ ᴠᴄᴛ·l ɒịgʀɛᴄş oꝼ şᴠꝼɛʀiŋ oʀ ɛnjoymɛnᴄ aʀ in ɛny şoʀᴄ ᴠᴄᴛˑl, ᴄhɪ jɒᴄa oꝼ şᴠꝼɛʀiŋ mᴠşᴄ ᴠlwɛyş bɪ pʀɛvalɛnᴄ, ɛᴄᴄ.

Figure 4.2. Bridges' alphabet as printed in his essay alongside an extract from *Phonetic transcriptions of English prose* (Bridges 1910: 65–66).

When I came on to the phonetic scene (or rather I think it may be better described as a battlefield) in 1907, I came in for quite an amount of criticism, just as my predecessors had done.

Jones says that he had been accused of advocating the speech of "costermongers and servant-girls" and that one critic had written to him complaining of Jones's "nauseating London simper". Going on to relate the story of his battle with Bridges, whom he describes with characteristic generosity as "my good friend" and "that very distinguished scholar", he says:

> In spite of the peculiar language in which his criticisms were couched, I don't think Bridges really considered my observations to be inaccurate—at least so I gathered from many a talk with him. What he did object to was that people should record in print the actual facts of speech. He held the view that the pronunciation of English ought to be altered in various particulars, and he actually devised a manner of writing what he deemed to be a suitable reformed pronunciation.

With gentle irony, Jones points out that Bridges' own speech was not at all consistent with his published views.

> ...he didn't speak with his reformed pronunciation; his pronunciation was very much like mine, except that he made rather freer use of the obscure vowel to which he took such strong objection. I and a friend once counted them at a meeting of this Association—the Annual General Meeting of Jan. 28th, 1911—at which he was one of the chief speakers.

Jones claims that Bridges "deplored the fact that phoneticians did not fancy becoming champions of reformed pronunciation", and that they were attempting "to stereotype degraded forms". Jones then responds:

> I hope that by now [1946] people have come to realise that we are not out to do this kind of thing. Nor have we power to do it if we could. The phonetician is an observer of facts. If the facts turn out to be distasteful to anybody, the phonetician cannot help it. He finds out how people speak, and his findings may be taken as a basis to work upon by people who desire to undertake the invidious task of reforming pronunciation, of deciding what is to be approved and what should be condemned.[59]

Jones goes on to say: "Personally I now find myself more loth than ever to make recommendations concerning pronunciation", and this assertion is an echo of statements to be found throughout his publications, for instance in the later editions of the *EPD*.

The English Association Lecture shows how far he eventually moved from his prescriptive elocutionary position of *Pronunciation of English*[1] in 1909 (see Sections

3.4 and 14.5). Jones would doubtless have altered his views sooner or later anyway—but the change was accelerated by the patent absurdity of the attacks by Bridges and Abercrombie on Jones's books.

Bridges' essay reappeared in book form in 1913, when he modified the content, and toned down some of the more outspoken passages. This version featured numerous appendices, the first of which is entitled "Apology to Mr. Jones". Bridges is in fact extravagantly apologetic in his retractions, and terms Jones "an unimpeachable authority" and says that his transcriptions are "absolutely faithful" (Bridges 1913: 37). Bridges' embarrassment is perhaps reflected in his contorted English style (p. 37):

> But I was writing mainly for those who would not agree with us, nor believe him; and in my appeal to them I took advantage of their prejudices in so far as I could sympathise with them: and this attitude, no doubt exaggerated, and my quarrel with him that I held him somewhat guilty of teaching this conversational style as "correct" and without seeking to improve it, led him to misinterpret me.

Bridges points out that he has amended several passages referring to Jones, and says (p. 38):

> ...though my opinion can be of little service to him, I wish for my own credit to say that I consider him such a trustworthy expert that I should be ashamed to appear to disagree with him.

He then remarks, oddly, that Jones "concurs with me in my opinion that some of the decaying sounds may be saved, and in my wish that they should be restored", so concluding "there is really no disagreement whatever between us" (p. 38). This last statement would suggest that Jones was either being remarkably diplomatic, or, possibly, somewhat pusillanimous, in his discussions with Bridges, since the conclusion is obviously false.

So what had occurred between the publication of Bridges' first outburst in 1910 and the second version in 1913? Bridges appears to have realised, or to have had pointed out to him, that Jones was a far more formidable opponent than he m ght first of all appear, with power-bases in London and Oxford, and a host of impr r .nt friends in the British academic establishment. In order to mend their relationship, Bridges decided to take the bold step of inviting the Joneses to stay at Chilsworth, his home near Oxford, in the early summer of 1912. Jones could hardly have contemplated refusing such an invitation: not only would he have offended Bridges further, but he would also have had to reject the prospect of meeting over dinner at Corpus Christi such luminaries as Henry Bradley (1845–1923), the philologist and lexicographer, and Sir William Alexander Craigie (1867–1957), the Oxford professor of Scandinavian Languages. Both men had been working on the *Oxford English dictionary*, Craigie being its joint editor from 1901 to 1933. Bradley was eventually unable to attend, but was informed by Bridges later that the visit as a whole had been a great success. It appears that Jones at last had managed to convince Bridges of his academic integrity, and had genuinely enjoyed his meeting with Craigie. Cyrille played her part appropriately, and succeeded in charming her host. Bridges wrote to Bradley:

> Daniel Jones and his wife, who is a very young Frenchwoman, came to us for 2 or 3 days. We got on well with them and I had great discussions about the points that I fight for—and he was not at all unsympathetic. He seems a really learned phonetician, very clearheaded and generally reasonable. His wife "quite a dear" [sic]—I got Craigie to come and dine at C.C.C. [Corpus Christi College] to meet him. Jones was very sorry for your absence, but got on swimmingly with Craigie, who was I knew just the man for him, because Daniel is just now prosecuting Scandinavian.[60]

Bridges seems even to have got on to first name terms with Jones (which would have been astonishing intimacy for a time when middle-class men were in the habit of addressing each other by surname even after years of close friendship). But Bridges' motives for extending hospitality to Jones are made clear later in the letter to Bradley:

> I think the sort of alliance that I have made with Jones may bring him to be more scrupulous about the tendency of his teaching: for he saw the point of my contention, and, as I said, he was not unsympathetic.[61]

Undoubtedly, in the atmosphere of apparent bonhomie which Bridges had managed to engender, Jones would have felt himself forced to make concessions to Bridges' linguistic fads. Nonetheless, Daniel Jones, too, was probably satisfied with the outcome of the encounter, and with Bridges' eventual published apology, even though he might have found the republication of the offending essay an irritant.

On the other hand, Bridges' true opinion of "the enemy Jones and Company", as he designated them in a letter to Lascelles Abercrombie six months later,[62] is probably reflected better in his later piece *On English homophones* (Bridges 1919). This, one of the tracts published by the Society for Pure English, an organisation which he, together with Bradley and others, had founded in 1911, was devoted to the hypothesis that degraded pronunciation standards had led to English having a superfluity of homophones and that this was endangering the intelligibility of the language. Jones's name occurs on no fewer than eighteen of its pages (well over a third of the total) and much of the text is devoted to attacking him, directly or indirectly, for failing to preserve standards in pronunciation—although Bridges scrupulously and repeatedly mentions Jones's professional competence in the most flattering terms. Gimson (1977: 154) picks out the following samples of his diatribes (Bridges 1919):

> The peril that we are in of having Mr. Jones' degraded pronunciation thus sprung upon us in England and taught in all our schools is really threatening. (p. 37 n.)

...the mischief is being encouraged and propagated by the phoneticians, and Mr. Jones' books are taken as an example of their method.

The reason why the work of these phoneticians is so mischievous is that they have chosen too low a standard of pronunciation. (p. 38)

I have been told that the German experts believe that the Cockney form of English will eventually prevail. (p. 45)[63]

Doubtless, Jones initially felt at risk under the assaults of figures such as Robert Bridges and Lascelles Abercrombie. Bridges was—officially at least—the leading poet in the land, and Abercrombie was a critic with a high reputation. No matter what their lack of expertise, and notwithstanding the absurdity of their arguments, or the ill-judged nature of their language, their opinions carried weight, particularly in academic circles where their influence was immense. However, with the support of more knowledgeable colleagues in the IPA and the SSS, Jones was able to survive the storm. It is indicative that when it came out, Bridges' (1919) polemic, despite its immoderate phrasing, caused scarcely a flurry and was soon forgotten.

By 1913, Jones's international status was established, his position in UCL was secure and likely to improve soon with promotion to a readership. Ironically, both Bridges and Abercrombie were to influence his life in other ways. Robert Bridges would later be appointed Chairman of the BBC's Advisory Committee on Spoken English (see Section 10.11). Lascelles Abercrombie's son, David, was eventually to be a student in Jones's Department and afterwards go on to found at Edinburgh the largest department of phonetics and linguistics within the British university system, becoming himself one of the leading advocates of Jonesian approaches to phonetics.

Chapter 5

Studying spoken language

5.1. *Phonetic readings in English*

Throughout this period, despite the strains of putting a home together, the foreign lecture tours, his academic battles and day-to-day difficulties of setting into motion a rapidly expanding department, Daniel Jones managed to find even more time than before to devote to writing books and articles. This was when some of his best work was produced—although, because of the war, some of it would not be published until several years later. *Phonetic readings in English* (Jones 1912b, henceforth *Phonetic readings*) is a book which is noteworthy chiefly for the huge number of reprintings which it has achieved. Though a modest work, *Phonetic readings* is certainly one of the most popular phonetic textbooks ever written, and is still sold today in a form little different from that in which it first appeared from the press of Carl Winter in Heidelberg more than eight decades ago.

For some time Jones had been publishing short passages of English in phonetic transcription, which appeared in the "partie des élèves" section of *Le Maître phonétique*. He bundled a number of these together, and added several more, bringing the total up to forty. The emphasis was on a light humorous touch—though many of the passages may seem rather lugubrious in their wit to a modern reader. In addition, Jones added a one act comedy (*Box and Cox* by J.M. Morton) and William Cowper's comic poem *John Gilpin*. Jones says in his introduction: "It is hoped that the comedy included in this book may be found specially useful in *schools* where English is taught on modern lines" (*Phonetic readings*: iv). It is doubtful whether Jones's choice of humour would ever have appealed to schoolchildren, but the book did have an immediate success in universities and teacher training colleges. The first edition rapidly sold out and a second edition was on sale before the outbreak of war in 1914. Jones later recorded the forty anecdotes himself on gramophone discs which were marketed by Deutsche Grammophon Gesellschaft.[1]

Phonetic readings is of significance in that it shows Jones becoming more realistic in terms of transcription as compared with the earlier *Phonetic transcriptions*. He abandons the division into three degrees of formality of style, and removes from his transcriptions the oddities in vowel representations that Savory (1908) had rightly found objectionable. The transcriptions are workman-like; and if often over-careful to a modern ear, in other places they appear to be daringly progressive in their representations of assimilated and elided forms. For example, he indicates as alternatives in footnotes [ˈdoump ˈbliːv] and [ˈpoultərəʒ ˈʃɔp] for "don't believe" and "poulterer's shop" (p. 9); the form [præps] is given as the preferred choice for "perhaps" (p. 10). Tie-marks are shown throughout before word-initial vowels, presumably because the book was aimed in the first place at the German market, and this would help avoid the typical German error of over-glottalisation as the onset to vowels in this context. No concession has been made to those such as Bridges who wished to see the representation of the vowels suggested by the orthography in unstressed syllables (see Section 4.11). Three passages are shown with intonation curves similar to those in the *Phonetic transcriptions* and the *Pronunciation of English*, but no discussion of intonation is included in the book.

In 1950, shortly after his retirement, Jones made slight emendations for a revised edition (the twenty-ninth) which was published in 1951. A few years later, in 1955, a more thorough revision was performed and in 1963, right at the end of his life, Jones was asked to make new recordings of the texts and these were published by Linguaphone (see Section 13.14). However, the book has remained unaltered in its essentials for over eighty years—and is perhaps most remarkable for that.

5.2. The *Cantonese phonetic reader* and the *London Phonetic Reader* series

The other phonetic reader to appear in 1912 was quite unlike *Phonetic readings*. Though its sales were tiny, its significance was great; nothing of quite this type had ever appeared before. This was the start of a series which was to be of great importance in the development of descriptive phonetics and its application to a wide range of languages, many of which had not been subjected to linguistic analysis of any sort previously. The *Cantonese phonetic reader* (Jones—Kwing Tong Woo 1912a) was written by Daniel Jones in collaboration with a Cantonese Chinese informant. It was the first of the numerous similar publications to appear under the imprint of the London Phonetic Readers. Jones had wished to find an outlet for the research which he was conducting on the sound systems of a number of languages. He also needed to show that phonetics had a useful role to play in language learning—not only for French, German, Italian and Spanish, but also for the languages of the Far East, India and Africa, which at this time were virtually unexplored areas of knowledge. A solution was found by means of an arrangement with the University of London Press—which had already produced *Chindau*. They agreed to publish a series of short readers which would include a concise description and analysis of the overall sound system of the language concerned—all to be carried out on strictly IPA principles. It was decided to cover a wide range of languages—some familiar, like French and German, some at that time virtually unexplored, like Tswana. Over the course of the next thirty years, up to the outbreak of the Second World War, sixteen further books on similar lines appeared.[2] The majority were never expected to make a profit, and needed subsidies from the University, the authors or other sources. (Jones incurred a debt of £90 for the *Cantonese phonetic reader*, which was not repaid until 1918, see Section 7.9)

It has already been noted (Section 3.9) that *Chindau* gives the impression of being a kind of forerunner to the London Phonetic Reader series. It is also interesting to notice that the form and content of *Phonetic readings* are similar to what one would expect from such a volume if it had appeared in the London Phonetic Reader series. It is possible that Jones had originally planned *Phonetic readings* as the first of the London Phonetic Readers, but changed his plans—possibly realising that sales of the book would be far greater, and of longer duration, if aimed at the German market rather than if it were the first of an experimental series produced by the University of London press.

In any case, the London Phonetic Readers got off to a good start with the publication of the *Cantonese phonetic reader*. Though Jones and Kwing Tong Woo appear on the title page as co-authors, it is actually clear from the Introduction (which is stated as being written exclusively by Jones) that Woo acted only in the role of informant, and that the organisation and theoretical aspects of the book are Jones's work. This is implied by the following portion of the Introduction (p. viii):

> The texts in colloquial style were specially written by Mr. Woo. The transcriptions were made by me from Mr. Woo's dictation. Mr. Woo speaks typical good Cantonese and his pronunciation may be relied on as an excellent standard. Moreover, the transcription of every word has been repeatedly checked, and in no case has the transcription of a word been finally settled until the word has been pronounced by me to Mr. Woo's satisfaction.

It is typical of Jones's intellectual generosity that he wished to share the credit for the book with his informant, when many academics might have relegated Woo's part in the work to a brief acknowledgement.

Jones makes the point in the "Introduction" to the *Cantonese phonetic reader* (p. v) that little previous work had been done on Chinese languages, but he mentions, together with other publications on Mandarin Chinese, an article which had appeared in *Le Maître phonétique* entitled "Cantonese Phonetics" (Seers 1908). This appears to have been, for its time, a very good summary of the Cantonese sound system and Jones must have found it a useful basis on which to develop his own analysis. In 1911, Jones had produced a brief article on Cantonese for *Le Maître phonétique* (Jones 1911g) for which he also employed Kwing Tong Woo as an informant. Additional assistance was provided by Woo's father Yik Nam Woo (whom Jones describes as a "famous literary man", and who provided a complete page (p. 83) in Chinese calligraphy. Later, in January 1912 a "spécimen" of Cantonese in a more informal colloquial style, consisting of a transcription of the "North Wind and the Sun" text appeared (Jones 1912g: 67).

The segmental system of Cantonese is represented in Figure 5.1. Though the presentation of the sound system in this form implies something analogous to phonemic analysis, there is really little in the description to indicate that Jones was thinking along phonemic lines. However, it is only to be expected that some contextual variation should be mentioned, as for example in the lowering of [ʊ] (represented as [u]) to [o] when pre-velar (p. xiii). The fricative nature of [i] following voiceless alveolar [s ts tsʻ] giving a realisation as [z] is noted—but Jones does not in any way expand upon what is today regarded as a remarkable example of phonetic variation within the same phoneme category (p. xii). Jones's interest appears to be mainly to achieve a reasonable mimicry of the segmental phonemic norms by the learner and not to be over-concerned about possible phonetic variation within the phonological system. It seems likely that Jones was hampered here by his lack of an appropriate methodology and terminology. It is interesting to compare this book (written apparently before

TABLE OF CANTONESE VOWELS AND CONSONANTS

The Cantonese vowels and consonants may be arranged in a table according to their mode of formation as follows:

		Labial.		Dental.	Palatal.	Velar.	Glottal.
		Bi-labial.	Labio-dental.				
CONSONANTS	Plosive	pʻ p		tʻ t tsʻ ts		kʻ k	
	Nasal	m		n		ŋ	
	Lateral			l			
	Fricative	w	f	s	j		h

		Front.	Mixed.	Back.
VOWELS	Close	i ɨ y		u
	Half-close	e		o
			ə	
	Half-open	ɛ œ		ɔ
	Open		a ɑ	

Figure 5.1. Table of Cantonese vowels and consonants (*Cantonese phonetic reader*, p. xix).

Jones became aware of the phoneme concept) with the *Sechuana reader*, which was produced after Jones had made contact with the East Europeans Ščerba and Benni. These scholars gave him the clue to phonemic analysis, and thus provided a foundation for an altogether more sophisticated and modern approach (see Section 6.8).

It is noteworthy that Paul Passy (1913: 72), in his review of the *Cantonese phonetic reader*, picks out for approval the author's treatment of tone. The attention paid to this topic is in contrast to the lack of any consideration of tone which is such a defect of the Chindau article (Jones 1910k) and *The pronunciation and orthography of the Chindau language* (1911a; see Section 3.9). Both of Jones's articles on Cantonese (mentioned above) and the *Cantonese phonetic reader* itself provide detailed analyses of the tonal system. With Cantonese, however, Jones had the benefit not only of Seers' work, but also of the traditional Chinese analyses—dating back, as Robins ([1979]: 106) has pointed out, to the fifth century—which had taken account of the tones of Chinese languages. The *Cantonese phonetic reader* provides a table of six Cantonese tones (see Figure 5.2), with their Cantonese nomenclature. Jones warns of the importance of the tone system to the student of Cantonese (p. ix):

> The necessity for acquiring the exact values of the tones cannot be urged too strongly. Cantonese pronounced with wrong tones is *absolutely meaningless*, and differs in this respect from Mandarin where it appears that it is possible to make oneself understood without troubling much about the tones.

In the *Cantonese phonetic reader*, the tones are indicated in the texts by a system of angled marks and in addition conventional musical notation is used as a means of indicating the pitches and speech rhythm (see Figure 5.3). The musical notation has the disadvantage of implying a fixed pitch for each tone, rather than the relative values which are the essential characteristic of tone languages—though Jones mentions this point adding that: "For ladies' voices (average) they should be transposed 8 or 9 notes higher" (p. xv). Jones says, optimistically: "I cannot help feeling that the difficulty of the tones is generally much exaggerated. Anyone who has a musical ear can learn them in a very short time by practising the following tune"; he then provides an illustrative piece in musical notation (p. ix); see Figure 5.4. Jones seems here to be underestimating the difficulties of learning tone languages, and regarding it from the point of view of an expert talented learner with an excellent ear for pitch (like himself) rather than seeing the problems faced by the average pupil.

The emphasis on musical notation is a reminder of Jones's musical interests and of his musical background—on his mother's side of the family (Section 1.2). His advice to those less musically inclined is brief: "Students who are ignorant of music should go to a singing master, preferably to one accustomed to teach on the Tonic Sol-fa system..." (p. ix).

Throughout his career, Jones continued to relate teaching tone systems closely to musical training—not always with success. Dennis Fry (at one time an amateur violinist) recalled an example of this Jonesian approach to tonetic analysis:

CANTONESE NAMES OF THE TONES

Number of tone according to scientific classification.	Scientific description (based on musical value, see Section IV.).	Cantonese Name.		Literal meaning of Cantonese name.
1st Tone	Upper falling (*with variant* uppermost level)	when syllable does not end in **p, t** or **k**	˗sœŋˌp'iŋ	upper level.
		when syllable ends in **p, t** or **k**	˗sœŋˌjɑp	upper entering.
2nd Tone	Upper rising	when syllable does not end in **p, t** or **k**	˗sœŋˏsœŋ	upper rising.
		when syllable ends in **p, t** or **k**	*wanting*	—
3rd Tone	Upper level	when syllable does not end in **p, t** or **k**	˗sœŋ-hœy	upper departing.
		when syllable ends in **p, t** or **k**	*wanting*	—
4th Tone	Lower falling		ˏhɑˏp'iŋ¹	lower level.
5th Tone	Lower rising		ˏhɑˏsœŋ¹	lower rising.
6th Tone	Lower level	when syllable does not end in **p, t** or **k**	ˏhɑ-hœy	lower departing.
		when syllable ends in **p, t** or **k**	ˏhɑˏjɑp	lower entering.

The 4th and 5th tones do not occur in words ending in **p, t** or **k**.

Figure 5.2. Table representing the tone system of Cantonese (*Cantonese phonetic reader*, p. xvii).

I remember that one Saturday morning I had to go to his house and try to reproduce Cantonese tones on the fiddle. I wasn't a very good fiddler and I can't say I made much of a fist of [it].[3]

See also the *Phoneme* (pp. 141–142 n.), where Jones explains aspects of pitch and prominence by reference to musical passages.

Jones's treatment of tone in the *Cantonese phonetic reader* (pp. xiv-xv) is neither innovative nor detailed, though at a phonetic level it appears to be largely valid. There is, of course, no mention of tonemics; but neither is there even any explicit statement that the tones have a function in distinguishing meaning (apart from what is implied

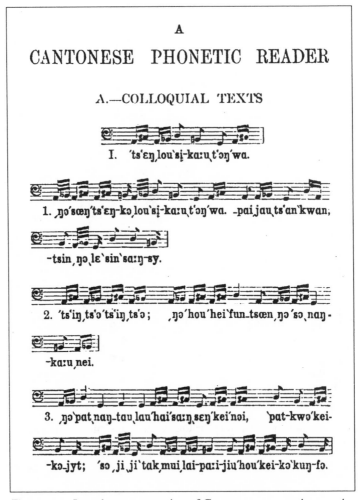

Figure 5.3. Jones's representation of Cantonese tones using musical notation (*Cantonese phonetic reader*, p. 3).

in the caveat on p. ix mentioned above). Jones came back later in the *Phoneme* (p. 154 n.) to re-analyse certain details of his treatment, in particular to establish a distinction between a high falling ("upper falling") and a high ("uppermost") level tone, claimed to be variants (p. xvii) in the *Cantonese phonetic reader*, see tone table (Figure 5.2); but he seems to have been in the main satisfied with the outline given in the *Cantonese phonetic reader*. (See the *Phoneme*, p. 251 n. for discussion of the number of tones in modern Cantonese.)

Despite the brevity of the treatment of tone in the *Cantonese phonetic reader*, it can be said that the book marks a step forward inasmuch as it made more Western European linguists aware of the way in which tone systems work. Furthermore, through his work on Cantonese, Jones had now become acquainted with the intricacies of a tone language—one of considerable complexity—and in so doing he had gained valuable experience which he had so obviously lacked when he was attempting to tackle Ndau (Section 3.9). The expertise which he thus acquired was to be especially useful to him in his later seminal work on Tswana in the *Sechuana reader* and "The phonetic structure of the Sechuana language" (Jones 1917c), since he would then be dealing with a tone language which, unlike Cantonese, was virtually unexplored in terms of linguistic analysis.

Jones was to look back later on his work with exotic languages as some of the most enjoyable and rewarding that he ever did, and Gimson (1968: 4–5) has noted that "of all his work, he was most proud of the pioneer studies he had written on such languages as Cantonese, Russian, and Tswana".

A postscript to the *Cantonese phonetic reader* begins with a paragraph in which Jones mentions that he is "hoping to supplement this reader shortly by a short treatise on Cantonese pronunciation in which the requisite phonetic theory will be found, and in which methods will be indicated for acquiring the difficult sounds" (p. vi). But this project was never to be realised in the form described. However, three years later, a slim pamphlet entitled *Supplement to the Cantonese phonetic reader* (Jones—Kwing Tong Woo 1916b) appeared, containing merely the *Cantonese phonetic reader* "texts in Chinese writing". This volume is not mentioned in the bibliography in Abercrombie et al. (1964: xi-xix), and correspondence between Jones and University of London Press shows that the book achieved minute sales (only 59, in total, from 1922 to 1932).[4] A letter written four years later, in 1936, contains marginalia from Jones where he assumes that all copies of the book must be lost. He accepted with *sang-froid* the total disappearance without trace of all this painstaking work: "This doesn't much matter as it seems that there are a good many mistakes in the Chinese characters."[5] In fact, at least one copy of this ill-fated publication did survive; it is held in the archives of University College London.

5.3. The Michaelis—Jones *Phonetic dictionary*

Though Jones took a personal pride in his research on lesser known languages, he was eventually to be much better known for the outstanding work he did in a specialised

The tone marks used in this book indicate by their form and position the musical value of the tones.

I cannot help feeling that the difficulty of the tones is generally much exaggerated. Anyone who has a musical ear can learn them in a very short time by practising the following tune, singing it on any vowel or on one of the consonants **m, n** or **ŋ** until it is firmly fixed in his mind :

For ladies' voices this tune might be transposed thus :

It is also useful to practise singing the tunes of the texts to which musical notes are added (Nos. I, II and VI) without any words. Students who are ignorant of music should go to a singing master, preferably to one accustomed to teach on the Tonic Sol-fa system, and be taught to sing the above tune and the tunes occurring in texts I, II and VI. (The

Figure 5.4. Extract on tone from the *Cantonese phonetic reader* (p. ix)

branch of lexicography which he was to dominate during (and after) his lifetime, namely the pronunciation dictionary.

In 1913, Daniel Jones produced his first attempt at a dictionary of pronunciation for English. His co-author was Hermann Michaelis, a headmaster of a "Mittelschule" from Biebrich in Germany, and a longstanding member of the IPA. The book was published in Germany under the title *A phonetic dictionary of the English language* (Michaelis—Jones 1913a, henceforth *Phonetic dictionary*). At the time, there was simply no reliable guide to the pronunciation of English words in existence.

The eighteenth century had witnessed the publication of a number of English pronunciation dictionaries (see Bronstein 1986 for an overall survey from the seventeenth century onwards). The best known are those of Sheridan (1780) and Walker (1791). The latter, Walker's *Critical pronouncing dictionary*, was far ahead of its time and, as Howatt (1984: 114) says, "contains a wealth of information on the pronunciation of standard English". It had gone through numerous editions and reprintings, and by the end of the nineteenth century was available only in much-modified versions, such as those produced by Nuttall as "Walker's pronouncing dictionary" and "Nuttall's standard pronouncing dictionary".[6] The great *Oxford English dictionary* (J. Murray 1933) was still not complete, and furthermore the representation of pronunciation was by far its weakest component. The task had been rejected by Sweet, who though a leading figure in the movement to publish the dictionary, thought that too little was as yet known about the subject to allow any indications of pronunciation. James Murray, the editor of the OED, took the task of devising a transcription system and eventually used a cumbersome version of Ellis's palaeotype. This combined with the difficulties that Murray, as a speaker of Scots, had in indicating southern English pronunciation rendered many of his entries either invalid or very difficult to interpret—a danger Sweet apparently foresaw in 1882 (K.M.E. Murray 1977: 190).

In 1909, a notable pioneering work had been produced in Sweden, Afzelius's *Pronouncing dictionary of modern English*. In a review, Jones considered this book "a praiseworthy attempt to carry out a work of extreme difficulty", saying that it was "an exception to the general rule…that the pronunciation recorded in most dictionaries is very different from that actually used by most educated people". Jones, however, criticises Afzelius for not choosing to employ IPA transcription, but using instead a modification of Sweet's Broad Romic. "The system in itself is unobjectionable, but we feel very strongly that the multiplication of phonetic systems ought to receive every possible discouragement" (Jones 1910l: 157).

In the preface to the *Phonetic dictionary*, Michaelis and Jones echo Jones's complaints in the Afzelius review concerning the deficiencies of the available dictionaries (*Phonetic dictionary* v-vi):

> In the past the *written language* has been looked up to by many as being the only form of the language worthy of respect. One result of this reverence for spelling has been that innumerable "spelling-pronunciations" are creeping into the language…. It is a regrettable fact that most pronouncing dictionaries definitely encourage many of the modern spelling-pronunciations. We feel that such artificialities cannot but impair the beauty of the language, and we hope that the present dictionary may do something towards convincing the educated public of the desirability of studying the spoken language in preference to the conventional written language, and so avoiding undesirable changes in pronunciation in the future.

In the above, one may also detect reverberations of Jones's quarrels with Bridges, Lascelles Abercrombie and the Society for Pure English (see Section 4.11).

The *Phonetic dictionary* strikes a modern reader as being most odd in one aspect of its arrangement. Its entries are reversed as compared with modern pronouncing dictionaries—or indeed as compared with pioneering efforts—the phonetic transcription comes first and the orthographic form second (see Figure 5.5). This system was used first by Michaelis and Passy for their *Dictionnaire phonétique de la langue française* (1897), which was originally conceived as the first in a series of similar dictionaries with Michaelis as the general editor. This is a work which shows very clearly the methods and approach of Passy with no discernible additional influence, and it is likely that Michaelis was not responsible for anything other than the routine work which would have been involved. The Michaelis—Jones *Phonetic dictionary* was planned as the second book in the series and is referred to as such in the preface to the revised edition of Michaelis and Passy's work (1897 [1914²]: x): "Notre dictionnaire, d'ailleurs, n'est plus seul de son espèce; il a été publié un dictionnaire anglais exactement parallèle."

---

aː

aː ah
aː* are (*from* be)
aː*, -z are (s.), -s
aː*, -z R (*the letter*), -'s
● aː'bʌθnət Arbuthnot
'aːbə* Árber
'aːbə*, -z 1) arbour, -s; 2) arbor (*axle, arbour*), -s
'aːbəlest [-list], -s arbalest, -s
'aːbəlestə*, -s arbalester, -s
'aːbəlist, -s arbalist, -s
'aːbəlistə*, -s arbalister, -s
aːbərӕl'zeiʃən,-s arborization, -s
aːbə'reiʃəs arboraceous
aːbə'resↄn|s, -t arborescen|ce, -t
'aːbəret [-rit], -s arboret, -s
'aːbərəs arborous
aːbə'riːt|əm, -əmz, -ə arboret|um, -ums, -ə
'aːbərikʌltʃə* arboriculture
aːbəri'kʌltʃərist, -s arboriculturist, -s
'aːbərist, -s arborist, -s
'aːbə'vaiti·, -z arbor vitæ, -s
'aːbitə*, -s arbiter, -s
aːbi'traːʒ ['aːbitridʒ] (arbi'traːʒ) arbitrage (*of stocks, etc.*)
aːbi'treiʃən, -z arbitration, -s
'aːbitreit, -s, -iŋ, -id, -ə*, -əz arbitrat|e, -es, -ing, -ed, -or, -ors
aː'bitrəmənt [-tri-], -s arbitrament, -s
'aːbitrər|i, -ili, -inis arbitrar|y, -ily, -iness
'aːbitridʒ arbitrage (*arbitration*)
'aːbitris, -iz arbitress, -es
'aːbjuːt arbute
aː'bjuːtəs, -iz arbutus, -es
'aːblӕst, -s arblast, -s
'aːblei Árblay

'aːbɔː* arbor (*tree*)
aː'bɔːri|əl, -əs arbore|al, -ous
'aːbrəm = 'eibrəm Abram
aː'brouθ [-ouð] Arbroath
aːbuː'kiə* [ə'buːkə*] Aboukir
● aː'dɛnz (ar'dɛn) Ardennes
'aːdə [aː'daː] Ardagh
'aːdə* ardour
'aːdən 1) Arden; 2) = 'eidən Aden
'aːdənsi ardency
'aːdənt, -li ardent, -ly
'aːdiŋ Arding
'aːdjuəs, -li,-nis arduous,-ly,-ness
'aːdli 1) Ardleigh; 2) Ardley
aː'driʃig Ardrishaig
aː'drosən Ardrossan
'aːdwik Ardwick
'aːdwin Ardwin
'aːdʒənt argent
'aːdʒəntain Argentine
aːdʒən'tifərəs [-dʒen't-] argentiferous
'aːdʒil argil
aːdʒi'leiʃəs argillaceous
aːdʒi'lifərəs argilliferous
● aːft aft
'aːftə* after
'aːftəbəːθ, -s afterbirth, -s
'aːftəgaːd, -z afterguard, -s
'aːftəglou, -z afterglow, -s
'aːftəkrop, -s aftercrop, -s
'aːftəmӕθ, -s aftermath, -s
aːftə'nuːn, -z afternoon, -s
'aːftəpiːs, -iz afterpiece, -s
'aːftəθɔːt, -s afterthought, -s
'aːftəwəd, -z afterward, -s
● aː'gail, -ʃɪə* 1) Argyle, -shire; 2) Argyll, -shire
'aːgӕnd [-gənd] (ar'gã) Argand
'aːgəlis Argolis

Michaelis & Jones, Phonetic Dictionary.   1

Figure 5.5. Extract from the *Phonetic dictionary*. Note the curious arrangement with words listed according to their phonetic representations. The sign • indicates the beginning of a new sub-group.

The *Phonetic dictionary* system of entry arrangement is, of course, most unwieldy, and, for most purposes, of little practical utility. It may originally have been based on the need to look up words when reading a phonetic transcription, such as those which appeared in *Le Maître phonétique*, and this is indeed one of the uses mentioned in the preface to the *Phonetic dictionary*. The authors suggest other possible ways of employing the dictionary, such as "a person hearing a word for the first time, and being in doubt as to how it should be spelt, may ascertain the correct spelling…" and "the dictionary may even be *read* with much profit" (p. vii)—both of which seem somewhat implausible. However, Michaelis and Jones are on stronger ground when they point out that their book could prove "useful to students of *linguistic science* in general" and go on to say (p. vi):

…many important questions relating to English linguistic science can be studied with far greater ease. Such are the comparative frequency of sounds, rules of pronunciation depending on the positions of sounds relatively to other sounds, various processes of derivation…

However, Jones probably realised the overall drawbacks of reversing the usual system for entering words. It is, for example, stated in the preface that "the fixing of a satisfactory *alphabetical order of the sounds* was a matter of no small difficulty, particularly in the case of the vowels". Michaelis and Jones solve the problem by arranging the vowels into five groups corresponding to the letter shapes of the alphabet (see Figure 5.6). Exact sequence was decided by other criteria, so that ʌ was placed with the **a** group "on account of its acoustic similarity to the sound **a**". The ordering of the consonants was arrived at by a similar system of compromise; **w**, for instance being placed immediately after **u**, so that the sequence **uː u w** would correspond with **iː i j** (pp. vii–viii). The final ordering was as shown in Figure 5.6.

Correspondences in the choice of words give the impression that the *Concise Oxford dictionary* (H.W. Fowler—F.G. Fowler 1911), which had recently appeared, was used as one source lexicon, though no direct acknowledgement is stated. However, the COD is quoted approvingly twice in the preface, and it is likely that it was used at least as a final check for omissions (p. vi).

Just before the *Phonetic dictionary* came out, another pronunciation dictionary was published in Germany, Viëtor's *Deutsches Aussprachewörterbuch* (1912). The general efficiency of the editing, combined with the comprehensive word list, but above all, the advantages of the more conventional system of orthographic entries followed by transcriptions, must have made Jones recognise the deficiencies inherent in the *Phonetic dictionary* even before the latter was on sale. It was possibly one additional factor which inspired him to begin work straightaway on a second pronunciation dictionary.

Tucked away in the bibliography of the pamphlet, containing the Principles of the International Phonetic Association (Passy—Jones 1912m: 37), is the information that Jones was already in the course of writing the *EPD* for the London publishers Dent,

```
The complete order of the sounds is consequently:
aː,  a, æ, ʌ  . . . . . .  b, d, ð,
eiꞌ), e, ɛ, əː, ə  . . . . .  f, g, h,
iː,  i  . . . . j  . . .  k, l, m, n, ŋ,
ouꞋ), o, ɔː, ɔ  . . . . . .  p, r, s, ʃ, t, θ,
uː,  u  . . . . . w  . . .  v, z, ʒ.
```

Figure 5.6. The sequence of sounds in the *Phonetic dictionary* (p. viii).

even before the *Phonetic dictionary* had been published. The *EPD* was to occupy him for the next four years, and when it appeared in 1917 it immediately became the standard work of reference, and the most successful book of its kind ever written. Perhaps the crucial significance of the *Phonetic dictionary* was not only that it was the first pronunciation dictionary of any distinction to be written by an English hand for over a hundred years, but also that it provided simultaneously the groundwork (through its virtues) and the incentive (through its deficiencies) for Daniel Jones to go on to produce the *EPD*.

5.4. Minor publications 1911–14

In addition to the major books which have been mentioned above, Jones continued in this period to publish numerous shorter pieces—mostly in *Le Maître phonétique*, but also in other language publications. In 1911, he produced an article on the importance of ear-training (Jones 1911q) for *Die neueren Sprachen*, and two short book notices for the same journal (Jones 1911r, 1911s). He also wrote two pieces for the *Revue de l'Enseignement des Langues Vivantes* (Jones 1911t, 1911u). Later, after his tour of India in 1912, several articles came out in Indian journals, namely the *Educational Review* (Jones 1913n) and the *Madras Christian College Magazine* (Jones 1913o); the latter, "Standard English Pronunciation", was subsequently reprinted in the *Hindustan Review*.

Though the appearance of these pieces shows that Jones was in demand, and also that more openings were available to him, yet his main work, both in terms of quantity and significance, continued to be found in the articles in *Le Maître phonétique*. In 1911–14, Jones published forty-four items in this journal. Some were only brief notes; others took the form of transcription passages for students, or brief reviews. Jones published much interesting work in the form of "spécimens" of various languages and dialects. These comprised Hungarian (Jones—Stern 1911f), Tyneside dialect (Jones 1911o), north west Lancashire dialect (1913e, 1913l), and Manx (1914j), in addition to the articles on Cantonese Chinese (Jones 1911g, 1912g) discussed in Section 5.2.

The short transcription of the Lord's Prayer in Manx is of particular interest since it is presumably the earliest competent phonetic transcription of the language by an expert phonetician, and was made at a time when Manx was still to a limited extent a living medium of communication on the Isle of Man.

5.5. The IPA *Principles*

A major contribution was made by Jones to the revision of the *Principles of the International Phonetic Association* (Passy—Jones 1912m), which appeared as a supplement to *Le Maître phonétique*. This could, in fact, be regarded as being effectively Jones's work, which Passy implied when he referred in 1911 to "l'Exposé anglais que Jones prépare".[7] The last (anonymous) English version of the principles had appeared eight years previously (IPA: 1904). Passy had also produced an (unsigned) *Exposé des principes de l'Association Phonétique Internationale* (IPA: 1908).[8] Jones did much more than merely rehash either of these; he added considerably to the explanation of the IPA system of transcription, and expanded the brief introduction to phonetic principles that Passy had produced. He also, naturally enough, removed the emphasis on French which Passy had in his *Exposé*; however, Jones did not choose to replace this with an unduly English bias, but decided instead to make his approach more truly one of a general phonetic character—with his examples culled from a wide range of languages.

After a brief introduction on the origins, history, and aims of the IPA, and the constitution of the organisation, the pamphlet goes on to consider linguistic problems. Sections follow dealing with "phonetic writing and its uses"; the International Phonetic Alphabet and the values of the symbols; narrow and broad transcription; and "principles of transcription for languages hitherto not transcribed". This portion closes with a section which speculates on possible future developments in the use of symbols, summarising various suggestions that had been made to the Association (Passy—Jones 1912m: 6–18).

The Jones-Passy version expands considerably on the number of "specimen texts" of transcription as compared with the 1908 "Exposé". Four varieties of English were included (termed "Southern", "Northern," "Scotch" and "American")[9] and eighteen other languages from Europe and elsewhere. The choice possibly reflected the availability of informants to Jones as much as any other consideration, hence the inclusion of "South African Dutch" (i.e. the forerunner of Afrikaans) rather than standard Dutch itself.[10] The full list of specimens is as follows: French, German, Italian, Spanish, Portuguese, Catalanian (sic), Welsh, Swedish, Russian, Polish, Czech, Hungarian, South African Dutch, Urdu, Panjabi, Cantonese Chinese and Burmese. In addition, a sample of English is given in "phonetic spelling…based on the principle that it should be capable of being easily read and written by speakers of any dialect" (pp. 19–32). The pamphlet also prints a full bibliography of books available at the time, covering many different aspects of phonetics and its applications (pp. 32–39).

Some of the changes made by Jones have become familiar features of modern approaches to articulatory phonetics. For instance, the grid of consonant articulations was changed so that the labials were placed on the left, and glottal sounds on the right; the 1908 "Exposé" has them running in the reverse manner. Other alterations have not been accepted. For instance, Jones introduces terminology employed by Sweet to describe places of articulation, e.g. "lip-teeth, point and blade, throat" etc. Although sensible and straightforward, these terms lost favour and were replaced by the Latin derived terminology which is familiar today (labio-dental, alveolar, pharyngeal, etc.).

The sections covering "Narrow and Broad Transcription" (pp. 14–15) and "Principles of Transcription for Languages Hitherto not Transcribed" (pp. 15–16) are noteworthy for the elegance and economy of the explication, which shows Jones's scholarly style at its best, combining pithy language with clarity of thought and well-chosen exemplification. Throughout, there is emphasis on the need for a broad transcription to indicate only those sounds which are "distinctive", an idea stated previously in the 1908 "Exposé" but repeated here much more forcibly (Passy—Jones 1912m: 15):

> The general rule for strictly *practical* phonetic transcription is therefore to *leave out everything that is self-evident, and everything that can be explained once for all*. In transcribing any given language it is in general sufficient to represent the *distinctive* sounds only.

And again, in the second principle for transcribing previously unanalysed languages (p. 16):

> It is necessary to ascertain what are the *distinctive* sounds in the language, i.e. those which if confused might conceivably alter the meanings of words. Shades of sound which are occasioned by proximity to other sounds, absence of stress and the like, very often do not require special symbols.

Examples are quoted from the French vowel system ("the regular rule that **r** has a lowering effect on preceding vowels") and clear and dark **l** in English *little*, in order to illustrate the points (p. 15).

It is not unfair to say that the significant principles inherent in the phoneme concept are contained here—although the word itself is not actually used. Indeed, if one excludes the qualifying phrases, "might conceivably" and "very often", the statement would pass as a reasonable summary of a structuralist approach to phonemic analysis—and in many ways closer to a mainstream modern viewpoint than Jones's later definitions of the phoneme. It is plain from Jones's own reminiscence that although he was aware of the word "phoneme" through Ščerba's (1911) article in *Le Maître phonétique*, it was only two years later, through discussion with Tytus Benni, that "the immense importance of the theory then became very clear to me" (*History and meaning of the term "phoneme"*: 6). How Jones could play the major role in producing such a clear statement of the phoneme concept, but also claim not to have realised the significance of it all for another two years, must remain something of a puzzle (see also Section 14.16 for detailed discussion).

5.6. Work for the IPA 1911–14

Apart from translating and revising Passy's *Exposé*, Jones shouldered an increasing burden of the work involved in running the IPA itself and editing *Le Maître phonétique*. As a direct result of his poor health, Passy suggested early in 1911 that Jones should take over the editorship of *Le Maître phonétique* and this was approved by the Council.[11] Jones was also responsible for running the elections in 1911 to 1912, and it is probable, given Passy's preoccupation with his health, that Jones had now taken over most of the day-to-day affairs of the IPA, though helped by Sophie Lund, who remained at Bourg-la-Reine to carry on as Treasurer of the Association. The list was expanding continuously, and in 1912 the 1500th IPA member was enrolled.[12] Of the total, about 400 were in Britain, and 350 in Germany. France now had only about 100 enrolled, and was surpassed by the United States with 120. Denmark had the surprisingly large membership of about eighty (probably owing to the efforts of Jespersen and Sophie Lund) while Austria-Hungary, Switzerland, Sweden, Canada and (remarkably) Chile, had between forty and sixty each. There were in addition members in twenty-four other countries dispersed all over the world—for instance, Iceland, Costa Rica and the Dutch Antilles. The growth in membership continued up to 1914, reaching a total of 1751,[13] and showing particular expansion in India (with more than fifty enrolled), probably as a direct consequence of Daniel Jones's lecture tour the previous year.[14]

India figured in another area where the Association was expanding its work. The number of students taking the Association's examinations was increasing yearly. In 1910, Daniel Jones had taken over as the Association's English examiner from E.R. Edwards on a temporary basis.[15] Following an IPA Council election, in 1911, he was confirmed in the post, beating his only opponent, Walter Ripman, by nineteen votes to one.[16] A call had come from an IPA Council member, J.A. Yates, who was an influential School Inspector in Madras, for an IPA examination to be held in India to save Indian students the journey to Europe. Later, Jones took up the idea with Yates in the course of his tour of India, and presented to the IPA a suggestion for a diploma in "Elementary phonetics for Indian Students", covering the same material, though at a lower level, and including some work in the mother tongue of the candidate. Yates was charged with running the new diploma, and the examination was officially instituted in June 1913.[17] Jones could count this as one more concrete result of his Indian experience, and another factor in helping to stimulate the development of phonetics in the most important country in the British Empire.

The IPA was now at its zenith of international influence. There was a large worldwide membership—concentrated in the richest and most powerful countries, Britain, Germany, France and the USA, but with rapidly expanding growth elsewhere. Among its members were important figures in education—such as university professors, school inspectors and headmasters and principals of colleges. Numerous libraries also subscribed; the British Museum took out a subscription for the first time in 1912.[18]

5.7. Transcription in *Le Maître phonétique*

Le Maître phonétique was still appearing regularly five times a year and in 1911 comprised 192 pages, plus 44 pages of supplements. In 1912, there were 156 pages, with another 84 pages in the four supplements. In 1913, 152 pages were printed of the regular journal, but plans were going ahead for a special supplement to celebrate the IPA's twenty-fifth anniversary; this came out the following year as *Miscellanea Phonetica I* (Passy—Jones 1914a). The increasing emphasis on supplements in this period is to be explained by the continued insistence by the Association on all material being submitted and published in the form of transcription; the only way in which articles could be presented in conventional orthography was for them to be issued as supplements.

In June 1912, Daniel Jones put forward the proposal that articles should be permitted to appear in normal spelling, and pointed out that this would allow the issue of offprints, which would also be useful for publicity. Passy immediately indicated his doubts: "Sans être absolument opposé, j'incline à limiter ce système aux suppléments...". Jones's suggestion stirred up considerable controversy amongst Council members.[19] Jones (1912l) stated his views forcibly:

> I am of the opinion that the time has now come when articles in ordinary spelling could and should be admitted into the m.f. Much of the work originally contemplated by the a.f. has now been accomplished. The alphabet is now incomparably more widely used than any other phonetic system...the a.f. could extend its influence far more rapidly by admitting current spelling into the body of the m.f. Not only would the journal appeal to a far wider circle of readers, but there would be a considerable saving in the cost of printing...

Jones goes on to say that he is concerned that "many valuable articles are simply lost to the world" and deplores the fact that off-prints are not available. He states that the problem cannot be solved by the printing of supplements: "It is not possible whenever we have an interesting article to issue it as a supplement." He concludes by advocating a "journal in ordinary spelling (in which of course a.f. script would be compulsory in all cases where phonetic symbols were required)".

Jones had the support of Jespersen, who wrote brusquely: "On ne peut pas discuter sérieusement en écriture phonétique."[20] In the vote, they were joined by Sophie Lund; the Grenoble professor, Rosset; and the Czech, Frinta. However, twelve voted against, including Passy himself, Viëtor (who was now President of the IPA following Sweet's death), Ščerba, Edwards and Grandgent. The discussion continued into the following year, with Jones's idea receiving considerable backing in the form of a pungent article by Camerlynck (1913) arguing for freedom of choice, and detailing the problems caused to contributors and readers by the use of phonetic transcription. Palmer also wrote a brief note allying himself with Jones.[21]

Le Maître phonétique had achieved astonishing success as a journal, considering the handicap that was imposed upon it by the ban on articles in conventional spelling. As it was, the slim issues, in their dowdy green covers, with articles in five languages, in a variety of transcriptions, managed to reach more than sixteen hundred subscribers all over the world. If Jones's far-sighted proposal had been accepted, the audience would have been even greater, and the influence of the journal far wider in the academic world. The decision to change to orthography was not eventually taken till after Jones's death, when *Le Maître phonétique* began a new life in 1971 as the *Journal of the International Phonetic Association*.

Despite this defeat, Jones could feel proud of his work for the IPA. He had held the organisation together at a time when Passy was unable to cope, and furthermore had seen its membership, influence and recognition at their peaks.

5.8. University College 1912–14

By the beginning of the new academic year in the autumn of 1912, Daniel Jones's new Department was flourishing. His Departmental Report for that year states: "The number of classes held this session has been considerably greater than in any previous session."[22] The expansion was due in part to the success of Noël-Armfield's courses in Spoken English (see Section 4.5), but in addition Jones had organised classes in the phonetics of English, French and German. Now, thanks to Jones's research with Kwing Tong Woo, Cantonese Chinese was added to the list. The classes in English for foreign students were attracting students from all over the world. Jones lists eleven countries—including Chile and Japan.

A potential obstacle to the progress of Jones's career came in 1913 when it was mooted in the Senate that as part of the projected co-ordination of the work of University College and King's College "the question of the place at which the teaching in Phonetics shall be provided [will] be considered at a later date". [23] This appeared to leave the status and the location of phonetics teaching in London University uncertain. However, nothing more seems to have ever come of the idea—probably much to Daniel Jones's relief.

In the summer of 1913, Jones ran his research class, which was clearly more successful than ever before. Seven papers are cited in the report, including work on Russian, Chilean Spanish and Mauritian Creole. A woman student, M.L. Annakin, read a paper on the dialect of Nidderdale in Yorkshire—later to be published by the IPA (Annakin 1922)—and the names of two students who were eventually to be members of Jones's staff appeared here for the first time. H.O. Coleman, who was shortly to write a pioneering article on intonation in *Miscellanea Phonetica I* (Coleman 1914), read a paper on "Emphasis in Speech"; S. Jones, soon to be appointed as the first supervisor of the new phonetics laboratory, dealt with "Vowel Resonance". Jones says: "The work of these students attained a remarkably high standard of excellence" and he mentions that he is arranging for "at least two of the papers" to be published (some eventually appeared in *Miscellanea Phonetica I*). As a result of these successes, Jones decided to hold the following year's research classes throughout the session, rather than only in one term.[24]

An area where Jones was beginning to see new possibilities for phonetics was in missionary work. At this time this was a rapidly expanding field. Religious belief was still firm among the general public in Britain, and there was felt to be an obligation to preach the gospel to the native populations of the vast British Empire, on which it was proclaimed the sun never set. Scientific advances had made it a less hazardous task than it had been in Victorian times, but the difficulties of learning exotic languages of Africa and Asia were known to be a formidable obstacle to progress. Though he never appears to have had any strong Christian beliefs himself (even before coming under the influence of theosophy; see Section 10.8), Jones rapidly realised that there was a good opening for applied phonetics in the need for missionaries to learn to pronounce languages in an intelligible manner. In 1912, a course of lectures was put on for "Missionaries and others likely to be concerned with the writing down of languages hitherto unwritten".[25] Jones also contributed a section on phonetics to a *Bibliography for missionary students*, which was published by the Board of Study for Preparation of Missionaries (Oliphant—Anderson—Ferrier 1913) and in 1913 the first classes aimed specifically at missionaries were started at UCL.[26]

5.9. Jones at Oxford

In May 1913, Jones was offered a part-time post at the world-famous Taylorian Institute for Modern Languages at Oxford University.[27] Sweet's death in April 1912 had left a gap to be filled, and at first the University had been undecided about whether to try to re-establish Sweet's readership, or to create a lecturer's post instead.[28] Oxford was to discover that Sweet was virtually irreplaceable and that "the only good phonetician available for the work", to quote the words of the Curators of the Taylorian Institute, was Daniel Jones.[29]

Even though the position would be very well paid compared with his London job, Jones was only willing to take the job if it could be built around his busy schedule at UCL. He therefore stipulated that he "would be unable to lecture and give instruction for more than four hours during each week of Full Term owing to the large number of lectures and classes he had at the University of London".[30] Furthermore, Jones's teaching hours were to be arranged on one day of the week. For this, Oxford agreed to pay him £100 a year plus all his expenses.[31] However, the Curators of the Taylorian Institute discovered that the regulations did not permit them to appoint a lecturer to teach so few hours.[32] Perhaps it was for this reason that just eleven days later, Jones was invited to take up a full-time post at Oxford. This would have given him £300 pounds a year—a fifty per cent increase on his basic London salary.[33] Given also the prestige of the Taylorian Institution, and the fact that he would be seen to be taking over the mantle of Sweet, the offer must have been very tempting. Yet, nevertheless, Jones turned it down.

The background to his decision cannot be completely determined, but it can be conjectured that it gave Jones an enviable position from which to negotiate his personal situation at UCL. Provost Gregory Foster was undoubtedly concerned at the possibility of the loss of one of his most promising young staff, who was in charge of a department which was unique in Britain. He may have held out promises of promotion and even the prospect of a chair. This could have tipped the scales for Jones, since although the full Taylorian lectureship would have offered more immediate prestige, the chances of advancement to a professorship would have been more problematical. In any case, it is unlikely to be coincidental that shortly afterwards, in December 1913, Jones's name was put forward to the Board of Advisors, this being the first step towards his readership.[34] And, in his recollection of the affair just over twelve years later, Jones tellingly juxtaposes his rejection of Oxford's offers and his later promotion at UCL (see below).

Eventually, the Taylorian Institute, desperate as it was to secure his services, changed the regulations so as to permit Jones to take up a part-time post on his own conditions.[35] Jones accepted the position and travelled up to Oxford each week for two terms.[36] His courses were highly successful and heavily subscribed; it has been recorded that no fewer than 113 students attended his lectures and classes in phonetics (C.H. Firth 1929: 87). Jones claimed to find the extra work (despite the good salary) too much: "In 1914, owing to over-strain, I was obliged to give up the work at Oxford, but University College was generous to me and raised my status and salary" (Jones 1926e: 398). But it could also be that Foster was applying some pressure to Jones to persuade him to give up his Oxford connection in exchange for better prospects at London. Jones arranged for H.O. Coleman, at that time still his student, to take over from him at Oxford for the summer term,[37] and in June, Jones eventually resigned.[38] Coleman was appointed to take his place,[39] but on the outbreak of war, the phonetics courses were discontinued (C.H. Firth 1929: 87), which incidentally meant that all Henry Sweet's connections with Oxford University were finally severed.

So ended Jones's flirtation with Oxford. By the end of it, he knew that his future in UCL was secure, and that he had a much sounder financial and professional footing on which to work. It is interesting, however, to speculate on what might have happened had he made a different choice and decided to use the Taylorian Institute at Oxford, rather than University College London, as the springboard for his academic ambitions.

5.10. Stephen Jones and the Laboratory

In total, Jones's Department had no fewer than twenty-seven different courses on offer in the session of 1913–14.[40] However, one area is noted as being of especial significance for Jones, as he makes clear in the opening sentences of that year's Departmental Report: "The most important development has been the establishment of the Experimental Phonetics Laboratory, and the appointment of an Assistant to supervise this branch of the work."[41]

The assistant who had been appointed was Stephen Jones —the same S. Jones who had read a paper on vowel resonance in the 1912 research class. Stephen Jones was in no way related to Daniel Jones, and was a Welsh-speaking Welshman employed as a physics master at Haberdashers' School in Cricklewood, Middlesex. His UCL post was part-time and he continued to share his time between the two jobs for several years, eventually joining Jones's full-time staff in 1921.[42] Apart from his work in the laboratory, Stephen Jones began using his native-speaker Welsh background to research and teach the phonetics of that language. He published a "spécimen" of Welsh in *Le Maître phonétique* the following year (S. Jones 1914) and gave two public lectures on Welsh in October of that year. Later on, he wrote the *Welsh phonetic reader* (S. Jones 1926), which is regarded today as a classic work, and together with Sweet (1884), the best early study of the phonetics of Welsh. Stephen Jones was to remain at University College until he retired in 1937, being remembered with affection by Abercrombie (1980: 1): "Steve, as he was always known—was a nice, kind, generous man, and a fine teacher." He died in 1941.

Setting up the equipment for the new laboratory was a time-consuming task but Stephen Jones proved his worth from the start. Despite his Cambridge mathematical background, Daniel Jones was not happy with scientific machinery, and grew to be more unwilling to have anything to do with instrumentation as the years passed. Although he was certainly very enthusiastic about the idea of being in charge of a phonetics laboratory, he appears nevertheless to have left most of the work of installing the equipment to Stephen Jones. In his Report, he gives full acknowledgement to his new assistant:

> Great credit is due to the Assistant Mr Stephen Jones, for his untiring energy in supervising the construction; it may be mentioned in particular that owing to his efforts we are now in possession of what I believe to be the largest and most accurate Phonetic Kymograph in existence.[43]

Daniel Jones also revealed that most of the equipment had never been made in England before, and this meant that construction and testing took considerable time. One item arrived as a gift—a device known as a "sirène à ondes", enabling the production of artificial vowel sounds; this had been donated by Dr Marage of the University of Paris (see above, Section 4.9, for the mention of this in *Pygmalion*).

Though Jones rightly regarded the establishment of the laboratory as a great step forward, resources and experience were still limited. Compared with the laboratories already in existence in Europe, such as Hamburg or Grenoble, the facilities of UCL were pathetically small. The vast resources of Hamburg, particularly, rankled with Jones; and he was to comment later on the imbalance between the funding of phonetics in England and Germany. Writing in 1919, Jones said:

> We believe that in spite of their fine installation, the methods of phonetic analysis used by the Hamburg staff are inferior to those followed in this country. Nevertheless, during the first four years of its existence (1910–14) that establishment, owing to its superior equipment, attained a great reputation.[44]

In April 1914, Jones was able to see just what progress was being made at Hamburg for himself when he attended the Congress of Experimental Phonetics held there. He was accompanied by Stephen Jones, and by W. Perrett, who was a member of the UCL German Department but who gave lectures on phonetics (Jones 1914h: 50). Though he was disappointed by the apparent lack of interest shown by linguists and philologists—"it is to be hoped that before the next Congress they will have come to realise... that phonetics has its uses for them"—Jones was impressed by the "wonderful exhibition of apparatus". He cast (Jones 1914h: 50) envious eyes on "some of the chief attractions" such as:

> ...the "Lioretgraph" (the most perfect instrument yet devised for enlarging the curve of a phonograph record), stereoscopic photographs of the interior of the larynx, Struycken's apparatus for showing and photographing speech vibrations, and last but not least cinematographic pictures of the vocal cords in action.

Jones records that "the municipality of Hamburg ... entertained the members in great style" (Jones 1914h: 51). It was probably with very mixed feelings that he and Stephen Jones returned to their own meagre recently acquired equipment in the overcrowded accommodation of University College.

5.11. The outbreak of war

Daniel Jones was to make one further trip to Germany in 1914. In June, he travelled to Bremen to act as the representative of University College at the sixteenth *Allgemeiner Neuphilologentag*.[45] He could not have known that it would be his last chance for several years to visit a country with which he had built up close connections and where he had numerous good friends, some of many years' standing. One of these, Wilhelm Viëtor, who had given him such important help at the outset of his career, he was never to see again. The First World War was to create a gulf in the world of international scholarship and nowhere more so than in phonetics, which of its very nature had to be the international science *par excellence*. It was particularly ironical that the first issue of *Miscellanea Phonetica*, advertised as a *Festschrift* to celebrate the twenty-fifth anniversary of the foundation of the IPA, had Viëtor at the head of its list of contributors. The collection did not actually appear until many years later in 1922 (though still bearing 1914 as its publication date), by which time Wilhelm Viëtor himself had died (in September 1918)—just a few weeks before the signing of the Armistice.

Jones not only had ties in Germany through his own friendships and scholarly relations, but he had also attracted many students from that country to his new Department. For instance, in the summer term of 1914 there were twenty-six students attending the classes in Practical English Phonetics; of these, no fewer than nineteen were of German nationality.[46]

Moreover, the nature of the membership of the IPA was a further witness to the significance of Germany, both for phonetics generally and for Jones personally. Germany claimed more IPA members than any country except England (see Section 5.6), and there were important groups to be found in Austro-Hungary, and also in other countries soon to be allied to the so-called Central Powers. It is not surprising that, on the outbreak of the war, *Le Maître phonétique* suspended publication. The final number to appear (July-August 1914) gives no hint from its contents that there was any sign of international tension; on the contrary, it contains the usual mix of contributions from scholars throughout Europe and the world. The journal remained out of circulation for the duration of the war and for several years thereafter, resuming publication in 1923 (see Section 10.9).

There was much activity planned for the members of Jones's new Phonetics Department in the summer of 1914. Noël-Armfield was going to Germany, to the University of Marburg, presumably at the invitation of Viëtor, to hold "a course of Phonetics for foreigners...early in August", which was undoubtedly abandoned once war was declared.[47] The name of Ida Ward (see Section 9.2) occurs for the first time in a departmental report at this point, where it is stated that she is going to hold a "course of phonetics for foreign students at the Letchworth Holiday Course in August".[48] Jones himself had been asked earlier in the year to run a vacation course in phonetics at UCL for students from training colleges.[49] For this, he engaged the help of Noël-Armfield and also his old friend, Douglas Savory, now holding the chair of French at Queen's University, Belfast. Surprisingly, given the chaos into which Britain was plunged by the declaration of war, this vacation course did take place, possibly because many of the participants were young women. In the first week of August, Jones had agreed to give a lecture on phonetics at a conference for teachers of English to be held in Stratford-on-Avon.

It is difficult to imagine that either Jones delivering the talk, or the audience listening to it, would have been able to give it whole-hearted concentration. Since the end of June, when the Archduke Ferdinand and his wife had been assassinated in Sarajevo, events in Europe had moved towards confrontation at frightening speed. Throughout July the nations had lined up, either behind Germany and Austro-Hungary, or in alliance with France and Russia. On Saturday, August 1, when Daniel Jones might have been checking through his notes for Stratford, Germany announced general mobilisation. In the stifling heat of a Bank Holiday weekend, the British began to realise that their government's commitment to defend the neutrality of Belgium would involve them in a war which would cause upheaval to their own country and every other nation in Europe. Each day crowds waited at post offices (before the era of domestic radio) so as to get the latest news of the developments on the Continent. On Tuesday, August 4, German troops marched into Belgium, and Britain issued an ultimatum to Germany. *Punch*, for once quite serious, reported the parliamentary announcement in these words:

"We have asked," said the Premier as quietly as if he were mentioning [a] request for early reply to a dinner invitation, "that a satisfactory answer shall be given before midnight". House knew what that meant. On the stroke of midnight Great Britain and Germany would be at war.[50]

Chapter 6

Not adversely affected by the war (1914–17)

6.1. Adjustments to wartime

"The Phonetics Department has not been adversely affected by the war."[1] Daniel Jones's opening sentence of his Departmental Report for the year 1914–15 indicates with phlegmatic understatement how Jones (like many others not directly involved in the fighting) found that he had to cope with the routine of his job. The additional problems produced by wartime conditions would not be allowed to interrupt the work of his staff and students.

Jones neglected to put down on record his attitude to the war; but one may be certain that he did not share the jingoistic responses of so many of his British contemporaries. Unlike most Englishmen of his generation, Daniel Jones had spent his early adult life either living abroad, or otherwise in the company of people from many different countries. Because of his connections with Germany, he might have recognised the essentially militaristic nature of the Kaiser and his government, but he could never have joined in the general vilification of all things German which reached a point of hysteria during the war years.

Coming as he had under the influence of Paul Passy, who had firm pacifist views, it is probable that Jones realised early on that the war was a calamitous waste of the lives of Europe's young men. There appears to have been no thought ever in his mind of enlisting in the forces (where his linguistic skills would presumably have been welcomed). Nor is there any record of his having worked for the intelligence services in any kind of capacity.[2] He could no doubt have parried any suggestion that he should join up by pointing out the contribution his Department could make to language learning, an important potential to develop in wartime. In any case, although he was of the right age to go to the front, his poor health record was such that he would probably have been rejected for active service of any sort.

But there is evidence that during the war Jones (perhaps influenced by Passy) became sympathetic to the pacifist cause, and apparently attended the tribunals arranged to test the sincerity of those claiming to be conscientious objectors.[3] This could have given rise to tension within the Jones family. In contrast, Jones's half-brother, Arthur Daniel, had embarked on a notable military career, gaining the Military Cross and a Distinguished Service Order (with Bar), and being wounded on three occasions.[4]

One of the best indicators of Jones's lack of sympathy with the general war hysteria in Britain was the fact that he continued to have contact with his German publishers Teubner during the period 1914–18, He sent his communications through Switzerland.[5] Possibly he used one of his Swiss students as a go-between for this purpose (perhaps G. Bonnard, who is mentioned in the 1915–16 Departmental Report). In any event, maintaining the links with Teubner through the wartime years had its reward as the *Outline* was published almost as soon as the war ended (see Section 8.2).

Many of Jones's colleagues at University College joined the armed forces, as did a vast number of students and former students. Wartime issues of the *University College London Union Magazine* often read as one long obituary column, noting briskly the tragically curtailed lives of so many young men. In all, a total of three hundred and one members of the College died during the war (Harte—North 1978: 142). One effect on Jones may have been to make him more concerned with philosophical and religious matters but also to render it impossible for him to accept the conventional western religion of Christianity, whose spiritual leaders were backing the governments of the nations involved in the conflict. Eastern religions, with a strong emphasis on pacifism and international brotherhood running through them, might have had more appeal at such a time, and indeed it was to this type of faith, as interpreted by organisations like the Theosophical Society, that Jones turned after the war ended.

6.2. The Department in the early war years

Equipped as he now was, with two part-time members of staff, and with the services of Perrett from the German Department, Daniel Jones had made ambitious projections for the session 1914–15. The advertised programme promised a total of thirty-nine courses in all (twelve more than the previous year). There were to be a number of innovations. A special practical class was on offer to Indian students of English (to cater, presumably, for those entering for the new IPA certificate, see Section 5.6). Public lectures were announced on the pronunciation of Cantonese Chinese, Hindustani and Welsh. French and German were, of course, covered, and special classes were set up for missionaries and students of philology. Experimental phonetics was to receive even more attention, with the new laboratory available to students every evening of the week except Saturday. In the third term, a "Research Class for Advanced Students desirous of doing original work in any branch of Phonetics" was offered, and Jones had also included for the first time a course of "Advanced General Phonetics for those desiring to qualify as Teachers of Phonetics".[6]

Surprisingly, Jones's claim that the work of the Department was unaffected by the war seems to be borne out by the facts. In the event, he was able to report that "23 full courses of lectures and practical classes have been held during the session, besides 4 short courses of public lectures". He goes on to detail the topics covered: "…English Pronunciation, French Pronunciation, German Pronunciation, Chinese Pronunciation, Hindustani Pronunciation, Welsh Pronunciation, Phonetics for Missionaries, Advanced General Phonetics, and Experimental Phonetics".[7] So, Jones's programme would have survived almost intact.

Jones was especially proud of the success of his classes in French phonetics, and the reasons for this were twofold. Firstly, French phonetics still provided him with more students than any other single area (almost two hundred and fifty in 1914–15). For the other factor, we have to consult a special report Jones prepared on the French classes of the spring term of 1914:

> Owing to the large size of the practical classes in French phonetics and the conse-
> quent impossibility of giving adequate individual attention to the students, it ap-
> peared desirable to subdivide one of the classes. As additional assistance was
> required for this purpose, on the suggestion of the Provost I tried the experiment
> subdividing the General Practical class, taking one group myself and leaving the
> other groups to be taken by my wife.[8]

Jones goes on to report that the attendance for his classes was seventy-eight per cent, but that Cyrille had managed to achieve an attendance figure of eighty-six per cent for her groups. It was cause for satisfaction since not only had he managed to find a way of incorporating Cyrille into the framework of the Department, but this had been at the instigation of Gregory Foster himself. Furthermore, he obviously felt that his wife had in no way let him down by her performance. In the 1914–15 Report, Jones singles out the classes in French Phonetics as "particularly successful owing to the additional assistance which has been provided this session", only mentioning later that French phonetics was in the hands of Mrs Daniel Jones.[9]

The success of Jones's Department at this time is even more remarkable if seen in the context of University College as a whole. Student numbers plunged with the out-break of war, soon falling to just over a thousand—roughly half of what they had been pre-war (Harte—North 1978: 201). Yet, there were some beneficial sides to the war as far as Jones was concerned. As emerges from the 1915–16 Departmental Report, the loss of the large contingent of German students, who had formerly made up such a substantial proportion of the English phonetics courses, was in part redressed by an influx of refugees. However, Jones was forced to concede that "the number of Foreign Students is, of course, much smaller than before the war".[10]

6.3. A readership

Jones's Department was by now being recognised as a "valuable auxiliary to all the Language Departments", as the College Committee Report commented, noting the expansion of the work in phonetics.[11] Soon, Daniel Jones was to be awarded the prize he had long awaited. In November 1914, he was appointed a member of the Council of the Faculty of Arts.[12] February 1915 saw the Professorial Committee commend conferring the title of Reader,[13] and in March of the same year the Senate finally ap-proved Jones's new status, at the same time designating him an "Appointed Teacher".[14] A brief note in the College Committee Report states: "The work of Mr. Daniel Jones has obtained further recognition, the title of 'Reader in Phonetics in the University of London' having been conferred upon him by the Senate."[15] It had taken just over eight years to progress from being a temporary assistant teacher employed for only a couple of hours each week to an appointment as one of University College's senior staff, at the head of his own Department, which unlike virtually every other section of the College was actually managing to grow during the wartime years. Jones was still only thirty-four years old.

From this secure position, and in the knowledge that Gregory Foster would give him complete backing, Jones must have realised that it was only a question of waiting for the war to end for a new period of general expansion in education to begin, making his own prospects excellent. It would certainly have crossed his mind that a university chair might be his within the foreseeable future.

6.4. The appointment of Harold Palmer

The programme advertised for the session 1915–16 was expanded yet further, and for this year the Phonetics Department had planned a total of fifty-two advertised courses. The college prospectus gives a good indication that by this time Jones's approach had settled down into a formula which provided a pattern for his work throughout his career. "English Phonetics for Foreign Students" now comprised the following components: General Practical Work; Pronunciation Exercises; a set of lectures on "English Speech Sounds"; Phonetic Dictation and Ear-Training Exercises; and various courses described as "Practical Work". The emphasis on the practical element, and the use of the techniques of phonetic dictation and ear-training—these last resulting from the influence of Paul Passy and, indirectly, his brother Jean (see Section 2.3) —were to become the basics of the Jonesian approach to the teaching of foreign language pronunciation. The programmes for the highly successful courses in the phonetics of French—which were again taught partly by Cyrille during that year—were similar in their concept. However, the material for English Phonetics for English students still retained some of the old-fashioned elocutionist approach, and a course of lectures was put on claiming to deal with "The Sounds of Educated Southern English, Dialectical Forms, curing of Cockneyisms, Assimilation, Intonation".[16]

The expansion did not involve many new courses. Hindustani was no' 'termed Urdu —but this merely reflected the background of the informant. As before 1'.ere was little apparent interest in German (which had only one class); this can be explained by the anti-German feeling at this time. Experimental phonetics continued along the lines already established. The notable expansion was once again in the courses for missionaries. As Jones points out in his Report for 1915–16, after starting with a single course for just four students in 1912–13, and reaching a total of nineteen in 1914–15, spread over two courses, the Department now ran three courses with fifty-three potential missionaries in attendance. Furthermore, more than half of these were now officially nominated by the Board of Study for the Preparation of Missionaries.[17]

The major change in the departmental personnel is noted briefly by Jones at the very end of his report: "Mr H.E. Palmer was appointed temporarily to assist the department during this session."[18] Harold Palmer's presence in London was a direct consequence of the war. In 1902, Palmer had left his family home in Kent with the idea of spending a period of time abroad. He had obtained a post as a teacher at the Berlitz Language School in Verviers in Belgium. He became fascinated with the problems of language teaching, and had joined the International Phonetic Association.[19] He corresponded with Jones, and had also exchanged views with him through the columns of *Le Maître phonétique* (see Section 3.8.); and on one occasion the two men had met on a cross-channel steamer.[20]

On the outbreak of war, Palmer found himself stranded in Belgium as the German troops advanced. He managed, with his Belgian wife and his young daughter, to survive, undetected for a period of six weeks and then determined to escape to the Netherlands, which was neutral territory. To do so, Palmer chose a method smacking of spy-novel romance. Hiding himself, his wife and his daughter under the covers of a vegetable cart, they managed to slip past the border guards. Once in the Netherlands, they quickly obtained a passage to England. They had been forced to abandon all their possessions in Belgium, and when he arrived at his parents' home in Folkestone, he was quite penniless (Jones 1950c: 4–5). His daughter, Dorothée, later recalled: "When we arrived in England, we had literally only the things we stood up in—we were truly refugees!" (D. Anderson 1969: 140).

After a brief period of teaching, Palmer contacted Daniel Jones, who, since he had already formed a high opinion of Palmer's talents, was very willing to help him get employment (Jones 1950c: 5).

> In October 1915 he was, on my recommendation, invited to deliver a course of evening lectures on methods of language teaching at University College, London. These lectures attracted large audiences, mainly school teachers, and were the forerunners of many other successful courses.

In fact, Jones stated at the time that Palmer also "conducted most of the Spoken English classes" and confirmed the success of his work, and the interest shown in it.[21]

This was the beginning of a valuable period of association between Palmer and Jones at University College which was significant for them both. In 1916, Palmer was appointed to the regular part-time staff at University College, "a position which he occupied with distinction" (Jones 1950c: 5). He remained there till 1921 and it was over this period of time that Palmer produced some of his most important contributions to applied linguistics and phonetics. For his part, Jones had working for him a man whose lively independent intelligence was an inspiration to his students and to his colleagues. Howatt (1984: 232) states:

> ...the following year, 1916, Palmer began giving the lectures on language teaching methodology to local foreign language teachers which formed the basis for his first major work, *The Scientific Study and Teaching of Languages*, published only one year later. To make the transition from refugee English language teacher to

the authorship of a classic text in the field inside three years was a phenomenal achievement. Obviously, it would not have been possible if he had not thought deeply about the issues while working in his school in Belgium, or without the stimulus of his contacts with Daniel Jones and his colleagues in the Phonetics Department at University College.

6.5. Death of Jones's father

The year 1915 was in many ways another turning-point in Daniel Jones's life. The progress in his career, and his professional acclaim, were now offset by personal grief when his father, Daniel Jones Senior, died on December 4th at the age of eighty-one. His death was sudden, even unexpected; he had enjoyed good health all his life and his terminal illness lasted a mere twenty-four hours. Jones's father was mentally and physically active into his eighties (like Jones himself in old age).[22] In 1915, owing to the war, for the first time in many years, there were no Wimbledon championships, but the magazine *Lawn Tennis*, displaying Dan Jones's photograph on its front cover, claimed:

> ...we may be quite sure that, if there had been a Wimbledon, and no war, in the blank season of 1915, he would have been there—watching with unimpaired alertness the progress of a meeting over which in by-gone days he had presided as referee, and in the evolution of which he had played so unostentatious, and yet so vitally important, a part.[23]

Apart from the trauma of his first experience of close family bereavement, the loss of his father must have meant much to Jones. Dan Jones was remembered by a great number with warmth and affection. He was by all accounts a master of legal argument, though it is also said that in everyday matters he was notoriously indecisive.[24] Though his interests were far removed from those of his son, he undoubtedly had considerable influence on Daniel Jones's early life and the initial stages of his professional career. It could not have been easy for a man with a brilliant academic performance behind him, and with a passionate interest in games, to understand the problems of a sickly youngster, who had been miserable at school, was mediocre at university and had grown up to have no interest either in tennis or any other game. It is also easy to imagine Dan Jones's concern when his son, and namesake, showed a noticeable lack of enthusiasm for the idea of following his father in a legal career, and instead seemed intent on spending his youth living abroad picking up foreign languages.

Jones Senior appears to have reacted sensibly in these matters and was certainly not the stereotype of the stern Victorian father. He wisely removed his son from Radley and sent him to University College School, where his talents were better able to develop. However, there is also a streak of obstinacy in his determination that Jones complete his Bar examinations before devoting himself to phonetics, not to mention his apparently petty insistence on young Daniel's walking long distances to school (see Section 1.5).

Yet he did not stand in his son's way when Jones wanted to pursue what must have seemed a bizarre fringe subject, and supported him financially up to 1907. Jones, of course, rapidly restored himself in the esteem of his father by his evident industry and his progress in his career. His father's willingness to undertake the journey to Brittany for the wedding when he was seventy-seven years of age is perhaps an indication of his regard. Undoubtedly, it was pleasing to Daniel Jones that his readership arrived when his father was still alive to witness his success.

Dan Jones left over twenty-six thousand pounds in his will—an enormous sum of money at the time—and owned eight houses in central London. The property was divided among his sons, and Daniel Jones inherited two houses, both in Bayswater, which he appears to have disposed of shortly afterwards.[25]

6.6. The Jones family

Daniel Jones seems to have had little family feeling for his two half-brothers, Arthur Daniel and Wilfred, but was much closer to his mother and his one full brother, Arnold. Viola Jones also seems to have favoured her own sons, and in 1916 made a will leaving all her estate to be divided between Arnold and Daniel, with nothing at all going to her stepsons.

She is remembered as a woman of extreme vanity ("unable to pass a glass without arranging her hair, or doing something")[26] though her photographs show her to have been of rather plain appearance. Viola was far younger than her husband, but her influence on him is not to be underestimated. It is worth remembering that she may well have been responsible for the decision to send Daniel Jones to University College School. Viola Jones eventually went to live with Arnold, who did not marry; she died in 1926.

Daniel Jones was devoted to Arnold, even though the two were completely different in character. Arnold is recalled today by members of the family as a bluff, hearty man, constantly making jokes or telling amusing stories; he combined this with a profound religious conviction as a member of the Church of England. (Daniel Jones appears to have had little contact with the church even before he became involved in theosophical beliefs.) After an unsettled period in his youth, Arnold took up teaching as a profession, and it is possible that his first post was obtained as a result of Jones's influence. He became a master at the Eagle House prep school which was run by Robert Bruce Lockhart Senior—the father of the Robert Bruce Lockhart whom Daniel Jones had met when staying with the Motte family at Bourg-la-Reine.

Arnold was the only other member of the Jones family who shared his brother's interest in phonetics. He joined the International Phonetic Association in 1908, soon after Daniel Jones returned from France, and in the following year contributed a competent review of Ripman's *English, French and German sound charts* (A. Jones 1909) to *Le Maître phonétique*; indeed, the criticism is so polished that one suspects the hand of his brother was involved in the writing, or at least in its revision. In 1911, an article appeared in *Le Maître phonétique* by Daniel Jones under the heading "Phonetics in English Schools; Eagle House School, Sandhurst" (Jones 1911b), which reviewed two plays—one in English and the other in French—performed by the young schoolboys "under the direction of our colleague Mr Arnold Jones, who has for some time past used phonetic methods in this school for teaching the pronunciation of foreign languages". The review is most laudatory, terming the pronunciation of the actors in the French play "nothing short of marvellous" with "excellent intonation and characteristic stress". The English play also contained "evidences of careful phonetic training"; the broken English of "a German count and a French waiter" was very convincing, although it was conceded that "the American young lady" was "a trifle overdone". Once again, the suspicion remains that Arnold may have had not a little help from his brother in training his boys for this play.

In any case, Arnold certainly assisted one aspect of Daniel Jones's work, albeit in a humble way. Arnold was used as a model for the lip-shape photographs in the 1918 edition of the *Outline* (*Outline*[1]: vii) and several of these were retained for subsequent editions (see, for example, *Outline*[3]: iii). As a result, his moustache, lips and jaw became familiar to many thousands of students all over the world.

Arnold Jones was appointed to be a headmaster (of Marlborough House School in Reading) during the war, and it was to his care that Daniel and Cyrille entrusted the education of their son, Olivier (see below). Arnold was a devoted son and cared for his mother till her death. She had become a demanding and, it is said, dominating old lady; quite possibly, Arnold's greatest contribution to his brother's career was merely to relieve him of the task of looking after her. Arnold died after contracting lung cancer in his early forties; his death, coming so soon after that of their mother (see Section 10.4), affected Daniel Jones deeply and may have been a triggering factor in producing the depressions from which he suffered in later life.[27]

6.7. Solomon Plaatje

The war, which stopped the publication of *Le Maître phonétique* and made it impossible for the IPA to carry on its usual functions, proved to be an upheaval in the development of the organisation from which it perhaps never fully recovered. Nevertheless, events could be viewed positively in one respect. Jones was now freed of what had become a tremendous burden of editing, writing, proofreading and correspondence and was able to devote himself more to ensuring that the works which he was writing were completed. It allowed Jones to concentrate his mind on writing *books*— and he is unquestionably better remembered today for his books than for the many articles which he wrote in the years up to 1916. It was in this period, during and just after the war, that his book publishing reached its peak.

Several of these publications had already been in preparation for a number of years. We have seen that the *Outline* was virtually complete and set up in print before the outbreak of war; another book which was in a fairly advanced state was the *EPD*. But some of Jones's books were actually conceived in the war period, and one of the most significant of these was the *Sechuana reader* (Jones—Plaatje 1916a).

The year 1915 was also when Jones began his analysis of the Tswana language—or Sechuana as it was then generally known.[28] This research formed the basis of some of his most notable contributions to general phonetics and phonology, and it is certain that Jones himself considered this as one of his most important areas of work, as has been confirmed by Gimson (1977: 151).

Jones (*Sechuana reader*: v) himself recalls the way in which the *Sechuana reader* originated:

> Early in 1915 it was my good fortune to make the acquaintance of Mr. Solomon Plaatje, a native Bechuana, and as I found him to possess unusual linguistic ability, I suggested to him that a useful purpose would be served if we were to make an analysis of his native language on modern phonetic lines. He readily agreed, and between May 1915 and September 1916 we had constant meetings…

Solomon T. Plaatje (1876–1932) his informant, and co-author, also put on paper his first impressions of his meeting with Jones (p. viii):

> I had but a vague acquaintance with phonetics until early in 1915, when Miss Mary Werner took me one day to the Phonetics Department of University College, London, where Mr. Daniel Jones was conducting a class. After some exercises I gave the students a few Sechuana sentences, which Mr. Jones wrote phonetically on the blackboard. The result was to me astonishing. I saw some English ladies, who knew nothing of Sechuana, look at the blackboard and read these phrases aloud without the least trace of European accent. The sentences included the familiar question, "leīnā ɟā-xɑxo īmāŋ?" ("What is your name?"), and it was as if I heard the question put by the Bahurutshe women on the banks of the Marico River.

Plaatje was obviously impressed both by Jones and with the possibilities of phonetics. But Daniel Jones was also aware that in Plaatje he had no ordinary informant but a person of unusual talent and intelligence.

Solomon Tshekisho Plaatje—known generally as "Sol"—was born in 1876. By the time he first met Jones, he already had an interesting life behind him. Plaatje had an excellent command of Tswana, English and Afrikaans (or Cape Dutch as it was then termed) and, according to his biographer, "spoke eight different languages, European and African, and wrote regularly in half of these" (Willan 1984: vii). Plaatje's brilliance as a polyglot is indicated by his performance in an examination in secretarial studies held in his youth. He gained top place, beating all European candidates, despite the fact that at the time educational opportunities for Africans were sparse. In the Boer War, Plaatje acted as an interpreter, and his diaries provide an interesting and unusual view of the conflict as seen by a black nonparticipant (Comaroff 1973). He had published a small book of Tswana proverbs and was the editor of a paper aimed at an African readership, the *People's Friend* (Willan 1984).

Jones acknowledged his debt to his informant in the Missionaries' Lecture (see Section 6.9 for full discussion), written at the time:

> My work on this language [Tswana] was done under rather favourable conditions, namely with an intelligent and observant native, Mr Plaatje, who is a good linguist and knows English well, and (most important of all) soon understood what I was driving at and was able to help very materially in the investigation.[29]

Most of the *Sechuana reader* texts were written by Plaatje and based on Tswana proverbs or folktales. One of these stories relates that whilst one can easily crack a single stick, it is impossible to break a tied bundle, and ends with the proverb: "Alone I am not a man; I am only a man by the help of others" (*Sechuana reader*: 14). The aphorism appealed strongly to Jones and from then on he is known to have quoted the words frequently to his colleagues and friends.[30]

Sol Plaatje returned to London in 1919–20 and 1922–23, each time resuming his contact with Jones for a series of informant sessions (Willan 1984: 253, 284) although it appears that Jones completed his later work on Tswana (Jones 1928a) without further assistance, only sending his work to Plaatje once it had been published (Willan 1984: 338).

Plaatje can be considered one of the most important figures in the early history of African nationalism, being one of the first black activists, and arguably the most influential spokesman for African peoples in his lifetime. His cogent protests against the treatment of his black fellow-citizens, and his disgust with, for example, the introduction of the notorious pass laws, are stated at length in a newspaper interview (Anon. 1917: 170)—long before most of the world was aware of deteriorating conditions for South African blacks.

> ... "the screw is tightening round the black man," said Mr. Plaatje. "Political rights? Well, we have the right to pay our taxes with the utmost regularity and a poll tax for the colour of our skin. This money is used among other things for the maintenance of public schools for white children, from which our own children are excluded."

There can be little doubt that Jones's meetings with this remarkable man would have reinforced his enlightened attitudes—remarkable in the context of the time—towards people of all nationalities and races. But it was not an unequal debt. Willan (1984: 193) notes:

...his collaboration with Daniel Jones...gave Plaatje, quite apart from much needed income, an interest in phonetics that he was to retain for the rest of his life.

Plaatje was noted for his "unrivalled ability as a public speaker, a man whose wit and humour could hold any audience" (Willan 1984: 381). He was able to make brilliant speeches in several languages and undertook lecturing tours of Britain, the USA and Canada, explaining the position of the black population in South Africa. In addition, he was an outstanding journalist and author, writing books, editing a succession of magazines, and producing *Mhudi* (Plaatje 1930), the first full-length novel by a black South African. Towards the end of his life—partly under the influence of his contacts with Jones—Plaatje took up a fight for a proper recognition of the status of the Tswana language and for the reform of the non-phonemic system of spelling introduced by the missionaries (Willan 1984: 324–348). He died in Kimberley in 1932. Willan (1984) provides a detailed biographical study of one of the earliest and least recognised figures in the struggle for racial equality.

6.8. The *Sechuana reader*

The *Sechuana reader* appeared in the London Phonetic Reader series and follows the same general plan as the other volumes (see Section 5.2) in containing a brief phonetic/phonological description plus a set of reading passages with phonetic transcriptions and literal translations; see Figures 6.2. and 6.3.

Jones and Plaatje (p. xi) state their aims clearly at the outset:

> The object of this book is threefold. It is intended (1) as a collection of reading-matter suitable either for native Bechuanas or for foreign learners of the Sechuana language, (2) as a guide to the pronunciation of the language, and (3) to demonstrate the desirability and feasibility of writing African languages on the "one sound one letter" basis.

These aims are carried out quite systematically. The native Tswana speaker is catered for both in the selection of stories which would be suitable for use in schools and also by the fact that the title page (see Figure 6.1), the contents table and the page headings are given in Tswana. The authors presumably realised that it would be important for the African user to see his native language used in written form for the first time. Jones and Plaatje emphasise throughout the *Sechuana reader* the vital significance of the need for the orthography of African languages to be soundly based on what are, in essence, phonemic principles (though the word phoneme is never employed in the *Sechuana reader*). However, the description of the pronunciation of Tswana is naturally the chief preoccupation of the authors.

The phonetic/phonological analysis of Tswana is based on Plaatje's own idiolect, which is considered to be typical of the Barolong tribe (i.e. the Serolong dialect);

ᴅipalɔ tsā-sɪcɣàːnɑ

ka-litļhāka tsā-ꜰonētike ĕā-merāꜰɪrɒːꜰɪ

(lɪ phetolɛlɔ tsā-seɲēsɪmɑːnɪ)

lɪ-kwālĭlwe kɪ
dænjəl dʒoʋnz
riːdər ɪn fonetɪks ɪn ðə juːnɪvəːsɪtɪ əv ʟʌndən

lɪ
sōlomon tshēkīɣɔ plàːki
morŭlāxaɲi wā "tsāla ĕā-bāthô," kŏ-kɪm̄bɒːlɪ,
mokwāli wā "lĭanɪ tsā-sɪcɣānā lɪ maēle ā-sekxòːɑ."

kxātĭɣɔ ĕā-ɟunivēsiti ĕā-lōntɒːn.

1916

Figure 6.1. The title page of the *Sechuana reader*.

36   A SECHUANA READER

XIII.—WIND OF–SOUTH AND SUN

Wind of-South | once-upon-a-time took dispute | with-Sun, that he-who is strong | between-them both | is who. Thereupon | there-appears traveller | being-dressed-in cloak which is warm. Wind and Sun | agreed-mutually | that he-who can take-off-from traveller cloak first | is himself he-who is strong.

Wind of-South | blew-violently with-force ; no-matter-how-much-it blew-violently, traveller continued wrapped-himself-up | with-folds of-cloak his; at-length | Wind of-South | despaired. Thereupon Sun shines (*lit.* pierces), it-is-hot (*lit.* it weeps), so-that-there-is warmth, traveller so-much-so-that-he took-off cloak ; so Wind of-South surrendered | it-said Sun is himself he-who is strong.

XIII.—THE SOUTH WIND AND THE SUN

The South Wind and the Sun were once disputing which was the stronger, when a traveller came along wrapped in a warm cloak. They agreed that the one who first made the traveller take off his cloak should be considered stronger than the other. Then the South Wind blew with all his might, but the more he blew, the more closely did the traveller fold his cloak around him ; and at last the South Wind gave up the attempt. Then the Sun shone out warmly, and immediately the traveller took off his cloak ; and so the South Wind had to confess that the Sun was the stronger of the two.

Figure 6.2. Extracts (*Sechuana reader*, p. 36) showing (1) literal translation of Tswana text; (2) English text.

Figure 6.3 Phonetic Tswana text with representation of tones by musical notation (*Sechuana reader*, p. 37).

Plaatje had spent most of his life in the town of Mafeking (p. xiv). Tswana segments are said to consist of "twenty-four elementary consonant-sounds...and ten vowel-sounds" (p. xiv). The idea of the phoneme is never far away from Jones's mind, as is obvious from the passage below (p. xiv):

> Of these [consonants and vowels] the consonant-sounds c, ɟ, ɥ, and the vowel sound ʉ are probably "non-distinctive" in respect to the sounds t, l, w, and u. By this we mean that the substitution of the sounds t, l, w, u, respectively, for the sounds c, ɟ, ɥ, ʉ would probably never change the meaning of any word. At the same time c, ɟ, ɥ, ʉ are so distinct in sound from t, l, w, u, that the substitution of the latter sounds would constitute mispronunciations; it seems, therefore, desirable to assign special letters to the sounds c, ɟ, ɥ, ʉ. (In simplified orthography the sounds might, if desired, be represented by t, l, w, u.)

Nevertheless, Jones avoided using the actual word "phoneme", which is surprising in view of what he later stated in his article on the history of the phoneme concept, where the claim is made that "by about 1915 the theory [of the phoneme] began to find a regular place in the teaching given in the Department of Phonetics at University College". The explanation given for avoidance of the term is that "the theory was still in the process of being clarified, and the terminology was incomplete" (*History and meaning of the term "phoneme"*: 6). Jones adds, "I used to manage at that time without using the term" and goes on to refer to the passage from the *Sechuana reader*, p. xiv, quoted above) saying: "A year or two later I would have said that the sounds c, ɟ, ɥ, ʉ 'belong to' or 'are members of' the t, l, w, u phonemes" (*History and meaning of the term "phoneme"*: 258). It is to be inferred, therefore, that the work which led to the *Sechuana reader* came at a crucial time in Jones's development of his concept of the phoneme, and it is significant that his first recorded use of the actual term "phoneme" was also to be in a piece devoted to Tswana (Jones 1917c); see Section 7.5.

In the *Sechuana reader*, Jones and Plaatje provide a detailed description of the consonantal system of Tswana. Their analysis gives an inventory of twenty-four consonant sounds plus five affricates which are treated as consonant sequences (p. xiv). The description is a fine example of Jones's ability to reduce data to a description which is economical and concise. The articulations are frequently compared with corresponding consonants in English—which is understandable given the fact that most of the potential readership of the book might be expected to be English-speaking. It is possible to criticise certain aspects of the description, for instance the lateral ejective [tl] is termed "not a true click, but an 'implosive' sound". In a footnote, this is amplified by the statement: "In a true click air *enters* at the point of primary articulation; in an implosive sound air *passes outwards* at the point of primary articulation" (p. xviii). In fact, since Jones specifies that both this sound, and also certain varieties (i.e. allophones) of [p t k], are articulated with closed glottis, it is clear that he understood the nature of the articulations, and indeed had discussed the topic many years earlier in his article "Implosive sounds and clicks" (Jones 1907m). However, he was still hampered by the inappropriateness of the term "implosive" for ejective articulations. In a later description of Tswana, unsigned but almost certainly from Jones's hand, which appears in the *Principles of the International Phonetic Association* (IPA 1949: 48–49) the description is much simplified, and [tl] and the stops are specified as ejectives.

The symbol F is used for the bilabial fricative [Φ], which is in accordance with IPA practice at the time.[31] Jones introduces two other symbols, ɺ and ɭ. The former is used for the lateral flap which constitutes an allophone of /l/ before close vowels (p. xx). The articulation of [ɭ] is described thus (pp. xx–xxi):

> ɭ is a breathed sound, having approximately the tongue-position of j combined with a particular kind of lip-rounding. The essential feature of the lip-rounding is that the chief narrowing is made by a point of the inside of the lower lip against the upper teeth; this point is between ¼ and ½ an inch behind the edge of the lip. When the sound ɭ is pronounced with emphasis there is considerable protrusion of the lips. The lip-position is similar to that used in producing a lip-teeth whistle.
>
> The tongue-position appears to vary between true palatal and palato-alveolar position. The tongue-tip is always kept down, near the lower teeth.

The description exemplifies well the attention to detail, and the clear precision of Jones's style. But he does not seem to have realised that the sound [ɭ] is in fact a labialised counterpart of /ʃ/ comparable to other labialised consonants which the *Sechuana reader* treats as sequences of consonant + [w]. Again, in the 1949 IPA treatment, this is clarified (IPA 1949: 48):

> **w** following a consonant letter denotes labialisation of that consonant, e.g. **xw** = x͡w. **ʃw** is a single sound having a peculiar type of lip-rounding involving an articulation by the inside of the lower lip against the upper teeth.

For a discussion of the status of [ɭ], its representation as **ʃw**, and its distribution in Tswana, see the *Phoneme* (pp. 44–45), where Jones also discusses the representation of the sound in the orthography.

All in all, as pioneers, Jones and Plaatje produce a good phonetic analysis of the extremely complex consonant system of Tswana, and also go most of the way towards providing an adequate basis for a phonemic analysis. The description of the vowel system in the *Sechuana reader* is a landmark inasmuch as it is the first published attempt by Jones to utilise his Cardinal Vowel system (see Section 7.3 below). Somewhat enigmatically, the concept is introduced thus: "The vowels [of Tswana] are best described by comparing them with the eight "cardinal vowels" (i, e, ɛ, a, ɑ, ɔ, o, u) described in books on phonetics" (p. xxiii). The "books on phonetics" are not specified and it is puzzling to know what Jones could have had in mind at this particular time. None of the works mentioned in the bibliography to the *Sechuana reader* contain

TABLE OF SECHUANA SOUNDS.

		Labial.	Alveo-lar.	Retro-flex.	Palato-alveolar.	Palatal.	Velar.	Glottal.
CONSONANTS	Plosive	p b	t			{c} ɟ	k	
	Plosive-Lateral		ƫ					
	Affricate	(oʾ)	ts tɬ		cʃ [cʾɬ]	oʾ	kx	
	Nasal	m	n		[ɲ]	ɲ	ŋ	
	Continuant-Lateral		l l					
	Rolled		r					
	Flapped			l				
	Fricative	ғ (ʾ)	s		ʃ [ʾɬ]	ʾ	x	h
	Semi-vowel	ww{ɥ}				{ɥ}{(ɥ)}	(w̥)(w)	

						Front.	Mixed.	Back.	
VOWELS	Close	(u)				i	{ʉ}	u	
	Half-close	(ʊ)/(o)				ɪ / e		ʊ / o	
	Half-open	(ɔ)				ε	{ə}	ɔ	
	Open						a		

The secondary articulation of sounds having double articulation is shown by the symbols in ( ).
The alternative position of sounds with variable articulation is shown by the symbols in [ ].
Non-essential sounds are shown by symbols enclosed in { }.

Figure 6.4. Table of Sechuana sounds (*Sechuana reader*, p. xvi)

any reference to Cardinal Vowel theory; indeed, the first outline of the model, sketchy though it is, appeared first in the *EPD*[1]—a book which was completed by 1916, even though it did not come out till the following year. One must assume that Jones was anticipating the publication of the *EPD*, and perhaps also of the *Pronunciation of Russian*. This last book, which contains a full explanation of Cardinal Vowel theory, was being written in 1916 and was apparently completed in 1917, but suffered considerable delays before its eventual publication in 1923 (see Sections 7.3, 7.6 and 14.14 for further discussion).

So it is that the Cardinal Vowel system (perhaps still the most influential model of vowel description in use even today) modestly makes its debut in the *Sechuana reader* —this concise but significant publication. In fact, the references to the theory are slight in the extreme; there is no explanation of the underlying principles, and not even a vowel diagram. Though Jones and Plaatje provide so little to help their reader, the following footnote appears (p. xxiii n. 1):

A mastery of the cardinal vowels is an indispensable preliminary for anyone who wishes to analyse with accuracy the pronunciation of foreign languages. These vowels are best learnt by oral instruction from a phonetically trained teacher.

Such an injunction could scarcely have been cheering to those attempting to use the *Sechuana reader*, who found themselves unable to contact the few persons who could claim expertise in the Cardinal Vowels in 1916. In fact, the description leans heavily on references to other languages, as can be seen from this extract (p. xxiv):

> The Sechuana **o** is very nearly cardinal vowel No. 7 (the French sound of *ô* in *tôt*); the tongue-position is, if anything, a shade lower than this. The sound does not exist in Southern English, but may be heard in the Scottish pronunciation of words like *home*, *go*. It must be carefully distinguished from the diphthongs heard in the various English pronunciations of such words.
>
> Italic *o* means that either **o** or **u** may be used, **o** being probably the more frequent.

The Tswana vowel system (see Figure 6.4) is analysed by Jones and Plaatje as containing nine vowels (i.e. [i ɪ e ɛ ɑ ɔ o ʊ]) though the vowels [ɪ] and [ʊ] are problematical in status, as Jones makes clear in his preface: "It appears that in some words ɪ is an essential sound, in others **e** is essential, but in a very large number of cases ɪ and **e** are interchangeable; similar considerations apply to **u** and **o**" (p. vi). Jones expresses here the hope that later it will be possible to simplify the transcription by finding "general principles" to determine the occurrence of these two vowels which will allow the transcription "to dispense with the letters ɪ and **u** altogether". As an ad hoc procedure, italics are employed to show where [ɪ] and [e], and [ʊ] and [o], respectively, are in free variation. In addition, Jones and Plaatje show two central vowels ([ʉ] and [ə]), stating these to be "non-essential". It turns out that these sounds are extra allophonic variants of /u/ and /e/ respectively (p. xxv). The analysis in this respect is one more indication of what is to all intents and purposes a phonemic approach. In a later work, *The tones of Sechuana nouns*, (Jones 1928a: 2 n.), Jones stated that he intended to ignore all the extra vowels. However, [ɪ] and [ʊ] are reinstated in the 1949 IPA Principles treatment, being shown with what were then alternative IPA symbols ι and ω. For further discussion, see Tucker (1929; 1971: 630).

The segmental analysis is intended to provide a basis for a consistent orthography for Tswana and it is clear that at this time, probably because of his work with missionaries (see Section 5.8), Jones was preoccupied with the question of providing writing systems for languages which lacked alphabets, or had only recently been provided with them. He seemed especially impatient at the efforts previously made to devise alphabets for African languages, including Tswana, particularly where the final results were orthographic systems which oversimplified the phonological system of a language by obscuring essential phonemic contrasts. Such simplifications might come about either as a deliberate strategy in order to render the difficulties of the language less apparently formidable for Europeans—or, more commonly, because linguistically unsophisticated missionaries, or others, could not hear crucial sound differences. Hence, a section in *Sechuana reader*, entitled "A few maxims for the transcriber of

African languages" (pp. xxxv–xxxvi) provided an opportunity for Jones to give vent to his feelings.

The "maxims" warn the prospective linguist against believing that he will find similarities with his own language ("You will be fortunate if the language you are studying contains as many as six consonants and three vowels identical with those of your mother-tongue") or instructing in terms of English sounds ("the English word *day* is pronounced in at least four easily distinguishable ways"). Jones recommends ear-training for accurate observation, and warns against the flattery of informants: "If your native teacher tells you that you pronounce beautifully or 'almost like a native,' don't believe it." The conventional orthographies of African languages "official or otherwise" are to be regarded as unreliable; and the transcriber is told: "Don't speak of *letters* when you mean *sounds*. Languages are made up of SOUNDS." The crux of the matter is summed up in the eighth maxim, the first sentence of which is printed in bold type (p. xxxvi):

Don't imagine that a difficult language can be turned into an easy one if you only clothe it in an inaccurate but familiar-looking orthography. You cannot by any device abolish the difficulties of a language. You may *conceal* many of them by an apparently "simple" orthography, and the result will be that in practice you will ignore the concealed difficulties and will therefore speak the language badly.

Jones's final instruction is for the prospective analyst to bear in mind that African languages are, for the most part, tone languages and this should be allowed for in the orthography.

Plaatje, in his preface also emphasises the importance of tone in Tswana (p. viii):

…what a blessing it would be if missionaries were acquainted with phonetics. They would then be able to reproduce not only the sounds of the language, but also the tones, with accuracy. Their congregations would be spared the infliction, only too frequent at the present time, of listening to wrong words, some of them obscene, proceeding from the mouth of the preacher in place of those which he has in mind (which have similar conventional spellings but different tones).

The treatment of tone in the *Sechuana reader* is another noteworthy aspect of the work of Jones and Plaatje (see Figure 6.5). It is the first systematic tonal analysis of Tswana (though not the first of an African language, see Section 14.13). As has been pointed out by Cole (1955: xxvii), and also by Jones himself (*History and meaning of the term "phoneme"*: 16, n. 53), the approach to tone in the *Sechuana reader* is phonetic and not phonemic (tonemic). The *Sechuana reader* (p. xxvi) treats Tswana as possessing six "essential" tones: high level (marked ⁻), semi-high (ˣ), mid-level (unmarked), low-level (_), high-falling (ˋ), low-falling (ˌ). In later work, Jones (the *Phoneme*: 154–155) reduced this to a system of two tonemes, plus a modification of tone lowering. This corresponds to a modern analysis of Tswana as two tone

terraced-level with downstep—a pattern which is commonly found in the Bantu languages (for discussion of such languages, see, for instance, Welmers 1973: 77–159).

Yet it would be wrong to dismiss the analysis of Tswana produced by Jones and
Plaatje in the *Sechuana reader* as ignoring all aspects of tonemic analysis. For in-
stance, several cases of allotonic variation are noted, such as: "When a sentence begins with two consecutive high-level tones, or when two high-level tones follow a
mid-tone, there is a tendency to lower slightly the first of the high tones" (p. xxvii).
The phenomenon of "down-drift" (Hyman 1975: 226) is also noted here: "...in most
Sechuana sentences the average pitch gradually descends as the sentence proceeds"
(*Sechuana reader*: xxx). Most importantly, however, Jones and Plaatje appear to have
been the first analysts to have observed the feature of downstep (Hyman 1975: 227)
and stated its occurrence as part of a tone system. They do not use the actual term
"downstep" but the phenomenon is mentioned in the course of the discussion on the
"semi-high" tone (pp. xxvii–xxviii):

> The use of ˣ means that from this point onwards the high-level pitch is slightly
> lower than what it was before. A glance at the musical notation on p. 37 [see Fig-
> ure 6.3] will show the working of this curious system of tone-lowering.... The
> tone ˣ has a grammatical significance.

Jones does not appear to have got proper recognition for this work which, subsequent to the pioneering—but succinct—work of Christaller (1875), must be considered the most crucial early contribution to the analysis of tone languages. Welmers
(1973: 85) does not even mention Jones's name—though he does refer to the analysis
of Igbo contained in the IPA Principles (IPA 1949: 45), which he considers to be
written probably by Ida Ward, as the "earliest valid analysis of a tone system of this
type". But Welmers has ignored the quite similar sample of Tswana three pages further on, which is almost beyond doubt the work of Jones, derived as it is from the
analysis presented in the *Sechuana reader*. It is likely that Jones either wrote the Igbo
piece, or at the very least that Ward conferred with him about it.

Tucker (1964: 597), on the other hand, rightly credits Jones with introducing the
raised exclamation mark to show downstep in his 1928 treatment of Sechuana (Jones
1928a: 3); this replaced the sign ˣ of the *Sechuana reader*, and afterwards became
generally accepted amongst Africanists (it was only in 1989 that a different symbolisation gained the approval of the IPA). And Stewart (1971: 190) pays full tribute to
Jones: "...there are three scholars to whom we appear to be chiefly indebted, namely
Christaller, Jones, and Welmers". See further, Section 14.13.

6.9. Jones's methods of linguistic fieldwork

Another interesting aspect of the *Sechuana reader* is that Jones has left us some details
of the way in which the material for the book was obtained and analysed. These are
in the form of notes for a lecture bearing the title "How to use phonetics in connexion

with little known languages". Given at the beginning of the 1916–17 session—apparently to a group of students who were prospective missionaries—it will be referred to henceforth as the "Missionaries' Lecture". [32] The contents are interesting both for the light they shed on Jones's own data gathering techniques and for the advice he gives to others on learning languages which were regarded at the time as exotic.

Jones warns of the difficulty of learning "little known" languages—as opposed to the relative ease of acquiring familiar European languages, such as French, where a large amount of reliable teaching material existed. He emphasises (p. 3) the importance of linguistic and phonetic training as a preliminary:

---

54. The following are the essential tones :—
   1. A high-level tone, indicated thus, ā.
   2. A lowered variety of high-level tone, indicated thus, ằ. The term " semi-high " is suggested for this tone.
   3. A mid-level tone, which is left unmarked.
   4. A low-level tone, indicated thus, a̱.
   5. A high-falling tone, indicated thus, à.
   6. A low-falling tone, indicated thus, a̱.

55. There also exists a rising tone, which arises in all cases from a juxtaposition of a mid-level and a high-level tone. It is here indicated thus, aā (as in tɬhaā, p. 13, l. 1), but it might also be written thus, á.

56. An exceptionally high tone (marked with =) occurs once (p. 13, l. 14); for details see note 2 on p. 13.

57. An idea of the musical values of the six essential tones and the limits within which they may vary in simple narration may be gathered from Text No. XIII, in which a musical notation of the tones (for male voice) is given. The music may, of course, be transposed up or down to suit individual voices. For the female voice the music should be transposed about a sixth higher. In animated conversation the range of tone is often considerably extended.

Figure 6.5. Extract dealing with tone system (*Sechuana reader*, p. xxvi).

The student must prepare himself beforehand with a thorough grounding of general linguistic theory. He must be quite clear in his mind what he wants to learn, and must know what are the best methods to pursue.

A decision must be made as to whether the priority is to learn the oral or (if one exists) the literary form of the language; predictably, Jones (pp. 4–5) recommends the former, suggesting that pronunciation must be mastered first:

> ...the first thing to be done is to acquire a thoroughly good pronunciation. This comes before vocabulary, grammar, syntax or anything else ...whenever a person starts with a bad pronunciation, that pronunciation generally sticks; attempts at correction later are generally failures. The idea that pronunciation will get right all of itself is fatal to success.

Jones emphasises that for "an out-of-the-way language you can't make use of information already supplied by expert phoneticians. Such information doesn't exist." It is therefore essential for the student to "get this knowledge before you go out to the country" (p. 9). He also underlines the significance of ear-training, "which some students are apt to overlook. If you haven't had proper ear-training, you will never be able to determine with accuracy the nature of the sounds you have to learn" (p. 10). "Mouth-training" is then essential, and Jones's phonetic expectations for the missionaries are high (pp. 11–12):

> I should say that a good control over about 100 well assorted sounds would do well enough for ordinary purposes...perhaps about 40 vowels (including some formed by such modifications as nasalisation) and 60 consonants.
> To learn all these sounds you must have a <u>phonetically trained teacher</u>. It is not the slightest use learning them wrong...you can't learn them for certain from a book.... Notice also that your native teacher won't tell you whether you are doing the things right or not. He will generally say that you are doing them right when you are not.

Jones (p. 7) shows himself to be very suspicious of native informants—perhaps through bitter personal experience.

> It is moreover extremely difficult to find out <u>whether you are pronouncing accurately or not</u>. Your native teacher simply regards you as a fool, and his teaching is entirely based on the assumption that you are not clever enough to learn to make any of his speech-sounds properly. He simply takes for granted that it is an impossibility. If you ask him whether you are pronouncing a sound correctly, he is sure to say that you are pronouncing beautifully or "almost like a native".
> You must <u>never</u> believe him when he says that. He probably only means that you have got as near to the right sound as he thinks you are ever likely to.

These remarks are very similar to portions of the "Maxims" in the *Sechuana reader* (pp. xxxv–xxxvi).

To overcome the problem of incompetence, or deliberate flattery, on the part of the native speaker teacher, Jones (p. 12) recommends the "invaluable device of intentional mispronunciations".

> When you have doubts about one of your sounds, pronounce the word you are practising making slight deviations from what you believe to be the correct sound. You mispronounce on purpose, and notice whether your native is just as well satisfied with your intentional mispronunciation as he is with your attempt at the right sound. If he is just as well satisfied, you may be quite sure that your attempt at the right sound is still very wide of the mark. If your attempt at the right sound is a really good one, the native will certainly prefer it to your intentional mispronunciation.

After a considerable space devoted to the need to employ rational orthographies, using arguments similar to those found in the *Sechuana reader*, Jones compares the romanised systems of African and Indian languages, and in approving of the latter gives credit solely to the insights of the ancient Indian linguists (see also Section A.1). In so doing, Jones reveals incidentally considerable knowledge of the work of the ancient Sanskrit phoneticians—possibly acquired during his Indian tour in 1912–13 (see Section 4.7). At this point in his life, perhaps under the influence of Walter Ripman and others in the Simplified Spelling Society, Jones had developed a marked distrust of the conventional spelling systems of European languages—not only of English. In addition, he obviously despises the faith in conventional spelling shown by the layman. He describes his experiences with an unfortunate Portuguese informant when taking down phonetic transcription (p. 17):

> ...much to his disgust, because of course he couldn't make out head or tail of what I was doing—he simply thought I was a fool and wasting the time of the lesson. Then towards the end of the lesson, after I had been writing a lot of this, he used to say: "Now let's do some Portuguese".... He didn't seem to understand that I was paying him in order to learn to <u>speak</u>, not in order to learn to spell... I need hardly say I never looked at the things he insisted on writing out for me; I only worked at my phonetic transcriptions. He said to me one day that I seemed to have the knack of picking up the pronunciation very well; I felt very much inclined to tell him that it wasn't any knack, it was simply a matter of attending to the pronunciation systematically instead of expecting it to come of itself, and that I should have learned to pronounce still better if he hadn't wasted so much of each lesson trying to teach me how to spell.

Jones's recommendation to his students is "to insist that their teacher shall <u>not show them any writing at all</u>" (p. 18, Jones's emphasis). He states adamantly:

22. Walter Ripman

23. Sol Plaatje

24. Harold Palmer

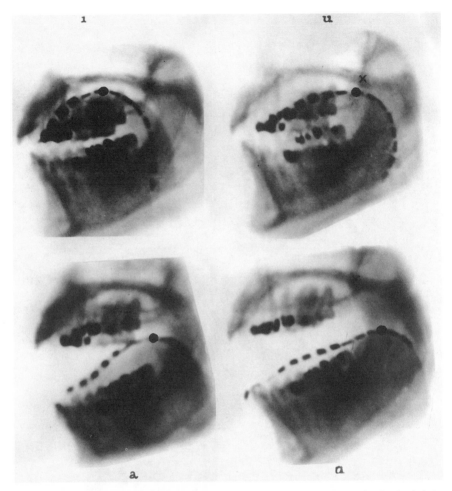

25. The original X-ray photographs of the Cardinal Vowels (see Section 7.6). The thin lead chain indicating the configuration of the dorsum of the tongue is clearly visible. Jones has added a black dot to indicate the highest point of the tongue.

...you can't learn pronunciation out of books. <u>Make your teacher give you what you can't get out of books</u>...you must <u>make your own phonetic transcriptions</u>.

In order to achieve competence in this area, a student must have adequate training with a phonetically trained teacher (p. 18).

The art of writing phonetically does not come of itself any more than the art of painting. The average English person can't paint his own portrait, nor can he write his own language phonetically or anything approaching it...he is always thinking he says one thing when he really says something else; besides which...he is always wanting to write down what he thinks people ought to say (which has nothing to do with the case).

Jones recommends his students "to include in your transcriptions of the foreign language certain sound-attributes such as length and shortness, stress or lack of stress" (p. 19). He emphasises that to begin with the student should "<u>not strive after simplification</u>" since this could eventually prove self-defeating, but "rather aim at recording the pronunciation with minute accuracy". He goes on to say (p. 19):

...later on in your investigation you are certain to come across many principles and rules of pronunciation which will enable you to simplify your very minute transcription (by adopting some conventions).

Once again, here, it is obvious that phonemic conventions must be what Jones has in mind—even though the actual term is not employed.

By way of illustration, Jones provides, a detailed account of his data gathering for Tswana. He begins by excluding Plaatje from his general diatribe against informants (see above), and reveals that he started off the investigation by getting Plaatje to dictate to him whilst he transcribed phonetically (p. 22).

...I generally find it best to <u>begin straight away by transcribing</u>. Some people have a great idea of getting the native to talk to you a bit in his language first, and you just listen to the general effect, to get some sort of general idea of what the language sounds like...I don't find that listening to the general effect helps me much; I like starting straight away into the details of the pronunciation.

Jones reports that he then set to work using a method based on assigning "to each sound the letter of the nearest cardinal sound in the general phonetic system" (p. 22). (The cardinal vowels are discussed briefly on the following page, p. 23, but here he appears also to have had the consonants in mind.) Sounds which are "near cardinal sounds but yet distinguishable from them" should have a special mark attached to them, while "sounds which are quite distinct from anything you have ever heard before (and you must expect to find several such sounds in any language you have to deal with), write them provisionally with large numbers 1, 2, 3, ..." (p. 22).

Jones acknowledges that he was not anticipating anything like the complex tone system of Tswana; as might be suspected from his deficient analysis of Ndau (see Section 3.9), he was not aware of the importance of tone in Bantu languages (p. 23).

> One of the first things that became apparent was something I was not at all expecting at the time (though I know now that it must be looked out for in every African language), namely the existence of significant "tones".... Later investigation showed that the pitch of every syllable in the language is of importance...

His surprise at his discovery of tone in Tswana derives, Jones claims, from the fact that previous descriptions of the language had ignored the feature (although he later on (p. 28) admits that one linguist, Endemann 1876, actually does mention tonal phenomena). Furthermore, Jones himself must by this time have been aware of the general prevalence of tone in the languages of the world. Apart from his work on Cantonese for the *Cantonese phonetic reader*, he had also quite recently contributed to research on Igbo carried out by N.W. Thomas (1914). This involved the use of gramophone disc recordings: "The values of the tones were ascertained by Mr. Daniel Jones and myself in collaboration. The method followed was that described in Mr. Jones' 'Intonation Curves'..." (Thomas 1914: 40). Thomas's study must count as one of the very earliest applications of instruments as an aid to research on tone languages—but it was undoubtedly Daniel Jones who devised the procedure.

The tone system was, as far as Jones was concerned, "the part of the pronunciation which gave far more trouble than anything else" (p. 28). He goes on to describe in detail his working methods (pp. 28–29).

> This is the way to set about analysing tones. Write out phonetically long passages of the language on music paper, and write as well as you can by means of musical notes (or curved lines, or tonic sol-fa if you prefer) the tunes that you hear your native "singing" when he talks. Get him to repeat each sentence or portion of a sentence over and over again. If you have had your ear trained to observe differences of pitch, you will have no difficulty in getting down at any rate a very fair approximation to his tune.
>
> You should do an enormous amount of this. I had to do something like 10 sheets of music paper before I began to get the hang of the tones. This necessarily takes an immense time, but it's the only way of doing it.

It might be said in fairness to Jones's informants that if he typically worked with such thoroughness and dedication to detail, but at the same time gave them no real explanation of what he was doing—merely posing as someone interested in learning the language out of general interest—then it is not surprising that some of his native speakers lost interest, or considered him "a fool". Undoubtedly, Jones worked far more happily with perceptive, intelligent informants such as Plaatje, or Kwing Tong Woo, who were also aware of what he was trying to discover.

Jones claims to have obtained "a fairly accurate general idea" of the Tswana tone system after about ten "sittings" (to use his term), but new features kept cropping up "causing us to modify some of the conclusions we had come to previously; so that it was a very long time before we really got the thing straight". However, "one fact about the tones was not brought to light until we had well over 50 sittings!" but Jones ends by saying "I hope and think that we have now got the analysis quite accurate" (p. 29). It is, incidentally, noticeable that Jones refers constantly to "we" at this point, indicating perhaps the degree to which Plaatje was able to help him in his analysis. There appears to have been a felicitous combination of Jones's phonetic training and sharp ear for pitch with Plaatje's native-speaker intuition (activated by his intelligent perception of what information Jones wished to have supplied).

Downstep was apparently the chief complicating factor. Jones (p. 30) describes the feature in detail:

> ...at certain points in the sentence, determined by grammatical considerations, the value of the high-level tone has to be slightly lowered *and during all the rest of the sentence it never goes back again....* The high level stays at the lowered position unless another point of lowering arrives in which case it goes a semi-tone lower still. The other tones move downwards to match...

Here Jones appends the diagram represented in Figure 6.6.

The description of downstep in the Missionaries' Lecture is somewhat fuller than that in the *Sechuana reader*, and shows that Jones was many years ahead of his time in his understanding of tone at this point. Furthermore, he appears to have worked out the system entirely on his own (with, of course, Plaatje's invaluable aid) since he does not appear to have been aware of Christaller's (1875) researches on Akan. The Missionaries' Lecture also contains the precursor of the raised exclamation mark referred to in Section 6.8. A list of transcription symbols shows the downstep marking ˣ which Jones had used in the *Sechuana reader.* This symbol has been circled by Jones and the handwritten addition "or '" placed just beneath it (p. 32). Presumably, this raised vertical mark was later converted to a raised ! to avoid confusion with stress markings. See also the Philological Society Lecture, Section 7.5.

Jones also describes his fieldwork methods in his research on the segmental system of Tswana, and shows how he combined his vast experience with sharp observation.

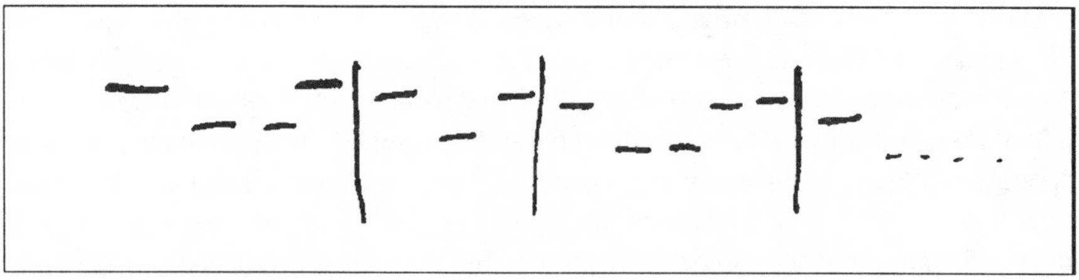

Figure 6.6. Extract from Missionaries' Lecture illustrating downstep.

I soon spotted the phenomenon of *aspiration of plosive consonants*...I was accustomed to that in other languages. I also soon saw (because I happen [sic] to be on the look out for it) that the unaspirated plosive consonants were often pronounced with *simultaneous glottal stop*.... I was of course on the look out for clicks, but it turned out that there were not any. (p. 24)

Jones goes on to explain his difficulties with the Tswana centralised vowels [ɨ ʊ]: "...it required a good deal of listening practice to learn to distinguish them from other vowels" (p. 25)—and two "awkward" consonants, the Tswana /l/, which has retroflex flap allophones, and the labialised [ʃʷ]. The first posed difficulties because at slower speed the flap allophone is articulated as [d]. Jones (p. 25) comments:

I should probably have noticed it earlier, if I had consulted some of the existing books on Sechuana; not because the sound is accurately described anywhere, but because some authors write it with a *d* and others with an *l*; whenever you find such an alternation, you may be quite certain that the true sound is neither one nor the other. I purposely did the investigation without consulting any books for fear of being mislead [sic] by the inaccurate observations of other people.

The detail of Jones's articulatory approach to phonetics is well brought out by his description of his attempts to imitate this sound (p. 26).

...by dint of looking at Mr Plaatje's tongue and trying experiment [sic] myself, we found that in order to make it the tip of the tongue must be curled backwards and must touch the left hand side of the roof of the mouth. It is one of the most difficult sounds to make I have ever come across; I practised it off and on for some months while Mr Plaatje was here, and in the end got it very nearly well, though even now I cannot always make it to my entire satisfaction.

The peculiarly labialised [ʃʷ] merits even more articulatory precision in its description, with instruction given on tongue position similar to that already quoted from the *Sechuana reader*. Jones says: "I am in no doubt whatever about the formation of this sound; anyone who follows these instructions can learn to pronounce it absolutely correctly" (p. 27).

The Missionaries' Lecture displays clearly the strong points and also some of the weaknesses of Jones's approach to phonetics and particularly to linguistic fieldwork. His painstaking thoroughness and attention to articulatory detail are clearly revealed. Jones was a perfectionist, and he was willing to devote a great deal of time to reaching a final result which satisfied his own high standards; Jones's own estimate of the time spent with Plaatje on informant sessions was between a hundred and a hundred and twenty hours, though he considered that, having tackled one Bantu language, he could deal with another of the same family more rapidly (p. 34). The analysis of tone indicates Jones's remarkable ear for pitch, and the analysis of downstep shows that he was not lacking in theoretical insights. Throughout, Jones insists that he is determined to arrive at his ideas as a result of his own efforts and does not wish to have to rely on the work of others.

The last point, however, shows simultaneously a weakness in Jones's approach, and one which was to re-emerge throughout his career. He was always unwilling to read the work of others (cf. Section 14.10), but in this case could certainly have speeded up his fieldwork had he done so. Though most previous writers on Tswana showed complete ignorance of tone, Endemann (1876), as already mentioned, is an exception. Had he read more widely, Jones might also have encountered Christaller (1875) with its penetrating analysis of downstep in Akan. There is a hint of arrogance in his determination to work independently, and this has other manifestations in his determination to avoid being influenced by orthography, and in his reluctance to let his informants in on the exact nature and purpose of his work—unless, like Plaatje, they are bright enough to work it out for themselves.

Furthermore, it is questionable whether the students for whom the Missionaries' Lecture was intended would have been able to utilise much of Jones's advice, since they lacked his knowledge and abilities in practical phonetics. It should, however, be stated in Jones's defence that he did advise them to read the work of other linguists (p. 34):

> ...get hold of any reliable book you can find on the pronunciation of any language belonging to the same family as the one you want to learn; study that carefully and notice the peculiarities in the pronunciation; it is highly probable that many of the peculiarities of the language you have to learn are similar to those which you find in the cognate language.

The notes for the Missionaries' Lecture are invaluable since they not only provide information about Daniel Jones's research methods from his own pen but also shows that he passed these ideas on to his pupils. We can see much that is written here reflected in the work of many of Jones's distinguished followers—such as Armstrong, Beach, Doke, Ward and many more (see Section 10.13). The fieldwork method described is that which was to be the foundation of the most important research carried out not only at University College, but later at the School of Oriental and African Studies, and in other centres all over the world where students trained in Jonesian techniques passed them on to others.

Chapter 7

A sort of mission

7.1. Ripman's influence

There was really no chance that the Michaelis—Jones (1913a) dictionary, *A phonetic dictionary of the English language* (henceforth *Phonetic dictionary*), could ever be a commercial success. Everything was against it. The reverse arrangement of the entries with the transcription coming first (see Section 5.3) was a tremendous handicap in itself, but on top of that there was little possibility of large sales for a book on English pronunciation, published in Germany, which had the misfortune to appear so shortly before the outbreak of war. In fact, even before the *Phonetic dictionary* came out, Jones was already engaged on his own dictionary, and by 1913 the book was in a sufficiently advanced state for it to be mentioned in the list of Jones's publications at the end of the *Phonetic dictionary* (p. 444) as being "in preparation". By December 1916, Daniel Jones had at last completed all the work for this second dictionary to which he had given the title *An English pronouncing dictionary* (Jones 1917a, referred to in this volume as *EPD*) and it finally appeared in the following year.

It is possible that the *EPD* was begun as another Jones—Michaelis project. In his introduction to the dictionary, Michaelis receives acknowledgement (p. xii) for having given "considerable help...during the initial stages of the work". In addition, Jones mentions a number of other colleagues who have assisted him, including Noël-Armfield, Coleman (now a lieutenant in the army) and Savory (who had succeeded to a chair at Queen's University, Belfast). He had also consulted two lecturers in training colleges for help on Scottish pronunciations (William Grant at Aberdeen and Bessie Robson at Edinburgh), and Raymond Weeks, an American. But Jones makes clear that the person to whom he feels most indebted is Walter Ripman (who at the outset of the war had felt prompted to delete two letters from his too Teutonic-sounding name in deference to British anti-German feeling of the time).

Ripman's contacts with Jones had grown closer over the years in part through their work together for the Simplified Spelling Society. Jones held him in high regard and Ripman was obviously a significant influence on him at this point in his career. In 1905, Ripman had been appointed a Staff Inspector of Schools for London University. This powerful position, together with his work as an examiner for modern languages and his editorship of *Modern Language Teaching* (the organ of the Modern Language Association), enabled Ripman to be a major proponent of the use of phonetics in schools.

He comes over as a dynamic figure, of whom Jones (1947b: 2) was later to say: "Ripman had a colossal store of energy. For many years he never worked less than fourteen hours a day, and he took only very brief holidays." Ripman's tireless industry and his linguistic interests—phonetics, language teaching, simplified spelling—show him to have had many things in common with Jones, even though in other respects the men were quite dissimilar. Unlike Jones, Ripman had enjoyed a brilliant career as a university student, working on his own for a London BA, which he gained at the age of eighteen, and then taking no fewer than three triposes at Cambridge—Classical, Modern and Oriental Languages. Yet he did not devote himself to writing and then forge an academic career for himself as did Jones. Once he had completed numerous short textbooks, including two on English phonetics (Rippmann 1906, 1908), he subsequently concentrated to a large extent on editorial work. Nevertheless, much of his writing, even if limited in scope, is interesting for its time, and his last important publication, *Good speech* (1922), is notable for its use of numerical pitch level intonation marking. Apart from editing *Modern Language Teaching*, Ripman also produced the *Pioneer* journal for the S.S.S, and was responsible for the official version of their reformed orthography (Rippmann—Archer 1910); see Section 4.10. He was the editor of a collection of language teaching texts for the London publishers, Dent's, called "Dent's Modern Language Series". Most of these volumes were textbooks on French and German but Ripman had introduced a strong phonetic bias and eventually produced a separate phonetics section—which included an adaptation (Rippmann 1903) of Viëtor's (1897) *Kleine Phonetik*.

It was within this series that the *EPD* was to find a home. In his "Editor's Preface" (*EPD*[1]: v), Ripman pays a tribute to Jones's work, and it is notable that he chooses to emphasise the importance of the book as an archive of contemporary spoken English:

> It is a great satisfaction to me that I am privileged to include in my Modern Language Series an English Pronouncing Dictionary by Mr. Daniel Jones, whose reputation as a phonetician extends far beyond the limits of this country. It is a work of permanent value as the record, by a competent and careful observer, of a certain type of English speech at the beginning of the twentieth century.

When Jones was working on the *Phonetic dictionary*, Ripman gave very considerable assistance—acknowledged fully by Jones in the introduction to that book (pp. ix–x). With the *EPD*, Jones makes clear (p. xii) that Ripman assisted him at every stage:

> My chief debt is to Mr. Walter Ripman…whose help dates from the time when the work was in contemplation. The plan of the work was settled very largely in consultation with him; later on he revised the whole of the manuscript with great care, and supplied me with much information that I lacked and with innumerable suggestions for improvements.

Ripman also "rendered invaluable assistance by collaborating in the uncongenial task of hunting for words inadvertently omitted from the manuscript". In addition, Ripman indulged Jones's perfectionist tendencies by assisting in a thorough revision of all the material—"those who have had experience of dictionary work will know what that means" is Jones's weary comment—so enabling the author to declare (p. xi):

> ...it is too much to hope that errors have been entirely avoided, though every effort has been made to render the information accurate, and the whole of the proofs have been revised three times by me and once by Mr. Ripman.

Jones's acknowledgement is much more than the formal thanks of a writer to his editor. Ripman had clearly not only taken a genuine interest in the book but even done much of the donkey-work involved.

7.2. The *English pronouncing dictionary*

Unlike his first pronouncing dictionary, the *EPD* was a success from the outset and a reprint was needed within two years. In 1924, an enlarged version was published, and 1926 saw a third revised edition. From then on Jones brought out numerous further editions (the most important revision being the *EPD*[11] in 1956) and only handed over the task of editing to A.C. Gimson in the 1960s, by which time Daniel Jones was over eighty (Wells 1985: 3).[1]

The *EPD*[1], as it appeared in 1917, contained four hundred and nineteen pages of text plus a further thirty pages of introductory matter. The dictionary gave the pronunciation of almost fifty thousand words including eleven and a half thousand proper names. The total would have been even larger had Jones included the inflected forms of words and alternative spellings (*EPD*[1]: xxvi). Later editions of the *EPD* increased the number of entries, and the current fifteenth edition has around eighty thousand —with a considerable rise in the number of proper names recorded (*EPD*[14]: viii).[2]

The introductory portion of the *EPD*[1] was divided into two parts headed "Introduction" and "Explanations". The former includes a discussion of the pronunciation model "Public School Pronunciation", or PSP, as Jones termed it. This is defined—in similar terms to those used in the *Pronunciation of English*[1] (p. 1)—as the speech of "the families of Southern English persons whose men-folk have been educated at the great public boarding-schools" (p. viii). However, Jones concedes that such pronunciation is also used by ex-public school pupils not hailing from the South of England, and also widens the definition to include "persons of education in the South of England who have not been educated at these schools" (*EPD*[1]: viii). Jones retained much the same view of the British English pronunciation standard all his life; but, significantly, he later dropped the label "Public School Pronunciation". In a subsequent edition (*EPD*[3] [1926]) he was responsible for reviving and popularising the phrase "Received Pronunciation". This term had originally been used by Ellis (1869–89: 23) in his *Early English pronunciation* (see Section A.3 for a discussion of Ellis' work) at a time when "received" was in general use as a synonym of "socially accepted".

In the *EPD*[3], Jones also coined the abbreviation "RP", which has remained the only widely recognised term by which linguists refer to this type of speech—despite other more recent suggestions.[3] He was undoubtedly influenced here by Wyld's (1914: 235–236) use of the phrase "Received Standard" to refer to the same kind of pronunciation; Jones was not particularly happy with the term, saying that it was only "for want of a better" (*EPD*[3]: viii). For discussion, see Windsor Lewis (n.d.).

Jones goes on to explain the utility of the dictionary to various types of users—necessary information in 1917, when a modern pronunciation dictionary was still a novelty. He discusses transcription (see below) and then two sections follow where Jones, characteristically, defends himself, in advance, against attack by potential critics: "Apparent Inconsistencies" (p. x) and "Errors and Omissions" (p. xi). The former section is an interesting statement of Jones's approach to linguistic observation and his lack of compromise in dealing with empirical research. Jones complains that critics ("particularly foreign critics") fall into the "inconsistency fallacy", and says that in the "best type of book on phonetics, viz. that which aims at recording accurately, there may be errors of observation, but there can be no such thing as inconsistency" (p. x). He goes on (pp. x–xi):

The word "inconsistency" presupposes the existence of rules or principles. The accurate record is not concerned with rules; it furnishes materials from which rules may be deduced, and if the material is complete or nearly so, the principles deduced therefrom will probably be correct.

Jones claims that since "the materials hitherto available have not been complete, readers must not be surprised if they find that certain principles which they had previously seen formulated, or had tacitly assumed, will require modification". To those critics who may question apparent inconsistency of pronunciation as compared with orthography, Jones comes out with this straightforward justification: "Because it appears to me that *the forms given are those which are as a matter of fact heard in PSP*" (p. xi, Jones's emphasis).

The second part of the introductory material, "Explanations", covers matters directly relating to the use of the dictionary, including the explanation of the transcription system and conventions for representing alternatives and variant forms of stressing. Certain sections here make fairly severe demands on the phonetic awareness of the user; no fewer than twenty symbols (all IPA) are introduced for the representation of foreign loanwords. The descriptions of the variant values of the realisations of English vowels—described in terms of the Cardinal Vowels (see Section 7.3)—would also have required a good knowledge of articulatory phonetics.

It is interesting that here Jones mentions in passing many phenomena which are often thought of as having been first observed at a much later date. For instance, he notes the fronting of [ʌ] and of the first element of [ou]; the reduction of the second element of [aiə] and [auə] and the potential levelling of the contrast of these with [ɑː]; the susceptibility of the alveolar consonants to assimilation and elision; and the tendency for [ə] to replace [i] in medial unstressed syllables, e.g. abili*t*y, eas*i*ly (pp. xix, xxii).

Whilst Jones's first attempt at a pronouncing dictionary, the *Phonetic dictionary*, might strike the modern reader as quaint, or even bizarre, the first edition of the *EPD* is, in contrast, remarkable only for its familiarity. At first sight, a page of the *EPD*[1] looks similar both in arrangement and overall approach to the [1988] reprinted four-teenth edition (see Figures 7.1 and 7.2). The resemblance to the [1967] *EPD*[13], which was the last to retain Jones's original form of transcription more or less intact, is even more striking. It is only in 1997 with the arrival of the long-awaited fifteenth edition of the *EPD* that there has been a drastic change in its layout and overall arrangement.

But, in this context, the odd appearance of the *Phonetic dictionary* is misleading. If one examines these books more closely, it becomes obvious that much of the format and content of the *EPD* was established already in the *Phonetic dictionary*. In fact, if allowance is made for the awkwardness of the reverse arrangement of the entries, and all the problems this brought about, then the *Phonetic dictionary* could almost be regarded as a pilot version of the *EPD*. As has been shown, the *Phonetic dictionary* was based on Michaelis and Passy's (1897) *Dictionnaire phonétique*. This was the first pronouncing dictionary to use an IPA model of transcription and to be founded firmly on articulatory phonetic principles. Although the *Dictionnaire* has joint author-ship, the main inspiration was undoubtedly Passy's since it carried out the ideas that he was expressing elsewhere at that time in his publications, and especially in the pages of *Le Maître phonétique*. So once again, we observe yet another influence of Passy on Jones's work in that the *EPD* has its origins in the *Phonetic dictionary*, but the latter is itself modelled on Michaelis and Passy (1897).

It is noteworthy that certain crucial matters determined first of all by Michaelis and Passy and then repeated in the *Phonetic dictionary* were carried over into the *EPD*. For instance, the *Phonetic dictionary* had no definitions and concentrated entirely on pronunciation. Previous English pronunciation dictionaries had included brief defini-tions; their absence from the *EPD* saved considerable space, which could be devoted to a fuller treatment of pronunciation. The *Phonetic dictionary* also established that there was some demand for a dictionary which made no compromise in terms of pho-netic transcription or a general organisation based on an articulatory phonetic frame-work. Up till then, pronunciation dictionaries produced in Britain had employed some modification of conventional orthography (though the great *Oxford English dictionary* had employed Ellis's somewhat impenetrable "Palaeotype"; see A.3).

Apart from the actual transcription system (see below), the *Phonetic dictionary* had also established other related matters, for instance, the use of an asterisk to indicate potential liaison in words ending in **r**. The stress marking system was also taken over from the earlier work. A three-term system was employed: ' was used to indicate primary stress, , secondary stress, whilst other syllables were treated as unstressed and left unmarked. In the *EPD*[4] ([1937]), following IPA recommendations, the original angled stress marks were replaced by verticals.

The transcription system of the *EPD*[1] follows exactly that used in the *Phonetic dic-*

ENGLISH
PRONOUNCING DICTIONARY

A

A (*the letter*), -'s ei, -z
a (*indef. article*) ei (*strong form*), ə
Aaron, -s 'ɛərən, -z   [(*weak form*)
Aaronic, -ally ɛə'rɔnik, -əli
aback ə'bæk
aba |cus, -ci 'æbə|kəs, -sai
abaft ə'bɑːft
abandon (*s.*) ˌæbɑ̃ːn'dɔ̃ːŋ [-bɔ̃ːn-,-bɑːn-,
 -bɔːn-, æ'bɑ̃ːnd-, æ'bɔ̃ːnd-, æ'bɑːnd-,
 æ'bɔːnd-, ə'b-] (abɑ̃ːdɔ̃)
abandon (*v.*), -s, -ing, -ed/ly, -ment
 ə'bændən, -z, -iŋ, -d/li, -mənt
abas|e, -es, -ing, -ed, -ement ə'beis,
 -iz, -iŋ, -t, -mənt
abash, -es, -ing, -ed ə'bæʃ, -iz, -iŋ, -t
abatab|le, -ly ə'beitəb|l, -li
abat|e, -es, -ing, -ed, -ement/s ə'beit,
 -s, -iŋ, -id, -mənt/s
abatis (*sing.*) ə'bæti, (*plur.*) -z
Abba 'æbə
abbac|y, -ies 'æbəs|i, -iz
Abbas 'æbəs [-bæs]
abbé, -s 'æbei (abe), -z
abbess, -es 'æbis [-bes], -iz
Abbeville 'æbviːl (abvil)
abbey (A.), -s 'æbi, -z
abbot (A.), -s 'æbət, -s
Abbotsford 'æbətsfəd
abbotship, -s 'æbət-ʃip, -s
Abbott 'æbət
abbreviat|e, -es, -ing, -ed, -or/s ə'briː-
 vieit [-vjeit], -s, -iŋ, -id, -ə*/z
abbreviation, -s əˌbriːvi'eiʃn, -z
abbreviatory ə'briːviətəri   [-vieit-,
abc, -'s 'eiˈbiːˈsiː ['eibiːˈsiː], -z   [-vjət-]
Abdera æb'diərə
abdicant, -s 'æbdikənt, -s   [-iŋ, -id
abdicat|e, -es, -ing, -ed 'æbdikeit, -s,
abdication, -s ˌæbdi'keiʃn, -z
Abdiel 'æbdiəl [-djəl]
abdomen, -s æb'doumen [-min, -mən,
 'æbdəmen], -z
abdomin|al, -ally æb'dɔmin|l [əb-], -əli
abduct, -s, -ing, -ed, -or/s æb'dʌkt
 [əb-], -s, -iŋ, -id, -ə*/z

abduction, -s æb'dʌkʃən [əb-], -z
Abdy 'æbdi
abeam ə'biːm
A Becket ə'bekit
abed ə'bed
Abednego ˌæbed'niːgou [ə'bednigou]
Abel (*English name*) 'eibəl, (*foreign*
 name) 'aibəl
Abélard 'æbelɑːd [-bil-] (abelaːr)
Abelmeholah 'eibəlmi'houlə [-mə'h-]
Aberavon ˌæbə'reivən [-bɔːˈr-, -ˈræv-]
Aberbrothock ˌæbəbrə'θɔk [-bɔːb-,
 -bro'θ-]
Abercorn 'æbəkɔːn [-bɔːk-]
Abercrombie 'æbəkrʌmbi [-bɔːk-,
 -krɔm-]
Aberdare ˌæbə'dɛə* [-bɔːˈd-]
Aberdeen, -shire ˌæbə'diːn [-bɔːˈd-],
 -ʃiə* [-ʃə*]
aberdevine, -s ˌæbədə'vain [-bɔːd-], -z
Aberdonian, -s ˌæbə'dounjən [-bɔːˈd-,
 -niən], -z
Aberdour ˌæbə'dauə* [-bɔːˈd-]
Abergavenny (*family name*) ˌæbə'geni
 [-bɔːˈg-], (*place*) ˌæbəgə'veni
Abernethy ˌæbə'niːθi [-bɔːˈn-]
aberran|ce, -cy, -t æ'berən|s, -si, -t
aberrat|e, -es, -ing, -ed 'æbəreit [-ber-],
 -s, -iŋ, -id
aberration, -s ˌæbə'reiʃn [-be'r-], -z
Abersychan ˌæbə'sikən [-bɔːˈs-]
Abert 'eibɔːt
Aberystwyth ˌæbə'ristwiθ
abet, -s, -ting, -ted, -tor/s ə'bet, -s, -iŋ,
abeyance ə'beiəns   [-id, -ə*/z
abhor, -s, -ring, -red, -rer/s əb'hɔː*, -z,
 -riŋ, -d, -rə*/z
abhorren|ce, -t əb'hɔrən|s, -t
Abiathar ə'baiəθə*
Abia (*biblical name*) ə'baiə, (*city*) 'æbiə
Abib 'eibib
abid|e, -es, -ing, abode ə'baid, -z, -iŋ,
abies 'æbiiːz ['eib-]   [ə'boud
abigail (A.), -s 'æbigeil, -z
Abijah ə'baidʒə

A

A

A (*the letter*), -'s eɪ, -z
a (*indefinite article*) eɪ (*strong form*), ə
  (*weak form*)
aardvark, -s 'ɑːdvɑːk, -s
Aaron, -s 'eərən, -z
aback ə'bæk
Abaco (*in Bahamas*) 'æbəkəʊ
abacus, -es 'æbəkəs, -ɪz
Abadan (*in Iran*) ˌæbə'dɑːn [-'dæn]
Abaddon ə'bædən
abaft ə'bɑːft
abandon (*s.*) ə'bændən (abūdō)
abandon (*v.*), -s, -ing, -ed/ly, -ment
  ə'bændən, -z, -ɪŋ, -d/lɪ, -mənt
abas|e, -es, -ing, -ed, -ement ə'beɪs,
  -ɪz, -ɪŋ, -t, -mənt
abash, -es, -ing, -ed ə'bæʃ, -ɪz, -ɪŋ, -t
abatab|le, -ly ə'beɪtəb|l, -lɪ
abat|e, -es, -ing, -ed, -ement/s ə'beɪt,
  -s, -ɪŋ, -ɪd, -mənt/s
abatis (*sing.*) 'æbətɪs [-tiː]
abatis (*plur.*) 'æbətiːz
abatises (*plur.*) 'æbətɪsɪz
abattis, -es ə'bætɪs, -ɪz
abattoir, -s 'æbətwɑː* [-twɔː*], -z
Abba 'æbə
abbac|y, -ies 'æbəs|ɪ, -ɪz
Abbas 'æbəs [-bæs]
abbé, -s 'æbeɪ (abe), -z
abbess, -es 'æbes [-bɪs], -ɪz
Abbeville (*in France*) 'æbviːl (abvil),
  (*in U.S.A.*) 'æbvɪl
abbey (A.), -s 'æbɪ, -z
abbot (A.), 'æbət, -s
Abbotsford 'æbətsfəd
abbotship, -s 'æbət-ʃɪp, -s
Abbott 'æbət
abbreviat|e, -es, -ing, -ed, -or/s ə'briː-
  vɪeɪt [vjeɪt], -s, -ɪŋ, -ɪd, -ə*/z
abbreviation, -s əˌbriːvɪ'eɪʃn, -z
abbreviatory ə'briːvjətərɪ   [-vɪət-,
  -vɪeɪt-]
abc, -'s ˌeɪbiː'siː:, -z
Abdera æb'dɪərə
abdicant, -s 'æbdɪkənt, -s
abdicat|e, -es, -ing, -ed 'æbdɪkeɪt, -s,
  -ɪŋ, -ɪd
abdication, -s ˌæbdɪ'keɪʃn, -z
Abdiel 'æbdɪəl [-djəl]

abdomen, -s 'æbdəmen [æb'dəʊmen,
  -mɪn, -mən], -z
abdomin|al, -ally æb'dɒmɪn|l [əb-], -əlɪ
abduct, -s, -ing, -ed, -or/s əb'dʌkt [æb-],
  -s, -ɪŋ, -ɪd, -ə*/z
abduction, -s æb'dʌkʃn [əb-], -z
Abdulla, -s æb'dʌlə [əb-], -z
Abdy 'æbdɪ
Abe eɪb
abeam ə'biːm
abecedarian ˌeɪbiːsiː'deərɪən
A Becket ə'bekɪt
abed ə'bed
Abednego ˌæbed'niːgəʊ [ə'bednɪgəʊ]
Abel (*biblical name, English name*)
  'eɪbəl, (*foreign name*) 'ɑːbəl, ɑː'bel
Abelard 'æbəlɑːd ['æbɪ-]
Abell 'eɪbəl
Abelmeholah ˌeɪbəlmɪ'həʊlə [-mə'h-]
Aberavon ˌæbə'rævən [-bə:'r-] (*Welsh*
  aber'avon)
Aberbrothock ˌæbə'brɒθək [-bɑː'b-]
  Note.—This place-name has to be
  pronounced ˌæbəbrə'θɒk [-bɑːb-] *in*
  Southey's 'Inchcape Rock'.
Abercorn 'æbəkɔːn
Abercrombie [-by] 'æbəkrʌmbɪ[-krɒm-,
  ˌ-'--]
Aberdare ˌæbə'deə* (*Welsh* aber'daːr)
Aberdeen, -shire ˌæbə'diːn, -ʃə* [-ˌʃɪə*]
aberdevine, -s ˌæbədə'vaɪn, -z
Aberdonian, -s ˌæbə'dəʊnjən [-nɪən],
  -z
Aberdour ˌæbə'daʊə*
Aberdovey ˌæbə'dʌvɪ (*Welsh* aber'dəvi)
Abergavenny (*family name*) ˌæbə'genɪ,
  (*place*) ˌæbəgə'venɪ (*Welsh* aber-
  ga'veni)
Abergele ˌæbə'gelɪ (*Welsh* aber'gele)
Abernethy ˌæbə'neθɪ [*in the S. also*
  -'niːθɪ]
aberran|ce, -cy, -t æ'berən|s [ə'b-], -sɪ,
  -t
aberrat|e, -es, -ing, -ed 'æbəreɪt [-ber-],
  -s, -ɪŋ, -ɪd
aberration, -s ˌæbə'reɪʃn [-be'r-], -z
Abersychan ˌæbə'sɪkən (*Welsh* aber-
  'səxan)
Abert 'eɪbɜːt

1

Figure 7.2. The first page of the fourteenth edition of the *English Pronouncing Dictionary* (1977).

tionary; it was the same transcription that Jones had originally used in his first articles published in *Le Maître phonétique* in 1906 and had employed frequently from then on. As Windsor Lewis (1974: 1) has pointed out, "it had already existed in one or other of several very slightly different forms" dating from 1888 when the IPA agreed on the principles for their new international alphabet. One attractive feature of the transcription was that it was relatively economical in terms of symbols, and included few exotic character shapes. It might therefore be thought less off-putting to non-specialist readers. There was a further advantage to its use in a dictionary; it was economical in terms of space—always an important consideration in lexicography. The use of the length mark to indicate the vowel contrasts [i iː ɔ ɔː u uː] allowed brackets to be employed to indicate alternatives such as [ru(ː)'meinjə].

In the introduction to the *EPD* (p. xi), Jones states:

> The phonetic alphabet used is that of the *International Phonetic Association*. I have adopted this system of transcription not merely because it is more widely used than any other, but because I consider it the best at present in existence.
>
> The simplified ("broad") form of transcription usually employed for practical purposes has been adopted; it is the form which uses the minimum number of symbols consistent with avoiding ambiguity.

This was not, of course, true. It was perfectly possible to avoid ambiguity (presumably Jones means in the sense of showing phonemic contrasts, although he does not use the term phoneme in the *EPD*[1]) and still employ several fewer symbols. Thus æ and ɑː could have been replaced with a and aː. In addition, o , to represent the "reduced" form of [ou] in words like *molest*, was not only allophonic, but probably old-fashioned even in 1917. The "variant" diphthongs [oi ɔə eə oə ui] in *going, four, they're, Samoa, fluid* were superfluous to the needs of a dictionary of this sort (p. xxv).

Jones could also have managed without the symbols ɛ and ɔ. The end result would have then been similar to the transcription Jones used in his writings in the forties and fifties, notably in the *Phoneme*, and which he referred to as the "Simplified IPA Transcription" (see, for instance, *EPD*[11] [1956]: xviii).

But Jones did not want to confine himself to representing solely phonemic distinctions in his dictionary. This is shown by his indication of the lengthening of [æ] in certain items, such as *bad, bag*, etc, and by his use of [ç] to indicate the variant of [hj] in *here, human*. Furthermore, he wished to draw attention to the reduction of the diphthongs [ou ei] in certain sequences. Consequently, the *EPD*[1] was intended to display a certain degree of allophonic variation in its transcription forms in addition to phonemic contrasts, and this would have been Jones's defence for these extra symbols. Later on, he came to acknowledge the inconsistencies (*EPD*[10]: xii):

> Broad transcription of the chief kind of English here recorded would need only eight vowel letters, namely **i e a ɑ o u ʌ** and **ə**. ... It should, however, be pointed out that in transcribing a simple type of English with fewer variants than are here

given (i.e. a type such as is suitable for foreign learners to acquire) the symbols ɛ and ɔ can be dispensed with; the letters e and o can be written in their place. The reduction of **eiə** to a diphthong and **ou** to a monophthong are refinements with which the foreign learner need not concern himself, and they can in any case be implied in transcriptions of a simple and consistent form of the language. æ is also not essential for the purposes of this dictionary; **a** could be used in its place without giving rise to ambiguity, and I hope to make this substitution some day when circumstances permit.

It is perhaps an indication of the success and influence of the *EPD* over the years that this transcription system has become firmly associated with Daniel Jones, and with the dictionary itself; until recently, it was indeed often referred to informally as the "EPD transcription". Jones eventually used this term himself (*Outline*[8]: 340–341) though he did not claim credit for inventing the system, or indeed for popularising it. Nevertheless, it was undoubtedly as a result of Jones's employment of this transcription in his early writing in *Le Maître phonétique*, and then more particularly in the *EPD* and the *Outline*[1], that it became so widely accepted, especially in the field of teaching English as a foreign language.

But paradoxically, Jones was never enthusiastic about the system which was thought of as his creation, and almost as his property. Shortly after the *EPD* appeared, he began to favour a more elaborate scheme of transcription (*EPD*[10]: xii, xii n.):

> Some critics have urged me to adopt a still narrower form of transcription, introducing at least four further letters (to differentiate the qualities of short and long **i, u, ɔ** and **ə**). At one time I was attracted by this type of transcription. I used it in writing for *Le Maître phonétique* from 1923 to 1928, and I experimented with it in practical teaching for some years. I also encouraged others to use it, with the result that several books appeared in which it was employed, including Armstrong's *English Phonetic Reader* and Ward's *Phonetics of English*.

In his later career, both for practical and theoretical reasons, Jones had become convinced "that a strictly broad type, being the simplest, is the best for most purposes" even though he qualified this by saying that "a certain limited degree of narrowing is useful in comparative work" (*EPD*[10]: xii). However, as far as the *EPD* was concerned, he was probably the prisoner of his own success, and he could never bring himself to risk the sales of the book by going over to a simpler transcription. When changes did come to the *EPD*, they were not of the sort he would have favoured.

Jones's colleague, A.C. Gimson, took over the revision of the *EPD* for the twelfth edition ([1963]) and the thirteenth ([1967]). At first, the transcription changes were few, as Gimson himself (1977: 156) states:

> The thirteenth edition of 1967, which I edited and which appeared only a few days before Daniel Jones's death, introduced some changes (notably, on the phonetic

level, the more realistic notation /əu/ for the older /ou/ in a word such as *go*), but the base remained hardly different from that laid down by Jones in 1917.

In his final revision, *EPD*¹⁴ [1977], Gimson replaced the original transcription with a qualitative/quantitative transcription for vowel contrasts, this being a modified form of the transcription used in his *Introduction to the pronunciation of English* (Gimson 1962). Ironically, this system, often called "Gimson transcription", is very similar indeed to that which Jones invented and employed during the 1920s for his teaching and research and later rejected in favour of a simplified broad form. Gimson commented when interviewed about the matter:

> He [Jones] could never make up his mind about the transcription he wanted to use. He disliked the one which he had, which remained in the *Outline*, and still is in it, and in the Dictionary until I changed it. Not that he would have changed it to what I changed it to. He would have thought that was worse. He would have gone over to something like MacCarthy's system of doubling letters.⁴

For further discussion, see Section 14.9.

The *EPD* established itself rapidly as the only really reliable guide to the pronunciation of British English—a position which it retained effectively unchallenged for over seventy years until the appearance of Wells's (1990) comprehensive and authoritative *Longman pronunciation dictionary*. The *EPD* was admittedly helped in achieving this pre-eminence by the weakness of the representation of pronunciation in the otherwise redoubtable *Oxford English dictionary* (see Section 5.3). Despite the alterations by Gimson, and later by Ramsaran, and most recently by Roach and Hartman, even in its latest version it remains in essence the work of Daniel Jones. This dictionary is also today the most valid and living of all his publications; it is simultaneously a classic work and a current authority which is indispensable for anyone dealing with the pronunciation of English in Britain. The *EPD* is tangible proof of Jones continuing after his death to be a major influence in the world of phonetics.

7.3. The Cardinal Vowel model of vowel description

The *EPD* has one further significance: it is the publication where Jones chose for the first time to provide a full, explicitly labelled, diagram of the Cardinal Vowels. Consequently, this work has a crucial place in the development of Jones's model of vowel description.⁵

The search for some way of representing accurately the quality of vowel sounds did not, of course, begin with Daniel Jones. This is a problem which has vexed phoneticians throughout the history of linguistic science. It was, however, only in the nineteenth century that the work of Ellis, Bell and Sweet began to make real progress towards producing a viable model of vowel description within an articulatory phonetic framework, whilst in Germany the work of Helmholtz provided a firm foundation for an acoustic approach to the same problem (Ladefoged 1967: 62–75).

The actual term "cardinal vowel" seems first to have been employed by Henry Sweet (1877: 11–12) in the *Handbook of phonetics*, where he states:

> The movements of the tongue may be distinguished generally as horizontal and vertical—backwards and forwards, upwards and downwards.... From among the infinite degrees of height three are selected, "high", "mid", and "low".... These distinctions apply equally to back, mixed, and front vowels, so we have altogether nine cardinal vowel positions:

high-back	high-mixed	high-front
mid-back	mid-mixed	mid-front
low-back	low-mixed	low-front

Sweet's ideas find their origin in *Visible speech* (Bell 1867: 16), which refers to nine vowels which provide "the means of noting, as by lines of latitude and longitude, the precise *place* of any vowel in the mouth". Bell says that these nine vowels are derived from combining "cardinal degrees" of opening between tongue and palate and "cardinal degrees" of tongue position (front to back). But, as Abercrombie (1967: 151) has pointed out, Bell's ideas in turn lean on the writings of Ellis (1844: 52), who appears to have been the first phonetician to develop the concept of a set of reference vowels from which others might be described.

The pre-twentieth century history of the development of systems of vowel description has been set out by several scholars, including Viëtor (1884: 41–65), Raudnitzky (1911), Ladefoged (1967: 62–75), Butcher (1976, 1982), Nearey (1977: 38–56) and Wood (1982). Of these, Viëtor provides a particularly useful survey of nineteenth-century work, which includes schematic arrangements and diagrams by numerous early phoneticians from Hellwag (1781) onwards. Raudnitzky (1911), *Die Bell-Sweetsche Schule*, is an early piece of historiography on the contribution of Bell and Sweet to vowel theory;[6] interestingly, much of its content is in fact devoted to the work of Ellis.

The impact of Ellis, Bell and Sweet on Jones's work has been already noted (see also Section A.3) and is beyond dispute. Yet there is a more direct influence on Jones as far as vowel description is concerned than any of those mentioned above, and that is Paul Passy, who was a devout Christian and a dedicated socialist (see Section 2.3). Passy considered phonetics to be in great measure a useful tool in language teaching—a means by which human beings could establish better understanding with each other—and, consequently, found much in the directness and empiricism of Bell, Ellis and Sweet to attract him. He approved of their interest in linguistic observation and description, agreeing particularly with Sweet in his emphasis on the importance of phonetics as a component of second language acquisition. The essentially practical linguistic approach of the British school had more appeal for Passy than the more

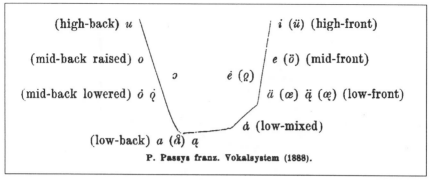

Figure 7.3. Passy's (1888: 18) vowel diagram (as printed in Viëtor [1898⁴]: 58).

objective, experimentally-based researches of his fellow countryman, Rousselot, or the "misplaced striving for physiological accuracy" which coloured the work of certain German phoneticians in the late nineteenth century (Kohler 1981: 172). Passy did not, however, fall into the trap of overloading his descriptions with excess detail and transcriptional complication, in the way that Bell, Ellis and Sweet were at times prone to do. Inspired by his Christian socialist beliefs, he sought to combine scientific accuracy with a clear exposition which could be understood even by people of humble background and limited education (Jones 1941c: 31–32). In the introduction to the (Savory—Jones 1907c [1913²]: iii) translation of his *Sons du français* (1906⁶), Passy expressly states that he had written "a popular work on scientific lines".

Passy had been working on his version of tongue-arch vowel theory, especially as applied to French, from the early 1880s onwards. In his study of the French sound system, Passy (1888: 18) represented the vowels as in Figure 7.3. Ladefoged (1967: 69) has written:

> Passy (1888)...devised the diagram of the French vowels shown [in Figure 7.3.]. This is probably the first example of this kind of vowel diagram; and certainly, in devising it, Passy was moving further towards the representation of auditory qualities rather than articulatory positions.

This may be true of Passy's position at this stage, but Ladefoged (1967: 70) oversimplifies when he goes on to say that "the next step was taken by Jones (1917) who instituted the well-known cardinal vowel system". It is possible to trace a number of intermediary stages which make clear that Passy himself in his later work preferred an articulatory model of vowel description—and it was this scheme which was later taken over and extended by Jones.

Passy produced a modification of the diagram for his *Changements phonétiques* (1891), where a table of the "voyelles normales" appears which bears remarkable similarities to Jones's subsequent work. Not only are the four degrees of aperture

	Vélaires	Palatales
Fermées	u	i
Mi-fermées	o	e
Mi-ouvertes	ɔ	ɛ
Ouvertes	α	a

Figure 7.4. Passy's (1891: 80) table of "voyelles normales".

shown, but even the symbols are exactly those which were later to be chosen by Jones for the Cardinal Vowels (Figure 7.4).

Passy (1891: 79) states explicitly that he is employing articulatory criteria in arriving at his system:

> D'abord, on peut ouvrir ou fermer plus ou moins le passage de l'air dans la bouche, en rapprochant plus ou moins la langue du palais. De ce chef nous distinguerons quatre degrés: *voyelles fermées, mi-fermées, mi-ouvertes* et *ouvertes*.
>
> Puis, on peut retirer la langue dans la bouche, en relever le fond vers le palais mou et le voile du palais; ou au contraire, l'avancer, en lever le milieu vers le palais dur; ce qui nous donne deux classes de voyelles, que nous appelons *voyelles vélaires* et *voyelles palatales*.

Passy then goes on to apply these descriptive criteria to vowels of a more complex nature:

> Des voyelles formées dans une position intermédiaire pourront porter le nom de *voyelles mixtes*.
>
> En troisième lieu il faut considérer la position des lèvres, qui peuvent être *neutres, arrondies* et projetées en avant, ou *écartées* en fente. En général, la position des lèvres correspond à celle de la langue: elles sont fortement *arrondies* pour les *voyelles vélaires fermées*, à peu près *neutres* pour les *voyelles ouvertes*, *écartées* en fente pour les *voyelles palatales fermées*.

This descriptive model must be seen as a direct precursor of that later to be used by Jones for the Cardinal Vowels. Furthermore, Passy regarded his system of vowel description and classification as one capable of universal application and certainly not merely confined to French. This is evident from the final table (reproduced as Figure 7.5), where he adds the "voyelles mixtes" to the "vélaires" and "palatales" in both "normale" and "anormale" forms.

Vélaires.	*Mixtes.*			*Palatales.*	
u	ɯ	ü	ï	y	i
o	ʌ	ö	ë	ø	e
ɔ	ʌ	ä		œ	ɛ
	ɑ		a		

Figure 7.5. The elaborated form of Passy's
(1891: 83) vowel table.

Passy goes on to include further modifications, specifying "voyelles relâchées"
[i.e. "lax"], "voyelles nasalisées" and, finally, "voyelles intermédiaires" and introducing a set of diacritics to show intermediate tongue and lip positions (pp. 84–85).
Passy claims (p. 85):

...nous pourrons représenter sans difficulté, non pas sans doute toutes les nuances
possibles de voyelles, mais du moins toutes celles que notre oreille est en état de
reconnaître.

Passy also makes clear that he is well aware of the controversy over acoustic as
opposed to articulatory ("organique") classification, and that any good system of
vowel description must combine aspects of both methods (p. 75):

Pourquoi, d'ailleurs, supposer a priori que les deux systèmes s'excluent récipro-
quement? Il semble, au contraire, qu'une bonne classification acoustique doit être
parallèle à une bonne classification organique; car des effets semblables doivent
être produits par des causes semblables.

Thus, in a sense, Passy anticipates the types of criticism of articulatorily-based vowel
classification systems that were later to be directed against Jones's Cardinal Vowels,
e.g. Russell (1928: passim) and Butcher (1982), to name only two.

Very similar tongue-arch models, applied mainly to the vowel system of French, can
be found in *Les Sons du français* (Passy 1887 [1899⁵]: 77–90). Certain sections clearly
foreshadow Cardinal Vowel theory, being couched in terms very similar to the language that Jones was repeatedly to employ in successive works dealing with this topic.
Two examples from the Savory—Jones (1907c) translation (p. 61 and p. 62, respectively) may suffice:

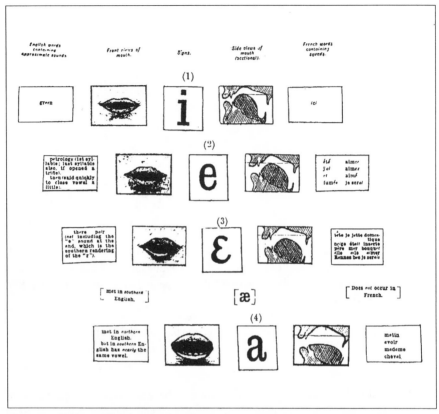

Figure 7.6. Dumville's (1904: interleaf 36–37) table of "Fundamental Vowels" (cont. on p. 179). The same work includes tongue positions for the French front rounded vowels [y ø œ] (p. 55).

It is hardly possible to lower the tongue beyond the **ɑ** position; we may therefore say that **ɑ** is the back vowel formed with the mouth as wide open as possible.

[i]. This vowel is formed by raising the front of the tongue towards the hard palate as high as possible without producing audible friction, and by spreading the lips so as to leave a long narrow opening.

Compare the above with two extracts from two later works by Jones, where he is describing his Cardinal Vowels (*Pronunciation of Russian*: 29, *Pronunciation of English*[3]: 19, respectively):

Cardinal vowel No. 5 is a sound in which the back of the tongue is lowered as far as possible and retracted as far as is possible with the sound being a vowel.

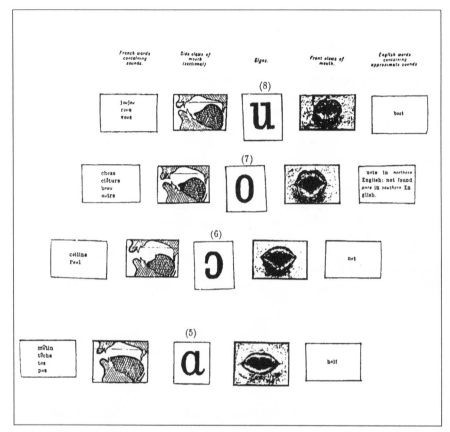

Figure 7.6. (*cont.*)

No. 1 is the vowel which combines the greatest degree of "closeness" with the greatest degree of "frontness". It is not possible to make a "fronter" vowel; and if the tongue were raised any higher, normal breath pressure would give rise to a frictional noise and the sound uttered would not be a vowel at all.

Passy's widespread influence on the phonetic world of this era—nowadays very much forgotten—may also be discerned in other publications of the time. One notable example can be seen in Figure 7.6, taken from the writings of another of Passy's pupils, Benjamin Dumville (1904: facing 37), illustrating what he terms the "fundamental vowels" of French. It is consequently possible to sympathise with Hockett, who has been criticised by Ladefoged (1967: 77) for claiming that the reason some of the French vowel phonemes are similar to the Cardinal Vowels is that "the French vowel system played a major part in the development of the original 'cardinal vowel' theory". This would indeed appear to be so, even if Jones himself later conveniently ignored it, stating that they had been "chosen on a scientific basis and are independent of the vowels of any language" (Jones 1956a: 6).

Passy, therefore, can be seen as the direct inspiration of Jones's version of tongue-arch theory, even if the final steps in the construction of a new model of vowel description which could be applied (in principle) universally to languages were taken by Jones himself. It was also Jones's works which spread and popularised the theory —at least in the English-speaking world. Nevertheless, it is largely thanks to Passy that phoneticians had access to what may still be considered to be an efficient, if very simplified, model, which manages to avoid the mass of minor auditory distinctions and over-detailed symbolisational complications with which Sweet (1908: 39) eventually encumbered his vowel description (see, for example, Figure 3.8 in Section 3.4).

Jones (1941c) freely acknowledged his debt to Passy, regarding him as the most important force shaping his views on phonetics. Indeed, Jones appears to have been influenced by the early British school to a large degree *indirectly*, i.e. via the filter of Passy's publications and teaching. Apart from taking over much of Passy's theoretical approach, Jones also admits that he was attracted to Passy's clear and direct methods of presentation. In his obituary of Passy, Jones (1941c: 33) puts on record his admiration for "Passy's clarity of style in writing and in speaking...a model of conciseness and lucidity".

Jones's own first sustained attempt at vowel description came with his *Pronunciation of English*[1] (Jones 1909b), see Section 3.4. Although the basis of his description is clearly derived from Passy, he has already moved closer to the eventual Cardinal Vowel model. For instance, unlike Passy, Jones emphasises the significance of the "highest point of the tongue" (pp. 10–11).

> In the production of most vowels the tongue is convex to the palate. Vowels may therefore be conveniently arranged *according to the position of the highest point of the tongue*.... Vowels are thus classed as front, mixed, and back, according to the horizontal position of the highest point of the tongue. They may also be classified according to the vertical position of the highest point of the tongue. Those in which the tongue is as high as possible consistently with not producing perceptible friction are called *closed vowels*. Those in which the tongue is as low as possible are called *open vowels*. We distinguish two intermediate positions, *half-closed* and *half-open*, in which the tongue is lowered from the closed position to about one-third, and two-thirds, of the total distance from the closed position to the open position.

Jones appends the diagrams which are reproduced in Figure 3.7, showing a vowel quadrilateral (and an accompanying sagittal cross-section to illustrate the tongue postures for the vowels [i ɑ u]). In terms of the development of Jones's model, this quadrilateral is a distinct advance on Passy's vowel tables. (It is manifestly a forerunner of the diagram (see Figure 7.7) which forms the frontispiece of the first edition (1917a) of the *English pronouncing dictionary*.) The accompanying sagittal cross-section serves to indicate the highest points of the tongue. A further interesting feature

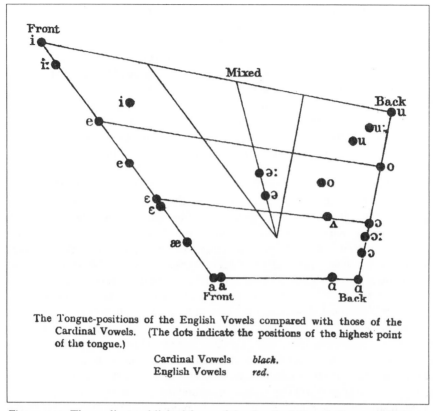

The Tongue-positions of the English Vowels compared with those of the Cardinal Vowels. (The dots indicate the positions of the highest point of the tongue.)

Cardinal Vowels *black.*
English Vowels *red.*

Figure 7.7. The earliest published form of the Cardinal Vowel diagram (*EPD¹*, p. ii). Note that, in the original, English vowels are printed in red.

is the introduction of a grid with lines linking the various tongue heights and marking off clearly the "front-mixed-back" divisions.

Apart from a set of vowel charts (Rausch—Jones 1911v) which break no new ground, the next stage in the development of the theory is to be found in the *Sechuana reader* (pp. xxiii–xxv), which contains Jones's very first (albeit brief) published mention of the term "cardinal vowels".[7] However, although he and his co-author indeed describe the vowel system of Tswana through the medium of the Cardinal Vowels, no explanation of the actual Cardinal Vowel model is offered. Jones and Plaatje, bafflingly, leave their readers in the dark as to the theory behind it, merely stating in a footnote (as quoted previously on p. 152) that a "mastery of the cardinal vowels is... indispensable".

As has been stated, the *EPD¹* (p. ii) contained an important innovation, namely the very first published version of a full explicitly labelled Cardinal Vowel diagram. This was used as a frontispiece illustration, and reference to it was made throughout the description of realisational variation of the English vowels. The Cardinal Vowel symbols are shown in black, with the English vowels depicted in red. The diagram is notable for the retention of the term "mixed", instead of the later label "central", and for the slightly sloping back line. The theoretical explanation in the text is minimal, though the dots on the diagram are said to be "representative of the positions taken up by the highest point of the tongue in forming the vowels" (p. xx). One later familiar feature was absent: arrows were not yet used to indicate changing tongue shape in the diphthongs. Once more, as in the *Sechuana reader* (see Section 6.8), the Cardinal Vowels are purported to be "described in books on phonetics" (p. xx). But again, as in the *Sechuana reader*, no indication is given of what books these might be.

The *EPD*, although therefore by no means having the place in the sequence of events allocated to it by Ladefoged (see above), did nevertheless include this crucial first version of the diagram, albeit with sparse elucidation. Jones's next significant publication, the (1918a) *Outline*, whilst containing a detailed section on vowel description, does not even mention the Cardinal Vowels, and is obviously written from a theoretical standpoint which *precedes* that of the *Sechuana reader*. This is not surprising, since although the *Outline* did not appear until just after the Armistice, it was in fact complete and largely set up in type before 1914 (see Section 8.2).

By 1917, therefore, Jones had gone much of the way towards the development of his theory of Cardinal Vowels. His inclusion of a diagram in the *EPD* was one indication of his confidence in the model. In 1917, he also took the more significant step of producing a recording of the eight Cardinal Vowels. This gramophone disc—now extremely rare—was in fact the first of three audio versions of the Cardinal Vowels that Jones was to make during his life. Furthermore, this first recording (1917) appeared with no proper backing explanatory literature to accompany it.[8] He made another on similar lines in 1943,[9] and in 1956 he produced a more elaborate recording in which the primary vowels are spoken on contrasting pitches and the secondary Cardinal Vowels (see Sections 7.6 and 13.12) are recorded for the first time.[10] It is this last version which is used as the standard today.

From the references to the Cardinal Vowels in Jones's publications from 1916 onwards, and from the remarks of Noël-Armfield (see Section 7.6), it seems not unreasonable to conclude that from this date on—possibly earlier—Jones was using Cardinal Vowel theory as a routine part of his teaching and research. Consequently, it is puzzling that such an important contribution to descriptive phonetics should have been left so long without its originator attempting a full exposition in published form, rather than letting the information dribble out by way of a reference here and a diagram there. The most probable explanation for this curious reluctance of Daniel Jones to inform the world about his Cardinal Vowel theory is outlined in Section 7.6.

7.4. The work of the Department in the later war years

The remaining years of the war saw the Phonetics Department continue to expand, running counter to the trend of contraction of activities that the remainder of University College was experiencing as a result of the war.

Cyrille Jones's name appears in the staff list in the 1916–17 session.[11] In the same year, she collaborated with Palmer in the writing of a short textbook *Colloquial French* (Palmer—Motte 1916). Jones's wife apparently helped, not only in the teaching of French phonetics, but also in lending a hand with secretarial work. Since at this time the Joneses were living at 40 Ridgmount Gardens—hardly any distance from University College—she could presumably combine her work for the Department with taking care of their flat.

Jones's 1916–17 Report describes the furious activity in the, as yet, still tiny Department.[12] Harold Palmer was given charge of what Jones calls the "Spoken English department". Palmer had evidently submitted a report on the work of the section, in which he had put in a plea for more publicity for the Spoken English courses.[13] Apart from his spoken English assignment, Palmer also gave lectures on language teaching methodology (termed in the Report "linguistic pedagogy").

Jones speaks optimistically of the way in which the Phonetics Department was coping with wartime difficulties:

> The number of students attending the lectures and classes in the Phonetics Department has been well maintained in spite of war conditions…. The number of foreign students taking English Phonetics has been about the same as last year.

However, he complains about staff shortages hampering research. Nevertheless, work had proceeded on several languages. A woman student, M. Björndal, had "done some excellent work on the analysis of Norwegian pronunciation by experimental and other methods". H.S. Perera—with whom Jones later collaborated on the *Colloquial Sinhalese reader* (Perera—Jones 1919a)—was stated to be investigating the pronunciation of colloquial Sinhalese. Jones mentions his own work on the grammar of Tswana, later to appear as *The tones of Sechuana nouns*. (Jones 1928a; see Section 10.6); Palmer ran "a research class for investigating the mathematical theory of grammar…[which] led to interesting results". Unfortunately, no further detail is given of the contents of this course.

It was in this year—summer vacation 1916, and Easter vacation 1917—that Jones organised his vacation courses in French for the first time. They were extremely successful, and Jones was authorised by the College Committee to continue with the "interesting experiment".[14] The experiment turned into an established annual event and these vacation courses marked the beginning of a long University College tradition of Summer Schools in French and later (even more successfully) in English as a foreign language. These courses provided an introduction to phonetics and applied linguistics to thousands who would otherwise not have encountered either subject. Jones also went on with his classes for missionaries, and it is in connection with an August vacation course for the preparation of missionaries that the name of Lilias Armstrong is mentioned for the first time (see Section 7.8).[15]

The extra responsibilities that Jones was assuming began to take its toll on his health and Cyrille also apparently suffered from illness at this time. Jones turned these misfortunes to advantage:

...the development of the work of his Department has been such that it is necessary for him to give practically his whole time and energy to it; that in order to do this Mr. Jones has relinquished paid work outside the College; that in order to increase his income last session he organised one vacation course in the Easter Vacation and two vacation courses in the Summer Vacation; that these courses, while of undoubted value educationally, had made it impossible for Mr. Jones to obtain the rest which he requires during the vacations, and that in consequence his health is impaired.[16]

As a result of this intervention, apparently made on his behalf by the Provost, Gregory Foster, Jones found his salary raised by £100; he would now receive £400 a year. The College Committee added the rider that he should from now on be involved in no more than one vacation course a year.[17]

The Provost then reported on Cyrille:

...that Mrs Daniel Jones, who is assisting her husband, has been receiving £30 a year for the practical classes which she is conducting; that the work of those practical classes has largely increased; that at the present moment Mrs Jones's health has broken down and that it is necessary to appoint a substitute for her until Easter...that the salary of Mrs Daniel Jones likewise appears to need consideration in view of the increase of the work entailed.[18]

Senate was recommended to double Cyrille's salary from £30 to £60 per year.[19]

The Joneses would appear—despite the blackness of the case presented by Gregory Foster—to be prospering in terms of the conditions of the time. The staff salaries for the part-timers at UCL were pitifully low. In the 1916–17 Session, Palmer was paid £45, Stephen Jones £40 and Noël-Armfield had to be content with £10 a year. All had other employment, although it was noted that Palmer found it difficult to manage.[20] Jones was always concerned over money matters, both for himself and others, and it seems to have rankled with him that in London University the work—at least for junior lecturers—was so badly paid. He later wrote (1926e: 398):

Unfortunately, the salaries of most of the teachers in the University of London were, and still are, preposterously small, and in many cases are less than the salaries paid for corresponding work in provincial Universities. The reason for this is not far to seek. In the provincial cities the local rich men have a local patriotism which induces them to give large sums to their Universities for the bettering of their teaching. In London there is no local patriotism, and it is very difficult to raise money for educational purposes.

26. Jones at about age 35

27. With baby Olivier

28. The entrance to Jones's home in Ridgmount Gardens (taken in 1997)

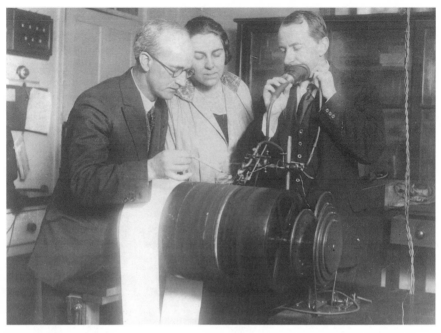

29. Stephen Jones, Eileen MacCleod and Arthur Lloyd James in the Phonetics Laboratory

30. The facade of University College (taken in 1997)

The striking lack of interest shown by the government in the activities of the Phonetics Department is still evident at this time. Palmer is noted as having given courses in spoken French "for members of His Majesty's Military and Naval Forces" but no mention is given of any other language work in connection with the war.[21] The absence of such activities may later have cost Jones dearly when he was rooting around for support in government circles for his Phonetics Institute (see Section 9.3). However, both Jones and Palmer gave evidence to the Government Committee on the Teaching of Modern Languages, and the UCL Phonetics Department was visited by a representative of the same Committee.[22]

Jones mentions that he has started to give courses in General Phonetics at the School of Oriental Studies—which he and others from his Department continued to do for several years. Jones also says that he delivered "one Friday evening discourse and two afternoon lectures at the Royal Institution".[23] These lectures, later published as "The use of experimental phonetics and its utility to the linguist" (Jones 1919c), were significant in that they gave a welcome stamp of recognition to phonetics in Britain, and to the work of Jones and his Department. The invitation to address the Royal Society was something which would allow Jones a new respectability among his scientific colleagues in other departments and also provide him with more leverage when it came to asking for finance—which was very much on his mind at this time.

7.5. The Philological Society Lecture and the term "phoneme"

In 1917, Jones was also invited to give an address to the Philological Society on his research on Tswana (henceforth, the Philological Society Lecture).[24] This can be regarded as an important event in the history of Western European linguistics in that it was in this lecture that the word "phoneme" was employed by Jones outside the Department for the first time, and as such was the first ever recorded use of the term in a public context in the English-speaking world. However, an important section on the general concept of the phoneme in Jones's lecture was deleted from the published version, as Jones recalled, forty years later, in his pamphlet *History and meaning of the term "phoneme"* (henceforth *HMTP*). He stated (*HMTP*: 9–10):

> I should like to put on record the fact that the first occasion on which I employed the term outside the class-room or in private conversation with my colleagues was in a lecture on *The Sechuana Language* given to the Philological Society on 4th May 1917. Unfortunately, the part of that lecture dealing with the general conception of the phoneme was omitted from the *Proceedings*. It may therefore be of some historical interest, as exemplifying the state of our knowledge of the phoneme at that date, if I reproduce here the words I used on that occasion. They are copied from the lectures (sic) notes which I happen to have kept.

The validity of Jones's claim is proved by examination of the notes, part of which are reproduced in Figure 7.8. Yet, just why Jones allowed such an important portion of his address to be left out of the published transactions (Jones 1917c) must remain a question for speculation. It would seem that he later felt unhappy with his definitions

2

When people are seeking information regarding the sound-system of a language, the first thing they generally ask is 'How many sounds are there?' (I am assuming we are not dealing with one of those benighted individuals who starts by asking how many letters there are in the alphabet of that language.) Well, it is rather difficult to say precisely what the number of speech-sounds is in Sechuana. It depends how you define a speech-sound. We know that in every language certain so-called speech-sounds vary in value to some extent according to their surroundings. (Eng. k in key, call, n in bun, month, e in get, well). But in counting up the Eng. sounds, we do not generally count these varieties as separate sounds; we ignore such incidental variations, because they are not what is called 'significant'; the meaning of words does not in any way depend on them.

In order to make matters clear, it will be found convenient in dealing with any language to make a distinction between 'speech-sounds' proper and what may be termed 'phonemes' or the significant phonetic elements of speech. Speech-sounds should be considered as definite sounds incapable of variation; a phoneme might be defined as a normal sound of the language together with all its incidental variants. These two k's in English [in key & call] are different speech-sounds but the same phoneme.

In such languages as English and French, phonemes do not as a rule differ greatly from speech-sounds. Incidental variations are on the whole slight. But in other languages cases may be found where very different speech-sounds count as

Figure 7.8. Extract from Jones's notes for the Philological Society Lecture showing references to the phoneme.

and so chose to edit the published text by omitting the whole portion concerned— rather than by rewriting the text of what was the record of a public lecture, which he might have considered dishonest. It is significant that a marginal note in the Philological Society Lecture manuscript states "terminology unsatisfactory", and that when he published the section in *HMTP* he provided both an exact record of what he said (taken from his notes) plus footnotes to accommodate his later reassessment of his views.

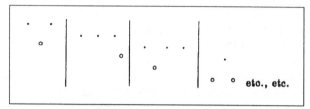

Figure 7.9. Illustration from the published version of the Philological Society Lecture showing downstep (1917c: 104).

Nevertheless, the diffident phrasing that Jones uses in *HMTP* could be thought to imply that the published Philological Society Lecture does not contain any reference to the phoneme at all. But this is far from the truth. Even in its truncated form, the report of this lecture provides numerous examples of the first recorded uses of the term "phoneme" in English, and, furthermore, a brief definition: "The Sechuana language appears to contain twenty-eight phonemes, i.e. twenty-eight sounds or small families of sounds which are capable of distinguishing one word from another" (p. 99). The text of the Philological Society Lecture is the first explicitly phonemic analysis of a language in English, discussing Tswana vowels and consonants in terms of the phoneme concept, mentioning variation dependent on phonetic context, and using the actual word "phoneme" in total on seven occasions.

Jones did not at this point make the mental leap of dealing with Tswana tone on a phonemic basis, though he does state clearly that tone has a meaning differentiation function: "If the pitch of a syllable is changed, the word may be converted into another totally different word" (p. 103). He did, however, move towards a tonemic approach in that the number of tone categories was reduced from the total of eight mentioned in the *Sechuana reader* to five—high level, mid-level, low-level, high-falling and low-falling.[25] Another notable advance on the *Sechuana reader* is the refinement of the description of downstep (pp. 103–104).

At certain points in sentences (these points being apparently determined mainly, if not entirely, by grammatical considerations) the whole of the tones have to be made slightly lower than what they were in the previous part of the sentence, and during all the rest of the sentence the tones do not return to their original level.

They continue to the end of the sentence at the lower pitch, unless there comes another of these special grammatical points, in which case the tones all go down another stage. The amount of descent may be taken for practical purposes to be one semitone, but it is really often less than this.

Jones illustrates his text with a clear diagram (see Figure 7.9), showing generalised pitch features, instead of the music notation which he used in the *Sechuana reader*. He employs black dots to represent high-level tones and circles for mid-levels (cf. the diagram in the Missionaries' Lecture, Figure 6.6). He also alters the symbol used to indicate downstep from ˇ to ' , later to be changed again to ¦, see Section 14.13. Cf. Jones's statements in the Missionaries' Lecture, Section 6.9.

For both tone analysis and the phoneme concept, the Philological Society Lecture can be viewed as a crystallisation of Jones's theories and also the most important stage in his views being made available to a circle wider than immediate colleagues and pupils. The lecture is therefore of paramount importance in the history of the development and dissemination of Jones's ideas.

7.6. Jones's experimental interests and the Cardinal Vowels

From about 1912 onwards, when the first phonetics laboratory in Britain was set up in University College, Jones began to take greater interest in experimental phonetics. In February 1917, he was invited to address the Royal Institution, delivering a paper entitled "Experimental phonetics and its utility to the linguist", which appeared later that year in *Nature* (Jones 1917e).

Jones must have felt that this article (one of two papers published by him in a single year in that prestigious journal) signalled acceptance by the wider scientific world both for phonetics as a discipline and for himself as a scholar. The paper, dealing with various methods of determining tongue postures, particularly (though not exclusively) in vowel sounds, came out at a point when Jones appears to have been very concerned with the problems of substantiating his theory of Cardinal Vowels by means of objective instrumental data. Crucially, it contains the first publication of X-ray photographs showing the tongue postures for cardinal vowels 1, 5 and 8 [i ɑ u]; these had been produced for Jones by H. Trevelyan George, a radiologist at St Bartholomew's Hospital, London, using a technique pioneered by Meyer (1910) whereby a thin lead chain was placed over the surface of the dorsum of the tongue so as to provide a material opaque to X-rays thus enhancing the resulting image.[26] The photographs (together with one for Cardinal Vowel 4) were subsequently to become familiar to linguists when they were reproduced over thirty years later in the third edition of the *Pronunciation of English* (Jones [1950³]).[27]

The appearance of these X-ray photographs and the references here to Cardinal Vowels is one more element in the strangely evasive attitude of Jones to his own

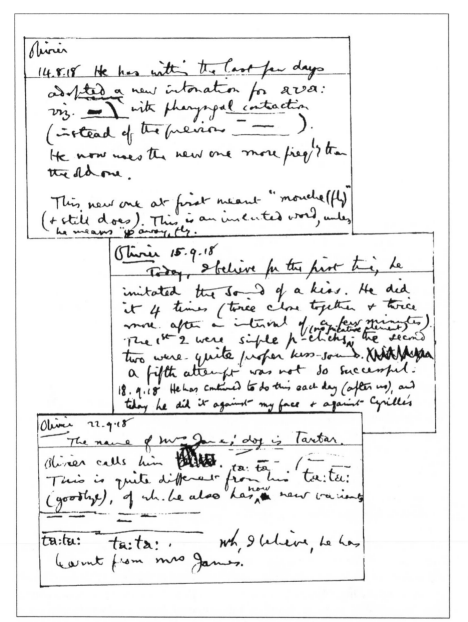

Figure 7.10. A small selection from Daniel Jones's card index recording the speech development of his son.

theory at this time. Jones had mentioned the Cardinal Vowels as being described in "books on phonetics" without specifying any further information (see Section 7.3). This phrase is used again in the *Colloquial Sinhalese reader* (Perera—Jones 1919a: 6), which deals with the topic of the Cardinal Vowels briskly, although it does include a diagram of the vowels of Sinhalese shown alongside the Cardinal Vowels, and makes reference to the availability of the HMV recordings (see Section 9.4). The second edition of the *Outline* (Jones [1922]: ii) provides even less in the way of detail, dismissing the topic in 13 lines. In fact, from Jones's initial reference to the Cardinal Vowels in 1916, no fewer than seven years were to elapse until the appearance of the first full treatment of Cardinal Vowel theory from Jones's own pen in the *Pronunciation of Russian* (Trofimov—Jones 1923a: 27–41).

Yet already, by 1919, Jones's colleague, Noël-Armfield, had introduced a new appendix discussing the Cardinal Vowels for the second edition of his *General phonetics* (Noël-Armfield 1916 [1919²]: 117–120). This made available the first reasonably thorough description of the principles behind the theory—far more comprehensive than anything written up till then by Jones himself. Noël-Armfield presented a total of twelve Cardinal Vowels, including a brief mention of front rounded [y ø œ] and back unrounded [ɯ]. These four vowels were later fully described for the first time in the *Pronunciation of Russian* (p. 40). They were not as yet called secondary Cardinal Vowels—a term which seems not to have been used in publications before the third edition of the *Outline* ([1932³]: 35–36).

Noël-Armfield also indicated that other developments were taking place, stating (p. 119): "It would be an advantage if three cardinal mixed vowels [i.e. central] were established, but up to the present this has unfortunately not been done." It is clear, therefore, that the Cardinal Vowels were by this time a familiar feature of phonetics as practised in Jones's Department. Jones and his colleagues also appear to have been engaged on work on other aspects of research concerning his theory, as Noël-Armfield ([1919²]: 120) makes clear:

> Investigations are being made to determine the absolute musical pitch of the cardinal vowels, and when this is done the result will be invaluable in fixing for all time their acoustic value.

Why then did Jones not provide a fuller treatment of his theory at an earlier date? One indication that something was amiss is Noël-Armfield's reference to "careful and prolonged research (unfortunately *not completed* at the time of writing) by Mr. Daniel Jones and his colleagues at University College, London" (p. 118, our emphasis). Another clue is to be found in the nature of Jones's acknowledgement to Trevelyan George, "who has displayed much ingenuity and patience in getting over the numerous difficulties which present themselves in the course of work of this nature" (Jones 1917e: 97). All in all, it leads to the suspicion that Jones was concealing the fact that he was encountering unforeseen problems, obtaining negative results from the efforts of Trevelyan George to produce suitably clinching data in the form of corroborative X-ray photographs. Perhaps the best evidence we have of the reasons behind Jones's reluctance to communicate his theory is to be found hidden away in Noël-Armfield's short footnote (p. 119 n.) referring to the radiographic material.

> Exact pictures of the tongue positions of the cardinal vowels have not yet been secured; therefore, for the present we have to be content with the equi-distant divisions.

By 1923, Jones was forced to reconcile himself to the facts, and though maintaining that the extreme vowels [i a ɑ u] were based on X-ray tracings, he had to admit the uncertainty surrounding the rest (*Pronunciation of Russian*: 29–30):

> The tongue-positions of Cardinal vowels 1, 4, 5, and 8…are drawn from X-ray photographs. The drawings of the remainder are only approximate.

He eventually rationalised his position and retreated to a weaker version of the theory, stating that the vowels had been chosen to be "acoustically equidistant"—by which one must infer that he meant *auditorily* equidistant (cf. Ladefoged 1967: 72; Ashby 1989: 86–87). Nevertheless, he continued to claim that the tongue was raised and lowered "through approximately equal intervals" (*Outline*[8] [1956]: 32).

Jones would have found the job of proving the existence of such "approximately equal intervals" an impossible task, and undoubtedly the X-ray photographs of the intermediate Cardinal Vowels contradicted his ideas rather than supported them. Evidence from the 1920s onwards has shown no confirmation of the neat steps from one tongue posture to the next that Jones's hypothesis demanded. Research, carried out in his own Department by his close colleague, Stephen Jones, was also to prove, in the main, negative. Citing Stephen Jones's (1929) work, Ladefoged (1967: 71) has commented:

> …it is readily apparent that the tongue positions are very different from the theoretical description of the articulations of the cardinal vowels. In addition, it seems that the tongue does not move in a series of even approximately equidistant steps when a set of cardinal vowels is pronounced.

The results of most contemporary and later work on the tongue-arch theory in general, and Jones's model in particular, has revealed it to be resting on very shaky foundations (see, for instance, Russell 1928: 133–156; Wood 1982).

The whole affair was doubtless a blow to Jones's professional pride since clearly he had not wished to put forward his theory without the radiological evidence to back it. This, of course, he was never to obtain. So he delayed, eventually allowing his ideas to emerge almost grudgingly to the world in what at first sight appears to be an inexplicably inconsequential, piecemeal manner. But, given the crucial lacunae in his data, the procrastination in the presentation of the Cardinal Vowel theory is perhaps not so difficult to explain.

7.7. Work of the Department 1917–18

Jones's Departmental Report for 1917–18 is terse, saying at the outset that work "has been carried on on the same lines as in the Session 1916–17, but has been enlarged by the addition of some courses of General Phonetics conducted by the Department at the School of Oriental Studies".[28] Yet, it is clear from what he says in recalling this period almost thirty years later, that this was a crucial era for the Department and also for Jones himself.

Amongst Jones's lecture notes are those prepared for a talk with the title "The London School of Phonetics", given first at Zürich University in 1946, and referred to henceforth as the Zürich Lecture.[29] The Zürich Lecture was later developed into the 1948 article, also entitled "The London School of Phonetics" (Jones 1948f, referred to henceforth as the *London School*). But certain passages—one marked by Jones in the margin as "too personal"—were omitted from the published version; it is, in fact, these deleted sections which reveal most clearly how Jones considered the development of his career.

Jones (Zürich Lecture, pp. 1–2) looks back on the early days in the Department and his problems finding the right staff and giving them suitable training.[30] He complains about being forced to manage with part-timers. He then goes on (p. 2):

> Gradually things improved. Improvement seemed to go parallel with the gradual realisation that came to me of the place of phonetics in educ[atio]n & its function as a factor in human relations. You know how a young man starts his career. He thinks "I've got hold of a good thing here; I think I'll make a nice pos[itio]n for myself". This gives place in due course if he is wise to "I've got a good thing here; I can make myself v[ery] useful to other people by means of it". I gradually came to see that Phonetics had *an important bearing on human relations*—that when people of different nations *pronounce* each other's l[an]g[uag]es really well (even if vocab[ulary] & grammar not perfect), it has an astonishing effect of *bringing them together*; it *puts people on terms of equality,* & a *good understanding betw[een] them immediately springs up.* (Jones's emphasis)

These words may indicate that it was about this time that Jones's interests deepened in the religions and philosophies of the East, particularly as these were interpreted by the Theosophical Society (see Sections 10.8 and 13.2).

In the Zürich Lecture, Jones (pp. 2–3) goes on to connect his new philosophy of life and work with the rapid growth of his Department in this period:

> So I came to see that phonetics was a sort of mission, & not merely a way of earn-

ing a living or making a nice pos[itio]n. You may think it a coincidence (I don't), but it is a fact that when I came fully to realise this (ab[ou]t 1917) & to treat the subject as a mission, the Dep[artmen]t began to enlarge itself in an extraordinary way. Instead of carrying on with difficulty with a few part time assistants to help with evening work, means quickly became forthcoming to enable me to have full time assistants—with the result that within a comparatively short time (1922) the Dep[artmen]t grew to the size that it now is...namely 9 full time assistants. The Coll[ege] also gave a house for the Dep[artmen]t (about 1920). Well, with a staff of 10 it is possible to get useful work done, & shortly after 1917 it became possible to get started on a large programme of work (teaching & research).

Jones later stated that he regarded this period as a turning point in the history of his Department (see below). Furthermore, he attributed this not so much to the coming of peace and the funds that were consequently released for investment in education, or to the interest in language teaching at the time, but more to his own state of mind, and his new work ethic. Marginal notes in the Zürich lecture provide further evidence. Jones has pencilled in at the side of the extract above: "cause & effect, action & reaction", and "things of the mind & spirit as well as in purely physical happening" (p. 3).

Though the Report for the year is brief, the College Calendar shows that Jones's Department continued to expand its work. Palmer, particularly, appeared to be making a contribution far beyond what might be expected from a part-timer on a minuscule salary. In addition to his "Spoken English for Foreign Students", he expanded his series of classes on "Methods of Foreign Language Teaching",[31] and also organised a German interpretership course held "at the request of the War Office" for twenty British army officers. "All the officers satisfied the test at the end of their course, most of them attaining a high standard."[32] The course was run in co-operation with the University College Professor of German, Priebsch, and it is odd that something similar was not tried earlier in the war—especially since Phonetics shared one member of staff (W. Perrett) with the German Department. It may be that Jones was not enthusiastic about becoming engaged in work connected with the war because of his pacifist sympathies; and it is notable that he (unlike J.R. Firth and his colleagues) also indicated no desire to be involved closely with the armed forces during the Second World War (see Section 12.1). Perhaps the only instance of Jones being involved with the military occurred after the Armistice had been signed. In the Christmas vacation of 1918 he is noted as having undertaken a fortnight's tour of Belgium lecturing to the troops.[33]

Palmer was also the most prolific contributor to the departmental publications, producing two books: *A first course of English phonetics* (Palmer 1917a) and his classic work *The scientific study and teaching of languages* (Palmer 1917b). Both of these were largely based on his lectures at University College; the former deriving from his phonetics classes and the latter from his work for his course on Spoken English and Methods of Foreign Language Teaching. It is also known that Palmer was busying himself in other aspects of the research of the Department. Jones (1950c: 6) says:

"The subject of intonation first attracted him [Palmer] in 1917"; and in his unpublished preparatory notes for the Philological Society Lecture (Section 7.5), Jones remarks (p. 10):

> The subject of Sechuana grammar has been investigated in a masterly fashion by my colleague Mr. Palmer. I supplied him with the phonetic materials, and he applied to them his unique knowledge of general grammar. The result is that he has collected grammatical information of the highest interest and importance.[34]

This would indicate that much of Jones's work on tone declension (Jones 1927f, 1928a) owes its inspiration to the insights which Palmer gave him into grammatical analysis at this time. Palmer's debt to Jones was his exposure to the best teaching of practical phonetics available anywhere in the world and the freedom and encouragement Jones gave him to develop his theories on language teaching. (See Howatt 1984: 230–244 for further comment on Palmer's work in this period.)

7.8. Lilias Armstrong and H.S. Perera

If the dominant personality in Jones's Department at this time was the forceful figure of Palmer, with his dynamic approach and inventive linguistic talents, a new member was added to the UCL staff, who would, in the long run, and in a quieter way, have an even more important influence on the development of phonetics in London University. Jones was soon to appoint his first full-time assistant, Lilias Armstrong.

Lilias Eveline Armstrong (1882–1937) was born in Salford in Lancashire. She took her BA at the University of Leeds and then moved to the South East of England. At the time when, in her mid-thirties, she first attended Jones's Department as a part-time student, she held the post of senior mistress at East Ham Central School in metropolitan Essex. She had been highly successful in her career as a teacher and was widely tipped for promotion to headmistress.[35] Even before Lilias Armstrong had her first experience of teaching phonetics on the 1917 summer vacation course for missionaries (see above), Jones had plans to offer her a full-time post. The London County Council had provisionally decided to demand more work from Jones and his staff, and to increase the payment made to the Phonetics Department to £400 a year. This splendid news came just before the summer vacation in 1917. Jones planned rises for all his colleagues, but most of the money (£180) was to be used for the salary of a full-time assistant, and Miss Armstrong was named to take up the post.[36] But by October, Jones was informed that the LCC had now had second thoughts and that the payments would not, after all, be made.[37]

This announcement must have been shattering for Armstrong, who was planning to give up a secure job on the strength of the original decision. In November, perhaps by way of compensation, she was put forward by Jones for a temporary lectureship. He had courses planned for the School of Oriental Studies, and Lilias Armstrong was down to take the practical classes.[38] In February 1918, she was finally approved for a temporary part-time lectureship,[39] which provided small comfort since the salary was a meagre £10 per annum. However, it was at least a footing enabling her to work within Jones's Department. She had to wait until the beginning of the next academic year before she obtained a full-time appointment; and Jones had his long anticipated first full-time member of staff. He noted in his Report for 1918–19:

> ...a marked improvement in the attainments of the students of the Phonetics Department this year as compared with former years. This is to be attributed to the excellent work done by Miss L.E. Armstrong who was appointed as a full time assistant at the beginning of the session.[40]

Jones's high opinion of Lilias Armstrong was never to alter in the twenty years she remained in the Department up to her death in 1937. At the outset, she obtained rapid promotion and became a Senior Lecturer by 1920 although she was then not appointed to a Readership until shortly before her death. Jones always regarded her as occupying a special place among his members of staff, and as we shall see, when he was ill in 1920, she was nominated by him to run the Phonetics Department in his absence (see Section 9.7). A great personal and professional bond existed between them and he is said to have been deeply affected by her relatively early death.[41] Her importance within the structure of the Department would be difficult to overestimate and she was to become the doyenne of the "devoted band of ladies" by whom Jones "was shielded from the world, and from all exhaustion and worry" throughout his later career (Abercrombie 1980: 2). See Section 10.13 for an overview of her publications.

Another appointment made by Jones during the 1917–18 Session was that of H.S. Perera, a student from Ceylon, who was working with Jones at this time on the phonetics of Sinhalese. Part of this research was later published in 1919 as the *Colloquial Sinhalese reader* (see Section 9.4). Apart from the work on his mother tongue, Perera was useful to the Department in another way, having been trained in psychology. Jones reports that Perera had "been making a special study of the psychology of speech, and his work is beginning to show useful practical results".[42] Characteristically, Jones shows himself to be really convinced of the usefulness of academic work only when it can be judged to have "practical" value. However, the project which Perera was undertaking, together with Palmer's pioneering approach to applied linguistics, could be considered sufficient to rebut the criticism sometimes made of the London School that no attention was ever paid to anything other than narrowly defined articulatory phonetics. In fact, the Department always contained a variety of research, and Jones made a point of encouraging all aspects of phonetic study.

Perera was appointed as an "honorary assistant"— this meaning presumably that there was no money to provide him with a salary. He remained in the Department for two years and afterwards became an important member of the Ceylon Schools' Inspectorate. After a lapse of nearly twenty years, Perera and Daniel Jones would co-operate once again in a publication on the romanisation of Sinhalese (Perera—Jones 1937k). See Section 9.4.

7.9. The birth of Jones's son

Whilst Jones was engaged on producing the most influential books of his career, and also preparing his Department for the post-war expansion he was expecting, there was also a significant happening in his personal life. In the early summer of 1916, Cyrille had discovered that she was pregnant. The news would have been welcomed by the couple, the more so since she had previously suffered a miscarriage.[43] The pregnancy continued without mishap, and on January 3, 1917, she gave birth to a healthy baby boy. They called the child Olivier Daniel.

Very unusually for this era, Cyrille appears to have carried on with her work at University College throughout her pregnancy and to have resumed work shortly after Olivier was born. However, as noted above, she did have a period of ill health in 1917, following which her salary was doubled at the personal intervention of Provost Foster. Jones managed to get the size of Cyrille's classes reduced to a maximum of six (instead of eight) students, and a note in the 1917–18 College Prospectus states explicitly that her classes (of "Pronunciation Exercises") would be conducted in French. Though the actual work could not have been arduous, she was scheduled to teach at awkward hours—two evenings a week and also on Saturday mornings. In the context of the time, for a woman to go on with a job whilst pregnant and then when caring for a young baby was quite remarkable and it says much for the force of Cyrille Jones's stamina and personality. Daniel Jones must also have been far ahead of his time in his view of the contribution that women could make to society. Not only did he have this attitude towards his wife, but later on he was to employ large numbers of female staff at a time when women were still something of a rarity in the academic world.

Olivier, who was later to be a strikingly handsome young man, was apparently "a very ugly baby and very small";[44] nevertheless, his father was quite devoted to him. A photograph shows Jones cradling the infant Olivier in his arms, and members of the family confirm that Jones had strong paternal feelings. His interest in his son's development is borne out furthermore by other evidence. During Olivier's early childhood, Jones kept a record of his language acquisition, using a card index for the purpose. Many index cards have survived (see Figure 7.10), and a selection of these can give an indication of Jones's fascination with child language at this time—an aspect of his linguistic interests which is not otherwise apparent from his published work:

1.7.18   The most noticeable thing about his speech is his inability to make vowels. He can hardly say any vowels except **a æ ə**. He occasionally makes a diphthong of the **ai** (prob[ably] rather **aɛ**) type.
Today I heard him sustain the top F# of the piano (in calling to Mrs Stafford).

He is beginning to put different syllables together, instead of merely repeating the same syllables. I haven't yet been able to catch any examples sufficiently accurately to note them; but I fancy he said something like n<u>æsæ</u> this morning (?Louisa).

Since he learnt to imitate ʀa he has been saying it to himself a good deal (with a variant gʀa. The ʀ is scrapy and rather forward.

7.7.18   When he makes words containing 2 cons[onants], those cons[onants] appear to be generally artic[ulated] at same place.

He is beginning to understand a great deal more. He undoubtedly <u>understands</u> who papa and māmā are, though he often doesn't use the words appropriately.

If we say apɔrt sa a māmā or a papa he generally does it right.

If he hears the postman put letters into the box & we say va ʃɛrʃe le lɛtr he will do it.[45]

Jones also discussed child language with colleagues, as is clear from the following:

20.7.18   I have always thought that Olivier's inability to make a back a̰, or in fact any back vowels, was due to the fact that the mouth was still too small to make the required low resonance.

But Ripman tells me that his little daughter (age 1) can make a back a̰ quite well and often causes amusement by repeating such syllables as pa̰-.[46]

He shows a particular interest in Olivier's command of pitch and intonation:

[N.d.]   Hums a little now. But his tunes are not recognisable.

He will hum to order (either to French [ʃɑ̃ːt] or English [sɪŋ]).

14.8.18   He has within the last few days adopted a new intonation for avaɪ viz. ⌒ with pharyngal contraction (instead of the previous ‾‗).

He now uses the new one more freq[uent]ly than the old one.

This new one at first meant "mouche (fly)" (& still does). This is an invented word, unless he means "go away, fly".

19.9.18   When he wants someone to do something (such as giving him something, opening a box or a packet) he says æ̰ pointing at it. He goes on saying æ̰ until we have done the thing he wants. He sometimes replaces æ̰ by m̰.

æ̰ means yes. His invention of this word enormously facilitates communicating with him.[47]

Several of the observations would indicate that Jones was interested at this time in the semantic use of pitch. It was, of course, at this point that he was investigating, together with Palmer, the tonal base of the grammar of Tswana (see Section 7.7).

21.7.18   He seems to attach meaning to certain intonations (apart from sounds).

22.9.18   The name of Mrs James's dog is Tartar. Olivier calls him taː taː. This

is quite different from his taː taː (goodbye), of wh[ich] he has now new variants

taː taː taː taː wh[ich], I believe, he has learnt from Mrs James.[48]

The index cards provide, additionally, interesting sidelights on the Jones's life in their Ridgmount Gardens flat—it is perhaps as near as Jones ever got to keeping any sort of diary. The apartments in which he lived were spacious and generally regarded as luxurious. They had been recently built in handsome Edwardian redbrick, and were situated not far from the area in which Jones himself had grown up. Though surrounded by busy streets, there were the squares and open spaces of Bloomsbury where little Olivier could be taken each day. All the occupants of the flats employed domestic staff and Olivier is noted as saying "la bɔn" (la bonne) (the servant in the opposite flat)".[49] There is a reference to feeding chickens, presumably on one of the Jones's visits out of town, perhaps to see one of Cyrille's three sisters, who all had married Englishmen and were now living within a relatively short distance of London. Such visits were frequent, according to Jones's niece, Mrs Meryl Phillips.[50]

The cards quoted below exemplify Jones's combination of paternal pride with a nice record of phonetic detail:

15.9.18   Today, I believe for the first time, he imitated the sound of a kiss. He did it 4 times (twice close together & twice more after an interval of a few minutes). The 1st 2 were simple p-clicks (no fricative element)—the second two were quite proper kiss-sounds. A fifth attempt was not so successful.

18.9.18 He has continued to do this each day (after us), and today he did it against my face & against Cyrille's.[51]

Jones must have later looked back on this period as one of the happiest times of his long life. He was financially prosperous, with a comfortable income supplemented by his earnings from vacation courses and (increasingly) by royalties from his publications. Furthermore, he had received a substantial inheritance from his father. In addition, Cyrille was earning a considerable sum each year. An indication of his lack of financial worries is that he was able to undertake paying the University of London Press a sum of £90 (not uncommon as an annual wage at the time) out of his own pocket to settle his liability for publication costs of the *Cantonese phonetic reader*. ULP allowed him 12½% royalties on future sales of the book. The transaction indicates also that there was a considerable author's contribution involved in the original publication deal in 1911.[52]

Together with secure finances, he had a happy marriage to an intelligent young wife—who, he might have hoped, could be groomed one day into making an academic career for herself teaching the pronunciation and phonetics of French. Though Cyrille's health had failed in 1917, she had made a good recovery, and was back teaching at University College the next session. His own health—after the problems reported in 1917—also seemed to be going through a relatively stable period. And, in addition, Jones was now the father of a baby son, in whom he took great delight as the youngster grew into a remarkably good-looking and intelligent little boy, able to talk equally fluently in French and English.

The Joneses were happily settled in their Bloomsbury accommodation. They found Ridgmount Gardens so much to their liking that they stayed there for ten years, not moving to their next house (in Golders Green) until 1924—two years after their daughter, Michelle, was born. Jones always loved London and it obviously suited him to be so close to University College. Bloomsbury was a prosperous and leafy part of town, which he had been familiar with since his childhood, and which was popular with artists, writers and intellectuals generally. At the same time, both he and Cyrille had relations living in the South East of England, so it was possible for Olivier to spend time away from them in the country, or at the seaside, since Cyrille's sister, Irène, lived at St Leonards-on-Sea on the Sussex coast. Soon, once peace came, there would be the prospect again of holidays in France—either at Cyrille's home in Bourg-la-Reine, or at Trégastel, to spend part of the summer on the coast of Brittany.

The war in Europe was still raging—Jones's index cards refer to a new sight in the London skies, when Olivier produces the neologism [hapaŋ] as his version of "aéroplane".[53] However, the Zeppelin raids were now a thing of the past, and by August 1918 it became apparent that German resistance would soon collapse. It was no longer unrealistic to make plans for the prosperity which it was assumed would be coming with peace. Daniel Jones was no exception to the general feeling of optimism. He had great plans for transforming his Department, and was already hard at work trying to ensure that this scheme would come to fruition.

7.10. The idea of an Institute of Phonetics

As early as 1914, there had been indications that Jones felt some dissatisfaction with the small size and limited resources of his Department at UCL. He considered that it was restricted in terms of finance, accommodation and staffing, especi: lly when compared to the richly endowed departments, such as Hamburg and Gr r ble, that had recently been established on the continent of Europe.

This came over clearly in Jones's reactions to his visit to Hamburg in April 1914 for the Congress of Experimental Sciences when he was so obviously impressed by what the German institute had in the way of resources and staff. There is no doubt that from this point on, Jones retained a hope that he might one day, when the war was over, enable phonetics in London to compete with its continental rivals on a more equal footing. The difficulties of coping with the situation brought about by the war, together with the amount of work he was putting into his publications, perhaps restrained Jones's ambitions in this area for some time. But by 1916, Jones was already thinking ahead and feeling the need to plan for the future; he presented a memorandum to the College Committee with an outline scheme for expanding the teaching of phonetics.[54] The memorandum itself has not been preserved and the only indication of its contents is contained in a brief note in the College Committee Report for 1917 stating that:

> The College Committee have received from Mr Jones an important scheme for the development of a Practical Research Institute in Phonetics on the lines of the Phonetics Institute at Hamburg.[55]

The reference to the Hamburg Institute is a significant confirmation of the deep impression made on Jones and his UCL colleagues by their visit in 1914; it was without doubt a prime influence on his expansion plans throughout this period. Given the strength of anti-German feeling at this time, it is perhaps surprising that Daniel Jones chose even to mention the fact that he was modelling his proposed Institute on one in Germany.

The "important scheme" is the first inkling we have of the grandiose plans for a London Phonetics Institute that were to play such a crucial part in Jones's life over the next few years. However, at this point the hoped-for expansion was still modest: "The possibility of giving effect to this scheme depends upon the provision of special funds, amounting to about £850 a year."[56] It was also noted that the Institute could play a role in helping the training of deaf children.

Nothing seems to have come directly of the idea, but it appears to have sown the seed for the far more ambitious project that Jones was shortly to devise.

7.11. The coming of peace

The First World War eventually ended with the signing of the Armistice on November 11, 1918. It is generally agreed by commentators (for example, A.J.P. Taylor 1966: 86–99) that the four years of war had produced greater changes in the life of Britain than anything hitherto. The soldiers returning to England after the war—who must be counted as fortunate young men, since it has been reliably estimated that there were as many as ten million European deaths in the conflict and many millions more seriously wounded (A.J.P. Taylor 1966: 53)—would have noticed the radically altered appearance of the towns. Motor cars had ceased to be a curiosity and were now a commonplace. The streets of London still smelt—but increasingly of petrol fumes rather than horse dung.

Different social attitudes had also come about with the war. Women had been forced to take over many of the jobs formerly done only by men and this meant that some reappraisal of the role of women had taken place. More female students would shortly be enrolling at University College London, and Cyrille Jones would soon no longer be considered so unusual in wishing to carry on her career after marriage—and even after child-bearing. The work of Jones's colleague, Marie Stopes, who worked in the Biology Department of UCL for several years in propagating birth control and pioneering woman's liberation would also be a significant factor. The changing idea of women's place in society and their needs in education would have special significance for the UCL Phonetics Department, which had always had a large number of women students and was shortly to appoint numerous female lecturers.

The war had—ironically—done something towards breaking down the traditional isolationism of Britain with respect to the Continent of Europe. Before 1914, few British ever left their own country; hardly anyone took holidays abroad—not even the upper classes. There was no reason, or opportunity, for most English people to travel overseas and certainly no need to learn foreign languages. By 1918, however, a vast number of young men had lived for months, even years, in France, Belgium, Germany or elsewhere, and if they had endured the horror of the war, they had also had the benefit of meeting people from other countries with different languages and cultures. This could only be of benefit to the UCL Department of Phonetics, which was dependent on foreign language teaching and learning for its *raison d'être*.

Fighting a war had further increased Britain's awareness of her role as an imperial power; the British Empire had provided valuable resources of food and raw materials on which the nation had been completely dependent for survival. In addition, portions of the Empire had been theatres of war, and soldiers from the colonies and dominions had served in the fighting forces. The spirit of nationalism fostered by the war, and encouraged by the government, had laid great emphasis on Britain's imperial glories. Inevitably, with this concentration on the countries of the Empire, it became impossible to ignore the languages spoken by their peoples. This aspect was bound to be beneficial to the only academic centre in Britain which was in any true sense equipped to deal with research into what were at the time termed "little known languages" —namely Jones's Phonetics Department.[57]

University College would rapidly be feeling the beneficial effects of peace. The numbers of students rose dramatically from 1918 onwards, and by 1920 had topped three thousand (see chart of UCL student numbers, Harte—North 1978: 201). A period of rapid expansion would soon be under way for the British universities although government funding would be severely limited. The war had drained Britain's finances, notwithstanding the fact that she had entered the conflict as the richest country in the world.

But, all in all, on November 11, 1918, Daniel Jones might have had every reason to feel optimistic if from his Ridgmount Gardens flat he had heard the cheerful sound of the Armistice Day crowds moving down Gower Street to join the revels taking place in Trafalgar Square on that wet November evening. He might, amongst other things, have been looking forward to getting his hands on the first publication copies of a book which he had completed just before the outbreak of war for his Leipzig publishers Teubner. After four frustrating years, during which Jones had nevertheless managed to carry on with the proof-reading by channelling the copy through Switzerland (see Section 6.1), the book was now ready to be published just as soon as the war was over. It was to prove to be the most successful textbook Jones ever wrote and is still in demand even to this day; it was to be called *An outline of English phonetics*.

Chapter 8

The *Outline*

8.1. Introduction

An outline of English phonetics (Jones 1918a, referred to in this volume as the *Outline*) can be considered as Daniel Jones's most significant publication; together with the *EPD*, it is also undoubtedly his best known. Because of the renown of the *Outline*, and its importance as an expression of Jones's ideas on phonetics, phonology and pronunciation teaching, it is necessary to discuss the work in considerable detail. In addition, reference will be made here to the first edition of the *Pronunciation of English*, where the origins of many of Jones's statements and theories can be found. Consideration is also given at this point to the radical revision of the *Outline*, namely the third edition, published in 1932. The chief subsequent revision, far less significant in scale, is the eighth [1956] edition, to which reference is made in this chapter, and which is considered again in Section 13.11. An evaluation of the overall contribution of the *Outline* to phonetics is to be found in Section 14.6.

8.2. Opening chapters

Perhaps the first point of interest about the *Outline* is the doubt about its date of publication. No date appears on the first edition, but there is an note stating: "The greater part of this book was in print before 1914" (p. ii). The 1922 edition also contains no reference to the year in which the book first appeared, whilst the introduction to the [1932] *Outline*[3] (p. iii) states:

> This edition has been completely rewritten. It incorporates the results of my experience during the last eighteen years (since the book was originally prepared).

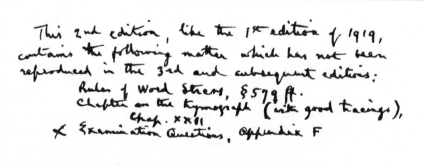

Figure 8.1. Jones's handwritten note on date of publication of the first edition of the *Outline*.

A later edition, *Outline*[8] [1956], gives 1918 as the publication date, and in the preface (written in 1955) Jones refers to the "thirty-seven years since this book first appeared". Consequently, 1918 has been accepted, and the *Outline* appears listed under this date in the bibliography of Jones's work in Abercrombie et al. (1964: xi). Yet it is highly unlikely that Teubner could have managed to get the book out in the month or so remaining in 1918 after the signing of the Armistice. Clinching evidence for 1919 as the true publication date, however, comes from Daniel Jones himself. In his personal copy of the first edition of the *Outline*, with marginal notes apparently intended for a future revision, Jones wrote, "This 1st edition (1919) ...",[1] making it virtually certain that the book did in fact appear in that year. Furthermore, on a copy of the second edition of the *Outline* a note appears in Jones's own hand (see Figure 8.1): "this 2nd edition, like the 1st edition of 1919".[2] However, to avoid contradiction with other authorities, the *Outline*[1] in the present volume is listed in the chronological bibliography of Jones's work under 1918.

In any case, it is also plain from the above that Jones thought of the book as actually representing his views in 1914 rather than any later date and, indeed, the *Outline*[1] does clearly reflect a less developed phonetic viewpoint than Jones had reached by the end of the war. It is especially noticeable in the lack of any mention of the phoneme concept and the virtual absence of reference to the Cardinal Vowel system (but see below). Even the second edition only remedies these omissions in the form of a very brief preface which manages to deal briskly not only with the eight primary Cardinal Vowels but also phoneme theory in the space of a single page. Jones (*Outline*[2]: ii) excuses himself in this way:

> Since this "Outline of English Phonetics" was written—and the greater part of it was in print in 1914 —, many new discoveries in the field of phonetics have been made, and many new devices for the practical teaching of pronunciation have been invented. To incorporate into this book, all the new material bearing upon English would require the rewriting of many parts, and this for various reasons is at present impossible.

One of the reasons was probably the state of Jones's mental health (see below) and, in fact, a major revision of the *Outline* had to wait until the third edition of 1932.

The *Outline*[1] is considerably shorter than the more familiar later versions of the work. It contains 221 pages of text (plus introduction) divided into 786 numbered subsections, whereas the (final) 9th edition (*Outline*[9] [1960]) has nearly 1,000 subsections and a total of over 380 pages.

The opening chapters cover transcription and standards of pronunciation. Jones employs the same transcription as in the *EPD*; this is something which has remained constant in all subsequent revisions of the book, as has the curious "alphabetic" arrangement of the symbols in the "List of English Speech-Sounds with Key Words" (p. viii) running from ɑ to ʔ, which was presumably derived from the Michaelis—Jones (1913a) *Phonetic dictionary of the English language* (see Section 5.3). Jones

(*Outline*[1]: v) defends his choice of "broad transcription" on the basis of practicality rather than theoretical motives:

> Some teachers have objected that the "broad" form of transcription is simplified to an unnecessary extent. Considerable personal experience in the teaching of foreigners has, however, convinced me that this is not so. For two years I tried the experiment of using in my foreigners' classes at University College a "narrower" form of transcription, but the results were not satisfactory; the students who had no great aptitude for learning pronunciation could never remember the symbols, while those to whom the subject came more easily had no need of the elaborate transcription, because they knew or learned readily the rules of pronunciation which make it possible to simplify the transcription.

Jones had a particular interest in his early career in providing rule systems for the conversion of broad transcription to narrow, and one example of such a scheme is to be found in Appendix A (*Outline*[1]: 183). It provides an interesting early example of the application of an algorithmic approach to a phonological problem. The following extracts give some idea of the scope of Jones's rules intended to "simplify transcription":

(7) the rule that "dark" l is only used finally and before consonants.
(8) the rule that voiced liquid consonants and semi-vowels are partially devocalized when preceded by breathed consonants in the same syllable.

The second part of Appendix A provides appropriate modifications for incorporating the above statements within a scheme for narrow transcription:

(7) using ł finally and before consonants, and l elsewhere,
(8) marking partial devocalization of liquids by ̥

An additional point of interest in Appendix A concerns the fleeting references, without explanation, to "'cardinal' (continental)" vowels. It is probable that this is not a pre-1914 mention of Cardinal Vowels, but rather that Appendix A is a late addition to the book. At this time, Jones was going through a particularly intensive period of experimentation with transcription. In later editions (e.g. *Outline*[8]: 343–345), in the corresponding but totally revised appendix on transcription, Jones discusses at length his changing views, saying that "at one time (around 1918) I made considerable use of narrow transcription." He goes on to mention his own use of such systems in the early twenties, and his encouragement of Armstrong to produce a book of narrow transcription suitable for learners (Armstrong 1923a). It might be inferred that had the *Outline* been published either a little earlier—or a little later—it would have appeared using narrower symbols. (See also below for comments on transcription in the "Length" section of the *Outline*[1]: Chapter XVIII.) Though the *Outline*[1] does not explicitly use the phoneme concept, the definition of broad transcription (p. 3) is essentially phonemically based:

> …a transcription obtained by using the minimum number of symbols requisite for representing without ambiguity the sounds of the language in question (without reference to other languages).

It is notable that throughout the book, Jones uses square brackets to enclose narrow transcription.

> Broad transcription of English is used throughout this book, narrow forms being occasionally added in cases where it might be helpful. Such narrow transcription is in every case enclosed in square brackets [ ].

This would appear to be the first time that this convention (later applied to phonetic as opposed to phonemic transcription) was ever employed in a published work.[3]

At this point, the first extensive change is made in the revised [1932] version, *Outline*[3], in the form of a series of sections on the problems faced by the foreign learner of English (pp. 2–10). In the first of these, "Difficulties of Pronunciation" (pp. 2–3), Jones considers the problems of the language learner under six headings which may be summarised as (1) recognition, (2) articulation, (3) correct distribution, (4) suprasegmental features ("length, stress and voice-pitch"), (5) catenation and (6) the relationship between orthography and pronunciation.

In the following section, entitled "How to surmount the Difficulties of Pronunciation" (pp. 3–9), he emphasises the importance of a good linguistic ear and how this may be acquired by means of ear-training (p. 3):

> To cultivate a good linguistic ear requires systematic practice in listening for sounds. There is only one effective exercise for this purpose, namely dictation of isolated sounds and meaningless words by a teacher who can pronounce the foreign sounds accurately.

Jones defines articulation as the "gymnastics of the vocal organs". To cope with articulatory problems, Jones states (p. 4) that "the language learner should (1) study phonetic theory, and (2) do, when necessary, exercises based on that theory". Jones's third listed difficulty, the order and distribution of sounds, is where he believes phonetic transcription can be of greatest assistance to the learner, whilst supra-segmental problems, in Jones's view, require "accurate information". He says of these last with surprising confidence (p. 8):

> Generally the student will be able to pronounce correctly in the matter of length, stress, and pitch, if accurate information as to the foreign usage in regard to these matters is supplied to him…There is as a rule nothing particularly difficult in

carrying out such instructions. The main difficulty in connexion with them is to bear them in mind—again a question of memory.

Catenation exercises (see Section 8.9 below) are prescribed for students who have problems in connecting sounds in context.

Jones rounds off by distinguishing those areas of pronunciation training where a teacher is essential (pp. 9–10). The teacher is required to be a model of pronunciation, and to provide ear-training exercises. Furthermore, he is needed to judge the success, or otherwise, of the learners' efforts. Jones notes that books cannot predict all the possible errors of pronunciation. He also advocates "a good gramophone or phonograph" which can supplement the teacher's instructions.

In the first edition of the *Outline*, a short chapter follows on "Standard Pronunciation". This is defined as "the form which appears to be most generally used by Southern English persons who have been educated at the great English public boarding schools" (p. 4) and, all through the book, is referred to merely as "English". Jones draws again on his early distinction (in *Phonetic transcriptions of English prose*) of Style A, B and C (see Section 2.7); style B, "the pronunciation used in conversation when speaking carefully and not too rapidly", is "recommended for the use of foreigners" (p. 5). A vast change is obvious between the prescriptive approach to standard pronunciation which characterised the *Pronunciation of English*[1] (see Section 3.4) and Jones's attitude here. He says (p. 4):

> Many suitable standards of English pronunciation might be suggested, e.g. educated Northern English, educated Southern English, the pronunciation commonly used on the stage, etc. It is convenient for present purposes to choose as the standard of English pronunciation the form which appears to be most generally used by Southern English persons who have been educated at the great English public boarding schools.

He also emphasises in the *Outline*[1] Preface (pp. vi–vii):

> ... it is not the object of this book to set up this particular style of pronunciation as a standard. Its object is to record accurately *one form* of English pronunciation, and to give to foreigners methods of acquiring that form if they wish to do so.

In the *Outline*[3], this chapter was retitled "Types of pronunciation", and the more liberal approach to pronunciation standards emphasised further. His recommendations to foreign learners remained unaltered, namely that they should learn what he now termed Received Pronunciation. Jones says (p. 12) he uses this term "for want of a better". He goes on to state: "I wish it, however, to be clearly understood that other types of pronunciation exist which I consider to be equally 'good'."

A brief simplified exposition of the organs of speech (*Outline*[1], pp. 5–7) is notable only for its familiarity; apart perhaps from Jones's retention of the spelling "vocal

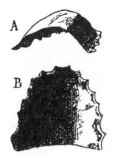

Fig. 9.

Palais artificiel.

A. Le palais artificiel est vu dans sa position naturelle. La face supérieure est en haut; quelques alvéoles des dents de devant apparaissent en dessous.
B. Le palais est posé à plat, la face concave tournée vers le spectateur.
On peut le construire rapidement et à peu de frais de la façon suivante : avec du *godiva*, préparation employée par les dentistes, ramolli dans l'eau bouillante et placé en boule à l'extrémité d'une règle plate que l'on introduit dans la bouche, on prend l'empreinte du palais. Sur ce moule légèrement huilé, on estampe avec soin une feuille de papier filtre mouillé. Puis on fait un mastic avec de la poudre de craie ou de kaolin et une colle forte, la *sercotine* par exemple, que l'on étend en couche mince sur le papier. Enfin on applique une nouvelle feuille de papier mouillé que l'on estampe aussi. La pièce une fois sèche est découpée suivant le contour des dents et enduite d'un vernis noir. On peut augmenter son imperméabilité en la plongeant dans de l'huile bouillante.
Quand on veut étudier une articulation quelconque, on blanchit la face intérieure du palais artificiel au kaolin, on l'introduit dans la bouche en ayant soin que la langue ne l'effleure ni avant, ni après l'expérience . Une fois le son produit, on le retire. La langue a enlevé partout où elle a touché la légère couche de poudre et les régions de contact apparaissent nettement dessinées en noir sur le fond blanchi du palais. Au préalable, on en a reporté sur du papier les contours exacts et on a établi avec soin des points de repère. Pour cela, on a percé le palais artificiel de trous et on a obtenu sur le papier une projection très exacte de ces trous et un contour tout à fait correct, en posant l'appareil à plat et en répandant au-dessus une pluie de poudre de minium. Un décalque fait sur papier transparent permet de prendre le dessin renversé. Il suffit ensuite de le retourner pour avoir à l'envers une image directe représentant la voûte palatine orientée suivant sa position réelle.
Le tracé obtenu, il ne reste plus qu'à le reproduire sur le patron ainsi préparé, en s'aidant des points de repère, des échancrures des dents et du compas.

Figure 8.2. Extract from Rousselot—Laclotte (1902: 22) on the artificial palate.

chords", it would not be really out of place in a modern introductory handbook on articulatory phonetics.

This is followed by Chapter IV, entitled "Experimental Methods", which is introduced thus (p. 7):

> It is not suggested that experimental phonetics is a necessary study for all those who wish to pronounce a foreign language correctly, but demonstrations by means of special apparatus are often found helpful by students as fixing in the memory that which they have previously learned by the ordinary methods of practical phonetics. The parts of this book relating to experimental phonetics may be entirely omitted by those who have not time or opportunity to take up this branch of the subject. Paragraphs which may be so omitted are marked with an asterisk *.

8   CHAPTER IV. EXPERIMENTAL METHODS

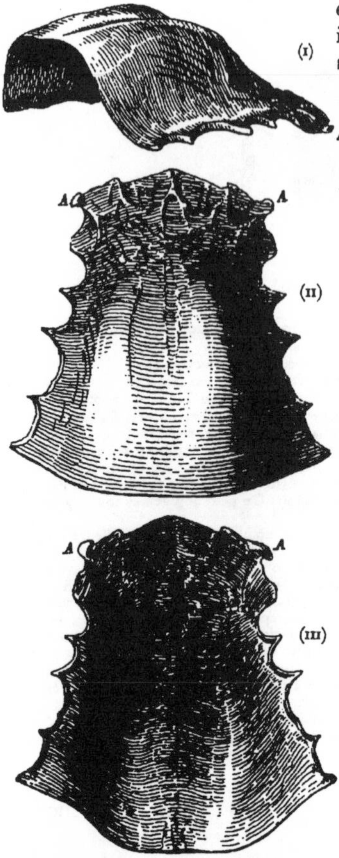

Fig. 3. The Artificial Palate.
(I) Side View. (II) Seen from above.
(III) Seen from below.

exactly, and it must be so made that it will keep in position by itself; it should be provided with little projecting pieces in the front so as to admit of its being removed from the mouth easily (AA fig. 3).

If the material is not black the under side should be blackened with varnish.[1]

*40. An artificial palate sufficiently good for ordinary purposes may be made as follows. Soften some dentists' wax by putting it in water, warmed to a temperature of about 60° C. (= 140° Fahr.). Spread it on a dentists' mouth-tray and introduce the tray into the mouth; then press it upwards so that the soft wax becomes moulded into the shape of the palate. Remove from the mouth, and allow the wax to cool. When quite hard, oil the surface of the model thus obtained. Then cover the surface carefully with a piece of damp filter paper, taking care that no air-bubbles are left between it and the wax. On the top of this place a thin layer of seccotine or other strong gum well mixed with precipitated chalk. Apply a second piece of damp filter paper taking care as before not to leave any air-bubbles. When the whole is thoroughly dry, the paper may be removed from the wax and cut out along the line marking the edge of the teeth. The under side of the artificial palate thus obtained should be covered with black varnish.

*41. The artificial palate is used as follows. The under side of the palate is first covered with a little finely powdered chalk and inserted into the mouth. A sound is then pronounced and the palate is with-

---

[1] Suitable palates may be made by any dentist. Prices vary considerably, the cheapest are those made of prepared paper and these answer quite well for ordinary purposes. M. Montalbetti, 4 Rue de Goff, Paris, makes them at the price of 5 francs. Palates in metal or vulcanite are more expensive.

Figure 8.3.   Extract from *Outline*[1] (p. 8) on the artificial palate to show the similarity with Rousselot and Laclotte's treatment of the same topic.

Whilst it must be remembered that the *Outline* was intended essentially as a handbook for foreigners wishing to learn English, and this is stated clearly in the preface (p. iii), nevertheless, the quotation shows that even at this time, when Jones's enthusiasm for instrumental work was presumably at its height, he consigns experimental phonetics to a subsidiary place as compared with articulatory and auditory approaches.

Jones goes on to list the main types of apparatus (p. 7): "the artificial palate, the kymograph, the laryngoscope, the mouth measurer, the gramophone and other talking machines, and a number of other less important instruments". See also Sections 8.3 and 8.8.

Chapter IV deals almost exclusively with the traditional method of palatography, with full instructions for the manufacture of artificial palates. The subsequent chapters contain numerous palatograms illustrating consonant and vowel articulations.

The passages on experimental phonetics in the *Outline*[1] often bear striking similarities to portions of Rousselot—Laclotte's (1902) *Précis de prononciation française*. This can be seen by comparing the section on the artificial palate in the *Outline*[1] (p. 8) with the similar section in Rousselot—Laclotte (1902: 22); both have been reproduced (Figures 8.2 and 8.3). There is some similarity in the illustrations (even though the *Outline* drawings are far superior to the rough sketches found in the French work) but it is the text which seems to have too many correspondences for mere coincidence. It would appear that Jones has partially paraphrased—and, in fairness, expanded—Rousselot and Laclotte.

The *Outline*[1] shows other similarities to Rousselot and Laclotte notably in the illustration throughout with palatograms and lip photographs (see Section 8.4). The final chapter of the *Outline*[1], "The Kymograph", must also be regarded as leaning to an extent on the earlier book.

Surprisingly, no mention of the French work, or its authors, is to be found anywhere in the *Outline*[1]. This is doubly remarkable, for Jones rarely borrowed directly from the work of others, and when he did, he appears always to have been scrupulous in his acknowledgement. No record exists of any contacts Daniel Jones may have had with Abbé Rousselot or Laclotte themselves; and if Jones ever attended any of the Abbé's lectures or courses in Paris whilst he was at Bourg-la-Reine, it has not been noted. Yet it is quite likely that Jones would have found Rousselot and Laclotte's book useful for the lectures he gave to his students on experimental phonetics from 1910 onwards; and he may have used the illustrations as a basis for the preparation of the lantern slides he employed in the early days at UCL before the laboratory proper was in being. It is just conceivable that Jones failed to keep in mind just how much the experimental portions of the *Outline*[1] owed to Rousselot and his colleague.

Yet it is noticeable that among the text which was removed, or altered most radically, for the [1932] revised third edition of the *Outline* was much of the material which had been taken from Rousselot and Laclotte. For instance, the section on the artificial palate was completely rewritten; and, as we shall see in Section 8.8, the chapter on the kymograph was removed. Although his ideas may have been changed by the work in his own laboratory, and he may well have felt that experimental approaches were largely out of place in a book of this type, it is also very likely that Jones wished to eliminate those sections of the *Outline*[1] which were not entirely his own work. (It is conceivable that this is one of the reasons for Jones's strange habit of advising those contemplating publishing to avoid reading the work of others;

TABLE OF ENGLISH SPEECH SOUNDS

This table is for reference only. It should be used constantly in connexion with the detailed descriptions of the sounds, Part I, §§ 29 ff.

		Labial		Dental	Palatal	Velar	Glottal
		Bi-labial	Labio-dental				
Consonants	Plosive	**p b**		**t d**		**k g**	
	Nasal	**m**		**n**		**ŋ**	
	Lateral			**l**		**(l)**	
	Rolled			**r**			
	Fricative	**w**	**f v**	**θ ð, s z,** **ʃ ʒ, ɹ**	**j**	**(w)**	**h**
Vowels					Front Mixed Back		
	Closed	**(uː)(u)**			**iː, ɪ uː, u**		
	Half-closed	**(o)**			**e o**		
	Half-open				**ɛ əː ʌ** **ə**		
	Open	**(ɔː)** **(ɔ)**			**æ ɔː** **a ɑ ɔ**		

The sounds underlined in the table are breathed, all others are voiced (§ 9).

Sounds which appear twice in the table have a double articulation, the secondary articulation being shown by the symbol in ( ); see the sections relating to each of the sounds in question.

Figure 8.4. Table of English speech sounds (*Pronunciation of English*[1], p. xiii).

TABLE OF ENGLISH SPEECH-SOUNDS

		Labial		Dental	Palatal	Velar	Glottal
		Bi-labial	Labio-dental				
CONSONANTS	Plosive	*p* b		*t* d		*k* g	
	Nasal	m		n		ŋ	
	Lateral			l		(l)	
	Rolled			r			
	Fricative		*f* v	θ ð, *s* z, *ʃ* ʒ, ɹ			
	Semi-vowel	w			j	(w)	*h*

					Front	Mixed	Back	
VOWELS	Close	(u:) (u)			iː i		uː u	
	Half-close	(o)			e	əː	o	
	Half-open				ɛ	ə	ʌ	
	Open	(ɔ:) (ɔ)			æ a	ɔː ɑ ɔ		

The sounds in Italic Letters in the table are breathed; all others are voiced. Sounds which appear twice in the table have a double articulation, the secondary articulation being shown by the symbol in brackets ( ).

Figure 8.5.   Table of English speech sounds (*Outline*[1], p. vii).

see Section 14.12 for Blandford's comments on Armstrong and Ward 1926.)

Chapter V is concerned with phonation ("Breath and Voice") and again refers to simple forms of apparatus, for example, the laryngoscope and Zünd-Burguet's "Voice Indicator"—a type of sensitive rattle for placing against the larynx; this information is retained in later editions of the *Outline*. No types of phonation other than voiced and voiceless are described, though whisper is mentioned briefly (p. 10).

8.3.   Classification of consonants and vowels

The chapters which follow (VI–XV), which deal with the classification and description of the sounds of English, must be considered to be the core of the book. By English, Jones means in effect "Standard Pronunciation", since only the briefest references are made to other varieties.

Chapter VI opens with a section entitled the "Classification of Sounds" (pp. 11–12). A vowel is defined as a "voiced sound in which the air has a free passage through the mouth, and does not produce audible friction"; other types of sound are classed as consonants, i.e. unvoiced sounds; sounds where the air has an impeded passage

	Labial		Dental	Alveolar	Palatal	Velar	Glottal
	Bi-labial	Labio-dental					
Plosive	p b			t d		k g	
Nasal	m			n		ŋ	
Lateral				l		(l)	
Fricative		f v	θ ð	s z, ʃ ʒ, r			h
Semi-vowel	w				j	(w)	

CONSONANTS

		Front	Central	Back
Close	(uː) (u)	iː i		uː u
Half-close	(o)	e	ə	o
Half-open	(ɔː)	ɛ	əː	ɔː
Open	(ɔ)	æ a	ɐ	ʌ ɑ

VOWELS

Figure 8.6. Table of English speech sounds (*Outline*³, p. x).

		Labial		Dental	Alveolar	Post-alveolar	Palato-alveolar	Palatal	Velar	Glottal
		Bi-labial	Labio-dental							
CONSONANTS	Plosive	p b			t d				k g	
	Affricate					tr dr	tʃ dʒ			
	Nasal	m			n				ŋ	
	Lateral				l				(l)	
	Fricative		f v	θ ð	s z	r	ʃ ʒ			h
	Semi-vowel	w						j	(w)	

								Front	Central	Back
VOWELS	Close	(u:) (u)						i: i		u: u
	Half-close	(o)						e	ə:	o
	Half-open	(ɔ:)						ɛ	ə	ɔ:
	Open	(o)						æ a	ʌ	ɔ ɑ

Table of English Sounds

Figure 8.7. Table of English speech sounds (*Outline*[8], p. xvii).

through the mouth; sounds where the air does not pass through the mouth; and sounds in which there is audible friction. Jones goes on to relate this basic division to the concept of sonority, placing sounds on the following scheme (from most to least sonorous): open vowels; close vowels; voiced liquid consonants (nasals, lateral, rolled); voiced consonants; voiceless consonants. This scale is also outlined in the *Pronunciation of English*[1] (p. 55).

The section on the "Classification of Consonants" (pp. 12–15) shows Jones to have reached a stage close to his final system of consonant classification, as shown in the tables which illustrate the progression from the *Pronunciation of English*[1] (1909b) to the *Outline*[9] [1960]; see Figures 8.4 to 8.7. It will be seen that the chief differences between the *Outline*[1] and Jones's final classification lie in the consideration of [r] in the earlier editions as a roll (with fricative variants), and the omission of [tʃ] and [dʒ], which are treated by Jones as consonant sequences.

A considerable drawback of Jones's system of consonant classification in the *Outline*[1] is that in his "Table of English Speech-Sounds" (p. vii) no fewer than twelve of the English consonants are classified as "dental" (Figure 8.5); furthermore, two others are labelled "labio-dental". Even in the slightly more refined version of the consonant section, to be found in Chapter VI (p. 15), as many as eleven consonants are consigned to the "post-dental" subcategory (Figure 8.8).

This confusion was cleared up to a certain extent in the third edition of the *Outline* by the employment of the terms "alveolar", "post-alveolar" and "palato-alveolar"

67. The classification of consonants is made clear by arranging them in a table, horizontal rows containing sounds articulated in the same manner, and vertical columns containing sounds articulated by the same organs. The following is a table of the English consonants so arranged:

| | Labial | | Dental | | Palatal | Velar | Uvular | Glottal |
	Bi-labial	Labio-dental	Pre-dental	Post-dental (alveolar)				
Plosive. . .	p b			t d		k g		
Nasal . . .	m			n		ŋ		
Lateral . .				l ɫ		(ɫ)		
Rolled . . .				r				
Fricative .		f v	θ ð	s z, ʃ ʒ, ɹ				h
Semi-vowel	w				j	(w)		

Figure 8.8. Consonant table from the *Outline*[1] (p. 15)

(*Outline*[3]: 44), but it is not until the appearance of *Outline*[8] ([1956]: xvii) that these improvements were carried over into the main table of English sounds (Figure 8.7). Jones's difficulties with place terms for fricatives in the *Outline*[1] are discussed in Section 8.4.

Even in terms of Jones's traditionalist view of phonetics, the *Outline*[1] classification of vowels (pp. 15–21, see also the Table in the *Outline*[1], p. vii, reproduced here as Figure 8.5) must be regarded as conservative in its approach. Firstly, Jones does not treat the English diphthongs as discrete units, but instead describes them as modifications of their initial vowel elements; neither does he illustrate the glides on his vowel quadrilateral (Figure 8.5). From the theoretical standpoint, such a view can be defended, but this approach (retaining the scheme of the *Pronunciation of English*[1]), so going back to 1909, poses some descriptional difficulties for him (see Section 8.5). Secondly, the Cardinal Vowel system is not utilised, even though the description obviously draws on similar principles. Jones starts from the concept of a vowel triangle, elaborating this into a Cardinal Vowel-type quadrilateral (see Figure 8.9), unusual only in its sloping back line. The vowel triangle is almost identical to that to be found in the *Pronunciation of English*[1] (see Section 3.4, Figure 3.7).

The description and classification of vowels in the *Outline*[1]—based on the parameters of tongue height (open, half-open, half-close and close), portion of tongue raised (back or front), and lip shape—is not actually in its essentials different from that in the *Pronunciation of English* (see Section 3.4). As in the second edition of the *Pronunciation of English* ([1914]: 11), "closed, half-closed" is replaced by "close, half-close".

As in all his earlier publications, Jones employs the term "mixed" for what were later to be called "central" vowels. There is, however, one significant change in

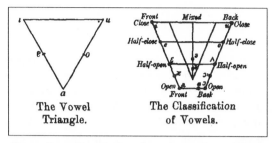

Figure 8.9. Vowel triangle and vowel quadrilateral (*Outline*[1], pp. 16-17).

Jones's viewpoint. He states (*Outline*[1]: 17) that: "The positions of the tongue in the formation of the different vowel sounds may, to a large extent, be felt, and in many cases they may be seen by means of a looking-glass", and then adds: "They may also be determined experimentally in various ways." To support his classificatory system, Jones brings in elementary instrumentation to provide aid in gauging the posture and height of the tongue, including direct palatography, and two mechanical means of estimating the extent of the space within the oral cavity, Atkinson's "Mouth Measurer" and Zünd-Burguet's "quadrant indicator". Jones was particularly enthusiastic about the Mouth Measurer, the use of which he had been advocating for some time previously.[4] None of this was, of course, innovative work on Jones's part, but it does show that he was interested in backing up his vowel theory with empirical data and had been working along these lines. By 1932, when the *Outline*[3] was published, X-ray data had made the use of the Mouth Measurer largely superfluous. In fact, even in the first edition, Jones (*Outline*[1]: 19) shows that he is aware of the contribution that radiology was making to speech science:

> Dr. E.A. Meyer of Stockholm has obtained excellent diagrams of the tongue positions of vowels by means of a row of fine leaden threads attached to an artificial palate along its centre line. He has also arrived at valuable results with X-ray photographs.

Jones claims that Meyer's (1910) work is "of the very highest interest and importance" and it was by utilising Meyer's methods that he was to arrive at his own theory of Cardinal Vowels. Cf. Section 7.6.

Jones discusses, briefly, the tense/lax distinction (p. 20), expressing his doubts about its validity.

> The two vowels, iː, i (in *seat, sit*) are commonly described as corresponding tense and lax vowels, it being considered by many that the main part of the tongue is raised to much the same extent in each case and the difference between the vowels is mainly one of tenseness of the muscles of the tongue.

The author of the present book is not completely convinced of the correctness of this mode of describing the sounds.

Jones considers that a better description of [i] would state the tongue is "lowered and somewhat retracted from the normal close position". However, he decides to retain the traditional terminology (close/lax) as a convenient way of neatly express- ing this lowering and retraction. In addition, for the vowels [u] and [uː], he consid- ers that for the former there is "lowering of the tongue and a wider opening of the lips". He proposes confining the contrast tense/lax to the close and half-close vowels and [əː].

It would appear here that Jones is searching for a means of confining his vowel description within the parameters of tongue height and lip shape. Given that the book actually represents Jones's views of 1914 rather than 1919, this could be considered as evidence that the *Outline*[1] can be regarded as the last exposition of an earlier model on which Jones based his later Cardinal Vowel system (see Sections 7.3, 14.14).

Jones's dissatisfaction with the *Outline*[1] is perhaps indicated by the fact that the diagram reproduced as Figure 8.9 was subject to one of the very few alterations he effected in the [1922] edition of the *Outline*, the line of the back vowels being made to "slant from left top to right bottom" (*Outline*[2]: ii).

Chapter VII (pp. 21–23) consists of a discussion of the syllable in terms of sonority, utilising the sonority scale mentioned above. Jones states (p. 21) that: "When two sounds of a group are separated by one or more sounds less sonorous than either of them, the two sounds are said to belong to different syllables." This section is a devel- opment of the brief treatment of the syllable in the *Pronunciation of English*[1] (55–56) (cf. also Sweet 1890a: 60–64). Jones (*Outline*[3]: 54–56) was later to develop his con- cept of the syllable into a more clearly defined theory of prominence based on se- quences of peaks (vowels and syllabic consonants) and valleys (consonants) with the latter being regarded as potentially ambisyllabic. Jones also provides (*Outline*[1]: 22) a definition of diphthongs as two vowels "which do not form more than one syllable".

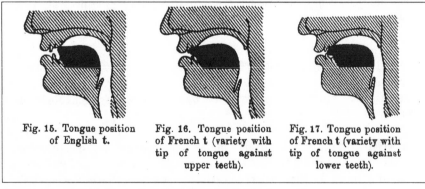

Fig. 15. Tongue position of English **t**.

Fig. 16. Tongue position of French **t** (variety with tip of tongue against upper teeth).

Fig. 17. Tongue position of French **t** (variety with tip of tongue against lower teeth).

Figure 8.10. Sagittal cross-sections for [t] (*Outline*[1], p. 26)

Fig. 18. Palatogram of the English word *two*.

Fig. 19. Palatogram of the French word *tout*.

Fig. 20. Palatogram of the English word *tea*.

Fig. 21. Palatogram of the French word *type*.

Figure 8.11 Palatograms for [t] (*Outline*[1], p. 27)

8.4. Description of consonants

Jones then proceeds to the painstakingly detailed description of English consonants and vowels which has probably been the most significant single source of the book's success—both academically and commercially. He begins with the plosives (Chapter VIII). His style is completely appropriate to the subject matter—concise, lucid and precise; Jones does not set out to impress the reader, either by an unnecessary display of erudition, or by cloaking explanation in complex academic verbiage. This brief extract from the description of [k] (pp. 29–30) will serve as a representative sample of these portions of the book:

> In pronouncing the sound **k** the air passage is completely blocked by raising the back of the tongue to touch the soft palate, the soft palate being also raised so as to shut off the nose passage; the air is compressed by pressure from the lungs, and when the contact of the tongue with the palate is released by lowering the tongue, the air suddenly escapes through the mouth and in doing so makes an explosive sound; the vocal chords are not made to vibrate. The formation of the sound **k** may be expressed shortly by defining it as the BREATHED VELAR PLOSIVE consonant.

Jones's language is ideal for his purpose. The careful accuracy perhaps owes something to his early legal training. However, the clarity of expression and the avoidance of anything smacking of the deliberately arcane still remind one most strongly of Passy's limpidly clear French. The influence is perhaps more obvious when Jones's (1941c: 33) own view of Passy's writing is recalled:

> Passy's clarity of style in writing and in speaking...was conspicuous even in

France, the country where clear expression is the rule. In his writings, his lectures and equally in his impromptu speeches in debates his style was a model of conciseness and lucidity. A Frenchman of my acquaintance compared it to that of Pascal.

These words reveal Jones's admiration not only for French writing in general but for Passy's French in particular. Yet the tribute (as far as written language goes) could be applied equally well to Jones's own work. Although Jones always wrote with distinctive clarity, yet possibly the excellence of his writing and the competence of overall presentation are nowhere better than in the *Outline*.

The treatment given to each consonant is comprehensive and includes sagittal cross-sections as illustrations (Figure 8.10) and (where possible) palatograms. The selection of palatograms shown in Figure 8.11 is that used for the description of [t].

In addition, sound-spelling relationships are dealt with in detail, and considerable space is devoted to the potential errors of foreign learners of English. Jones spends most time on the problems of French speakers; German speakers' difficulties also receive considerable space, followed by Scandinavians and other Europeans. Little is said about any non-European languages, and this remarkable imbalance in Jones's treatment could be considered a major criticism of the book. It might be excused by the more limited *Weltanschauung* of Britain in 1914 and it is noteworthy that within a few years Jones was going to be attempting to stimulate interest in the languages of the Empire (see Section 9.3). The allocation of space probably simply reflects numbers of students from overseas arriving at UCL to take part in Jones's courses in the period before the war. It was an imbalance which Jones appeared to find hard to correct, as can be seen from an examination of the later revised editions; for example, the *Outline*[8] contains no fewer than seventy-seven references to French and German mispronunciations plus a further eighteen allusions to the sounds of those languages. In contrast, only four Indian problems are dealt with; whilst not a single Chinese or Arabic difficulty is even mentioned.

The chapter on plosive consonants includes a section on [ʔ]; this deals mainly with the occurrence of [ʔ] as an onset to vowels and German learners' errors which are associated with it. There is no mention of the possibility of glottal reinforcement or replacement of fortis plosive consonants (cf. Gimson 1962: 158). Wells (1982: 282) has pointed out that in the conservative upper-class variety which he terms "U–RP"— the type of modern pronunciation probably closest to what Jones calls "English" in the *Outline*[1]—glottalisation is rare. Yet, even though this feature was not as common in pre-1920 English as it is in present-day RP (see Eustace 1967: 303–304), nevertheless, audio-recordings provide evidence that pre-glottalisation and glottal replacement were firmly established in the upper-class English of Edwardian times (Collins—Mees 1996). Gimson (1977: 155) has mentioned "the old-fashioned nature" of Jones's own speech instancing "the avoidance of glottalisation of final /p, t, k/", but this is not confirmed by listening to recordings of Jones's voice dating from as early as 1924 and 1929. These reveal Jones glottalising final fortis stops fairly consistently.[5]

Consequently, it is surprising that in the first edition of the *Outline* glottalisation of this type goes entirely without mention.

Jones first noted the occurrence of consonantal glottalisation in non-standard English as early as 1909 in the *Pronunciation of English* (Jones 1909b: 16, 19). The first mention of glottalisation in RP is to be found in the *Pronunciation of Russian* (1923a, see Section 10.5), but it was left to the revised edition of the *Outline*³ ([1932]: 139 n.) to deal with the matter in more detail.

> Many educated speakers of Southern English use ? for **t** at the termination of a syllable when a consonant follows, especially before **m, n, r, j** and **w**...; the use of ? for **t** before a vowel must be regarded as exclusively dialectal.

The section on "Breathed Plosives" (*Outline*¹: 34) deals chiefly with aspiration.⁶ Jones distinguishes two degrees of aspiration (comparing English with Danish and German) and two degrees of breath force in plosives (comparing the relatively strong French unaspirated voiceless plosives with the "feebly articulated" (p. 24) voiceless plosives of southern German).

"Implosive Sounds" (pp. 34–35) does not in fact describe *implosives* but *ejective plosives*. See Sections 2.11 and 6.8 for discussions of this terminological ambiguity. In the *Outline*³, Jones retitled this section "Ejective Sounds".

"Voiced Plosives" (*Outline*¹: 35–36) is mainly concerned with devoicing in English stops. Whilst it is not stated explicitly here, Jones is presumably using information derived from kymographic investigations (see Section 8.8), and the same applies to the following short sections: "Incomplete Plosives" (pp. 36–37), covering plosive sequences where one member lacks audible release; "Faucal Plosion" (p. 37), which is Jones's term for nasal plosion; and "Lateral Plosion" (pp. 37–38). All show a degree of precision in terms of timing which could hardly be obtained from auditory and articulatory phonetic techniques alone, and in this respect contrast sharply with the lack of such sophistication in the description of plosives in the *Pronunciation of English*¹ (pp. 15–18).

The chapter closes with a section on "Affricative Consonants" (pp. 38–39). Jones distinguishes between "clean-cut" plosive articulations and those in which "when the organs articulating the plosive are separated more slowly, the ear perceives distinctly the effect of the corresponding fricative". The latter he terms "affricative or assibilated consonants" (p. 38); his distinction corresponds well to a modern idea of plosive and affricate. However, as stated previously, Jones does not choose to regard the English consonants [tʃ] and [dʒ] as affricates, arguing that "for the purposes of practical teaching of English it is more convenient to regard these English sounds as double" (p. 39). In the revised *Outline*³, he changes his mind on this point, and in a chapter entitled "The English Affricate Consonants" (*Outline*³: 145–154) he includes not only [tʃ dʒ] (which are classed as unit phonemes) but also the sequences [ts dz tr dr]. The *Outline*¹ can therefore be seen as a halfway stage between the *Pronunciation of English*¹—where the term affricate is not even mentioned and [tʃ dʒ] are regarded only as sequences—and Jones's later systems of phonetic description where the affricate is an important subcategory of the stop consonants. Jones was possibly influenced here by the results of his kymographic research (*Outline*[1]: 175–176), see Section 8.8.

Chapter IX (pp. 40–51) is entitled "The English Liquid Consonants". Jones takes "liquid" as a cover term for nasal, lateral and rolled consonants (from the *Outline*[3] on, Jones dispenses with the use of the traditional category of "liquid", dealing with the nasals and laterals in separate chapters and regarding [r] as a fricative).

In the section on "The l Sounds", Jones is greatly preoccupied with the distinction between clear [l] and dark [ɫ] and the problems this poses for foreigners; in particular, much space is taken up with the correct articulation of dark [ɫ]. Once again, the balance of the book is questionable here, since although this is indeed a problem for German and French students, no question of blurring of phoneme contrast is involved. Apart from a brief reference to the Portuguese, no advice is given to learners who find clear [l] a difficulty or, like the Dutch, produce an [ɫ] which is too dark. Much more surprising, however, is that the frequent errors of confusing /l–r/, typical of millions of speakers of Far Eastern languages, is not even mentioned, either here or in the following section on [r]. The *Outline*[3] corrects this imbalance only in part; the Japanese confusion of /l–r/ is referred to but no other nationality is discussed. The omission of any mention of Cantonese in this context is particularly remarkable given Jones's previous experience with the language when writing the *Cantonese phonetic reader*.

The treatment of English [r] is in many ways one of the most unsatisfactory parts of the first edition of the *Outline*. Jones is forced to admit that his decision to class it as a "voiced post-dental rolled consonant" (pp. 48–49) is not borne out by facts:

> This sound is regularly used in the North of England as the pronunciation of initial *r*, and it is generally regarded by English elocutionists as the most correct pronunciation of the letter *r* when followed by a vowel.
>
> This form of **r**-sound, however, is not generally used by Southern English speakers. In Southern English the sound is usually replaced by the corresponding fricative (narrow phonetic symbol [ɹ] ... The use of this fricative consonant is practically universal when the preceding consonant is a dental (e.g. in draw drɔː, *Henry* ˈhenri), and extremely common in other cases.

The deficiency of the description can only partly be explained by the pressure that Jones still felt himself to be under from elocutionists to prescribe a rolled [r], and that this conflicted with his observations that a roll was an oddity in colloquial educated English. His attitude could be thought pusillanimous, and the comment on northern English, though it was the accepted wisdom of the time (Lloyd 1899), flies in the face of the observable facts, unless it is reinterpreted to mean a tap-[ɾ] (Wells 1982: 368). Remarkably, this analysis is, in its essentials, retained throughout all the revised editions of the *Outline*, e.g. *Outline*[8] ([1956]: 195).

Jones attributes the error of substituting a uvular *roll* to "most French people and

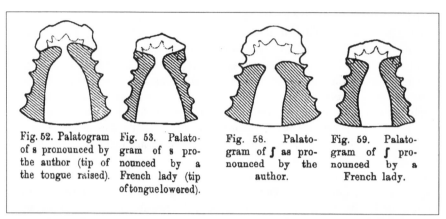

Fig. 52. Palatogram of s pronounced by the author (tip of the tongue raised).

Fig. 53. Palatogram of s pronounced by a French lady (tip of tongue lowered).

Fig. 58. Palatogram of ʃ as pronounced by the author.

Fig. 59. Palatogram of ʃ pronounced by a French lady.

Figure 8.12. Palatograms of [s] "pronounced by the author (tip of the tongue raised)" and "by a French lady (tip of tongue lowered)"; and similar pair for [ʃ] (*Outline*[1], pp. 55, 59)

most Germans" (*Outline*[1]: 49). Again, Jones's observation lets him down since their typical substitution is a uvular fricative—mentioned as an afterthought by Jones—or, more commonly, an approximant. Roll articulations were prescribed by elocutionists, particularly for use in the theatre; yet, it is very unlikely that they were still, as late as 1918, the norm in either standard French or German. Furthermore, the suggested exercises for the foreign student attempting to acquire English /r/ (pp. 49–50) are elaborate but unconvincing (more involved, but still rather reminiscent of those in his early Paris lecture; see Section 4.6).

> Keep the mouth very wide open by placing the bent knuckle of the thumb, or better still a cork about an inch in diameter, between the teeth, and try to pronounce the sound ʒ with the tip of the tongue raised. The resulting sound is very nearly the English fricative [r] .... Some foreigners obtain the sound more easily by trying the same exercise with z or ð instead of ʒ. The sound may be improved by pushing back the tip of the tongue with the end of a pencil (the end of the pencil being placed underneath the tongue).

In dealing with liaison forms of /r/, Jones covers "linking" r but omits to mention the almost equally common "intrusive" r (the latter is dealt with by Jones for the first time in the revised *Outline*[3]). Jones's restrictions on the occurrence of the r-link, namely that linking-r does not occur "when the vowel of the final syllable is preceded by r" and "when a pause is permissible between the two words (even though no pause is actually made)" (p. 48) would seem to hold true only for certain speakers, and not for all as is implied. See Windsor Lewis (1975) for a detailed discussion of English r-liaison, with mention of Jones's changing attitudes; see also Wells (1982: 224).

Chapter X, "The Fricative Consonants" (pp. 51–63), is less detailed but in general better organised and balanced. It is noticeable that Jones treats the whole topic of fricatives more briskly—perhaps because he considers these articulations less complex than plosives and "liquids". The increase in tempo cannot be related to the relative difficulty of the sounds involved for the language learner, since [ð]—which is a notorious problem for foreign students of English from many language backgrounds—is disposed of in just over half a page (p. 54). Here, when dealing with [f], we find the first instance of any problems of a non-European group (the Japanese) being considered (p. 51). However, Jones still gives virtually all his attention to the French, Germans and Scandinavians.

Jones is particularly interested in contrasts between French and English, and uses palatograms to show the differences in tongue shape between the auditorily similar French and English forms of the sounds [ʃ] and [ʒ]. The palatograms—of an unnamed "French lady", perhaps his wife, Cyrille—may be derived from one of the experimental phonetic research projects undertaken either by Jones or by one of his advanced students (Figure 8.12).

Apart from palatograms, as has already been noted, Jones illustrates his text with numerous photographs of lip positions. This particular use of photographs would appear to be more extensive than in any comparable practical phonetic textbook on English up to the date of publication of the *Outline*, or indeed (to our knowledge) since. In Brown's (1981) opinion, one possible effect of this use of photographs is that Jones in this way hit upon the significance of lip shape in consonant articulations (other than those primarily classified as labial consonants).

Brown (1981: 69) regards Jones as being virtually unique in the history of British phonetics in recognising this importance of consonantal lip-rounding:

Daniel Jones (1962, first published 1918) provides the most extensive discussion I have encountered of lip position in consonants that are not primarily classified as labial. His verbal descriptions are frequently accompanied by small inset photographs, which illustrate the type of pronunciation under discussion.

Brown (1981: 69) goes on to discuss the significance of the illustrations in this section of the *Outline*; although she is referring to the later *Outline*[8], her remarks apply equally to the *Outline*[1].

These photographs necessarily draw our attention to labial features. It is instructive to compare the verbal description with the photographic illustrations.

The photograph illustrating [ʃ] (*Outline*[8]: 190) is picked out by Brown (1981: 69) as showing: "the corners of the lips compressed, the lips protruded, and the soft inner surface of the lower lip displayed". The same photograph appears in the *Outline*[1] (p. 58, Figure 57) but there it is one of a pair and is labelled "The consonant ʃ pronounced with exaggerated distinctness" whilst the other photograph (p. 58, Figure 56) shows less obvious and non-everted lip-rounding. It would seem that, for later editions,

Jones chose to use only the photograph with more clearly displayed lip-rounding, and exclude the other, because he considered this would be more useful as a model for foreign learners. See Section 8.5 for a discussion of lip photographs of vowels.

Brown (1981: 69) then quotes Jones's comments in *Outline*[8]: "there is protrusion in the lips" and mentions that he recommends to Danes that for English [ʃ] "the lips should be rounded and protruded". The *Outline*[1] puts it thus: "The sound ʃ is usually accompanied by a certain amount of rounding and protrusion of the lips, though this is not essential" (*Outline*[1]: 58) and also suggests that the Danish learner should add lip-rounding to his [ʃ] (*Outline*[1]: 59).

Brown (1981: 70) goes on to list further examples of Jones's perceptive remarks with reference to other consonant articulations, and sums up:

> In general, then, Jones recognises lip position as being relevant to the description of a group of consonants that are not primarily classified as labial consonants. He positively identifies /ʃ/ and /ʒ/ as normally being produced with lip protrusion (and so, we must surely suppose, would describe what he regarded as the sequences /tʃ/ and /dʒ/ as having the same characteristic protrusion). [In fact, though Brown does not seem to have noticed, Jones states this both explicitly (*Outline*[8]: 161) and, by implication, in an instruction to Danish learners (*Outline*[8]: 163).] He recognises /r/ and /w/ as rounded. [The comment on [r] is missing from the *Outline*[1] and is to be found first in the *Outline*[3].] He allows that /s, z/ have "lip-articulation" in some people's speech and, although he does not recognise this in /f, v/, the photograph of the articulation of /f/ also demonstrates this feature.

Brown (1981: 70) regards Jones as effectively the only British phonetician to have accorded lip position an appropriate degree of significance in consonant articulations:

> I can find no other writer on English who pays the same amount of attention to lip-rounding on consonants as Jones does. Most twentieth century writers...ignore the feature completely, even when they pay what may seem to be excessive attention to lip-rounding on vowels.

Jones is compared favourably by Brown (1981: 71) with his predecessors, "the great phoneticians of the nineteenth century", Bell, Ellis and Sweet. Whilst acknowledging Sweet's well-known innovative comments on inner and outer lip-rounding, Brown (1981: 72) points out that he "has little to say on rounding in consonants". Furthermore, Brown (1981: 74) considers that Jones is far superior to later writers such as Ida Ward and Gimson (actually, of course, Jones's own pupils), who to a large extent play down, or ignore, the lip shape in consonants.

Brown (1981: 74) conjectures that the decision to illustrate the *Outline* so profusely with photographs of the lips might have forced Jones to become more interested in labial characteristics, but concludes that:

> ...it is more reasonable to suppose that he decided to include the photographs because he thought that lip posture was an important and relevant feature.

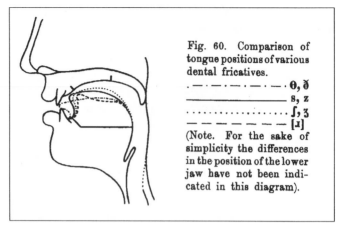

Figure 8.13. Diagram illustrating tongue positions of "dental fricatives" (*Outline¹*, p. 60).

It would seem at first sight that Brown's surmise is correct. Jones shows himself interested in lip shape throughout his writing. For instance, in the *Sounds of the French language* (p. 82) a sentence is added to the original French, stating: "In English the sounds ʃ, ʒ are often pronounced with lip-rounding." Again, the *Sechuana reader* (pp. xx–xxii) reveals Jones (and his co-author) paying considerable attention to lip shape in the articulation of consonants.

It is possible that the main reason for Jones's preoccupation with lip shape was simply that it was a phenomenon which was easily observed and recorded; for it must be remembered that we are still dealing with an era when most aspects of the speech process could only be deduced with difficulty from introspection, or gauged approximately from the primitive instrumentation then available. See Section 8.5 for Jones's attention to lip shape and tongue-tip in vowel description.

Printing techniques had reached the stage by 1914 where it was easy, and not prohibitively expensive, to include halftone blocks in the text, providing relatively high quality paper was used, and so there was really no technical obstacle to the use of photographs. Nevertheless, Jones had to spend time getting the lip positions posed and photographed (all those in *Outline¹* were of his brother Arnold's mouth) and he obviously would not have gone to this trouble, had he not thought that these illustrations would contribute to the value of the book.

He may also have been swayed by Jespersen's (1897–99) influential *Fonetik*, better known in its German translation as *Lehrbuch der Phonetik* (Jespersen 1904b). This included a fold-out table which reproduced (using wood-block engravings) a sequence of early cinefilm frames showing the lip positions for the utterance "Je vous aime".[7] (It is interesting that the company responsible for Jespersen's *Lehrbuch*, namely Teubner of Leipzig, were also the publishers of the *Outline¹*.)

However, there is a more plausible reason for the *Outline*[1] being illustrated so lavishly with photographs showing lip shape. It has already been shown that a significant influence on Jones in certain sections of the *Outline*[1], albeit an unacknowledged one, is Rousselot—Laclotte's (1902) *Précis de prononciation française*. This is the only other book (of a non-specialised nature) that is to be found which has the same kind, and quantity, of illustration with photographs of lip position as the *Outline*[1]. It is noteworthy that the descriptions of lip positions of not only vowels but also consonants are accompanied by photographs. The likeliest interpretation would appear to be that Jones took over the idea from Rousselot and Laclotte (together with much else) and that we may trace much of Jones's preoccupation with lip shape back to this source.

As mentioned above, Jones gets into considerable difficulty with his place terminology in the use of the term "dental". Seven of the fricatives fall into this category: [θ ð] (pre-dental); [s z] (blade post-dental); [ʃ ʒ] (blade-front post-alveolar); and "fricative [r]". It is perhaps no wonder that Jones is forced to introduce an explanatory diagram (p. 60, reproduced as Figure 8.13), saying apologetically: "The formation of the various dental fricatives will be made clearer by comparing the tongue positions shown, and a comparison of the palatograms" (p. 61). In fact, Jones does use the term "alveolar" for [s z ʃ ʒ] in the *Outline*[1] but only as a bracketed alternative to "post-dental" (pp. 54, 57, 58, 60).

Jones's treatment of "fricative r" (pp. 60–61) is slight, referring the reader to the main discussion under "liquids" (see above). Another small section is devoted to [ç] as a frequent realisation of the sequence [hj] (p. 61). The chapter on fricatives closes with a small section on devoicing in initial and final voiced fricatives in which Jones points out the extent of complete devoicing of final voiced fricatives (p. 63).

The concluding consonant section is Chapter XI (pp. 64–67), dealing with the semivowels, which Jones defines both as "vowels used in the capacity of consonants" and "fricative consonants in which the friction is practically imperceptible" (p. 64). Interestingly, as well as [w] and [j], Jones (p. 64) considers types of [r] as falling within this category:

> The English sounds **w** and **j** are usually semi-vowels, being vowels of the **u** type and **i** type respectively, pronounced in such a way as to give to the ear the effect of consonants. Many English persons pronounce **r** as a semi-vowel, namely the vowel ə (i.e. ə pronounced with simultaneous "inversion" of the tip of the tongue) used in the capacity of a consonant.

Such a description is somewhat closer to the phonetic reality of the typical articulation of RP English /r/ than most of what Jones states in the [r] section itself.

Jones deals in detail with lip shape in [w], particularly in relation to the problems of German learners, pointing out that lip-rounding is variable according to the degree of emphasis and is especially obvious before [uː]. Jones considers the "breathed fricative" [ʍ] in the semi-vowels section, as a variant of the sequence [hw]. He points out that the use of either [ʍ] or [hw] in words spelt with *wh* is "regular in Scotland, Ire-

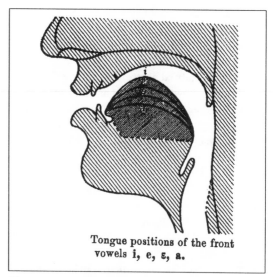

Tongue positions of the front
vowels **i, e, ɛ, a.**

Figure 8.14. Diagram illustrating "tongue positions of the front vowels **i e ɛ a**" (*Outline*[1], p. 68).

land and the North of England", but that in the South the forms with [w] are "more
usual", though he concedes (p. 65) that [ʍ] or [hw] "may also be heard, especially
from ladies". (Apart from the comment on the North—where the use of [ʍ] or /hw/
is most unusual in unaffected speech—Jones's comments seem reasonable today; see
Wells 1982: 228–230.) Jones feels confident enough to resist any pressure from elocutionists to retain the spelling pronunciation, saying (p. 65): "Foreigners may use
whichever pronunciation they prefer." But he also mentions in a note (p. 65 n.) that,
according to the editors of the *Concise Oxford Dictionary*, such pronunciations in the
South of England are confined to "purists in pronunciation". Similarly, in dealing
with the use of [u] following [j] in words like *lute*, Jones (p. 67) says:

> ... the forms with **j** are generally recommended by elocutionists, but the forms
> without **j** are, if anything, the more usual in ordinary speech, at any rate in the
> commoner words.

8.5. Description of vowels

Jones then devotes three chapters (XII, XIII and XIV) to a similarly exhaustive discussion of the English vowel articulations. The ordering of his description is based entirely on criteria of place of articulation, and the chapters are entitled "The Front Vowels", "The Back Vowels", and "The Mixed Vowels", respectively. "Short" and
"long" vowels are treated wherever they come in the sequence (going from close front

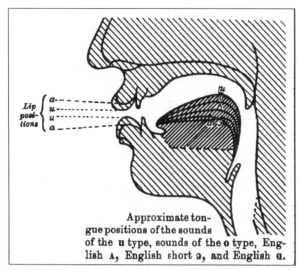

Figure 8.15 Diagram illustrating "approximate
tongue positions of the sounds of the u type, sounds of
the o type, English ʌ, English short ɔ, and English ɑ"
(*Outline¹*, p. 80).

to open back and ending with "mixed") whilst diphthongs are ordered on the basis of
the starting point. In the revised *Outline³* (p. 60), Jones established a new sequence by
ignoring the place categories, but separating the monophthongal vowels from the diphthongs; it was the second ordering which became widely popular as a system of numbering for the English vowels; it is still employed extensively to this day.

Jones's use of illustration by diagrams, and especially by photographs, is even more
extensive here than in the consonant treatment. Just as in the consonant section, lip
shape in vowels is a constant preoccupation with Jones. Certain of his observations in
this respect are most perceptive, for example, his description of the strong lip-rounding
associated with /ɔː/ and the emphasis he places on this in his advice to foreign learners. Each vowel has at least two accompanying lip photographs, one showing the articulation in "normal speech", and the other as "pronounced with exaggerated distinctness". Diphthongs have three, or even four, such photographs to demonstrate changes
in lip shape inherent in the glides. Revised editions from the *Outline³* onwards reduce
the numbers of photographs to one per vowel sound. As in the case of consonants (see
Section 8.4), Jones retains the form used in emphatic speech, presumably because he
considered this would be most helpful for practical teaching purposes. Palatograms are
also shown (where it is possible to derive one from the vowel articulation)—and Jones
in addition includes the two elaborate overlaid cross-sections illustrated in Figures
8.14 and 8.15. These diagrams are of interest in that they indicate a stage in Jones's
progression towards an "equal interval" approach to vowel description—as he was

to term it in later works such as the *Pronunciation of Russian* (p. 30) and the *Outline*[3] (p. 32). It was to become a crucial aspect of his Cardinal Vowel theory (see Section 7.3). In the preface to the second edition of the *Outline* [1922], Jones (p. ii) mentions the vowel diagram shown in Figure 8.16 as requiring improvement. By 1932, in the *Outline*[3], the whole of the section on vowel description was radically revised in the light of Jones's Cardinal Vowel theory (see Sections 7.3 and 14.14).

The following extract from the section on the vowel [ɔ] (p. 81) serves as a sample of Jones's articulatory descriptions of the English vowels.

> In pronouncing the English short ɔ the tongue is as low down and as far back as possible ... ; the lips are slightly rounded ... ; the soft palate is raised; the tip of the tongue is generally, though not necessarily, somewhat retracted from the lower teeth; the lower jaw is considerably lowered. The sound gives no palatogram. The vowel may be defined shortly as the FULLY OPEN BACK ROUNDED vowel.

However, in a book which is otherwise notable for clear style and presentation, Jones does not always appear to be at ease when dealing with the small differences in tongue shape which are crucial to vowel description; or in presenting these in a way which will be meaningful to the reader unable to hear a demonstration of the sound in question. He obviously feels the need for a well-ordered descriptive scheme like the Cardinal Vowel system. Indeed, writing the *Outline* could possibly have been the stimulus which made Jones realise the advantages of such an approach.

At times, he tends to get over-involved in the small detail of minor articulatory movements. For instance, he appears much preoccupied with tongue tip posture (exemplified in the extract above), and the only good reason for this would seem to be that it is a phenomenon which lends itself to close, accurate observation—even though for most vowels, at least in RP English, the tongue-tip is of minimal significance. Some portions of Jones's descriptions, whilst accurately observed (given the state of knowledge at the time), seem involved and excessively complex—perhaps more suited to the phonetics specialist than the foreign learner of English, for whom the book was supposed to be written. Take, for example, the description of the vowel [e] (p. 72):

> In pronouncing the vowel e the front of the tongue is raised considerably in the direction of the hard palate, but not quite so high as for the i sounds ...; the more usual English variety of the sound is not a very close one; it is described as lax by many writers, and this term will be retained here as denoting "a variety with tongue somewhat lower than the normal half-close position".

It is clear that Jones was unhappy with this aspect of his book; it is certainly noticeable that among the parts of the *Outline*[1] which underwent most drastic revamping in the revised editions were the articulatory descriptions in the chapters on vowels. The changes were mainly ones of simplification, aimed at providing a more orderly descriptive approach, based in part on the Cardinal Vowel system. Jones obviously felt the student would find this easier to absorb than what had existed in the *Outline*[1]. The tongue shape description in the *Outline*[8] (p. 70) is restated thus:

> The tongue-position for the principal English **e** is shown by the dot [in the vowel diagram] .... The following is a formal description of the manner of forming the sound:
> (i) *height of tongue*: intermediate between half-close and half-open;
> (ii) *part of tongue raised*: the "front".

Jones (*Outline*[8]: 28) summarised his views in these words:

> There is only one way of making written descriptions of vowels intelligible to a large circle of readers of different nationalities, and that is to describe the sounds with reference to a scale of "Cardinal Vowels," i.e. a set of fixed vowel-sounds having known acoustic qualities and known tongue and lip positions.

Jones runs into some organisational difficulties which derive from his decision to consider the English diphthongs as sub-categories of their initial vowel elements, rather than treating them as separate units. This means, for example, that [ei] is regarded by Jones as being derived from [e] in *get*. Though this is clearly defensible as a theoretical position (for discussion, see Swadesh 1947, Cohen 1952: 89–107, Sommerstein 1977: 30–35, Wells 1982: 48–50), Jones does not make it sufficiently clear that certain English diphthongs behave as functionally significant speech sounds (i.e. as phonemes, were he working within a phonemic framework) whereas others are the result of a reduction process of monophthongisation in sequences, which Wells (1982: 238) has termed "smoothing". For instance, it is not stated clearly that [oi] in *boy* (p. 84) has totally different linguistic status from the [ɔi] resulting from the smoothing of the original diphthong plus vowel in *going* (p. 87). (Note that in the *EPD*[1] (p. xxv) such diphthongs are clearly designated as "variants".) This may be the reason why, in the *Outline*[1] (p. 84), [ɔi] is dismissed in a few lines tucked away at the end of the [ɔ] section; in the *Outline*[3], and later editions, all the diphthong phonemes are given proper status and sections of their own whilst the diphthongs resulting from smoothing are mentioned only in passing.

Wells (1982: 241) rightly gives credit to Jones for first mentioning the phenomenon of smoothing (in the *Pronunciation of English*[1] in connection with [aiə]). It is, however, here in the *Outline*[1] (p. 78) that Jones develops the concept more fully.

> In pronouncing this triphthong, the tongue does not really reach the full **i** position with most speakers; **aeə** or **aɛə** would really be a more accurate representation of the pronunciation usually heard. The assimilation is often carried so far that the triphthong is simplified into **aə** or even simply becomes a lengthened **a** (repre-

sented phonetically by **aː**); thus *fire* often becomes **faə** or sometimes even **faː** (distinct from *far* **faː**); *empire* is often pronounced ˈ**empaə** or ˈ**empaː**. This levelling of the triphthong is especially common when a consonant follows, e.g. *fiery* ˈ**faːri**, *society* sə**ˈsaːti**, *entirely* **inˈtaːli**, *violin* **vaːˈlin**, *higher up* ˈ**haːˈrʌp**, etc.

Similar remarks are applied to [auə] (p. 78):

> . . . the usual pronunciation being rather **aoə** or even **aɔə**. The levelling is often carried so far that the triphthong is simply reduced to a single long sound, namely a variety of **aː** tending towards **ɑː**. This retracted **aː** may be represented phonetically by **àː**.

Jones appears to have coined the term "levelling" in this passage. Wells (1982: 241) points out that this term is used in the *Pronunciation of English*⁴ ([1956]); it is perhaps worth noting that Jones first employed the word in this sense almost forty years earlier.

It is surprising that Jones does not note the occurrence of monophthongisation of [ɛə], either in the *Outline*¹, or in later revised editions. This is in contrast to Gimson (1962: 144) and other descriptions of present-day RP, e.g. Brown (1977: 36) and Windsor Lewis (1969: 21). Jones does concede in the revised third edition of the *Pronunciation of English* ([1950]: 63): "Occasionally one hears a monophthongal long ɛ (ʃɛː, bɛː, skɛːs, stɛːz)." See Ball (1984: 40–44) for the increasing frequency of monophthongal realisations of /ɛə/ in modern RP.⁸ One might conclude that [ɛː] is a recent phenomenon, but at the turn of the century, it was being treated as the norm in the context preceding /r/ by Soames (1899²: 48–49). Presumably, Jones chose to ignore it, perhaps feeling that it was unsuitable for teaching purposes, or believing that [ɛː] was not truly part of RP (or "standard English" in *Outline*¹ terms). (It is interesting that Wells (1982: 299) still doubts the acceptability within RP of monophthongal [ɛː] for /ɛə/ in final stressed syllables.) However, the replacement of [uə] by [ɔː] is noted by Jones, even though foreign learners are warned against it (*Outline*¹: 91):

> Thus it is by no means uncommon to hear *poor, sure* pronounced as **poə, ʃoe, pɔə**, **ʃɔə** or even **pɔː, ʃɔː**. There is no objection to the forms with **oə**, but the forms with **ɔə** and **ɔː** are not recommended for foreigners.

In later editions, Jones modified this advice (*Outline*⁸: 118):

> The forms with **uə** are generally taught as being the most "correct"…and on the whole they seem the best for foreign pupils to learn.

Jones goes on to mention that foreign learners should know of the existence of the reduced forms "since they are used by large numbers of people whose speech must be regarded as Received English."

Some features of the vowel description in the *Outline* can indeed be traced to the process of evolution of different speech habits. For instance, [ʌ] is treated as a back vowel (*Outline*¹: 84–85), whereas today it is more commonly heard with front/central vowel quality (see Gimson 1962: 111). But often one finds qualifying remarks which show that Jones also recognised a more up-to-date variant. With [ʌ], for example, in his advice to foreign learners Jones (*Outline*¹: 85) says: "If all efforts to obtain the precise sound ʌ fail, the best substitute is **a** ... , which bears a considerable resemblance to ʌ." Similarly, Jones is usually thought to have regarded [ou] as having a "half-close back" starting point, whereas today, following Gimson's (1962: 134–136) lead, the diphthong is written əʊ and is thought of as beginning unrounded mid-central. But Jones (pp. 86–87) qualifies his description: the vowel is "lax" and "slightly advanced" and points out that foreigners "fail to advance the tongue sufficiently", going as far as to recommend them to start with [ə].

Again, [æ] is described (pp. 75–76) as having a vowel quality which sounds surprisingly up-to-date: "front unrounded vowel, open but slightly raised" and the advice to the learner "in practising the sound the mouth should be kept very wide open" and "it is better to err on the side of **a** rather than on the side of ɛ". The description is more in keeping with the typically more open modern versions of /æ/ (see Wells 1982: 291–292) than is, for example, Gimson (1962: 108–109).

Jones occasionally exhibits somewhat snobbish sensitivity to pronunciations typical of London dialect, providing echoes of his proscriptive treatment of London English in the *Pronunciation of English*¹. For example, he says (pp. 87–88): "foreigners should avoid replacing **ou** by forms like ɔu, ɑu, au, ʌu all of which may be heard in London" and claims that "it is better to use the Continental **o:** than any of these forms", rationalising this by stating that **o:** is used in standard Scottish. And he says of [i:] (p. 69):

> It is not necessary for foreigners to use the diphthongic [sic] pronunciation. Any exaggeration of the diphthong sounds vulgar. (In Cockney an exaggerated form of diphthong, approaching **ei** or **əi**, is used; thus the word *sea*, which is pronounced in standard speech **si:** or **sij**, becomes in Cockney almost **sei** or **səi**.)⁹

In Chapter XIV, "Mixed Vowels", Jones includes within the section on [ə] a two-page table of strong and weak forms (pp. 96–97). Brief though it is, this is, remarkably, the most attention that Jones had given to the topic in his work up till then. The *Pronunciation of English*¹ has no specific section on weak forms, and the phenomenon is only mentioned cursorily in the *EPD*¹ (p. xix). Jones's treatment of the topic suffers from the fact that it is covered under [ə], and hence only weak forms containing [ə] figure in the table. This has the odd consequence that frequent words such as *be, been* are not covered; but, on the other hand, Jones includes unimportant weak forms of words such as *madam* [məm] and even *times* [təmz]. Later editions beginning with the *Outline*³ (pp. 115–126) devoted a separate section to strong and weak forms, and featured a far longer table and more explanation. Nevertheless, Jones retained most of the unimportant weak forms, and indeed added more.

There follow two brief chapters on "Nasalisation" and "Cacuminal Sounds".

"Nasalisation" (pp. 99–100) is in essence proscriptive (similar in tone to the section in the *Pronunciation of English*[1]: 48–49), and implies that the student should avoid the nasalisation of vowels preceding nasal consonants. Yet, in another section of the *Outline*[1] (p. 176), Jones produces evidence from kymographic recordings to show that:

> …vowels are to some extent nasalized when followed by nasal consonants in English, and that vowels (especially short vowels) may become completely nasalized when situated between two nasal consonants.

It is interesting to compare with the above the following paragraph in the *Outline*[3] (p. 198):

> It can be shown by experimental methods that slight nasalization of vowels occurs in English when nasal consonants follow. Such nasalization is, however, not sufficient to give to the vowels the characteristic nasal tamber. For the purposes of practical teaching it is therefore necessary to state definitely that vowels are not nasalized in English.

One may detect here one reason why Jones eventually became disenchanted with experimental phonetics (one of the indications of this being his decision to remove almost all the instrumental material from the revised editions of the *Outline*, but see also Section 8.2 above). The experimental evidence provided too many contradictions to the elaborate articulatory phonetic edifice which he had found so effective in his experience of teaching English as a foreign language. (See also Sections 7.6 and 8.8.)

The section on cacuminal sounds, Chapter XVI (pp. 100–101), is even more proscriptive in tone, describing the use of retroflex sounds (consonants and vowels) and stating that these do not exist in "standard English". The advice is particularly directed to Norwegians and Swedes, no mention being made of the difficulties of Indian speakers (see Section 8.4 for Jones's neglect of his non-European readership). Warning against "cacuminal modification" of vowels (i.e. retroflexion), Jones (*Outline*[1]: 101) states that this feature "may be observed in English dialectal speech. It is common in the North and South-West of England, and in America, but it is not recommended to foreigners."

Later revisions of the *Outline* are written in a far less hectoring tone. The change in Jones's approach to varieties other than RP is striking. The corresponding chapter in the *Outline*[3] (pp. 199–201) treats the sounds referred to above in this way (p. 200):

> The use of retroflexed vowels…is not confined to local dialects, but may be heard in the speech of many educated English people, and particularly of those who come from the South-West of England; retroflexed vowels are also a characteristic feature of Irish and American English.

The sections on vowels perhaps show the *Outline*[1] most clearly as the stage in

Jones's development between the *Pronunciation of English*[1] and the later revisions of the *Outline*. In the *Pronunciation of English*[1] we encounter the young Daniel Jones's somewhat sketchy, rather shallow, treatment; this is modified and expanded by the experienced phonetician in the *Outline*[1]; that version is, in its turn, revised and polished by Jones in the period of his maturity—not only in the extensive 1932 revision of the *Outline* but again, in minor refinements, in the years of his retirement.

8.6. Supra-segmental features

The subsequent portion of the *Outline*[1] deals chiefly with supra-segmental features, beginning with assimilation in Chapter XVII (pp. 101–104).

Jones's definition of assimilation (p. 101): "when a sound is influenced by another near it, it is said to undergo an *assimilation*" must be considered very lax. Indeed, the treatment of the topic here is much briefer and less rigorous than that found in later editions of the *Outline*. In the *Outline*[1], for example, we find no distinction made between historical and contextual assimilation (as in the *Outline*[8]: 218), both types being lumped together. This distinction is first encountered in the *Outline*[3] (p. 203), where the latter is, however, termed "juxtapositional assimilation".

Assimilations are of two kinds, historical and juxtapositional. By a "historical assimilation" we mean an assimilation which has taken place in the course of development of a language, and by which a word which was once pronounced in a certain way came to be pronounced subsequently in another way. By a "juxtapositional assimilation" we mean one which is occasioned when words are juxtaposed in a sentence or in the formation of compounds and by which a word comes to have a pronunciation different from that which it has when said by itself.

Neither does Jones in the *Outline*[1] utilise his later distinction of "assimilation" versus "similitude"—a categorisation which he also did not introduce until the *Outline*[3], where he defined (p. 202) assimilation as being the "process of replacing a sound by another sound under the influence of a third sound which is near to it in the word or sentence". Similitude was stated to be where "a particular sequence of two phonemes involves the use of a certain subsidiary member of one of them which has a greater resemblance to the neighbouring sound than the principal member has" (*Outline*[3]: 202). Since the definition of similitude is dependent on the phoneme concept (similitude can only "be used in reference to subsidiary members of phonemes"), it is not surprising that no hint of it is to be found in the *Outline*[1], which did not recognise the phoneme.

Furthermore, Jones does not mention directionality of the assimilation process; his distinction of progressive/regressive assimilation also appears for the first time in the revised third edition (*Outline*[3]: 212). However, in the *Outline*[1], Jones does distinguish voicing assimilation as against place assimilation (p. 101) and the occurrence of co-

547. The differences of length caused in this way may be made very evident by representing the rhythm by means of musical notes. Thus if we take a quaver ♪ to represent the length of time between two consecutive stresses in *eight, nine, ten* the first two of the above groups will appear thus:

́eiti: n´nainti: n´twenti   ́eit´nain´ten

548. It is clear from this that the diphthongs **ei, ai** are something like twice as long in the second group as they are in the first. In like manner the other two groups appear thus:

ðɛəz´noubədi´ðɛə   ðɛəz´nou´taim

Figure 8.16. Extract on rhythm from *Outline*[1] (p. 106)

alescent assimilations (p. 103). Chapter VII includes examples of assimilations found in colloquial speech, confirming Jones's obvious interest in such speech forms, e.g. [aiʃtf´θɔːtsou] *I should have thought so* (p. 102). A striking omission is that no mention is made of elision; a chapter covering this topic was introduced only in the *Outline*[3] (p. 214).

The treatment of assimilation and elision in the *Outline*[1] is somewhat shallow, since so many distinctions are skated over or ignored; it is therefore not surprising that this is a section which underwent considerable change in the *Outline*[3]. Jones's later revisions show much more awareness of the analytical difficulties in dealing with this topic. Yet, nevertheless, even in the *Outline*[3], much of his classification is defined with unnecessary complexity, and his writing here, unusually for him, is over-involved and convoluted. The similitude/assimilation distinction, as Jones defines it, marks an important dichotomy, but does not come completely to grips with the essential distinction, namely that some assimilation sound changes are merely allophonic, whilst others are more radical inasmuch as a sound is shifted, through phonetic conditioning, from one phonemic category to another.

However, the most striking contribution here is, in fact, Jones's excellent observation of many features of colloquial English. This comes to the fore in the *Outline*[3], and it would appear that his abilities in this area actually improved with maturity. Jones notes for the first time many phenomena—albeit referring to them (p. 211) as occurring in "careless speech"—which are normally thought of as being innovations of the late twentieth century. Much of which is to be found in later works (e.g. Gimson 1962: 271–275) is either directly borrowed, or at least has its origins, in Jones's perceptive comments made three or four decades earlier.

In the chapters which follow, "Length" (Chapter XVIII) and "Stress" (Chapter

XIX), Jones builds upon the much briefer treatment which he had already produced for the *Pronunciation of English*[1]. The influence of Sweet is particularly noticeable in these sections.

Chapter XVIII (pp. 104–110) covers the topic of duration under the title "Length". Jones accepts that several degrees of length, "say five or six", are distinguishable, but believes that two degrees (long vs. short), plus the occasional use of an intermediate degree ("half-long"), are all that are required "for practical purposes". The treatment is strikingly reminiscent of Sweet (1877: 59, and 1890a: 43). Jones goes on to provide a number of rules, largely refined from material that had already been included in the *Pronunciation of English*[1]: 52–54), in order to determine vowel length. He distinguishes the vowels (/iː ɑː ɔː uː əː/), which together with the diphthongs may be regarded as "long", but then points out that these are subject to a number of conditioning processes which affect their length; such processes also affect the "short" vowels but these are "not sufficiently great to be of practical importance". Once again, one sees here that Jones is essentially concerned with practicalities in his *Outline*[1] treatment and is determined to highlight the features which are most salient for the foreign learner. The length rules include shortening before (1) a "breathed" consonant; (2) before another vowel; (3) in unstressed (as opposed to stressed) syllables (pp. 104–105).

In addition, he mentions that short vowels— in particular [æ]—may undergo lengthening, a phenomenon which is also recorded through entries in the *EPD*[1] (see Section 7.2). He points out that [æ] may suffer optional lengthening before [d] in certain adjectives, e.g. *bad, sad*, and before other voiced consonants in a number of nouns, e.g. *man, bag, jam*. Jones appears to have been the first to have noted this phenomenon, but it is also observed and discussed by, amongst others, Gimson (1962: 109) and Wells (1982: 130); see also Fudge (1977: 207–210). The lengthening of [e], in words like *bed, dead, yes*, which is also observed by Jones, does not appear to have received notice elsewhere (p. 106). In the *Outline*[3], Jones gives further examples and notes that in his view the tendency to lengthen "short" vowels appears to be on the increase, citing its prevalence in London dialect and also in American English.

In a short section entitled "Effect of Rhythm on Length", Jones mentions the important principle of the apparent isochrony of intervals between stressed syllables in English (p. 106):

> There is a strong tendency in connected speech to make stressed syllables follow each other as far as possible at equal distances. The result is that when a syllable containing a long vowel or a diphthong is followed by unstressed syllables, that vowel or diphthong is shorter than if the syllable were final or followed by a stressed syllable.

Jones goes on to give examples, using systems of musical notation, e.g. the extract given in Figure 8.16. He points out the variation in the length of the vowels in monosyllables as opposed to disyllables in the case of counting, and the differing lengths of [ou] in the second example; he also refers to the musical notation indicated throughout Chapter XXI (misprinted in the text as Chapter XX).

In the *Outline*¹, Jones successfully provides, for its time, a most succinct summary of the chief features of English rhythm (inasmuch as these can be appreciated using non-instrumental procedures). Abercrombie (1967: 171, n.7), whose ideas on isochrony were particularly influential in the fifties and sixties, stated that "many writers since the eighteenth century have pointed out that in English stressed syllables tend to be isochronous". Nevertheless, it is Jones's (considerably expanded) section in the *Outline*³ (pp. 220–226) that Abercrombie took as his starting point for the seminal article "Syllable quantity and enclitics in English" (Abercrombie 1964: 216). The principles of isochrony and stress-timing, for which excessive claims were made by Abercrombie's followers in the 1960s and 1970s, see Gimson—Cruttenden (1994: 227), are no longer held to be true in a literal sense, having been disproved by numerous instrumental investigations from O'Connor (1965) onwards. However, Jones's comments in the *Outline*³ and later editions are on the whole valid, and it is noteworthy that he explicitly states (*Outline*⁸: 242–243) that the topic is not capable of forming the basis of any generalised theory.

Jones adds a section on consonant length (*Outline*¹: 107) and a section on foreigners' errors (pp. 108–109). Here again he shows considerable indebtedness to Sweet (1908: 49–50) in his treatment of Germans' errors (discussing one of Sweet's examples, the incorrect length of the vowel in Germans' pronunciation of "all right", and adding information on the intonational difference, p. 108 n.). Jones indicates by his statement that "French persons usually fail to reproduce correctly the English rhythm" his awareness of the differences between English and French speech rhythm, and provides some typical examples of French errors made with repeated ♪♪♪-type rhythm. Disappointingly, he fails to take his analysis any further than this, and the *Outline*³ (p. 226) only adds that Japanese speakers have "the greatest difficulty of all".

Jones closes this chapter with a "general note on the representation of length in phonetic transcription" in which he summarises the inadequacy of length marking in transcription (*Outline*¹, p. 109):

> ...the custom of regarding certain vowels as long and certain others as short is, to say the least of it, unsatisfactory. The length of the long vowels is very variable, and depends on a variety of circumstances; the so-called "short" vowels on the other hand are sometimes quite long, and no definite rules can be laid down for the use of the long forms.

Jones states that the main motivation for his choice of a transcription with length marks is that of "uniformity of method and transcription...for encouraging the spread of phonetics...even at the sacrifice of scientific accuracy". He concludes (p. 110):

> Though adhering in this book to the conventional distinction between long and

short vowels…the author desires to call the attention of phoneticians to the unsatisfactory nature of the current system of transcription in view of the actual facts in regard to the length of English sounds. It is much to be desired that all writers on English phonetics should come to an agreement to adopt a system of transcription for English independent of length-marks.

The above quotation, and indeed the whole of this section, must be taken as further evidence for Jones's doubts about the efficacy of the transcription system with which his name is today associated (see Section 8.2 above). In the *Outline*[3], by which time his views on length marks had completely changed, this section was removed.

In Chapter XIX (pp. 110–135), Jones deals with the topic of stress. As with other sections of the *Outline*[1], it is possible to trace a sketched-out basis in the *Pronunciation of English*[1] (pp. 57–58); in this case, there has been considerable expansion into a long chapter with much exemplification.

The treatment in the *Outline*[1] is interesting because it is apparent that Jones was now at a crux in his whole view of stress, which had altered radically under the influence of his colleague, Coleman. Yet this change came about too late for it to be included in the *Outline*[1], which had been completed in advance of Coleman (1914). Jones's position is indicated in the preface to the *Outline*[1] (p. v):

It has for practical reasons been found convenient to treat stress in the conventional manner in this book. It is undoubtedly a fact, however, that much of the effect commonly described as stress is in reality a matter of intonation. It has been well observed by Coleman [1914]…that stress is generally accompanied by a change in the direction of intonation, and that this change in the direction of intonation is of greater importance than any increase in the force of the breath.

Jones emphasises that intonational direction change is enough to "produce on the ear the effect commonly described as stress" without any increase in force, and hopes that experimental approaches can provide information to prove this effect, but he concludes that since the relationship between stress and intonation had not yet been fully investigated "there is nothing for it but to treat stress in the conventional manner" (p. v).

Following his earlier book (*Pronunciation of English*[1]: p. 57), Jones recognises five degrees of stress, illustrating this categorisation with the word *opportunity* (*Outline*[1], p. 111).

ɔpətjuːniti

The system appears to be ultimately derived from Sweet, who in his *Handbook* (1877: 92) shows the word *impenetrability* with no fewer than seven degrees of stress. Jones states of his own five-degree system (p. 111): "such accuracy is not necessary for practical purposes; it is generally sufficient to distinguish two degrees only, *stressed* and *unstressed*" (cf. *Pronunciation of English*[1], p. 57, with very similar wording). The

Outline[1] marking system is a slight elaboration of that found in the *Pronunciation of English*[1]. Stress is indicated as in *Pronunciation of English*[1] by an acute accent preceding the stressed syllable. In the *Outline*[1] (p. 111), Jones adds the extra refinement of marking secondary stress with a lowered grave accent preceding the stressed syllables, giving the example *examination* [ig‚zæm'ineiʃn]. In the *Outline*[3] (pp. 228–229) Jones's treatment is similar except that the acute and grave are replaced by raised and lowered verticals, respectively.

Jones proceeds to a long and involved series of "rules of stress", covering simple and compound words, and distinguishing single and double stressing. The treatment is, in the main, morphologically based and Jones deliberately excludes historical considerations because, as he says disarmingly, "most of those who wish to learn English are not philologists" (p. 111 n). Jones starts out with this caveat (p. 111):

> The rules regarding the position of the stress in English words of more than one syllable are very complicated, and most of those which can be formulated at all are subject to numerous exceptions. Many students find the best way of learning the stress of English words is simply to learn the stress of each individual word as they come across it; others prefer to study the rules.

In an appendix (pp. 184–186) Jones provides "lists of words stressed according to rules, in cases where the exceptions are numerous".

Jones (p. 123) takes account of the effect of rhythm on double stress producing stress shift (e.g. 'Princess Vic'toria vs. a 'royal prin'cess). He also has a short section covering the errors of foreigners—predictably only of French and German learners.

In total, Jones's rules for word stress cover no less than sixteen closely printed pages, with nineteen systematic rules for simple word stress alone; the whole is crammed with examples and counter-examples. A further six pages (pp. 128–135) are devoted to rules for sentence stress. Yet, in the revised *Outline*[3], Jones radically rewrote the whole of the chapter on stress and in so doing threw out his whole edifice of rules for predicting word stress (with the exception of double stress, for which he retained a selection of rules). He restated his position thus (*Outline*[3]: 229):

> English word-stress cannot be learnt by means of rules. In most cases there is no rule as to the incidence of the stress, and when rules can be formulated at all, they are generally subject to numerous exceptions. It is therefore necessary for the foreign student to learn the stress of every word individually.

It is unfortunate that Jones—presumably out of the frustration arising from the numerous exceptions to his rule schemes in the *Outline*[1]—decided to abandon a systematised approach to this aspect of stress; if only because his enterprise in this area is today largely unknown. Although it came out no fewer than forty years later, Kingdon's (1958b) *Groundwork of English stress* seems generally to be regarded as the pioneering work in the field. Few scholars appear to have considered it necessary to track down Jones's early editions, and consequently take Kingdon's (1958b: xii) comment at face value: "The field of English stress is practically virgin soil, it having been generally held it follows no rules." For example, Chomsky and Halle (1968) and Halle—Keyser (1971) list only the *Outline*[8], whilst Fudge (1984) does not mention Jones at all.

Chapter XX (p. 135), entitled "Breath-groups", is a mere sixteen lines in length. As in the *Pronunciation of English*[1] (p. 58), Jones defines breath-groups as "groups of sounds which are pronounced without pause", adding (p. 59) that "pauses for breath should always be made at points where pauses are necessary or permissible from the point of view of meaning…. The proper divisions between breath-groups are generally made clear in writing by the punctuation marks." The *Outline*[1], like the *Pronunciation of English*[1], makes no attempt to relate a definition of the breath-group implicitly to intonation; nor do later editions of the *Outline*. Jones suggests a marking system of ‖ to indicate obligatory breath-group pauses, and | to show optional pauses; but claims that "a more accurate method is not to leave any spaces between consecutive words in a breath-group" (p. 135). It is this latter system that Jones employs in his transcribed examples throughout the *Outline*[1]. In subsequent editions, from the *Outline*[3] onwards, he recognised the disadvantages of this method, both because it produces unwieldy chunks of transcription and because it runs counter to his ideas on the phonetic significance of the word (Jones 1931k). The *Outline*[3] (p. 254) also introduces the concept of "sense-groups", which are defined as "the shortest possible … groups … which are not capable of being further subdivided by pauses"; he recommends | as a marker of sense-group and ‖ for breath-group boundaries.

As early as in the first edition of the *Outline*, it can be seen that Jones has here laid down an important foundation for handling the segmentation of discourse intonation on which much subsequent work has been based. To give but two examples, it is obvious that Halliday's (1963) concept of "tonality" derives in part from the Jonesian "sense group"; O'Connor and Arnold's (1961) "word group" also has its roots in Jones's work.

8.7. Intonation

Chapter XXI (pp. 135–168), "Intonation", is of special interest inasmuch as it provides what is certainly the most developed statement of Jones's independent thought on this subject. This is because in the revised post-1932 editions of the *Outline* Jones chose to present a markedly different view of intonation largely based on the published work of his colleagues Armstrong—Ward (1926).

Here, as with many other sections of the work, it is clear that the *Pronunciation of English*[1] (pp. 59–64; see also Section 3.4) provided the basis from which the *Outline* treatment was developed. In this instance, the *Pronunciation of English* section seems quite skeletal in comparison with the *Outline* (only five pages as against over thirty) and can really only be considered a springboard for the much more elaborate description which appears in the later book. Indeed, no discussion of English intonation published up to this time—if one discounts Jones's own *Intonation curves* and Coleman (1914)—had covered the subject with anything approaching the detail, or provided the wealth of exemplification, found here. The limitations of *Intonation curves* have already been discussed in Section 3.3. Jones mentions in the preface (*Outline*[1]: p. iv) that he had not had the chance to consult Coleman's work before the *Outline* was complete, and this is borne out by the obvious lack of similarity in their approaches.

The chapter on intonation in this book was unfortunately in print before the

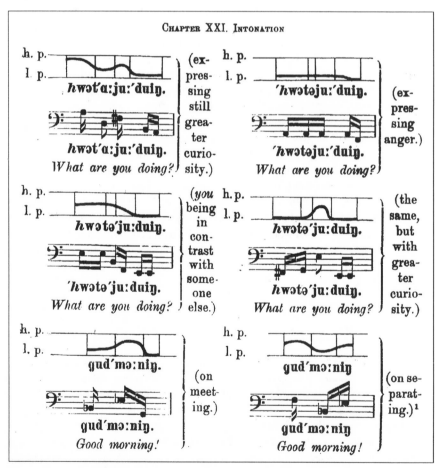

Figure 8.17. Examples of Jones's interlinear intonation curves and musical notation (*Outline*[1], p. 138).

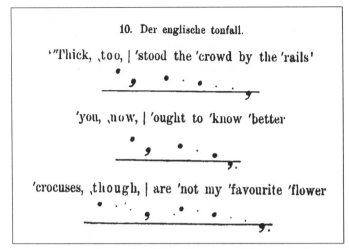

Figure 8.18.   Klinghardt—Klemm's (1920: 66) intonation marking.

appearance of the excellent article on the subject by Coleman; his discoveries have suggested to me various ways in which this chapter might be improved.

In fact, the only noteworthy study of English intonation prior to this date was the short (though perceptive) passage in Sweet (1877: 93–97), the content of which is largely repeated in his subsequent work (e.g. Sweet 1890a: 64–67; 1908: 13, 52–53). However, despite its interesting ideas, this was extremely compressed and simplified, and lacked sufficient marked examples (only to be found to any extent in Sweet's 1885a [1904³]: 43–45 *Elementarbuch*). So whilst Sweet's contribution is not to be undervalued, it should nevertheless be recognised that here Jones was largely breaking new ground and it is in the light of its pioneering approach that the "Intonation" chapter of the *Outline*[1] should be judged.

After an introductory section providing a simple definition ("variations in the pitch of the voice, i.e. the variations in the pitch of the musical note produced by vibration of the vocal chords", p. 135), Jones goes on to deal with marking systems. He favours a system of interlinear curves similar to that used in the *Pronunciation of English*[1] but with the addition of vertical bar lines to indicate syllable boundaries (Figure 8.17). Jones supplements this with musical notation which is used concurrently throughout the chapter. It is probable that what appears today to be a peculiarly involved approach was in the context of the times perfectly sensible. The intonation curves are obviously drawn by hand—something which was possibly time-consuming but in an era of cheap German labour not prohibitively expensive. The musical notation graphics would have been a resource available to virtually every publishing house of the period.

It is noteworthy that in the *Outline*[3], and for subsequent editions, Jones abandoned

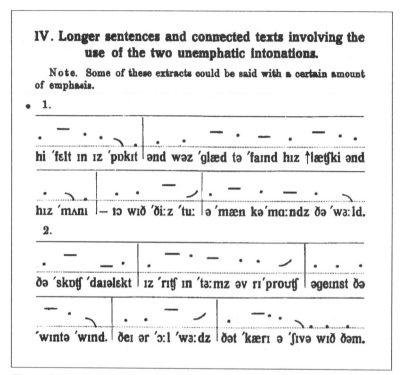

Figure 8.19. Armstrong and Ward's (1926: 36) intonation marking.

both the curved lines and the musical notation in favour of a slight modification of Armstrong and Ward's (1926) interlinear dot and dash system (Figures 8.19 and 8.20); the latter itself finds its origins in the work of Klinghardt—Klemm (1920); see Figure 8.18.

Crystal (1969: 35) is not accurate in his comment that "Daniel Jones continued to use a musical notation in his *Intonation curves* (1909a) with a syllable for every bar— a notation which he retained for the first two editions of the *Outline of English phonetics*." *Intonation curves* had a curve employing a musical stave (see Section 3.3) whilst the *Outline*[1] uses an interlinear curve supplemented by parallel musical notation approximating the pitches of an average male voice (p. 137). Jones was aware of the disadvantage of musical notation, namely that the "notes merely show the salient points of the true intonation" (p. 137, n.); but presumably considered that the familiarity of this system to his readers, at a time when probably most educated people would have been able to read music, was a great asset in presentation. A notable lack in the scheme, however, is that no indication is made of stress in the "intonation curve", even though this is shown in the adjacent phonetic transcription.

Jones's *Outline*[3] system differs from Armstrong and Ward's only in one minor detail; an extra horizontal is inserted between the top and bottom lines to aid clarity.

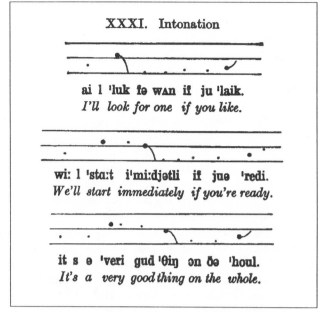

Figure 8.20. Jones's intonation marking (*Outline*[8], p. 296).

Armstrong and Ward's system had two obvious advantages over *Outline*[1] musical notation. It was easier than drawing a long continuous line and, furthermore, it enabled the stress to be indicated by means of a convention whereby stressed syllables were shown by a line and unstressed syllables were indicated by dots. See Section 14.12 for influence of Jones on Armstrong and Ward.

Jones then proceeds to formulate his description of English intonation as a set of rules, each rule being modified by a list of significant exceptions. These rules are stated in terms of complete intonation patterns—thus Jones adopts an essentially holistic rather than analytical approach to intonation. Each rule is stated in terms of containing either a terminal rise or fall, thus providing a clear antecedent to Armstrong and Ward's (1926: 4, 20, *et passim*) Tune 1 and Tune 2. Jones's rules are drawn up primarily in terms of grammatical categories, though, as will be seen, some attention is given to attitude variation and to considerations of discourse.

The first two of Jones's rules (pp. 144–145) specify terminally falling intonation patterns as being typical of statements and imperatives. He notes the following exceptions: statements "equivalent to questions", or which "suggest a continuation or rejoinder", "doubt" or "regret on the part of the speaker", and "reservation". Terminal rises are also attributed to statements which involve "antithesis", and where there is reference back to the person addressed, or to material previously mentioned. This last exception is also applied to imperatives; and in addition, imperatives which can be interpreted as "a request or entreaty" are stated to have terminal rise (pp. 144–145).

Rule III (pp. 145–148) in Jones's scheme covers "direct questions capable of being answered by 'yes' or 'no'". These are regarded as generally bearing a terminal rise with several exceptions. The exceptions include "antithesis (expressed or implied)", "invitations", under which Jones subsumes types of tag-questions with falling intonation, stating that these constitute "an invitation to assent"; and cases where a question is "equivalent to a statement" (pp. 145–148).

Jones's Rule IV regards a terminal fall as being typical of questions "not capable of being answered by 'yes' or 'no'", and mentions "requests for repetition" as constituting an exception. Series of "alternative questions" are said to carry terminal rises, with a fall on the final question in the set (pp. 148–150).

Interjections and exclamatory phrases are specified as taking the intonation of the complete sentences to which they are equivalent (Rule V). He notes the effect of intonation on "thank you", which typically has a rise, but if said with a fall indicates "acknowledging an unexpected favour" (p. 152).

Rule VI (pp. 153–154) discusses "expressions of a parenthetical nature", which have low level intonation in non-final position, but which vary in final position following the pattern of the sentence which precedes them. These would largely be covered by tails and parenthetical groups in more familiar terminology (O'Connor—Arnold [1973]: 287; Cruttenden 1986: 78). Rules VII and VIII deal with the intonation of initial dependent clauses, which are claimed by Jones to take an intonation opposed to that of the main clause they precede (pp. 154–155).

Jones's Rule IX (pp. 155–158) considers a number of disparate matters. He deals firstly with dependent clauses following a main clause, which he claims take the pattern which the main clause would bear if standing alone. Final clauses expressing reservation are noted as taking rises. These must be interpreted as a compound tune of a fall plus rise type (O'Connor—Arnold [1973]: 28–29). Jones remarks on the intonation typical of lists (p. 158): "in enumerations of things a rising intonation is used for each item except the last".

He goes on to discuss the "compound rising" intonation, a term borrowed from Sweet (1877: 94), by which he means a fall-rise. Jones notes the frequency in English of this pattern, and claims that it is used in terminal rises "when the final word is emphasised for contrast". Though he does not use the idea of contradiction, or reservation, his examples show that this is really what he intends, e.g. " 'That is what he said' implying 'though I don't know if that is what he meant'." Within this section, Jones also considers the phonetic realisation of fall-rise patterns, stating, for example, that in monosyllables the rise can take place over a single lateral or nasal consonant; during the "stop" (i.e. hold stage) of a voiced stop; or in the middle of a vowel. In other cases, the "compound rising intonation" may be spread over two or more syllables (pp. 158–159). Jones does not mention Sweet's other compound pattern, the "compound falling", i.e. rise-fall, presumably because of its relative rarity, though later editions of the *Outline* treat rise-falls under "Emphasis for Intensity" (*Outline*[3]: 288–290).

The last of Jones's rules, Rule X, (pp. 161–162) also deals with the phonetic characteristics of intonation contours. Jones states that in falling intonation patterns "the first important stressed syllable has the highest tone and the other syllables form a descending series of notes". Here, Jones shows that he has grasped the idea of a falling head together with the concept of an "onset" (Crystal 1969: 143, 229–230).

In the revised *Outline*³, as mentioned above, Jones changed the whole of this chapter, reorganising his ten rules along the lines of Armstrong and Ward's (1926) "Tune 1" (falling) and "Tune 2" (rising). In the process, his material presumably gained in terms of appeal to the average student, but, regrettably, numerous interesting observations were eliminated along with the undesirable vagueness and ambiguities of the *Outline*¹ treatment. In fact, Jones's *Outline*³ presentation is on the whole far more direct and clear than the explanation to be found in Armstrong and Ward's own book. See Cruttenden (1981: 37–41) for a critique of the Armstrong and Ward whole tune approach. Nevertheless, it may be considered unfortunate that Jones chose to retain their holistic view of intonation patterns rather than to adopt the more advanced analytical framework of Palmer (1922), who based his approach around the concept of the nucleus. This work, together with Coleman (1914)—whose contribution Jones did take into account, in a limited way—would probably have provided a far more fruitful basis for intonation description. Since the section appears almost completely unaltered in all subsequent editions, we may infer that Jones personally felt well satisfied with his presentation of intonation in the *Outline*³. See Section 14.12 for Jones's overall contribution to intonation theory.

A section on error analysis follows (pp. 162–167), which, typically for the *Outline*¹, relates to the intonation problems of Europeans exclusively, no other nationalities being considered. In fact, Jones restricts himself to the problems of French and German learners, with a solitary mention of Swedes (p. 167). Later editions do nothing to correct this imbalance.

The chapter is rounded off by a brief consideration of "methods of recording intonation" (pp. 167–168). Jones characteristically recommends a simple auditory approach, revealing that all the musical notation and curves in the chapter "have been obtained entirely by ear" (p. 167). He also describes his use of the gramophone (as in *Phonetic transcriptions of English prose* and *Intonation curves*, see Sections 2.7 and 3.3) and refers his readers to the instrumental methods involving the kymograph, which he deals with in the final chapter; see Section 8.8.

8.8. The kymograph

Chapter XXII (pp. 168–182), the final chapter of the *Outline*¹, is concerned entirely with the description of the kymograph, and an exposition of its use in contemporary experimental phonetics. Although Jones had described simple forms of apparatus earlier in the book (see Section 8.2), he must have believed the kymograph to hold a special place in phonetic science by virtue of the amount of valuable information which it was capable of yielding to the phonetic researcher. Hence he decided to devote a whole chapter of a non-specialist book to a single item of instrumentation.

The preface to the *Outline*[1] (p. iv) indicates the conflict that Jones felt in including this and the other earlier material on experimental phonetics:

> For the benefit of those who are accustomed to instrumental methods or who wish to study these methods, a certain amount of information regarding experimental phonetics has been included.... Experimental phonetics is a highly interesting study in itself, but it must not be regarded as an *indispensable* study for those who wish to learn to pronounce a foreign language correctly.

In fact, Jones merely regards experiments as being useful for "students who have by nature a special difficulty in hearing the differences between similar sounds" (p. iv) and goes on to say:

> In most cases, however, the experiments should be regarded merely as corroborative of the results obtainable by the ordinary methods of practical phonetics—that is, by direct observations made by a trained ear—and as a means of helping to fix them in the student's memory. Experiments which go further than this can hardly be considered as of practical value to language students.

It was by this let-out (and indicating with asterisks the portions of the *Outline* dealing with experimental material which could be "entirely omitted" by those with no interest in experimental phonetics) that Jones managed to include the chapter on the kymograph in a book intended primarily as an aid to learners of English as a foreign language. It may be that these statements in the preface, and the similar passage on p. 7, were late insertions made after his early enthusiasm for instrumental work was cooling down.

The kymograph was developed as a tool for the phonetician largely through the work of Marey and Rousselot (see Section A.5). The *Outline*[3] (pp. 168–171) describes the apparatus in some detail. It consisted of a "Marey tambour", a drum-like device capable of registering small movements, linked to a continuously revolving drum covered with a layer of smoked paper. By means of an "embouchure" (i.e. a mask placed over the mouth) and a nasal olive inserted in the nostril, the device was then capable of registering details of articulation and phonation such as changes in nasal and oral airflow. A "larynx recorder", in the form of a rubber membrane attached to a pressure pad which could be pressed firmly against the exterior of the larynx, was used to pick up vocal fold vibrations. "Exploratory bulbs" (i.e. hollow rubber bulb-like attachments) were used in order to detect (to some degree) changes in the height of the tongue and the pressure in the buccal cavity. As Hardcastle (1981: 52) has pointed out:

> These basic recording techniques were quite accurate but had, of course, relatively slow response times due mainly to the inherent characteristics of the materials used. However, one could study many aspects of the dynamics of speech using these techniques, such as the timing of voice onset associated with plosives, the

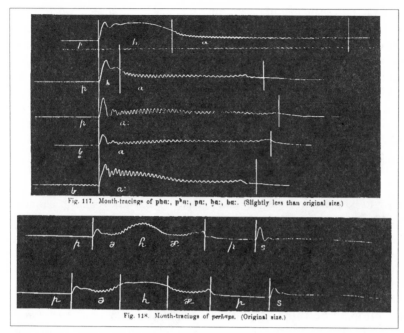

Fig. 117. Mouth-tracings of pɑː, pʰɑː, pɑː, bɑː, bɑː. (Slightly less than original size.)

Fig. 118. Mouth-tracings of perhaps. (Original size.)

Figure 8.21. Diagrams to illustrate aspiration (*Outline*[1], p. 172).

degree and timing of nasalisation, the manner of articulation (e.g. stop versus fricative), relative duration and extent of voicing etc.

For further description and critique of the early techniques of kymography, see Rousselot ([1924[2]]: 47–109, *et passim*), Hardcastle (1981) and Panconcelli-Calzia (1957).

It is most likely that Jones was engaged on writing this chapter in the years 1913–14, around the period when he would have been supervising the establishment of the new Phonetics Laboratory at University College (see Section 5.10), and he would recently, for the first time, have gained access to relatively elaborate instrumentation. It is certain that the final version was written after the establishment of the UCL lab, since Jones states (p. 170) that the accompanying illustrations "were made on the large kymograph in the Phonetics Laboratory at University College London", adding proudly: "It is driven by an electric motor." It was at this point, when he was also greatly impressed by his visit to the 1914 Hamburg Conference (see Section 5.10) that Jones's fascination with experimental phonetics was at its height, though he maintained a strong interest in instrumental work up until the years immediately after the war (see below).

Jones's explanation of the use of the kymograph is typically lucid and thorough, and would have provided the English-speaking phonetics student of this era with the best summary of the capabilities of the instrument available. However, it would appear to be derived at least in part from Rousselot and Laclotte's (1902) *Précis de prononciation française*. This little elementary treatise on French, as has been indicated in Sections 8.2 and 8.4, seems to have had a considerable influence on the experimental sections of the *Outline*, and this is seen obviously here. Rousselot and Laclotte include a clearly written short summary of the kymograph, and kymographic techniques, together with numerous kymograms illustrating various phonetic phenomena in French. Several of the illustrations in the *Outline*[1] seem to parallel those in the French work, even though the engravings in the *Outline* are far more elaborate and realistic than the simple line sketches of the French researchers (cf. *Outline*[1]: 170–171, and Rousselot—Laclotte 1902: 16). The photograph of Jones himself, seated at a "small portable kymograph" (*Outline*[1]: 169), is obviously similar to the simple line drawing to be found in Rousselot and Laclotte (1902: 14). As has been indicated above (Section 8.2), it could well be that it was to remove any suggestion of plagiarism that Jones, for the *Outline*[3] and subsequent editions, expunged most of the experimental portions, including the chapter on the kymograph *in toto*. Whatever his dependence on original sources, Jones appears in his treatment of the kymograph to be completely in command of his subject.

With the exception of the articles directly relating to experimental phonetic topics (Jones 1917b, 1917e, 1918b, 1919c; see Section 7.6), this is the nearest that Jones ever came to a hard scientific approach to phonetics. Whilst it lacks the sophistication of Rousselot or Scripture, the content is entirely appropriate for non-scientific students, and it would have been these that Jones had primarily to consider when writing the *Outline*. It is sometimes forgotten in estimates of Jones's scientific abilities that he had completed a mathematics degree at Cambridge, and obviously his university training

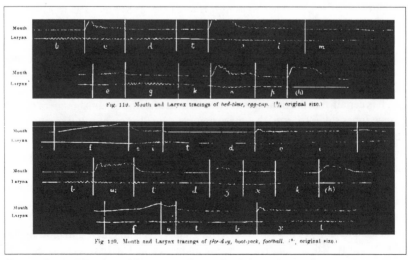

Figure 8.22. Mouth and larynx tracings of voicing (*Outline*[1], p. 173).

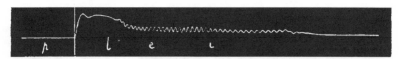

Fig. 122. Mouth-tracing of *play*, p.onounc.d by the author. (³/₄ original size.)

graphically. Fig. 122 is a mouth-tracing of the word *play* **plei** pronounced by the author; it will be seen that the voice-vibrations do not begin until quite an appreciable time after the explosion. Fig. 123

Fig. 123. Mouth and Larynx tracings of *play*, pronounced by a Flemish-speaking Belgian. (³/₄ original size.)

shows simultaneous mouth and larynx tracings of the same word pronounced by a Flemish-speaking Belgian whose pronunciation had not been corrected; here the voice vibrations begin at the instant of the explosion. The l in this Belgian's pronunciation produced on the ear the effect of being syllabic, and the complete voicing of the l caused the preceding **p** to sound somewhat like a **b** (to English ears).

Figure 8.23. Mouth and larynx tracings of *play* as pronounced by Jones and by a Flemish-speaking Belgian (*Outline¹*, p. 174).

would enable him to cope easily with the elementary physics involved with speech research at this period. Furthermore, Jones manages to adopt a style which is most suitable for a presentation of such material to students with little scientific background. As always, Jones here displays the virtue of writing to inform, rather than to impress, his audience.

After an explanation of the construction of the kymograph, and the principles on which it operates, Jones goes on to demonstrate a number of applications of the instrument, beginning with the detection of voicing and aspiration. Jones demonstrates the delay in voice onset in aspirated [p] (Figure 8.21), and the extent of voicing in voiced-voiceless and voiceless-voiced stop sequences (Figure 8.22). Using kymograms, Jones is also able to show the devoicing of [l] in initial clusters such as [pl] in *play*; at the same time, he is able to bring over a contrastive point, namely that this does not occur in the English of certain foreign learners, as in the case of a Belgian Flemish speaker (Figure 8.23).

Referring to his treatment of the affricates [tʃ dʒ] as sequences of sounds rather than units (see *Outline¹*: 38–39), Jones then provides (pp. 175–176) kymographic evidence in support of the alternative possibility of considering them as single speech sounds:

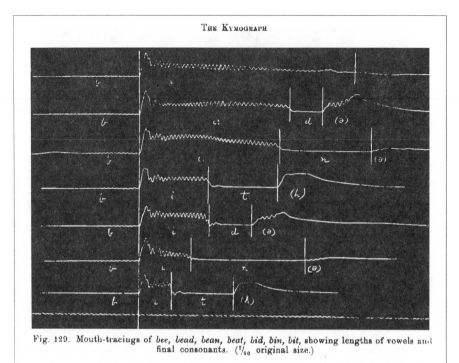

THE KYMOGRAPH

Fig. 129. Mouth-tracings of *bee, bead, bean, beat, bid, bin, bit,* showing lengths of vowels and final consonants. (⁷/₁₀ original size.)

Figure 8.24. Mouth tracings of *bee, bead, bean, beat, bid, bin, bit,* showing vowel and consonant duration (*Outline*[1], p. 179).

It will be seen that the tracings of English **tʃ** and **dʒ** are quite distinct from those of **t, d**, but approach very closely to those of **tɹ, dɹ** and **ts, dz**. This fact lends support to the view...that if **tʃ** is to be considered as a single sound then several other groups now generally regarded as double must likewise be considered as single sounds.

This is in fact the way in which Jones treated the affricates of English in later editions of the *Outline* (e.g. *Outline*[8]: 47, 158–167) and it is probable that in so doing he was influenced by his kymographic research.

Kymograms are also used to depict (pp. 176–179) the relatively slight nasalisation of vowels following nasals, and the complete nasalisation of vowels between nasal consonants. Differences in vowel and consonant duration are also demonstrated with kymograms, which illustrate particularly the shortening of vowels before (voiceless) /t/.

The tracings in Figure 8.24 are interesting in that Jones appears to have omitted the length mark in *bee, beat,* and also in that the obvious voicing off-glide following [d] probably indicates an over-careful articulation in the production of the kymograms.

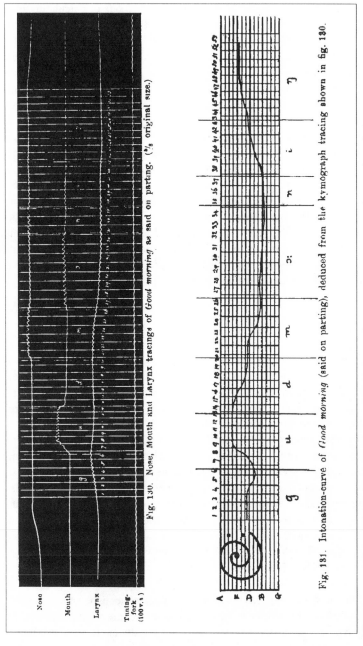

Fig. 130. Nose, Mouth and Larynx tracings of *Good morning* as said on parting. (²/₃ original size.)

Fig. 181. Intonation-curve of *Good morning* (said on parting), deduced from the kymograph tracing shown in fig. 130.

Figure 8.25. Tracings illustrating the derivation of "intonation curves" (*Outline*¹, pp. 180–181)

Jones completes the chapter by explaining the methods of calculating intonation patterns from kymograms by means of comparing these with the known frequency of vibration of a tuning fork. From kymograms, Jones thereby demonstrates that it is possible to produce relatively accurate "intonation curves" using specially prepared music paper, as is shown in Figure 8.25.

In this section, Jones shows clearly how valuable the kymograph was to early phoneticians and how ingenious Jones and his colleagues were in their exploitation of its resources, notwithstanding its obvious limitations. The criticisms that can be directed against the instrument—apart from the clumsy mechanics of its operation, and the slow response times involved—were that the utterances produced were probably far removed from natural speech, since the subjects had to submit to the mouth being covered with a mask and nasal olives inserted in the nostrils. However, such criticism can be directed at many experimental procedures in operation today.

Jones certainly does not appear to have contributed any innovations to kymographic techniques. However, this part of the *Outline*[1] did serve to present a view of phonetics as being in part a discipline based on hard data and relatively accurate scientific approaches, and probably reached a wider audience than many other more complex books concerned with experimental phonetics.

8.9. Appendices

Jones rounds off the *Outline*[1] with no fewer than seven appendices. Appendix A deals with rules for converting broad to narrow transcription. The chief point of interest lies in the casual references made, without explanation, to "'cardinal' (continental)" values of vowels (see Section 8.2). Appendix B lists words covered by stress rules "in cases where the exceptions are numerous" (see Section 8.6).

In appendix C, Jones provides sets of ear-training exercises based mainly around the idea of "nonsense words". This is the first sample we have of this crucial component of Jones's system of ear-training, which he developed at University College, and which has been copied in phonetics departments in Britain (and those elsewhere following the British tradition). Jones did not invent the idea of using meaningless sequences of sounds as a method of phonetic training. As stated in Section 2.3, it appears to have been devised by Jean Passy, and it was used extensively by Paul Passy in his teaching. However, Jones was to become known as the best exponent of the technique, which he advocates thus (p. 187):

> For cultivating the capacity to recognize instantaneously and accurately the sounds of the foreign language, ear-training exercises are required. The only satisfactory type of exercise for this purpose is for the student to write down phonetically isolated sounds and nonsense words dictated by the teacher.... Ear-training exercises should in the first instance only include the sounds of the language studied. As the student advances, other sounds may with advantage be introduced; he should pay special attention to the sounds of his own language.

The extract shown in Figure 8.26 gives some idea of the powers of recognition that
Jones was demanding from his student. Jones ends—with understatement (p. 188):
"Any student who can write the whole of the above exercises to dictation without
mistake may be satisfied that his ear has been very well trained."

Appendix D demonstrates cursive forms of phonetic symbols, whilst Appendix E
is a booklist extending over three pages. This covers not only books on phonetic theory, phonetic readers, and pronouncing dictionaries, but also books on the history of
English pronunciation and one treatise on versification. In addition, there are lists of

---

III. MORE DIFFICULT MONOSYLLABLES CONTAINING ONLY ENGLISH SOUNDS

tnəð, skrɔːndʒd, tʃrɔːld, ɡɲɔldʒ, ɲɘlpstʃ, zweɪldð, mlʌh, ʒdriːlg, zmæunʒ, tʃuɘʃθ, dðɑːmg, zðaɪmj, dʒvɪɘb, ʃkeŋgʒ, ɡɲʌθʃt, ʃtrɪndʒ, tsnævk, ʃɲjupt, ɒmdsk.

IV. DISYLLABLES CONTAINING ONLY ENGLISH SOUNDS

njʌrvɘːʒ, zɪxtælɒ, dzwaɪmɪɲzɡ, bmɘnʃsɛɘ, hedʃændʒ, sprædɘθs, tʃʌŋktjuɘʃ, mwɔːsmɪksθ, lɘmðaɪŋkʃ, jɔɪmɒθɪːʒ, æsklɘːndz, ʃɘkpuɪθ, moʊtɡɑːntʃt, strɛɘzneɪɡ, ɲɒptʃɘːŋ, ʒdneɪr, ɲɪvæh, tnzelp, psʌðɡlɘːb, xksezbrɛɘ, mjɔnʒdou, ɲθmɛɘk, bmuktn, krouzʒlʃ, mlɡŋ, sklɔɪdʒkeɪʃ, shɔːʃʃɘ, dʒuuːɲvɪɘ.

V. WORDS OF THREE OR MORE SYLLABLES CONTAINING ONLY ENGLISH
SOUNDS

vlæpeɪsez, ʃɘːʃwiːsleɪd, rɪzdfuɘʒɪɘ, ɲoumrɘːʃveɪl, zmjuːɘːskeʃ, ʒiʒɡrɔvɱɛɘʒ, ɡwiːɪʃtouɲl, θɛɘzmʌktaɪl, sɘðɘɲme, tueɪzdʃɑːlrʌnɘt, xlɘvzæʃɑuɪ, mʌɲdʃuɘnʃhoɪ, fsounlɡreh, zleɪvolɪkdɘ, daɪsɪbɘðkeɪl, suːjɪtnɘk, zɘzɑːtxtɘnaɪʃ, dɘlkɲiːuːt, nɔːðɪklɪmɘu, stɪrtseɪθnjɑːl, nɪɲɪdnerɘv, ɡolɘnɪʒdɑːm, nɘkeɪvzdɔːlæɡ, tnwɑːnɔːdjɘdɘθ, zwaunlːrɑːznʌ, sɘðpʌkɲɪleɪ, ɡɲɑːɲeɪðɲɪkɲauk, priːɲweɲθɘl, blædnɪplɔʒl, zɛɘseɪθlɔɪdɑː, lubʃkrauɲeʃ, ɪrpluɘwoumbɘ, tiːuːnæɡɪnæm, snɪsɲɘlɘvenɪfɘ, zliːvtsɪteɪɡɘð, niːbvɔzʌkɪddug, nɘdzuɪpdɪbɘteɪðɘtɘ, sjuːniːdʒɘːlɘtʃl, ɘbsʌnvɪɡzl, znɛɘrɘpʃrɘlɔːðɘkous, kɘːmɘɲuːtɪnɘk, ɲlɪwɔːpnevɪkʌlmfɘt, slɘzɘnæɲɪskwou, ʃenɪɬɱɑːɡlufɘʃtsoumɪ, tjuɘrɘsiːnɪdɘlæs, hiːaɪbjʌlefʌɲtou, ntlɑːɲktsxɘbjoɪldn, ænɘːmɪdreklæɔːnl, haɪhuːθnɬjɪdʒɘɲɘnplɪs, lldrefɘzɘstʌdʒ, wɘθsɪɘkɲɘt, oubeɪnðɪdzaul, lɪɘkniːsvɛɘznɘːd, txɪfaɪbtælzmiːb, mʌtɘbdɘːɲɪntaɪlɲɔːt, xkrɒmdlɡz.

VI. WORDS CONTAINING NON-ENGLISH SOUNDS

prɪːxsʃsuɘ [1], dlɪstyːntʃ [2], fɛɘndʒʌɲzeɪ [3], ɲʃeʃndɵːtaɪlpʃ [4], θouxtɘːɡyx, tjɪɘçlɑːtnɪxʃ [5], kɲæðɵyskrʌpt, hɘxyɲɡuʃyu, rɪmʒɔçuauð, ɲœheɪxoɲkɛɘθ [6], dʒuɘtʃɵx, æntyɲɡwedʒɪðz, ɔtluːθsɲʌʋiː [7].

In the following exercise i, u are to be taken to have "tense" values in all
cases, when short as well as when long; e, o, ɔ are to be taken to have their
"cardinal" values (as in French *thé, tôt*, German *Gott*); r is to be rolled.

pmɑːʀeːvɛ [8], tʌːɡondʒœl [9], ɡɪçmaɪt [10], ʌɲɡɑːlɘɘryusθ [11], ʀɑ̃ːkɲe [12], pmtɡadnʃɵːʀdɪrp [10], ɡzɪʔɔklunœsʃ [13], ɛ̆xoɪdlçɪu, ɡɪːjɵɲk [14], dɵzɡeːɪhœʃ, nzcyʀtɑ̃ːwʌɛɘ [15], mjækklɶːʀou, eɪnɡyʔar, θɪɪeːznɪɛu, ʒuyxɔlɛ [16], tnɔːðssrûç, fmɛyzɲɡɲlç, sɲurʀiːɡuɪ, syzwæɛ̆ɡhuɡ, tʰataɱeʃrwɛx [17], zblʲorxɲɘl [18].

Any student who can write the whole of the above exercises to dictation
without mistake may be satisfied that his ear has been very well trained.

Figure 8.26. Ear-training exercises from *Outline*[1] (p. 188).

Appendix C

iːlθ llθ elθ ælθ ɑːlθ, etc.
iːlð llð elð ælð ɑːlð, etc.
iːlv llv elv ælv ɑːlv, etc.
iːŋ lŋ eŋ æŋ ɑːŋ, etc.
ŋiː ŋl ŋe ŋæ ŋɑː etc.

Various combinations such as: θiːlx xllθ θees ræsθ wɑːθs θsɔsθ θsɔːθs sθsθs xuːðx xðʌðx xðɔːxð xðəl ðveilθ vðouls wallðx raulv θrɔilð ðrieθ ðlousθ ðwalls ðrauθl vrɔixð xnɔːŋ xŋɔːn ðnɔːŋx θŋɔːnθ, and so on, substituting other vowels and diphthongs.

θæθex sexæθ ðæθes xʌðæð θesɑːð xæθʌs . . . wævex vewæθ væweð wʌvæθ wewɑːx vɒvʌð . . . θθθɔːx sɔːxθθ ðθθɔːs xouðɔð θɔːsouð xɔːðous . . .

After practising systematic exercises of the above description, the learner should practise pronouncing miscellaneous invented words such as those given in Appendix B.

Figure 8.27. Extracts from the "Catenation exercises", Appendix C (*Outline*³, pp. 308–309).

phonetic charts, models of speech organs, and gramophone records. The whole provides a most interesting survey of the phonetic materials available at the time. Appendix F is a compilation of examination papers set in UCL between 1911 and 1914, which provide interesting insights into the work of Jones's Department in the period just before the outbreak of war (we reproduce a selection of these in an appendix to the present volume).

In the *Outline*³, Appendix A is retained, but with considerable modification. Appendix B is removed. Ear-training exercises as in the *Outline*¹, Appendix C are now spread over Chapter XIII (p. 61) and Appendix B (pp. 306–307). In a new Appendix C, Jones provides exercises in catenation "which should be practised by learners who can make the sounds but have difficulty in pronouncing sound-groups" (*Outline*³: 308–309); see Figure 8.27.

The aim of these exercises appears to have been to help learners of English who had difficulties with syllable structure, and is perhaps evidence of the greater numbers of students coming to his Department from outside Europe. See Section 9.3 for Jones's greater preoccupation with learners of non-European origin. The remaining material in the appendices in the *Outline*¹ is abandoned with the exception of the booklists which, suitably updated, are retained as Appendix D.

Chapter 9

A Professor of Phonetics (1919–21)

9.1. Work of the Department 1919–21

By 1919, the UCL Department of Phonetics had taken on much the form which it was to retain for the next twenty years, up to the outbreak of the second World War. Jones had set up the framework within which he wished to operate and had attracted a nucleus of staff who shared his view of phonetics and were capable of living up to his severe demands, particularly concerning their practical linguistic abilities.

The day-to-day work of Jones's Department was mainly the purveying of short non-degree courses. No attempt appears to have been made to start any kind of BA degree programme, either alone or in cooperation with other departments. In many ways, Jones could be viewed as running a "service department to the modern language departments" (Abercrombie 1980: 7), and much of the work was based on the teaching and learning of foreign languages. The performance element of the subject was all-important, which implied an insistence on the need for all students to develop their skills in recognising and producing exotic sounds. Even at an elementary level, UCL students had actually to be able to *pronounce* (though not necessarily to *understand*) words and utterances in any foreign languages they intended to study.

These languages were, for most students, still the familiar English and French, together with some German, though by 1919, Italian and Welsh (taught by Daniel Jones and Stephen Jones respectively) were also on offer. In addition, the prospectus for that year stated: "Special Classes for the study of the Phonetics of certain other languages, such as Russian, Cantonese, Urdu, Sechuana, Sinhalese, will be formed if not less than three students apply."[1]

The teaching philosophy of Jones and his colleagues, which Abercrombie has described as he first encountered it in 1930 (see Section 14.7), was therefore essentially already established at this time. The emphasis was on learning to read from phonetic texts, and to recognise sounds and sound sequences dictated for transcription. General phonetic theory was subsidiary to what were regarded as the essential skills of performance and recognition of sounds; whilst any phonological theory was directed primarily towards the aim of achieving accurate and economical transcriptions.

Under Palmer, the courses in "Spoken English" were also flourishing and well-supported, leading students to a "College Certificate of Proficiency in Spoken Language". Palmer had also introduced public lectures on applied linguistics under the heading "Theory of Language Study", which he expanded later (1921–22) into an evening course of twenty lectures.[2]

Compared with continental Departments of Phonetics, one branch of the subject was, of course, seriously under-represented, namely experimental phonetics. Stephen

Jones, now on a full-time appointment, was responsible for whatever work could be undertaken in the laboratory with the equipment available. Although funds for expansion were limited, Jones was still keen on encouraging experimental work, and the feeling of distance between the two sections of the Department—which Abercrombie (1983) was aware of in the thirties—had not yet set in (see Section 11.7).

The UCL Phonetics Department was notable among British universities at this time in pioneering so enthusiastically the idea of vacation courses. No year passed without these being organised, and they appear to have been from the outset a success, attracting numerous participants even at the height of the war. Jones was able to pay his staff high fees—even part-time assistants were given ten shillings an hour (a large sum in days when many workers still found as little as thirty shillings in their weekly pay-packets). Several of Jones's staff found their way into their careers via this route, which gave them experience and Jones a chance to see how they performed as practical teachers—something which he always rated more highly than either paper qualifications or research potential.

By far the largest part of the teaching work of the Department was still undertaken in the evenings. In 1919, only one class was specified as beginning earlier than 5.30 p.m., and that was Jones's Saturday afternoon class in Italian. These times were quite reasonable in view of the nature of the courses and the needs of the students, but it could possibly have given the idea to other academics in London that Jones was effectively catering merely to part-timers and his Department was not something to be taken really seriously. Furthermore, he had staff who possessed great talent but had acquired few, or no, recognised academic qualifications, the prime example being Harold Palmer. In addition, many people in the pre-1920 social climate might still have viewed with deep suspicion any university department which was eccentric enough to have equal numbers of men and women on the staff. This was the case in the sessions 1919–20 and 1920–21; by 1921–22 there were actually for the first time *more* female than male members of staff—and two (Lilias Armstrong and Ida Ward) held senior posts.[3] Nevertheless, if sexism of any sort did play a part in the University's view of the Phonetics Department, Jones took no notice and he continued to appoint women whenever he felt they were the best people for the job.

He was now rapidly becoming determined that this tiny Department, with its meagre resources and mainly part-time student body, would soon be transformed into the centre of phonetic research for the whole world, once his plans for an "Institute of Phonetics" were under way.

9.2. Ida Ward and Hélène Coustenoble

In 1919, two important newcomers, both women, came to join Jones's staff. They had each been connected with the Department for some time, but now Jones was able to take the chance to offer them teaching posts. Ida Ward and Hélène Coustenoble were to become two of Jones's most loyal colleagues, leading figures in the "London

31. Lilias Armstrong

32. Ida Ward

33. Arts Annexe 1, 21 Gordon Square
(taken in 1997)

34. Hélène Coustenoble

35. Sophie Lund

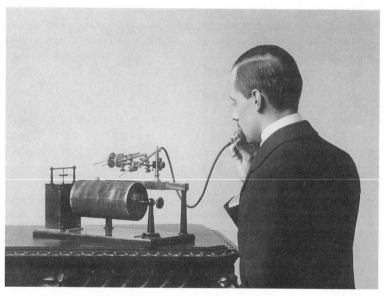

36. Jones using the kymograph

School of Phonetics", and both would play a crucial part in propagating Jones's view of phonetics by their teaching and publications.

Ida Caroline Ward was born in Bradford in 1880, being the eighth child of a York-shire wool merchant.[4] She took her B.Litt. degree at Durham University, going on to teach in secondary schools, firstly in the North of England, but soon moving to a post in Putney in south London. Her early background is reflected linguistically in her *Phonetics of English* (Ward 1929), which contains numerous examples from York-shire and Cockney, the accents she explicitly states (1929: v) she knew best.

She first had contact with University College London in 1913 when she started attending evening classes and gave a clear indication of her phonetic talents. However, it was not till 1919 that Jones was able to offer her a full-time post, for which she was prepared to give up any prospects she might have had of a headship of a school. She soon settled down in the Department, and was, in Jones's (1950b: 2) words, at "the commencement of an astonishing career".

Ida Ward specialised initially in teaching English phonetics, and also became inter-ested in speech defects, publishing her first book on this topic, *Speech defects, their nature and cure* (Ward 1923). She was to publish two other successful books on Eng-lish (Armstrong—Ward 1926; Ward 1929), but soon was devoting all her research energies to African languages, providing the first thorough phonetic analyses of Efik, Igbo and Yoruba (Ward 1933, 1936a and 1952, respectively). She included in all of these a thorough and systematic analysis of tone, on which she eventually became the world's leading authority.

She was to stay with Jones for the next thirteen years before leaving, in 1932, to join Arthur Lloyd James (see Section 9.5) at the School of Oriental Studies. There she continued to teach and research along largely Jonesian lines, and obtained a chair in 1944. It could be said that, of all Jones's many students, Ida Ward was the scholar who produced the greatest contribution to phonetics in her own right.

Hélène Coustenoble was born at Bezons in the south of France in 1894—which accounts for her later interest in Provençal (Coustenoble 1945)—but her parents origi-nated from the north of the country.[5] Her father took up a post in Lille, and it was there that she spent her youth. She later attended college at Abbeville, where she ob-tained a good general education, but no further qualifications. As she explains (Coustenoble 1964), she then decided to come to England to improve her English and learn something of phonetics, and so encountered Jones:

> Ayant été vaguement initiée à la phonétique par un de mes professeurs d'anglais, en France, et ayant vu une annonce relative à l'Association Internationale de Phonétique dans le *Journal of Education*, je me suis mise en rapport avec lui. En avril 1917, je suis venue à Londres suivre un cours de vacances dirigé par lui, et à partir de ce moment, je suis devenue son élève. Depuis, je n'ai jamais cessé de travailler avec lui et pour lui.

From the start, she impressed Jones with her sharp personality and quick intelligence, and she was asked to teach on the Easter vacation course on French phonetics which had been arranged for the following year. Jones, noting how competently she performed her tasks, employed her again on other similar work. When, in 1918, a request came through from Birmingham University asking UCL to arrange courses in the phonetics of French for their students, Jones requested a permanent appointment for Coustenoble, who by now was teaching in Maltman's Green School at Gerrards Cross in Buckinghamshire—the town where Jones himself was later to make his home. The Birmingham courses fell through, but instead she was offered part-time work at UCL, and her name appears on the full-time staff lists from 1919 onwards. She was to remain in the Department for over forty years, making it her life. Coustenoble retired in 1962 and died just one year later.

Of all his staff, "Cou"—as she came to be called by everyone—was the most devoted to Daniel Jones. Her admiration for him was boundless, and she was almost fanatical in her professional and personal loyalty and her jealousy of rivals. On her retirement, she wrote this tribute:

> ... If I have achieved anything as a phonetician, then it is to Professor Daniel Jones that I owe it. Not only is he *the* outstanding phonetician in the world—because of his exceptional natural gifts and his unremitting labour, coupled with a genuine love for his subject—but he has, to a very high degree, that most important quality of knowing how to inspire his pupils.
>
> I realised all this when I became his student, deciding as a result, to give up my career in France so that I might follow him. It has been my privilege to be trained by him, and his advice and learned encouragement have always been invaluable to me.[6]

Hélène Coustenoble produced scholarly work of distinction (notably her *Studies in French intonation*, Coustenoble—Armstrong 1934, and *La Phonétique du provençal moderne en terre d'Arles*, Coustenoble 1945), but she was valued from the outset by Jones particularly for her practical teaching ability (Jones 1963: 24). Jones considered it essential that his staff should all be highly proficient in colloquial French; he wanted them not only to have near-native pronunciation, but also to be able to converse effortlessly in the language (see also Abercrombie 1980: 5). As the teacher in charge of French phonetics, Coustenoble was in a position of peculiar power and influence. An apparently casual comment from her on the French of students or members of staff could seriously affect their future prospects with Jones for good or ill.

Her importance in Jones's scheme of things, particularly after Ida Ward left the Department, and Lilias Armstrong had died, was attested by Gimson:

> He was very much influenced though by the members of his staff, especially the ladies, Ida Ward ... Lilias Armstrong and, more particularly—in later years certainly—Hélène Coustenoble, who was really responsible for getting *me* on the staff and O'Connor and Arnold, because we had all been *her* students and he accepted her opinion of us.[7]

Hélène Coustenoble was the person who more than any other, except perhaps Jones himself, impressed her personality on the Department in its halcyon years. More than two decades after her death, numerous famous academics who passed through UCL still remembered Coustenoble's classes in French pronunciation with reverence mingled with awe. She was respected by all for the high standards she demanded from herself and others but dreaded for her acid sarcasm when crossed, frustrated, or even merely disappointed.

9.3. The proposed Institute of Phonetics

By 1917, the concept of an Institute of Phonetics was much in Jones's mind, and this proposal had been noted in the college report for that year (see Section 7.10). However, what is described there appears to be more in the nature of a modest extension and reorganisation of the work of the Phonetics Department. The "Practical Research Institute in Phonetics" was estimated as costing no more than £850 per annum; although we have to multiply that sum by at least a factor of about 50 to reach present-day values, it would nevertheless seem a relatively conservative piece of planning that was envisaged. But between 1917 and 1919, Jones continued to plan his Institute, and in the process the concept grew out of all proportion to his original ideas.

In 1918, Jones began to busy himself with writing letters to a number of persons who might be expected to have some interest in the proposed Institute. His correspondence at the time includes letters to such figures as the High Master of Manchester Grammar School (actually his old University College School headmaster, J.L. Paton),[8] the renowned conductor and founder of the English promenade concerts, Sir Henry Wood (who replied enthusiastically saying that he was "intensely interested", and with praise for Jones's *EPD*: "a monumental work ... I am finding it most useful and instructive").[9] Backing also came from a member of the government (Sir Stanley Leathes), and high-ranking civil servants such as the Secretary of the Scottish Education Department (Sir John Struthers) and the Chief Inspector of the Welsh Department of Education (Sir Owen Edwards). Jones must have been relieved to discover that the Director of the School of Oriental Studies (Sir E. Denison Ross) was fully in favour of the scheme and, with the aid of Provost Sir Gregory Foster, he was also able to marshal the support of the Vice-Chancellor of London University and the Principals of both King's College and Bedford College.[10]

Foster backed Jones all along, and from the surviving correspondence it is clear that Jones turned to him for advice in organising and running the propaganda campaign. The nature of the operation was in many ways far from Jones's style of doing things, and it may be owing to the Provost's over-enthusiastic encouragement that the plan suddenly expanded to elephantine proportions from its original modest base.

By January 1919, a report entitled "Scheme for an Institute of Phonetics" (henceforth *Scheme*) had been prepared for presentation to the College Committee.[11] The proposal was passed by the Senate in March,[12] and the first meeting of the new committee which had been set up to supervise the establishment of the Institute met a fortnight later.[13] By June of the same year, a slightly revised *Scheme* had been produced,[14] which included a personal defence by Jones (p. 7) of the size and scope of the project. This addition indicates that the plan was already, understandably, under attack as a utopian project which would be far too expensive for the resources available.

The *Scheme* begins by stating the reasons why an Institute of Phonetics is needed, concentrating on the requirement to analyse accurately the languages of the British Empire, and pointing out that the study of phenomena such as tone had been largely neglected. Jones, presumably helped by Foster, seems to be the person largely responsible for the text (*Scheme*, p. 1).

We believe that the University of London could easily be made *the recognised world centre for phonetic study* if proper funds were available. Great Britain is the original home of phonetics, and the practical applications of that science in education have been more fully developed here than in any other of the countries mentioned.... There are many good phoneticians in this country, and it is only through lack of financial support that we have fallen behind other countries in the matter of phonetic research.

The report underlined the way in which at the time London was lagging behind continental universities in phonetic research—and claimed that the poor showing of UCL was owing to inadequate funding. It is known that the account of the new Phonetics Department at Grenoble in 1909 (Section 3.7), and the visit he made just before the war to the impressively equipped Hamburg Department (Section 5.10), had made a marked impression on Jones; this seems to be reflected in many of the ideas contained in the *Scheme*. The writers of the report are also not above deliberately playing on jingoistic prejudices and fears of a resurgent post-war Germany, pointing out that (p. 2) "but for the War, the Germans would have derived considerable commercial profit from their phonetic analysis of languages of our portions of Africa".

The work of the proposed Institute was seen to include a vast area—all aspects and applications of phonetics that were current, or foreseeable, in that era. The first aim was scarcely modest: "The phonetic analysis of all the important languages and dialects of the Empire" which "would require the aid of all the most modern apparatus". Further related activities would be the "reduction of unwritten languages to writing" and the "reconsideration of some of the existing orthographies of Africa, etc." (p. 2). The imperial theme, reiterated throughout the *Scheme*, reflects the mood current at the time that Britain should exploit its vast empire more effectively as a source of wealth —a feeling which was going to be emphasised in the run-up to the Wembley Empire Exhibition in 1925.

The *Scheme* also envisages "the establishment of a Phonographic Museum" to record languages and dialects; this was to have a "special section devoted to the dialects of the British Isles". Linguistic atlases were to be prepared (based on the *Atlas linguistique de la France* (Gilliéron—Edmont 1902–10); these were to start with the

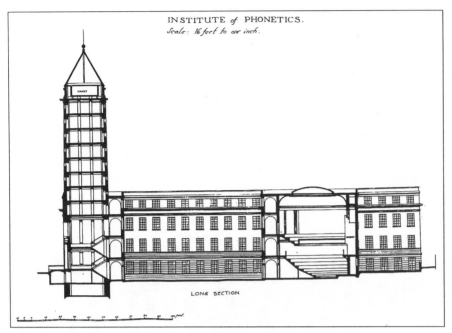

INSTITUTE *of* PHONETICS.
Scale: 16 feet to one inch.

LONG SECTION

Figure 9.1. Architect's drawing for projected Institute of Phonetics ("Long Section").

British Isles, but were eventually planned, somewhat ambitiously, to cover "various parts of the Empire" (p. 3).

The actual contemporary work of Jones and his colleagues is mirrored more closely in the plans for "advanced research in general phonetics by experimental and other methods" with special attention to "speech acoustics and speech psychology"; "philological research"; "curing certain kinds of speech defects"; and "training teachers of phonetics" and the encouragement of "independent phonetic research". "Teaching English people how to pronounce with accuracy all the most important foreign languages" and "teaching foreigners how to pronounce English" might be expected to occupy a higher place in the list. These come almost last of the stated aims—which might lead to the conclusion that the *Scheme* was slanted towards the need to conjure up financial support for the Institute rather than reflect Jones's own view of the relative significance of the various aspects of phonetics (p. 3).

Again, in the summary of the benefits to be gained from the Institute, the imperial theme is emphasised. The work would "promote the cause of education among the uneducated or only partially educated peoples of the Empire"; "political benefits" will arise from better communication by "those whose work brings them into contact with native peoples" (p. 3). The "economic benefits" receive special emphasis:

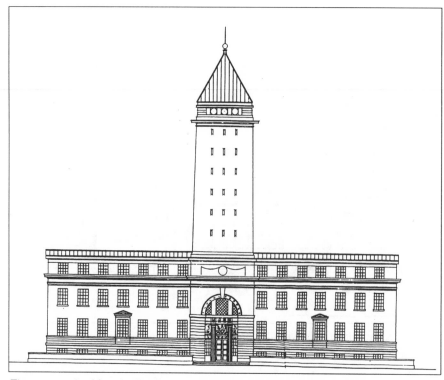

Figure 9.2. Architect's drawing for projected Institute of Phonetics (frontage).

Those who have to learn languages for commercial reasons will find that their relations with the people with whom they deal will be improved when they can speak the native languages better, and that their trade will be stimulated in consequence. We think it probable that in this way alone (leaving out of account the still more important educational and political benefits) the expenditure on the Institute of Phonetics would be covered in a few years by the profits to the nation arising out of our closer commercial relations with the native peoples of Asia and Africa. (p. 3)

The expenditure referred to above would indeed have been vast. Architect's drawings for the Institute have survived (see Figures 9.1–9.3) and illustrate the lavish facilities and accommodation that was envisaged. The Institute would have spread out over a prime site of about three quarters of an acre in Bloomsbury. Jones was later to reveal in correspondence to Foster that he favoured as a location Gordon Square just to the east of the main college buildings: "By far the best [possible site] would be the block of houses forming the north side of Gordon Sq. together with the first 6 adjoining

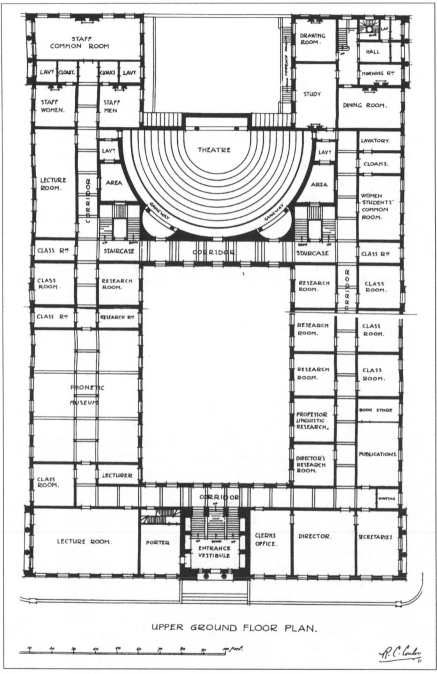

UPPER GROUND FLOOR PLAN.

Figure 9.3. Architect's plan for projected Institute of Phonetics (ground floor).

houses in Gordon St and the first 5 houses in Tavistock St."[15] Ironically, this was very close to where the UCL Phonetics Department eventually ended up—albeit on the opposite side of the square and in a single converted family house, rather than the palatial edifice planned by Jones and Foster.

The Institute was to be provided with a theatre to seat an audience of no fewer than six hundred. There would be five large lecture halls, twenty smaller class rooms, seven laboratories, and other facilities such as a dark room, X-ray room and a "photo-micro" room (what exactly this last was remains unexplained). In addition, there were plans to include a huge "phonographic museum" with storage for a quarter of a million gramophone records (in duplicate, together with the original matrices) "to illustrate as many languages and dialects as possible" (p. 3). There would be five "nearly sound-proof Phonographic Research Rooms", and a "Chart Room, where all kinds of linguistic charts would be prepared and kept" (p. 4).

Some of the plans seem to show considerable foresight on Jones's part in anticipating modern audio-visual techniques of language learning. For instance, there is mention (p. 4) of a "large room containing 20 fairly sound-proof compartments (for language learners using phonographic records)" and also (p. 3) a "Phonographic Class Room" which "would have table accommodation for 40 students, that is to say, there should be 40 phonograph receivers connected to the phonograph at the head of the table". In his survey of the history of mechanical media for language teaching, L.G. Kelly ([1976²]: 244) cites nothing of this kind until the construction in 1924 by Ohio State University of a room containing "sixteen sets of headphones linked to a single output". The *Scheme's* "Phonographic Class Room" preceded Ohio by several years and is therefore possibly the very first surviving plan for what would today be termed a language laboratory. Jones's concepts of applying audio equipment to language acquisition were many years ahead of their time, and are a reminder of his early enthusiasm for the gramophone when he published *Intonation curves* (1909a). It is interesting to speculate how this aspect of the history of language teaching would have been altered had Jones's grand plan ever been carried out (cf. Howatt's 1984: 219 discussion of the pioneering use of the gramophone and wire-recorder in language teaching).

A library of fifty thousand volumes was planned to "contain all books in which any information regarding the pronunciation of any language is to be found". Jones could also be considered as anticipating the modern realisation of the importance of linguistic historiography, since the *Scheme* (p. 4) specifies that "a special section of the library should be devoted to the history of speech" with "as complete a collection as possible of early printed grammars and other treatises dealing with the pronunciation of languages in early times".

The future Director of the Institute—a post which Jones presumably had in mind for himself—would have been well provided for under the terms of the *Scheme*. Apart from being paid a salary of £1,000 a year, the *Scheme* states that "it would be to the advantage of the Institute if a residence for the Director could form part of the building, as is the case at the Royal Institution" (p. 4). Though Jones's ambition was now to dedicate his life entirely to this work, he nevertheless expected to be recompensed fittingly. The staff provision would have been generous—with two professors (one for experimental phonetics and one for linguistic research) in addition to the Director, thirty research staff, and in excess of twenty-seven full-time teaching staff, plus part-time assistants, eight administrative staff, and an unspecified number of "servants" (pp. 4–5). The capital expenditure was estimated to be £120,000 and the annual costs of running the Institute were to be £38,000 (after revenue from sales of publications and other sources of income were taken into account).

Jones's personal note, which was added to the second version of the *Scheme* (p. 7), defended the plan as a "well-proportioned and co-ordinated whole" which should be carried out without any reduction in anticipated size, facilities or staffing, and pointed out that the Institute was to be thought of as occupying a special position (p. 7):

> It will be a national institution, and it is intended to meet the needs of the whole of the British Empire.... If we are the first in the field, and set up an Institute which shall answer all our requirements, our position will be established as the recognised world-centre for this kind of research.... We now have a good opportunity for securing the leading position, as the idea of founding a large Institute does not yet appear to have occurred to any other University. Moreover, the reputation of our present Phonetics Department would give us a good start.

The presentation of the *Scheme*, and its successful passage through the Senate, marked the high point of the history of the ill-fated Institute of Phonetics. From this time onwards, the campaign ran into trouble; unluckily for Jones it was to slow down, halt—and finally peter out. He continued throughout 1919 to attempt to attract backing for the venture, receiving only some degree of lukewarm support. He devised leaflets for propaganda and ensured that the press were made aware of the Institute plans. For example, an article on the Institute appeared in the *Observer*.[16] Jones advocated that "one of the first things the Committee ought to issue" was a "booklet or series of leaflets explaining in language that the ordinary businessman will understand *what is the use of the Institute of Phonetics*".[17] He went on to produce a number of (unsigned) propaganda leaflets with titles such as: "How the Institute of Phonetics will help benefit trade" (leaflet 2); "How the Institute of Phonetics will help missionary work" (leaflet 6), etc. He wrote numerous letters and attempted to get the Committee together for a meeting. This proved to be no easy task, since Foster and Jones had made the error of packing it with so many eminent persons that it was well nigh impossible to get them all together on any one occasion—even for the vital matter of electing a chairman. "I am still endeavouring to get the Phonetics Institute Committee to meet, but it is extraordinarily difficult", Jones wrote to Sir Stanley Leathes in November.[18] At last, late in December, Jones managed to persuade most of the Committee to assemble again and work proceeded on the approval of the propaganda sheets Jones had devised, and the first steps were taken towards organising an appeal for funds.[19]

It was intended that the business community was to be the major source of funds for the Institute, but Jones seems to have been out of his depth in dealing with the non-academic world. Amidst all the elaborate plans for public appeals and press campaigns, he wrote to Gregory Foster suggesting that he might put on a shortened version of *Twelfth Night* in the original pronunciation. The performance was to be staged by his brother Arnold's prep school pupils—something which might appeal to the academic mind, but which was hardly likely to draw the hundreds of thousands of pounds required from the business community.[20] The play never materialised, and it would, in any case, have been one more time-consuming job for someone already burdened with the tasks of running a developing academic department, completing a full programme of research and publication and also planning a major publicity campaign.

Jones had put all his considerable energy and his hopes into the Institute idea and was perhaps beginning to construct his life around his ambitions to be its Director. Predictably, the strain was eventually to prove too much. Within only a few days of the December committee meeting, Jones fell ill, and, by the beginning of 1920, he was the victim of a sudden and severe nervous breakdown. There can be little doubt that the major cause of his collapse was the stress of the hectic year of pressure in the period 1918–19 when the Institute scheme had begun to dominate his life. Once Jones had been forced to rest and take a prolonged period of sick leave, the campaigning for the Institute came temporarily to a standstill, and though it was later resumed, the operation never again recovered the original momentum. However, the idea remained hanging in the air for several years, and the eventual demise of the Institute campaign did not come about until 1925.

Even then, it would seem clear that Jones continued to hang on to a faint hope for the realisation of his dream. Nevertheless, he ultimately recognised that he would not himself ever be the man in charge. As late as 1944, he put these thoughts into an internal UCL report on post-war planning:

> I would recall that the importance of developing phonetic studies on a large scale was recognised by the College and by the University in 1919, when a scheme for raising funds for an Institute of Phonetics (to be attached to University College) was approved.... An appeal for funds was in fact launched, but it met with no response from private donors, and it was discontinued. ... it would be well to keep the plan in mind for reconsideration at some future time when someone much younger than myself can be found who would be competent to undertake the direction of a large Institute.[21]

9.4. *A Colloquial Sinhalese Reader*

The *Colloquial Sinhalese reader* (Perera—Jones 1919a), was the last of Jones's major publications to appear before he obtained a professorship. Although it does not form part of the London Phonetic Reader series, the *Sinhalese reader* is obviously (both in terms of form and content) in the same mould. Indeed, it is something of a mystery why this book should have appeared under the imprint of Manchester University Press and Longman Green and Company, rather than being published by University of London Press.[22] Perera takes first place in the authorship; so it must be assumed that he, as a colleague in Jones's Department, albeit with an honorary status, had the phonetic knowledge to play a major part in the actual linguistic analysis of Sinhalese. It is stated at the outset that the book aims to record "one form of colloquial Sinhalese... that used by the first author in ordinary talking". The book thus fulfils Jones's ideal for phonological analysis, which he considered to be best achieved by examining a single individual's speech, which could then be considered representative of a wider speech community (Jones 1944d: 126–127; *Phoneme*: 9.) Perera goes on to claim that "he has reason to believe this style of speech to be fairly representative of the colloquial language of the better educated inhabitants of Colombo". Recognising that diglossia prevailed in Ceylon, Perera points out that the type of Sinhalese dealt with is "quite different from the literary language" (*Sinhalese reader*: 1).

Despite Perera's taking first place in the authorship, Jones's overall direction of the book is, nevertheless, obvious on every page. The organisation and layout of the *Sinhalese reader* is exactly like that of the London Phonetic Reader series, with a brief phonetic introduction, followed by a practical phonetic description and rounded off by a large number of texts presented in transcription together with an orthographic version. If for no other reason, the *Sinhalese reader* would be outstanding amongst Jones's publications in that it is the first of his books to be written incorporating fully two vital aspects of Jones's contribution to linguistics—namely, phoneme theory and the Cardinal Vowels.

In a section entitled "Sounds and Phonemes" (pp. 1–2), the *Sinhalese reader* provides a clear, specific statement of Jones's views. Perera and Jones begin by defining a speech sound (p. 1):

A *speech-sound* is a sound of definite acoustic quality produced by the organs of speech. A given speech-sound is incapable of variation.

The authors go on to say that languages have large numbers of distinguishable speech sounds but that these can be reduced in "phonetic writing" because "many of the sounds fall into groups called phonemes" (pp. 1–2), and then define a phoneme in these terms (p. 2):

... a group of related sounds of a given language which are so used in connected speech that no one of them ever occurs in positions which any other can occupy.

These sections encapsulate Jones's two essential ideas on the phoneme, namely the concept of a "group of sounds" (later, "family of sounds") and the requirement of complementary distribution. In addition, the *Sinhalese reader* provides an early summary of the idea of the speech-sound as a concrete entity—even though the opposing abstract nature of the phoneme is not mentioned. This was not fully discussed until Jones's paper "Concrete and abstract sounds" (Jones: 1938a), which, interestingly, is introduced by Jones quoting from a recent informal conversation which he had held with Perera. Illustrative examples of allophonic variation are provided, firstly from English, with advanced and retracted varieties of /k/ in "keep" and "call"; and also from Sinhalese, with varieties of /n/ before alveolar and retroflex consonants, in /kanːdə/ "hill", and /kanːdiə/ "mound" (p. 2).[23]

> Speech-sounds which belong to the same phoneme cannot distinguish one word from another; failure to distinguish them on the part of a foreign learner may cause him to speak with a foreign accent, but it will not as a rule make his words unintelligible. On the other hand, if the foreign learner confuses one phoneme with another, he will confuse different words of the language.

Finally, Perera and Jones state their view of the relationship of the phoneme concept to models of transcription (p. 2):

> It is generally only necessary in phonetic writing to have symbols for the phonemes. The use of the different sounds belonging to any given phoneme is, in most languages, determined by simple rules which can be stated once [and] for all, and which can be taken for granted in reading phonetic texts.

The importance of this section of the *Sinhalese reader* is underlined by the fact that Jones quoted large portions verbatim in his 1957 survey of the development of the phoneme concept with these comments (*HMTP*: 11–12):

> By 1918 the terminology was straightened out, as will be seen from the short but very nearly adequate explanation of the phoneme [in the *Sinhalese reader*]... [the] explanations with a few verbal amendments to the definition...hold good to-day, and the theory as it then stood has formed the basis of the phonetic work at University College ever since.

Consequently, it may be said, on the authority of Jones himself, that the *Sinhalese reader* provides the first effectively complete statement of Jones's phoneme theory to appear in print. It is, even more significantly, the first clear summary of phoneme theory ever to be published in the western world, pre-dating the work of American phonemicists by almost a decade. In fact, it was chance which gave this distinction to the *Sinhalese reader*, since another of Jones's publications containing information on the phoneme had already been completed, namely, the *Pronunciation of Russian* (see Section 10.5), which was in manuscript form by 1917, but which, owing to delays, did not finally come out until 1923.

Furthermore, the *Sinhalese reader* constitutes a landmark in the history of phonology as the first complete overtly phonemic description of the sound system of any language. Here, Jones is not merely working roughly along phonemic lines (as in the *Sechuana reader*, for example) but is explicitly using phonemic concepts and termi-

TABLE I.

CHART OF SINHALESE PHONEMES

		Bi-labial.	Dental.	Alveolar.	Alveolar with Front Raising.	Retroflex.	Palatal.	Velar.	Glottal.
CONSONANTS	Plosive . .	p b	t d			ʈ ɖ		k g	
	Affricate .				ʧ ʤ				
	Nasal . .	m		n				ŋ	
	Lateral . .			l					
	Flapped .			r					
	Fricative .	f		s	ʃ				ɦ
	Semi-vowel .	ʋ					j		
VOWELS	Close . .	(u) (o)					Front. i e	Mixed. ə æ ǽ	Back. u o
	Open . .							a ᴂ	

Figure 9.4. Chart showing the Sinhalese phonemes (*Sinhalese reader*, p. 4).

nology. De Silva (1969: 239) therefore errs when he refers to a later work (Perera—Jones 1937k) as "the first attempt towards a phonemicization of Sinhalese". As will be demonstrated here, the phonemicisation of Sinhalese was not only attempted, but largely achieved, almost twenty years earlier in the *Sinhalese reader.*

Perera and Jones's description of the segmental system of Sinhalese is based on an inventory of twenty-eight "essential phonemes" and two "non-essential phonemes" (see Figure 9.4). By the latter, the authors mean the marginal phonemes /Φ/ (represented here by the symbol F in common with the contemporary IPA practice) and /ʃ/ found only in loanwords and not employed by all speakers. The phonemic analysis of Sinhalese is by no means clear-cut; in the *Sinhalese reader* solution, Jones and Perera appear to be attempting to reduce the sound system to the smallest possible number of segmental elements. In so doing, they are forced to permit numerous combinational permutations.

For instance, Sinhalese is shown to contain in its consonant system sequences of stops preceded by a brief nasal element [mb nd nɖ ŋg nʤ]. In the *Sinhalese reader,* these are regarded as combinations of phonemes; but Perera and Jones reveal that it is possible also to have sequences of full length nasal plus stop, giving contrasts such as: [kanːdə] "hill" and [kaňdə] "trunk". Perera and Jones solve this problem by invoking a length distinction which can be applied to vowels and many consonants: "In most cases length is a 'significant' element of speech in Sinhalese; its use is not regulated by any rules" (p. 12). However, the authors admit when considering the structure of the Sinhalese syllable that the nasal/stop sequences "count as single consonants" (p. 14). In later work—for instance Perera—Jones (1937k) and in the *Phoneme—*

Jones came back to the problem of the Sinhalese nasal stops, taking a different view (*Phoneme*: 78–79):

> …they are regarded by Sinhalese speakers as single sounds, but analysis shows them to be of a compound nature…. A case of this nature raises the question whether one is at liberty to divide into two parts a sound which is regarded by native speakers as indivisible, and whether, if one does divide it, the parts can properly be assigned to other phonemes existing in the language.

Jones declares (*Phoneme*: 79) that "the view of the native speaker as to what constitutes a 'single sound' should be regarded as important, though not necessarily conclusive" and goes on to say that:

> If the Sinhalese people regard m̐b, n̐d, etc., as being indivisible, we should give their view serious consideration, even though it should conflict with the ideas we have derived from European languages; we should be open-minded enough at least to examine the possibility of regarding these sounds as constituting separate independent phonemes. My personal opinion is that they should be so regarded.

A likely interpretation of the above is that it represents the last echo of a difference in view between Jones and Perera over the analysis in the *Sinhalese reader*. Jones may well have wished for an elegant linguistic analysis with the segmental system reduced to as small a number of phonemic elements as possible, whilst Perera considered that such a solution went against his native speaker intuition. Jones appears to have won as far as the *Sinhalese reader* was concerned, but he felt eventually that he had taken insufficient notice of his fellow author's intuitive insights into his mother tongue.

Another indication that Perera certainly did not act passively, but took a full part in the writing of the work, can be deduced from the treatment of the symbolisation of the retroflex consonants /ṭ ḍ/. These are shown here with the symbols ʈ ɖ rather than the contemporary IPA ṭ ḍ; a footnote states that "these signs can be shown on psychological grounds to be superior" (p. 3 n.), reflecting presumably the results of Perera's research.

The affricate phonemes /tʃ dʒ/ are treated here as unit phonemes and not as sequences of two sound elements (p. 7). (Cf. the discussion in the *Outline*[1] of the similar sounds in English, Section 8.4) The following description of /n/ shows the extent to which Jones is now thinking along phonemic lines (p. 7):

> This Sinhalese phoneme includes four distinct sounds. The most typical sound is alveolar (as in English). A dental variety is used when ʈ or ɖ follows. A post-alveolar variety is used when ʈ or ɖ follows. A somewhat palatalized variety is used in the group nj.
>
> The presence of these varieties being always determined by the nature of the following sound, it is not necessary to indicate them by special signs in phonetic transcriptions.

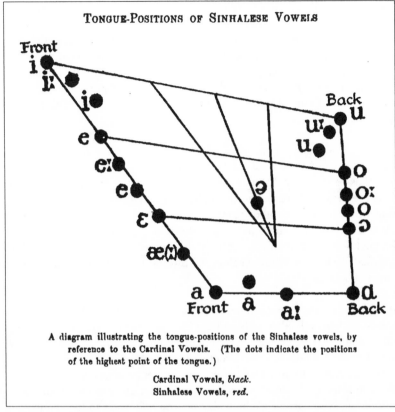

A diagram illustrating the tongue-positions of the Sinhalese vowels, by reference to the Cardinal Vowels. (The dots indicate the positions of the highest point of the tongue.)

Cardinal Vowels, *black*.
Sinhalese Vowels, *red*.

Figure 9.5. Vowel diagram, with original caption, from the *Sinhalese reader* (p. 5). Note that the Sinhalese vowels were picked out in red.

Jones's description of the Sinhalese vowels is preceded by a section on the "Tongue-position of the Sinhalese Vowels", including the diagram reproduced here (Figure 9.5). If compared with the vowel diagram which appeared in the *EPD*[1], it will be seen that the *Sinhalese reader* version has a more "modern" look about it. The word "mixed" is omitted, and the back line now slopes slightly forwards rather than leaning back. It is, essentially, the same kind of diagram as that found in the *Outline*[3] [1932] onwards.

The student is referred briefly to the Cardinal Vowels and recommended to learn them by "oral instruction from a teacher who knows them" though it is pointed out that "the student may with advantage supplement this by a study of the gramophone records" (p. 6). The section ends by saying that:

A thorough knowledge of a system of Cardinal Vowels is indispensable for anyone who wishes to acquire a first-rate pronunciation of languages for which phonetically trained teachers are not to be had.

Though the Cardinal Vowel system was still only partly developed, Jones was prepared at this point to make a strong claim for its efficacy—a position from which he did not deviate for the rest of his career: "Any student who is familiar with the Cardinal Vowels will get from this diagram a good idea of how the Sinhalese vowels are formed and what they sound like" (pp. 5–6). In the description of the Sinhalese vowels, as will be seen from the sample below (p. 10), the *Sinhalese reader* refers throughout to the Cardinal Vowels, the model obviously being regarded as capable of a high degree of precision.

When long, Sinhalese u has a tongue-position rather lower than and probably slightly advanced from Cardinal Vowel No. 8.... The lip-rounding is weak. It must thus be carefully distinguished from the numerous English ways of pronouncing oo in *too*. In particular, the Sinhalese u, unlike the English phoneme, has no tendency towards diphthongization.

When the vowel is short, the tongue-position is probably a little lower still, and the lip-rounding is still less than for the long sound... The Sinhalese short u is something like the Southern English vowel in *put*, but it has rather less lip-rounding than this.

As a practical descriptive technique, the combination in the *Sinhalese reader* of reference to the Cardinal Vowels and the English vowels (with which it might be assumed that most of his readers were familiar) is quite effective. It is odd, however, that the Sinhalese diphthongs (no fewer than sixteen in number in the *Sinhalese reader* analysis) are merely listed with no attempt at further description.

We have some evidence of Jones's later reconsideration of the *Sinhalese reader* description of Sinhalese, since he makes several references to the language in the *Phoneme*. For example, he has an updated version of the Sinhalese vowel diagram, showing slightly different placings in some cases (*Phoneme*: 29). The question of vowel length is also discussed (*Phoneme*: 131), with the same description as in the *Sinhalese reader*, but treated in terms of a chroneme distinction. A more radical revision is made in respect of the treatment of stress.

Stress, in several aspects, e.g. word stress, sentence stress, articulation of unstressed syllables, forms a major part of the phonetic introduction to the *Sinhalese reader*, though it is recognised and clearly stated that: "Stress (force-accent) is not a 'significant' element of speech in Sinhalese" (p. 13). The *Phoneme* (p. 138), however, reevaluates Sinhalese as "stressless", and Jones adds this note (*Phoneme*: 139 n.):

I have come to the conclusion that the view expressed by me (in 1919) on page 14 of that book [the *Sinhalese reader*], that there is a tendency to put stress on long syllables of Sinhalese words, is incorrect. I believe I mistook prominence for stress, and am now very doubtful if there are any real stress distinctions in the Sinhalese language.

The introduction to the *Sinhalese reader* closes with a brief consideration of intonation. The authors point out that, in Sinhalese, intonation is not "significant", i.e. that the language is non-tonal (*Sinhalese reader*: 16). The claim is also made that "intonation is not even used to any large extent for conveying 'expression' or subtle shades of meaning, as in English" because of the existence of a system of particles for this purpose (*Sinhalese reader*: 16).

The marking system used in the *Sinhalese reader* (see Figure 9.6) is of interest since it represents an advance upon the methods previously employed by Jones to show pitch patterns (p. 16).

> Intonation is best represented by a system of dots and lines placed in reference to two horizontal lines indicating the upper and lower limits of the ordinary speaking voice. The dots represent approximately level pitches, and the lines represent rising or falling pitches. Each dot or line has reference to one syllable.

The extract reproduced in Figure 9.6 shows that the system appears to foreshadow *mutatis mutandis* the intonation marking scheme for English produced by Armstrong —Ward (1926), but no acknowledgement of any debt to Jones is mentioned in that work (although Armstrong and Ward dedicate their book to him). In fact, their only acknowledgement is to Klinghardt—Klemm (1920), whose system of intonation marking is in many ways quite different from that used by Armstrong and Ward; cf. the examples of intonation marking illustrated in Section 8.7, Figures 8.17, 8.18 and 8.19. Ironically, as we have seen, Jones borrowed Armstrong and Ward's scheme for his 1932 revision of the *Outline*. It seems that he was effectively borrowing back what his students had borrowed from him.

The *Sinhalese reader* would certainly be regarded a pioneering work of prime significance if considered solely on its merits as "the first book to describe the sounds of spoken Sinhalese" (De Silva 1969: 239). But it is much more than that. The *Sinhalese reader* is clearly (notwithstanding its modest length and lack of pretension) a landmark study where new ground was broken, and where several of Jones's ideas reached a crucial stage of development.

Though much in the *Sinhalese reader* was to be repeated later in a more advanced and elaborate form in the *Pronunciation of Russian*, it is here, in this short reader, that it first reached the world. As such, the *Sinhalese reader* must be regarded as one of Jones's most important—if nowadays little read—publications.

9.5. Dorothy Parkinson and Arthur Lloyd James

In 1920, two more colleagues, who were both to play an important part in Jones's life, though in quite different ways, appear on the staff list. One was Dorothy Parkinson, who was given the post of Departmental Secretary. She was soon known to all in the Department as "Parky"—except Jones who believed in formality in names as in much else, and always addressed her as "Miss Parkinson".[24] She came to UCL with no experience of universities, or any other academic work, and up to that time had been working in an insurance office. But Jones's distrust of paper qualifications meant that he would always appoint people on the basis of his personal assessment of their future potential. On several occasions he was to employ people with few or no scholastic achievements behind them, and in most cases his judgement appears to have been proved right. To begin with, Dorothy Parkinson not only occupied herself with secre-

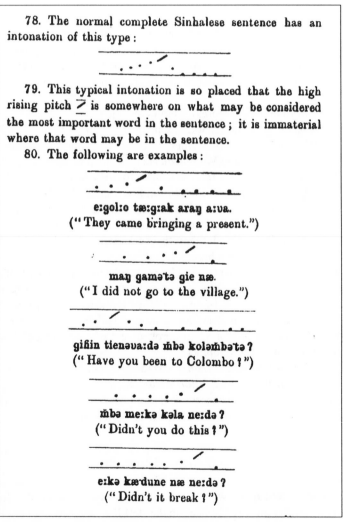

78. The normal complete Sinhalese sentence has an intonation of this type :

79. This typical intonation is so placed that the high rising pitch ⟋ is somewhere on what may be considered the most important word in the sentence ; it is immaterial where that word may be in the sentence.

80. The following are examples :

e:gol:o tæ:g:ak araŋ a:ʋa.
("They came bringing a present.")

maŋ gamətə gie næ.
("I did not go to the village.")

giɓin tienəʋa:də m̂bə koləm̂bətə ?
("Have you been to Colombo ? ")

m̂bə me:kə kəla ne:də ?
("Didn't you do this ? ")

e:kə kæ·dune næ ne:də ?
("Didn't it break ? ")

Figure 9.6. Perera and Jones's intonation marking system for Sinhalese (*Sinhalese reader*, p. 17).

tarial duties, but also helped out with the odd conversation class for Palmer's course in spoken English, but after a few years gave up all teaching and concentrated on administration. She was to remain with Jones right up until the year he retired—and when he went, she left too (see Section 12.12).

The other newcomer was the Department's second Welshman, Arthur Lloyd James, who had, for this era, a somewhat unusual background for a phonetician.[25] He was born in 1884, in Pentre, a mining village in the Rhondda, where his father was manager of the local colliery. Unlike Stephen Jones, Lloyd James was not himself bilingual, but he was nevertheless the son of two Welsh-speaking parents, and remained proud of this fact all his life. As he wrote of himself: "Welsh was the daily speech of his father and mother and the Mabinogion first opened his eyes to the beauty of Mediaeval Romance" (Lloyd James 1935: 199). Audio recordings show that although he transformed his speech into something very close to RP, he nevertheless always retained faint traces of his native Welsh accent.

After going to the University of Wales at Cardiff (where he managed only to achieve a third-class degree in French), Lloyd James later enrolled at Trinity College, Cambridge, as an advanced student taking a degree in languages and specialising in Old French. He then taught French and phonetics at a London teacher-training college before joining Jones's Department at University College in 1920. He soon proved himself a highly successful teacher and researcher, and moved on from French and English phonetics to specialise in West African languages. He parted company from Jones in 1927 to become head of the Phonetics Department at the School of Oriental Studies. In 1933, he was awarded a chair, thus becoming Britain's second Professor of Phonetics. At the School, together with Ida Ward (see Section 9.2), he was notable for propagating Jones's view of phonetics as applied to African and Asian languages. However, he was to become better known nationally for his work for the BBC as Honorary Secretary of the Advisory Committee on Spoken English, and later on, in 1938, as the first BBC linguistic adviser. Probably more than anyone else, apart from Jones himself, Lloyd James was responsible for the spread of the concept of "BBC English"—really RP in another guise—and was foremost in interesting the general public in pronunciation, and popularising phonetic ideas. See Section 12.2 for details of the tragic end of his life and the effect of this on Daniel Jones.

9.6. Unpublished lectures on Italian, Spanish and French

Amongst the most important of the works not intended for publication which Jones has left behind are three collections of lectures on the phonetics of Italian, Spanish and French (henceforth the Italian Lectures, the Spanish Lectures and the French Lectures, respectively).

That Jones himself thought this material to be of more than passing significance is indicated by the fact that years later he arranged for them to be professionally bound in handsome black cloth decorated in gilt.[26] All three collections date back to the pre-

1920 period; Jones has added in his own hand "about 1914" on the flyleaves of both the Italian and the Spanish volumes, and "written about 1919" on the French collection. Unlike the majority of his surviving lectures which are in manuscript, these are all typewritten. (The typing—judging by the numerous errors, corrections and over-strikings—is Jones's personal effort rather than being the work of his secretarial staff.) All three contain many emendations added in Jones's handwriting. In addition, each has illustrative vowel diagrams and rough sagittal cross-sections.

Dating is assisted to an extent by the contents. The lectures on Italian and Spanish, for example, contain mention of the Cardinal Vowels. In fact, if Jones's own estimate of the date is accepted, these sections may well be the very first written evidence we have of Jones's system of vowel description. In the Italian Lectures (p. 26), after having dealt with the basics of the tongue-arch theory of vowel description and arriving at the vowel quadrilateral, Jones notes:

> On the circumference of this figure it has been found necessary to choose certain points called "cardinal" vowels to serve as a standard or scale from which all other vowels may be measured. These vowels are a close **i**, a close **e**, an open **ɛ**, 2 varieties of **a** (front **a** and back **ɑ**), an open **ɔ**, a close **o**, and a close **u**. The vowels of any language can be placed with reference to these cardinal vowels. For instance I can place the Italian vowels or the English vowels on this figure, and if I were to do so it would show very clearly the most important differences between them.

The Spanish Lectures (p. 26) contain similar information, albeit in more concise form. The French Lectures (p. 30), on the other hand, deal at length with the Cardinal Vowels, mentioning the fact that "they have known tongue-positions and known acoustic qualities which have been recorded on gramophone records". This of itself reveals that the French Lectures are of later date than the others (the first recording of the cardinal vowels having appeared in 1917). Further confirmation of Jones's suggested date lies in the fact that although several mentions are made (for example on p. 248) to Passy's (1914) *French phonetic reader*, no mention occurs of Passy's (1920) *Conversations françaises*, making it very likely the lectures were written before 1920.

Additional evidence of a date around 1919, later than the other two collections of lecture notes, comes from the fact that while the phoneme is not mentioned either in the Italian or Spanish Lectures, in the French material, the following somewhat clumsily phrased explanation occurs (p. 35):

> A *phoneme* is then the name given to a small family of related sounds which may be regarded as variants of one, for a given language, the variant used in any given French word being determined by the nature of the surrounding sounds.
>
> Therefore when the ordinary person speaks of the English or French vowel so-and-so, he generally means the English or French *phoneme* so-and-so. People

generally simply leave it to be regarded as an understood thing that sounds vary in quality according to their position in the word or sentence.

This is a similar (even if more loosely formulated) definition to those in the *Colloquial Sinhalese reader* and the *Pronunciation of Russian* (see Sections 9.4 and 10.5) and echoes the phrasing "a family of sounds", which first occurred in the Philological Society Lecture (see Section 7.5), but which was not revived until Jones's (1931) "On phonemes".

All three sets of lectures are written in the same style—very much in a colloquial kind of English, with much use of the first person and contracted forms, which makes them pleasant to read, but quite different from the precise lucid language typical of Jones's books and articles. However, the three sets of lectures vary considerably in depth. The Spanish and Italian Lectures are brisk, somewhat superficial treatments (64 and 71 double-spaced quarto pages, respectively) whereas the French Lectures are much more expansive.

The introductory general phonetic sections of both the Italian and Spanish Lectures are very similar, often virtually word for word, apart from the choice of examples. As is typical of Jones's works, though more unusually for linguistic works of their time, they are synchronic and contrastive in their approach. Little mention is made of philological matters; they are typically Jonesian in their concentration on the practicalities of helping the English-speaking learner to pronounce the languages concerned. There are, however, some conservative aspects to Jones's approach. For example, his description of Spanish ll in *calle* allows only for a palatal lateral articulation [ʎ]; no mention is made of what, even in 1914, is likely to have been an important, if not the commonest, form in colloquial Castilian Spanish, namely [j]. Jones's lack of confidence in his command of spoken Spanish is reflected in the fact that he appears to have used a native speaker for his lecture performances. Constant reference throughout the lecture notes is made to a certain Mr Pla who to pronounced the examples for him.

The French Lectures consist of over 320 pages of material. It is a perceptive treatment which can be read with interest even today, despite being astoundingly old-fashioned in parts. One example of this is the description of /r/, where the lingual trill [r] is recommended as a first choice to the learner, and the uvular fricative [ʁ] is condemned as being "considered not very good" and belonging "chiefly to the vulgar Parisian dialect" (p. 160). In other areas, such as the analysis of assimilation and elision, and the discussion of mute e, Jones emerges as progressive in comparison with other textbooks of the time.

The question arises of why Jones did not decide to evolve publications from this mass of material. As far as Italian and Spanish were concerned, it is not so surprising since he may well have felt that his knowledge of the languages was not sufficient for him to work in isolation and he may not have been able to find a native speaker whom he trusted like Plaatje, Perera or Trofimov.

The case of the French material is at first sight more surprising. The notes are detailed and extensive, the result of a great deal of careful thought and close observation. In the context of its time, it is reasonable to say that all significant aspects of the sound system of the language needed by the learner of academic background are dealt with. The obvious comparisons are with the *Outline* and the *Pronunciation of Russian*. Given Jones's reputation and position, it is scarcely credible that such a full treatment could not have found a publisher. Furthermore, a work on French could certainly have been produced with far less cost in terms of Jones's energies than the *Pronunciation*

155

so rapid that we commonly regard the sequence of sounds as one sound.   (3) Soft palate raised.   (4) Vocal chords vibrating and producing voice.

   Here is a diagram showing the action of the tongue.

   Many English people possess this sound and use it in English, It is a regular sound of the Scotch pronunciation of English.

   But the majority of English people do not possess it and have considerable difficulty in learning it.   The usual English sound of r, at any rate in the South, is ɹ—a fricativ It is made by the tongue-tip against the hinder part of the teeth ridge, but the air comes out in a continuous stream and there is no vibration (ɹ, r).   Listen to my pronunciation of draw, ride; I don't say drɔ:, raid, but dɹɔ:, ɹaid.

Figure 9.7. Types of /r/ from (a) Jones's French Lectures (p. 155) and, on p. 279, (b) Armstrong (1932: 110–111).

English Fricative *r* [1]

288. Description

1. The tip of the tongue is raised to the back part of the teeth-ridge.

2. The passage is narrowed at that point, but not sufficiently to cause much friction.

3. The sound is voiced.

DIAGRAM 52—English fricative *r* (ɹ)

1. Lingual Rolled *r* (r)

290. Description

1. The tip of the tongue is raised to the teeth-ridge and so held that it vibrates up and down against the teeth-ridge as the air-stream passes through the mouth.

2. r is generally voiced.

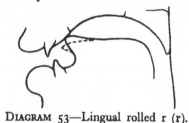

DIAGRAM 53—Lingual rolled r (r).

Figure 9.7. (cont.)

of Russian. As far as native-speaker informants, or collaborators, were concerned, Jones had available not only his wife, Cyrille, but later on his new young colleague, Hélène Coustenoble. In many ways, the French Lectures are the skeleton of a missing work on the phonetics of French (perhaps *The pronunciation of French* would have been its obvious title). This was a book Jones might have been expected to produce at some time around 1920. So why was it not forthcoming?

One possible reason is that Jones feared that a book of this sort could have damaged his relationship with Passy. Jones might have felt that too much of the material had been derived either from Passy's lectures or his *Sons du français*, and this might lead to suspicions of plagiarism. There also might have been the severely practical consideration of not wishing to threaten the sales of the *Sounds of the French language*. Jones may also have been uneasy about writing on the phonetics of French (as opposed to English or other languages) because Passy considered the phonetics of French as personal territory and brooked no opposition. In the lecture room, Jones clearly felt it safe to express his doubts over certain aspects of Passy's at times conservative approach to French phonology—as in the extract below (pp. 248–249).

> If you look through Passy's French Phonetic Reader you will notice an extraordinary amount of variation in the lengths of the nasalised vowels in non-final syllables. I suppose it is a matter of subtle shades of emphasis. At any rate it does not seem to me to matter in the least for practical purposes if you make them all short and put no length marks in your transcriptions.
>
> With some French speakers it appears that non-final length may be significant: Passy gives ti·rɑ̃ (tirant), tirɑ̃ (tyran).... But I can't help thinking that a good many French people do not make these distinctions. My impression is that in practical language teaching you need not trouble about length in non-final syllables, and it is really not necessary to mark these lengths in phonetic transcriptions. In most, if not all, the cases where lengthening is possible it also seems possible to keep the vowel short. So why trouble about it?

But this material was intended to be disseminated to small groups of students, and Passy would be most unlikely ever to hear of it. On the other hand, Jones might not have wanted even such mild insubordination to appear in print for all to read.[27]

Yet the French Lectures can be seen as being a precursor of two significant later publications. Firstly, much material (for instance, the sections on intonation), after editing and revision, appears in refurbished form in the excellent and greatly underrated *Colloquial French* (Stéphan—Jones 1927a); see Section 10.7. Secondly, there is much in Armstrong's (1932) *Pronunciation of French* which is reminiscent of the French Lectures. To give one example, we may cite the sections on the French stop consonants and glottal stop in the French Lectures (pp. 112–127) with the corresponding sections in Armstrong (1932: 20–21, 89–100), where very similar material is covered, albeit more economically, by Armstrong. Again, the sections on [r] have some similarities, but the treatment in Armstrong is more up-to-date in its approach. Although she describes a lingual trill [r], and says that it is frequently recommended, she comes down on the side of uvular articulations, in particular (pp. 113–114):

> ... uvular fricative r [which] is nowadays very commonly heard in Paris and other large towns of the north. Many use it in unemphatic speech in all positions ... The widespread use of ʁ among educated speakers marks it as very French, and for that reason it commends itself to many English learners.

The diagrams which accompany the text are often very similar to those found in Jones's French Lectures. Striking examples are the illustrations of types of /r/ taken from Jones's lecture notes (p. 155) and Armstrong (1932: 110–111); see Figure 9.7.

Lilias Armstrong can in no way be accused of pirating material; every section is reworked, written in her own words and provided with new exemplification; nothing (apart, perhaps, from the illustrations) is lifted or copied directly. But in contents, arrangement, approach and overall tones, there are constant echoes of Jones's approach. Armstrong would not only previously have attended Jones's lectures herself when a student, but clearly when preparing the book was also given sight of these actual notes. And doubtless Jones would have encouraged his protégée to borrow any ideas which she felt might be useful. In the preface to her book, Armstrong (p. v) writes: "I here express my indebtedness to Professor Daniel Jones for much more than permission to use Diagram 1, taken from the 1932 edition of his *Outline of English Phonetics*." This was her restrained way of acknowledging the influence of Jones which is so all-pervasive in this work.

Jones's Spanish and Italian Lectures may also be considered to have had some influence on future published work. Stirling's (1936) *Pronunciation of Spanish* produced a concise but most competent contrastive study of Spanish and English which was very much in the Jones mould. An acknowledgement to Jones appears in the preface. He mentions (p. x) "the invaluable assistance which [Daniel Jones] has so generously given me in preparing this book for the press". Much later, Marguerite Chapallaz's (1979) *Pronunciation of Italian* appeared—perhaps the last work of this kind ever to come from the Jones stable.

9.7. Health problems

The new decade did not begin auspiciously for Daniel Jones. On New Year's Day, 1920, the Department Secretary, Dorothy Parkinson, had to inform a correspondent that Jones was "unfortunately suffering from a breakdown, the result of over-working, and his Doctor has ordered him to take a complete rest".[28] The strain of the hectic campaign to obtain backing for the Institute project had predictably taken its toll of Jones's health.

Jones had had constant problems with his health, in one form or another, since his youth when the symptoms of chest disease had been the original reason behind his stay in Bourg-la-Reine. Later on, the main cause of his ill-health were problems related to nervous conditions. He lived constantly under the threat of a nervous breakdown—a tendency which worsened with age.[29] One indication of his poor mental state is that it was around this time that Jones decided to abandon playing chess, which was, together with music and reading detective stories, one of his few interests apart from his work. He gave up playing after a particularly exciting game with his brother-in-law, Philip Dannatt, which had resulted in Jones suffering a minor physical collapse.[30]

In part, his problems were brought on by his compulsion for excessive work—he was what might be termed today a "workaholic". Jones was normally well aware of this defect in his character and was careful to take adequate relaxation during the vacation periods. And in 1917, when Jones had organised three vacation courses, the Provost complained to the College authorities on Jones's behalf that the extra classes in the vacation would be liable to damage his health (see Section 7.4). However, the dream of the Institute, and the spur it formed to his ambition, seems to have resulted in Jones's succumbing completely to work pressure, and taking no proper rest breaks.

Originally, Jones had hoped to take a short period of time away from the Department, and his initial request "for leave of absence...in accordance with medical advice" was for one term only.[31] Lilias Armstrong was delegated to take over from him, and ran the Department for the remainder of the term. However, later in the year it was reported that Jones would be "unable to resume his full duties during the Third Term, but will be able to undertake part of his work".[32] The 1920 College Report commented on the absence of the head of the Phonetics Department:

> Mr. Daniel Jones has worked too arduously and has had to apply for leave of absence for the current term. Miss Armstrong is acting as Head of Department and, by means of additional assistance, is carrying on the full programme of work. The work in Phonetics is, thanks to the energy and whole-heartedness that Mr. Jones has always given to it, so progressive that its leader is greatly missed and his return in full vigour will be welcomed.[33]

One of the part-timers appointed to help out was Emile Stéphan, who assisted in the teaching of French phonetics. Stéphan was later to cooperate with Jones in writing one of the earliest audio-lingual courses (see Section 10.7).

As it turned out, Jones only finally returned to work (even then not to full-time duties) in October of the 1920–21 session,[34] and so, effectively, he was absent from the Department for a period of nine months. However, incredibly, in the interim he applied (successfully) for permission to spend the 1920 summer vacation in South Africa "in order to undertake a special piece of research work". This meant that he would not be able to take part in the vacation courses as advertised and it is noteworthy that, since Jones could now appear to be regarded as a potent attraction in this type of course, the College Committee instructed that all intending students should be informed of the change so that they could withdraw if they wished.[35] It appears that Jones never went on his proposed research trip; nothing more is recorded of it, and no mention of it is made in any report, or in any of Jones's publications; it seems likely that he called things off at the last minute—possibly on the advice of his doctor.

It is probably not coincidental that Jones's breakdown marks a noticeable halt to the progress of the expansion of the Department. After this point, Jones seems to have lost the impetus which had been driving him on, and the Institute, whilst it remained as an idea, did not seem to grip him in the way it had previously. Indeed, he handed over much of the work to Lloyd James before the collapse of the project in 1925.

Perhaps even more importantly, Jones's research and publication can be seen to undergo an alteration at this point. There is no longer the compulsive urge to publish which is characteristic of his performance prior to his breakdown. Instead, his work entered upon a period of quiescence lasting about five years when little of note appeared—apart from the long delayed publication of the *Pronunciation of Russian* in 1923. And when Jones did start producing again, his output in the years up to the war was to a great extent—though not entirely—the re-writing and consolidation of previous material. Jones's inventiveness, and his capacity to probe new avenues of research, were no longer so much in evidence. In compensation, as we shall see in Chapter 10, this would be eventually replaced by an industrious capacity to rearrange, extend and generally improve work of his own which had already been published, and to stimulate the research of his students and colleagues.

9.8. A Professor of Phonetics

In 1919, Daniel Jones was re-appointed Reader in Phonetics, as was the practice in London University at this time, for the customary five-year period. His financial position at this time was remarkable, since he was being paid a total of £700 a year, which was a full hundred pounds more than any other University College Reader—more than several of the professorial staff. Actually, Jones was receiving even more than this, since he was paid £40 each term for the lectures which he undertook (together with other members of his staff) for the School of Oriental Studies.

However, Jones was still, despite his high salary, without the power and status which would be accorded to a professorship. Promotion would undoubtedly have been mooted to Jones earlier by Provost Sir Gregory Foster, as a recompense for his work in establishing and running the Department; but, not surprisingly, no record exists of the point when it was first mentioned. There may well have been a connection between Jones's overloading himself with the work connected with the proposed Institute and the promise of a chair. As noted previously, it is possible that the professorship may have been discussed as early as 1914, which may have been a factor in Jones's decision to turn down the offer from Oxford University (see Section 5.9).

In the summer of 1920, Jones again received an invitation to work elsewhere—this time in India. Jones took the trouble of reporting to the College Committee, when returning to his post in October 1920, that during the vacation he had been offered the Professorship of Phonetics in the University of Dacca "on attractive terms", adding that "after careful consideration, he decided to refuse the offer".[36] The announcement was presumably intended to goad the College into making a decision to provide a chair for Jones, but perhaps foreknowledge of its contents had already had the required effect. At the same meeting, a resolution was passed requiring that "the necessary steps be taken for the conferment upon Mr. Daniel Jones of the title of Professor of Phonetics".[37] In January 1921, Jones's salary was raised to £800 in anticipation of his new status.[38]

In June 1921, as part of a general revision of personnel in University College, several of his staff received promotion, including Ida Ward, Harold Palmer and Arthur

Lloyd James. Lilias Armstrong became a Senior Lecturer and Stephen Jones was appointed "Superintendent of the Phonetics Laboratory", on the grounds that "such an officer has become essential in view of the growth of the Laboratory". He was to receive the remarkably high salary (for a non-professional post) of £600 a year.[39] Although Palmer was soon to depart for Japan, the others would remain to form the nucleus of the Department for the period of the twenties. Financially, things were certainly looking brighter in all ways, and in September the University Grants Committee decided to provide the Department with a recurrent annual grant of £2000.[40]

However, for Jones the most crucial piece of news came in the meeting of the Senate on July 20, 1921, when his appointment as "Professor of Phonetics" at last received official confirmation.[41] He was the first person in Britain to have that title—though he might well have mused upon the fact that Shaw's Henry Higgins had been his fictional forerunner. Whilst he had been thwarted in the matter of the Institute, he had achieved his other, and older, ambition of obtaining the first University Chair in Phonetics ever to be established in Britain. He was not yet forty years old—remarkably young to have gained a professorship in the nineteen twenties. Not only had Jones been given personal recognition, but, just as significantly for him, he could feel that in Britain the discipline of phonetics had finally come of age.

Chapter 10

They do nothing but phonetics (1921–30)

10.1. The later career

By 1921, Jones had written most of what would later be considered his major publications. All his books, apart from the *Pronunciation of Russian* and the *Phoneme*, had now appeared and the former was already complete in manuscript. Jones had previously shown himself capable of assuming the chief responsibility for the editorship of a significant (if modestly produced) journal, *Le Maître phonétique*. This periodical had flourished under the editorship of Jones and Passy in the years 1907–14, and had become a major force in the rapidly developing world of phonetics and linguistics of that era. Jones would soon start the journal up again and, whilst it never again achieved the dynamism of the pre-First World War period, it was nevertheless to publish numerous short but influential contributions to the advancement of phonetics and phonology.

Similarly, though the International Phonetic Association was never again to regain the momentum of the years between 1907 and 1914, when the youthful and ambitious Jones was effectively in charge, nevertheless the organisation went on taking an important part in the promotion and spread of phonetic ideas. It was also notable for the development of the IPA alphabet, which became widely accepted by phoneticians and linguists throughout the world, at least outside the USA (see Abercrombie 1983: 6–7). In this, as will be seen, Jones played the main role.

Yet the time from 1921 onwards cannot be reasonably regarded as fallow years. True, he was never again to achieve the tempo or the massive output of the extremely productive period from 1907 to 1921; however, it would have been difficult for anyone to keep up such a pace. Nor did his publications ever again have the freshness and originality of the pre-1921 period. But such originality is characteristic of the work of the young academic. It is not unusual in a scholar's later years for the contribution to take on the less dynamic, but potentially just as useful, role of consolidating his or her own work combined with the stimulation of the efforts of others, and this was certainly true in Jones's case. Viewed in this light, we may consider the years from 1921 to 1967—the whole period, since Jones went on working until the year of his death—as a time of mature reassessment of his own earlier contributions, and provision of encouragement and valuable guidance to his colleagues and pupils.

10.2. The Department in the early twenties

The Phonetics Department was still housed in cramped accommodation in the main building of University College. One of the enthusiastic young students who crowded into Jones's Department to learn from the exceptionally talented group of phoneticians that he had working for him at this time was a young Dutch woman, Johanna Schilthuis, later to be co-author of the *Dutch phonetic reader* (Quick—Schilthuis 1930). In 1984, shortly before her death, Mrs Talma-Schilthuis, as she now was, placed on record her impressions of the six months she had spent there in 1921.[1]

She was taught mainly by Arthur Lloyd James, "a perfect teacher", who inspired

Figure 10.1. A cartoon of Daniel Jones, which accompanied his article "In the days of my youth" (Jones 1926e).

his students with "eagerness to learn and to try to imitate", but also received tuition from Harold Palmer, Lilias Armstrong, Ida Ward and "on special occasions" from Jones himself, then recovering from his illness. Although the atmosphere in UCL was "friendly and homely", Jones demanded hard work from all his staff and students. In his classes (as was also noted of Tilly), everyone was treated alike. This could have disastrous consequences, as when the well-known Dutch linguist and lexicographer Prick van Wely (1867–1927) asked to sit in on one of Jones's lectures. Whenever Van Wely started speaking, Jones "kept correcting him, as he corrected anyone". After a while, Van Wely felt he could no longer accept what he obviously regarded as personal humiliation in front of a group of young students and pointedly left halfway through Jones's class.

Jones never obtained his desire for an institute devoted totally to phonetics and operating in its own magnificent buildings. The move, when it came in 1922, was to much more modest accommodation—a Victorian terraced house, backing on to the main buildings of University College and overlooking the gardens of a Bloomsbury square. Number 21 Gordon Square, known for many years in the College as "Arts Annexe I", was to be the home of the UCL Phonetics Department for the rest of Jones's career (apart from the interruption of the war years). Indeed, the non-experimental portion of the Department (now merged with the former Department of Linguistics, and renamed the Department of Phonetics and Linguistics) is housed there to this day.

Following the period of rapid expansion after the end of the First World War, the early twenties saw the numbers of the Department stabilise at around ten full-time staff including Jones himself. Jones (1926e: 398) wrote, with obvious satisfaction:

> Now I have nine assistants on full-time work. They do nothing all day and every day but phonetics; for students come to the department from every quarter of the world, and we have representatives of over twenty nationalities in our classes at the present time.

10.3. Vacation courses

In the 1920s, once Europe had got over the problems caused by the war, Jones's vacation courses (see Section 14.4) prospered, attracting students from all over the Continent and even wider afield. The most popular courses were those on French aimed at British teachers of the language, and English aimed at non-native speakers. Unlike most language training available at the time, Jones's courses dealt almost exclusively with colloquial speech and always had a considerable emphasis on pronunciation training. Furthermore, Jones was not frightened to include a large amount of phonetics in the programme (though always with a practical bias) and he was pleased to find this was no deterrent to the students—rather the reverse. Large numbers of registrations for the summer schools were proof of the success of the methods of pronunciation training he was advocating. Not surprisingly, the students were asked to use books written by Jones himself and by his staff. Naturally, for students of English, the *Outline* was always required reading.

We have a good idea of how the English vacation courses were received by the students thanks to a magazine report written in 1921 by a Dutch participant, J.P. Prins, just a week after his return to Holland in August of that year.[2] A wide variety of participants attended. Prins (1921: 140) describes how some students arrived having learnt nothing of phonetics in their native countries and having to start from scratch. Others, for instance the Dutch and the Swedes, having already strong phonetic traditions in their own countries, achieved a higher standard of pronunciation—which on this occasion had apparently been noted in one of the London daily newspapers.

Daniel Jones and Lilias Armstrong had decided to divide the lectures between them —Jones dealing with the English vowels, and Armstrong with the consonants. In addition, lectures were included on supra-segmental features; amongst those areas cited by Prins were length and intonation. Prins acknowledged that this component of the course might have been useful for other participants, but, for the Dutch contingent, all these plenary lectures were somewhat elementary. In fact, he valued (p. 139) mainly the opportunity of thus "acquiring a good, pure pronunciation and of hearing the language spoken by 'educated people'". Prins thought particularly highly of Lilias Armstrong's ear-training classes (p. 140):

> She wrote the vowels on the blackboard in phonetic transcription and then pronounced them clearly several times, so that people learnt to make a good distinction between the sounds. Then she produced the vowels and consonants in 'unusual combinations' which were totally without meaning, so that although they were composed of English sounds, no connection could be attached to the written image in one's mind…. If one had written down the combination incorrectly, then she pronounced it with the sound the pupil thought he had heard, in order to make him recognise clearly his mistake.

The practical classes, for which students were divided up into groups on the basis of nationality, also received particular praise from Prins. Ida Ward was one of his tutors for these sessions, which consisted of half an hour of reading practice and another half hour of practice in "fluency" and intonation. Prins found the classes "very entertaining, instructive and … useful".

10.4. Family and personal life 1921–30

By the autumn of 1922, Jones had recovered his mental health sufficiently to take charge of his Department once more for the new session. However, the problem of nervous strain was one which was to be recurrent from now on. His concern with his health became a dominating feature of his life, almost an obsession, and he frequently had to cope with periods of depressive illness. These were at times severe, and he was especially prone to long bouts of insomnia. Nevertheless, he carried on with his work at University College, cosseted by his senior staff, and although rarely actually absent, brought a sofa into his room, and not infrequently lay down to rest on it actually while seeing staff or students (Abercrombie 1980: 2).

In September of this year, the Jones's second child was born. To their delight, it was a girl, to whom they gave the name Michelle. Cyrille continued to visit her relations frequently. This close family connection is also shown by the fact that she chose to stay for the birth of her baby with her sister Irène at St Leonards. With a family of two young children—Olivier was now a bright youngster of five—Jones felt unable to remain in his London flat, notwithstanding the convenience of Ridgmount Gardens for his work. He decided to move to less cramped surroundings, and ultimately settled on a house in what was then the rapidly developing suburb of Golders Green in north London. Oddly, for someone troubled by a nervous condition and insomnia, Jones chose to live on a busy portion of what was later to be designated the North Circular Road; the address was at that time 90 Lyttelton Road (though the name of this section was later changed to Falloden Way).

The Jones family was to remain in this house for twelve years whilst the children were growing up. They had been joined by a former member of the Bourg-la-Reine *ménage* who had moved to England when Cyrille's father, Henri Motte, died in 1922, namely Sophie Lund. She moved in with the Joneses at Golders Green and so became "Marraine" to a second generation. Sophie Lund also shared with Jones an interest in theosophy and related beliefs, which was now a major part of his life. Jones managed to find a job for her in University College, where she worked until 1934 (as mentioned by Abercrombie, see Section 11.7).

In this decade, Jones suffered two significant family bereavements. His mother died in 1925 at the age of 77. Her will provides evidence that old family quarrels and divisions had deteriorated further after Dan Jones's death. Mrs Jones left all her money to her own children, Daniel and his brother Arnold, and nothing to her stepsons. It would appear that virtually all contacts were eventually lost with Jones's half-brothers and they played no part in his later life. Whatever effect his mother's death had on Jones, it is certain that he was far more distressed at the loss of Arnold only four years later in 1929, who, in his early forties, succumbed to cancer after a long struggle against the disease. Although he was quite unlike his brother in temperament, the bonds between them had remained firm. Without doubt, Arnold's death had a worsening effect on Jones's mental health and exacerbated his bouts of depression.

10.5. *The pronunciation of Russian*

Even for Jones, who had become notorious for delays with his publications, the time-lag before the eventual appearance of *The pronunciation of Russian* (Trofimov—Jones 1923a) was remarkable. The authors claim that the book was, in effect, complete before the end of the war (p. v):

This book was prepared during the years 1916–17, and the manuscript was sent to the printer on Dec. 31st, 1917. For various reasons the printing and proof-correcting have taken far longer than was anticipated, with the result that it has not been possible to issue the book before this year (1923).

In a sense, *The pronunciation of Russian* therefore belongs to an earlier period of Jones's development; nevertheless, as we shall indicate below, there are certain portions which seem to have been inserted, or at least rewritten, at a later stage. Even though the Revolution of 1917 had meant that most of the phonetic texts were "not applicable to present conditions in Russia" (p. v), the material was retained apparently unaltered; the authors clearly felt themselves unable to face the amount of rewriting this would have involved, and contented themselves with an apology in the preface (p. v).

Whatever Trofimov and Jones's "various reasons" were for the delay of almost six years is not made clear. Abercrombie (1983: 6) has described Jones's obsessive "concern for typographical appearance" and the notoriously perfectionist demands which he made of printers. Jones's interest in typography and presentation of material meant that his later books were commendably free of errors and attractive in appearance, compared with the average linguistic publication of the period. His realisation of his readers' limitations ensured that Jones's books were far more approachable than, for example, those of Sweet. On the other hand, as Abercrombie points out, this also meant that he had long arguments with printers and publishers.

In the event, the *Pronunciation of Russian* proved to be an exceptionally pleasing book in terms of its presentation with clear, well-arranged vowel diagrams and cross-sections. Reading the *Pronunciation of Russian* today, one is struck by how up-to-date the book appears in its printing and lay-out. It contrasts sharply with the ugly typography and old-fashioned arrangement of the *Pronunciation of English*[1]. Indeed, Jones must also have been highly satisfied with the end result since the *Pronunciation of Russian* seems to have been the typographical model for his revision, almost thirty years later, of the *Pronunciation of English*[3]. The cross-section diagrams in the *Pronunciation of Russian* (themselves enlarged versions of those in the *Outline*[1]) are clearly forerunners to the *Pronunciation of English*[3] (see Figure 10.2); some in fact seem to have been transferred virtually unchanged from the earlier to the later book.

Remarkably for someone who was eventually the author of two major works on the language, Jones himself did not speak the language—apart from an ability to produce phonetically perfect imitations of a selection of words and phrases. Many years later, in a candid self-admission of his own limitations, he wrote : "... I...don't know any Russian except some isolated words".[3] It must therefore be assumed that virtually all the information about Russian was provided by his co-author. As was the case with all his other works on languages other than English, Jones operated in conjunction with a reliable native speaker—in this case, M.V. Trofimov.

Michael V. Trofimov (1884–1949) was born in Archangel, and graduated from St Petersburg. He had taught Russian at Liverpool and was Reader in Russian at King's

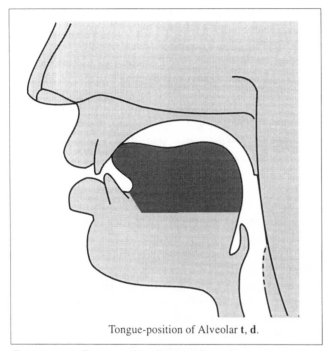

Tongue-position of Alveolar **t, d**.

Figure 10.2. Cross-section diagram from the *Pronunciation of Russian* (p. 45) illustrating alveolar /t, d/. An almost identical diagram of English /t, d/ is to be found in the *Pronunciation of English*³ (p. 67).

College, London in 1914. Five years later, he obtained a chair at Manchester—a post which he held until 1945. Trofimov was himself no mean phonetician and had co-authored a *Handbook of Russian* (Trofimov—Scott 1918), a book which claimed to be "the first attempt in English to deal comprehensively with the Russian sound system" (p. vii) and devoted sixty-eight pages to the topic. For the *Pronunciation of Russian*, however, Jones appears to have had the upper hand in matters of phonetic theory. For instance, in his earlier work, Trofimov had favoured an idiosyncratic terminology, derived in part from Sweet, but this is abandoned in favour of a Jonesian system of description. A footnote also indicates, diplomatically, that Trofimov lost at least one battle over the use of a term: "Palatalisation is also known as "jotation"; the first author [Trofimov] prefers this latter term" (p. 84 n.). In fact, Trofimov and Scott (1918: 30–31) rejected palatalisation as a "confusing term", arguing, rather pedantically, that: "the palate stretches from the uvula to the upper gums; how then can a consonant be 'palatalised'?"

The *Pronunciation of Russian* takes as its standard for pronunciation Michael Trofimov's own idiolect—a *modus operandi* which conforms to Jones's later views on phonemic analysis (*Phoneme*: 9). Although Trofimov was a native of Archangel, his Russian seems largely to have reflected the contemporary educated usage of St Petersburg and as such could be regarded as "typical of the speech of a large number of educated Russians" (*Pronunciation of Russian*: 13). A short section is devoted to the chief differences between this type of Russian and that of Moscow, e.g. the replacement in Moscow of the sequence /ʃtʃ/ by /ʃʃ/ (cf. the discussion in Comrie—Stone 1978: 26–29). For English, Jones and Trofimov (p. 14) take as their model the pronunciation "which we believe to be most usually heard from educated Southern British persons". For detail of this type of English, they refer their readers to the *EPD* (Jones 1917a), where Jones describes what he at that time called "Public School Pronunciation". See Section 7.2.

The *Pronunciation of Russian*, a book of just over 260 pages, was published in the Cambridge "Primers of Language" series, of which Jones had been designated the editor, and which had also included the *Pronunciation of English*[1] and Grant's (1913) *Pronunciation of English in Scotland*. Trofimov and Jones begin with an overview of general phonetic theory, covering the speech mechanism, phonation and the classification of vowels and consonants. This section appears to have been written by Jones alone, with little or no assistance from his co-author, and represents in published form the earliest complete survey of Jones's fully developed view of general phonetics. In its statements on the principles of description and classification of vowels and consonants, the *Pronunciation of Russian* is clearly ahead of all Jones's published work thus far, and in many ways it can be seen forming the basis of much of Jones's later books, in particular the revised third edition of the *Outline* [1932]. Therefore, apart from the contribution that it makes to Russian descriptive phonology, the *Pronunciation of Russian* must also be seen as being important as a culmination of the development of Jones's ideas on phonetics and phonology. It would also seem clear that (despite Jones's statements in the preface) this portion of the book was a late addition, since much of the content appears to be in advance of Jones's theoretical position in 1917 (cf. Section 7.5), and is also somewhat fuller than that of the *Sinhalese reader*.

Seen in this light, one of the most significant portions of the book is that dealing with vowel description, and in particular the summary given of Cardinal Vowel theory (pp. 27–41). The principles of the theory are presented on the lines which had already been previously established in the *Sinhalese reader* but Jones now provided a clearer explanation with more detailed exemplification. The *Pronunciation of Russian* also has illustrative diagrams of the assumed tongue positions of the Cardinal Vowels (see Figure 10.3), together with eight photographs showing lip shapes of the primary Cardinal Vowel series (see Sections 8.4 and 8.5 for Jones's overall interest in lip shape). No such comprehensive statement of Jones's Cardinal Vowel theory was to appear before the revised [1956] edition of the *Outline*[8] (pp. 29–41), and most of that seems in fact to be derived from the *Pronunciation of Russian*.

In one important respect, Jones carries his theory of vowel description a stage further than in the *Sinhalese reader*. A section entitled "Subsidiary Cardinal Vowels" (*Pronunciation of Russian*: 40–41) deals with "vowels derived from the eight primary

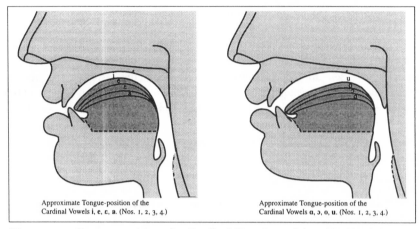

Figure 10.3. Tongue positions for Cardinal Vowels as claimed by Daniel Jones in the *Pronunciation of Russian* (pp. 28–29). These diagrams are also to be found in the *Pronunciation of English*[3] (pp. 19–20).

cardinal vowels by changes of lip-position"; these were later to be termed the "Secondary Cardinal Vowels" (see, for example, *Outline*[8]: 35–36) . Jones indicates the vowels [y ø œ ɒ] derived from adding lip-rounding to unrounded vowels, and he also shows [ʌ] and [ɯ] derived from unrounding rounded vowels. He omits rounded Cardinal 4 [ɶ], thus anticipating later pronouncements of the IPA that such a vowel did not occur in any known language (IPA 1949: 6). Strangely, Jones does not include the unrounded Cardinal 7 vowel [ɤ]—perhaps because he had not yet hit upon a suitable symbol.

In addition to allowing for a "centralised" diacritic ¨, the *Pronunciation of Russian* also shows a number of central vowels (p. 40):

close mixed unrounded ɨ , rounded ʉ
half-close mixed unrounded ǝ , rounded ɵ
half-open mixed unrounded ɜ , rounded ɞ.

Of these, only [ɨ ʉ] were finally retained as Cardinal Vowels, whilst of the remainder, ɜ ɵ have been quite commonly used as central vowel symbols, whereas ǝ ɞ were until recently generally defunct. Jones appears to have gone on for some time using these symbols in his own teaching, and the whole set (with ɞ reversed as ɷ) cropped up again in Abercrombie (1967: 161; 177 n. 7), who stated, however, that "not all these six vowels are acknowledged by Daniel Jones". Kingdon (1964) also revived these vowel symbols (see Figure 14.1, Section 14.14). Recently, with the latest 1993 revision of the International Phonetic Alphabet, these symbols have achieved a second wind, and Jones could hardly have guessed that they would appear on the current

1993 IPA chart in exactly the same form as he had devised them precisely 60 years previously.

The general phonetic description of consonant sounds (pp. 41–48) is also in keeping with Jones's final view of consonant articulation, as found in his later works, and indeed the *Pronunciation of Russian* could be viewed in this respect as the precursor of the revision of the *Pronunciation of English* (*Pronunciation of English*³ [1950]). In the *Pronunciation of Russian*, for instance, there is none of the havering over the status of affricate consonants found in the *Outline*¹ (see Sections 8.4 and 8.8), these being clearly defined and indicated for both Russian and English (*Pronunciation of Russian* 45; 105–113). Jones's distinction between consonant and vowel description, familiar to the present-day reader, is also clearly stated in the *Pronunciation of Russian*. Consonant description is to be based essentially on articulatory criteria; but vowels require a combination of these and auditory judgement, thereby invoking the need for the Cardinal Vowel system.

In passing, it may also be noted that a significant observation on English is tucked away in a note (*Pronunciation of Russian*: 94 n.), where Jones and Trofimov make the very first mention of the occurrence in educated English of glottal replacement of /t/, stating that "very many English speakers do not use **t** at all in words of this kind [i.e. those involving the sequence **tn**], but replace it by the 'glottal stop'". This has been passed over by Andrésen (1968: 12–35) in his otherwise very thorough historiographical survey of glottal stop in English. See Collins—Mees (1996: 179).

The chapter "Principles of Transcription" (pp. 49–53) provides a complete statement of Jones's views on the phoneme at this period but this is not in any important respect different from the *Sinhalese reader* (see Section 9.4). Again, as in the *Sinhalese reader*, Jones's position is much the same as that put forward by him throughout his later publications (see Section 13.4). The phoneme is defined as follows (*Pronunciation of Russian*: 49–50):

> ...a group of sounds consisting of an important sound of the language (i.e. the most frequently used member of that group) together with others which take its place in particular sound-groups.

Again, doubt is cast on the authors' claim that the *Pronunciation of Russian* was completed in 1917 (p. ii), since the above extract seems (as compared with the *Sinhalese reader*) even closer to the concept as stated in the *Phoneme* (p. 7):

> ...small families of sounds, each family consisting of an important sound of the language together with other related sounds which, so to speak, "represent" it in particular sequences or under particular conditions of length or stress or intonation.

Though the *Pronunciation of Russian* states that generally it is only necessary to use the phonemes in "practical phonetic writing", Russian is argued to be an exceptional

CHART OF RUSSIAN PHONEMES

		Bi-labial	Labio-dental	Dental	Alveolar	Dental-palatalized	Alveolar-palatalized	Post-alveolar	Palato-alveolar	Palatal	Velar
CONSONANTS	Plosive	p b		t d		t d					k g
	Affricate				ʦ ʣ				ʧ ʤ		
	Nasal	m			n		ɳ				
	Lateral				l		ʎ				(l)
	Rolled				r		ɼ				
	Fricative		f v		s z		ş ᶎ	ʃ ʒ			x g
	Semi-vowel									j	
VOWELS	Close	(u)								Front i Central ɨ Back u	
	Open	(o)								ɛ ə o a	

Sounds which have a marked double articulation appear twice in the chart, the place of secondary articulation being shown by the symbol in brackets (). Palatalized p, b, m, f, v are regarded as subsidiary members of the p, b, m, f, v phonemes (see §§ 338, 339, 382, etc.).

Figure 10.4. Chart of Russian phonemes, according to Trofimov and Jones (*Pronunciation of Russian*, p. xii).

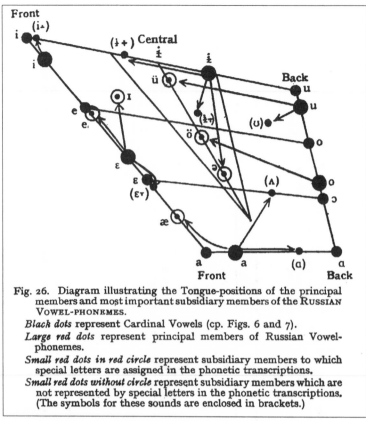

Fig. 26. Diagram illustrating the Tongue-positions of the principal
    members and most important subsidiary members of the RUSSIAN
    VOWEL-PHONEMES.

Black dots represent Cardinal Vowels (cp. Figs. 6 and 7).

Large red dots represent principal members of Russian Vowel-
    phonemes.

Small red dots in red circle represent subsidiary members to which
    special letters are assigned in the phonetic transcriptions.

Small red dots without circle represent subsidiary members which are
    not represented by special letters in the phonetic transcriptions.
    (The symbols for these sounds are enclosed in brackets.)

Figure 10.5. Vowel diagram showing the analysis of the Russian
vowel phonemes (*Pronunciation of Russian*, p. 55).

language in that "many of the phonemes have unusually numerous subsidiary members" (p. 51). Consequently, the *Pronunciation of Russian* is provided with a relatively narrow transcription in order to indicate some of this allophonic variation.

A remarkable feature of the work is that throughout the main body of the book,
examples are shown in transcription *only*, and conventional Russian orthography is
relegated to the appendices at the end (pp. 210–252). This system must be regarded
as a brave token of faith in the efficacy of phonetic transcription (though it is worth
noting that in the subsequent version, *The phonetics of Russian*, the principle was
abandoned, and Jones and Ward ensure that Russian orthography appears throughout
the text alongside transcription; see Section 13.15).

The Russian sound system is described in detail and subjected to a contrastive
analysis in which it is compared with the sounds of English; the chart reproduced in
Figure 10.4. shows the Trofimov—Jones view of the phonemic system of Russian.

This section, which forms the core of the book, is noteworthy for being one of the earliest attempts at a thorough contrastive analysis of a language for English learners. The *Pronunciation of Russian* is Jones's most ambitious attempt ever at a work of this type, being far more elaborate and detailed than any of his books on languages other than those on English. (However, evidence exists in the form of correspondence, lecture notes and index cards that a book of similar type and length was envisaged for French, but this appears never to have got beyond a rough planning stage. See also Sections 9.6 and 10.7.)

The vowel system of Russian is analysed as consisting of six vowel phonemes /i ɛ a o u i/ (p. 54); in addition, the *Pronunciation of Russian* recognises a number of diphthongs, all terminating in [i]. The distribution of the chief allophones is illustrated in the vowel diagram reproduced in Figure 10.5. The analysis of [i] and [i] as two separate phonemes, instead of regarding them as being in allophonic relationship was later to cause Jones considerable concern, and seems to have been a matter of continuing regret, almost obsession. It was perhaps the chief reason for Jones's great dissatisfaction with the *Pronunciation of Russian*, and his eagerness many years later to accept Dennis Ward's offer to collaborate on a revision. It is curious that the *Pronunciation of Russian* is not referred to at all in the *Phoneme*, and appears to have been deliberately excluded from the personal bibliography at the end of the book (*Phoneme*: 255). Jones later discussed the matter several times in letters to Dennis Ward; on one occasion when advising the latter on the content of the bibliography for another work, he wrote:

> If not too late, I suggest that you delete the title of the book by Trofimov & me from your list.... Not only is that book hopelessly out of date in many respects— & will no doubt be disapproved of by the present authorities. But it also contains that gross inaccuracy about the phonemic status of i , & I don't want the fact that I ever thought i & i to be separate phonemes to be perpetuated. Baudouin & Co knew that they were allophones of the same phoneme years before.[4]

It is odd that Jones should have been so embarrassed over this point, since although the status of [i] as an allophone of /i/ is today regarded as being fairly clear-cut, as stated explicitly by Boyanus (1947), the weight of evidence was by no means as clear in 1923. In any case, the *Pronunciation of Russian* contains an "escape clause" in the form of a note stating (p. 54 n.): "Some students of Russian phonetics have suggested that i may be regarded as a member of the i-phoneme. The matter merits further research."

Another feature of the *Pronunciation of Russian* vowel analysis which might be regarded as dubious is the assignment of [e] to the /ɛ/ rather than the /i/ phoneme (p. 55); this was amended in the *Phonetics of Russian* (p. 29); cf. the discussion in the *Phoneme* (pp. 104–106) on the Russian vowel system.

The Russian consonant system is subjected to a similar detailed articulatory description and contrastive analysis with English (see chart, Figure 10.4). As will be seen, the

Pronunciation of Russian (p. 86) considers certain of the palatalised consonants, i.e. [p̡ t̡ m̡ f̡ ɣ̡], as allophonic variants (although not employing that term), whilst the remainder are regarded as phonemes in their own right. However, in the *Phonetics of Russian* (p. 197) the more elegant, and generally accepted, solution of regarding all the non-palatalised and palatalised consonants as opposed phonemic pairs is opted for, and this is also the treatment suggested in the *Phoneme* (pp. 25–26). In addition to this segmental analysis, the *Pronunciation of Russian* contains sections covering assimilation of voice and place in Russian (pp. 155–161); vowel and consonant length (pp. 161–165); stress (pp. 165–169) and intonation (pp. 169–173). The intonation section is extremely brief, and as Trofimov and Jones in effect confess, it is merely an impressionistic view of a few aspects rather than an attempt to tackle the topic in any depth (p. 170):

> The formidable task of discovering the principles of Russian intonation has not yet been attempted, and all it is possible to do at present is to give some examples of Russian usage.

However, the section is interesting in that the three-line interlinear marking, though not distinguishing stressed from unstressed syllables, could be considered as a kind of precursor to the Armstrong and Ward (1926) intonation system (see Section 14.12). At the same time, the mention (p. 169) of a "convenient notation for the intonation of single syllables" (level —, fall \, rise /, rise-fall ∧, fall-rise V, level finished off by rapid fall ⌐, level preceded by rapid fall ∟, level finished off by rapid rise ⌐, level preceded by rapid rise ⌐) would seem to show the influence of the work of Harold Palmer (cf. Palmer 1922: 7–8).

The first part of the *Pronunciation of Russian* closes with ear-training exercises (Chapter XXII), catenation exercises (Chapter XXIV) and lists of exemplifications of Russian sounds cited in isolated words (Chapter XXV). In a manner reminiscent of the *Outline*, the remainder of the book (Part II) consists of phonetic texts and two appendices dealing with Russian orthography.

The *Pronunciation of Russian* appears to have been a book which Jones came to hold in no high esteem, and eventually regarded even with embarrassment—at least as far as its linguistic content was concerned—even if he approved of its appearance. He must undoubtedly have considered that he knew too little about the Russian language to write about it with confidence, and had been forced to rely too much on Trofimov for his information. It may also be that, years later, he suffered from the criticisms of Simon Boyanus when the latter was working in London University (see Section 11.12).

In fact, Jones was being hard on himself and his co-author. It is true that the *Pronunciation of Russian* cannot be considered a pioneering work on Russian in the way that the *Sechuana reader* was for Tswana, or the *Sinhalese reader* was for Sinhalese, since so much research of exceptional quality on Russian phonology had already been done in Russia and Poland (see Section A.6). Nevertheless, the book is of value in at least two respects. Firstly, the *Pronunciation of Russian* provided the fullest statement yet available of Jones's views on the phoneme and on Cardinal Vowel theory. Secondly, it was the first example of a book produced in Britain which subjected the sound system of a foreign language to a lengthy contrastive analysis, and while Jones's linguistic theory may be faulted, his detailed articulatory description and contrastive phonetic work was, as always, thorough and on the whole remarkably accurate.

In the 1950s, Jones began work on a radical revision of the *Pronunciation of Russian* in collaboration with Dennis Ward, eventually to be published two years after Jones's death under the title *The phonetics of Russian* (Jones—Ward 1969). This turned out to be essentially a different book, rather than merely a new edition; see Section 13.15.

10.6. Shorter publications and revisions 1921–30

In the 1920s, Jones's output was much reduced as compared with his activity in the pre-war and war years—a pace he was only once ever going to approach again, namely in his later 1950s productive period after his retirement. In the years immediately following his breakdown, there are, quite uncharacteristically, three almost blank years. In 1920 and 1921, he appears to have produced nothing and in 1922 merely brought out the second, scarcely changed, edition of the *Outline*. Indeed, in the first four years after he obtained his chair—if one excludes the *Pronunciation of Russian* (1923a), which had been virtually completed considerably earlier—Jones's writings consisted only of a sample of Cornish English (Jones 1923b) and some "spécimens" of Chinese Hwa Miao (Jones 1923c), Korean (Minn—Jones 1924a) and Gã (Jones 1925)—all of which appeared in *Le Maître phonétique*.

But by the second half of the decade, Jones was again writing more consistently. In 1926, in addition to another "spécimen", this time of Gujarati (Jones—Kabraji 1926b), more general writing appeared. Jones wrote two perceptive short papers on symbolisation (Jones 1926a, 1926c). The first of these argues against the use of a separate vowel symbol to indicate the lowering of final /ɪ/ in contemporary RP (as in the second vowel in *city*).[5] The second article is notable for its discussion of juncture (the actual term is not employed), anticipating the more detailed treatment in Jones (1931k), and the later work of the American structuralist school on this topic, e.g. Trager—Bloch (1941). He also produced a review of Doke's work on Zulu (Jones 1926d) and wrote the brief, but revealing, autobiographical piece "In the days of my youth" (Jones 1926e).

By 1927, Jones had returned to full activity. That year saw not only the appearance of the massive *Colloquial French* (see Section 10.7 below), but also the publication of the first of two papers based on Jones and Plaatje's earlier research (see Sections 6.7 and 7.5) on Tswana, "Words distinguished by tone in Sechuana" (Jones 1927f). A second study, *The tones of Sechuana nouns* (Jones 1928a), was issued as a monograph by the International Institute of African Languages and Cultures. Both of these are nowadays regarded as classic works in the early study of tone (see Section 14.13) but the latter is also especially interesting as being one of the first detailed treatments of the tonal morphology of the declensions of a Bantu language.

Jones's work in this area received notably approving comment from one significant authority. His erstwhile informant, Sol Plaatje, commented thus in an internal report probably intended for the University of Witwatersrand and quoted by Willan (1984: 338) in his biography of Plaatje:

> ...Professor Jones of University College, London, has recently brought out a pamphlet illustrating "The Tones of Sechuana Nouns". It may interest you to know that Professor Jones, writing alone in London, has in his little brochure 126 Sechuana nouns not included in Brown's big Sechuana Dictionary (the official Dictionary of that language), and he has rendered correctly 30 other nouns which appear but are mistranslated by Brown. One wonders how many untranslated words the Professor would have given us, supposing he had dealt with all the nouns and perhaps the verbs too.

In the same report, it is noted (p. 338–339) that the work on Sechuana was completed by Jones himself without the assistance of Plaatje and that the number of translation errors ("only three words") are remarkably few.

Jones's (1928h) "Principles of practical orthography for African languages.—II" takes the form of an addendum to Carl Meinhof's (1928) article bearing the same title. It follows directly on from Meinhof's piece, which is a rejoinder to the Memorandum on *Practical orthography of African languages* (Anon. 1927, but probably largely the work of Jones and Arthur Lloyd James). Jones states that "the authors" agree with many of Meinhof's views, e.g. that orthography intended for Africans ought not to take into account the needs of Europeans. Furthermore, he refers to the necessity for "simplicity and clearness" and the avoidance of diacritical signs. He also draws attention to the implicitly phonemic principle: "that it is only necessary to be precise when misunderstanding might occur through a confusion of sounds", and the importance of "the provision of good cursive forms of letters" (1928h: 237). In addition, he points out that they accept the need for digraphs in certain circumstances, but not for /ʃ/, which might cause confusion, especially if written "sh" in English colonies and "ch" in French territory (1928h: 238). Jones goes on to point out that the IPA has both a system of transcription and orthography for each language, and concludes by emphasising the need for aesthetic considerations when designing typefaces, where all symbols must fit harmoniously with other Roman letters.

In addition to the 1922 edition of the *Outline* (see above), Jones also produced revised editions of the *EPD* in 1924 and 1926. These involved few changes in content: six hundred new words were added to the 1924 edition and a revision made to the preface in 1926. The latter is notable for its introduction of the term "Received Pronunciation" and the abbreviation "RP". This replaced Jones's coinage "Public School

KEY BOOK

to the Practical Course of

COLLOQUIAL FRENCH

FOR THE ENGLISH

with the aid of

"His Master's Voice"

GRAMOPHONE RECORDS

BY

E. M. STÉPHAN

SENIOR LECTURER IN FRENCH, UNIVERSITY COLLEGE, LONDON

AND

DANIEL JONES

PROFESSOR OF PHONETICS, UNIVERSITY COLLEGE, LONDON

LONDON
THE GRAMOPHONE COMPANY, LTD.
EDUCATION DEPARTMENT
1927

Figure 10.6. Title page of the Key Book to *Colloquial French* (1927).

Pronunciation" and "PSP", which he had been using in the *EPD* up till then. It is striking that these changes were not made thoroughly throughout the book. By what seems to have been uncharacteristic carelessness, Jones retained "PSP" in the "Explanations" section and the abbreviation continued to appear (with no explanation whatsoever) in subsequent reprints until 1937 when Jones undertook a more extensive revision of the text (see Section 11.3).

10.7. *Colloquial French*

Since his student days, when he had spent the happiest period of his youth in France, Jones had been fascinated by French. Unlike most of the languages he wrote about, this was one he spoke fluently to near-native standard and used every day in his family circle. His very first books had dealt with French— *100 Poésies enfantines* and the Savory—Jones (1907c) translation of Passy's *Les Sons du français*—so it was not surprising that he would want eventually to write a book of his own on the pronunciation of French. As has been stated earlier (Section 9.6), he already had accumulated extensive lecture material and had a large card index of information on the colloquial language, which he had collected over the years—and the absence of a book on the topic is one of the mysteries of his pre-professorial era. But when his long-awaited work on French finally appeared, it was quite different in form from anything he had written previously—or that he was ever to do again. Entitled *Colloquial French* (Stéphan—Jones 1927a), it was a language course with accompanying gramophone records.

Jones was now firmly in the habit of writing any book on languages other than English with a reliable native speaker; despite knowing French so well, this was also his policy on this occasion. His co-writer was Emile Stéphan, a French native speaker of Breton stock, but with standard educated French pronunciation; he was a talented phonetician.[6] Stéphan was attached to the University College French Department, but since 1919 had been assisting in teaching the phonetics of French to Jones's students. In fact, it must be assumed that Stéphan did the greater part of the work involved with the course; not only does his name appear out of alphabetical order on the title page, but the innovative treatments of grammar and lexis which underpin *Colloquial French* are likely to have been his contribution; Jones never displayed talent or deep interest in such areas. However, the sections on pronunciation, which form a major component of the book, are completely Jonesian in approach.

Colloquial French is a hefty work consisting of over 560 pages, plus an additional short key to exercises (see Figure 10.6). It is, in fact, in sheer volume, the largest publication that Jones ever produced. In addition, it has the accompanying set of fifteen gramophone discs, with up to 90 minutes of spoken material. This must have made *Colloquial French* a most comprehensive audio course by the standards of the day, several decades before the invention of long-playing records and domestic tape-recorders made the provision of listening material in this way commonplace. For the recordings, Stéphan used Hélène Coustenoble's and Cyrille Jones's voices in addition to his own.

The authors were at pains to point out the novelty of this audio component (p. xiii):

> In the past, various Gramophone Records have been published exemplifying literary French. But the records with which this book deals are designed to illustrate the type of speech used by educated Northern French people in *ordinary talking*.

Furthermore, they stressed the need for using the recordings for intensive listening and speaking practice, thus anticipating by several decades the aural-oral approach, with its emphasis on "overlearning"—a phrase used by Bloomfield (1942: 16), but associated particularly with the language teaching techniques fashionable in the late 1950s and early 1960s. See Howatt (1984: 265–269) for discussion. Stéphan and Jones state (p. xii):

> To ensure success in learning to speak and understand French it is necessary that the learner should listen to every record a large number of times…. The learner should not, however, content himself with listening to the records solely at those places in his course of study which are recommended in this book. He should supplement these auditions by playing the records frequently at other times. After playing a record a great number of times, he will find he knows it so well that it is practically impossible for him to forget the words.

At the time they were produced, the records would have been a huge advance on anything else available; in the words of one educationist, Robson (quoted in Davies 1930: 33): "they represent at this moment the acme of method".

Stéphan and Jones state at the outset (p. ix) that they intend to follow the "principles advocated by the foremost authorities in language teaching (Sweet, Jespersen, Palmer, de Saussure, etc.)".[7] In fact, it is the influence of Palmer which seems to be dominant, as is witnessed by the adherence to a limited, strictly graded vocabulary and the frequent use of the substitution table as a teaching device. Although the authors underline (p. ix) their preoccupation with utility rather than mere frequency in the choice of items, nevertheless the rigidity with which they stick to the principle of vocabulary grading is remarkable. This has some weird consequences, particularly as far as certain familiar grammatical items are concerned: for example, on the basis of word-frequency lists, "nous" is not introduced until Chapter 33, "because on examination we find the first person plural to be much rarer than the other persons". Even more surprisingly, "tu" and its other grammatical forms are omitted altogether, since these are regarded as "not being essential to an English learner with a vocabulary of 1,000 words" (p. ix n.).

It is not made clear whether the authors used already existing word-frequency lists for French.[8] There are acknowledgements to Hélène Coustenoble and E. Quick "for help in preparing the word lists", so it is likely that these were devised by Stéphan and

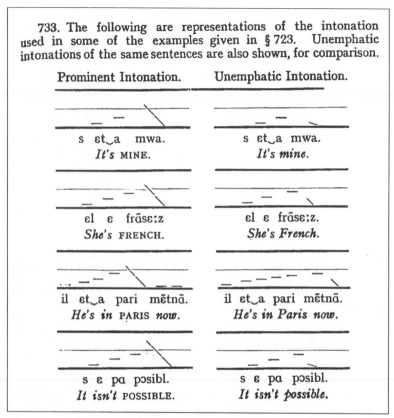

733. The following are representations of the intonation used in some of the examples given in § 723.   Unemphatic intonations of the same sentences are also shown, for comparison.

Figure 10.7. Examples of intonation patterns shown in *Colloquial French* (p. 296).

Jones themselves with the help of UCL staff; in which case, this would count as a notable contribution to the development of vocabulary control in second language teaching, particularly in the teaching of French, anticipating the concept of "français fondamental" by over twenty-five years. For a general discussion of word frequency and vocabulary control in second language teaching, see Howatt (1984: 245–259).

It is clear that Jones must have played the major role in devising the treatment of pronunciation, since it clearly follows what had by now become the UCL tradition. Nevertheless, perhaps in the interests of allowing the book to appeal to a wider non-academic readership, an attempt appears to have been made to limit the extent of pho-netic/phonological concepts and terminology. For instance, no mention is made of the phoneme, which is instead replaced by the term "essential sound" (p. xv), and there are no vowel diagrams or sagittal cross-sections. However, IPA phonetic symbols are used throughout, and the vowels of French are explained by Cardinal Vowel theory, accompanied by illustrative photographs of lip positions.

A criticism which can be directed at Stéphan and Jones is that certain sections of *Colloquial French* betray a reluctance to move away from established dogmas in language teaching, and that some pronunciations are recommended which are outdated or, at best, old-fashioned (even for 1927). For example, for French /r/ (pp. 154–155), students are recommended to adopt either a uvular or an alveolar roll. Outside the artificial elocution of the French stage, the former would be unusual, whilst the latter would have been confined to peripheral dialects, e.g. those of the Midi. The typical French uvular approximant [ʁ], here termed "throat-r", is in effect proscribed (p. 154), even though it is acknowledged to be employed by Stéphan himself.

Other examples of conservative usages are the insistence on maintaining the vowel contrast /ɛ̃–œ̃/, which was probably largely absent from educated Parisian French by the late twenties. Similarly, even though it is admitted that Stéphan "in common with many other French people" (p. 36) reduced the contrast /a/ and /ɑ/ in words such as *table* and *bas*, nonetheless the English learner is advised against this merging. Excluding old-fashioned Parisian speech, such levelling was undoubtedly normal for the educated French of the time, and would certainly have rendered the students' task of acquiring the essentials of the French vowel system much easier.

On the other hand, Stéphan and Jones are quite radical in their advocacy of elision forms in speech. For instance, a pronunciation of *il/ils* without final /l/ is recommended to the learner (p. 35), whilst *ne* is noted as being "often omitted" in "rapid colloquial speech" (p. 115). Furthermore, much emphasis is placed on the importance of elision, liaison and vowel epenthesis.

Very unusually for the era, suprasegmental features such as stress and intonation receive detailed attention. Stress is considered on a three-term scale—"unemphatic", "prominent" and "intensive" (pp. 293–294). The last of these is the most extreme category and includes the displacement of stress from the terminal syllable of polysyllabic words. Intonation (pp. 295–309) is treated on a similar three-term scale, and is illustrated by means of an interlinear marking system, with an intermediate line, as shown in Figure 10.7. (Later in the book, from p. 299 onwards, for no stated reason, the intermediate line is frequently abandoned.) There is a clear relationship between this approach and the interlinear whole tune approach made popular for English by Armstrong—Ward (1926); see Section 14.12.

Stéphan and Jones insist on their readers' learning the normal colloquial forms of typical educated French, and being able to recognise the vast differences that exist between the spoken and the written language. Making available the means and materials for students to achieve this lifted *Colloquial French* into a different class from its contemporary rivals. Nevertheless, Stéphan and Jones realised that their teaching in these areas might cause some consternation (p. xiii):

> Some French people on reading the texts, and especially the phonetic transcriptions, of these records might at first be surprised at their appearance, and may even be tempted to say that they represent a vulgar or dialectal form of French. This is because the colloquial language is seldom written, so that the written form

of it looks strange as compared with the familiar literary language; also because many people do not realise how wide the difference is between the colloquial language and the literary language, or between the pronunciation used in reading aloud serious literature or in a carefully prepared discourse and that used in every-day talk. Those who feel inclined to criticise the texts in this book have only to listen carefully to a few of the records to be convinced that the texts are accurate representations of the ordinary speech of educated people of the North of France.

Colloquial French has not yet had the recognition it deserves as a pioneering effort in the history of language teaching—it is not even mentioned by Titone (1968), for example—but it was appreciated by numerous teachers of French and several genera-tions of students. Commercially, it appears to have been most successful, going into several subsequent editions. Abercrombie (1980: 5), who learnt from it himself, called *Colloquial French* "much the best introductory course in a language ever written".

10.8. Involvement in theosophy

By the 1920s, Jones had already been preoccupied for some considerable time with eastern religion and philosophy. He was attracted, more particularly, to "theosophy", a modified form of Hindu and Buddhist doctrines, interlarded with much western re-interpretation and innovation. It was a fashion, almost a fad, in America and Europe at this time. This movement, claiming roots going back far into history, was in reality largely an invention of the second half of the nineteenth century, coming to world prominence after the founding in 1875 of the Theosophical Society in New York. The whole faith was effectively the inspiration of one woman—a fierily eccentric Russian, born in the Ukraine, and claiming aristocratic forebears, H(elena) P(etrovna) Blavat-sky (1831–91). She collaborated with an American, Colonel H.S. Olcott, and in 1878, the pair left America, arriving in India in January 1879. In 1882 they established a branch at Adyar, near Madras, which eventually became the world headquarters of the Theosophical Society.

Later, in the early twentieth century, the chief centre of theosophical activity moved to Britain. The leader of the British movement from 1907 onwards was the charis-matic Annie Besant (1847–1933), who earlier had achieved fame as a pioneer of femi-nist socialism and trade unionism; she was also subsequently to be a significant force in the drive for Indian independence, founding the Indian Home Rule League in 1916.

Today, theosophy survives only as a peripheral cult with relatively few adherents, and it has been largely forgotten just how powerful a force it was in the first decades of the twentieth century. The movement had its own press, the Theosophical Publish-ing House, and achieved notable sales for some of the numerous books and pamphlets which it printed (many of which today gather dust on the less accessible shelves of second-hand bookshops). Mass meetings, often held at the Queen's Hall in London, were able to attract huge crowds reminiscent of revivalist religious gatherings. In

38. H.J.Uldall

37. Jones on the steps of UCL (1934)

39. Jones's house at 3 Marsham Way, Gerrards Cross

40. Maud MacCarthy
(later Swami Omananda Puri)

41. Jones with Arthur Lloyd James

42. With colleagues outside UCL;
l. to r. Jones, Dennis Fry, Eileen Evans, H.J. Uldall and ?

America, the meetings were even larger and Mrs Besant's followers more numerous. She travelled throughout the world, frequently addressing enormous audiences, being feted and lionised, and converting thousands (at least temporarily) to what would have seemed a novel alternative philosophy of life. Many people were tired of the dogmas of conventional Christianity but not willing to retreat into total atheism or agnosticism. Theosophy, drawing as it did on aspects of many eastern and western religions, yet not requiring total commitment to any of them, possibly provided a way of dealing with the problems of living in the troubled inter-war period. Theosophical beliefs were even espoused within some intellectual circles—one example of a sympathiser being Aldous Huxley. Another declared theosophist, the British High Court judge Christmas Humphreys (1966: 19), wrote of the original success of H.P. Blavatsky:

> She aroused new interest in comparative religion. She taught in Karma and Rebirth a twofold doctrine which many, with fading faith in the Christian God, found an excellent substitute, more reasonable and more complete, and more acceptable to the average Western mind.

Although theosophy is noted for tolerating diversity of belief amongst its followers, nevertheless there are certain features to which all its members adhere. Theosophists emphasise the dichotomy of esoteric as opposed to exoteric doctrine in religious writing, and are prepared to subject many of the religious literatures of the world to exegesis—for example, Hindu and Buddhist texts, the Old and New Testaments, the Kabbalah and the Koran—in an attempt to discover hidden meanings within them. There is a preoccupation with the importance of mystical experience, which can be best gained through meditation. Furthermore, a very high significance is placed on the occult in all its forms, and theosophists exhibit a fascination with the supernatural, although spiritualism as such is despised. Theosophy stresses monism, namely that everything is derived from a single unifying principle to which all in our experience can be traced. Reality is constituted in this single ultimate spirit and all-encompassing unity. In all their theories and speculations, most theosophists claim oriental religions, and in particular the writings of the ancient Indians, as their chief inspiration; in fact, it is also possible to trace many theosophical ideas to western authors, and some concepts appear to be merely the invention of the early founders of the movement, especially Blavatsky and Olcott.

Well before the turn of the century, theosophy had moved on from its origins as a kind of eclectic philosophy, and was rapidly on the way to developing many of the trappings of a religious cult. It was Blavatsky and Olcott who elaborated and transformed the basic tenets, adding considerably to the supernatural element, as can be seen in Blavatsky's (1877) *Isis unveiled* and (1888) *The secret doctrine*.[9] Theosophists were now expected to believe in a complex cosmogony, which regarded the universe as a series of seven planes of existence. These were all clearly defined, ranging from the lowest "physical plane" to the highest "divine plane". Crucial to a being's progress from one plane to another are the two concepts of reincarnation and "karma".

Whilst the latter may be considered as a kind of fate, theosophists insist that there is nothing fatalistic about a being's passage between the planes. All actions in life influence the nature of any future existence, so that one is effectively able to decide the nature of one's future incarnation; similarly, one's predicament in this existence has already been determined by one's actions in the past.

Much of the above, whilst perhaps difficult for non-believers to accept, is nevertheless an accepted part of conventional Hinduism and Buddhism. More controversial was Blavatsky's assertion, elaborated further by her followers, that there was already in existence a group of immortal "Adepts", known variously as the "Masters" or the "Brothers", who had actually passed through various planes but who were nevertheless present on Earth. It was thought that it was possible to establish contact with these beings, and indeed Blavatsky and others claimed to have met and conversed with them. The *Mahatma letters* (Barker 1923) were actually purported to have been written to A.P. Sinnett by the Brothers themselves.

How Jones first became drawn into theosophy is fairly clear. The first impulses may even have come from within Jones's own family circle. After all, the Cartes had an interest in Swedenborgian ideas, which was doubtless one reason why Jones was sent to University College School, well-known for its non-Christian education. As Jones himself acknowledged, Paul Passy was significant in Jones's development morally as well as linguistically. But, as a devout Christian, Passy would certainly not have had any truck with fringe religions, although he undoubtedly would have engaged with Jones on wide-ranging discussions of a philosophical nature. However, there is a much more likely candidate as the crucial influence, close to Passy and sharing many of his moral concerns, but not his Christian faith. It is known that Sophie Lund was a convinced theosophist and it is probable that it was she who first stimulated Daniel Jones's interest in theosophical ideas during his stay at Bourg-la-Reine (see Section 2.2).

Some time afterwards, Jones found himself in contact with Henry Sweet, who (as Jones himself pointed out, Section 4.8) was not only fascinated by the linguistic contributions of the ancient Indians, but also by Hindu philosophy and religion. Later reinforcement of Jones's inclination towards theosophical ideas would have come from his visit to India, not only because of the importance of native Indian religion and philosophy, but also possibly because the headquarters of the theosophical movement were located at Adyar (near Madras—one of the towns which Jones visited on his 1912 tour).

Much later in his life, the deaths of his mother and brother were an additional spur to his already profound involvement in this type of religion. In particular, his brother Arnold, a deeply religious Christian, is reported as having undergone, shortly before he actually died, what would nowadays be dubbed a "near-death experience" with a vision of a radiantly exquisite after-life, saying on his return to consciousness: "It was beautiful what I saw." It is claimed that this episode made a tremendous impact on Jones.[10] But whatever may have channelled Jones towards the movement, or deepened his later commitment, there is plenty of evidence that by his fortieth year Jones was already fully involved in quasi-theosophical beliefs and that this interest later expanded into what must be regarded as virtually an obsession towards the end of his life.

Nevertheless, Jones for all his preoccupation with theosophical ideas, never appears officially to have joined the British Theosophical Society. Such a position was not at all unusual since the official theosophists were in fact almost proud of the large number of extra sympathisers at the fringes of the movement. In Jones's case, his non-membership may have indicated either his own doubts about any type of organised religion, or his more direct concerns about the sincerity of certain persons at the centre of the theosophical movement. Like many others, Jones eventually became disillusioned with the personality cult around Mrs Besant, and with the apparently corrupt activities of some of her immediate followers. He made this clear in the letter (previously quoted in Section 4.8) discussing Sweet's philosophical interests, stating that Sweet had taken an interest in theosophy "before distortions of the original teachings began to creep in".[11]

However, his fascination with the writings and philosophy behind theosophy in no way diminished and he began to become actively involved in groups interested in offshoots of oriental religion. It is perhaps not coincidental that it was at this point that he invited Sophie Lund to stay as a long-term guest in his house, and found her a post at University College. From this period on, Jones was ever more clearly committed to theosophical ideas, and fell particularly under the spell of Maud MacCarthy (see Section 13.2). By the 1930s, these beliefs had begun to play the dominating role in his own philosophy of life, even extending into influencing his views on phonetics and phonology (see Section 11.4).

10.9. The IPA and *Le Maître phonétique* in the 1920s

By 1923, both the International Phonetic Association itself and its journal *Le Maître phonétique* were in an almost comatose state. There had been no issue of *Le Maître phonétique* since the outbreak of war nearly nine years previously, and because the activities of the IPA depended so much on the frequent appearance of the journal—there were no recurrent conferences, or any such thing as an annual general meeting—the Association itself was moribund.

About the only activity which continued to take place was the examination of students for the IPA certificate (Passy 1923: 1–3). In addition, there was a trickle of publications. Even during the years of the war, one or two pamphlets had come out—and from 1921 onwards, an annual collection of texts in various languages was published under the title "Textes pour nos élèves".

Now, a decision had to be made either to finish off the IPA and its journal, or face the daunting task of rebreathing life into them. Paul Passy still nominally held the post of Secretary but was now in retirement and fully involved with his Christian Socialist commune, Liéfra, situated in a remote corner of rural France (see Section 2.3). Having only recently recovered from his nervous breakdown, and still not publishing on a regular basis, Daniel Jones might have considered himself ill-fitted for the massive lə

mɛːtrə fɔnetikə

ɔrganə

də l asɔsjasjoŋ fɔnetikə ɛŋternasjɔnalə

traŋtɥitjɛmə aneː də l asɔsjasjoŋ

trwazjɛmə seriː.—prəmjɛrə aneː·

ʒaŋvje—mars 1923

sɔmɛrə

artiklə də foŋ.—viː nuvɛlə (P. Passy).

koŋtraŋdy.—O. Jespersen, *Sprogets logik* (P.P.).

spɛsimɛn.—tʃainiːz (ðə Hwa Miao laŋgwedʒ ɔv wɛstərn tʃainə) (D. Jones).—patwa sɥisə rɔmaŋ dy *Val-d' Illiez* (P. Passy). —wɛst raidiŋ ɔv jɔrkʃiər (I. C. Ward).—kɔrniʃ (D. Jones). **parti: administrativə.**—nɔtə.—egzamɛŋ də fɔnetikə. **syplemaŋ.**—tɛkstə pur noz elɛvə.

viː nuvɛlə [1]

apɾɛ ply də ɥit aŋ də mɔr aparaŋtə, lə mɛːtrə fɔnetikə rənɛ a la viː! vwala la ʒwajøzə nuvɛlə, k avɛk no mɛʃœr swɛ, nuz aŋvwajoŋ a tu le maŋbrə, aŋsjɛŋ e nuvo, də nɔtrə vjɛʎə e ʃɛrə asɔsjasjoŋ.

l asɔsjasjoŋ fɔnetikə, ɛlə, n a paa resysite, kar ɛlə n a ʒamɛ sɛːse də vivrə. purtaŋ, sa viː ete laŋgisaŋtə, e ɛlə sɔr bjɛŋ mœrtriː də la krizə moŋdjalə, kɔmə taŋ d otrə, kɔmə nu mɛːmə. plyzjœɾ də se ʃɛf le plyz ilystrə oŋ disparyː sitoŋ Storm, Viëtor, Vianna, Rambeau, Spieser, doŋ nu salɥoŋ rɛspɛktɥøzəmaŋ la memwarə. . . . də noŋbrø

[1] ekri, noŋ aŋ traŋskripsjoŋ, me aŋ ɔrtɔgrafə fɔnetikə.

Figure 10.8. The first page of the revived *Maître phonétique*. Note the use of Passy's "Orthographe phonétique".

organisational and editorial work involved in reviving *Le Maître Phonétique*. Two things were essential before restarting the journal could be contemplated; the editorial and administrative headquarters had in effect to be moved to London (although Passy would still remain nominally in charge of editing the Romance language articles), and a firm of printers had to be found who were prepared to take on the difficult task of typesetting the phonetic texts, with all the exotic symbols and diacritics involved. The choice fell on the firm of Stephen Austin, based in Hertford, who continued to function as the IPA printers until well after Jones's death, in fact until the mid-1980s, when the journal was adapted to computerised technology. A crucial factor was that in London there was also someone who was energetic, competent and willing to mobilise the process of restoring the journal and the Association to life. This was Jones's trusted assistant, now a senior lecturer, Lilias Armstrong.

In 1923 the first issue of the revived journal appeared in its third series, with Jones and Passy's names on the cover, and looking at first sight astonishingly similar to the pre-war publications. Passy (1923: 1–3) wrote a cheery article, under the title "Vie nouvelle" (see Figure 10.8):

Après plus de huit ans de mort apparente, *Le Maître phonétique* renaît à la vie! Voilà la joyeuse nouvelle, qu'avec nos meilleurs souhaits, nous envoyons à tous les membres, anciens et nouveaux, de notre vielle et chère association.

Contributors were allowed possibly even more latitude than before in the choice of transcription and language, provided they kept to IPA principles. For instance, Passy (1923) had written his article in a form of French simplified spelling called "Orthographe phonétique", which horrified certain veteran IPA members, such as Jones's old Edinburgh colleague Bessie Robson, who wrote in to say that she felt that she could no longer allow students to borrow her copy of the magazine.[12] Stephen Jones was asked to review a textbook on Spanish, written in English. He chose to submit the review (S. Jones 1923) in his mother tongue—Welsh. So the tradition of linguistic and transcriptional variety in the IPA journal was maintained, if perhaps sometimes at the expense of the reader.

Lilias Armstrong's name does not appear on the cover until the July 1923 issue, where she is listed as "Secrétaire de Rédaction", a post which she held until 1936. Possibly under Armstrong's influence, *Le Maître phonétique* became in this period very much the property of the University College staff, and their contributions dominate. Another who is known to have given Jones considerable assistance was Sophie Lund, who was by this time working in UCL and living with the Jones family; her contribution to the IPA was later acknowledged in her obituary (Jones 1948b). By 1925, the editorial staff had managed to keep to the guidelines stated cautiously in the 1923 first issue (p. 7): "Nous ne pensons pas pouvoir publier plus de quatre numéros cette année; il nous faut marcher avec prudence. Nous ferons mieux dès que nous les pourrons." Initially, four issues had appeared per year, even though some of these were painfully thin, and with material which could have appealed only to a very limited audience. Nevertheless, the reappearance of *Le Maître phonétique* was essential for any revival of the IPA itself.

The year 1925 saw Jones and Armstrong managing once again to produce six issues. In January of that year, full details of IPA membership were published—the first time for over a decade. Remarkably, given the recent history of the organisation, over four hundred members, many of them recently acquired, were listed, and, as in the old days, they came from all over the world, representing a wide variety of interests. Jones could be pleased that despite all difficulties both the IPA and its journal were now back in business.

In 1927, Passy was elected President of the IPA, replacing the deceased Viëtor.[13] Jones succeeded Passy as Secretary of the Association in 1928, a post he was to hold until his retirement.[14] Throughout this period, he was largely responsible for editing *Le Maître phonétique*; Passy, though officially joint editor, seems to have played little part in the actual production of the journal.

In addition to his editorship, Jones took on other tasks on behalf of the IPA. In 1925, he attended the International Conference on Phonetic Transcription, which made important changes in the use of symbols—and where Jones played a crucial role in emphasising the need to fit the alphabet to phonemic principles. He also acted as the IPA delegate to the First International Congress of Linguists, held in The Hague in April 1928 (see Jones 1928f). Some of the most useful work that Jones undertook was the publication of pamphlets which restated the principles of the IPA and provided exemplifications of transcription systems for various languages. It was these pamphlets, written firstly in German (Jones 1928b),[15] subsequently in Italian (Jones—Camilli 1933a) and finally in Spanish (Jones—Dahl 1944b), which provided the model for the well-known revision of the IPA Principles in English (IPA 1949), which, judging by content and style, is clearly from Jones's hand, though it does not actually bear his name.

10.10. Otto Jespersen and the Copenhagen Conference

Although the men had met briefly before, it was not until 1926 that Jones was to encounter at close quarters one of the major figures of twentieth century European linguistics, the Dane Otto Jespersen. The great Scandinavian linguist proved to be a formidable opponent and Jones may have found the confrontation more exhausting than he ever expected.

The two men had much in common. Like Daniel Jones, Jespersen came from a family with strong legal traditions and, under parental pressure, began to read law; he, too, gave this up because he developed an interest in languages. He travelled to England and Germany, where he met, amongst others, Sweet, Ellis, Viëtor and Sievers. A short but memorable episode in his life was the two months spent in Paris in 1887 when he stayed with the Passy family, and established a close relationship with Paul Passy and his brother Jean. Jespersen describes the deep impression made on him by the Passy household in his autobiography *En sprogmands levned* (Jespersen 1938 [1995]: 70–71) and recalls how he frequently spent whole mornings talking to Passy about phonetics. He would then go to Paris with Passy to attend his classes or other lectures at the Sorbonne. Twenty years later, Daniel Jones was to follow very much the same pattern when he stayed at Bourg-la-Reine with Passy's brother-in-law, Henri Motte. After obtaining his doctorate, Jespersen taught in schools, and in 1893 was appointed to the first professorship in English at the University of Copenhagen; he remained there as Professor of English until his retirement in 1933.

Jespersen has left an extensive record of his personal and professional life, both in his detailed autobiography and also in his "Farewell Lecture" (Jespersen 1933a). Regarded as one of the most important of the general linguists of the early twentieth century, Jespersen, like Passy and Jones, was a master of lucid explanation. He was a convinced believer in the importance of applied linguistics, especially in language teaching. Nevertheless, he took exception to Jones's (1937j) "Aims of phonetics" for its excessively practical and non-theoretical bias (Jespersen 1938 [1995]: 253). In contrast to Passy and Jones (but like Sweet), Jespersen is also notable for a breadth of his interest in language; he published not only on phonetics and phonology, but also on philology, syntax, semantics, child language acquisition and stylistics. He even constructed his own artificial language ("Novial") and furthermore retained a considerable interest in literature. These facets of his linguistic interests are reflected in his influential work on general linguistics *Language* (Jespersen 1922).

Nevertheless, Jespersen's early work was based mainly on phonetics and language teaching. At the beginning of his career in 1886, he was one of the founders of a Scandinavian movement for language teaching reform, "Quousque Tandem", which took its name from Viëtor's famous pseudonym (see Section A.4). He was one of the first members of the International Phonetic Association and later became a Vice-President. His first notable phonetic work was *Articulation of speech sounds* (1889), where he introduced his analphabetic notation, consisting of strings of symbols representing the various articulatory features. His greatest phonetic work was *Fonetik* (1897–99), written in Danish, but reaching a much wider audience when translated into German as *Lehrbuch der Phonetik* (1904b) and *Phonetische Grundfragen* (1904a); he also published a work on English phonetics, *Engelsk fonetik* (1912). Furthermore, in many of his later linguistic publications, a strong underlying interest in phonetics is often apparent, reflecting his belief that speech should be primary in linguistic studies.

In addition to his other contributions, Jespersen produced the pronunciation component for Brynildsen's (1902–07) dictionary, *Engelsk—Dansk—Norsk Ordbog*. This was a landmark in that it was the first to use a system based on the recommendations of the IPA, thus anticipating Jones's *Phonetic dictionary* and the *EPD* by over a decade. See Sections 5.3 and 7.2. Jespersen has recently been the subject of a full-scale assessment; see Juul—Nielsen (1989).

In April 1926, at Jespersen's invitation, Daniel Jones set off for Denmark to attend a conference in Copenhagen, called to discuss the various forms of phonetic transcription currently in use at the time, and the feasibility of amalgamating these into a single universally accepted alphabet.[16] The proposals were later published in the form of a report entitled *Phonetic transcription and transliteration* (Jespersen—Pedersen 1926). The idea of organising a convention of this sort had originally been conceived in Brussels at the 1922 meeting of the Union Académique Internationale at a time when the IPA was still in a state of post-war somnolence and before *Le Maître phonétique* had resumed publication. The scheme appears to have been essentially Otto Jespersen's with backing from several Danish and other European colleagues. In 1924, Jespersen and his associates sent out a questionnaire to about a hundred linguists, the answers to which "were so widely divergent and partly so indefinite that nothing could be built on them" (Jespersen—Pedersen 1926: 4). It was presumably to avoid problems of this sort that the numbers attending the Copenhagen Conference had been deliberately restricted to a select twelve, all of whom were acknowledged experts in a particular area of linguistics. Even though it was stated explicitly that nationality was not a consideration, there was a noticeable preponderance of Germans and Scandinavians—no fewer than three were actually drawn from the staff of Copenhagen University. Not only was Jones the sole representative of the English-speaking world, but he was also the only prominent member of the IPA—apart from Jespersen himself.

Proceedings continued for a week and Jones must early on have realised that he had been invited to what Jespersen intended as the funeral wake of the IPA in its role as arbiter of international phonetic symbolisation. Jones's lack of rapport with the other conference members, together with Jespersen's generous acknowledgement of his practical gifts, is revealed by Jespersen's (1938 [1995]: 215) own retrospective account in his autobiography: "Daniel Jones's over-utilitarian views ('I'm no philologist') rather irritated the rest of us; but we were impressed by the sureness of his mastery of many different sound systems in practice, and were grateful to him for his exposition of his 'system of cardinal vowels'."

Eventually a large number of decisions on symbolisation were put to the vote and approved apparently without opposition. Jones undoubtedly felt himself outnumbered and doomed to fight a losing battle—although he is significantly noted as abstaining in an otherwise unanimous vote on at least one occasion (Jespersen—Pedersen 1926: 17). The conference decisions envisaged a transcription system broadly on the same lines as that of the IPA, but with sweeping changes to letter shapes and the application of diacritics. Were these to have gained general acceptance, they would have proved the most radical revolution in transcription since the alphabet was put into its 1889–90 form shortly after the founding of the IPA. Copies of Jespersen and Pedersen's report were delivered to Jones for him to send out, free of charge, to every single member of the IPA; Jespersen and his collaborators had arranged for this too to be subsidised by a Danish academic foundation, the Rask-Ørsted fund. Jones invited members to give their reactions whilst the Council of the IPA were also asked to vote on whether they were prepared to accept the complete Copenhagen programme of revisions.[17]

Whatever frustrations Jones may have had about the Copenhagen Conference, he was undoubtedly delighted with the reaction of other IPA members to the proposals. With the predictable exception of Jespersen, the IPA Council voted unanimously to reject the Copenhagen plan. Jones at last had a chance to state his own misgivings publicly:

> The Copenhagen scheme appears to me to fail in several respects through not taking sufficiently into consideration such matters as ease of writing, legibility of connected phonetic texts, and harmony with the ordinary Roman type. Thus, the system proposed for palatalisation is very awkward in current writing. It is difficult to imagine a more cumbrous way of writing a click than with the proposed letters with triangles above or after them. The symbols ʇ, ʖ, ɕ, which have excellent script forms, are clearly better than any such contrivances. The form ϑ of Greek θ is in my view unsuitable because it cannot be made to harmonise with Roman type.[18]

Other members of the Council were even more adamant in their rejection. The American, Charles Grandgent, considered the recommendations "a great disappointment", and declared the scheme "manifestly inferior" to the IPA alphabet; another American phonetician, John Kenyon, said that the "attempt to be more logical and systematic is an excellent feature of the report; but it is not well exemplified in the arguments used…"; whilst Jones's earliest phonetic mentor, William Tilly, responded bluntly with: "to this monstrous proposal an emphatic no".[19]

Nevertheless, several of the Copenhagen recommendations were approved by the IPA Council and these have become common phonetic symbolisations. They include the use of Φ and β to replace the old signs F and υ for bilabial fricatives, and new signs for retroflex consonants, e.g. ʈ ɖ ɳ etc, instead of the subscript dot formerly employed. The old stress mark ´ was replaced by a vertical line ', and diacritics, such as that for labialisation ̫, dental ̪, closer ̣ and more open ̠, were introduced for the first time.[20]

In 1928, a separate round of changes was circularised and put to the vote, including what later became familiar usages like ʇ ʖ ɕ for clicks;[21] ɬ ɮ for lateral fricatives; ɓ ɗ ɠ for implosives; χ for the voiceless uvular fricative; ɕ ʑ for the "alveolo-palatal" fricatives of Polish; ħ ʕ for pharyngal fricatives; ɨ ʉ ɵ for central vowels; and the diacritics ̡ for palatisation and, on the model of dark-l, ~ for velarisation or pharyngalisation. Changes which proved less generally successful were the use of special symbols ɭ ʒ for labialised ʃ ʒ and the use of ɟ for the ill-defined sound "intermédiaire entre l et d fréquent dans les langues africaines."[22] A second 1928 circular allowed the Council to approve the vowel symbols ɒ and ɤ.[23] Undoubtedly, these subsequent changes were made chiefly on Jones's instigation—several of them are to be found in books written previously by him or by his close colleagues. All were passed with minimal opposition from the Council. It cannot be proved, but it is very likely that one non-consenting member was Otto Jespersen.

This was the end of the Copenhagen episode in the history of the IPA. It must have appeared to Jones at one stage that Jespersen and his associates were indeed about to wrest the authority for setting standards for phonetic symbolisation from the IPA. In the end, Jones was able to turn potential misfortune to his advantage and put through the most radical set of innovations since the early days of the organisation. Jespersen's wily manoeuvres ironically made Daniel Jones's job easier, since the realisation that there was a challenge to the Council's status would have made its members more prepared to accept the need for changes and the necessity to preserve unity in the face of opposition.

10.11. Involvement with the BBC

Daniel Jones's involvement with radio, and the question of standards of pronunciation in national broadcasting in Britain, goes back to even before the time when the BBC was first established as a public body in the form that we know it today. In 1927, following a decision of a parliamentary committee, the former British Broadcasting Company was dissolved and replaced by a public corporation which was renamed the British Broadcasting Corporation. One year previously, Daniel Jones's connection with the BBC had begun.

The part played by the BBC in the establishment of a standard of pronunciation has been examined exhaustively by Leitner (1982). In this context, over the years, one can distinguish a change in Jones's significance from the period before the Second World War—when he was really peripheral, and his influence derived largely from his publications and academic status—to the time during and after the war, when Jones was, by virtue of his function as the paid Consultant Adviser to the Corporation, one of the most important direct influences on pronunciation within the BBC itself.

In 1926, he became one of the founder members of the Advisory Committee on Spoken English (see Figure 10.9), set up by the first Director General, John (later Lord) Reith, in order to regularise the pronunciation used in broadcasting, particularly by announcers (Armstrong 1926). Jones's fellow committee members included his colleague Arthur Lloyd James, and two powerful personalities with eccentric views on pronunciation, George Bernard Shaw and the Poet Laureate Robert Bridges—both of whom had figured previously in Jones's professional life (see Sections 4.9 and 4.11). Bridges was chairman of the Committee until his death in 1931, when he was replaced by Shaw.[31]

Jones took a relatively small part in the early work of the Committee, leaving the major role to Lloyd James, who had developed a considerable interest in the language of broadcasting (see Lloyd James 1935; Leitner 1982; Jones 1958). Under Shaw's chairmanship, the committee was enlarged to no fewer than twenty-two members, chosen for their eminence in public life rather than their competence to make decisions on pronunciation. Jones, though he agreed to become one of the four paid advisory experts, sensibly remained in the background, avoiding conflict with the often opinionated but on the whole ill-informed lay-members of the Committee.[32]

T H E

BRITISH BROADCASTING COMPANY

ADVISORY COMMITTEE on SPOKEN ENGLISH

MINUTES OF FIRST MEETING.

The first meeting of the Committee was held at
Savoy Hill on Monday July 5th, 1926 at 2.30 p.m.

There were present:-

Mr. Robert Bridges (Poet Laureate) in the Chair.

Sir Johnston Forbes - Robertson.

Mr. Daniel Jones (Professor of Phonetics in the
University of London)

Mr. Logan Pearsall-Smith (Society for Pure
English)

Mr. Lloyd James (Lecturer in Phonetics at the
School of Oriental Studies,
London)

Mr. J. C. W. Reith (Managing Director, B.B.C.)
Mr. J. C. Stobart {B.B.C.}
Mr. B. E. Nicolls {B.B.C.}
Miss Somerville {B.B.C.}

The Minutes of the Preliminary Meeting on June
25th were read, amended on two points, and adopted
(as attached.)

The Chairman put the following propositions
before the meeting.

ARTICULAR   That recommended pronunciations should be in
RONUNCIA-
IONS.   three classes.

(a)   Place names.

(b)   Words which have not yet encountered
speech-rub. (These are inconvenient long
literary words and scientific terms.)

(c)   Words in common speech use.

lace Names.   After discussion the Committee decided that no
definite principle could be applied to the pronunciation
of place names, but that each should receive individual
consideration as need arose.

Figure 10.9. Page 1 of the minutes of the first meeting of the BBC Advisory
Committee on Spoken English. Note that, at the time, the BBC was the British
Broadcasting Company.

10.12. Travels to the USA and elsewhere

In early October 1924, Jones went to Berlin to attend the first post-war "Neophilologentag", an event attended by over 700 German academics and language teachers. He was given the honour of addressing the conference on behalf of the foreign delegates. Jones then travelled to Switzerland, where he gave three lectures on "Phonetics applied to the teaching of English".[33]

Apart from his eventful journey to India (see Section 4.7), Jones had not, up till this point, travelled outside Europe. In the summer of 1925, accompanied by Cyrille, he made his only visit to the United States. There he gave "an intensive course of phonetics, with special reference to English", at Smith College (Northampton, Massachusetts) during the first three weeks of June. The course attracted "about sixty students from various parts of America". There is a record of his having given a guest lecture at Hunter College, New York, on June 22.[34] The Joneses also visited Odette, the only one of Cyrille's sisters who had not settled in England. Somewhat to the shock of her French protestant family, she had married a black American clergyman and emigrated to the USA. Although she apparently suffered much opposition to the match from the Mottes, it appears that Daniel Jones and Cyrille made a point of visiting her and her husband.[35] It provides yet another example of Jones's complete lack of any hint of racism—something quite remarkable for a man of his generation.

In November of the following year, Jones—perhaps now having regained a taste for long distance travel after his successful American experience—embarked for Kenya where, according to an announcement in *Le Maître phonétique*, "...he intends to spend about two months. He hopes to make a phonetic analysis of Kikuyu".[36] But Jones only travelled as far as Genoa before being struck down by illness and had to return to England with his research plans unfulfilled.[37]

Jones was a notoriously bad traveller, being prone to seasickness, and hating even the thought of a channel crossing. The ill-fated journey to Kenya appears to have marked a watershed. From this point on he seems to have confined his journeys to the Continent of Europe. Within these limits, he travelled frequently, making trips to France nearly every year to stay with Cyrille's relations, and take the children to Trégastel. On one occasion, they brought Jones's colleague, Hyacinth Holdsworth, along with them. Half a century later, she was still able to recall clearly the house close to the sea, with its bare wooden floors and rough, simple items of French peasant furniture. Jones, even on holiday, kept a watchful ear on her French, occasionally correcting her uncertain intonation.[38]

In April 1928, the First International Congress of Linguists was held in The Hague, and proved to be a "remarkable gathering of some 200 specialists in various branches of linguistics ... many of the most famous linguists, phoneticians and phonologists in the world". Jones had been nominated as the official representative of the IPA and, in addition, numerous other members of the Association were present, including Tytus Benni, Otto Jespersen, Etsko Kruisinga, Arthur Lloyd James, and Ernst Meyer. According to the report in *Le Maître phonétique* (unsigned, but presumably from his own hand), Jones was able to circularise to the Congress members the new German language version of the IPA Principles (Jones 1928f) which "appears to have created a favourable impression upon those who have hitherto been insufficiently acquainted with our system". The matter of transcription provided a "very interesting debate", but Jones was probably relieved that "it was resolved not to make any formal decisions on any points of detail".[39]

10.13. The Department in the 1920s

Jones produced relatively little new work in the twenties, but his staff made up for this by their hectic academic activity. Lilias Armstrong, who had acted as Jones's deputy when he fell ill, had been appointed Senior Lecturer in 1921. But whilst her organisational role would have been of prime importance during this period, she also published a large volume of work, both on her own and in co-operation with others. She wrote two books for Jones's "London Phonetic Reader" series, one on English (Armstrong 1923a) and the other dealing with Burmese (Armstrong—Pe Maung Tin 1925). However, undoubtedly her best known contribution in this period was the slim *Handbook of intonation*, written together with Ida Ward (Armstrong—Ward 1926). Although this book has been criticised for its simplistic approach (see Section 14.12), their treatment of intonation was extremely influential for several decades with phoneticians working within the British English tradition, especially in the field of English language teaching (Cruttenden 1981: 40).

Ida Ward herself wrote the *Phonetics of English* (Ward 1929), a straightforward presentation which was for many years the only real rival to Jones's own descriptions of English. Ward's book is a very competent piece of work for its time, marred only by its frequently proscriptive approach to dialect features.

During this period, apart from the work of Jones's full-time staff members, a great deal of phonetic research in the Jonesian mould was undertaken by advanced students, sometimes employed as temporary staff, passing through the Department. Some titles appeared many years after the authors had left UCL, but nevertheless retained in large degree the influence of the Jones school. Only a selection of the most significant are mentioned here.

Douglas M. Beach, an American who studied at UCL in the 1920s, after writing a thesis on Chinese tone, *The phonetics of Pekingese* (Beach 1923), went on to become a professor at Cape Town. Another pioneering study of a South African language was Clement M. Doke's *Phonetics of the Zulu language* (1926), reviewed by Jones (1926d). An Indian student, Suniti Kumar Chatterji, completed a thesis on Bengali before being appointed to a chair at Calcutta University; he was eventually elected President of the IPA. His *Bengali phonetic reader* (Chatterji 1928) appeared in the London Phonetic Reader series.

Jones wrote no more of these little handbooks himself, but continued to edit the series. Produced on a stringent budget, sometimes with a subsidy from the country where the language concerned was spoken, sometimes with a contribution from the author, the London Phonetic Readers provided useful publicity for the descriptive phonetic research going on in the UCL Department. The list was balanced, as before the war, so as to include not only popular languages such as Italian (Camilli 1921), but also less well-charted areas like Polish (Arend 1924) and Czech (Frinta 1925) and Welsh (S. Jones 1926). More volumes in the series were to be added in the 1930s (see Section 11.6).

10.14. John Rupert Firth

Jones's links with the School of Oriental Studies had always been strong, and up till 1926 his Department continued to service the School with phonetics teaching. In that year, with Jones's blessing, Arthur Lloyd James left to take up a post as lecturer in phonetics at the School, and from then on traffic between the two institutions increased further.

But Lloyd James's departure created a gap in the Department which had to be filled as rapidly as possible. It was no easy task, since Lloyd James was, after Lilias Armstrong and Stephen Jones, probably Jones's most trusted and experienced member of staff. It could not be, as sometimes in the past, just a question of Jones going out and finding an apparently talented youngster who spoke good French; there was a need for a person with considerable phonetic knowledge and teaching experience. News came to Jones of someone who appeared ideal—a highly-regarded teacher of English, with an interest in phonetics and a reputation for original ideas, who already held a senior academic post in India but was eager to return to Britain. His name was John Rupert Firth.

Firth was born in Keighley, a small country town in Yorkshire, in 1890. In contrast with Jones's privileged background, Firth was of humbler origin and came from the lower—rather than the upper—middle class. He was the son of a bookkeeper and had been educated at the town grammar school before reading history at the University of Leeds. All through his life, Firth remained proud of his North Country background and in his behaviour epitomised the bluntness and rough humour often thought characteristic of the North of England in general, and Yorkshire in particular. Unlike Jones, Firth was a man who loved socialising, preferably with a glass of beer in his hand, and was never happier than when he was animatedly discussing linguistic matters with friends and colleagues.

At Leeds, he obtained a first-class degree and went on to take an MA. For a short time, Firth taught at Leeds Training College, but uprooted himself from Yorkshire in 1916 in order to join the Indian education service. His career was soon interrupted by the First World War and his military service took him not only to India, but also to Afghanistan and Africa. In 1919, he was appointed to the University of the Punjab at Lahore, where he held the post of Professor of English, and "achieved a considerable personal and academic reputation" (Robins 1961 [1966]: 543). Firth was devoted to

India, an attachment which he retained all his life, but by this time, he was tired of his work at Lahore, and was desperately trying to get back to Britain.

The decision to give Firth a job was made very rapidly, and he joined University College for the 1926–27 session as a "Senior Assistant". Firth appears, only a few months later, to have concluded that he had made a terrible mistake, when it was reported that "Mr J.R. Firth...having decided to resume his work in India, does not seek reappointment on the college staff as from the end of the current session".[40] For the session 1927–28, Firth was replaced by three part-timers. But Firth was rarely predictable in his actions, and he changed his mind yet again. In 1928, he returned to University College, this time with the much more desirable status of Senior Lecturer.[41] Firth was later reported to have always declared his gratitude to Daniel Jones for allowing him to return to England,[42] and it does seem as if Jones was either particularly tolerant of Firth's vacillation, or perhaps was forced to recognise that Firth's talents were too good for the Department to lose.

From this point on, Firth was to become an increasingly significant force in University College. Initially, without doubt, he must have made an important contribution and filled the significant gap of the lack of a lecturer with a bias towards theoretical aspects of phonetics and phonology. Jones indeed may have seen him in this role as something of a replacement for the brilliant innovatory ideas of Harold Palmer (even though Firth and Palmer had quite different interests and approaches to linguistics).

It was many years before it became clear that Firth was at heart frustrated at University College; that he would eventually despise what he considered to be the Department's old-fashioned approach to phonetics, and the general apathy towards the theoretical developments in phonetics and linguistics which prevailed with Jones and his senior staff. Nobody, at this point, could have guessed exactly where Firth's frustration would eventually lead.

Chapter 11

Upstairs and downstairs (1931–39)

11.1. Changes in University College

Even in 1926, when University College was in festive mood for its centenary, Jones may have had some slight forebodings. It was known that the man at the centre of those celebrations, his powerful friend Sir Gregory Foster, had for some time been the victim of ill-health, and was constantly in severe pain; it could only be a matter of time before he would be forced to leave his post. As Provost, Foster had presided over radical changes, and despite the war and periods of financial strain, these were mostly beneficial. H.E. Butler has said of Foster:

> Foster during his long term of office (1904–1929) steered the college with wisdom, vigilance, and courage through all these difficulties. Many important new departments of study were established; the college buildings were increased threefold; and the number of students was trebled. It would be difficult to overrate the part which he played in this development. He may well be regarded as the second founder of the college.[1]

Foster, who had been knighted in 1917, and who during his last two years, from 1928 to 1930, was also Vice-Chancellor of the University of London, stayed on only until 1929, retiring at what was, for this era, an unusually early age. He died soon after, in 1931.

Jones had always maintained a close relationship with the Provost, and he must have realised that future hopes of achieving any of his ambitions for his Department would depend very much on the person who was to replace him. He was perhaps relieved when he heard that Sir Gregory's successor was to be not a scientist—science being something which Jones was already starting to regard with suspicion—but an arts man, seemingly very much in the mould of Foster. The new Provost, Allen Mawer, was a UCL graduate—a dedicated, brilliant scholar with a glittering academic record in the field of English philology.

Mawer, who took up the appointment in 1930, was a Londoner, born in 1879. After taking his BA at UCL, he went on to Cambridge, obtaining a first-class degree with double distinction. He then held university posts at Cambridge (Gonville and Caius), Sheffield and Newcastle, and afterwards succeeded H.C. Wyld as Professor of English Language at Liverpool. His work and reputation was recognised by a knighthood awarded in 1937. See Ekwall (1942) for an appreciation of Mawer's life and career.

Mawer's area of specialisation was the etymological study of English place-names, and he rapidly became the world's leading scholar in his field, being the founder of the English Place-Name Society. He might have been expected to favour a linguistically-oriented discipline such as phonetics. In fact, for no clear reason, and whilst there is no record of any open disruption, the atmosphere between the two men appears to have been cool from the start. Mawer's letters to Jones sometimes have a sharp, peremptory tone that gives the impression of a brusque note written to an errant young teacher—rather than correspondence addressed to a senior professor with a world-wide reputation.

The relationship between the two men appears to have become more distant rather than closer as the years progressed. Jones doubtless missed the direct access to authority which he had enjoyed over the years with Provost Foster. Mawer perhaps regarded the Phonetics Department—with its lack of undergraduates and odd mixture of part-time students and postgraduate researchers—as an eccentricity which did not fit happily into what he, with his tidy mind, considered a university department should properly be.

11.2. A house in Gerrards Cross

In 1934, Jones decided for the first time in his life that he was going to live permanently outside London. He was proud of being a native Londoner, and had a deep affection for the city of his birth so it was certainly not a decision which he took lightly. Jones had an uncanny foresight of the advent of the Second World War. He had been convinced of the inevitability of an approaching holocaust since the beginning of the 1930s, having received "warnings" to this effect at the seances organised by the mystic Maud MacCarthy and her medium "the Boy" (see Section 13.2). His daughter has confirmed that this was the reason that he came to the conclusion that it was imperative to move away from metropolitan London.[2] Sophie Lund did not go with them. In 1934, having been troubled by ill health for some time, she gave up her post at University College, left the Jones household, and returned to her native Denmark.

Although he was determined to leave London, Jones could not bring himself to go far. In the end, he decided to move to Gerrards Cross in Buckinghamshire—a dormitory town only about 20 miles from central London, with a fast train service. He may well have been recommended to the place by Hélène Coustenoble, who had herself spent some time there when she first arrived in Britain. Jones bought a detached house in Marsham Way, a quiet side road within easy walking distance of the railway station. It was roomy but unpretentious, built in the undistinguished 1930s British architectural style typical of tens of thousands of other houses put up in the inter-war period. Surrounding the house, there was a large area of garden, which Jones and Cyrille were later to put to good use in the lean war years, and after, for growing their own vegetables and keeping chickens.

Gerrards Cross was conveniently placed on a direct railway line into Marylebone

Station, from where Jones could travel by underground to Euston Square (in fact, the same station, now bearing a different name, that he had used at the turn of the century when he was a schoolboy). He would then walk the few hundred yards to University College entering through the rear of 21 Gordon Square (the front door was kept permanently locked to deter unwelcome visitors). For the next twenty-five years of his life, and longer, his routine was based around this rail journey. For example, he became well known for his curious habit of meeting and entertaining distinguished visitors at the buffet at Marylebone Station, rather than asking them either to his home, or to the senior common rooms in University College.[3]

Jones gradually took to spending less and less time in college, generally arranging his week so that he needed to come to London on just three days, knowing that he could rely on Lilias Armstrong, Hélène Coustenoble, Dorothy Parkinson and the rest of his staff to cope with day-to-day departmental matters. Much of the remainder of his week was spent in his study at Gerrards Cross where he could concentrate on the book which was to occupy much of his intellectual energy from about 1937 onwards, and which he hoped would be considered his magnum opus—a lengthy treatise which was later to emerge as the *Phoneme*.

11.3. Revision of the *Outline* and the *EPD*

Daniel Jones published no other new books in this period, but he did finish his radical revision of the *Outline*—virtually a completely rewritten book. It appeared in 1932 as the third edition, and continued at this stage to be printed and published by Teubner of Leipzig. For discussion of the content, and differences with the *Outline*[1], see Chapter 8.

In 1937, Jones produced another extensively revised version of a previous success, in this case a fourth edition of the *EPD*.[4] This book had sold in good numbers throughout the twenties and thirties, and Jones had produced two new editions with minor additions and revisions in 1924 and 1926. But he now felt that it was time to update both the contents and the way in which these were handled (*EPD*[4]: vi):

> It has been evident for some years past that this dictionary was in need of enlargement and of detailed revision. Many new words have entered the language and many rare words have become common since the book was first published (1917). Moreover, many words have undergone changes of pronunciation during that period: new pronunciations have appeared, and pronunciations which were previously rare have now come into common use.

However, he retained the most significant element of the earliest edition, namely the transcription system (see Section 7.2). Minor emendations were the replacement of diagonally sloping stress marks by verticals, and the substitution of a straightforward colon for the clumsy, albeit IPA approved, length mark consisting of a "colon with triangular dots". Jones pointed out that "it was found that the latter symbol becomes indistinct in reprints" (p. vi).

Jones added several thousand new words to the body of the dictionary, so that it now contained almost 55,000 in total. In so doing, he made clear that, apart from his own usage and his personal observations of the speech of other educated speakers, which remained overwhelmingly his principal sources of information, he had also "derived considerable help" from Wyld's (1932) *Universal dictionary of the English language* and the BBC's series containing recommendations to announcers, published as a series of seven booklets under the title *Broadcast English* (Lloyd James 1928–39), commenting that "the authors of these works are excellent phoneticians and their observations can be relied upon" (p. vi). (Characteristically, reflecting his suspicion of work by writers not known to him personally, Jones then adds that "other reference books have been used as sparingly as possible".) It is interesting that the mention of Lloyd James's publications was the first clearly stated connection between the *EPD* and the BBC, which was later to develop into a significant symbiotic relationship. After Lloyd James's death in 1941, Jones was to make an important contribution as pronunciation adviser to the BBC, to be helped in return by Elizabeth Miller in his compilation of entries for the *EPD* (see Section 12.9).

A noteworthy difference from the *EPD* editions of the 1920s is that Jones, following his own practice established in the *Outline*³ (see above), at long last replaced his use of "Public School Pronunciation" (PSP) by the term "Received Pronunciation", abbreviated to RP.

11.4. The phoneme (and the Joneme)

The concept of the phoneme was now beginning to play a large part in Jones's work, as is clear from the number of articles which he published on this theme from 1929 onwards.

"Definition of a phoneme" (Jones 1929c) is an attempt to clarify his statements in the *Pronunciation of Russian*, where he first set out his views. In essentials, this repeats his 1923 position, but he admits that "it doesn't seem possible to give in a single sentence a comprehensive definition which leaves no loopholes for misunderstandings" (Jones 1929c: 43). It is in this article that he first introduces his restriction of a "language" to "the speech of a single individual speaking in one particular style" (p. 44). He also emphasises his distinction between his "essentially ... phonetic conception" and the fact that substitution of one phoneme "for the other in a given situation *may* alter the meaning".

Jones (1931a), entitled "On phonemes", provides a definition which emphasises once again the significance of phonetic similarity and complementary distribution: "a family of sounds in a given language, consisting of an important sound of the language together with other related sounds, which take its place in particular sound-sequences" (p. 74). He supplies extensive exemplification of these features from numerous languages. Similarly, as in Jones (1929c), the semantic function of the phoneme is regarded as a consequence of the above and emphatically not a part of the definition itself. The same approach figures in his "Theory of phonemes, and its importance in practical linguistics" (Jones 1932a), the paper which he gave to the First International Congress of Phonetic Sciences at Amsterdam. This very brief treatment is written on similar lines to his previous phoneme articles but is significant for taking the definition one stage further, stressing the importance of the word: "a family of sounds in a given language, which are related in character and are such that no one of them ever occurs in the same surroundings as any other in words" (p. 1). In addition, this paper introduces the concepts of the "diaphone" and the "variphone". The diaphone represents the range of sounds heard as realisations of a particular phoneme across language varieties, for example between different regional dialects. The variphone covers the possible variation in the realisation of a phoneme within a single idiolect—in other words, free variation. Both of these terms are treated more extensively in the *Phoneme*; see Section 13.8.

One of the most influential of Jones's articles in the inter-war period is "The word as a phonetic entity" (Jones 1931k) which, apart from its defence of the word as a phonetic reality (in contrast to Jones's earlier views), is chiefly notable in being one of the first explorations of the concept of juncture. Although the term "juncture" is not actually employed, Jones's treatment pre-dates the American structuralists' preoccupation with this topic in the forties and fifties.

In "Concrete and abstract sounds" (Jones 1938a), a paper read at the Third International Congress at Ghent, Jones attempted to apply a philosophical theory of "abstractness" to the idea of the phoneme, linking this ultimately to ideas on the nature of human existence. The paper is probably the first published evidence of Jones's deepening interest in theosophical ideas, and, indeed, its contents cannot be interpreted without recourse to such concepts.

Jones deals here with a favourite theme of theosophical work, namely the relationship between the physical material world and the non-physical world of abstractions. Jones draws upon a frequent theosophical device to illustrate the relationship between the physical and the non-physical, namely the analysis of emotional states, such as anger. Deriving his ideas to a large extent from the views of the Japanese linguist K. Jimbo, as interpreted by Jones's own former colleague Palmer (1930: 39–48), he classifies speech sounds according to the following scheme, invoking four degrees of abstraction. It is to be noted that this idea of classification in layers of progressively more abstract systems is a commonplace in theosophical thinking (see, for example, Besant 1897 [1924²]: *passim*; Leadbeater [1907]: *passim*).

Concrete sounds: the actual sounds uttered.
1st degree of abstraction: sounds pronounced by an individual "in a similar manner" (or "speech-sounds").
2nd degree of abstraction: phonemes as realised by a single speaker.

3rd degree of abstraction: phonemes as realised by a group of speakers of similar speech style (or "diaphones").
4th degree of abstraction: wider differences in sound quality or usage of phonemes (or "diaphonemes").

Jones (1938a: 6) summarises finally in these terms:

> Lastly, the categories have, in my view, an importance for the development of the general theory of sound. I have put before you the suggestion that abstract sounds (at any rate those of the 1st degree) are really in perpetual existence. We are not perpetually perceiving them objectively, but this is because most people are only conscious of one dimension of time. We have, however, means of projecting these perpetually existing sounds into our one dimension (by "making concrete sounds").

Jones was normally circumspect about linking his profound interest in theosophy with his professional career in phonetics. But this was a period of deep involvement with Maud MacCarthy (alias Swami Omananda Puri) and her medium Bill Coote (alias the "Boy"), see Section 13.2, so it is perhaps not surprising that theosophical ideas were creeping into his work.

In the closing section of this paper, Jones (1938a: 6–7) gives the clearest statement of his theosophical beliefs to be found in his writing:

> Perhaps in the distant future the human race may develop a faculty of consciousness in two or more time-dimensions. There appear to be in fact already a few people who have some sort of conception of such dimensions. And besides it is to me, and no doubt to others, very unsatisfactory to envisage an eternity of time in a single dimension; it seems to me that one gets a much more hopeful view of life if one expects some ultimate expansion of consciousness which will include other dimensions of time, and in which therefore abstract sounds will be concrete. Of course in such a state of existence communications by sound would be carried on in some new way, and there would doubtless be a science of super-phonetics which we need not speculate about at the moment.

It is actually interesting to speculate on what the linguists gathered in Ghent might have made of this, but probably Jones left his audience (apart possibly from the odd fellow theosophist) completely puzzled. The "few people" referred to here are the group of "adepts" ("Masters" or "Brothers") who, theosophists assert, have managed to reach a semi-immortal state of existence from which they are capable of exerting tremendous influence on human affairs (see Besant 1897 [1924²]: 3–4 *et passim*; Humphreys 1966: *passim*). Jones obviously feels that the phoneme is "one aspect of phonetics [which] leads in the direction of metaphysics into regions which merit profound exploration" (Jones 1938a: 7). He returns to these ideas in the *Phoneme* (p. 217), where the concluding paragraph of the preface states that "phoneme theory has a certain bearing upon philosophy, and in particular upon questions relating to the 'existence' or 'non-existence' both of material phenomena and of ideas" (p. vii). In fact, Jones's theosophical background may account for his insistence on the split between the totally practical definition of the "physical" phoneme and the possibility of expansion along numerous lines of thought to account for the linguistic function of the phoneme—including the invocation of meaning, the "psychological" concept of the phoneme, and the elaboration of various abstract phonemic concepts as indicated above. Such a split would reflect the division between the materialist nature of the everyday world and the multi-layered spiritual planes of existence postulated by theosophists.

This paper, together with portions of the *Phoneme* (see Section 13.8), provide the best evidence that Jones was attempting to forge links between his academic, in a sense, existential, interest in phonetics and linguistics and his preoccupation with philosophy and transcendentalism, as interpreted by theosophy—and this link was through the phoneme concept.

It is therefore not true to say, as some critics have done, that Jones was interested only in a limited practical view of the phoneme, which excluded theoretical approaches, being based exclusively on phonetic and distributional criteria, the whole being dismissed disparagingly by the joke term "Joneme" (Abercrombie 1983: 8). Even though these criticisms could be applied to his actual definition, Jones was, in fact, involved in his own (essentially non-linguistic) theorising, whilst also extending the range of his overall phoneme concept as a means of escaping from its original limitations. See Collins and Mees (1997) for further discussion.

11.5. Shorter publications

In addition to this sequence of papers on the phoneme and related matters which appeared in the thirties, Jones produced a number of short papers dealing with other topics.

Two pieces, which deal with reconstructions of Shakespearean and Chaucerian English (Jones 1937i and 1938c), appear to have been triggered largely by his work for a set of gramophone records, *English pronunciation through the centuries*, which Jones produced together with the philologist H.C. Wyld for Linguaphone. Wyld wrote most of the material in the accompanying booklet, but Jones was responsible for the text of the Shakespearean English (passages of dialogue from four plays) and for the accompanying notes (Jones 1937i). These are of interest since they reveal Jones's sources for his Shakespearean reconstructions. He quotes a number of authorities (Ellis 1869–89; Sweet 1874 [1888]; Viëtor 1906a/b;[5] Jespersen 1909; Zachrisson 1913; and his own co-author, Wyld 1920 [1936]), but claims that his "conclusions correspond in the main with Zachrisson". The texts and Jones's comments are an interesting intermediary step in his Shakespearean work, between the early attempts (see Section 3.2) and his later efforts, in the fifties, for the *Pronunciation of English*[3] (see Section 14.15). Jones also mentions, in passing, and probably for the first time in print, an important dialect feature in modern English, namely the lack in some varieties of English of what Wells (1982: 234–236) has termed the NORTH—FORCE merger. Jones notes correctly that certain regional accents maintain a distinction between words such as *story*, with a close vowel [o:], and *morning*, with an open vowel [ɔ:]. He considers this contrast to be widespread in so many types of English (even being indicated in some dictionaries) that it must "go back to ancient times" and concludes that the phenomenon was certainly prevalent in the sixteenth century.

A further collaboration with his old colleague and co-author, H.S. Perera, resulted in a suggested revised alphabet for Sinhalese (Perera—Jones 1937k). This was the first in a series of such projects for orthographies for languages with non-Roman writing systems which Jones was to undertake in the 1940s (see Section 12.7). Jones's fascination with exploring the sound systems of less familiar languages is reflected in the numerous brief samples which he wrote up for the *Spécimen* section of *Le Maître phonétique*, working together with native-speaker informants: Sindhi (Jones 1933k), Assamese (Jones 1933l), literary and colloquial Marathi (Jones 1934g; 1935c), Bulgarian (Jones—Moskowska 1937f) and Greek (Jones 1937g). These pieces came mainly as a result of Jones's classes in phonological analysis of non-European languages, which were by now a regular feature of his teaching to advanced students. Another publication, the *Chinese–English phonetic dictionary*, co-authored by Jones and published in Shanghai, appears to have been produced in this decade.[6]

However, Jones also maintained his interest in more familiar matters. His article "On 'Received Pronunciation'" (1937a) probably stemmed from his thorough revision of the *EPD* (Jones [1937⁴]); see Section 11.3. Here, Jones (1937a: 1) once again states clearly his view that the phonetician should be "an impartial recorder of the facts of speech, and not an advocate of any particular style". Jones claims that the only recommendation he would make is "that people should speak in such a way as to be intelligible to their hearers" (p. 1), and holds that there is no case as such for teaching RP exclusively. Other accents, such as Scottish or south-western English, would be just as acceptable in his opinion and that even talking with a foreign accent would be reasonable, "if he [the foreign learner] does not find it worth his while to speak more intelligibly" (p. 1).

Jones considers that RP is to be favoured as a model for foreign learners only because of the ready availability of descriptions and the widespread acceptability of the accent. As far as native speakers of English are concerned, he states his views in this form (p. 2):

... no attempt should be made to impose one particular form of speech upon anyone who prefers another form. Above all it appears to me important that *no person should ever disparage the pronunciation of another*. (Jones's italics)

Such views would seem commonplace today in linguistic discussion (even if still openly contested by laymen); in that era, they represented a notably forthright expression of liberal ideas from someone who was by this point getting to be accepted as the most important British authority on such matters. See Section 14.5 for discussion.

Jones had expressed somewhat similar opinions earlier in a paper "Speech training: the phonetic aspect" (Jones 1935f). Here he distances himself from those concerned with "voice-production" and does not regard value judgements on pronunciation as falling within the remit of the phonetician (1935f: 28):

> In fact, it is his function to take up a rather detached attitude in regard to such questions. By doing so he finds that much of what is sometimes called "beautiful" or "ugly" in speech is not intrinsic beauty or ugliness at all, but is merely convention. The use of a certain sound recalls an unpleasant circumstance or reminds us of somebody we do not like or whom we despise, and (often without realizing the connexion) we attribute ugliness to the *sound* instead of to the circumstances recalled by it.

Jones's views are advanced for the period (1935f: 29):

> If one is trying, for instance, to teach the sort of English I am now using to a class of Cockney schoolboys, and if one is intolerant about their speech and tells them that their way is "wrong" or "bad" or "ugly", it simply antagonizes them. They do not like being told that the kind of English they have always used and which is used by their parents, their brothers and sisters and friends, is "bad." But if the teacher takes up a more tolerant attitude and explains that they have a language which serves its purpose well for home use, but that there exist many other ways of talking; that some of these ways are only understood well in restricted areas, say London, or South Lancashire, or the neighbourhood of Dundee, while others are readily understood over much wider areas—some, in fact, over the whole of the English-speaking world: that it often comes in very usefully if a man can talk a kind of English which is easily understood everywhere, and that is why a special kind of English is taught in school; then the teacher can get the boys on his side, and they become willing to learn the school pronunciation instead of thinking it silly and affected.

One of the papers published by Jones shortly before the outbreak of war was a general survey of the subject under the title "The aims of phonetics" (Jones 1937j, 1938b). Sensing undoubtedly the growing movement in favour of instrumental approaches, Jones here wrote a spirited defence of traditional auditory-articulatory phonetics, and the importance of the practical applications of the discipline: "... phonetic science is of value in so far as it is studied with a view to applying it to constructive ends" (p. 7). It remains one of the best summaries of Jones's viewpoint on the value of phonetics and linguistics "as a means to an end" (p. 1), and his views changed little from this point on until his death. Nevertheless, Jones's practical approach struck

UNIVERSITY OF LONDON, UNIVERSITY COLLEGE

—

SESSION 1933-34.

—

DEPARTMENT OF PHONETICS

———

STAFF :

DANIEL JONES, M.A., University Professor of Phonetics.

Miss LILIAS E. ARMSTRONG, B.A., Senior Lecturer.

J. R. FIRTH, M.A., Senior Lecturer.

STEPHEN JONES, B.Sc., Superintendent of Phonetics Laboratory.

W. PERRETT, B.A., Ph.D., Lecturer (German Phonetics).

Miss HÉLÈNE COUSTENOBLE, Lecturer (French Phonetics).

Miss EDITH E. QUICK, B.A., Lecturer (General and Dutch and Spanish Phonetics).

Senior Assistants :

Mrs. HYACINTH M. DAVIES (Spoken English).

Miss SOPHIE LUND (French Phonetics, Danish Phonetics).

Assistants :

Miss A. DOROTHY PARKINSON.

Miss EILEEN M. EVANS, B.A.

Honorary Lecturer :

A. LLOYD JAMES, M.A., University Professor of Phonetics at the School of Oriental Studies.

Temporary Assistant :

Miss E. MARGUERITE CHAPALLAZ.

Figure 11.1. Extract from the departmental Prospectus 1933–34 showing a list of staff members.

many scholars of the day as being extremely limited and unduly antagonistic towards theoretical developments. One of the most devastating counterblasts came in the autobiography of the respected veteran Otto Jespersen (1938 [1995]: 253), who claimed to be shocked by Jones's article:

> ...in which only the practical usefulness of phonetics was emphasized without any kind of understanding of the value of the theoretical or historical study of language. Very much in my books and articles—and perhaps that which is in itself most valuable—is aimed exclusively at pure disinterested theory, at merely penetrating the essence of language (and language sounds) in order to expand our theoretical insight.

The point was taken up by Jones's friend Uldall, who was in the throes of a correspondence with Jones, in which he was attempting to explain to Jones, with little apparent success, the involved theory of glossematics, which was being developed by himself and Hjelmslev. In addition to quoting Jespersen, Uldall wrote:

> Your letter made me rather sad, because it brought home to me how very different our views are, or rather how much your views differ from those of other scientists.... The greatest possible benefit for humanity cannot be achieved merely by attempts to solve existing practical problems, because we know from past experience that new benefits are recognized only as the means of supplying them come to hand.... If science had limited itself to supplying the immediate needs of the [sic] existing society, we should still be busy perfecting flint tools.[7]

Jones responded to Uldall by saying that he was in favour of a wide variety of academic views:

> What I find so often among academic people is that they do so much investigation & re-hashing of other people's ideas. This surely is not civilization. Is not a really civilized community one in which all the individuals are creative and spontaneous, & do not allow themselves to be bound by what others say or have said? So I don't mind in the least if your ideas differ from mine. We are all different from each other, & whatever the goal of human existence may be, we all approach it by different paths.[8]

11.6. Work of the Department in the thirties

The departmental prospectuses for the thirties show that the UCL Phonetics Department flourished in the inter-war period as a centre for teaching. Despite limited facilities, cramped accommodation and some staff with few qualifications, or indeed none at all, Jones's students were well catered for. A wide range of classes were provided

UNIVERSITY OF LONDON, UNIVERSITY COLLEGE.
1935.
DEPARTMENT OF PHONETICS

IN
SPOKEN ENGLISH
FOR FOREIGN STUDENTS
will be held
under the general direction of
Professor DANIEL JONES and Miss L. E. ARMSTRONG
from 29th July to 12th August, 1935.

The Lectures and Classes will be held on each week-day, except Monday, 5th Aug. (Bank Holiday).
The Course will include

(*a*) **Twelve Lectures,** by Miss L. E. Armstrong and Mr. J. R. Firth.

(*b*) **Twelve Periods of Ear-Training Exercises,** by Prof. Daniel Jones and Miss L. E. Armstrong.

(*c*) **Practical Classes** { (*i*) **Pronunciation Exercises.**
(*ii*) **Intonation Exercises.**
Conducted by Miss E. E. Quick, Miss E. M. Evans, Mr. J. R. Firth, Mr. D. B. Fry, and other assistants.

(*d*) **Three Lectures on the Grammar of Colloquial English,** by Mrs. H. M. Davies.

(*e*) **Five Periods of Readings with Explanations,** by Mrs. H. M. Davies.

For the Pronunciation Exercises the Students will be divided into groups, each containing **not more than eight Students.**

Teachers of English Nationality are eligible to attend the Course ; they are invited to participate in the practical classes as observers, in order to see how the methods described in the lectures are put into practice.

Fee for the Full Course - £5 10s. 0d.
Morning Course only   - £4 10s. 0d.

Students will assemble for the opening of the Course at **9.25 a.m. on Monday, 29th July,** *in Henry Morley Annexe, Room No.* 1, *University College.*

Figure 11.2. An advertisement for a 1935 vacation course.

not only in phonetics but in more general English language teaching, together with some linguistics. There was always a strong emphasis on practical applications, as diverse as foreign language learning, speech therapy and romanisation. Jones and his colleagues also managed between them to deal with a remarkably large number of languages. All members of staff were expected to play their part as teachers of English or French pronunciation and to teach practical phonetics and ear-training. In addition, the by now very well established tradition of annual vacation courses was upheld and all members of Jones's staff were called upon to participate (see Figure 11.2).

The prospectus for the Session 1933–34 (see Figure 11.1) is representative of the rest of the decade. It lists four courses in the phonetics of French, two in German and single courses in the phonetics of no fewer than seven other European languages: Italian, Spanish, Modern Provençal, Swedish, Danish, Dutch and Welsh.[9] In addition, tuition was on offer in the phonetics of a number of more geographically distant languages, reflecting the Department's research interests, and ranging from Russian and Cantonese to Tswana and Somali; these would be taught provided at least three students showed an interest.

English was, naturally enough, the language which proved to be the chief focus of attention, with three courses aimed at native speakers and four for foreigners. Apart from the phonetics of English, courses were also given in "Spoken English", in which training was provided in "Grammar", "Composition", and "Conversation". Speech pathology was also included in the form of six "Lecture-demonstrations on Methods of Correcting Defects of Speech". These were conducted by Jones and Lilias Armstrong, and students were permitted to observe "the practical application of these methods." In addition, treatment was available for "Lisping, Lalling, Retarded Speech, and Defective Speech consequent upon illness or operation for cleft palate".[10]

Classes of a somewhat more theoretical nature included a course on general phonetics "adapted to the needs of students desirous of undertaking Research Work". Jones himself taught a course "for advanced students who wish to qualify as teachers of Phonetics, or to analyse the phonetic structure of lesser-known languages". These sessions, where Jones worked with native-speaker informants, conducting on-the-spot phonetic and phonological analysis by auditory methods, rapidly became famous, and his own amazing skills in the area of recognition and imitation became the subject of anecdote, if not of legend.

Stephen Jones was responsible for a brief course of six lectures on experimental phonetics, which was the only scheduled teaching in this area. However, it was stated that "Instruction in Practical Experimental Phonetics can be arranged to suit the convenience of students".[11]

J.R. Firth taught two lecture courses in linguistics and was responsible for the tutorials which accompanied them. He also conducted the "Principles of Speech Training" course, which laid considerable emphasis on child language acquisition, and gave a set of six lectures on "Romanic Orthography for Asiatic Languages".[12]

Research was also thriving in Jones's Department, as can be witnessed by the following paragraph headed "Research in Linguistics" and placed, somewhat oddly, in the general list of courses:

Special arrangements can be made for the guidance of linguistic research dealing with actual forms of speech such as regional, class, or occupational dialects, linguistic geography, the speech of children, and other special forms of language, spoken or written.[13]

Numerous publications were produced by Jones's staff in the course of the decade. In 1932, Lilias Armstrong produced her *Phonetics of French* (Armstrong 1932); then, together with Hélène Coustenoble, she published what is now regarded as a classic work on French intonation (Coustenoble—Armstrong 1934). Other publications on various European languages by members and ex-members of the Department included a textbook on Spanish (Stirling 1935) and the last books in the London Phonetic Reader series, on Dutch (Quick—Schilthuis 1930), Danish (Uldall 1933) and Serbo-Croat (Fry—Kostić 1939). Most of the earlier phonetic readers remained in print and the series was still being advertised in the post-war era.

Work on African languages included Armstrong's research on Somali (1934), whilst Ida Ward shortly after leaving for the School of Oriental Studies (SOS) produced her famous *Practical phonetics for students of African languages*, written in cooperation with Westermann in 1933. She later wrote important studies with an emphasis on tonal features of Efik (Ward 1933) and Igbo (Ward 1936a). Douglas Beach, now occupying a chair at Cape Town, published his brilliant study of Khoisan, *The phonetics of the Hottentot language* (Beach 1938). In the field of Far-Eastern languages, Sun-Gi Gim wrote a notable thesis on Korean under Jones's supervision (1937). Other more general publications included Abercrombie's (1937) historiographical study of Isaac Pitman, and two popular general introductions to linguistics by Firth (see Section 11.8).

11.7. Upstairs and downstairs

The atmosphere of the Department in the inter-war period has been nostalgically recalled by David Abercrombie, who spent seven years from 1930 onwards as a part-time post-graduate student there. He depicts the rundown, cramped accommodation of 21 Gordon Square and contrasts it with the lively energy of the academic activity which it contained. A complete university department of world-wide reputation was run from a Bloomsbury terraced house almost as if it were an extended family—complete with Jones himself as *pater familias*. Yet, as Abercrombie (1980: 1) indicates, the cosy ambience of Arts Annexe 1 cloaked fundamental divisions within:

…you entered it from the College, through the back door,…at the ground floor level, where the Department Office was, presided over by the formidable Miss Parkinson, or Parky, as she was known to every one…. From there you could go down by a dark staircase to what had been the kitchens of the original house, but which now constituted the Phonetics Laboratory, of which Stephen Jones was Superintendent. Or you could go up by another staircase to the lecture rooms and the rooms of the rest of the staff, with Mlle Coustenoble and Miss Ida Ward right up at the top. Daniel Jones's room was on the first floor. J.R. Firth and Miss Sophie Lund ("Marraine" as she was called) had rooms on the ground floor...one could go *upstairs* to Daniel Jones and most of his colleagues, or *downstairs* to Stephen Jones and his lab, and a different world.

Abercrombie's phrase "upstairs and downstairs" sums up neatly the dichotomy which developed in the Department. "Upstairs" was where Daniel Jones, surrounded by his, mainly female, senior staff refined an approach to linguistic research and teaching with techniques rooted in the principles of articulatory phonetics, carrying on the traditions established by Bell, Ellis, Sweet and Passy. The downstairs basement had "the original kitchen range in it, with a fire burning most of the year with a kettle on it and a teapot on the hob". This was where Stephen Jones and J.R. Firth ("spiritually he belonged to downstairs") would gather the younger members of staff around them "gossiping... about the present state and current problems of Phonetics".

From the young Abercrombie's (pp. 1–2) viewpoint, "the gossip was most educative". There was much discussion about topics such as a motor theory of perception, the significance of the syllable as a phonological unit, and alternatives to Jones's theory of the phoneme. Upstairs such matters were largely ignored; Abercrombie (p. 2) claims:

> Almost no general phonetic theory was taught in the Department, at least not formally. There were no classes in general phonetic performance, except for the Cardinal Vowels, which I was taught by Daniel Jones.

But, as we have seen, the prospectuses of the period show that in fact lectures on general phonetics were being given (by Armstrong, Ward and Jones himself). Furthermore, as Abercrombie (pp. 2–5) himself states, classes were being taught on Speech Therapy (by Ward), General Linguistics (by Firth), and Experimental Phonetics (by Stephen Jones). Abercrombie was nevertheless undoubtedly correct in claiming that the stress was laid on practical phonetic accomplishments in individual languages.[14] The emphasis given to applied phonetics—interpreted very narrowly, in the sense of direct application to the learning and teaching of foreign languages—meant that theoretical matters were to a large extent neglected.

Abercrombie relates how dissatisfied Firth and Stephen Jones were with this state of affairs. Although admiring the practical talents of Daniel Jones and his upstairs colleagues, they objected to "the lack of interest in theory, to the fact that students were never recommended to read books, and to the disregard of what was being said elsewhere by other people...to the very segmental approach...and their neglect of, and lack of interest in, the syllable" (p. 2).

Jones tended to judge his staff and students largely in terms of their practical abilities (p. 2):

The assessment of people upstairs was thought to be curiously limited. Firth was most amused when he said to Daniel Jones, after I had been working in the Department a while, "What do you think of Abercrombie," and Jones answered "Well, his Cardinal Three's not very good."

Abercrombie (p. 2) maintains, however, that while he was mainly sympathetic to downstairs views, and largely in agreement with Firth and Stephen Jones about the shortcomings of the Department, he nevertheless found a great deal that was "exciting and stimulating" in the intensive practical training he received from the upstairs staff. For Abercrombie, much of this came in the form of individual tuition from Jones himself, as he describes (pp. 2–3):

> I took a lot of classes with Daniel Jones and he taught me alone in nearly all of them. He sometimes taught lying down; he had a large leather-covered couch in his room for that purpose. It was always said that he was a chronic invalid.... Learning the Cardinal Vowels from Jones was a long and painful process, and it did not include learning how to use them in phonetic description of languages. That was left to Ida Ward...and very well she did it.

That Abercrombie was given private tuition is not in itself unusual, since Jones appears quite often to have taught students whom he considered particularly talented on a one-to-one basis; for example, Eugénie Henderson recalled being picked out for similar treatment.[15] Once Jones had spotted someone with potential amongst the young students, he took care that he or she was given good practical training, and also tried to provide work which would enable them more easily to pursue a career in phonetics. Abercrombie (pp. 3–5) relates how a number of part-time jobs were channelled towards him in this way, and how Jones also arranged for him to stay in France and take his IPA Certificate under the aegis of Paul Passy himself.

Abercrombie's amusing picture of the "upstairs and downstairs" division, and the gentle mockery of Jones by Firth and his younger associates, was however indicative of the beginnings of a deeper and more serious rift. A little later, the activities of J.R. Firth were to cause Jones the greatest pain and disappointment over a period of many years.

11.8. Firth's growing influence

It was clear that by now Firth was becoming a major force in the circle of phoneticians at University College. After having returned from India in 1928 to take up a post in University College, he was beginning to show that he would become a rival to Jones himself.

Firth was by now already in his forties, but was nevertheless nearly ten years younger than Jones. Once he had settled down in London, Firth did not confine himself to his work in University College, but also obtained a series of part-time posts at the London School of Economics, the Indian Institute at Oxford and at the School of Oriental Studies. At LSE, he came into contact with the social anthropologist, Bronislaw Malinowski (1884–1942), and a friendship grew up which was to prove a significant influence on Firth's later development, and move him further away from Jones's view of linguistics.

During this period, he published two short books—*Speech* (J.R. Firth 1930) and *The tongues of men* (J.R. Firth 1937). Indeed, these were the only complete books he ever actually got round to writing. Both are simple, straightforward expositions aimed at the intelligent non-expert and Firth's approach might in many ways have recommended itself to Daniel Jones—being wide-ranging and generally non-technical. Firth makes clear in them his interest in the work of earlier linguists, including people like Pāṇini and Wilkins, a fascination he shared with Jones. Firth, however, shows himself to have much wider interests than Jones, being able to regard phonetics as only one part of the wider discipline of linguistics.

In 1937, Firth went back to India for a period of fifteen months on a Leverhulme scholarship and on his return in 1938 he moved across to the Department of Phonetics and Linguistics at what was now the School of Oriental and African Studies (SOAS), where he worked under Jones's former colleague Arthur Lloyd James, specialising in Indian languages. Jones might have been pleased to see the back of his outspoken colleague, but once at SOAS, Firth began to lay the ground for establishing a rival to the UCL Department that was to make him the bane of Jones's latter years.

11.9. Dennis Fry

Dennis Fry was another scholar who first entered the Department during this period. Fry was born in Stockbridge in Hampshire in 1907, and throughout his life his voice retained echoes of the rhotic speech of that neighbourhood. He joined University College London as an undergraduate in 1928, and was still in his early twenties when he came as a student to the Phonetics Department in 1931, hoping to do an MA in the subject. Jones required him, like all other students, to attend elementary general courses in French and English phonetics. But Jones soon picked out his aptitude for the subject and three years later, in 1934, he appointed Fry to the full-time staff as an assistant lecturer. He was then groomed by Stephen Jones so as to be able eventually to take over the job of running the Phonetics Laboratory.[16]

On Stephen Jones's retirement in 1937, Fry duly assumed his position as supervisor of the lab. With only a brief break during the war, when he was in charge of the Acoustics Laboratory of the Central Medical Establishment of the Royal Air Force, investigating the problems of communication among aircrew, he stayed in University College for the rest of his career, in total over forty years. He later became Daniel Jones's direct successor as head of the Department in 1949 (see Section 12.12).

Once he took charge, Fry set about reorganising the laboratory, with Daniel Jones's support. The lab was still housed in the cellar of 21 Gordon Square, in the same cosy but cramped surroundings that Abercrombie had relished. The equipment which had been purchased in the early 1920s, or earlier, was now largely outdated, since there had been little money coming for replacements in the lean depression years. The work centred almost entirely on kymography and palatography, using techniques which had first been developed at the end of the nineteenth century. It was not until just before Stephen Jones left that the Department managed to acquire a cathode-ray oscillograph, which, for the first time, enabled the direct examination of the speech waveform, replacing the primitive manometric flames (see Section A.5) which had been the only means available until then.[17]

Nevertheless, despite all the limitations and under-funding, University College still possessed the only phonetics laboratory in Britain. Thanks to its position in central London, the Department regularly at this period attracted the attention of newspaper reporters although the articles which appeared were often more based on fantasy than fact as far as speech analysis was concerned. From the outset, Fry had to work with one disadvantage, namely Jones's ideas of the nature of experimental phonetics. At this point, Jones was not opposed to experimental ideas, as he later on became, but nevertheless he always had taken the view that experimental phonetics was essentially an adjunct to auditory phonetics. In Jones's opinion, the main task of the experimentalist was to *confirm* what the ear had heard. Fry was more modern in his approach, regarding phonetics as essentially "multifaceted", and taking account of the fact that the trained ear of the phonetician was only one possible source of information—albeit a very significant one—which could contribute together with many others to the analysis of the processes of speech and hearing.[18]

Fry immediately began building up the resources of the laboratory. (It is notable that around this time the Department is mentioned as overspending its allowances.)[19] Fry also busily cemented the relationships which had already been established with London University science departments and with London hospitals. In the session 1938–39, he worked with Phyllis Kerridge of the University College Physiology Department on the reception of speech by the deaf, but declared himself hampered by the limited resources of the phonetics laboratory.[20] Fry's plans for installing a proper up-to-date laboratory for the Department were, like so much else, to be completely disrupted by the outbreak of the Second World War and had to be held in abeyance until after 1945 (see Section 12.11).

11.10. The 1935 Conference

Dennis Fry was also co-editor, with Jones, of the proceedings of the Second International Congress of Phonetic Sciences (Jones—Fry 1936a), an event which provided the climax for Jones's Department during the thirties. London had been chosen as the centre for the Second International Congress of Phonetic Sciences, due to be held in 1935, and Daniel Jones had been nominated as Congress President. Preparations were made for the conference throughout the first six months of the year. University Col-

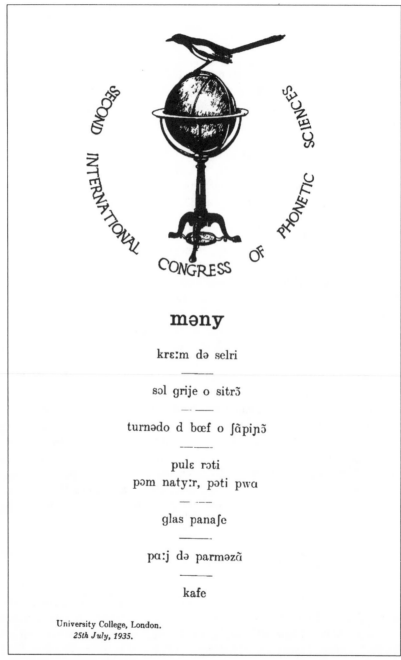

məny

krɛːm də selri

sɔl grije o sitrɔ̃

‒ ‒‒

turnədo d bœf o ʃɑ̃piɲɔ̃

‒‒‒

pulɛ rɔti
pɔm natyːr, pəti pwɑ

‒ ‒‒‒

glas panaʃc

‒‒‒‒.

pɑːj də parməzɑ̃

‒‒‒‒

kafe

University College, London.
25th July, 1935.

Figure 11.3. The menu for the dinner of the Second International Congress of Phonetic Sciences.

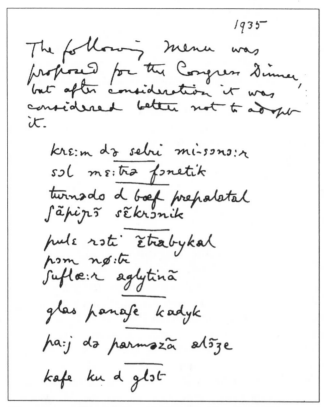

Figure 11.4. The suggested alternative menu for the conference (in Jones's handwriting).

lege was to host the whole proceedings, and plans were made by an organising committee which included Daniel Jones, Provost Allen Mawer, Sir Richard Paget and H.C. Wyld among its members.

The conference opened on June 22 and continued for a week, with 250 participants from all over the world. The programme was crowded, with over 70 papers and demonstrations, and the scholars involved ranged from veterans such as Scripture and Paget to younger figures such as Firth, Jakobson, Hjelmslev and Uldall. Firth's growing influence was indicated by the fact that he was the only UCL staff-member, apart from Jones himself, to chair a plenary session. The participants were honoured by a government reception at Lancaster House, entertained by a visit to the Mansion House, a special performance of *Pygmalion* and a conference dinner—where the menu was printed entirely in phonetic transcription (Figure 11.3).[21] Jones, in his speech to the participants, mentioned that an alternative menu had been devised, and this is illustrated in Figure 11.4. Harold Palmer then proceeded to entertain by giving a piece of mock Gilbert and Sullivan, "The Modern Phonetician" (see Figures 11.5 and 11.6).

The conference was notable for the emphasis on the importance of experimental phonetics, on the one hand, and for the numerous papers dealing with the concept of the phoneme on the other. The narrow view of the phoneme advocated by Jones (see Section 14.16) was still influential and had many adherents, but newer and more powerful linguistic models were now being put forward by the Prague and Copenhagen Schools. The conference could in some ways be seen as another indication of the rapid development of the two significant influences, namely experimental phonetics and theoretical phonology. These two aspects of the subject were eventually to overtake the primacy of the kind of traditional, practical, articulatory phonetics advocated by Jones and the majority of his colleagues in the British school at this time.

The conference was hailed as a great success—in terms both of content and organisation. And Jones, as the leading personality responsible for running the congress, could feel well-satisfied with the final result.

11.11. The rise and fall of the Simplified Spelling Society

The burst of activity which the Simplified Spelling Society went through in its early years was followed by a period in the twenties and thirties when the organisation was noticeably less active.[22] Jones, although remaining officially a member, played little part in its affairs. For some years, the lack of interest was largely owing to the action of SSS's most wealthy supporter, the millionaire Sir George Hunter, who had been elected President. In 1928, to save money on London office premises, it was decided to move the headquarters of the Society to Wallsend, on Tyneside, in the North East of England, where Hunter lived. From here, Hunter, together with a full-time paid secretary, T.R. Barber, appears to have run the Society almost as his own property. Jones may have resented this appropriation of the society by an individual, particularly one who was a businessman having no academic connections. Furthermore, as a Londoner, born and bred, Jones never seems to have relished travel to the North of England. In any case, even though the meetings in Wallsend were irregular and few, Jones does not appear to have attended a single one.

Despite inconveniencing Jones and other members by the move to the North, Hunter's overall usefulness to the SSS should certainly not be underestimated. Lloyd James called him "the veteran shipbuilder, who in the latter years of his life kept the cause alive with his zeal, and indeed with his money" (Ripman—Archer [1940[5]]: 5). Apart from his financial assistance, Hunter was also largely responsible for the organisation of a huge petition for spelling reform containing the signatures of hundreds of academics, numerous MPs and several bishops, together with representatives of a number of powerful professional bodies, thus arousing the greatest single expression of influential public support for simplified spelling ever witnessed in Britain, or anywhere else.[23] He also ensured financial solvency for the SSS for many years after his death through a large bequest made in his will.

Hunter died in 1937, and the centre of activity of the SSS moved back to London, even though the official headquarters, and the professional Secretary, remained in Wallsend until after the war—somewhat to Jones's annoyance, since he had attempted in 1939, without success, to get things changed. However, from this point on, the chief influences on the progress of the Society were once again academic, and Jones was to play a major part. He became a member of a small subcommittee which was charged with reorganising the SSS and revitalising its work. The chairman was Gilbert

S<small>ECOND</small> I<small>NTERNATIONAL</small> C<small>ONGRESS</small> <small>OF</small> P<small>HONETIC</small> S<small>CIENCES</small>
LONDON, 1935
C<small>ONGRESS</small> D<small>INNER</small>, July 25th.

TOASTS
The King
Phonetic Sciences
Proposed by Professor Lloyd James

ENTERTAINMENT

Recitation
(Professor T<small>HUDICHUM</small>)

A Phonetic Experiment
(Sir R<small>ICHARD</small> P<small>AGET</small>)

Recitation: Chaucer's 'Pardoner's Tale'
(Professor J<small>ONES</small>)

Demonstration of Sign Language
(Sir R<small>ICHARD</small> P<small>AGET</small>)

Song: 'The Modern Phonetician'
(Dr. H. E. P<small>ALMER</small>)

Figure 11.5. Programme for toasts and entertainment for the Second International Congress of Phonetic Sciences.

THE MODERN PHONETICIAN.*

A fluency Exercise—30 lines in 15 seconds.

I.

I wish to be the pattern of a modern phonetician
To know the sounds of languages, and also in addition
The sum of their varieties, ancestral or collateral
Arranged upon the triangle, the square or quadrilateral,
To know the different ways to utilize the nasal cavity
To measure its dimensions and its net specific gravity;
I wish to show by means of mathematical equation
The mysteries of Cockney vowels with stress and intonation.

CHORUS:
  The mysteries of Cockney vowels with stress and intonation
  The mysteries of Cockney vowels with stress and intonation
  The mysteries of Cockney vowels with stress and intona- - -tion.

I wish to be acquainted too with matters phonological,
Embracing their phenomena in order chronological.
In short it's my decision and my mission and ambition
To be the very pattern of a modern phonetician.

2.

I wish to lecture weekly to phonetical societies
On vowel sounds in all their combinations and varieties;
I wish to write some volumes on phonetical analysis
Exposing all the weaknesses of orthographic fallacies;
I wish to call attention to the tactics and the strategy
Exemplified in all the work produced by Dr. Chatterji,
To ascertain what happens at the back of people's pharynxes
And analyse the vocal chords in artificial larynxes.

CHORUS:
  And analyse the vocal chords in artificial larynxes
  And analyse the vocal chords in artificial larynxes
  And analyse the vocal chords in artificial lary-larynxes.

I'm so enthusiastic on the whole phonetic business,
I do my exercises till I fairly drop with dizziness.
In short it's my decision and my mission and ambition
To be the very pattern of a modern phonetician.

* By H. E. Palmer. Tune—"The Modern Major-General" from Gilbert & Sullivan's "The Pirates of Penzance."

3.

I've read the works of Daniel Jones, of Ripman, and of Viëtor
(Who tells us how the Germans speak in every German theatre);
I'm anxious to attain success in fluent catenation
In Palmer's book I've practised every blessed combination!
I've come to know the only word that really rhymes with *vinegar*
Is represented by the name of our illustrious *vosinoks* *
I've studied the phonetic chart and memorized the lines in it;
The alphabet I use is one with 15,000 signs in it.

CHORUS:
  The alphabet I use is one with 15,000 signs in it
  The alphabet I use is one with 15,000 signs in it
  The alphabet I use is one with 15,000 funny signs in it.

I've analyzed the sounds contained in tongues of every nation;
I've mastered all the tricks connected with articulation.
In short it's my decision and my mission and ambition
To be the very pattern of a modern phonetician.

4.

If I could only hear the differences in acousticity
And work my lower jaw with some degree of elasticity,
If I could only form my sounds without such artificiality,
If I could learn precisely what is meant by pure nasality,
If I could only cure myself of my bizarre propensity
To muddle up the attributes of glottal stop and tensity,
If I could only learn to roll my uvula mechanically
And not pronounce French sentences so awfully Britannically.

CHORUS:
  And not pronounce French sentences so awfully Britannically
  And not pronounce French sentences so awfully Britannically
  And not pronounce French sentences so awfully
                        Bri-tanni-tannically.

If I could only get myself to isolate successfully
Instead of making screeches that affect you so distressfully,
If half the sounds I made when speaking French were more Parisian,
I'd be the very pattern of a modern phonetician.

* van Ginneken.

Figure 11.6. Palmer's fluency exercise "The Modern Phonetician" for the conference dinner (based on Gilbert and Sullivan's "Modern Major-General").

Murray, lately retired from the chair of Greek at Oxford, who was a scholar of international renown. The other members included two of Jones's friends and colleagues—Arthur Lloyd James and Walter Ripman—together with Harold Orton, later to become the leading British dialectologist of his day. Jones was soon playing an important role in diverse activities of the Society. For instance, together with Harold Orton, he was mainly responsible for the revised sixth edition of the Ripman—Archer "Proposals", republished under the title *New Spelling* (Ripman—Archer [1948[6]]).[24] In 1939, Jones also took on the organisation of the Society's battle to defend its right to the Hunter legacy, which had to be fought in the High Court. The SSS won the case, and perhaps for once Daniel Jones was glad of his early legal training.

11.12. Honour and bereavement

In 1936, Jones received a welcome and completely unexpected honour. According to Ida Ward's (1936b) report of the event, Jones found himself invited to "a rather mysterious luncheon party" at University College, together with a group of his phonetic colleagues, the Provost and the Vice-Rector of the University of Zürich. It emerged

KENYATTA

UNIVERSITY COLLEGE, LONDON

GOWER STREET, W.C.1

Telephone : Euston 4400
Please Quote :

DEPARTMENT OF PHONETICS

11.6.1938

Dear Mr Kenyatta,

     In answer to your letter, I have undertaken
on behalf of Professor Boyanus to see Miss Armstrong's
book through the press, and Miss Honikman has very kindly
consented to help me in this rather difficult work.

     The question of putting your name on the title-
page does not arise. Miss Armstrong is the sole author
of the book, and grants to make publication possible
have been made to her by the University and by the
African Institute on the ground that it is her book.
You were the informant employed in connexion with this
piece of work. You did your work well, and full credit
will be given to you for everything you have done.
Authorship is quite a different matter; and I am afraid
you do not yet realise the nature of the work which an
author of this kind of book has to do.

     I hope you will try to understand the situ-
ation and accept it in the proper spirit. I hope too
that when occasion permits, you will continue to work
with us as before for the benefit of your language and
your people.

     I should be glad to have a talk with you
some time, if you would like it.
                 Yours sincerely,

Mr J. Kenyatta, 15 Cranleigh Houses,
Cranleigh St., n.w.1

Figure 11.7. Departmental file copy of letter written by Jones to Jomo Kenyatta.

that the Zürich authorities wished to recognise the centenary of London University (which was being celebrated that year) by the award of an honorary doctorate to a member of its staff. They had chosen Jones, "who had been so long connected with the oldest and biggest college of the University, and whose distinguished contributions to the study of phonetics were so well known and appreciated in Switzerland". Jones had been told nothing of what had been planned but was delighted to receive recognition of his work from such a distinguished European academic institution. From then on, as a matter of course, he placed the honorary degree after his name on the title pages of his books.

Lilias Armstrong retained her unofficial position as Jones's most trusted colleague. It was still she whom he turned to in an emergency or if he had reason to leave the Department for any period of time. She continued to be known as "Miss Armstrong", even though she had married the Russian phonologist Simon Boyanus, who taught at the School of Slavonic Studies but also had close links with the staff at UCL. Having at last obtained her readership, for which Jones had been pressing for a long time, she appeared to have reached a happy and productive period of her career. A book on the phonology of Kikuyu was in its final stages, based on informant work done with a young African student, Jomo Kenyatta—who was one day to become the first Prime Minister of Kenya. He could prove a somewhat demanding employee, as is indicated by a letter from Jones to him pointing out that working as an informant does not automatically give author's rights (see Figure 11.7).

In 1937, in the midst of this activity, Miss Armstrong was suddenly taken ill. A postcard (Figure 11.8) in November gave no hint to the Department that anything was seriously wrong—she merely complained of an annoyingly persistent attack of influenza. Within a month she was dead. The news came as a great shock to Jones, who had relied on her support for nearly twenty years, and he reacted almost as if it were a family bereavement; his obituary notice (Jones 1938d) bears moving witness to his regard for Lilias Armstrong and her work. It was arranged that her book on Kikuyu

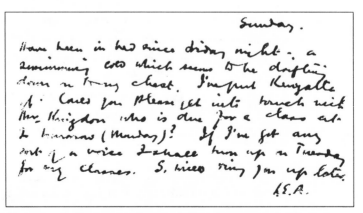

Figure 11.8. Postcard written by Lilias Armstrong shortly before her death. "S." is her husband, Simon Boyanus.

should be completed by a former UCL student, Beatrice Honikman (later a member of staff at SOAS, and afterwards a lecturer at Leeds University), who had also been working on Kikuyu with the same informant, Kenyatta.

11.13. The IPA in the 1930s

By 1930, both the IPA itself and *Le Maître phonétique* had gone some way towards recovering the ground lost in the war years. The membership list for 1932 contained 552 names, including notable contingents from Germany (47 members) and Japan (23 names)—the strong Japanese following was perhaps evidence of Harold Palmer's growing influence in that country. France was by comparison but poorly represented with a mere 14 listed. Britain was the leading European country, with 141 subscriptions but, surprisingly, the British had now been overtaken by the USA, which boasted no fewer than 147 members. Possibly, this was an indication of the way in which the centre of activity of linguistics was later to move away from Europe and find its home in America. Jones remained effectively totally in control of *Le Maître phonétique*, although still assisted by Lilias Armstrong as *secrétraire de rédaction*.[25]

Passy, though officially joint editor, seems to have played little part in the actual production of the journal even in the twenties; later on, his deteriorating health would have in any case prevented him playing any sort of useful role. Jones himself said, "in actual fact I have practically acted as sole secretary since about 1910".[26] Nevertheless, Jones, with the generosity and modesty which was typical of him, continued to retain Passy's name in the "Rédaction" panel on the front cover and allowed it to take precedence over his own. When he died, Passy's name was given an even more prominent position as "fondateur" and remained on the cover until 1971 when the name was changed to "Journal of the International Phonetic Association", and the whole appearance and format was revamped.

The Jones—Uldall correspondence is particularly revealing in the light it throws on Jones's editorship of *Le Maître phonétique* and the difficulties that he had experienced in this position over a number of years. In November 1935, Jones wrote to Uldall, apparently quite unexpectedly, saying that he was intending to give up both the secretaryship of the IPA and the editorship of *Le Maître phonétique*. He had decided to ask Uldall to take over from him.

> I have too much to do, & my health is not over good; clearly the thing should be taken on by a younger man. *Would you do it...?*[27]

Jones went on to say that he had chosen Uldall for the task because of his understanding of "the phoneme idea & the importance of broad transcriptions". That their views differed on so many other linguistic matters was not of importance, claimed Jones. Another factor was that Uldall was living in Denmark, which was, as Jones saw things in 1935, unlikely to be drawn into any future war—the grim prospect of which was increasingly preoccupying Jones at this period: "I think also it would be an advantage in the future for the I.P.A. to have its head-quarters in a 'neutral' country."[28]

Uldall replied, agreeing in principle to take on the responsibilities once he had obtained a permanent academic post: "I am very happy to know that you feel you can entrust the I.P.A. to me—I know of course what that means to you."[29] Jones proceeded to put the idea to the Council that Uldall should take on the posts of Assistant Secretary of the International Phonetic Association and Assistant Editor of *Le Maître phonétique*. By February, he had received enough replies to tell Uldall: "...you may take it as certain that you will be elected to the position of Assistant Secretary of the *a.f.* and Assistant Editor of *m.f.*."[30] Jones promised to announce Uldall's election in the 1936 April issue, and Uldall's name appeared on the cover from the July 1936 number onwards.

Jones indicated to Uldall some of the difficulties which had beset him over the years:

> Comparatively few contributors send manuscripts which are sufficiently correct and legible that they can be sent straight to the printer without correction or comment. You will soon get to know who are the meticulously accurate contributors, e.g. Camilli, Stirling, and one or two of the Americans. The first article of the MS I am sending is an object-lesson. Look how I have had to touch up the writing of Frinta and Thudichum.[31]

Surprisingly, possibly because of the small number of subscribers in France, Jones had trouble finding French texts for the *partie des élèves*: "French is always somewhat of a difficulty. Sometimes I ask Miss Coustenoble, but more often I just do it myself." Certain regular contributors could also prove problematical:

> [Paul] Menzerath will provide German texts, but only those of his own brand —ultra-narrow and showing his Western German peculiarities (which he seems to think are nearly universal). Westermann and E.A. Meyer, the two most practical German phoneticians, assure me he is mistaken. Also his renderings do not correspond at all with what I learnt as student [sic], viz. the pronunciation indicated by Viëtor and by Siebs.[32]

Nevertheless, in this matter, Jones reveals that he was at times quite prepared to moderate his linguistic demands for the sake of maintaining good personal relations. He adds: "However, Menzerath is an enthusiast, and a member of our Council, so we cannot refuse what he sends."

In July 1935, as an adjunct to the Second International Phonetics Conference held at UCL, Jones arranged a General Meeting of the IPA, which was intended to function not only as a business meeting, but also to celebrate the fiftieth anniversary of the foundation of the Association. The chair was taken by one of the most senior members of the IPA council, Jones's old school-master E.R. Edwards. Although Passy, Tilly

43. The 1935 Phonetics Congress in London. Front row (l. to r.) J. van Ginneken, Otto Jespersen, Allen Mawer, Daniel Jones, the Vice-Chancellor of London University, Prince N. Trubetzkoy. In the row behind can be seen far left Harold Orton, J.R. Firth directly above Jespersen, Dorothy Parkinson between Jones and Mawer.

44. Another view of the participants at the 1935 Phonetics Congress. The following have been identified. Front row (l. to r.) Eileen Evans (far left), Eugénie Henderson (far right). Row above (l. to r.) Arthur Lloyd James (first from left), Richard Paget (second from left). Top row (from l. to r.) Lilias Armstrong, Simon Boyanus, Ida Ward, A.N. Tucker, Beatrice Honikman, Dennis Fry.

45. An informal group taken at the 1938 Ghent Phonetics Congress.
L. to r. E. M. Stéphan, Beatrice Honikman, Daniel Jones,
Elizabeth Uldall (née Anderson), Ida Ward

46. Jones with son and daughter on Helvellyn in the Lake District (1939)

and Charles Grandgent were all unable to attend because of frail health, another veteran, Otto Jespersen, was present for the occasion. It was only the second general meeting of the Association, the previous one having been held in 1888. Jones, in his capacity as Secretary, addressed the members, giving a historical survey of the Association's work, and dealing at length with the question of symbols; he also read a message sent by Paul Passy (see Jones 1935d). The occasion provided some recognition for Jones's labours over a long period dating virtually from the day he joined in 1906.

11.14. The outbreak of war

Throughout the thirties, Jones had maintained regular publishing activity. The year 1939 stands out as one in which no new publications are recorded. The reasons for this disruption are undoubtedly to be traced not to Jones himself but to the build-up of political tension in Europe, which finally exploded in the autumn of that year. In the period just before the outbreak of war, the University College Phonetics Department was remarkable for having on its staff a large number of junior lecturers and research students who were later to become well-known scholars in phonetics and linguistics, both in Britain and elsewhere—and several of whom were to occupy university chairs. Apart from those already mentioned, they included many names which would become famous in the world of phonetics and phonology. Roger Kingdon, Miss Armstrong's replacement, was later to be acclaimed for his pioneering books on intonation and stress. Jean Paul Vinay was to move to Canada and produce important work on the phonetics of French. A.C. Gimson would stay on in London to become Jones's eventual successor at UCL and carry on work in the Jonesian tradition into the 1980s. Eugénie Henderson, J. Carnochan, Eileen Whitley (née Evans) and N.C. Scott were all to join Firth at SOAS and develop prosodic phonology. Two more junior staff—David Abercrombie and Peter MacCarthy—were to head phonetics departments at Edinburgh and Leeds, respectively. J.C. Catford later emigrated to the United States, producing crucial work on aspects of articulatory phonetics; while Elizabeth Uldall (née Anderson), after her husband's death, was to play an important part in the development of the phonetics department at Edinburgh.

Jones was now in charge of the most remarkable spawning ground of future talent and achievement in the history of British linguistics. Its only possible rival to this title was to be Firth's department in the post-war period at SOAS (itself an offshoot of Jones's school). It would have seemed incredible to anyone at the time that such a bubble of activity could burst and vanish in a few weeks, but this was indeed exactly what happened in September 1939. Once war broke out, Jones was faced with the harsh truth that for an indeterminate period his Department would, in all but name, cease to exist.

Chapter 12

In the Blitz and after (1939–50)

12.1. The phoney war and evacuation

The First World War descended unannounced on an apparently peaceful world, but the Second World War came as no surprise to anybody. Even the Daily Express had six months previously ceased printing optimistic messages on its front page promising that there would be no war in Europe. It had become too obvious that Hitler could not be stopped in his ambitions by Chamberlain's diplomatic efforts at Munich in 1938—nowadays derided by historians, but greeted by the British people with joyous relief at the time. Even more than most of the population, Daniel Jones had been anticipating the declaration of war. For almost a decade he had been convinced that war was inevitable, and had to an extent arranged his life, even down to his choice of residence, around the dreadful prospect. But when war came, it was not immediately the kind of holocaust which perhaps Jones, along with many others, had imagined. As A.J.P. Taylor (1966: 159–160) has put it:

> The transition from peace to war was less startling in 1939 than it had been in 1914. This time men's minds were prepared for war, though not necessarily for the war which actually happened. The institutions of war did not have to be improvised while the war was going on; they were all prepared, according to precedents.... No fuss, no excitement were indeed the features of the Second World War in its early stages.

During the first few months, for those not in services, the war proved an anti-climax—referred to at the time as the "phoney war"—with relatively little disruption of life, apart from dimmed lights, blacked-out windows and some early sporadic air-raid scares. Taylor (1966: 160) observed:

> Other measures of war-regulation, such as rationing, direction of labour and, even in Great Britain, the indignity of identity cards, were introduced without fuss, almost without being noticed.

However, for Jones and the members of his Department, and indeed for everyone in University College, the declaration of war on September 3, 1939, meant a complete upheaval in their professional and personal lives.[1] The 1938 Munich crisis had led to contingency plans being drawn up for the evacuation of the whole College in the event of war, and in 1939 these were put into operation. New entrants for the 1939 session were turned away and the remaining students and staff were split up in departments scattered all over the country, the majority finding temporary homes with the four constituent colleges of the University of Wales at Cardiff, Swansea, Aberystwyth and Bangor (Harte—North 1978: 174).

Some departments virtually ceased to function, and Phonetics was one of these. Effectively, Jones was left with nothing to administer. What work still existed was servicing for language departments, particularly for French. Hélène Coustenoble (who left London against her will, and returned to live in her London flat amidst the Blitz every vacation) continued to teach at the newly established remote outposts of University College, firstly at Aberystwyth and subsequently Bangor. Miss Coustenoble was in fact the only member of the Department who was retained in a teaching capacity. All the bustling research activity of the immediate pre-war period came abruptly to a halt. Of Jones's staff, most of the men had been conscripted into the forces whilst the women had been persuaded to seek war work outside the university.

A few students were still applying to join Jones's courses and at least one staff member, Eugénie Henderson,[2] was eager to continue with research,[3] but the Provost, Sir Allen Mawer, wrote to Jones from Aberystwyth, late in September, prohibiting him either from starting the formation of any classes or encouraging research.

> If we start undertaking obligations of that kind, members of the staff will be prevented from doing what is so important, namely securing paid national or other work in such a way as to help the nation, the College and their colleagues.... The College is unluckily unable to suggest that any member of its staff is doing best at the present time if they are simply carrying on their research work.[4]

When an offer came from Newcastle to help provide facilities for the Phonetics Department, Mawer again turned it down, saying that "most of Professor Daniel Jones's staff ought by reason of their linguistic equipment to be able to get good war work which would take them off the College pay-roll".[5]

At least one forceful protest was made about the situation; in December, the Head of the British Council wrote to the Provost that he had "learned with dismay that the work of the Department of Phonetics is to be suspended during the war" and stated his misgivings about the supply of properly qualified staff for the Council's work in the future.[6] But Allen Mawer was adamant, replying that there was no need and, perhaps more importantly, no money, for the Phonetics Department in wartime and that "the best service that the staff of the Department could render to the Nation at the present time would be by offering themselves for National or other service where their varied linguistic talents would be of active use to their country".[7]

At the beginning of the following session, though Jones was now reluctantly allowed to do some teaching, the Provost was still persistently reprimanding him for not giving sufficient encouragement to his staff to join in paid non-academic war work.

> I hear that you are taking a few pupils in Phonetics (that of course is all in order), and that Mrs. [Hyacinth] Davies and Miss [Eileen] Evans are assisting you. That,

of course, is also in order, provided that there is no idea that they are in any way released from their obligation to seek national or other service.... The fees of a few Phonetics students would not justify us in continuing to pay the full salaries of these two teachers if they could get other work.[8]

Jones was frustrated by the College, more particularly by Sir Allen himself, in any attempt to keep even a semblance of departmental work going. He must have looked enviously across to SOAS where J.R. Firth had taken full advantage of war conditions in order to begin crash courses in languages—particularly Japanese—with ample government funding. Most of the time Jones spent at his home in Gerrards Cross working on publications and the interests which remained to him. The *Phoneme* was now beginning to take shape and within a year or two would be complete, even though its publication would be long delayed (see Section 13.4). He managed to continue to produce *Le Maître phonétique* despite the war, and now became increasingly involved in the revitalised Simplified Spelling Society. Most stimulating of all, he took over Lloyd James's role at the BBC, and this provided him with trips to London, with generous expenses, a challenging new type of work and possibly the feeling that even he (a dedicated pacifist) was playing a public role in the national war effort.

Jones went to Aberystwyth in the 1939–40 session to conduct oral examinations and to give a lecture to the students taking phonetics,[9] but for the most part he appears to have left things to Hélène Coustenoble, and seems to have had little to do with the exiled remnant of his Department. On one of his rare trips to Wales, Jones was busily checking his phonetic transcriptions for the examinations, noting snatches of the Welsh conversation in the carriage, and practising "nonsense words" to himself. He was quite unaware that some perceptive passengers had been distressed by the strange activities of an elderly gentleman who was not only apparently muttering odd noises in a strange language which was neither English nor Welsh, but also writing down peculiar signs and symbols in his notebook. On his arrival at his destination, Jones was alarmed to find the local constabulary waiting to arrest him on suspicion of being a spy. Once at the police station, his credentials were rapidly established and Jones took things in good part. He told the story to family and colleagues for years afterwards.[10]

12.2. In the Blitz

Ida Ward wrote these lines to Hélène Coustenoble in June 1940.

I wonder what you are going to do this summer? Isn't life hard! And your country is suffering again and even worse than before I should imagine. I do hope we can get more men out to help & that our air force won't be too much occupied in defending these coasts to give effective help. I go up to Cambridge on Sunday for the last time this term. It has been disturbing living in two places.... What is to happen next Session we don't know. In the meantime I shall settle down at

Peaslake and hope to get some of the work I have in hand done—if only the war news will let us get on with the job.[11]

The war was beginning to affect the lives of everyone. Nevertheless, the evident lack of danger to civilians in the period of phoney war had led to plans being made for University College to move back to London. The return from Wales, and elsewhere, was well underway when the German bombardment of London began. As a result, any thoughts of coming back to the capital had to abandoned. University College was suffering the worst damage from German bombing ever to be inflicted on any university buildings in Britain. Harte—North (1978: 174) have described the catastrophic effects in this way:

> In September 1940 a bomb hit the buildings, entirely destroying the Great Hall and the Carey Foster Physics Laboratory. The Gustave Tuck and the Applied Mathematics Theatres were gutted, as was the Library north of the Dome. Serious damage was also done to other parts of the building. In April 1941 another air-raid led to considerable destruction by fire of the main building south of the Dome, and of the Dome itself.

When Jones looked at the stark outline of the skeleton of the ruined dome, and the burnt-out blackened remains of the other buildings he had known since his schooldays, he must have felt that his worst nightmares of war were coming true.[12] Amidst reports coming in of the damage from incendiary bombs, the whole process was put into reverse, and UCL was re-evacuated to Wales once more.[13] This time, Miss Coustenoble, along with the UCL French Department, was sent to Bangor, to the University College of North Wales.[14]

The phonetics component of the UCL library suffered appallingly in the air raids, necessitating almost complete restocking.[15] Beatrice Honikman—a former UCL student, and now on the staff at SOAS—had just completed (with Jones's backing and encouragement) the complex task of editing Lilias Armstrong's manuscript of *The phonetic and tonal structure of Kikuyu* (Armstrong 1940) and the work was now in print. Jones, symbolically, presented the College with a copy of the book which had been written by the person he had regarded as his closest colleague "as a fitting start in the reconstruction of the Phonetics Departmental Library".[16]

The war was by now the dominating factor in day-to-day activities. The choice of words for the transcription assignment for the Certificate of Proficiency in English examination, given on the morning of August 8, 1941, shows clearly what was preoccupying the examiners' and the students' minds as much or more than academic matters: "...Lease and Lend Act; Herbert Morrison; interment; casualties; mercantile marine; bomber squadron; ration coupons".[17]

It was at this point that the war faced Jones with a tragedy of a completely unexpected kind. His old friend and colleague Arthur Lloyd James had been evacuated along with other staff and students from the School of Oriental and African Studies from London to Cambridge. As Jones (1958: 430) later noted, the upheaval of the move together with "the stress and anxieties of war" caused Lloyd James to fall "a victim to depressive insanity". In 1941, after spending some time in a nursing home and making the appearance of a recovery, Lloyd James suffered a sudden total relapse, culminating in his making an attack on his wife and killing her.

The case was reported at length in the national press and Lloyd James eventually came up for trial at the Old Bailey. He was duly found guilty of murder, a plea of insanity being accepted as mitigating circumstances. He was subsequently committed to Broadmoor, the special hospital for the criminally insane at Camberley, where Jones went to visit him on several occasions—visits which made a profound impression on Jones, as he in later years related many times to his friends and family: "He said what a terrible experience it was to be under the roof of [sic] so many murderers...it affected him very much."[18] Jones maintained contacts with him in Broadmoor until March 1943, when Lloyd James, still in detention, finally succeeded in taking his own life by hanging himself.[19]

The whole episode was without doubt the greatest horror of the war for Jones personally, but Lloyd James was not the only London academic of Jones's acquaintance whose life was to be ended by the strains of the conflict. In 1942, Sir Allen Mawer died suddenly, on his way to a committee meeting, collapsing in a railway carriage after sustaining a heart attack. He had been running with a heavy bag, attempting to catch a train; two soldiers had attempted to revive him, but to no avail. The Provost's wartime period had been difficult and unhappy, and his death was put down largely to the strain of overwork and the stress of constant travelling around the creaking transport system of wartime Britain, trying "to hold the scattered fragments of the College together" (Harte—North 1978: 181).

The new Provost was a Cambridge scientist, David (later Sir David) Pye, who in 1943 took over the ruins of what had been London University's largest and most prestigious college, in which now "there was hardly a square foot of glass" (Harte—North 1978: 182). From his correspondence, Pye comes over as a much warmer, less tetchy personality than Mawer, and straightaway Jones was able to strike up a warm rapport with the new man. This good relationship soon bore fruit once it was suggested that Phonetics should be the first department to take in students again on the Gower Street site.

Pye was keen to bring University College back into operation once more in London—apparently, an utterly hopeless task. Although the war was now starting to turn in favour of the Allies, nightly German bombing raids were still an ever-present threat. The Gower Street buildings were largely in ruins and there were no students and hardly any staff remaining within reach of London. But Pye had to begin somewhere and, from his point of view, Phonetics was ideal as a starting point. It was a small department, running short courses and had no full-time undergraduates. Furthermore, it had been virtually closed down as a result of the war, and so there was no need to worry about any dismembered portions—apart from Hélène Coustenoble's work in Bangor. But she was, in any case, only too eager to come back to London again.[20]

To Jones's delight, after the years of frustration with Mawer, there was suddenly a genuine prospect of getting back to serious university work once again. He set about the task with enthusiasm, and advertisements were placed for courses to begin in the academic year 1943–44. In October 1943, Pye was informed by Jones that there had been a "very satisfactory" response.[21] With the help of Miss Coustenoble (who had achieved her desire of getting back to her London home), N.C. Scott,[22] and, as always, with the devoted support of his secretary, Miss Parkinson, Jones was able to lead the return of UCL to London with Phonetics as the "first teaching department to reopen in Gower Street".[23]

12.3. The feud with Firth

The success of the venture was greater than Jones could ever have hoped. Seventy people attended the opening public lecture and soon a number of classes were flourishing, so that Jones had immediately to start looking for extra teaching help.[24] He began to make plans for the following session, but eventually ran into unexpected difficulties in his attempts to recruit suitably qualified teachers.

Most of Jones's pre-war colleagues were by now enlisted in the armed forces, or working for various government departments; because of Allen Mawer's negativism, there had been no chance of keeping even a token core of staff busy on phonetic research. After a struggle with the Foreign Office, Hyacinth Davies was recalled from her government duties.[25] Also within easy reach, it appeared, were those staff who had temporarily joined J.R. Firth at SOAS. Jones now assumed that he could expect them to return to University College for what he viewed as the exciting challenge of starting up the Department once again in the middle of wartime. But Firth's own Department was expanding rapidly (he had obtained the Chair of General Linguistics in 1944) and his theory of prosodic phonology was beginning to take shape and find support amongst his junior colleagues. He encouraged two promising young phoneticians—Eugénie Henderson and Eileen Evans[26]—who had come over to him from Jones to undertake research on prosodic lines. He offered them permanent posts at SOAS and even promised the same status to Scott, who was still working as one of Jones's full-time assistants. Jones was shocked when he heard, as late as July, and only indirectly from a SOAS lecturer, A.N. Tucker, the news that three of his staff whom he had been hoping to employ in the 1944–45 session had been lured away by SOAS.[27] He was even more hurt when, to his surprise, all of these former colleagues and pupils proved keen to accept the SOAS posts, attracted by Firth's charisma and his innovative theories—combined, of course, with the better career prospects he was holding out to them. Jones naïvely refused to believe at first that his young staff were unwilling to return to UCL, and the situation left him deeply embittered.[28] His relationship with Firth, which had never been a happy one, was now permanently soured.

Jones was ultimately forced to reconcile himself to the loss of these staff-members, and tried to recruit elsewhere. Ivar Dahl was offered a temporary post;[29] and Olive

Tooley—a family acquaintance with no knowledge of phonetics, but with an obvious talent for the practical side of the subject—was asked to join the Department, Jones undertaking, together with Miss Coustenoble, to train her from scratch.[30] Julian Pring was brought back on a priority passage from Cairo, where he was serving in the RAF, and began work in the 1944–45 session.[31] Shortly after the end of the war, Jones and Pye managed to engage two young men who had formerly been two of Hélène Coustenoble's most talented students, and who now also had successful army careers behind them. They were Major A.C. Gimson and Major J.D. O'Connor. In the winter of 1945–46, the classrooms in University College were often so cold that "the two Majors" (as they were sometimes referred to at the time) were forced to teach in their army greatcoats.[32]

Jones could be satisfied that he now had the nucleus of a talented—if largely inexperienced—staff and excellent numbers of student enrolments for his courses. His Department was housed in rooms which, if cramped, old-fashioned and ill-heated, were only much the same as he had been forced to tolerate before the war. There was plenty of interest in his subject and the prospect of reasonable research funding now that peace had at last come. Apart from his feud with Firth, only one thing threatened Jones's hopes of putting the Department on a sound basis for the future and recovering the effervescent spirit and drive that had pervaded UCL Phonetics during the twenties and thirties—lack of time. For Jones knew that, according to University of London regulations, he would be forced to retire in less than two years. He dreaded the prospect.

12.4. Return to Gordon Square

By September 1945, the war in Europe had been over for three months and a battered Britain was learning to cope with the problems of peacetime recovery. The Blitz had left the whole of central London pockmarked with bomb sites, on which weeds were already starting to spread. Young men were being demobilised from the forces and so there was no shortage of students.

Accommodation was a continuing problem. In 1943, Jones had taken over a few rooms in the Law Department. But he was soon forced to move across to Foster Court and Crabb Robinson—outlying extensions of the main college where the buildings had not been damaged too badly by bombs or fire.[33] Because of the appalling conditions, with already damp rooms made worse by the lack of decent heating, and shortage of space to store books and equipment, Jones felt his staff and students were suffering. Eventually, it was mooted that the Department could return to the old Victorian terraced house at 21 Gordon Square ("Arts Annexe I"). Only in 1944, Jones had told Pye that he never wanted to go back there again because "it is such an inconvenient place",[34] and even brought up again in a report his old unrealised dream of a Phonetics Institute (see Section 9.3). But, just a year later, he accepted the offer of the premises gratefully, and his only concern was in the meantime to find a relatively dry room to store equipment and somewhere for Miss Parkinson to do her work undisturbed.[35]

In a letter, Dorothy Parkinson gave an indication that by the end of the 1945–46 academic year, the Phonetics Department was beginning to recover something of the spirit that it had generated in such remarkable measure in the period before the Second World War.

> We are all very glad to be back in Arts Annexe No. 1 again and the house begins to feel like "home" once more.[36]

The upheavals had been great. So much so that Daniel Jones attempted—with characteristic thoughtfulness, but without any success—to obtain a special honorarium for his hard-pressed secretary who had been forced to oversee two moves of a complete Department within a year.[37]

By this time, Dennis Fry had been released from his war work. Miss Parkinson noted:

> I hope it will not be long before Fry has the Laboratory in working order; he is having a very busy time just now.[38]

It was indeed a hectic period for everyone in Jones's Department. By 1945, the total student enrolment for phonetics courses had exceeded 250—far more than pre-war. In October 1946, Jones had been forced to turn away fifty prospective students; a further forty had to be refused admission to courses in January 1947.[39] Even so, Jones reported that "the number accepted has been such as to render it difficult for members of the staff to produce much in the way of research work", though he also felt that he could at last say:

> The Department of Phonetics has now largely recovered from its war-time difficulties of staff and accommodation and it has been possible to resume work on a considerable scale.[40]

12.5. The Zürich Lecture and "The London School of Phonetics"

Despite the pressure at University College, Jones allowed himself to snatch a fortnight in late September 1946 to travel to Switzerland, where he read two papers, one to the University of Geneva and the other to the University of Zürich (referred to in this volume as the Geneva Lecture and the Zürich Lecture, respectively). This was his first trip abroad since before the war, and it was a resounding personal triumph. On his return, he wrote to Pye:

> You may like to know that the proceedings at Zürich were of a particularly gratifying description. The lecture was attended by about 150 people, & was followed

by a dinner at which numerous distinguished professors from different parts of Switzerland were present.... I was bombarded with questions from 9 to 11 p.m.![41]

Jones's Geneva Lecture, read in French on September 28 to the Société Genevoise de Linguistique, appeared written up later as "Chronemes and tonemes" (Jones 1944c, see Section 12.6), confusingly bearing a date two years previous to its delivery (see Jones 1944c: 1, n. 1).

The Zürich Lecture, read on 11 October, was later published in revised form as "The London School of Phonetics" (Jones 1948f), and has been widely quoted for the historiographical interest of its short opening section, in which Jones discusses the history of phonetics in the University of London, mentioning both his own Department and the later offshoot, under first Lloyd James and later J.R. Firth, at the School of Oriental and African Studies.[42] Confusingly, Jones's term the "London School" was later taken over by Langendoen (1968) for his critique of the work of the Firthian group published under the title the "London School of Linguistics", leaving no convenient name—other than possibly the Jones School—to cover the work of the University College phoneticians. The remainder of Jones's article covers the teaching and research that were going on in the University College Department in the post-war period, and as such forms a useful source of information about the activities of Jones and his colleagues at this time. However, the published paper is very much shorter than the original lecture, which contained certain parts which Jones appears to have considered over-personal, possibly too revealing, to allow to go into print. As mentioned elsewhere (Section 7.7), one of these is actually marked "too personal" in the margin. Jones includes in the Zürich lecture a long section on the history of phoneme theory, some of which was later absorbed into *HMTP* (1957a). In addition, he has a lengthy treatment of the relationship between the phoneme concept and wider philosophical problems of an existentialist nature. Parts of this discussion carry on from "Concrete and abstract sounds" (Jones 1938a) and lay the foundations for portions of the *Phoneme* (Jones 1950a, see Section 14.16).

Several pieces produced in this period relate to the history of phonetics and its personalities. Perhaps, inevitably, most are obituaries (Passy, Jespersen, Lund, Ščerba, Edwards, Palmer, Ripman and Ida Ward). Jones also produced a tribute to Bernard Shaw, "G.B.S. and phonetics" (Jones 1946a), which appeared in the commemorative volume published on Shaw's ninetieth birthday. Jones's historiographical interest in pioneering phoneticians of an earlier period emerges in his series of broadcast talks "Our changing speech" (see Section 14.15 for further discussion).

12.6. Publications on the phoneme

Two major articles which are devoted to the development of Jones's conceptual approach to the phoneme can be considered as leading on from "Concrete and abstract

47. Bomb damage to UCL (1941)

48. Jones feeding his hens

49. With a group of English and Scandinavian colleagues outside Skovriderkroen (an inn at Charlottenlund, Denmark). Identifiable from l. to r. (1) ? (2) ? (3) Eli Fischer-Jørgensen (4) ? (5) ? (6) Daniel Jones (7) ? (8) Louis Hjelmslev (9) ? (10) C.A. Bodelsen (11) ? (12) ? (13) Knud Schibsbye (14) ? (15) Paul Christophersen (16) J.D. O'Connor.

50. J.R. Firth, David Abercrombie and Jones (l. to r.)

sounds" (Jones 1938a). Both bear the date 1944, though one of them was in fact produced later than this would imply. "Some thoughts on the phoneme" (Jones 1944d), a published version of a lecture given to the Philological Society, repeats Jones's preference for a physical view of the phoneme, and presents a number of postulates for phonemic analysis. Jones states here his view that for such analysis a "language" should be defined as "the pronunciation of a particular person speaking in one particular style" (pp. 125–126). The "particular style" is specified more clearly as "consistent" rather than "erratic"—which Jones takes to exclude such factors as idiosyncratic variations resulting from accent mixing, or the effects of "rapid colloquial…with its multitude of contractions and assimilations" (p. 127). Jones therefore proposes that the term language should be further restricted to "the speech of an imaginary 'average' person speaking consistently in a particular style". In so doing, he anticipates largely the position taken up by generativists in the 1960s of an idealised speaker-hearer (Chomsky—Halle 1968: 3–4).

Jones goes on to suggest that analysis should concern isolated words, and then, drawing partly on Jones (1931k), provides examples of phonetic markers of word boundaries (i.e. "juncture", although, as in the earlier article, that term is not employed). A further "proposition" states that the term "phonetic context" should take account of stress, length and (where necessary) tone of adjacent, or near-adjacent sounds (pp. 132–133). Jones lays down that "it is absolutely inadmissible that a sound should belong to more than one phoneme". Yet, he allows that there may be cases of phoneme "overlap", "where there is no more reason to assign a phoneme to one sound rather than another" (p. 133). Finally, Jones states the principle that the component sounds of a phoneme "must have some sort of fairly near relationship to each other", but admits that this is not easy to define, adding weakly that "we have to use common sense about it" (pp. 133–134). These "propositions" form a most important statement of the principles behind the Jonesian view of the phoneme, and remain largely unaltered in the *Phoneme* itself.

"Chronemes and tonemes" (Jones 1944c) appears to have been written much later than its nominal dating, and is a revised form of the Geneva Lecture of 1946 (see Section 12.5). Jones argues here for an extension of the idea of the phoneme to length ("chroneme") and tone ("toneme"), and provides considerable exemplification to back this theory. Though his views on the significance of tonemes were largely in agreement with contemporary opinion, Jones's ideas on the nature of chronemes within phonemes, and in particular the application of this theory to English, were to bring him into conflict with many scholars, including some of his own colleagues.

Over this period, Jones also wrote numerous minor articles, including "spécimens" of a variety of languages: Shan—a Burmese language (Jones 1942c), Georgian (Gugushvili—Jones 1944f), Oriya (Deo—Jones 1945b), Norwegian (Grøndahl—Jones 1946c) and Swedish (Mesterton—Jones 1946f). Numerous sections of *Le Maître phonétique* contain his views on symbolisation and other transcriptional matters—

much is to be found in published circulars to Council members or additions to other writer's articles, either as footnotes or as brief responses to points raised.

12.7. New alphabets

The early war years provided Jones with a period of time when he was largely free from the responsibilities of running his Department. Although he maintained production of *Le Maître phonétique*, continued his work for the Simplified Spelling Society and developed new interests at the BBC, he must have had far more time available to devote to writing. No new books appeared, but Jones produced several pamphlets and some notable articles. Doubtless he spent a great deal of his time on the writing of the *Phoneme*, which was virtually complete by the end of the war (see Section 13.4).

This was indeed a period when Jones was much preoccupied with the concept of the phoneme. He was especially concerned with the problems of applying theoretical phonemic principles to the practical problems of producing phonemic transcription and constructing new systems of orthography for a variety of languages. Much of this work can be regarded as a spin-off from his writing of the *Phoneme*. However, Jones had for many years exhibited interest in inventing orthographies for non-written languages and, as mentioned in Section 10.6, it is very likely that the booklet *Practical orthography of African languages* (Anon. 1927) came at least in part from his pen. A similar undertaking, co-authored by Jones and his old colleague Perera, was a proposed adaptation of "World Orthography" to Sinhalese (Perera—Jones 1937k).

In 1941, Jones read a paper at a tea-party for a group of Indian students at Cambridge, which had been followed by a discussion in which Firth "spoke at some length" (Jones 1942a: cover). As a direct result of this occasion, Jones produced a pamphlet entitled *The problem of a national script for India* (Jones 1942a) in which he attempted to deal with all the languages of the Indian sub-continent, both Indo-European and Dravidian, under one alphabetic system. Jones outlines his reasons for choosing a Roman alphabet as a basis, and mentions his admiration for the "Rômazi" system devised for Japanese (see below, Jones 1949a). He points out the difficulties of adapting the twenty-six symbols of the Roman alphabet to the richer sound systems of the various languages concerned and the means by which this could be achieved. Jones comes down firmly on the side of "properly designed new letters" rather than diacritics, and, predictably, recommends those of the IPA (pp. 10–11). He then introduces Firth's scheme for "a consolidated All-India Alphabet from which is drawn whatever is necessary for each language" (p. 12). Proposed alphabets follow for Hindustani (i.e. Hindi-Urdu), Marathi, Gujarati, Tamil, and Telugu (see Figure 12.1). The pamphlet is interesting in that it records possibly the last occasion when Jones and Firth could be observed co-operating harmoniously on a project before the rupture in their relationship in 1943 (see Section 12.3).

Jones was to return to this area in his work on the romanisation of another Indian language, Oriya (Deo—Jones 1945b; Jones 1949b). In 1949, he also provided a survey

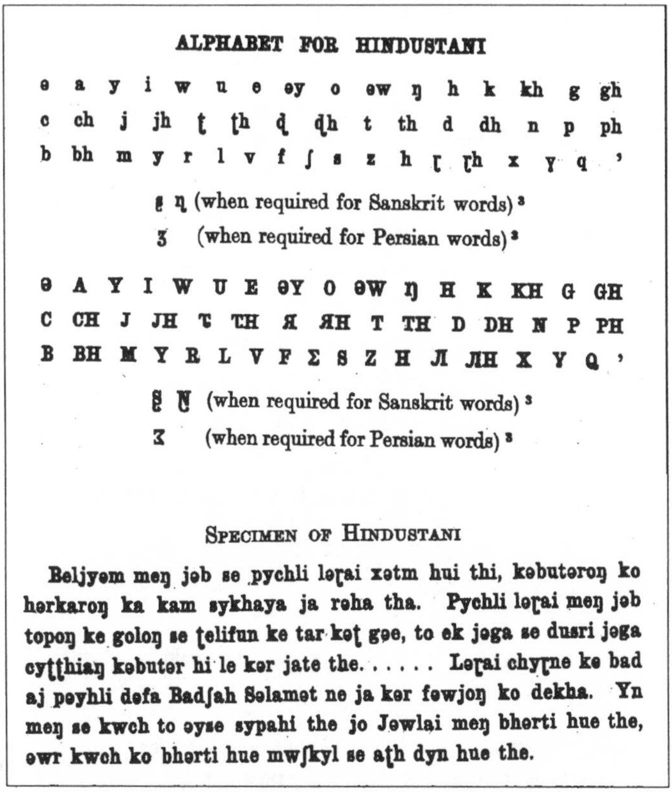

ALPHABET FOR HINDUSTANI

ə a y i w u e ey o ew ŋ h k kh g gh
c ch j jh ṭ ṭh ḍ ḍh t th d dh n p ph
b bh m y r l v f ʃ s z h ɽ ɽh x ɣ q '

ɛ ṇ (when required for Sanskrit words) ²
ʒ (when required for Persian words) ²

ə A Y I W U E EY O EW Ŋ H K KH G GH
C CH J JH Ṭ ṬH Я ЯH T TH D DH N P PH
B BH M Y R L V Σ S Z H Л ЛH X Ɣ Q '

ɛ Ṇ (when required for Sanskrit words) ³
ʒ (when required for Persian words) ³

SPECIMEN OF HINDUSTANI

Beljyəm meŋ jəb se pychli ləɽai xətm hui thi, kəbutəroŋ ko
hərkaroŋ ka kam sykhaya ja rəha tha. Pychli ləɽai meŋ jəb
təpoŋ ke goloŋ se ṭelifun ke tar kəṭ gəe, to ek jəga se dusri jəga
cyṭṭhiaŋ kəbutər hi le kər jate the. . . . . . Ləɽai chyɽne ke bad
aj pəyhli dəfa Badʃah Səlamət ne ja kər fəwjoŋ ko dekha. Yn
meŋ se kwəh to əyse sypahi the jo Jəwlai meŋ bhərti hue the,
əwr kwəh ko bhərti hue mwʃkyl se aṭh dyn hue the.

Figure 12.1. Extracts from *The problem of a national script
for India* (Jones 1942a, pp. 12–13, 15–16) showing alphabets
for (1) Hindustani (above) and (2) Tamil (on p. 362).

of the developments in Japanese in his article "The romanization of Japanese" (Jones
1949a). Here Jones reiterates his admiration for the latest "Kokutei Rōmazi" system,
this being the last improvement on the "Nipponsiki Rômazi" scheme, to which Jones
had given his support in 1922 (p. 69). He comes down firmly against the "Hepburn-
ian" romanisation dating from the middle of the nineteenth century, since this interpreted Japanese phonemes through the filter of the English sound system, i.e. excessive numbers of symbols were given to sounds which were merely allophones rather
than phonemes. Jones explains that the "Nipponsiki Rômazi" scheme "was in fact
based on one letter per phoneme" and "worked out by Japanese scholars who evidently had an instinctive feeling for the phoneme idea, although at the time the theory
of phonemes was unknown to them" (p. 68). Jones mentions that much of the information in the article is derived from Palmer (1930), which confirms that Palmer (together with Firth and Perera) was a most telling influence on Jones in the question of
devising new schemes of orthography.

Jones's interest in such matters at this point is also reflected in his renewed interest in the Simplified Spelling Society, for whom he published a pamphlet (Jones 1944a), see Section 12.8. A little later, Jones produced another short pamphlet, *Differences between spoken and written language* (Jones 1948e). Written in simple terms, and aimed at the layman, this piece explains the concept of phonetic redundancy (although this phrase is not used). In addition, Jones underlines the importance of such phenomena as stress, weak forms and intonation, which are not reflected in spelling, and the need for an enlarged alphabet to represent adequately the phonemic system

---

ALPHABET FOR TAMIL

a aa i ii u uu e ee ai o oo au

k ŋ c ny[1] ʈ ɳ t ɳ p m y r[2] l v

ɹ ɭ

(For loan-words g, j, ɖ, d, b, h, ʃ, and ʒ could be added)

A AA I II U UU E EE AI O OO AU

K Ŋ C NY Ʈ ɳ T ɳ P M Y R[2] L V

ɹ Ꭻ (or Ł).

(For loan-words G, J, Ɖ, D, B, H, Σ, and ʒ could be added).

SPECIMENS OF TAMIL

Paal kuʈikkaata puunai uɳʈaa entru raajaa tennaali raamaniʈam keeʈʈaar. Tennaali raaman uɳʈu entru patil connan. Appaʈiyaanaal koɳʈuvaa entru uttaraviʈʈaar.

Tennaali raaman tan viiʈʈuku pooy puunai ontrai piʈittu atan munnaal kotittukkoɳʈirukkum paalai vaittaan. Paalai kuʈikka poona puunaiyin mukam ventu pooyittru. Ippuʈi iraɳʈorutaram naʈanta pin, anta puunai eppootu paalai kaɳʈaalum oʈʈam piʈittatu. Kaʈaiciyaaka puunaiyai raajaaviʈam kaaɳ pittaan. raajaa mikavum aacoariyappaʈʈaar.

Kʂeemam, Aaciirvaatam,[1] unniʈamiruntu rompanaaaļaaka ļeʈʈer varavillai. Ꭻicempar maatattil irupattayintu pavun anuppiyirunteen. Atu vantu ceerunta viparam eɹutavum. Iŋke elloorum caukkiyam, unnuʈampai caukkariyamaaka paarttukoļļavum.

Veeɳum aaciirvaatam.[1]

Figure 12.1 (cont.)

of English. Jones then provides a sample of English in "World Orthography", which he claims is "already in use for the current writing of many languages in Africa and...well adapted to the needs of languages in India" (p. 6). He also reproduces a passage in the "New Spelling" of the Simplified Spelling Society. Another aspect of this general concern with problems of symbolisation can be seen in Jones's Spanish version of the IPA Principles (Jones—Dahl 1944b) and the last complete revision of the IPA Principles (IPA 1949), for which he appears to have been largely responsible.

12.8. The SSS and Bernard Shaw

During the war, despite the difficulties of printing, the SSS published more new material than ever before, producing a series of pamphlets covering various topics related to spelling and spelling reform. Jones wrote one of the booklets in this series entitled *Dhe fonetik aspekt ov speling reform* (Jones 1944a); see Figure 12.3. Actually written throughout in the orthography advocated by the SSS, the pamphlet deals briskly with the main differences between phonetic transcription and reformed orthography and indicates the contribution that phonetics can make to the problem of reorganising the spelling system. Jones points out that most phoneticians are not spelling reformers—but also indicates the exceptions to this statement, such as Ellis, Sweet, Ripman and, interestingly, his own mentor Paul Passy (p. 1). He relates the problem to the phoneme concept, and in fact uses the word "foeneem" (p. 2), summarising thus (p. 5):

> It iz kleer dhat dhe best tiep ov speling iz a sistem baest on dhe prinsipl ov wun leter for eech esenshal sound.

But he makes it clear that other considerations must play a part, and mentions particularly dialectal and idiolectal variation; the difficulty of designing acceptable new letter symbols; the desirability of distinguishing certain homophones; and, particularly for English, the need to cope with the problems posed by vowel gradation.

Jones ends with the following statement of his own moderate position on spelling reform (pp. 5–6):

> It wil be seen from whot haz been sed dhat a foenetishan mae suport dhe iedea ov reforming our speling not meerly on akount ov dhe partikuelar interest he taeks in fonetik siëns, but on jeneral eduekaeshonal, eekonomik and soeshal groundz. If he haz a kleer jeneral outlook, he wil see dhat dhe prinsipl ov rieting fonetikaly shood not be slaevishly ad-heerd to, and dhat dhe proesesez ov understanding spoeken wurdz and ov rekogniezing riten wurdz ar soe diferent dhat an orthografy for kurrent purpozez kanot be a kompleetly akueret reflekshon ov dhe wae in which peepl speek.

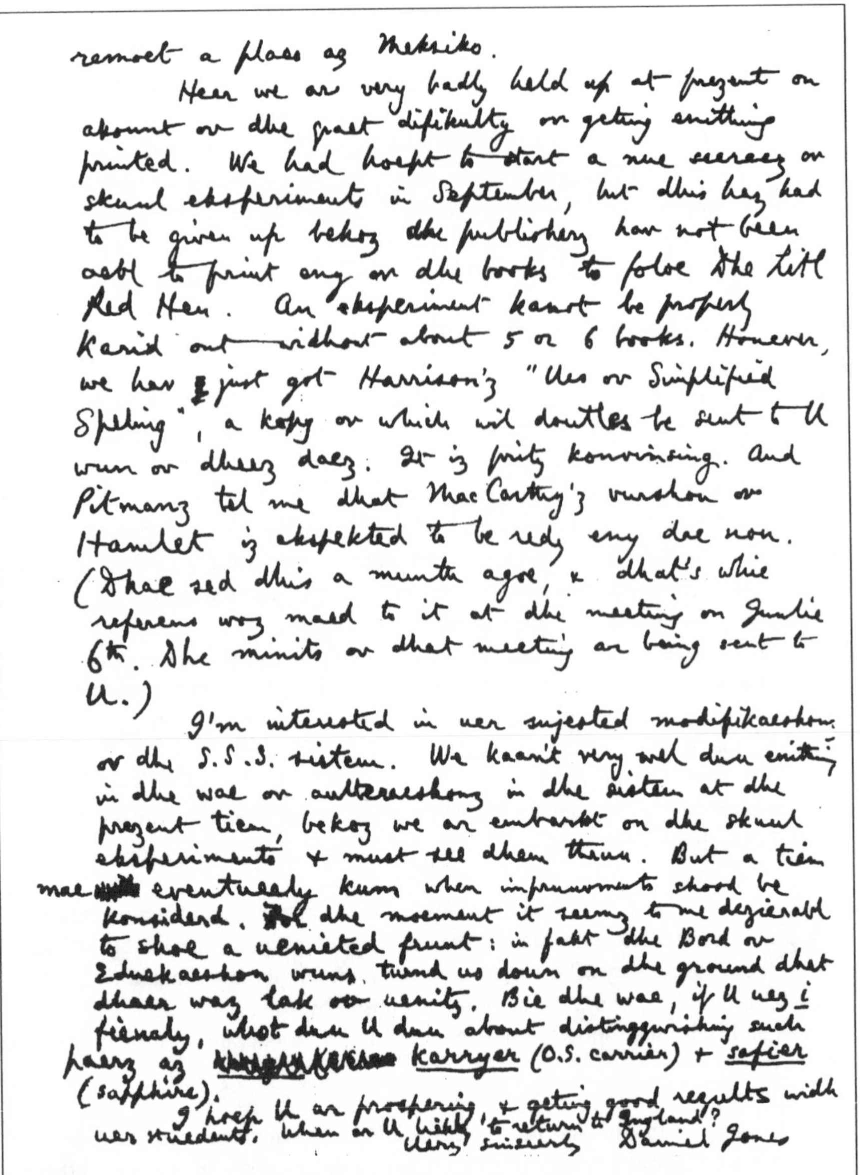

remoet a plaas az Meksiko.

Hear we ar very badly held up at prezent on akount ov dhe graet difikulty ov geting enithing printed. We had hoept to start a nue seeraez ov skuul eksperiments in September, but dhis haz had to be given up bekoz dhe publisherz hav not been aebl to print eny ov dhe books to folloe Dhe Litl Red Hen. An eksperiment kanot be properly karid out widhout about 5 or 6 books. However, we hav just got Harrison'z "Ues ov Simplified Speling", a kopy ov which wil doutles be sent to U wun ov dheez daez. It iz prity konvinsing. And Pitmanz tel me dhat MacCarthy'z vurshon ov Hamlet iz ekspekted to be redy eny dae nou. (Dhae sed dhis a munth agoe, + dhat's whie referens woz maed to it at dhe meeting on Juulie 6th. Dhe minits ov dhat meeting ar being sent to U.)

I'm interested in uer sujested modifikaeshonz ov dhe S.S.S. sistem. We kaan't very wel duu enithing in dhe wae ov aulteraeshonz in dhe sistem at dhe prezent tiem, bekoz we ar embarkt on dhe skuul eksperiments + must see dhem thruu. But a tiem mae eventuealy kum when impruuvments shood be konsiderd. For dhe moement it seemz to me dezierabl to shoe a uenieted frunt: in fakt dhe Bord ov Edukaeshon wuns turnd us doun on dhe ground dhat dhaer waz lak ov uenity. Bie dhe wae, if U wez i fienaly, whot duu U duu about distingwishing such paerz az Karryer (O.S. carrier) + safier (sapphire).

I hoep U ar prospering + geting good rezults widh uer stuedents. When ar U likly to return to England?

Yours sinserly Daniel Jones

Figure 12.2. Extract from a letter written by Jones to Roger Kingdon in Nue Speling.

This was the point when Jones's enthusiasm for spelling reform seems to have been greatest; he even for a brief period wrote some of his personal correspondence in "New Spelling" (see Figure 12.2). In 1946, Gilbert Murray resigned and Jones was asked to become the SSS's new President, and to accept the position of Chairman of the Committee; he agreed to take on the tasks. In the meantime, more of Jones's friends and colleagues had joined the ranks of the SSS. Among the new members of the Committee was Peter MacCarthy, a former UCL student, who was now a lecturer at SOAS. And the Vice-President was Professor Sir Douglas Savory, MP—the same Douglas Savory who had been Jones's companion and co-author in Bourg-la-Reine days.

Shortly after the end of the war, public interest in the question of spelling reform again mounted. Efforts were made to interest the man considered at the time the greatest living literary figure, Bernard Shaw, in "New Spelling" and to persuade him to give a portion of his estate to the SSS. Shaw had been advocating spelling reform for many years but was convinced that only a radical change to a completely new alphabet, with over forty letters, all of totally new design, could provide any sort of solution. This was anathema to Jones and the SSS membership. Nevertheless, together with another leading figure in the Society, James Pitman—the grandson of Isaac Pitman, and now MP for Bath—Jones visited Shaw to persuade the aged dramatist round to their view. Jones could perhaps have been hoping to benefit from Shaw's earlier moral indebtedness to him over the business of *Pygmalion* (see Section 4.9). Later, in the preface to a collection of Shaw's (1965: xiv–xv) writings, Pitman took the chance to describe the occasion of his and Jones's visit:

The iron gate of Shaw's Corner was open, and we were made by the great man to sense that we were most welcome and important visitors...His attentiveness to our needs and the charm of his manner have been a memory ever since. So too was the devastating argument and his determined obstinacy! His eyes and beard, his knickerbocker suit, his refusal to join us even in a cup of tea, and his whole presence made defeat, and certainty that there never would be even hope of success, a stimulating and indeed exciting experience.

So Jones and Pitman failed in their attempt, and Shaw went on to leave his vast wealth to the funding of his revolutionary but quite impractical alphabet, and landed the SSS with the problems of trying to fulfil the provisions of his will—which ran counter to their own most cherished spelling reform principles.[43]

A further development was the attempt to get a private member's bill on spelling reform through Parliament, supported by Pitman, and sponsored by Mont Follick, another MP with a diehard enthusiasm for spelling reform. The bill failed, but was rejected by only a small margin, and there was great propaganda value to the SSS resulting from the discussion in Parliament and the coverage in the press.[44] Shortly afterwards, in 1950, Jones resigned from his position as Chairman of the Society on the grounds of ill-health, and from then on played a far less prominent role. He was

DHE FONETIK ASPEKT

OV

SPELING REFORM

BIE

DANIEL JONES, M.A., Dr.Fil.

Profesor ov Fonetiks, Ueniversity Kolej, Lundon

PUBLISHT ON BEHAAF OV DHE
SIMPLIFIED SPELING SOSIËTY

BIE

SUR IEZAK PITMAN & SUNZ, LTD.

LUNDON

1944

Figure 12.3. Title page of Jones's booklet on spelling reform.

suffering more from arthritis and was undoubtedly also feeling the strain of having taken on too many commitments in his old age. He may also have felt the need to concentrate on a last period of writing.

Jones retained the office of President and continued to hold that position until his death. The last meeting which he attended was in 1962 when he was over eighty. By chance, owing to the indisposition of the then Chairman, Sir Graham Savage, Jones was asked to take the chair. He might well have considered this a fittingly active farewell to the Society he had supported so vigorously from the first years of its existence.

12.9. Work for the BBC

In 1939, the BBC replaced the largely unpaid Advisory Committee which it had set up in the inter-war period (see Section 10.11) by a small full-time professional Pronunciation Unit. It was staffed at the outset by just one woman, G(ertrude) M. Miller (or "Elizabeth" Miller as she preferred to be called by her friends), but her efficiency ensured that the Unit operated far more constructively than in the days of the Advisory Committee. It continues to function to this day. For a brief period, Arthur Lloyd James worked as an adviser to Miss Miller, but in 1941, when Lloyd James was in the midst of the tragic events which led to his death, Daniel Jones took over.

This was in the period when Jones found himself without a department to administer, and so had time at his disposal. He felt a duty to carry on where his colleague Lloyd James had left off, and perhaps also considered that working for a public body such as the BBC was as near to helping the war effort as his pacifist convictions permitted. Jones could also have thought, and with some justification, that the new Pronunciation Unit would be less difficult to deal with than the unwieldy and bigoted Advisory Committee; Gimson (1977: 154) has commented that Jones's "association with the BBC's Advisory Committee on Spoken English cannot have been an easy one". In any case, from this point on, Jones became the BBC's chief consultant, entering enthusiastically into the job, and working closely with Elizabeth Miller and the head of the announcing department, John Snagge.

Jones's long and cordial co-operation with Elizabeth Miller was particularly fruitful. Their prolonged correspondence (preserved in the BBC archives) reveals the thoroughness of their research on pronunciation variation, especially in proper names. Jones had found someone who was able to share with him his enthusiasm for this by way of phonetics, and who was prepared to undertake the detective work necessary to discover all the variants of family and place names. The findings were incorporated in later revisions of the *EPD*, in particular the eleventh edition of 1956. In an unusually gushing acknowledgement, Jones gave his thanks to Miss Miller and her Pronunciation Unit for "their immense and indeed unique experience and knowledge of pronunciation problems" (*EPD* [1956[11]]: xi). A further product of this co-operation is to be seen in the *BBC pronouncing dictionary of British names* (Miller 1971).

Jones also gave assistance to the BBC on the tricky question of anglicising foreign proper names. In 1946 he produced "a phonetic version of all the syllables of the Pekingese dialect of Chinese to serve as a basis for suitable anglicisations to be used in broadcasting".[45] His letters to Miss Miller contain much detail on the appropriateness of various anglicisations in a variety of languages.

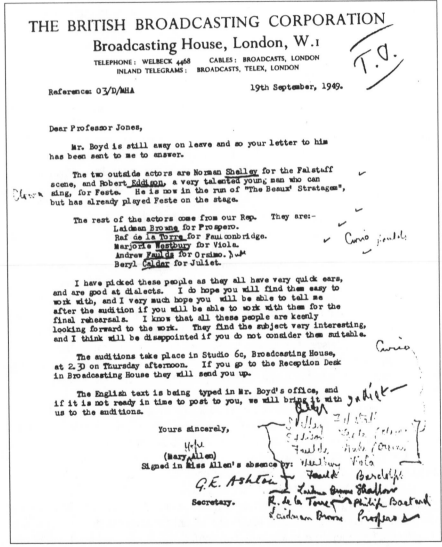

Figure 12.4. Letter, with annotations by Jones, from the BBC to Jones with arrangements for casting the Shakespearean performances.

Jones's other valuable contribution as pronunciation consultant was to carry on Lloyd James's role of helping in the training of announcers. In 1941, Jones started to monitor the performance of announcers so as to check on the standards of their speech, and was provided with a radio by the BBC for this purpose. He continued with this work, on and off, throughout the forties and up until the late fifties, filling exercise books with comments, transcriptions and impressionistic intonation patterns. His views on the speech of individual announcers have thus been preserved,[46] and as Gimson (1977: 154) has indicated, they reveal that Jones's personal opinions on pronunciation were not always as liberal as the image he presented to the world through his publications; indeed they sometimes hark back to his pre-1910 elocution-influenced views (see Sections 3.4 and 14.5).

Jones's work for the BBC appears to have been one of the most rewarding aspects of his life, both during the otherwise frustrating period of the early war, and in his years of retirement. He continued to act in a consultancy capacity for the BBC right up to the time of his death. For his part, Jones ensured that the question of maintaining a degree of uniformity in pronunciation in national broadcasting was interpreted in what must be regarded as a more enlightened way—certainly, as compared with the days of Reith's Advisory Committee. He prepared the way for the more liberal approach to pronunciation that prevails in the BBC today. Gimson (1977: 155) has commented on Jones's contribution:

> Above all, he urged consistently that the speech style of the announcers should be as natural and colloquial as possible. This attitude corresponds with his insistence in his textbooks and his *Dictionary* that he is concerned with the ordinary, colloquial pronunciation of the language.

In his contacts with the BBC, Jones did not confine himself solely to his role as pronunciation adviser. In 1949, in a novel experiment, Jones agreed to train a group of actors to present extracts from Shakespeare in a reconstruction of Elizabethan English pronunciation (see Sections 3.2 and 14.15 for Jones's interest in this topic). Previous work of this sort, such as Jones's amateur performances which he arranged in his early years at UCL before the First World War, or his 1937 recording for Linguaphone, always involved phoneticians, or students with phonetic training, and this was the first time that Jones had worked with ordinary actors (the BBC promised to have players who "all have very quick ears, and are good at dialects");[47] see Figure 12.4. The result was a successful radio programme which was put out under the title "The Elizabethan Tongue" for the BBC's cultural channel (the Third Programme, as it was then known); see Figure 12.5. Jones introduced the extracts with an explanatory talk, in which, unusually for him, he demonstrated evidence of some feeling for literary analysis:

> But it's reasonable to suppose that there is in his style something more than what is furnished by what we may call the bare dictionary meanings of the words he

Figure 12.5. The actual cutting which Jones kept from the *Radio Times* as a souvenir of his 1949 Shakespeare broadcast. The date is in his handwriting.

uses. I think we may properly assume that Shakespeare wrote in some measure—perhaps in a very considerable measure—for the *sound* of his lines: that much of what he wrote was intended to produce subtle effects of sound—one might perhaps say "magical" effects, effects that may be compared to those produced by music.[48]

He also wrote an article for the *Radio Times* explaining his methods of research for the reconstruction of Shakespearian English (Jones 1949c).

In addition, Jones took part himself in numerous programmes, contributing several talks to the BBC. A selection of the scripts dealing with the evolution of modern English pronunciation, together with tape recordings of Jones's voice, were later posthumously published as *Our changing speech* (Jones 1985). In 1961, the BBC went to Jones's home for him to produce his last broadcast. Entitled simply "A message from Daniel Jones", it was transmitted on the World Service a couple of days before

Jones's eightieth birthday. The programme was really more interesting for its commemorative significance than for its unexciting content, which consisted of simple advice on study strategies for language students (Jones 1961). It formed part of an entire programme (in the series "This English") which the BBC devoted to Jones's life and achievements.[49]

12.10. The IPA and *Le Maître phonétique*

The Second World War forced Jones to take the awkward decision of whether to continue with the publication of *Le Maître phonétique*, or to close it down, as had been done in 1914. He decided to attempt to carry on, and the journal continued to appear throughout the war years, with only two concessions to the hostilities raging in the world: from 1942 onwards, the number of issues was reduced to two each year and fewer pages were printed. Jones apologised to his readers for the need of these economies "en raison de l'inaccessibilité de beaucoup de nos membres",[50] and because of the stringencies of paper rationing.[51]

Curiously, there is no announcement in the pages of *Le Maître phonétique* of the decision to continue publishing; there was, in fact, virtually no mention of the war itself until it was all over. However, it is not difficult to work out Jones's reasoning in wanting to keep the journal going. In 1914, Germany and Austro-Hungary had provided a large proportion of the total IPA support; in 1938 (when the last pre-war IPA membership list was published) Germany, including annexed Austria, provided only 22 of the total IPA membership of about 450,[52] so carrying on without them was no disaster. He would have recalled how, when the journal ceased to appear in 1914, membership had slumped, and that even after two decades, membership was nowhere near pre-1914 figures; if *Le Maître phonétique* was removed from circulation again, might it not spell the end of the IPA? And in any case, unlike in 1914, Jones did not have to rely on liaising with Passy. He could work on his own from Gerrards Cross, and having temporarily lost his departmental duties he had time at his disposal. It is also possible that Jones thought of the IPA as one small unifying factor in a world torn apart by conflict.

After the war, Jones, with his usual self-effacement, thanked those who had written congratulating him on keeping *Le Maître phonétique* going during the war, and pointed out that he had received considerable assistance in the task (Jones 1947c):

> We are indebted to those who have contributed articles, and we are indebted in an even greater degree to a group of hitherto anonymous helpers "behind the scenes", without whose aid our journal would have had to be suspended indefinitely.[53]

In 1949, on leaving his post at University College, Jones gave up the secretaryship of the IPA and with it his editorship of *Le Maître phonétique*. In an open letter of resignation (Jones 1950d), in which he proposed A.C. Gimson as his successor, he also promised that he would continue to take an interest in IPA affairs. However, Jones's only actual publications in the pages of its journal were limited to a couple of reviews and some obituaries. By now Jones was firmly against any suggestion of changing the journal to conventional orthography and this may well have been one of the reasons for the paucity of his contribution. Like many others, he was probably deterred from publishing longer articles in *Le Maître phonétique* by the need to convert them into transcription. Nevertheless, he did choose the Association as the means of publishing his important and much quoted *History and meaning of the term "phoneme"* (1957a); see further Section 14.16. In 1950, Jones was elected to the Presidency of the IPA (vacant since Passy's death) in recognition of his services to the organisation.[54]

12.11. Final years at University College

Jones was now most concerned about his imminent retirement, since according to the London University regulations then in operation, he would be due to retire in 1947, once he had reached the age of sixty-five. Jones's relationship with the Department at this point was in some ways ambivalent. On the one hand, he was desperately reluctant to let go of control, fearing that things might pass into the hands of a dedicated experimentalist or, even worse, a Firthian epigone. On the other hand, Jones was so absorbed in completing or revising his publications that he did not wish to be concerned with the detail of departmental affairs, so that he became more and more reluctant to make the train journey from Gerrards Cross. A.C. Gimson remembered Jones's pre-retirement phase thus:

> He used to come in very infrequently, in fact; he used to arrive, when he did come in, about midday and depart soon after three. When he didn't come in, he used to telephone, or his secretary would telephone him at home at about three o'clock. Unless something special was on, I don't think he ever came in more than two days a week and in the end it was more like one day a week.[55]

Jones would have been quite remote from his staff had he not continued to hold regular weekly staff seminars, where he made a deep impression on his junior colleagues of the time. Gimson recalled that these informant sessions showed Jones in his element:

> He used to hold little staff meetings every Monday—it may have been Friday—morning and these consisted of having a native informant, usually Sechuana, Cantonese or an Indian language—languages which Daniel Jones had worked on. Sometimes more exotic ones, but these were the usual ones. And we used to take

down what these people had said and then read back our transcriptions to the satisfaction of the native informant, the idea being to produce ultimately a phonemic transcription, which was Daniel Jones's ultimate end...and Daniel Jones in these sessions showed great perception, enormous powers of perception, and, of course, he *knew* a lot about languages. He was absolutely reliable.[56]

In November 1946, to Jones's relief, the Professorial Board reported to the College Committee that it had been decided that "after an investigation of the field it appeared doubtful whether it would be possible to fill the Chair from the candidates at present available". Since there was no suitable successor to Jones, he was therefore to be allowed to prolong his tenure by a year.[57]

The experimental side of the Department was now beginning for the first time to become a recognisable force. Dennis Fry was acquiring equipment and resources, and making intelligent use of what government funding was available. For example, in 1947, £200 was allocated for work to begin on the construction of the anechoic chamber sited in the back garden of 21 Gordon Square; it was eventually completed in 1948, having cost over twelve times the original grant.[58] Jones, however, is reported to have found this building, and especially the "dead room" itself, quite repulsive, which reinforced his growing suspicion of experimental work.[59] Fry was also fortunate in having managed to recruit a talented young experimental phonetician colleague, with a background of electrical engineering, Peter Denes.[60] Research work was being undertaken on various aspects of deafness for the National Institute for the Deaf, and there was also a greater interest in experimental work from undergraduates. By 1947, UCL already had twenty students enrolled for Fry's new experimental phonetics course, and in the same year Fry was promoted to Senior Lecturer.[61]

However, Jones, rather than approving this build-up of a somewhat neglected aspect of the Department's activities, began to be increasingly wary of the instrumental approach to phonetics. His interest in experimental work—which up to about 1920 was considerable—had cooled over the years into indifference, and he had been quite happy to leave Stephen Jones to run the laboratory with virtually no interference. Now, his attitude changed to what can only be termed a kind of restrained antagonism, combined with a fear that the traditional practical basis of the work in the Department would be replaced by a concentration on experimental research and teaching.

Jones's *volte face* on experimental phonetics can be traced to two sources. One was his personal preference for practical articulatory phonetics, with a recognition of his own academic strengths and weaknesses—undoubtedly reinforced by a tendency to conservatism in his character which, predictably, increased as he grew older. However, there was also another perhaps more powerful factor. Jones was falling more and more under the influence of theosophical philosophy and persons interested in these religious ideas. This was making him come to regard machinery, in almost any form, as a hostile force which worked against the welfare of humanity, as opposed to co-operative social activities—such as practical ear-training, language teaching and informant-based research—which were an influence for good (see Figure 14.16 and Collins and Mees 1997).

12.12. Retirement

Jones made one more significant trip abroad in the years immediately before his departure from University College. In the Easter vacation of 1948, he went to Copenhagen to give a course of lectures. He was accompanied by his young colleague J.D. O'Connor, who was entrusted with the task of conducting practical classes.[62] It also gave Jones a chance to meet again some of the Danish linguists of the time, notably Louis Hjelmslev. Typically, what was to strike Jones most was Hjelmslev's practical abilities in English. Paul Christophersen remembers his visit well:

> In the spring of 1948 Daniel Jones and J.D. O'Connor spent a term at Copenhagen University.... Naturally I saw a good deal of the visitors. I remember in particular a debate in the Linguistic Circle, when Daniel Jones expressed surprise at hearing Hjelmslev speak English with great fluency and a good accent, and his surprise would no doubt have been all the greater had he known that Hjelmslev's preferred foreign language was French. The combination of practical and theoretical knowledge of languages struck Jones as unusual.[63]

Back home, Jones's reluctance to face retirement did not diminish. Neither did his fear that his Department would fall into the hands of experimentalists. He worked furiously in an attempt to persuade the higher echelons of University College to allow him a further respite from the threat. Thanks to the personal influence of the Provost, his wish was granted and Jones's period of tenure was extended for another year, so that he did not finally have to depart until 1949.[64] He went with the prospect of being awarded the honorific title of Professor Emeritus in the University of London,[65] and his retirement was marked by a dinner held in his honour on June 28, 1949, in the common room of the recently reconstructed main building of University College.

Jones's farewell dinner was from the official account (Gimson 1949) a most successful and moving occasion—"one of the nicest and best arranged that I have been present at" was the opinion of Provost David Pye.[66] It featured several speeches of appreciation—a sincerely affectionate tribute delivered by Hélène Coustenoble being reprinted in *Le Maître phonétique* (Gimson 1949: 18–21). Another eulogistic speech, ironically, came from the man Jones had long considered his arch-enemy, J.R. Firth. Messages also arrived from all over the world with greetings from colleagues and former students. For his part, Jones promised that he had no intention of either giving up his interest in phonetics or losing contact with the Department. Dorothy Parkinson, who had been his secretary for over thirty years, had decided to retire at the same time as Jones she is noted as having her name "mentioned many times in the speeches". This only underlined her value as a source of strength and continuity over the years, both for Jones and for the Department as a whole. In Wiktor Jassem's words:

Jones relied on Miss Parkinson entirely. She was definitely the backbone of the Department in all administrative matters, but she also helped him very extensively in his writings and seemed to fulfil the duties of an unofficial editor of what he wrote, and she seemed to be absolutely devoted to her work for him.[67]

The imminent departure of Parky, whose kindly efficiency had endeared her to generations of students and staff, would certainly have reinforced the impression among those present that an era in the history of the Department was coming to an end.

When Jones left, University College was still unable to make a final decision on his successor. He had managed to persuade the Provost and the College that he was effectively irreplaceable—which was, in terms of his personal prestige, true. The most senior member of his own staff, Hélène Coustenoble, had herself cherished ambitions of taking over the Department but she had been turned down. Jones managed to obtain a readership for Cou in 1948 but this had provided only meagre consolation for her wounded pride. The obvious person to follow Jones was Dennis Fry, but the UCL authorities did not consider Fry completely suitable as Jones's heir, perhaps because he was considered as yet too inexperienced for the job or, more likely, because Jones's suspicion of experimental phonetics had been communicated to Pye. Fry was eventually designated Departmental Head in 1949, but the chair was withheld; furthermore, his appointment was initially limited to a period of five years.[68] Fry was not in fact to obtain a professorship until another nine years had elapsed.

Any fears Jones may have had that Fry would swamp the Department with experimental work did not materialise. Under Fry, the UCL Phonetics Department, although it now indeed began to produce research of a high standard on the experimental side, continued to offer a balance of work, with a strong basis of articulatory phonetics in the Jonesian mould. In the meantime, new centres for phonetics had been established at two other British universities, and both of these would be headed by Jones's former students—David Abercrombie moved to Edinburgh in 1948 and Peter MacCarthy became head of Department at Leeds in the same year. Jones's period of retirement would certainly see changes but, as yet, no break in the traditions of what he now termed the "London School". In fact, the Jonesian approach to phonetics was, at least in terms of numbers of staff and students, growing more strongly than ever before.

Chapter 13

Final years

13.1. Jones in retirement

Once Jones retired, his publishing activity, far from ceasing or diminishing, actually considerably increased. This was partly because he already had numerous projects in hand—several at a point almost reaching completion—and also because about this time the restrictions on the use of paper which had been in operation since the war were fully lifted and so publishers were keener to produce books. Despite the fact that he was now troubled more and more by ill-health, especially painful arthritis, Jones was still able to proceed with a concentration that belied his years. Up to the age of eighty, he was constantly writing new material, or revising old, and showing the perception and energy worthy of a scholar in his prime.

He had in the meantime developed a pattern of work which turned to advantage one of the continuing problems of his life—insomnia. For many years, Jones had experienced difficulty in getting to sleep, a symptom linked to his recurrent nervous disorders. He put a bed in his study, claiming that since he could sleep for only about two hours, he would spend the rest of the night working. The room was piled high with the literature of phonetics, and he worked from a desk which was a cumulative disorder of books, papers, old notepads, journals and articles.

The house, decorated in the old-fashioned, sombre style of Jones's Edwardian youth, was dominated by massive pieces of furniture. On the walls hung several huge paintings by Cyrille's father, Henri Motte—the type of late nineteenth century art that later would recover much of its former reputation, but which in the 1940s and 50s would have been considered to be not merely outdated but positively bad taste. The Jones household was cluttered and ramshackle; the bathroom, especially, is remembered by visitors as being crammed with a confusion of flannels, towels, bottles, packets and medications. Downstairs, a piano and two organs bore witness to Jones's continuing love of music, in particular, the works of J.S. Bach. He occasionally took a minor part—playing the cymbals—in the local amateur South Buckinghamshire Orchestra; at home, for relaxation, he practised keyboard pieces.

Cyrille was now beginning to become almost a recluse, rarely venturing out of the house, and indeed spending much of her time in her bedroom, where she complained of a series of illnesses. "Your aunt *enjoys* bad health", Jones confided to his niece on one occasion.[1] Having never come to terms with what she considered to be the harshness of the British climate, she insisted on keeping the house heated to oppressively high temperatures, even in summer. Like many of her social class and generation, Cyrille was used to having servants and now found, with the war, that she had difficulty making do just with daily help. She neglected most housework, concentrating her domestic interests on cooking. Encouraged by her husband, she was engaged on writing a cookery book, motivated in this activity partly by her intense dislike of English food; but the work was never published, or even completed.

13.2. Theosophy and Maud MacCarthy

Throughout his life, Jones's fascination with theosophical ideas had grown, and had now come to play a dominant role in his thought and actions. Jean Overton Fuller, a friend and former student, shared his interests, having long discussions with him on such matters. According to her, by the time he reached old age, theosophical ideas and the like had become even more important to him than phonetics.[2]

By far the greatest influence on him was Maud MacCarthy (an Irish theatre orchestra musician, turned mystic), and her medium Bill Coote (a London East End ex-stoker and labourer, also known as "the Boy"). Jones made his first contacts with MacCarthy in 1929 and by the early 1930s he was deeply involved in her activities. The extent of his commitment is revealed in the autobiographical *The Boy and the Brothers* (Omananda Puri 1959) published by MacCarthy towards the end of her life. This book gives details of her relationship with Coote, with whom, after they had emigrated to India, she eventually entered into a form of celibate marriage. It also provides lengthy extracts from the seances in which she asserts that the Boy was in touch with the "Brothers" (the group of supernatural beings claimed to be able to foresee the future, and influence events on earth). Daniel Jones is mentioned several times, sometimes actually by name, sometimes as "our dear London professor". It is disclosed that he paid for MacCarthy and Coote's passage out to India in 1935 (pp. 93-94) and continued to help support them when they were settled there (p. 97). Jones even wrote a generous testimonial to Maud MacCarthy which appeared on the dustcover (MacCarthy had meanwhile obtained the Indian mystic title of "Swami", assuming the name "Omananda Puri").

> It's been my privilege to know Swami Omananda for close on 40 years. I'm therefore able to vouch for her integrity and the truth of what she's written. I also knew well her late co-worker whom she calls the boy, a man of high ideals for whom I had great respect. On several memorable occasions I've been present when teachings such as those recorded in Swami Omananda's book have been given out by him in the manner described.

Although members of Jones's own family knew about his contacts with MacCarthy, he avoided mentioning anything to the outside world (indeed most of his colleagues expressed astonishment when subsequently informed of his religious and philosophical interests). However, there were exceptions: A.C. Gimson was aware of Jones's beliefs; and at least one other phonetician, Suniti K. Chatterji ([1981]: 23), realised something of his religious predilections, and put this on record:

> He had one aspect of his personality which was not easily discernable [sic] from outside. He was something of a mystic and a philosopher, and as such he felt

attracted to India[n] philosophical thought also. I had several occasions to discuss with him the basic concepts of our Indian *Vedanta* philosophy. He seemed to be fully in accord with this system of thought and of interpretation of life and being.

13.3. Family life

Jones apparently received no sympathy for his religious ideas from his wife, who proved particularly antipathetic to Maud MacCarthy, so theosophical matters were not discussed in the house. However, two members of Jones's family, his son Olivier, and son-in-law Robert Stanbury, took considerable interest in unconventional religions and the occult.[3]

It provided an area of life—furthermore, a highly significant one—where Jones could feel a bond with his son, to whom he was devoted but who was much opposed to him in terms of personality, interests and way of life. Olivier had proved something of a shiftless personality, making little use of his obvious talents and intelligence, and never settling down in regular employment. He died of cancer in 1961 when only forty-four. Jones is reported to have been desolate at the death of his son, and perhaps never recovered from this premature bereavement.

Figure 13.1. One of Jones's New Year greeting cards (sent to Dennis Ward in 1955).

Jones's relationship with his daughter was much less troubled. Michelle had been educated at home in her childhood, and only sent to boarding school at the age of eleven. To her father's delight, she soon showed that she had an unusual talent for music, perhaps inherited from her Carte forebears, and eventually became a professional violinist. Jones derived enormous pleasure from attending her performances, undoubtedly feeling that his years of encouraging her to practise now had their reward.

By the late 1940s, Jones's ill-health, which had troubled him constantly for so long, was further exacerbated by arthritis, a condition which deteriorated throughout his old age and eventually crippled his hands, giving him tremendous pain. In 1952–53 he felt the progress of the disease had been halted as a result of treatment from a Viennese physician, Mona Rolfe, who employed spiritualist and faith healing techniques. Jones was much taken with her methods, and wrote to Elizabeth Miller describing the success of the treatment, even asking persistently if the doctor could be given a chance to give a radio talk (a request which was eventually turned down).[4] Jones's remission proved only to be temporary, and the arthritis proceeded to stiffen and twist Jones's hands so that in extreme old age he was unable to pour out his own tea, and found writing, or even turning the pages of a book, wearying and sometimes excruciatingly agonising tasks. Nevertheless, until quite late in his life, it was he, rather than Cyrille, who continued to do many of the household chores. Jones was a familiar figure in Gerrards Cross as he went to do his shopping. Few of his neighbours could have had any idea that this little, frail, old man, struggling to manage a bag crammed with groceries, was a scholar whose name was known to linguists and students of English world-wide—and Jones, who remained modest and self-effacing throughout his life, would certainly not have enlightened them.

13.4. The *Phoneme*: introduction

Jones's first post-retirement publication, the *Phoneme* (Jones 1950a), cannot in fact be regarded as a product of his retirement period since he had been working on the book for many years. McDavid (1952: 377), in his review of the *Phoneme* said, "taking advantage of his retirement from active teaching, he has collected his observations on phonetics and expanded them into this book", perhaps giving to many the impression that Jones had assembled the book casually, almost as an afterthought. Nothing could have been further from reality; producing the *Phoneme* had been a prolonged, almost painful process, which had dominated Jones's pre-retirement years.

It was, however, the first book to appear after he had given up his university post and, in a sense, an indication to the world that he did not intend to be inactive. During the long years of writing and rewriting, Jones had cherished the hope that the *Phoneme* would be considered as a major contribution to phonetics and phonology. He stated (*HMTP*: 14 n.) that he started writing the *Phoneme* in 1937 and that "the greater part of the manuscript was ready about 1941, but the conditions prevailing at the time prevented me from completing it until the end of 1945"; Jones's finished manuscript "was in the printer's hands in Jan., 1946". But, as was often the case with Jones— interesting parallels are the *Outline*[1] and the *Pronunciation of Russian*—there had then begun a series of delays which meant that the book's appearance was postponed for nearly four years (*Phoneme*[3]: vi). To what extent publication was delayed by the economic stringencies of the post-war period, and to what extent by Jones himself, is uncertain. In October 1947, Jones wrote to David Abercrombie, complaining about his publisher, Reuben Heffer:

> Heffer is terribly slow these days. (He has had the MS of my book on the Phoneme for nearly 2 years, & there are no proofs yet. This is not altogether Heffer's fault. There is a hold-up by the Monotype Corporation, who can't or won't produce various special phonetic types that are needed.)[5]

But Abercrombie (1983: 6) claimed later that the delays were owing, at least in part, to Jones's perfectionist demands in typographical details.

> It is said that he considered the dot over the i in the Gill Sans typeface, which he was using in the book for phonetic notation, was too high above the stem, and time had to be spent on re-cutting it. [6]

The publication was awaited eagerly by the linguistic world, who seem to have expected Jones to make a fundamental contribution to theoretical phonology and reveal how his ideas on the phoneme concept had developed since his early pronouncements.

They were disappointed. The *Phoneme* restated, essentially, a concept of the phoneme which Jones had put forward over thirty years earlier in the *Sinhalese reader* (see Section 9.4). What emendations there were in the *Phoneme* had in any case already been leaked in articles published years previously (e.g. Jones 1938a, 1944c, 1944d). Jones himself saw his task differently, and instructed his readers to look upon the *Phoneme* as "an unfinished collection of materials which may encourage them to progress by pursuing useful lines of investigation for themselves" (p. v). So the *Phoneme* broke no radically new conceptual ground, and it is clear that Jones felt himself under no obligation to do so (p. vii):

> ...the theory as presented by me was (and still is) the *original* theory conceived in the 1870's by Baudouin de Courtenay, though expounded mainly on "physical" (as distinguished from "psychological") lines, and I see no reason to deviate from it.

Jones revised the *Phoneme* twice but made no substantial alterations. The third edition, published in the year of his death, 1967, was enlarged by the addition of *HMTP* in the form of an appendix. This brought the *Phoneme*[3] to a total length of 285 pages, containing thirty-two chapters plus two appendices. It is this third—and effect-ively definitive—edition that we shall refer to here.

13.5. The *Phoneme*: opening chapters

In Chapter I, after defining concepts such as "speech sound", "simple", gliding and compound sounds" (pp. 1–6), Jones goes on to refer to a division into "concrete and abstract sounds", following largely the lines of his earlier (Jones 1938a) paper. Jones then proceeds in Chapter II to repeat his, by now familiar, definition of the phoneme as "a family of sounds in a given language which are related in character and are used in such a way that no one member ever occurs in a word in the same phonetic context as any other member" (p. 10). Previously, he had already emphasised (p. 9) that he is making the important restriction of confining his definition to a single idiolect, and to a single speech style, referring to Passy's concept of "prononciation familière ralen-tie", which he interprets as "slow conversational pronunciation".

Jones proceeds to examine further the "related in character" restriction in his defini-tion, pointing out that this may be either organic or acoustic in nature. He emphasises that the phoneme classification must be considered in relation to the word and not to larger units of speech. Furthermore, he asserts, one sound cannot normally be regarded as belonging to more than one phoneme—although Jones is forced later to admit that this aspect of his phonemic principles must often be qualified. Jones states that no way of defining the phoneme is unassailable but claims that his own gives an adequate working definition.

The *Phoneme* maintains Jones's constant emphasis on the importance of transcrip-tion, referring to broad transcription as an "infallible guide" (p. 220). He continues to use the distinction of "broad and narrow" forms, but admits that by the term "broad" he essentially means phonemic (p. 12). He uses here the same convention as he established in the *Outline*[1], namely showing any narrow transcription in square brackets, and regarding any unbracketed transcription as broad, i.e. implicitly phone-mic (p. 13). Predictably, Jones insists on the use of the IPA symbols for any kind of transcription.

As in his previous works on the subject, Jones's definition of the phoneme lacks reference to meaning. He regarded any semantic differentiation as essentially subsid-iary, and a corollary to the physical definition postulated (p. 14):

> The fact that sounds belonging to separate phonemes are capable of distinguishing words, while sounds belonging to the same phoneme are not, is thus not part of any "definition" of a phoneme as here conceived. It follows from our explanation of its nature.

To illustrate his case, Jones uses the familiar example of /h/ and /ŋ/, which are never capable of distinguishing the meaning of words, because they occur in complementary distribution. By virtue of their phonetic dissimilarity, however, they cannot intuitively be regarded as allophones of the same phoneme (p. 14).

13.6. The *Phoneme*: aspects of phonemic analysis

Jones now proceeds to a discussion mainly concerned with segmental phonemes and their analysis. He devotes Chapter VI to what he terms "minimal distinctions", that is, examples of minimal pairs providing instances not only of segmental variation, but also what could be analysed as phonemic distinctions of length, stress and tone (pp. 15–16).

Chapter VII provides numerous examples of "phonemic grouping", by which Jones means the grouping of allophones into phonemes and the factors inducing allophonic variation. Jones provides examples to illustrate phonetic conditioning, and the variation that may be brought about by duration, stress and pitch (pp. 18–32). Striking exemplification is given in Chapter VIII to show the degree of cross-linguistic differences in the extent of the range of allophones contained within various phonemes.

The subsequent chapters (IX–XI) are concerned with the difficulties of analysis. These include: (1) erroneous auditory analysis (treated under the heading "acoustic impressions"); (2) the difficulty of ascertaining phoneme contrasts; and (3) the dangers of either not recognising such contrasts or of mistaking allophones for phoneme contrasts. Again, many supporting examples are given from a variety of languages. Chapter XII discusses "difficulties in identifying sounds in special sequences" and deals mainly with problems arising from phonetic conditioning resulting in devoicing or assimilation. Jones takes examples from English such as the realisations of the morpheme <s> in plurals and verb endings, and the alveolar to palato-alveolar place assimilation of /s/ to /ʃ/ in phrases like "dre*ss* shirt".

Chapter XIII deals with clues to identification of phonemes to be found in the allophonic characteristics of neighbouring phonemes, dealing with cases such as the characteristic qualities of vowel sounds adjacent to palatal consonants in Russian, emphatic (pharyngalised) consonants in Arabic, and vowel length in relation to word-final voiced/voiceless consonants in English. Chapter XIV considers difficulties in establishing phonemic groupings in the light of what has been termed by Chao (1934 [1966]) the "non-uniqueness of phonemic solutions", and problems arising from cases where "the controlling principles are complex or difficult to ascertain" (p. 54). As McDavid (1952: 379) has noted, it is surprising that Jones does not refer to Chao's well-known paper at this point. For exemplification of the potential diversity of solutions, Jones includes discussions on problematical areas such as Korean plosives, Peking Chinese fricatives and the English central vowels. The complexity of underlying principles is illustrated by reference to the French and German vowel systems, and the German palatal and velar fricatives.

Chapter XV deals with "gliding sounds", under which Jones subsumes central approximants, e.g. English /j w/ and also diphthongal vowel glides. He examines allophonic variations which involve loss of the glide, and variation conditioned by tones as in Pekinese Chinese. He also considers here the difficulties relating to compound sounds, such as the Sinhalese /mb nd/, etc. Jones makes the significant statement (p. 79):

> I am disposed to think that in making a classification into phonemes the view of the native speaker as to what constitutes a "single sound" should be regarded as important, though not necessarily conclusive.

Jones considers vowel colouring in Chapter XVI, covering such features as nasalisation, r-colouring, breathiness, creakiness and sulcalisation, which last he considers to be a "'throaty' voice-quality" achieved by "raising the sides of the back part of the tongue and leaving a groove down the centre" (p. 82). Jones suggests that these types of vowel should be represented in transcription with digraphs rather than diacritics where possible.

Vowels and consonants as members of the same phoneme, as in one analysis of French, are considered in Chapter XVII. The following chapter deals with what Jones terms, rather vaguely, "manner of use". Within this category, he appears to include the distribution of the speech sound, together with its relationship to syntax and morphology. In determining phoneme categories, Jones invokes native speaker intuition, for example in the cases of the Japanese syllabic nasal (pp. 88–89).

Phoneme overlapping is considered in Chapter XIX, and defined as where two phonemes "contain a particular sound as a subsidiary member" (p. 92), i.e. where a particular allophone can be regarded as being held in common by two phonemes. Jones considers two types: (1) where a sound may be regarded according to context as belonging to one or another phoneme; (2) where a sound occurring in a given context may be assigned to either of two phonemes. The first case is illustrated with examples from the vowel systems of French, /œ ɔ/, and Russian, /e a/, and the potential overlap of flapped /t/ and /r/ in certain accents of English (pp. 93–96).

Chapter XX examines the second possibility, under the heading of "di-phonemic sounds", dividing these into two categories: (1) when the same sound occurs "incidentally" as well as "expressly" (examples of this categorisation are the occurrence of nasal vowels, not only as distinct phonemes, but also where they arise through the incidental nasalisation of vowels which occur in the proximity of nasal consonants, as, for example, in Hindi and Ewe); (2) where a sound is assignable to one of two phonemes with apparently equal justification (pp. 98–107).

Jones is not able to find watertight examples of the latter phenomenon in natural languages. He believes that if such a case were to occur, it would be best to assign the sound arbitrarily to one of the two phonemes rather than label it as di-phonemic (pp. 106–107).

13.7. The *Phoneme*: suprasegmental features

In the chapters which follow, Jones goes on to consider suprasegmental features. Chapter XXI begins by outlining certain linguistic functions of length, stress and pitch, with exemplification from a range of languages, including Russian, Hindi, Cantonese, Tswana and Igbo, and examines briefly cross-linguistic variation. Chapter XXII deals with significant length, i.e. "duration used as a means of distinguishing one word from another" (p. 115). Jones differentiates between length and "doubling" (more commonly termed "gemination", e.g. Trask 1996: 154), stating that although phonetically the phenomena may be similar, it is not possible to pronounce separately (i.e. with a brief intervening pause) phonologically long sounds, but it is possible to pronounce doubled vowels or consonants in this way. He then gives examples of what he considers to be true distinctive length (as opposed to doubling) in order to distinguish words, providing examples from Scottish English, where morphemic structure is indicated by means of length, and from varieties of English where frequently the only clue to distinguishing final /d/ from /t/ is the duration of the preceding vowel. Jones also shows how, in Tswana, length is employed with what must be considered a kind of grammatical function to distinguish statements from commands and questions (p. 122).

Chapter XXII continues with the theme of duration under the heading "Chronemes". Jones points out that phonetic length is always variable and then gives a summary of the chief factors affecting length. He terms "any particular degree of duration" a "chrone" (p. 126), stating that the relative values of chrones may be judged auditorily, whilst instrumental procedures must be employed to gauge durations more accurately. Groupings of chrones can be made to form "chronemes" analogously to Jones's phoneme/phone relationship previously postulated; variants within the chroneme may then be termed "allochrones". Jones again provides much exemplification including a reported three-term chroneme contrast in Estonian (pp. 132–133).

In Chapter XXIV, Jones examines stress and prominence, defining (p. 134) the former in terms of "force of utterance, abstracted from the other attributes of speech-sounds". He states that "stresses are essentially subjective activities of the speaker" perceived by the hearer in terms of loudness. Most languages, according to Jones, can be considered "stress languages" and, for the majority, the location of strong stress in polysyllabic words is an integral part of their pronunciation. One known language, Serbo-Croat, appears to employ varying types of stress, e.g level, crescendo, diminuendo, and crescendo-diminuendo, as an integral part of the pronunciation of words (pp. 136; 149–151). Other languages may employ strong stress in the sentence (e.g. French) whilst yet others again, Jones considers (p. 137), can be regarded as effectively stressless (e.g. Japanese, Hindustani, Marathi).

Jones distinguishes stress and prominence, maintaining (p. 137) that in contrast to stress, prominence is essentially "an effect perceived objectively by the hearer", and provides illustrative examples of prominence achieved by means of stress, tamber, length, intonation, and combinations of these phenomena. He emphasises the difficulty of distinguishing stress from other prominence attributes, and the tendency of speakers of stress languages to interpret all prominence in terms of stress. Jones believes that it is normally location of strong stress and not the type of stress which is linguistically significant. Consequently, the concept of a stress phoneme or "stroneme", composed of "strones", can have application only to Serbo-Croat—or any other language found to share its exceptional characteristics.

Jones deals with tone and tonemes in Chapter XXV, providing an analogous treatment of pitch phenomena to those already constructed earlier in the book for other features. He supplies (p. 153) the following definition of the toneme: "a family of tones in a given tone language which count for linguistic purposes as if they were one and the same, the differences being due to tonal or other context." The members of the toneme complex are termed "allotones". To illustrate his argument, Jones provides, in addition to a few examples from Cantonese, extensive exemplification from Tswana. He discusses the feature of downstep at length, although not employing the actual term. This portion of the *Phoneme* is derived from his work on Tswana. See Sections 6.8, 6.9. and 7.5.

"Distinction by complexes of attributes" is the title of the long Chapter XXVI. Jones points out that any minimal distinction is normally the result of a combination of a number of phenomena, providing here effectively a statement of redundancy in phoneme contrasts. Jones lists numerous possible dual combinations of tamber, stress, length, duration, pitch and voice quality (pp. 162–163). The remainder of the chapter is devoted to an examination of these combinations with copious illustrative data from a wide variety of languages.

13.8. The *Phoneme*: wider implications

Chapter XXVII moves on to what may be regarded as the third portion of the book, which discusses the wider implications of the phoneme concept. As early as 1932, Jones had introduced, in the *Outline*[3], a means of coping with dialect variation, namely the "diaphone", a coinage that has acquired a certain currency in modern linguistics. Jones begins by discussing aspects of individual variation, such as voice quality, distribution of phonemes (similar to what has been termed by Wells 1982: 79–80 lexical-incidential variation), vowel length, stress incidence and intonation. Jones ends the section by stating (p. 195) that "the actual sounds used by one person are often found to differ from the corresponding sounds used by other speakers of the same language". These last variations Jones terms "free variations", arguing that they must be distinguished from "allophones (members of phonemes)".

Jones then defines (p. 195) the diaphone as the "name for a family of sounds consisting of the sound used by one speaker in a particular set of words (said in isolation) together with corresponding though different sounds used in them by other speakers of the same language". As an example he shows a vowel diagram of the English vowel in "get" (reproduced as Figure 13.2), asserting that the area indicated shows

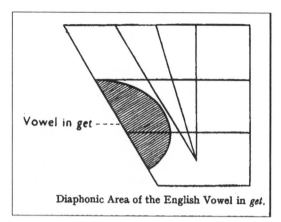

Figure 13.2. Diagram with explanation of the
diaphone (*Phoneme*, p. 195).

the range of the "various shades of **e** which may be heard from different English
speakers".[7]

Jones provides further exemplification from English accents and those of other
languages, covering both vowels and consonants. He then considers (p. 197) variation
resulting from styles of pronunciation ("formal", "slow conversational" and "rapid
familiar") and mentions the variation that occurs with weak and strong forms.

Jones points out that, by their very nature, diaphones frequently overlap although
in connected speech between speakers with radically differing ranges of diaphones
context plays a large part in ensuring intelligibility (pp. 199–200). He draws attention
to the capacity of human beings to disambiguate diaphonic variants, a phenomenon
nowadays termed "normalisation" (see, for instance, Clark—Yallop 1990: 246–247).
In Jones's model, a sound may belong to two (or more) diaphones; he provides examples from the English and Scottish English vowel systems and also the occurrence of
[ʔ] in English accents.

Jones relates the diaphone to the idea of free variation, finding that the only place
for incorporating free variants would be within a mentalistic definition of the phoneme
(p. 204) as "an 'ideal sound' which is 'realized' in one way by one person under a
given set of conditions, and in another way by the same person under other conditions
and yet in other ways by other persons". Because of the theoretical problems this
would involve, Jones is not prepared to accept such a view.

In chapter XXVIII, Jones considers the complications arising from what he terms
(p. 205) "erratic pronunciation", i.e. involuntary variations of pronunciation. He sub-
divides these into three categories: (1) where, because there are relatively few phonemes in the language, "absolute precision in the pronunciation of certain sounds is
not essential"; (2) variation resulting from dialect mixing; (3) where intentional
changes have been made in an individual's pronunciation (p. 205).

Jones gives the name "variphone" to the first type, defining (pp. 205–206) this as "'unstable' sounds...liable to 'variation' independently of their phonetic context". Jones provides considerable exemplification, including the Japanese /r/ phoneme, which varies between a post-alveolar fricative [ɹ], a lingual flap [ɾ], a retroflex plosive [ɖ] and an alveolar lateral [l]. He believes that Japanese speakers use these variants indiscriminately (although this statement is somewhat qualified in a footnote, p. 207 n.). He states (p. 207) that "variphones have a place in the phoneme theory" and that "the members of a variphone count as if they were a single sound, which may itself constitute a phoneme or which may be a member of a phoneme".

Jones also provides examples (several of them anecdotal in nature) of the two other types of pronunciation variation—dialect mixture and intentional changes of pronunciation—but does not attempt to fit them into his phoneme theory; today, most linguists would consider these phenomena as part of a sociolinguistic dimension related to "linguistic insecurity".

In Chapter XXIX, "Mentalistic and functional conceptions of the phoneme", Jones begins by a survey of views of the phoneme which are alternatives to the strictly physical view he has proposed. He first considers the mentalistic views of the phoneme as an "abstract" or "ideal" sound or a target at which the speaker aims. Jones then provides a brisk survey of the views of Baudouin de Courtenay, Sweet, Sapir, Trubetzkoy, Bloomfield, Twaddell and Hjelmslev, anticipating the much fuller treatment to be found in *HMTP*. The chapter concludes with Jones indulging in some curious philosophical speculation, the content of which (as with his earlier paper in the same vein, Jones 1938a) can only properly be interpreted when taken against the background of his theosophical convictions (see discussion, Section 14.16 and Collins—Mees 1997).

Jones's personal philosophy also comes to the fore in his introduction to Chapter XXX—entitled "The practical use of the theory of phonemes". He argues (pp. 217–218) here that "every man is endowed with certain abilities which he can use for the general good" and that those with an ability in applied phonetics (by which, of course, he implies Jonesian articulatory phonetics) are especially capable of "doing 'useful' work...'conducive to the ultimate well-being of humanity'". Jones emphasises his essentially practical view of phonetics, regarding it as being a particularly beneficial science since it can be used to improve human communication.

Jones goes on to argue (p. 218) here for the primacy of the phonemes in linguistics, declaring, in particular, that they constitute the "indivisible semantic units of which languages are composed", and which in sequence combine to form larger semantic entities such as morphemes, words and sentences. He moves from this to assert that "...it is the phonemic idea which forms the basis for the non-phonetic branches of linguistic science, i.e. semantics, morphology, grammar, etc".

In particular, Jones makes strong claims for the place of the phoneme in the learning of foreign languages (p. 219):

Phonemes in fact lie at the root of everything that is required for enabling language learners to use the right words, to put the words into their various forms and to use the forms appropriately. In fact, all practical linguistic attainments may be said to depend ultimately on the theory of phonemes.

Chapter XXXI returns to problems of transcription and the application of phonetic concepts to orthography. After restating the basic distinction of broad and narrow forms of transcription, and defining the former as one which "records the language by means of one letter to each phoneme",[8] Jones then goes on to discuss instances where it is justifiable to depart from the phonemic transcription by "narrowing" it for reasons of pedagogic convenience in language teaching (pp. 221–222) or to clarify points of phonology in comparative linguistic work (p. 223). However, in general, Jones advocates (p. 224) that in a transcription "the number of letters should be as small as practicable, and that each letter should have an elastic value".

For initial investigation of languages, however, Jones naturally enough believes that a very narrow transcription should be produced with no attempt to group sounds into phonemes until a later stage of research (p. 225); here he is restating ideas first put forward over two decades earlier in his unpublished Missionaries' Lecture (see Section 6.9). Since Jones believes that the word, and the establishment of word boundaries, are also crucial to phonemic analysis, he considers that the latter should be one of the first steps undertaken in informant research (see Jones 1931k).

Finally, Jones points out that although broad transcription is efficient inasmuch as it records the pronunciation of all the words in a language unambiguously, it has considerable limitations since it does not record many of the phenomena of connected speech, for instance, intonation, voice quality, gesture, and what he terms "special lengths and stresses". Devices such as punctuation, underlining, italics, etc. are inadequate for conveying this information and, consequently, Jones advocates (p. 226) that "the necessary information may be given…partly by rules and partly by special markings of length, stress and intonation".

Jones then moves to considering the application of phonemic principles to systems of orthography for universal use in writing languages, as opposed to transcription which is a tool of linguistics. What is said in this section (pp. 226–229) is largely a generalisation of his views stated elsewhere, in particular in Jones (1942a, 1944a, 1949a, 1949b). He points out that an orthography has to cater for a wide range of speakers with varying accents, and that variations such as rhotic as against non-rhotic pronunciation in English have to be taken into account. Features such as the existence of weak and strong forms (e.g. in English), liaison forms (e.g. in French) and the need to distinguish homophones also mean that it is often necessary to depart from the principles of phonemic representation. Nevertheless, given these constraints, Jones maintains (p. 233) that, for maximum efficiency, orthography should have a "one letter per phoneme" as its basis.

In the final chapter, XXXII, Jones discusses the significance of the phoneme in the historical development of languages. He cites numerous permutations of allophonic variation leading to changes in the phonemic structure of a wide variety of languages,

51. Paul Passy in his latter years

52. Jones speaking in the presence of the French ambassador at Linguaphone headquarters in London in 1956. The ceremonial dinner marked the unveiling of a
plaque to Paul Passy. At the far left is the Provost of University College, Sir B. Ifor
Evans.

53. Jones at home (1953)

54. With David Abercrombie (centre) at Jones's honorary
degree ceremony at Edinburgh University (1958)

and gives abundant exemplification. However, as Schubiger (1952: 43) points out, there is little attempt (she claims none) at explaining the underlying reasons for linguistic change. Despite these limitations, Jones's work here was important for the application of phonemic principles to what had previously been, in terms of more modern phonological approaches, a relatively neglected area. His numerous examples provided a source and stimulus to others coming later to the field.

13.9. Reactions to the *Phoneme*

In general, the reviews of the *Phoneme* were unfavourable or, at best, lukewarm. There was considerable criticism of its lack of innovative ideas, and Jones's overall unwillingness to sacrifice practical applications in favour of theoretical considerations. From the USA, in particular, came censure for his neglect of discussion within the structuralist paradigm, which at this time dominated American linguistics to the virtual exclusion of all other schools of thought.

A particularly damning review (McDavid 1952) appeared in the influential journal *Language*. Whilst it contained much valid condemnation, for example of Jones's restricted reading, and his "diffidence" in many of his linguistic statements, McDavid (1952: 379) went on to claim that the book's approach to the subject had been dictated by the "relative unfamiliarity of British readers with the concept of the phoneme" and that "Jones seems to worry about many details that American linguists take for granted". In discussing Jones's "family of sounds" definition, McDavid implies that Jones had borrowed his ideas from various American linguists but expressed them "not so tidily" (1952: 378).

The lack of American structuralist awareness of either Jones's own role in propagating the phoneme concept, or the primacy of the British school in the 1920s in pioneering the phonemic approach, did have one good effect. In an effort to put the record straight, Jones wrote *History and meaning of the term "phoneme"* (*HMTP*, Jones 1957a), which not only provides what is perhaps the best—certainly one of the most widely quoted—concise historiographical accounts of the phoneme, but also summarises his own position more succinctly than in any of his other works.[9] (See Section 14.16 for further discussion.)

Distanced as we now are from the linguistic battles of the time, it can be seen that, despite its theoretical limitations, the *Phoneme* can be considered successful within Jones's own criteria. Firstly, the book does indeed fill in lacunae in Jones's phoneme theory and takes certain sub-concepts, such as the diaphone and the variphone, further than in any of his previous publications. Secondly, he is able to develop the idea of the phoneme as a link between the concrete and the abstract—something which Jones himself may have regarded one of the most salient areas covered by the book. Thirdly, as has been pointed out by Cohen (1956–57: 321 n.) and Fischer-Jørgensen (1975: 58) amongst others, the *Phoneme* provided the best collection of examples of phonemic contrasts and allophonic variants available at the time, and it is arguable that it has not even now been surpassed. The exemplification was derived from over seventy different languages; overwhelmingly, the examples were not culled from the work of others, with all the questionable reliability which goes with such a procedure, but based either on Jones's own research or that of his close colleagues and direct pupils, all using native informants. The strength of UCL as a centre of excellence in the work of practical phonetic analysis, and Jones's own unrivalled gifts in this respect, guaranteed that the examples chosen by Jones were accurate, and not hearsay, secondhand, or the results of inadequate, skimped research procedures. Fischer-Jørgensen (1975: 58) has summed up Jones's contribution in this way:

> ...Jones always argues very cautiously. He hesitates to take definite standpoints, and he is generally sceptical about the possibility of proposing exact definitions. He is a practical man, not a theorist. However, the book is of great value because of the very extensive collection of examples, which derive from the author's life-long studies of a large number of languages, and which are therefore exceptionally reliable.

13.10. Revision of the *Pronunciation of English*

In the early period of retirement, a major part of Jones's work was the revision of books which he had written earlier in his career. The first to come out, in 1950, was a revised third edition of the *Pronunciation of English*.

The *Pronunciation of English*[3] consists of 206 pages, and is considerably expanded compared with the first edition. The sequence of chapters is similar to that in the *Outline*[3]. The first part of the book, entitled "Phonetic Theory", consists of sections on pronunciation models, the anatomy and physiology of the speech mechanism, the classification of segments, followed by a detailed treatment of vowels and consonants, with separate sections on plosive consonants and nasalisation. Supra-segmental features are covered in chapters on assimilation and elision, syllables, duration, stress and intonation. The last portion of Part 1 contains practical exercises and ear-training together with a brisk treatment of phoneme theory. As in the first edition, Part 2 provides texts in transcription, including twelve in RP, one of which shows intonation, and one, curiously, indicating the pronunciation of "those who lengthen traditionally shortened vowels" (p. 191). In addition, there are samples of South Western, Scottish, American and London varieties of English. Jones rounds off Part 2 with specimens of reconstructed Elizabethan and Chaucerian English.

By 1950, Jones had become ashamed of the fact that the *Pronunciation of English*[1] —though out of print—was still circulating. It had achieved remarkable success, despite its limitations. Indeed, in an introductory paragraph to an otherwise hostile review of the third edition, Henry Lee Smith (1952: 144) revealed that he had himself "cut his phonetic eyeteeth on the 1927 printing of the second edition". Since no revision had appeared since 1914, most of the ideas on phonetics and views on pronunciation which it contained were about forty years out of date. Jones now took the opportunity of revamping the work so completely and thoroughly that it became essentially a different book—retaining only the skeleton outline scheme of the original version.

The layout was reorganised throughout so that, visually, the *Pronunciation of English*³ bears a strong similarity to the *Pronunciation of Russian* (see Section 10.5). For instance, the stylised sagittal cross-sections of that book were clearly used as a model for those in the *Pronunciation of English*³. The vowel diagrams are similar to those in the *Phoneme*, and are particularly neat and elegant. Shortly after the publication of the third edition of the *Pronunciation of English*, Jones (1952c: 84) wrote in reply to a review by Wise (1952):

> I am very keen on certain details which many people would consider of little importance; I am particularly keen for instance on the general appearance and legibility of the printed page.

In fact, the *Pronunciation of English*³ might be considered of all Jones's publications the most pleasing to the eye—reflecting his great interest in typography and letter design.

Other less superficial revisions were just as radical. Jones's increasingly liberal attitude towards speech standards has already been noted in his revisions of the *Outline* and the *EPD* (see Section 11.5). In the *Pronunciation of English*³, he removed the elocution-influenced ideas which pervade the earlier editions, stating (p. v):

> ...a new attitude has been adopted in regard to the much-discussed question of standard pronunciation. I find that it can no longer be said that any standard exists, nor do I think it desirable to attempt to establish one. It is useful that descriptions of existing pronunciation should be recorded, but I no longer feel disposed to recommend any particular forms of pronunciation or to condemn others. It must, in my view, be left to individuals to decide whether they should speak in the manner that comes to them naturally or whether they should alter their speech in any way. Anyone desiring to modify his pronunciation will find in this book suggestions as to how changes may be effected, but I feel that the responsibility for putting any such suggestions into effect should rest with him.

Jones refers throughout the book to "RP", but claims that he considers this only as a "widely understood pronunciation" with no claim to authority. He states that the difference between "good" and "bad" speech should be based on "clear articulation", and that "a dialect speaker may speak well or badly" (p. 4). The *Pronunciation of English*³ represents the latest and, perhaps, the most complete statement of Jones's views on many aspects of English pronunciation, and is the only work where he provides any sustained description of dialect variation. Indeed, apart from the scattered details in Ward (1929), the *Pronunciation of English*³ was the only work of authority to contain any information on a range of English accents—a situation which held until the publication of Wells (1970). Nevertheless, this is probably the weakest aspect of the book, with many inaccuracies. For one variety, Scottish (*Pronunciation of English*³, pp. 193–194), numerous changes had to be made in the fourth edition (pp. 204–205).

An innovation in the *Pronunciation of English*³ was the inclusion of an attempt by Jones at a transcription of American English (cf. his addition of the appendix on American English in the *Outline*⁷). It turned out that some of the most biting criticisms in Smith's (1952: 146–147) unfavourable review were those taking Jones to task over his inaccurate and simplistic representation of American speech, in particular for lacking "an overall frame of reference to enable him to handle the vowel structuring of any dialect but his own" (Smith 1952: 145).

Jones changed the segmental transcription system so as to bring it into line with phonemic principles—although, surprisingly, the concept of the phoneme itself is only mentioned as an afterthought in a brief final chapter right at the end of the theory portion of the book (pp. 165–167); narrow transcription is consistently enclosed by square brackets (as Jones had been in the habit of doing ever since the *Outline*¹).

A striking improvement is the employment throughout of the Cardinal Vowel system as a means of vowel description (see Figure 13.3), rendering this section of the third edition immensely superior to its predecessors. For the first time in any of his publications, Jones included, as a frontispiece, the X-ray photographs of the tongue positions of [i, a, ɑ, u] which he had taken in 1917 in connection with his research into tongue posture in vowel articulations (see Section 7.6). These same photographs were later to be introduced as a frontispiece to the *Outline*⁹ ([1960]).

Jones's approach to supra-segmental features in the *Pronunciation of English*³ is greatly advanced from that to be found in the first edition. The treatment of stress is closest to that of the *Outline*³, but because of the different aim of the *Pronunciation of English*³, constant reference to foreigners' problems is avoided and instead discussion centres more on variation, dialectal and idiolectal, to be found in contemporary English.

Intonation is treated on a whole-tune basis, with patterns categorised into "simple fall", "simple rise", "normal fall-rise" and "emphatic fall-rise" (p. 147); in addition, a rise-fall pattern is mentioned (p. 154). The patterns are discussed effectively in terms of grammatical categories and discourse function; attitudinal function is also frequently mentioned. In all, the treatment shows some advances on that to be found in the *Outline*³ and must have benefited from Jones's earlier contacts with Harold Palmer (see 14.12) and the fact that Roger Kingdon was now a member of Jones's Department.

Nevertheless, Jones does not take any regard of either of these scholars with respect to the marking scheme, remaining loyal to the principles of the system devised by his former colleagues, Lilias Armstrong and Ida Ward (see Section 14.12). The single passage marked for intonation (pp. 185–191), since it contains the same text as that chosen for the *Pronunciation of English*¹ (pp. 87–97), provides an interesting comparison in terms of Jones's representations of pitch (see Figures 13.4 and 13.5). Jones's earlier system (taken over from *Intonation curves*) is far cruder and provides less information than the dot-dash interlinear scheme (very similar to that in the *Outline*[3] and modified from Armstrong and Ward 1926).

As in the *Pronunciation of English*[1], Jones included (pp. 198–200) samples of Chaucerian and Shakespearian English. These passages came in for considerable criticism (see Section 14.15) and underwent serious revision in the fourth edition (pp. 209–213).

The *Pronunciation of English*[3] is in many ways a neglected book, existing somewhat

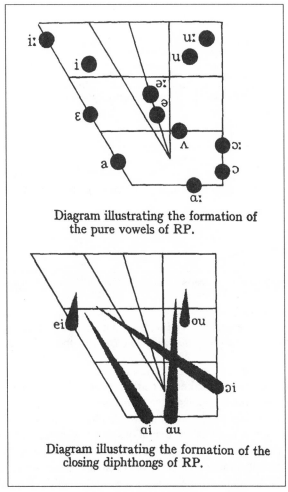

Diagram illustrating the formation of
the pure vowels of RP.

Diagram illustrating the formation of the
closing diphthongs of RP.

Figure 13.3. Vowel diagrams from the *Pronunciation of English*[3] (p. 23).

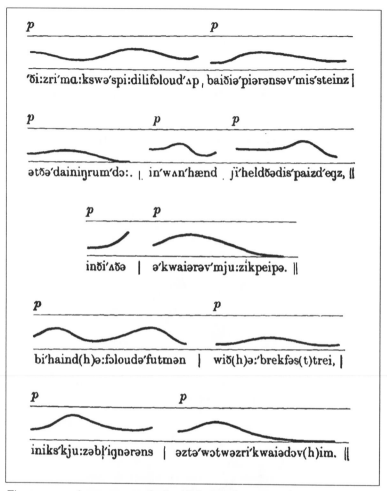

Figure 13.4. A passage marked with intonation curves in the intonation marking system of *Pronunciation of English*[1] (pp. 88–89).

in the shadow of the much better known *Outline*. Its reception may have suffered from Smith's (1952) harsh review published in *Language*. Smith berated Jones, rightly, for his avoidance of explicit phonemicisation in his phonetic texts, and for his lack of rigour and precision in many of the definitions and explanations of theoretical concepts. He also quite unfairly objected to Jones's treatment of intonation for failing to conform to American structuralist phonemic analysis, as set out in Trager—Smith (1951). Similarly, Smith denigrates Jones's presentation of the English diphthongal vowel system because structuralist units are not employed in the analysis. Now that structuralism can be viewed as merely one in a succession of linguistic paradigms, much of Smith's criticism seems arrogant and dated—but written, as it was, when the structuralists were at their zenith, the review was undoubtedly very damaging to Jones's reputation. It may also be that the linguistic world in the early 1950s was unwilling to accept anything which was a revision, no matter how drastic, of a work first written forty-one years previously.

As has been shown above, the content of the *Pronunciation of English*³ differs so completely from the *Pronunciation of English*¹ that it is fair to treat them as effectively different works. In fact, Jones would probably have done better to take the final step of scrapping the title (as he was later to do with the radical revision of the *Pronunciation of Russian*, see Section 13.15) so as to sever more completely the links with his outmoded first effort.

There are deficiencies in the *Pronunciation of English*³. It is regrettable that Jones did not go to others for advice on the samples of non-RP varieties. His decision not to introduce the phoneme concept at the beginning of the book—instead of merely as a tailpiece—is certainly odd. Furthermore, Jones should have gone further in embracing more completely Palmer's and Kingdon's views and adopted a more analytical view of intonation. Had he made these few changes to his last full statement on English pronunciation, its virtues of authoritative judgement, clear, concise presentation and abundant exemplification would have been even more evident.

13.11. Annus mirabilis

It is possible to regard the year 1956 as almost a minor "annus mirabilis" in Jones's life, since at an age when most people would be enjoying the leisure of retirement, he managed to produce no fewer than four revised books. It is perhaps no coincidence that this was Jones's seventy-fifth year and that he may have felt that he had to put his academic affairs in order before his death. The *Pronunciation of English*⁴ came out with significant revisions. David Abercrombie had been unhappy about the examples of Scottish English in the *Pronunciation of English*³, and Jones changed these to accord with Abercrombie's views, which are an anticipation of what was later to be known as Aitken's Law—also known as the Scottish vowel-length rule (Aitken 1962; Wells 1982: 400–401; 405–406). Abercrombie also supplied Jones with a new version of the Scottish English transcription passage. It is notable that Jones, unwisely, neglected to take any note of Smith's (1952) criticisms of the treatment of American English, as mentioned in Section 13.10, except to replace the ancient excerpt from the 1892 London *Daily Mail* with a piece of somewhat more up-to-date genuine American English from Sinclair Lewis's *Babbitt*.¹⁰ However, Jones did make revisions to the samples of Chaucerian and Shakespearean English—the latter being changed largely because of the criticisms in Kökeritz (1953: 50 and *passim*). In 1958, the fourth edition of the *Pronunciation of English* was reprinted once again with extra revisions in these areas, in particular to take account of the appearance of Dobson (1957a [1968]); see Section 14.15. Shortly after Jones's death, a "definitive edition" (subtitled as

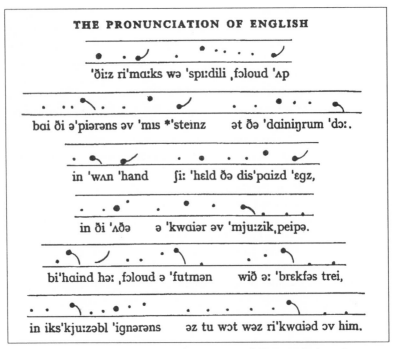

Figure 13.5. The intonation marking system of *Pronunciation of English*[3] (p. 186).

such) of the *Pronunciation of English* (1972) appeared, edited by A.C. Gimson, with a few corrections, but with no significant revision of the text.

The thirty-first edition of *Phonetic readings in English* bears the date 1955. However, it belongs in a sense to this group, since Jones appears to have regarded it as being a 1956 publication and it is stated to be such in the *Outline*[9] (pp. 368 and 379) and in Abercrombie et al. (1964: xi). *Phonetic readings in English* had been appearing in new editions but with relatively few changes since it first came out. Jones now to an extent updated it but retained the transcription system, without bringing in an explicitly phonemic framework. He also kept almost entirely to the same texts (though some of the more obvious archaisms were removed). However, as in the *Pronunciation of English*[3], he replaced the outdated "intonation curves" with an "Armstrong and Ward" type of marking system.

1956 also saw the new eighth edition of the *Outline*. This was the first time that the book had been completely in the hands of an English publisher; after years of co-operation, and despite two world wars, the Leipzig firm of Teubner amicably relinquished their interest in the book and handed over to Heffer of Cambridge, who had been printing editions for the home market for two decades.

As has been detailed in Chapter 8, Jones revised and rewrote the *Outline* very extensively for the [1932] third edition. The fourth edition [1934] contained only minor
revisions, and the fifth [1936] and sixth [1939] editions were virtually unchanged in
content. Only the seventh edition [1949] had seen a major addition in the form of a
section on American English, the first time that Jones had included more than a passing reference to any type of English other than RP.

For the *Outline*[8], a more thorough revision was needed, but nevertheless Jones preserved very largely the general form of the third edition, and even managed to retain
almost completely the original [1932] paragraph numbering. This he was able to
achieve not only by rewriting but also by employing numerous footnotes to accommodate the many "minor improvements ... too numerous to list ... to be found on most
pages" (p. vi). In addition, Jones wrote significant new sections on rising diphthongs
[ĭə ŭə ŭi] (pp. 118–125), derived largely from Jones (1954); and an extra chapter
XXXII on syllable division (pp. 327–330). The latter has, in part, its origins in his
earlier work on the word and junctural phenomena (Jones 1931k) and also relates to
his article on the use of the hyphen as a juncture marker, which was to appear later in
that year (Jones 1956d).

Furthermore, Jones rewrote and extended Appendix A, converting it into a short
treatise on the history of phonetic transcription together with a summary of his personal views (*Outline*[8]: 331–350); see also Section 14.9. Despite all these changes and
additions, the *Outline*[8] is still very much in spirit, and largely in content, as Jones
revised it in the 1930s. For the last edition, *Outline*[9] [1960], he made some further
changes, but none of significance; Jones himself dismissed this version, in a letter to
Dennis Ward, as "a new reprint (called a 9th edition)".[11]

The other major revision to appear in this fruitful year of 1956 was the eleventh
edition of the *EPD*. Jones had been working on this for several years, and his BBC
correspondence with Elizabeth Miller frequently refers to the progress of the "Dic.",
as Jones was wont to term it. About ninety thousand copies had been printed since
1937—a most successful sale for that era—and, in consequence, the plates were worn
and needed to be reset (p. vii). Jones took the opportunity to revise all the entries and
add many new words, bringing the total up to 58,000 (not counting inflected forms).
In this edition, he introduced the use of the hyphen as a means of indicating syllable
boundaries, following Jones (1956d), and employed the accent ˇ to indicate rising, as
opposed to falling, diphthongs, as discussed in Jones (1954). In essentials, the *EPD*
remained the same book as before, but there is no doubt that Jones invested a tremendous amount of work in what he probably considered would be the last revision of the
dictionary before he died.

In fact, the *EPD* was to undergo two more revisions in Jones's lifetime. The twelfth
edition undertaken together with A.C. Gimson appeared in 1963 and incorporated a
glossary of phonetic terms. In 1967, the *EPD*[13] appeared; this edition was produced
by Gimson working on his own, and saw rather more changes in symbolisations and
representations, the most obvious being the replacement of [ou] by [əu]. This was to
be the last version of the *EPD* that Jones himself would witness, and whilst Jones was

still alive, Gimson clearly had no inclination to make the sweeping alterations in transcription which were to be introduced in the [1977] fourteenth edition.

13.12. Shorter publications 1950–60

Jones also continued to produce important articles well into his seventies. "Falling and rising diphthongs in Southern English" (Jones 1954) deals with the problems of the prominence of the elements of English diphthongal vowels (particularly those terminating in [ə] such as /ɪə/ and /ʊə/) and the symbolisation needed to indicate this accurately. The article is indicative of Jones's preoccupation at this point with the deficiencies of conventional segmental phonemic transcription. A similar concern can be seen to be behind "The hyphen as a phonetic sign" (Jones 1956d), in which Jones developed further the ideas on syllable division which he had first propagated in "The word as a phonetic entity" (Jones 1931k). As has been stated, both of the 1950s theoretical articles had immediate practical application, in that the hyphen and the diacritic to mark the less prominent element of rising diphthongs were shown in the *EPD*¹¹ [1956].¹²

The most significant of the shorter publications of Jones's latter years was without doubt the IPA pamphlet *History and meaning of the term "phoneme"* (Jones 1957a, previously and henceforth *HMTP*). This gives Jones's view of the development of the idea of the phoneme, which he traces back to the fifteenth century Korean monarch Se-Jong. The origins of the word phoneme itself is noted by Jones as beginning with Mikołaj Kruszewski and Baudouin de Courtenay of the Kazan' School (see Section 14.16). He goes on to provide an overview of the work of the Prague School and the American structuralists in the 1930s and 1940s. In this publication, Jones was able to outline his own part in the popularisation of the phoneme concept, and the role of his immediate colleagues, such as Douglas M. Beach, in the spread of the term in Western European linguistic circles. He was also able to demonstrate (in a restrained way) that in Britain the employment of phonemic principles, and the recognition of their importance, antedated by many years—more than a decade—the interest in phonemics which characterised American linguistic writing in the thirties. *HMTP* was to become one of the most widely referred to and quoted of all Jones's works. It was later incorporated as an appendix into the last edition of the *Phoneme* [1967].

Apart from the above major articles, Jones also produced a number of minor works. In 1952, he wrote a long personal letter to C.M. Wise in response to a review of the *Pronunciation of English*³ which had appeared in the *Southern Speech Journal*. Wise decided to submit the contents for publication since "the letter contains so much valuable historical material, largely unknown to phoneticians, particularly in America".¹³ In his letter, Jones surveys the use of various means of transcribing the vowel system of English as represented in articles written in *Le Maître phonétique*. He also summarises his own changes of view on the value of broad and narrow systems of transcription, and the use he had made of these in his teaching and writing (Jones 1952b). Wise made the suggestion, in an open letter to the editor to the *Southern Speech Journal*, that Jones should write a monograph on the history of the IPA and its alphabet since "no one else could bring so much intimate knowledge and experience to bear on the subject".[14] Unfortunately, Jones never responded to this idea. Although another writer, Albright (1953), shortly afterwards produced a historiographical work on these lines, this lacked the authority which Jones would have brought to the task.

As he passed into old age, Jones was outliving many of his friends and former colleagues. He wrote the obituaries of the following: Simon Boyanus (Jones 1952a); H.J. Uldall (Jones 1957b) and, in co-operation with Marguerite Chapallaz, Amerindo Camilli (Jones—Chapallaz 1960). He also produced a brief life of Arthur Lloyd James, which appeared in the *Dictionary of national biography* (Jones 1958); although necessarily factual and concise, nevertheless Jones's sympathetic regard for his former colleague, and his distress at the manner of his death, is plain. Obituary notices form a considerable part of Jones's writing at this time. These, together with his articles on the "London School", and the development of the phoneme concept (*HMTP*), constitute Jones's major contribution to the historiography of phonetics.

Other minor articles include "Report on the Koreanisation of foreign words" (Jones—Skillend 1957d), and the article on "Phonetics" in *Chambers' Encyclopaedia* (Jones 1955). The latter, although containing no information which cannot be found elsewhere, is nevertheless a strikingly good example of Jones's ability to explain his subject lucidly and concisely to a lay audience.

Jones at this time also became remarkably active in recording and broadcasting studios, producing a considerable amount of audio material. He wrote a short booklet "Cardinal vowels" (Jones 1956a) to accompany his recordings of the Cardinal Vowels which appeared in that year.[15] This was the most elaborate version he had yet attempted, and included all the secondary vowels, with each one demonstrated on rising and falling pitch patterns. It is unfortunate that the uncertain, quavery voice quality reveals that Jones was suffering from studio nerves—perhaps forgivable in a man who was seventy-five when the recording was made. Nevertheless, for all its defects, it has become the reference version of the Cardinal Vowels and perhaps most phoneticians are unaware that two earlier recordings exist (see Section 7.3). Jones also produced several talks for the BBC (Jones 1957c); see also Section 12.9.

Jones's last significant piece of independent writing for a major journal (*Zeitschrift für Phonetik*) appeared in 1959—but in fact this was merely a reprint of "The use of syllabic and non-syllabic *l* and *n* in derivatives of English words ending in syllabic *l* and *n*" (Jones 1956c), which had already been published three years earlier in a Festschrift for Panconcelli-Calzia. It is a competent, if unexciting, treatment of English syllabic consonants, notable mainly for a large collection of examples, which are, as always with Jones, accurately observed.

13.13. The elder statesman of phonetics

One of the best-known examples of Jones's willingness to co-operate in phonetic research until late in his life was his help in the experiments set up by Peter Ladefoged in 1956 to estimate the validity of the Cardinal Vowel system. The work included the recording of sets of Cardinal Vowels by a number of professional phoneticians, and these were all scrutinised by Jones for authenticity. Ladefoged (1967: 51) observes: "It was an especially great privilege to be able to work with Professor Daniel Jones." Jones was undoubtedly pleased to hear that, although by no means infallible, his Cardinal Vowels, and the system of ear-training he had developed and propagated, appeared to emerge well from Ladefoged's research: "...the traditional rigorous training in the performance and use of known reference points remains essential for all who wish to make useful phonetic statements about vowel sounds" (Ladefoged 1967: 142). See, for further discussion, Section 14.8.

Throughout this final period of his life—indeed until shortly before his death— a steady flow of scholars and students sought Jones's advice on phonetic matters. He was noted right up to the end for his helpfulness and academic generosity to all comers. The surviving correspondence confirms his willingness to help fellow phoneticians and reveals his remarkable tolerance for the numerous cranks who wrote to him over the years. No matter how eccentric their views, or absurd their requests, all were answered courteously—sometimes with polite disagreement, or a firm refusal, but neither patronisingly, nor with irritation.

In professional terms, Jones had now assumed (rather like Sweet in his last years) the status of the "world's elder statesman of phonetics" as Pike later dubbed him (Abercrombie et al. 1964: 425). After the disappointment felt by many at the lack of new ideas in the *Phoneme*, few looked to him for fresh insights or innovative theories. However, he continued to be regarded as a final source of authority on the type of descriptive articulatory phonetics which he had made almost his own property. Thanks in part to the export of scholars from UCL to universities throughout the world, Jonesian phonetics now had, paradoxically, more adherents than ever—despite the imminent threats from instrumental approaches on the one hand and theoretical linguistics on the other. For even by 1960 many modern experimental techniques were only in a developmental stage, and the same held true for generative phonology.

So, in his last decade, Jones remained without rival as the most renowned of all living phoneticians. Eva Sivertsen (1968: 193) spoke for a multitude around the world when she claimed: "...he was very much alive to us as a legend and institution. Daniel Jones simply *was* phonetics to many of us."

13.14. Activities in last years

Jones, despite his ill-health, continued to be active professionally until his eightieth year, and beyond. His spate of publications in 1956 was followed by two recognitions of his academic achievements. He was made an honorary member of the Royal Irish Academy in 1957, and 1958 saw him visiting Edinburgh in order to receive an honorary doctorate. It must have been particularly pleasing to him to receive recognition of this kind from the University where a flourishing department of phonetics had recently been established by his former pupil David Abercrombie. Several of Abercrombie's staff had come to phonetics via UCL, and Edinburgh students (amongst others, Peter Ladefoged) were being encouraged to absorb the best aspects of Jones's approach to phonetics. Perhaps because of his lack of degrees, Jones set considerable store by these academic honours, and all were noted meticulously on the title pages of his later publications. He was, however, awarded no state honour from Britain, which, as Gimson (1968: 6) wrote, was "strange—and a matter of sorrow for his friends...it is true to say that he had greater fame in the world at large than in his own country".

In 1957, on January 22, Jones gave what was to be his final public university lecture (see Figure 13.6). Appropriately, it was held in the familiar surroundings of University College, in the Anatomy Theatre. A letter written to Dennis Ward reveals that the title, typically down-to-earth and Jonesian, was in fact not his own idea: "...I thought I would let you know that I am giving a public lecture at 5.30 at Univ. Coll. on 'Phonemes: what they are & what they do'—an expression which was suggested to me by you when you came here in the autumn."[16] Unfortunately, no record seems to exist of the content of Jones's last performance of this kind in public.

By this time, his visits to University College were getting to be very rare, and he took no interest in departmental business. Nor was he any longer very concerned with academic rivalries; even his long-standing feud with J.R. Firth seemed to peter out during retirement, though it perhaps only truly ended with Firth's death in 1960. Jones's final academic honour was the *Festschrift* (written to mark his eightieth birthday) entitled *In honour of Daniel Jones* (Abercrombie et al. 1964). It contained contributions from more than fifty distinguished colleagues from all over the world.

We have already noted that Jones also continued to be active in the sound studio until late in life, the last recording of the Cardinal Vowels being made when he was seventy-five. As detailed in Section 12.9, just before his eightieth birthday, Jones made his very last broadcast for the BBC, as part of a series which had been devoted to his life and work.[17]

In 1963, Jones was persuaded to take on an arduous recording session to produce new spoken texts for one of his most commercially successful books, *Phonetic readings in English.*[18] Gimson has revealed that Jones encountered considerable problems in the recording studio:

It was a very painful thing. I was with him when he did it at Decca studios. We rehearsed here [University College]. He sounded very muffled, mumbled and stumbled a lot, and so we had to edit them rather fiercely.[19]

Nevertheless, considering Jones's advanced age (he was eighty-two at the time) and his dislike of technical equipment, it could be considered remarkable that the recordings were ever made at all.

Even shortly after the grief of Olivier's unexpected death, Jones was still completing a vast amount of writing and rewriting—enough for a man many years younger. The spring of 1961 found him complaining about "masses of work before me—a revised edition of the *Phoneme*, a new supplement to my dictionary, etc, besides an incredible amount of correspondence".[20] Yet, in the following year, 1962, amazingly, he was obviously keen to resume the radical revision of the *Pronunciation of Russian* which

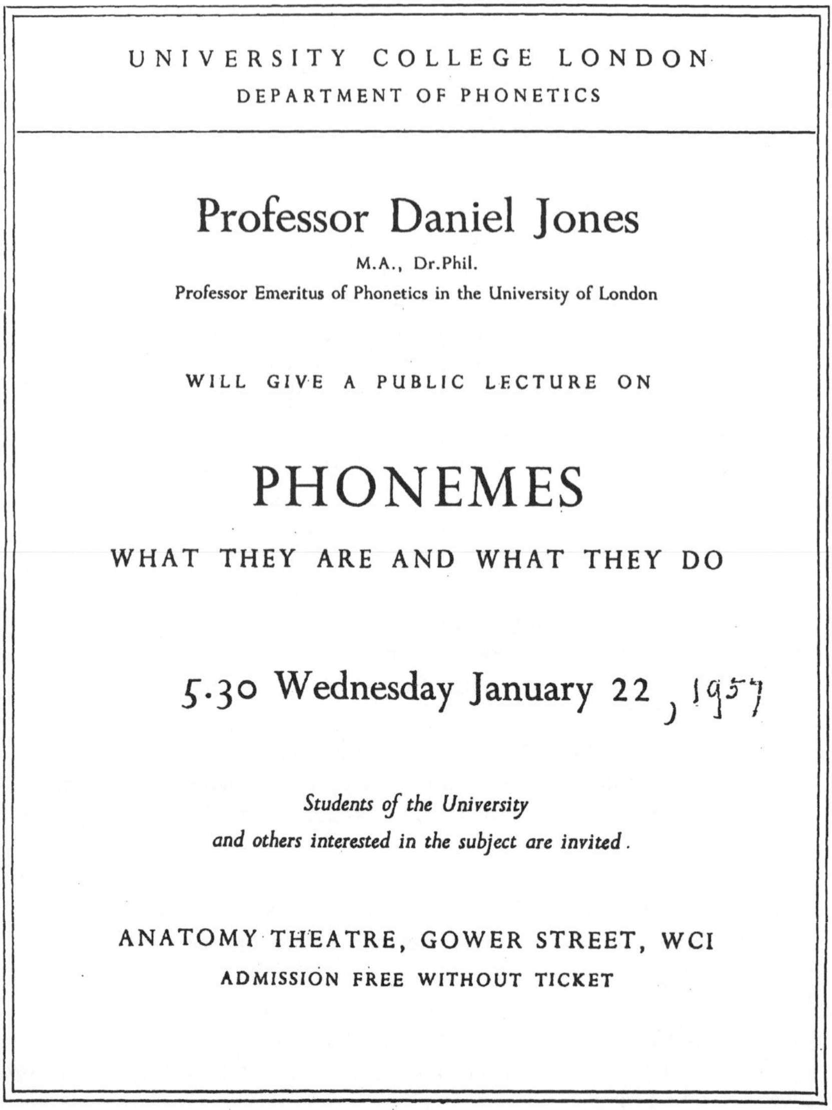

UNIVERSITY COLLEGE LONDON
DEPARTMENT OF PHONETICS

Professor Daniel Jones

M.A., Dr.Phil.
Professor Emeritus of Phonetics in the University of London

WILL GIVE A PUBLIC LECTURE ON

PHONEMES

WHAT THEY ARE AND WHAT THEY DO

5.30 Wednesday January 22, 1957

Students of the University
and others interested in the subject are invited.

ANATOMY THEATRE, GOWER STREET, WCI
ADMISSION FREE WITHOUT TICKET

Figure 13.6. A leaflet advertising Jones's last public lecture. Jones has added the year, 1957.

he had been engaged on together with Dennis Ward, and which eventually appeared after Jones's death, retitled *The phonetics of Russian*.

13.15. *The phonetics of Russian*

In reality, Jones, by his own admission, played only a minor part in the production of the *Phonetics of Russian* (Jones—Ward 1969). But this book is nevertheless interesting for the insight it provides on his methods of work. The contacts were almost entirely through letters; Ward acknowledges that he had very few face-to-face meetings with Jones in the fourteen years they collaborated on the task.[21] Thanks to the foresight of Ward, who carefully preserved not only Jones's correspondence, but also a manuscript in Jones's own writing, and numerous pages with his marginalia, far more pre-publication material for this book has survived than for all Jones's other published works put together.

The letters reveal that the idea of writing a revision of the *Pronunciation of Russian* came initially, in 1953, from Dennis Ward, then a young lecturer at the University of Edinburgh. Jones responded eagerly to Ward's suggestion:

> I was pleased to receive your letter. Pleased too with your proposal. I may say that the idea had also occurred to me when I saw you. I believe we could collaborate together well. What I need is someone who can fill in the gaps in my own knowledge, & it seems to me that you have just what is needed for this....We are not likely to get much in the way of royalties, if anything. But it will be a very worth while [sic] piece of work.[22]

From the start, Jones made it clear that "the lion's share of the work", as he put it, would fall on Ward.[23] Early on in their partnership, he indicated the main areas of the *Pronunciation of Russian* that he felt should be changed. He was concerned about deficiencies in the phonemic analysis, in particular, as mentioned in Section 10.5, the blunder he and Trofimov had made in the *Pronunciation of Russian* in mistakenly regarding [i] and [ɨ] as separate phonemes.[24] He wanted more information on intonation to be included in the new book and reminded Ward that not only should the orthography be modernised, but also that the old-fashioned type of Russian described in the *Pronunciation of Russian* should be replaced by a more up-to-date variety based on modern educated Moscow speech. The Jones-Ward correspondence indicates that the authors were in a quandary here about how far they should go in replacing traditional pronunciation with the spelling-influenced forms which had been adopted since the Revolution. Jones wrote:

> I am very glad to have your remarks on modern tendencies....Russian children are being *taught* to make a difference between unstressed i and e. What are we to do? To transcribe the pronunciation which is presumably still natural in Moscow (i.e.

unstressed **e** pronounced exactly like unstressed **i**), or to transcribe what is being taught in the expectation that it may some day become the regular thing? The case is, I suppose, comparable to the Southern English use of **i** in words like iks'pekt.[25]

The authors eventually decided to keep to the *ikanje* type of Russian (p. 27), this being the traditional Moscow-Leningrad prestige standard. Consequently, the *Phonetics of Russian* retains such conservatisms as the levellings of the unstressed vowels /iː/ and /e/ (pp. 44–46), as discussed in the above extract from Jones's correspondence, and equivocates on producing the conservative pronunciation of ⟨Щ⟩ as /ʃʃ/ rather than the more modern /ʃtʃ/. Nevertheless, despite their deliberations, it is this aspect of the book for which Akhmanova (1971: 298) took the authors to task, claiming that although their treatment did fittingly describe her own idiolect, and the speech of her contemporaries, as far as the younger generation was concerned, this variety was already "ancient history", characteristic of "the outgoing generation of 'intelligentsia' Moscovites".

After the early years, when he dispatched letters regularly full of ideas and suggestions, a noticeable change came about in Jones's attitude, and he began to put off reading Ward's work. This was the period when he had taken on some of the heaviest commitments of his career, and he was in the throes of preparing for all the revisions of his books which would appear in 1956. This extract from a letter is typical of many he was to write to Ward over a period of about six years:

> I'm quite excited to know that you have got a large batch of MS nearly ready. I fear it will be still quite a time before I shall be able to attend to it. I simply must get at least one of these other books off my hands first—there are 4 of them! And the work has been taking me a good deal longer than I expected.[26]

Ironically, once he had shifted the burden of work, Jones did not actually feel better able to cope, but instead seems to have been dragged down into a state of mental exhaustion:

> At the moment I am rather badly under the weather—seems to be a sort of reaction after completing the Dictionary—and am having to go very slow. It may be some little time before I can muster up enough energy to tackle your MSS. But I have confidence in your work....[27]

Ward was left to carry on more or less alone, and for a time the letters that came from Jones's side contained little except for encouragement and constant promises to read the manuscript when he was free of his other obligations.

Jones had sincerely believed that Cambridge would be willing to publish the *Phonetics of Russian*. It obviously came as a disappointment for him (but doubtless even more of one for Ward, who had put so much more work into the revision) to hear that Cambridge had decided to turn the project down, because "they had already on their hands too many books that will be published at a loss".[28] At the time, Russian was very much a fringe subject in Britain, hardly taught at all in schools and only in a very few universities. Ward then went to Edinburgh University Press, who also rejected the book—a frustration which Jones appeared to have accepted with resignation.

...I'm not particularly surprised, nor worried, by the fact that Ed[inburgh] U.P. won't take it on. Set-backs like that are to be expected with a book that obviously is not likely to pay its way.[29]

Ward continued with the task of rewriting, still receiving scant assistance, apart from encouragement and promises, from Jones.

But by the 1960s, the educational climate had changed and Russian suddenly became a focus of attention. Schools started appointing teachers in the subject. There was a shortage of suitably qualified candidates, and graduates in less fashionable languages, like French and German, attended accelerated conversion courses of training to teach Russian. The wave of interest was to last only for about ten years, but it was quite powerful enough for Cambridge to reconsider their position.[30] Yet before the *Phonetics of Russian*, as Jones and Ward had now decided that the book should be called (see Figure 13.7),[31] could be given the go-ahead, Cambridge University Press still had to be convinced that Daniel Jones, at eighty-one, was capable of making his contribution. John Trim, another former Jones pupil, then in charge of phonetics at Cambridge University, was able to reassure them that the problem was only one of finding sufficient space in Jones's crammed work schedule: "Professor Jones is still quite up to doing the job, if he has time to do it with his other commitments."[32]

From this point on, Jones worked on the book with amazing energy for a man of his years. Part I of the *Phonetics of Russian* (called "Phonetic theory and Transcription", pp. 3–23) is a considerably improved and compressed version of the corresponding sections in the *Pronunciation of Russian* (pp. 1–49). It covers with precision and clarity the basic introductory material, dealing with matters such as the organs of speech, phonation, and the description and classification of vowels and consonants, before going on to discuss briskly the principles of transcription and basic phoneme theory. That this portion is almost entirely Jones's effort is confirmed by the surviving original manuscript in his own hand.

The remainder of the book was all written by Ward and then submitted to Jones for his comments, suggestions and revisions. This far larger second part (pp. 27–247) is entitled "The Phonetics of Russian", and covers in detail the Russian vowels and consonants, assimilation, accent, stress and length, and intonation, all of which are very much altered from the corresponding chapters in the 1923 version. Ward makes it clear (p. ix) that many portions of Part II were not even seen by Jones, adding: "Any faults which the reader finds there should be laid at my door." In fact, Jones himself felt that his overall contribution was so small that this should be indicated on the title page by reversing the order of names—although this idea was eventually abandoned.[33]

It had already been decided to eliminate mention of the other original author: "There is no question of bringing in Trofimov's name. He died many years ago..."[34]

The book is rounded off with two appendices, covering ear-training and relationships between sounds and orthography. The ear-training material is taken over almost in entirety from Chapter XXIII of the *Pronunciation of Russian*, albeit with numerous changes in the examples to conform to Ward's revision of the vowel and consonant descriptions. Appendix 2, "Remarks on Russian orthography" (pp. 287–288), is vastly different from the corresponding section in the *Pronunciation of Russian* (Appendix I, pp. 210–228), and appears to owe virtually nothing to Jones.

One matter in which the *Phonetics of Russian* differed radically from the *Pronunciation of Russian* was in the use of Russian orthography. Instead of being excluded from the main text, as in the earlier book, Cyrillic script is only absent from Part I (except for a solitary instance on p. 22). Russian orthography is introduced early in Part II and then used consistently throughout. Jones commented guiltily in a letter to Ward on his own baffling limitations in this area:

I'm afraid I have been very remiss in never having learnt the Russian letters. When I started working with Trofimov, I decided not to learn them for fear that knowledge of Russian spelling might prejudice my aural observation. This turned out in the end to be a very bad plan.[35]

In fact, Ward himself has confirmed that Jones had no practical competence at all in the language: "He said he didn't know any Russian and I think that was perfectly true."[36] One letter discloses that when he was presented with a book by a Soviet academic (who not unnaturally assumed from Daniel Jones's writings that the latter was fluent in Russian), Jones was forced to ask Ward to come to his aid:

...what is it about? It looks like a treatise on English stress & intonation. A copy has been sent to me by the author with an inscription which I can't read.[37]

Jones's lack of any conventional grounding in Russian makes it all the more surprising that—as his letters clearly show—he had, with the aid of transcription, an amazingly good grasp of the finer points of the spoken language. His phonetic abilities in Russian doubtless matched those he achieved in languages like Cantonese, Sinhalese, Tswana, and others, which he managed to imitate with ease, and describe or analyse with assurance, even though he actually understood scarcely more than a few words.

The *Phonetics of Russian* is a remarkably pleasing book in visual terms and is also notable for its straightforward lucid presentation. Jones has left his imprint not only on the "admirably clear illustrations" (many of these were in fact taken directly from the *Pronunciation of Russian* with little or no modification) but also on the "mass of examples, the skilful use of type, and the attractive literary style", to quote Drage's (1972: 476) judgements. Akhmanova (1971: 298–300) also commends the "clarity of exposition" and comments that "at an age when the linguistic scene is suffused with

THE PHONETICS OF RUSSIAN

THE LATE
DANIEL JONES

Formerly Professor of Phonetics
University of London

AND

DENNIS WARD

Professor of Russian
University of Edinburgh

CAMBRIDGE
AT THE UNIVERSITY PRESS
1969

Figure 13.7. Title page of *The phonetics of Russian.*

vague and impracticable theories, one is happy to welcome the publication of a manual so competent, reliable and solid, so beautifully and carefully done".

Jones continued to play his part in the rewriting of the book, acting in a kind of supervisory role up to 1965 when he was at last forced to tell Ward that "for reasons of health, it will not be possible for me to do much more in the way of revising 'The Phonetics of Russian' ".[38] Yet, Ward and he continued to correspond on proof correction until only a few months before Jones's death. The last of these letters, written only a few months before he died, shows that despite a quavering hand, his sharpness of mind and perfectionist regard for detail, like his superb powers of sound recognition and performance, were with him until close to the end (see Figure 13.8):

> It seems to me that it [the proof] needs modifying in many respects. E.g. all the i and j ought to have high dots, thus i̇ j̇. And there are no doubt many errors which only you are competent to correct…. Please correct them & return them to me….[39]

13.16. Death

Yet, by this time, Jones's long life was inexorably coming to its close. He was bedridden for the last few months of his final illness and it was necessary for him to receive injections to relieve his pain. He remained at his home, in the care of his wife,[40] relatives and close friends, attended by a resident nursing help who lived with the Jones family for some time.[41]

Daniel Jones died on December 4th, 1967 (see Figure 13.9)—co-incidentally on the same day of the year as his father. One of his last requests was for a photograph of his son Olivier, to be placed near him. The funeral, on a bleak December day, was a private affair, attended only by a very few close members of his family, but in the following days and weeks, messages of condolence soon arrived at Gerrards Cross sent by colleges, universities, scholars and ex-pupils from all over the world. Obituaries appeared in due course in the leading linguistic journals. Not surprisingly, all are laudatory in discussing the outstanding nature of Jones's achievements in phonetics. Yet it is also notable that virtually every writer underlines the essential goodness and kindliness of Jones's character, which appeared to make an impression on everyone and remain in the memories of all who knew him personally. Few famous academics can have died as did Jones, having no apparent enemies and with so many of his colleagues holding him in high regard.

Apart from Jones's worth as a scholar, which will be examined in Chapter 14, it is perhaps fitting again at this point to note these more personal aspects. In the course of research on Jones's life, it was found that everyone who had actually met Jones remembered him for his modesty and sincerity. They stressed his helpfulness, his willingness to advise and spend time in providing guidance. Many could quote instances of how he had assisted them at some time in their careers. All were agreed on his dedication to phonetics and his determination to further its ends. But these were only facets of Jones's wider desire to do work which would be for the general good of humanity. A "gentle man of great integrity and rare singleness of purpose" was how Gimson (1968: 6) described him. And another of Jones's former students, S.K. Chatterji ([1981]: 25), wrote at the time of his death:

Scholars and Scientists there have been in plenty. But it is something which is a matter of special congratulation for mankind when we have a combination of a good man in his heart and in his inner spiritual aspirations who is at the same time

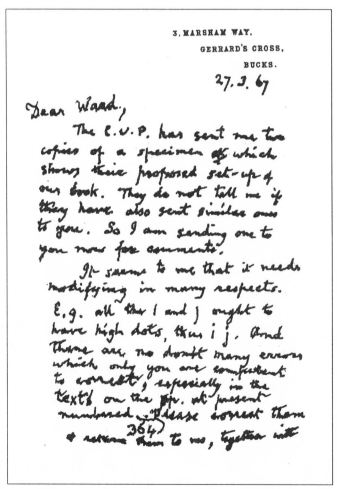

Figure 13.8. Extract from letter to D. Ward, written in Jones's last year.

JONES.—On December 4th, 1967, pecefully, at home in his 87th year, DANIEL JONES, M.A. (Cambridge), Dr.Phil. h.c. (Zurich), Hon. LL.D. (Edinburgh), Professor Emeritus of Phonetics in the University of London. Cremation private. No flowers, please, but if wished donations to Phonetics Dept. (addressed to Professor A. C. Gimson), University College, Gower Street, London, W.C.1.

Figure 13.9. The death notice in *The Times* (p. 18, December 6, 1967). ironically, considering Jones's well-founded reputation for accurate proofreading, a striking error crept in, namely the misspelling of "peacefully".

a great master of a particular branch of learning or science. Such a rare combination we had in the personality of Professor Daniel Jones.

Chapter 14

Jones's contribution to phonetics and linguistics

14.1. Introduction

In assessing Jones's contribution to phonetics, it is convenient to distinguish the following major divisions.

1. The organisational contribution (Sections 14.2–14.4).
2. The practical contribution (Sections 14.5–14.9).
3. The theoretical contribution (Sections 14.10–14.17).

Jones is remembered today by those who knew him as a mild-mannered, self-effacing individual devoted to his field of scholarship, and this is confirmed by published biographical record—for instance, Fischer-Jørgensen (1981: 68) recalls him in the last years of his professional life as "a quiet, reserved, polite and frail old English gentleman". Although Jones undoubtedly did have much of the introvert scholar in his mentality, and this was perhaps accentuated in his later years, yet he also had another striking aspect to his personality.

As noted in the previous chapter, Gimson (1968: 6) emphasised Jones's "rare singleness of purpose", and in the early period of his career, it is this trait which is predominant. At the outset of his professional life, Jones showed a determination to achieve his ambitions for himself and for phonetics, together with an obvious talent for management and organisation, and an ability to develop profitable relationships with his colleagues. This aspect of his character, though it diminished with the years, never entirely left him. Nor did his capacity for hard academic work abate, and right up to the last year of his life, he remained determined in his efforts to see projects through once they were embarked upon (see Section 13.14).

14.2. Establishing and running the University College Department

Perhaps the most significant organisational contribution from Jones was the founding of the first department of phonetics in Britain at University College, London. Though Jones was not the first person to teach phonetics in a British university—as we have seen, Alexander Melville Bell and Henry Sweet were two distinguished predecessors (see A.3, 2.5 and 2.9)—he was the first to establish and organise a department. Bell functioned as little more than a night-school instructor, whilst Sweet had fatal flaws in his personality which precluded any chance of his being allowed to establish a power base at Oxford. Jones, it could be argued, was lucky in arriving at UCL at a good moment. Nevertheless, he made the best use of all his good fortune, and expanded phonetics from a few tenuous part-time hours of teaching to a full department within five years. Thereafter, Jones was not only producing his own work but also encouraging, guiding and stimulating the efforts of others—and showing great talent and perception in this role. A rapid build-up of staff in the years leading up to 1920 ensured that the scene had been set for the remarkable output of research and publications within a Jonesian framework that was to emerge from UCL during the inter-war years. Many of these works are considered today to be classics in their field, and are still quoted as authoritative.

By 1921, when Jones obtained his chair, the UCL Phonetics Department had become recognised as a centre of excellence—at this time the most famous in the world. Furthermore, by these achievements, Jones did far more, since he obtained respectability and status for phonetics as an academic discipline. And it was Jones who first saw the need to found a phonetics laboratory in the United Kingdom, thus making up a little of the leeway between Britain and the rest of the world in experimental work. In addition, thanks to Jones's efforts, other phonetics departments were established, firstly at the School of Oriental Studies and, much later, in the post-Second World War period, at Edinburgh, Leeds and elsewhere.

Jones continued where Sweet had left off and speeded up what Sweet had started. It was Jones who accelerated the process of transforming phonetics in Britain from being an adjunct to philology pursued by a handful of individuals to being an important discipline, represented by numerous university departments, studied by a body of dedicated researchers and with a large corpus of published work. In so doing, he also eased the way for the later acceptance of linguistics as an academic study. All this might have occurred earlier had Sweet been of a more equable and accommodating temperament and consequently managed to make fewer enemies for himself in the scholarly world. Probably phonetics would have been established in British universities in due course even without the efforts of Jones; but it would have occurred later, and the development of the science in the United Kingdom would inevitably have followed a different pattern.

Jones may perhaps be criticised in one important respect. Once the UCL Department was established, he appears to have made no attempt to set up anything in the way of degree courses in phonetics or linguistics for undergraduate students leading to BA qualifications. This meant that the work of the UCL Department was always somewhat lacking in balance. There were numerous part-timers taking certificate courses for a few hours each week, and a large number of students coming in from other departments for phonetic training. Simultaneously, another, much smaller, body of students of post-graduate level were preparing for doctorates or master's degrees by thesis; but there was nothing in between the two. The lack of undergraduate courses meant also that the Department was rather an oddity and was therefore less likely to be taken seriously in the machinery of college administration. This did not matter as long as a supportive force was present in the form of Gregory Foster, but once he was replaced as Provost by the less amenable Allen Mawer, Jones's Department ceased to expand.

Whether it would in fact have been possible to set up phonetics or linguistics undergraduate courses before 1950 is debatable—but Jones did not press the issue. Abercrombie (1980: 7) has summed up the problems facing the discipline in Britain:

Another problem was that general phonetics was not considered to be a possible undergraduate subject (neither was linguistics). The greater part of academic phoneticians' time in those days was occupied with pronunciation teaching; the subject was almost entirely an ancillary one. A phonetics department, for the most part, was a service department to the modern language departments. "Pure", as opposed to "applied", phonetics was only taught at the postgraduate level, and then hardly ever in formally organised courses.

Abercrombie's personal ambition was "to try to make phonetics not only a *normal* subject, but also an undergraduate subject comparable in status to other undergraduate subjects"—something which Abercrombie eventually achieved at Edinburgh but which Jones never pressed for at UCL. The reason for his lack of dynamism in this area is undoubtedly in part owing to the suspicion that the academic world had for the novelty of phonetics and linguistics. But it is also probably rooted in Jones's breakdown in the early twenties and, crucially, with his disappointments over the scheme for a Phonetics Institute (see Section 9.3).

It is interesting to speculate on what might have happened had Jones been able to realise his visionary ideas for a major centre devoted to phonetic research and teaching. His error here was to have been ahead of his time. Such an institution, with a figure of Jones's reputation and abilities in charge, at the head of his unusually talented staff, might indeed have placed Britain in a position to lead linguistic research on an international scale in the inter-war period and possibly beyond. It is also possible that, had he reacted differently, Jones might have salvaged something from his disappointments—and this could perhaps have taken the form of a more stable base of undergraduate teaching.

14.3. The International Phonetic Association

When he was in his twenties, starting his career and making his first contacts with the phonetic world through Passy, Daniel Jones quickly revealed his remarkable industry and showed his capacities as a good organiser and an intelligent manager. These facets of his character were clearly demonstrated in his enthusiastic work for the International Phonetic Association in the years between 1906 and 1914 (Sections 2.6, 2.8, 3.10, 5.6).

Though Passy had laid the foundations, it was in large measure thanks to Jones's contribution that the membership of the IPA grew and *Le Maître phonétique* flourished. It was also because of Jones's efforts that the IPA gained a position of eminence in the world of linguistic scholarship. The First World War brought all this to a halt. Once peace came, Passy was more interested in other matters, namely his Christian Socialist commune Liéfra. It fell to Jones to restart the journal in the twenties, and build up the IPA into a going concern once more.

Jones can be criticised for certain failures. It would obviously have been better for the later success and influence of *Le Maître phonétique* if it had been converted to conventional orthography (ironically, Jones had early on been an advocate of articles in conventional orthography, see 5.7). Abercrombie (1980: 7) pithily summarises part of the problem:

> Another eccentricity was that articles in the subject's chief journal were printed in phonetic transcription, so that most people could not read them, and even those who could usually did not want to.

However, there was more to it than that. Setting a journal in phonetic type was time-consuming and costly. Scholars, particularly those outside the British school, neither wanted to take the trouble of transcribing nor welcomed having their transcriptions subjected to editorial scrutiny. Even Jones himself finally took to publishing his longer post-1940 articles in other journals—perhaps to avoid the same problem. The result was that *Le Maître phonétique*, being both a bother to read and a bother to write, never regained the position it had once held as the major organ for the exchange of views and opinions on phonetic matters. Increasingly, it came to be regarded as an oddity amongst academic journals.

Furthermore, in the first post-war version of the *Principles* (IPA 1949), Jones should have taken account of developments in phoneme theory. Since Jones's retirement, no revision of the *Principles* has appeared, although portions of a new *IPA Handbook* are printed regularly in the Association's journal.[1] Yet, despite these omissions, Jones's work for the Association was decisive in securing the predominance of the IPA alphabet world-wide (apart from the USA, see Section 14.9). It is also undoubtedly owing to the existence of the IPA that phonetics today has a widely recognised terminology, essentially derived from the tradition of Passy and Jones which was chiefly disseminated during the years when Jones flourished.

14.4. Other organisational activities

Jones was involved with several other activities with a large organisational or administrative component: work for the Simplified Spelling Society; his advisory function for the BBC; and, importantly, the establishment and running of vacation courses. Originally, Jones began short courses on an ad hoc basis as demand arose from groups of students such as missionaries and teachers in training (see Sections 5.8 and 10.3), but from 1915 onwards, the Easter and summer vacation courses became a regular feature of University College academic life. They were successful both with students and staff, the latter being glad of the chance to supplement their low salaries. Indeed, a major impetus for starting and expanding the courses was undoubtedly financial.

However, the vacation courses were eventually to play a valuable role in a wider sense. They were a means of bringing applied phonetics and linguistics to a far greater audience than would be reached by the normal means of university departmental teaching and academic publication. These courses popularised Jones's applied phonetic methods of pronunciation instruction among young language teachers in Britain and throughout Europe. Over the years, attendance at Jones's summer schools provided thousands of students with an introduction to twentieth-century phonetic and linguistic ideas. This would prove to be their initial contact with views of language acquisition which departed from the boredom of traditional translation-based approaches to language acquisition. For many participants, it fired an interest in the subject, which a good number managed to pass on to their pupils. Applied phonetics could be seen to be of real assistance in removing pronunciation difficulties and also in suggesting techniques which could be used in classroom teaching.

Of course, Jones did not invent the concept of vacation courses for language training—the idea was well established throughout Europe by the turn of the century. Jones had attended Tilly's inspiring courses at Marburg, which in their intensive content may have suggested much of what he was later to introduce into his own. He had also gained valuable experience at Edinburgh with the courses organised by John Kirkpatrick (see Section 2.10). The University College courses, because of their excellently devised programmes, the enthusiasm and talent of the staff, and the efficiency of their organisation, became models of their kind. Whilst many other educational institutions held summer schools which flourished for a brief period and were subsequently abandoned, those set up by Jones survived, and over the years educated generations of students. Indeed, one—the UCL Summer School in English Phonetics—is still thriving to this day.

14.5. Description and teaching of English

In any assessment of Jones's practical contribution to scholarship, pride of place must go to three major publications which together form his description of English pronunciation, namely the *Pronunciation of English*, the *Outline* and the *EPD*, which have, since their appearance, "served as indispensable source-books for every English language teacher" (Howatt 1984: 214).

The *Pronunciation of English*[1] was the first of these to appear, in 1909, and its importance is in great part derived from the fact that it is the earliest of Jones's major books. The *Pronunciation of English*[1] contains much which is oversimplified or inaccurate—and Jones was eventually ashamed of it himself (Section 3.4). But nevertheless, the *Pronunciation of English*[1] provided a brief, elementary description of English which was much needed at the time. To quote Burchfield (1986: 141–142): "He set down all that he concluded one needed to know about English speech sounds...in sixty-nine pages, with the utmost clarity." Because of its brevity, and simple pragmatic approach, the *Pronunciation of English* was in most ways more accessible to the non-specialist than the technically superior works of Sweet. The revised edition (*Pronunciation of English*³ [1950]) provided a much tighter, and linguistically competent description, though by this time there was no chance of the *Pronunciation of English* making any great impact, simply because the *Outline* was by then so well established as the standard description of modern British English pronunciation.

The importance of the *EPD*, "undoubtedly the major work on the pronunciation of the prestige form of British English" (Ladefoged 1975: 63), is difficult to overestimate. Not since Walker (1791) had any significant English pronunciation dictionary been published in Britain. Because of the awkwardness and unreliability of the *Oxford English dictionary* as far as pronunciation was concerned, this meant that the *EPD* provided the first easily accessible, scholarly record of educated British English pronunciation. Jones was also in large part responsible for the now generally forgotten pronouncing dictionary which had preceded the *EPD*—namely the *Phonetic dictionary*, which appeared in 1914. But this last, though important as a pioneering work, was effectively impossible for the non-specialist to use because of the difficulties posed by its arrangement and organisation (see Section 5.3).

The *EPD* was a landmark in English lexicography and the history of the description of the English language. It took the place of the Oxford dictionary as a final authority on the pronunciation of English words, and until 1990 it appeared unassailable. With the publication of the more up-to-date and comprehensive *Longman Pronunciation Dictionary* (Wells 1990), it was at last robbed of its unique position. Nevertheless, the *EPD* is still a famous and highly regarded publication, even now over eighty years after its first appearance. It is therefore all the more remarkable that the *EPD* was originally, and in all its revisions up to 1963, entirely the labour of one man, working on his own, without the aid of computers or any of the other modern apparatus of dictionary compilation.

As in the case of the *Pronunciation of English*, Jones ensured that his dictionary was easy to use and understand. Burchfield (1986: 142) has commented:

> Both [*Pronunciation of English* and *EPD*] were books that the general public, or the university student, could turn to with the certainty that one could find an uncomplicated answer to what one was looking for.

In view of the fact that Jones came under attack early in his career for his stand against the prescriptivist views of Robert Bridges and his associates (see Section 4.11), it is ironical that he should posthumously be criticised for allegedly pushing prescriptivist views of language, and attempting to impose a standard of his own creation on an unsuspecting public. Crowley (1989: 164–174), in his survey of the rise of standard English, devotes considerable space to a discussion of Jones's work, arriving at the judgement that there is "no doubt that [it is] prescriptive in its intent" (p. 165). In what is effectively a polemic, Crowley seeks to justify these views by means of selective quotation, largely from Jones's earliest works.

Crowley (1989: 169–170) cites Jones's introduction to the first edition of the *EPD* (p. viii): "The pronunciation used [*recte* represented] in this book is that most usually heard in everyday speech in the families of Southern English persons whose men-folk have been educated at the great public boarding-schools", and states that Jones "reveals a clear geographic, gender-specific and class-specific basis". This accusation is hardly fair to Jones, when in the context of his own time he was regarded as being, if anything, dangerously libertarian in his approach to pronunciation standards. Admittedly, at the outset of his career (as has been shown in Section 3.4), Jones took on the traditional prescriptive attitudes associated with elocution and its practitioners, possibly reflecting a need to find himself courses to teach and a market for his publications. However, what becomes evident from any thorough reading of his subsequent work is that the elocutionary approach was quickly abandoned, and that it formed no part of Jones's later concept of the role of phonetics and the phonetician. Jones was eventually ashamed of the prescriptivism of his earliest efforts; by 1917, when he produced his *EPD*, his attitude had altered fundamentally and this changed outlook was not only maintained but was reinforced throughout the rest of his professional career. He proclaimed himself to be, in his memorable phrase, a "living phonograph" (*EPD*[1]: ix) —that is, an objective observer of language who had no intention of correcting the speech habits of English native speakers, or of attempting to apply aesthetic judgements in any form to language. He later stated (*EPD*[3] [1926]: ix):

...I do not claim that RP is intrinsically "better" or more "beautiful" than any other form of pronunciation.... I wish to state that I have no intention of becoming either a reformer of pronunciation or a judge who decides what pronunciations are "good" and what are "bad"... I would add that I am not one of those who believe in the feasibility of imposing one particular form of pronunciation on the English-speaking world. If the public wants a standard pronunciation, I believe that a standard will evolve itself without any interference by phoneticians. If there are any who do not share this view, it must be left to them to undertake the invidious task of deciding what is to be approved and what is to be condemned.

Jones did indeed base his pronunciation model on social and (to an extent) geographical parameters; but after all, his main aims were to cater for the teaching of English to foreigners, and it was hardly possible for him to exclude regional and social considerations if he was trying to find a variety of English which was easily intelligible to large numbers of people worldwide. No-one would have treated him seriously—either then or today—had he attempted to teach foreigners the English of, say, working-class Bristolians; not because Bristol English is not a perfectly valid language variety within its own geographical area, but because it lacks any wider currency.

Yet there is no evidence whatsoever of any gender bias in Jones's attitudes. His use of the phrase "families of Southern English persons whose men-folk" in the above definition appears to be designed to get around the fact that his chosen standard ("Public School Pronunciation") would otherwise have effectively excluded much female speech. At the time, public school education was the norm for upper-middle class boys, but girls were still frequently taught at home by governesses. So Jones was not actually attempting to *exclude* women from this definition; in fact, the reverse is true, and it is certainly quite unreasonable to accuse him on this account of sexist attitudes. (It may be noted, incidentally, that in his professional life, Jones set himself firmly against sexism in a very practical way by flooding his Department with female colleagues at a time when women formed a minuscule minority of university academic staff.) In the [1926] third edition of the *EPD*, when defending his definition of what he now terms RP (still based on attendance at public school), Jones explicitly alters it to include women, saying "similar considerations apply to the modern boarding-schools for girls" (p. viii).

Crowley eventually admits towards the end of his peroration that Jones does not fit the role of prescriptivist that he is being forced into. Quoting Sweet's (1890a: 3) view that "it is absurd to set up a standard of how English people *ought* to speak, before we know how they actually *do* speak", Crowley says "the curious and contradictory thing is that Jones agreed with this assertion" (p. 173). Crowley is finally compelled to fall back on a weaker form of his argument, distinguishing (p. 174) between Jones's "conscious intentions" and the results which he achieved: "His intent may have been otherwise, but the effect of Jones's work was both prescriptive and proscriptive."

In reality, the status of a prestige model of British English pronunciation had been established many years before Jones's time—at least as long ago as the early nineteenth century, as is testified by the work of Melville Bell, Pitman and Ellis. As mentioned in Section 7.2, Ellis appears to have been the first linguist to use the phrase "received pronunciation" in print (recall that in Victorian English "received" commonly implied "socially accepted"). The concept of Received Pronunciation, although not the term, is also implicit throughout the work of Henry Sweet. All Jones did was to restate and clarify concepts which already existed and to revive a label which caught on amongst linguists.

The actual reinforcement of RP as a model in Britain unquestionably came from its use on BBC radio, where it was employed by most participants and was required of all announcers (see Mugglestone 1995: 323–328). Possibly, to a limited extent, the cinema also played a role; in pre-1960 British films and newsreels, a marked variety of RP is pervasive, often amusingly so. Jones might have been flattered by the suggestion that he foisted his ideas of standard pronunciation on the British populace; he would certainly have been realistic enough to know that such allegations were unfounded.

14.6. English as a foreign language

Another important aspect of the *EPD* was its contribution to the rapidly expanding interest in the teaching of English as a foreign language (EFL), as has been mentioned in Howatt (1984: 214). EFL was an area in which Jones had always showed the greatest interest and enthusiasm. As stated above, the *EPD* had its origins in the *Phonetic dictionary*—a dictionary written with a German co-author and published in Germany, and aimed largely at European students of English. From the moment of its first appearance, the *EPD* was obligatory reference material for all advanced non-native students of English.

But possibly even more important for EFL teaching was the publication of the *Outline*. With this book—more particularly in the later improved and revised versions from the [1932] third edition onwards—Jones managed to produce a surface phonetic/phonological description of a major variety of English which was not only thorough and scholarly but also written clearly and succinctly, so that its content could easily be absorbed by language teachers and their students. The completeness and reliability of the content, together with the excellent organisation and presentation of the material, meant that teachers of British English had at their disposal a pronunciation handbook which was the envy of those working on other languages—or, for that matter, other varieties of English. It is regrettable that no book of similar status was ever produced for American English.

Although aimed at the foreign learner, the *Outline* was much more than a mere foreign learners' aid. *Outline*[1] already represented a clear advance on the *Pronunciation of English* as a general description of English pronunciation, and became rapidly established as the standard work, superseding its rivals—and even, for all but specialist linguists, ousting the works of Sweet in this area. The [1932] third edition of the *Outline* reinforced its position, and it took many years for other writers, such as Gimson (1962) and Wells (1982), to provide studies of English RP which gave more information (and both of these authors acknowledged their debt to Jones). Of all Jones's books, the *Outline* is the most highly regarded, almost certainly the most quoted, and it has undoubtedly had the most influence on other writers.

Fry (1968: 198) has commented:

> It is safe to say that no single individual has ever had such a profound influence upon methods of language learning as Daniel Jones. Unlike many of his contemporaries in early days, he believed that it was not enough to be able to read a foreign language and that it was of tremendous importance how one spoke it. It was this conviction that led him to develop methods of teaching based on phonetic study which eventually revolutionized the learning of languages and particularly the study of pronunciation and intonation.

The writing of the *Pronunciation of English*, the *EPD* and the *Outline* would, in itself, have been a massive contribution to EFL teaching. However, the debt owed to Jones in this area is actually even greater than that.

In one of his early minor works, *Phonetic readings in English*, Jones provided a set of reliable phonetic transcriptions of colloquial English, including some with intonation marking, which have been extensively used over the years by teachers of English to foreigners. Though now outdated, the book filled a significant gap at the time, and is still in use to this day; furthermore, Jones's *Phonetic readings* provided the model for many books of the same type written in imitation by others. Finally, as noted above (Section 14.4), Jones also contributed to the expansion of EFL teaching through his organisation of summer schools.

Jones's other major contribution to EFL was the establishing of the UCL Phonetics Department. It played an all-important role in the propagation of techniques of applied phonetics and linguistics in foreign language teaching, and particularly of English. Lectures in Spoken English, essentially EFL classes, were begun in Jones's Department as early as 1912 and continued until after the Second World War. These are probably the longest continuous courses in EFL to operate in any British university. Howatt (1984: 171) refers to the "work of Jones, Palmer, and others at University College, London, out of which English as a foreign language emerged as an independent branch of practical language studies". In particular, Jones's help and encouragement to Harold Palmer resulted in a useful period of interaction and cooperation between the two (Howatt 1984: 232).

Jones's associates followed his lead in writing textbooks aimed directly, or partially, at the foreigner learning English. Howatt (1984: 264) picks out MacCarthy (1944), Christophersen (1956), and Gimson (1962) for their general surveys; and Kingdon (1958a, 1958b), together with Stannard Allen (1954), for works dealing with supra-segmental features. But other writers, who took a Jonesian approach, in greater or lesser degree, and were his pupils—or pupils of his pupils—could just as easily have been listed. Some examples are Ward (1929), Pring (1959), Windsor Lewis (1969), O'Connor (1967), Roach (1983)—who all produced general surveys. Schubiger (1958), O'Connor—Arnold (1961), W.R. Lee (1960), Cook (1968) provide examples of books dealing with intonation in the British tradition—although here the influence of Jones's colleague Palmer is more significant than that of Jones himself. Yet, this is by no means a complete list. Numerous authors borrowed Jones's ideas and imitated his approach, attempting to adapt these to the special needs of particular geographical areas. Although these books, which appeared in many different countries, were certainly of variable quality, on balance, they were an enlightening influence and served to correct outmoded ideas on English pronunciation and language teaching.

14.7. Description and teaching of French

Though Jones's research on other languages is considered elsewhere (Section 14.11) as part of his theoretical contribution, his own work on French—whilst of high quality—is not innovative or, in most respects, original. However, Jones did play an impressive practical role in helping to provide three excellent descriptions of French pronunciation for the English learner, namely the *Sounds of the French language* (1907c) and *Colloquial French* (1927a). His influence is also clearly detectable in the *Phonetics of French* (Armstrong 1932), and is indeed acknowledged by Armstrong herself (p. v). It is in Jones's work on French that we can see most obviously his direct debt to Paul Passy, and it was the Jones—Savory translation of Passy's *Sons du français* that provided the English student with a valuable summary of information which had previously been available only in French.

It is a matter of regret that Jones never completed his own independent work on French pronunciation (see Section 9.6). But apart from having provided the impetus to Armstrong and Coustenoble for their work on French and Provençal respectively (Armstrong 1932; Coustenoble 1945), he also made a notable contribution in his co-authorship of *Colloquial French*. This is important, not only for its success as the first description of educated spoken French easily accessible to the English-speaking beginner, but also as an extremely early example of a language course firmly based on an oral-aural approach.

In addition to the above, Jones was responsible for providing a centre for the teaching of French phonetics and pronunciation in UCL. The work of Jones's staff (in particular Hélène Coustenoble) has been much praised for its insistence on high performance standards from students. The same unrelentingly perfectionist attitude to language acquisition—especially as far as pronunciation was concerned—was encouraged at the annual summer schools in French which Jones ran each year at University College, largely staffed by Jones's colleagues and pupils.

David Abercrombie (1980: 2) has written of his own time as a UCL student in the thirties:

> I was taught to perform, that is to say to read aloud from phonetic texts, in French (above all: three or four hours a week), German, Danish, Urdu, Sechuana, Singhalese, Cantonese, and other languages that I have forgotten about. Almost all the teaching was tête-à-tête, and it was very intensive and rigorous—perfection was demanded. It was exhausting.

14.8. Ear-training techniques

The techniques of foreign language teaching at University College were largely based on Jones's view of the importance of ear-training. From the outset of his career Jones had been imbued with a conviction of the importance of recognition and performance both in learning foreign languages and also in phonetics itself. This had come about as a result of his training, firstly at the hands of Tilly (see Sections 1.7 and 1.8), then through his contacts with Paul Passy (Section 2.2) and finally through private tuition from Henry Sweet (Section 2.10).

Passy was the person who passed on the concept of ear-training by means of phonetic dictation to Jones, and in particular the ingenious technique of the "nonsense word". Passy's brother, Jean, was given credit by Jones (1941c: 33) for hitting upon this teaching device, and elaborating it into various methods for phonetic dictation (J. Passy 1894a, 1894b). Whilst Jones's earliest works make no mention of such procedures, the *Outline*[1] (pp. 187–188) contains the first printed examples of nonsense words, and emphasises (p. 187) the importance of ear-training and performance in phonetic training:

> For cultivating the capacity to recognize instantaneously and accurately the sounds of the foreign language, ear-training exercises are required. The only satisfactory type of exercise for this purpose is for the student to write down phonetically isolated sounds and nonsense words dictated by the teacher. A short exercise of this nature should form part of every pronunciation lesson.

Jones was not the first British phonetician to underline the significance of practical ability in phonetic training, since Sweet (1908: 124–125) had previously commented:

> The best training in the recognition of sounds by ear—apart from the still better but less systematic training afforded by language-study is—phonetic dictation. Phonetic dictation should, of course, always begin with the sounds of the native language....Phonetic training is stimulating to the pupils, and affords the teacher a ready and sure method of testing not only their ear, but also their general intelligence, as well as their knowledge of phonetics, and their power of handling symbols and notation, which is almost as important for the phonetician as for the mathematician.

Throughout his career, Jones always insisted on the importance of ear-training, and set a high priority on the practical recognition and performance abilities of his staff and students. His personal capacities in this area were of the highest level, as all who were taught by him testify. Harold Palmer (1930: 38) bracketed him in this respect with Sweet:

> A Henry Sweet or a Daniel Jones, with ears sharpened by intensive practice to an acuity that is the object of our envy, is the ideal phonetician.

Eva Sivertsen (1968: 197) said of Jones:

> He had a remarkable command of his own speech apparatus, and a very sharp ear for slight differences in sound quality and quantity.

And A.C. Gimson (1968: 5–6) recalled his abilities thus:

> Those of us who had the privilege of being his pupil or his colleague admired his patience as teacher and guide. Few of us could match the acuity of his ear or his remarkable powers of performance (talents which remained with him even in the last months of his long life), but we all benefited from his example. We remember with particular affection and profit the sessions spent with him analysing languages with the help of informants, as well as the constant insistence on an extremely high standard of auditory discrimination. D.J. had no time for those

55. Dennis Ward

56. A. C. Gimson, who on Jones's
retirement took over many of his roles

57. J.C. Wells, present Head of the
UCL Phonetics Department

58. Jones in 1964 (three years before
his death) still immersed
in his academic work

59. With Professor Masao Onishi
of Tokyo (1964)

60. One of the last photos of Jones,
taken at the age of 84

linguists (or linguisticians as he preferred to call them) who described the phonetic structure of languages yet were incapable of hearing with accuracy or of reproducing the sound of the language in question to the full satisfaction of a native speaker.

Jones's immediate successor, Dennis Fry (1961: 154) said of him:

It would be no easy task to analyse the gifts required to make a great phonetician. A most precise and very long-term memory for what things sound like would certainly be one of them....It is tempting to speculate whether Daniel Jones is perhaps endowed with "absolute quality" judgment just as Mozart was with "absolute pitch", for he is able to remember over long periods the quality of a speech sound once heard and to compare it with sounds heard subsequently.

Jones's demands on his students and the priority he accorded practical ability were almost legendary, as witness Abercrombie's (1983: 1) account of the first time he ever met Jones:

Jones answered the door himself, let me in, and said "How do you do? Come in and sit down. Would you please say a voiced bilabial implosive?" At that time I was not aware that he did not have much in the way of small talk. Fortunately I was able to produce the required implosive, and he then said "Thank you. Now will you please say a close back unrounded vowel." As it happened I could do so, and did; and the rigorous performance examination went on for some time. He put no theoretical questions to me at all.

Though Abercrombie, like others, found Jones's single-minded preoccupation with practical phonetics at times amusing, he has said elsewhere (Abercrombie 1980: 2) that in the 1930s (when he was a student) the UCL Phonetics Department was "stimulating and marvellous" and: "Daniel Jones's colleagues were marvellous phoneticians... I valued greatly the sensory training they gave me."
Peter Ladefoged, himself a product of the British School of phonetics, has emphasised that practical training is an essential part of its approach to the subject (Fromkin 1985b: 4):

A major characteristic of this [British] school is the emphasis on the ability to produce sounds oneself as well as being able to hear small differences in speech sounds. Daniel Jones was very good at this....In the British tradition, one is trained to become a practical phonetician in this sense.

At University College, Jones established in his Department a standard of excellence in training for practical articulatory phonetics which has never been equalled. Nor is it likely ever to be matched again, since there is now less demand for such abilities in a phonetician. Such emphasis on performance and recognition skills is today considered unfashionable, and many phoneticians would say that extensive practice in ear-training is now an unnecessary luxury given the leaps forward in instrumental techniques and the easy availability of electronic recording devices. As Butcher (1982: 69) puts it: "the days of the phonetician as human tape-recorder are over: magnetic tape does the job far more efficiently", adding (p. 70) "oral and aural acrobatics, though sometimes still useful, are no longer sufficient or even essential requirements in phonetics". Although Jones's insistence on high standards of performance and recognition through ear-training had a considerable influence in British (and Commonwealth) university departments, his methods have received less acceptance elsewhere. For instance, in the USA and continental Europe, practical phonetic training, as practised and advocated by Jones, is relatively uncommon (except possibly in certain departments headed by scholars who have themselves been taught by Jones or his pupils and become convinced of the efficacy of ear-training techniques). One important exception to this pattern is the work of Kenneth Pike and his followers in the Summer Institute of Linguistics, who have developed highly sophisticated methods of linguistic investigation of little-known languages, based on articulatory phonetics, with an emphasis on instruction by means of ear-training and performance and the reduction of impressionistic transcription to phonemic systems. According to Pike (1981: 182–183), although his approach was not derived directly from Jones, he is conscious of his debt to the British School, and was influenced by the works of Sweet, Ellis, Noël-Armfield and Jones himself; Pike also notes that he gained part of his training from the American dialectologist, Guy Lowman (1909–41), who wrote his doctoral thesis at University College under Jones.

14.9. Transcription

Abercrombie (1983: 5) has stated: "One of Jones's chief interests throughout his career was notation, with which he experimented a great deal". As Abercrombie goes on to say, it is ironical that Jones was in no way the originator of the transcription which is most often associated with his name, i.e. that used in the *EPD*[1] and all subsequent editions of that book until 1977. This was, in fact, the commonest form of transcription used for English in *Le Maître phonétique* by most IPA members in the 1900–14 period and Jones simply took it over. Whilst Jones was not involved in devising the system, he was unquestionably the most significant force in propagating this transcription and, indeed, IPA symbols in general, mainly through his three books: the *Pronunciation of English*, the *EPD* and the *Outline*. As Abercrombie also notes (1983: 5): "He had much to do with making the IPA alphabet widely used throughout the world."

In the course of his life, Jones's enthusiasm for different types of English transcription waxed and waned. To begin with he appears to have been happy with the "EPD" type mentioned above. In the 1920s, Jones experimented with a more narrow variety, which was revived by Gimson (1962) and is now often associated with the latter's name. Jones later returned to the *EPD* transcription, but at the end of his career advocated an extremely broad system with limited numbers of symbols, which he termed "simplified transcription" (*Outline*[8]: 346–349). This system also fitted in well with his ideas on the importance of "chronemic" distinctions, which saw length oppositions as being a crucial part of phoneme theory and a means by which the whole vowel phoneme system of English could be viewed as a small number of phonemes further differentiated by chronemic pairings (see Section 14.16). Jones has summarised his changing views on types of transcription in the useful appendix on the matter which he wrote for the *Outline*[8] (331–350). See also Section 13.11.

However, throughout Jones's various swings of opinion on transcription, one theme remains constant; all phonetic representations must adhere to the principles of the IPA. Apart from an isolated flirtation with an organic alphabet (see Section 2.11), he employed nothing else. Jones was adamant throughout his life in insisting on IPA transcription in his own work and in the work of others. Many of his book reviews, for example, either mention (with approval) the adherence of the author to IPA conventions or criticise any departures from them. It is notable that strict obedience to IPA Principles characterised the work of his pupils, and indeed of effectively all phoneticians and linguists working in Britain. On the continent of Europe, the IPA system also became well established and was used by virtually all working in the fields of phonetics and linguistics (apart from traditional dialectology). This was a result, in part, of the early work of Viëtor and Passy, but also undoubtedly owed much to Jones's influence.

The IPA dominance in Britain and continental Europe holds true today. In fact, the only part of the world where the IPA is less secure is the United States, where it has until recently been the choice of only a minority (see Abercrombie 1983: 6–7). This may be because of the traditional rivalry between linguistics departments (using for the most part non-IPA systems) and the more old-fashioned departments of speech (generally conforming to IPA transcription practice), as Abercrombie argues, but another factor must be that Jones's works had a less pervasive influence in the USA than elsewhere. (For a survey of the symbols widely in use at the moment within the IPA tradition side by side with those employed in the USA, see Pullum—Ladusaw 1986.)

In the post-1921 period, Jones made relatively few changes in his views on the IPA alphabet itself. He attended and played a significant blocking role in the 1925 Copenhagen conference, scuttling Jespersen's attempt to make radical alterations to the whole framework of the IPA alphabet (Section 10.10). After steering some significant changes of his own through the Council of the IPA in the aftermath of the conference, Jones, though recognising certain deficiencies, seemed largely satisfied with the transcription system. Perhaps because of Jones's lack of enthusiasm for change towards the end of his career, or because of the conservatism in the organisation itself, the IPA was slow to react to many of the advances that took place in the twentieth century, not only in terms of our enhanced knowledge of speech processes but also of the discovery of the existence of numerous "new" types of speech sound in previously unknown or undescribed languages (Maddieson 1987). A former President of the IPA stated bluntly (Ladefoged 1987b: 34):

> The present Alphabet is sadly out of date, both from the point of view of the principles underlying it, and with respect to the individual symbols and diacritics. There is no doubt that it should now be revised.

For nearly twenty years after Jones's death, although some gestures were made towards change—for example, Gimson (1973)—nothing materialised apart from a minor revamping of the IPA chart in 1979. In 1987, calls were made from within the IPA organisation itself for considerable reforms in the alphabet (see particularly, Ladefoged 1987a; Henton 1987), which led to the Kiel Conference in 1989. This meeting resulted in many important ongoing revisions to the IPA symbols—the first genuine updating since Jones pushed through his changes in the 1920s.

14.10. Jones's view of phonetics

Above all, Jones was a practical man, and eventually came to judge any aspect of phonetics in terms of whether it had direct beneficial application to human problems. It is therefore not surprising that much of Jones's contribution to the development of phonetics should lie in areas which are of outstanding practical value. Such contributions, whilst perhaps less spectacular than theoretical breakthroughs, have laid an important basis for scholarly work worldwide in the twentieth century.

Taken over the course of his long career Jones's organisational and practical achievements are impressive. However, Fry (1968: 198) was correct in pointing out:

> His reputation as a scholar was built, however, not only on this basis of practical study, but also on his outstanding achievements in the field of theory—the development of the cardinal vowel system and of phonemic theory, and also upon research into the sound systems of a wide variety of languages and into the history of the pronunciation of English.

Nevertheless, it must be admitted that Jones maintained a somewhat idiosyncratic attitude to the theoretical aspects of phonetics, which was remarkable for a linguist of his reputation. Jones did not value theories in themselves but considered any theoretical development useful only in how far it was likely to make a contribution to the practical side of phonetics, where his real interests lay. He appears actually to have treated with suspicion anything which smacked of theorising for its own sake. This attitude, which was to an extent apparent in his early work, developed and hardened as time went by. As he grew older, Jones became more hidebound in his ideas and increasingly restricted himself to pursuing relatively limited goals.

Such an attitude would today certainly be regarded as unscholarly. However, Jones's severely practical view of the subject could be defended far more easily in his own lifetime—particularly in Britain in the pre-1920 period when there was perhaps more admiration for a down-to-earth approach to science and scholarship generally. Ironically, as more theoretically orientated approaches came into fashion in linguistics in the twenties and thirties—both in Europe and the USA—Jones distanced himself still further from these linguistic trends. As a consequence, Jones, like many other scholars, hit upon his most valuable and perceptive ideas before he reached the age of forty; the remainder of his life was concerned with developing these ideas.

Another striking characteristic of Jones was his reluctance to read widely in his subject and his refusal to be influenced by more than a few of those authors that he did get round to reading. The restricted nature of his reading is dictated largely by the approach to phonetics that he favoured. He was especially unwilling to consider anything which appeared to him to have no direct application. In particular, Jones showed little interest in linguistic—as opposed to phonetic—publications.

A singular illustration of his attitude is to be found in this statement in a personal letter written to Antonie Cohen in 1952:

> To this day I have never read de Saussure, I am ashamed to say. But my life has been a particularly full one, & I have never had time to read many books that I should have liked to read.[2]

It is remarkable that a scholar of Jones's stature had, of his own admission, not read the most influential of all the early writers on modern linguistics.

Apart from his lack of interest in linguistics, and his suspicion of theorising, Jones had one other factor which limited his knowledge of the work of others. He was unhappy about accepting the validity of any data unless collected directly by himself, or by one of his immediate pupils. Consequently, his pioneering books on languages such as: Ndau (*Chindau*), Cantonese (*Cantonese phonetic reader*), Tswana (*Sechuana reader*) and Sinhalese (*Sinhalese reader*) are exclusively the results of the efforts of Jones and his co-authors. Jones also encouraged a similar attitude of suspicion towards published linguistic data and theories in his students and colleagues—as when Armstrong and Ward (1926: iv) state proudly that they "have purposely avoided consulting any other works on English intonation, and have made our analysis from personal observations only" (see also Section 14.12).

Seen from the viewpoint of today, Jones's attitude is inward-looking and mind-cramping—but such a standpoint was again much more understandable in the context of the time when most of the linguistic descriptions of non-European languages available were simply incompetent—especially from the phonetic point of view. In fact, it was not until the achievements of Jones and his UCL colleagues, followed later by the important work of the American structuralists, that reliable descriptions of non-European languages appeared (i.e. descriptions based on phonemic principles and capable, if necessary, of dealing adequately with tonal systems).

But this does not mean that Jones was totally lacking in theoretical influences. Far from it. Early on he was obviously deeply affected in his work by such figures as Tilly, Viëtor, Sweet and, above all, Passy. His awareness of the phoneme came mainly from the Kazan' School, through Ščerba and Benni (see Section 14.16). He was prepared to pick up ideas on instrumental phonetics from Rousselot, Laclotte, Meyer and others. And in due course, Jones would benefit from interaction with his own colleagues—for instance, Coleman, Palmer, Beach, Armstrong, Ward, and Kingdon. But, as time went on, Jones's lack of willingness to read the work of anyone outside his immediate circle meant that his influences were restricted to a very small group of scholars, many of whom were colleagues and friends.

14.11. Description of languages other than English

The first valuable theoretical contribution of Jones—which can in some ways be regarded also as a practical aid—lies in his description of non-European languages such as Cantonese, Tswana and Sinhalese (see also Section 14.6), on which little research had been undertaken and which were at the time effectively hardly known to western linguistic scholars. Certainly, Jones thought this was his best scholarly work, rating it above the world-famous and commercially successful books for which he is chiefly known today. Gimson (1977: 151) has stated:

> His phonetic transcriptions of foreign languages, often involving pioneer research, remain reliable and entirely valid statements today, e.g. those concerned with Cantonese and Sechuana. Indeed, it was his work on such languages whose phonetic aspects had been inadequately studied in Europe at the beginning of the century, which gave him most satisfaction. He always regarded his contribution to the phonetics of English, on which his international reputation was mainly based, as less original if of great practical value.

Jones, by insisting always on working with reliable native speaker informants, and refusing to be influenced by previous (and often inaccurate) work, ensured that his descriptions were of the authentic spoken language rather than outdated, or purely literary, usage; he took nothing another scholar said on trust. Jones always wanted to *hear* things for himself. Much of what he wrote as early as 1912 is notable for first-time observations and discoveries and indeed remains a useful source of information to this day. Jones's approach also provided a model for others who were to follow his methods, and develop them. He can be seen here to have been an enormous influence on researchers such as Ward, Armstrong, Coustenoble and Beach, who were his direct pupils, and numerous others who benefited either from contact with one of his students, or from his published work.

The part played by Jones's pupils (see Sections 9.5 and 12.3) in establishing the linguistics section of the School of Oriental Studies (later, the School of Oriental and African Studies) was also valuable since the language research and teaching carried on in that institution was begun on essentially Jonesian lines. Although this was later supplanted by a Firthian approach to phonological analysis, the data-gathering methods of phoneticians such as J. Carnochan, Eugénie Henderson, Nathalie Waterson, Harold Palmer, R.K. Sprigg, T.F. Mitchell and others were still largely based on Jones's ideas.

Jones's work on Russian (*Pronunciation of Russian*) was not pioneering in the way that, for example, the *Sechuana reader* or *Sinhalese reader* were. Nevertheless, the *Pronunciation of Russian* was the most reliable and easily accessible overview of the sound system of the language available at the time. It is therefore, in a sense, more of a practical contribution, comparable to Jones's work on French (see Section 14.7).

In addition to his major descriptive studies, Jones produced many short articles on the sound systems of a variety of languages for *Le Maître phonétique*. These brief sketches are of value since, given Jones's unquestioned expertise at this type of work, and his insistence on first hand information from native speakers, they often provided the first trustworthy transcriptions of the languages concerned.

14.12. Intonation of English

In the history of the development of descriptive theories of intonation, Daniel Jones played a leading role which is now in danger of being underestimated or even forgotten. For instance, Brazil—Coulthard—Johns (1980: 122), in the course of surveying various approaches to intonation, have the following as their only reference to Jones's work:

> Jones (1957) [i.e. *Outline*[8]] follows Armstrong and Ward (1926) in asserting that a "falling tone" is used in statements, wh-questions, commands and invitations, whereas a "rising tone is used in yes/no questions, dependent clauses, unfinished sentences and requests." It is not difficult to refute these generalisations.

Actually, it would be more accurate to say that Armstrong and Ward follow Jones (see below), but it is in any case easy to be fooled here by Jones's characteristic modesty in disregarding the influence of his own work on his junior colleagues (*Outline*[8]: 279). However, Brazil and his colleagues' discussion is also somewhat unfair inasmuch as Jones here clearly states that his treatment of intonation is "only a bare outline of the subject", and refers his readers to no fewer than eleven other authors (most of these being his own pupils or followers) for more elaborate descriptions. And Jones in fact provides his own modification to the quoted generalisations in the *Outline* only a few pages further on (*Outline*[8]: 286–319 *et passim*); he had also covered the topic in an earlier edition (*Outline*[1]: 135–167).

A realistic acknowledgement of Jones's crucial role in this area of phonetics is however to be found in the fullest historical survey of the development of intonation theory so far produced, Cruttenden (1981: 25), which points out the significance of Jones's contribution in *Intonation curves*:

> This early work of Jones was however chiefly important in making use of the newly invented gramophone.…[It] represented an important advance in the study of intonation, paving the way for future experimental underpinning of auditory analysis.

In fact, as we have seen, this is not the whole story, since these quasi-instrumental methods employed by Jones had first been mentioned and exemplified briefly in earlier works (*Sounds of the French language*: 116–117; *Phonetic transcriptions*: 41–44; see Sections 2.6 and 2.7). Furthermore, in the *Outline*[1], Jones gave wide publicity to pioneering advances in the use of the kymograph for registering and analysing pitch variation (Section 8.8).

It was this fuller investigation of an actual corpus of material, and the phonetic detail in the description, which gave Jones an advantage over Sweet, whose contribution to intonation theory, "while being extremely suggestive in his various hints about intonational distinctions, produced very little exemplification of the use and meanings of the various tones" (Cruttenden 1981: 24). In his treatment of intonation at this time, Jones can easily be criticised for unduly emphasising phonetic description as opposed to analysis; Cruttenden (1981: 26), indeed, views his contribution as a "regression from Sweet's work". However, *Intonation curves* is perhaps more usefully to be considered as a necessary response to the contemporary need for some type of data-based description of English intonation.

In his subsequent work, beginning with the *Pronunciation of English*[1], Jones started to develop his theory of intonation, moving towards somewhat more simplified and stylised systems of representing pitch change and providing an analysis of the semantic and grammatical implications involved (see Section 3.4). The *Outline*[1] elaborated this further into what was at the time the most detailed description of English intonation patterns available. This is, in fact, the peak of Jones's independent efforts in connection with intonation (see Section 8.7). However, notable though the achievement of the *Outline*[1] might be, as far as intonation is concerned, it is essential not to ignore a more weighty point. With the exception of Klinghardt's work in Germany, and Ripman's in England, virtually *all* the interesting developments at this time in this branch of English phonetics were taking place in University College and were being carried out by colleagues and pupils of Daniel Jones. Furthermore, Ripman was a close friend of Jones, and Klinghardt acknowledged at length his debt to Jones's works (Klinghardt—Klemm 1920: iv–vi), stating: "ohne dieselben hätte ich dieses buch überhaupt nicht schreiben können" (p. iv).[3] As Cruttenden (1981: 34) points out:

...in the early twentieth century a number of new ideas were being floated, some of which were to become the basis of more thorough intonational analyses. Studies of intonation during the remainder of the century have clustered round three types of analysis...

Cruttenden (1981: passim) distinguishes these as the "whole tune approach", the "nuclear approach" and the "pitch levels analysis". In one way or another, Daniel Jones was involved in all of these views of intonation through his working relationships with colleagues and pupils. We shall never know exactly how much these other writers owed to Jones's direct help, or to the benefit of the exchange of ideas with him in informal discussion. What seems obvious (perhaps most strikingly in the area of intonation) is that Jones was able to foster and maintain an atmosphere in UCL where research and publication could flourish, and where original theories were passed freely from one colleague to another.

To Jones must go the credit for encouraging Coleman, and publishing his seminal essay (Coleman 1914), in which is to be found not only the first attempt at marking intonation in terms of a "pitch levels analysis" but also, as Cruttenden (1981: 30–31) has indicated, the first inklings of concepts such as the nucleus, pitch change as the chief marker of prominence, and the importance of attitudinal and discourse markers in intonation.

... [Coleman's] article contained many seeds which were to germinate in later intonational studies....Ideas which have usually been ascribed to later writers can often be traced back to Coleman...

Harold Palmer was also a member of Jones's staff until 1921, and directly after leaving London for Japan, he published the first of his books on English intonation (Palmer 1922), in which he developed the original "nuclear approach" with its nowadays familiar analysis of intonation groups based on division into head, nucleus and tail—the most influential of all the British treatments of intonation. Finally, University College was the workplace of Lilias Armstrong and Ida Ward, who produced (Armstrong—Ward 1926) what Cruttenden (1981: 37) has termed the "most fully worked-out presentation of the 'whole-tune' approach" to intonation.

It is this last that Jones eventually favoured and returned to in his later revisions of his two most popular works, the *Outline*[3] [1932] and the *Pronunciation of English*[3] [1950]. As we have seen, he is today often regarded as merely taking over the work of his pupils, yet as Cruttenden (1981: 37) correctly emphasises, Armstrong and Ward's book was "heavily anticipated in Jones' two textbooks [i.e. the *Pronunciation of English*[1] and the *Outline*[1]]". The appeal of the Armstrong and Ward version of the whole tune approach is obvious to someone like Jones who was greatly interested in the application of phonetics to foreign language teaching. The distinction of just two main tunes allows for a quick grasp by the learner of essential intonation distinctions, and the over-simplification involved can later be modified by further elaboration. Yet the fact that Jones rejected Palmer's nuclear approach for inclusion in his own work must be seen in retrospect as a mistake, given that the most useful intonation research in Britain in the mid-twentieth century, e.g. Kingdon (1958a), O'Connor—Arnold (1961) and Halliday (1963, 1964, 1966, 1967), had its roots, to a greater or lesser degree, in Palmer's ideas.

Certainly, one phonetician, F.G. Blandford, Palmer's collaborator, thought even by the early thirties that Jones's views on intonation were outdated. He wrote to Palmer, concerning Jones and his colleagues in somewhat patronising terms:

> Now I can't help thinking that a fundamental weakness of D.J. and his School,— you know how I love and respect them and especially him and you won't misunderstand my criticism,—is that, with their wider international experience of I.P.A. propaganda, and perhaps the more immediately utilitarian aims of the teaching in London, they are unduly concerned with not frightening away the postulants and novices from the Phonetic Life...they sing "Tune I" and "Tune II" and imply that there is no more in English intonation than that; and, when they are forced to admit the imperfection of so simple a scheme, they fall back on "emphatic" and "unemphatic" intonations, as though these phenomena were merely quantitative and not qualitative and psychological. Poor dears! they must be missing all the fun.[4]

Blandford also has sharp reproaches for the Jonesians' lack of interest in the work of fellow scholars:

> ...I was so cross with Miss Armstrong and Miss Ward (N.B. they don't know that I was, but I did write a *lovely* review of their book and hadn't the heart to publish it) for saying in their Preface that they had purposely not consulted previous works on the subject. If that was true, it was disgraceful. They *should have* done so; as they were quite competent to estimate, adjust and arrange, with almost authoritative influence, the published work of Klinghardt, Jones, Palmer and Coleman in a valuable and scholarly whole, and to complete by their own research the gaps in yours [i.e. Palmer's]. They missed their chance of doing it.[5]

This letter somehow managed to slip into Daniel Jones's hands and he has noted brusquely in the margin that this was "not their [Armstrong and Ward's] object". What he thought of Blandford's criticisms apart from that is not revealed.

Jones showed himself privately to be by no means as negative towards Palmer's work as his public lack of interest might suggest, and incorporated some of Palmer's ideas into his teaching. The following is an extract from a personal letter to Palmer, in response to the latter's introduction of mnemonic terms for intonation patterns (Palmer 1933).

> As a matter of fact I like your nomenclature for the English tone-patterns (as far as I can tell from a rather hasty perusal of your booklet). I have recommended it

to several other teachers, including Blandford, but none of them seems to take to it.... Personally I don't find this difficulty with your terms. I have tried to extend the idea to French and German....I am completely mystified by your statement that your intonation patterns have practically nothing in common with the Armstrong-Ward tunes. I haven't been into the thing in detail, but the two systems look to me much the same but with a difference in nomenclature.[6]

By this time, Jones had completed his revised third edition of the *Outline*, otherwise it is conceivable that he might have incorporated some of Palmer's terminology. Had he done so, Jones might have seemed somewhat less rigid in his adherence to Armstrong and Ward's two tunes.

As far as intonation theory is concerned, Jones has been somewhat unfairly treated by several present-day observers. He has even been regarded by some as a peripheral figure, who contributed little and merely borrowed his pupils' theories. In fact, Jones can be said to have been the primary impetus of many of the most significant ideas on English intonation. His theories appear to have provided the stimulus to the work of Coleman, Klinghardt, Palmer, and Armstrong and Ward. Through these influential writers they were passed on to later generations of phoneticians working in Britain, America and Europe.

14.13. Tone languages

In his research on tone languages, Jones can certainly be regarded as a pioneer. Here he was dealing with an area where he was able to combine his talents for pitch recognition and description with his liking for working with undescribed languages. It is actually remarkable how little mention is made in present-day phonetic literature of Jones's part in the development of this area of phonetics, and how far ahead of his time he was in seeing the crucial importance of tone (see Sections 6.8 and 6.9). He contrasts sharply, for example, with Henry Sweet, whose treatment of the topic was cursory in the extreme (Sweet 1971: 175–180).

Although some of the ground had previously been broken by other workers, e.g. Christaller (1875) for African languages and Seers (1908) for Chinese, it was Jones who first managed to make the linguists of the early twentieth century aware of the variety and complexity of tone languages by providing a clearly written and phonetically accurate description of an African tone language in an easily accessible publication. Up till this time, tone systems had been considered only superficially and most work had concerned the languages of the Far East. Relatively little indeed was known of the wealth of tone systems to be found in the languages of the African continent.

Yet Jones's own initial attempt at dealing with a tone language was not at all perceptive; the articles on Ndau (Jones 1910k and *Chindau*) indicate that he recognised some differences in intonation but missed the nub of the matter. It is not until his work on Cantonese (*Cantonese phonetic reader*) that we have an idea of Jones's potential as a tone analyst. However, Jones's 1916 survey of Tswana (*Sechuana reader*) marks a milestone in tone analysis; an achievement not only for Jones himself but for linguistics as a whole. He had, admittedly, good fortune in finding in Solomon Plaatje someone who combined a sharp intelligence with native-speaker awareness, and whom Jones was able to consider as a colleague rather than a mere informant. The *Sechuana reader* provides the first accurate description and (within its limitations) reliable analysis of an African tone language, including the concept of downstep (even though Jones does not employ the term itself). Jones's further research on Tswana (1917c, 1927f, 1928a), with the help of the perceptive mind of Harold Palmer, took the analysis of the relationship of tone and grammatical meaning further than anyone to that date. His later work included a significant contribution to notation in his innovative use of the raised exclamation mark as an indicator of downstep.[7] Whilst the *Sechuana reader* was essentially phonetic rather than phonemic in tone analysis, Jones later came back to analyse Tswana and other tone languages in the *Phoneme* (pp. 152–160). Jones claims for himself the credit (*HMTP*: 12–13) for inventing the term "toneme", which appeared first in the work of his pupil Beach (1923: 79, 87–89).

Beach was only one of many of Jones's staff and pupils who were encouraged to undertake research on tone languages and publish the results, so that during three decades from 1920 to 1950 British phonetics led the world in research on tone linguistics. Jones's most distinguished *protégée* was Ida Ward, who, until her death, was widely regarded as the world's leading authority on African languages. Other well-known researchers on tone languages who were taught and influenced by Jones included Lilias Armstrong, Clement Doke, A.N. Tucker, Eugénie Henderson, and J. Carnochan (to name only a select few).

It is in this indirect way, by stimulating and fostering the successful and innovative work produced by writers such as those mentioned above, that Jones provided his last, and some might claim his greatest, contribution to tone linguistics. Though this also is rarely acknowledged today, it could reasonably be considered an achievement no less valuable than his own work.

14.14. The Cardinal Vowel system

It cannot be said, however, that Jones lacks recognition in the linguistic world for his chief contribution to vowel description and classification—namely the Cardinal Vowel system. In fact, for many of the younger generation of phonetics and phonology students, the Cardinal Vowels and the Jonesian phoneme concept are the only ways in which they even encounter his name. Yet, as we have seen, Jones was far from being the innovator of vowel descriptions of this type; by the end of the eighteenth century Hellwag (1781) was producing arrangements of vowels in a similar geometrical form of triangles or quadrilaterals. So Jones did not invent or discover this aspect of vowel classification; he was obviously indebted to the work of Bell (1867)—and even more directly to Paul Passy (see Sections 2.6 and 7.3). And there may have been other influences, such as the strikingly similar diagrams produced for French by Dumville (1904).

However, the final step in the construction of a new model of vowel description which could be applied (in principle) universally to languages was Jones's own. In what he eventually produced, he provided something which fulfilled the most necessary requirements of a simple scientific model. It was capable of taking in relatively complex data, and by means of simplification and schematisation, reducing these to a few significant parameters which could be subjected to further analysis. Working within an articulatory model of phonetics, the Cardinal Vowel system provided an excellent way of noting the essential factors needed for discrimination and reproduction of vowel qualities. Apart from being a first-class "shorthand" system for the linguistic fieldworker, it also allowed for a useful teaching method. As long as one was not in search of perfect performance imitation by students, the basic system was relatively easy to teach and to learn.

Where Jones failed was in not being readily satisfied with the virtues of the system seen in this light. When working on the Cardinal Vowel system, he began to view it as something which could add to the status of phonetics as a science. He hoped, by confirming his theory with hard evidence in the form of X-ray data, to show that there was a firm scientific basis for his largely hypothetical model of the equal intervals between tongue postures of the various primary Cardinal Vowels. Genuine support of this kind was never to arrive, and the X-ray material originally available was dubious, and in part contradictory to Jones's ideas (Section 7.6). Later research also failed to corroborate Jones's suppositions, and as Ladefoged (1967: 71) has commented: "It is readily apparent that the tongue positions are very different from the theoretical description of the articulations of the cardinal vowels." (See, however, Catford 1981: *passim* for arguments in favour of the Cardinal Vowels as articulatorily defined entities.)

Jones responded ineffectually to these disappointments. Rather than accept that he had a useful teaching and learning model with certain deficiencies —but nevertheless of tremendous general utility—Jones proceeded to make his original scheme far more complex and to insist on an inordinately long period of training before he was satisfied that anyone was fit to use the system. His perfectionist demands in this area have passed into the realms of phonetic anecdote, as Abercrombie (1983: 3) relates:

> It should be remembered that the Cardinal Vowel technique belongs to the art, and not to the science, side [of phonetics]. It is a technique which is time-consuming and difficult to learn. I was taught the Cardinal Vowels by Jones himself, and it was a lengthy and painful process. Cardinal Vowel Number One turned out to be the most difficult of all, rather unexpectedly, and it took a long time before Jones was satisfied with my version. I had trouble, too, with Cardinal Number Three, I remember.

David Abercrombie was, of course, to become one of the foremost articulatory phone-

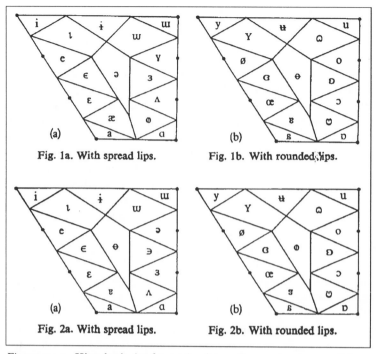

Fig. 1a. With spread lips.   Fig. 1b. With rounded lips.

Fig. 2a. With spread lips.   Fig. 2b. With rounded lips.

Figure 14.1. Kingdon's (1964: 144) scheme for rearrangement of the Cardinal Vowel diagrams.

ticians of his day; it poses the question of what sort of difficulties the average, or poor, student would have had. Such an approach could prove self-defeating—even though the demand for perfect imitation and production of sounds within the process of learning the Cardinal Vowels undoubtedly contributed to the well-deserved reputation of the British School as a training ground for first-rate practical phoneticians.

However, Abercrombie (1967: 151–162) in his own thorough exposition of the Cardinal Vowel system makes demands which are no less severe than those of Jones himself (p. 155):

> The specialist phonetician has first to learn to pronounce the cardinal vowels with infallible precision (as far as such a thing is humanly possible), and when that is done he must acquire the technique by which they are put to use in the description of vowels of actual languages.... It would not be reasonable to expect full command over their production without long training, and their successful application as a descriptive device comes only after considerable experience and practice.

Abercrombie's insistence on the long training necessary to use the Cardinal Vowel system, and the need for direct training by someone already familiar with the vowels,

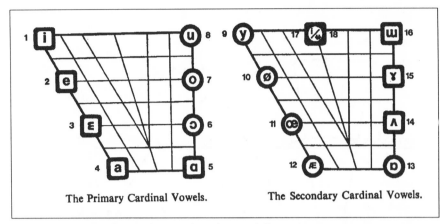

The Primary Cardinal Vowels.   The Secondary Cardinal Vowels.

Figure 14.2. Windsor Lewis's (1969: 16) vowel diagrams

is also found in much other British School phonetic work of the pre-1970s. And even later, it is notable that Ladefoged (1975: 197) states: "But the precise use of the cardinal vowel system as advocated by Daniel Jones can probably be achieved only by a group of phoneticians who have been in personal contact with Daniel Jones or someone taught by him."

For a period of about forty years within the British School, the Cardinal Vowels, despite the obvious deficiencies of portions of the system, were regarded with almost

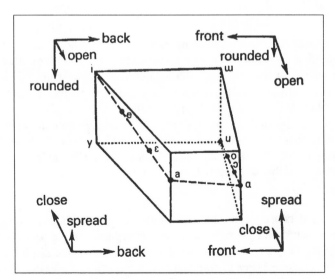

Figure 14.3. Ladefoged's (1967: 140) three-dimensional vowel diagram.

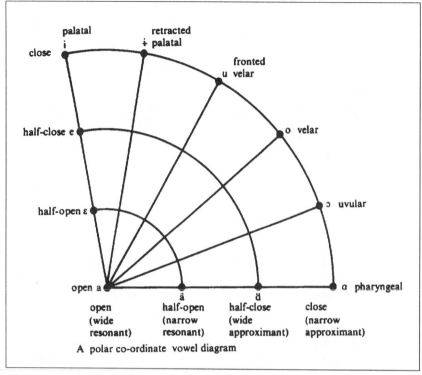

Figure 14.4. Catford's (1977: 185) "polar co-ordinate" vowel diagram.

religious respect and Jones's pronouncements on their validity accepted virtually without question. Nevertheless, strong doubts had been expressed by other scholars, beginning with Russell (1928: 325), who claimed that "phoneticians...are thinking in terms of acoustic fact and using physiological phantasy to express the idea", and this view was taken up later by Essner (1947) and Joos (1948: 49–56).

It was perhaps inevitable that a reaction should set in within the British School itself, where Jones's theory had gained its strongest adherents. Early in the 1960s, Jones's own pupil, Gimson (1962: 42), although generally approving of Jones's system, was nevertheless prepared to indicate his doubts about its articulatory basis:

It must be understood that this [cardinal vowel] diagram is a highly conventional-ized one which shows, above all, quality relationships. ...it has been shown that it is possible to articulate vowel qualities without the tongue and lip positions which this diagram seems to postulate as necessary. It is, for example, possible to produce a vowel of the Cardinal 7 ([o]) type without the lip-tongue relationship suggested.

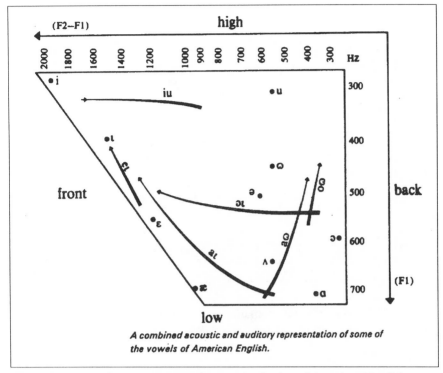

Figure 14.5. Ladefoged's (1975: 194) acoustic plotting of American English vowels based on formant values placed within a Jonesian Cardinal Vowel quadrilateral.

Gimson was probably influenced by reports of Ladefoged's (1967: 50–142) research into the nature of vowel quality and his experiments on the validity of the Cardinal Vowel system, the results of which were by this time already in circulation.[8] In this research project (which involved both Jones and Gimson) the Cardinal Vowels produced by a number of phoneticians (and passed as authentic by Jones) were subjected to instrumental investigation for analysis of formant structure. Considerable variation was discovered, indicating that vowels which were not acoustically similar could nevertheless be perceived as equivalents—a point taken up later by Butcher (1982: 65–66). In addition, Ladefoged asked fifteen phoneticians who had undergone traditional Cardinal Vowel training (though not Jones himself), together with three who had received no such training, to try to pinpoint on a vowel diagram the vowels of a language unfamiliar to them (a variety of Scots Gaelic).

It was found that although agreement was generally good over the front vowels, it was less than satisfactory as far as central and back vowels were concerned. Auditory judgements made on lip-rounding proved the greatest problem area and there was con-

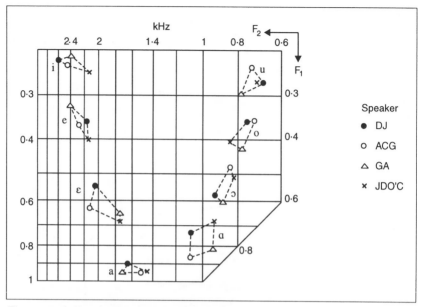

Figure 14.6. Butcher's (1982: 66) diagram showing formant plottings of Cardinal Vowels said by Jones and three colleagues.

siderable conflict between the judgements of different phoneticians. Nevertheless, Ladefoged's findings proved that those who had received traditional Cardinal Vowel training showed a far higher degree of agreement in their judgements of vowel quality than those without such experience (cf. Hammarström 1973: 25–26). Laver (1965) confirmed the reliability of trained phoneticians by a test given over a period of five days involving synthetic vowels. He found good agreement in judgements within his group of five subjects, all of whom had undergone a period of training in the Jonesian tradition.

Ladefoged (1967: 141) eventually came down in favour of the Cardinal Vowel system, stating that "these speculations...should not lead us to neglect the great value of the existing cardinal vowel system". But though he himself continued afterwards to advocate its use, in particular in his influential textbook (Ladefoged 1975: 194–199), even so, his findings made it impossible ever again to regard the Cardinal Vowel system as the finely tuned device with a firm physiological basis of supporting data that Jones (together with many of his followers) would once have had phoneticians believe it to be. From this point on, and increasingly during the seventies, the view was taken up that the Cardinal Vowels, though useful as a teaching aid, and serviceable as a device to speed impressionistic transcriptions, could only be regarded with suspicion as far as their theoretical basis was concerned.

At the same time, several writers suggested that changes could be made in their presentation. Some of these, such as Dietrich (1969), were, as Butcher (1982: 52) has stated, trivial alterations to the vowel diagram—but other ideas were more interesting. Kingdon (1964) presented a well-argued case for rearranging the vowel area divisions in a complex system of interlocking triangles (see Figure 14.1). He drew up two such vowel diagrams—one for rounded and one for spread vowels—considering this categorisation more logical than Jones's criteria for primary/secondary Cardinal Vowels. Additionally, he resurrected symbols little used at the time, and invented others so as to provide symbolisation for each portion of his diagrams; a second set of diagrams incorporates a minor reshuffle of the symbols to enable them to be more easily learnt. Kingdon (1964: 115) also tentatively suggested that it might be possible to simplify his scheme by using a "single symbol for each vowel position with auxiliary symbols to indicate lip spreading and lip rounding".

Windsor Lewis (1966; 1969: 15–23) revised the vowel diagrams for pedagogical purposes, using large vowel markers (incorporating useful indications of lip shape) on a 34 slot grid (see Figure 14.2). He claimed that his diagrams were "designed to bring out the broad differences between mother tongue and target language and to avoid unrealistically minute distinctions" (Windsor Lewis 1969: 16).

McClure (1972) criticised the concept of primary and secondary Cardinal Vowels, and following Kingdon (see above), demanded two new diagrams containing (1) all the spread, and (2) all the rounded, Cardinal Vowels.

Ladefoged (1967: 140) also came up with the interesting idea of a vowel diagram arranged in terms of points of three-dimensional auditory space in order to accommodate the parameter of lip shape (Figure 14.3).

Other linguists criticised, explicitly or implicitly, what they felt to be the English-cum-French bias of Jones's system. H.B. Lee (1968) produced acoustic evidence based on formant analysis (see below) to show that his own native Korean back un-rounded vowels were apparently more retracted than those produced by Jones in the last (1955) Cardinal Vowel recording. Hammarström (1973) also questioned Jones's renderings of front vowels from the viewpoint of a native Swedish speaker (though omitted to produce any hard evidence to back his views).

Windsor Lewis (1976: 29–30) returned to disputing the over-precision implied in many treatments of the Cardinal Vowels and also pleaded for the IPA to abandon the earlier sloping back line shapes designed to reflect supposed physically determined tongue height positions in favour of the more schematic forms with vertical back lines advocated by Jones from the 1930s onwards (as in the *Phoneme* and the *Pronunciation of English*³). Catford (1977: 165–187), in a spirited defence of the Jonesian Cardinal Vowels, produced a "polar co-ordinate vowel diagram" (Figure 14.4) to show how the information contained in the vowel quadrilateral could be presented in another geometrical form, namely as segments of a circle; however, he recognised that the idea lacked the convenience of the Jonesian arrangement.

Several critics took up Russell's point that the vowel chart was essentially based on

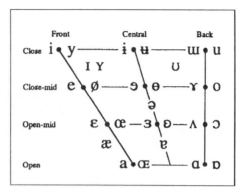

Figure 14.7. Jones's vowel diagram as
shown in the (1993) IPA chart.

auditory judgements rather than the physiological basis claimed by Jones. Essner
(1947) and Joos (1948: 49–57) were the first to show that a plot of the first and second
formants could be arranged to produce a diagram similar to that of the Jonesian cardinal quadrilateral. Joos claimed that his acoustic model corresponded better to the
Cardinal Vowel configuration than did articulatory postures as indicated by X-ray
data. The concept of formant plotting was examined by others, including Ladefoged
(1967: 75–115), and has gained wide acceptance. See Figure 14.5 for Ladefoged's
(1975: 194) diagram based on plottings of American vowels of English placed within
a Jones-type vowel figure (here the frequency of F_1 is plotted on the ordinate whilst
the difference between the values of F_2 and F_1 is shown on the abscissa). Catford
(1981: 23–27) also has an elaborate scheme for fitting formant plottings into the
Cardinal Vowel model.

One of the most devastating critiques of the Cardinal Vowels so far has come
from Butcher (1982). He attacked (p. 50) the model, sixty-five years after its conception, as outmoded and fallacious: "Daniel Jones's system...has reached retirement
age". Nevertheless, Butcher recognised its place in the development of phonetic
thought.

Since [1917], despite occasional criticism and suggestions for modifications, the
basic notion has continued to occupy a more or less central niche in the phonetic
orthodoxy.... Although the attitude of many academic phoneticians to Cardinal
Vowels might best be described as ambivalent, students on phonetics courses in
Britain will almost inevitably be introduced to the concept at an early stage and,
however healthy the degree of scepticism imparted, the impression is usually
given that this is still a basic element of the phonetics syllabus—an impression
which could only be strengthened by the treatment afforded the topic in quite recent introductory textbooks.

Butcher goes on to say that some of "the major practical and theoretical shortcomings of the CV system...have long been recognised" and claims that: "Continued use of the system has a positively dangerous effect in that it conditions phoneticians to an approach to their discipline which is theoretically inadequate and scientifically dishonest."

Butcher attacks the Cardinal Vowel system on several fronts. He is doubtful about the supposed arbitrariness of the chosen vowels, regarding them as likely to be derived from French (p. 53). He illustrates the fallacy of the direct relationship between the Cardinal Vowels and the tongue-height parameter and attacks the confusion in the model which has resulted through the need to include a lip-shape parameter (pp. 53–54). Butcher also indicts Jones for his neglect not only of the pharynx cavity (pharyngalisation) but also of other variables such as nasalisation and retroflexion, and tense/lax variation (pp. 54–55; cf. Catford 1981: 31). He also considers that it is difficult to judge the true physiological extent of vowel space and that this may be far greater than that considered by Jones in his theory (pp. 56–58). Butcher furthermore doubts the equidistance claimed for the Cardinal Vowels on a perceptual basis, showing that vowels are interpreted differently, not only by speakers of differing language backgrounds, but also even by native English-speaking trained phoneticians (pp. 62–64). He also claims that trained speakers show variation in the production of Cardinal Vowels (p. 66, see Figure 14.6).

Part of Butcher's rejection of the Jones Cardinal Vowel system must be accepted. There can be no doubt that claims were made for the model, either by Jones, or by his followers, which are impossible to maintain in the light of present-day knowledge. However, certain conclusions which Butcher draws are more open to question. His non-acceptance of Jones's specifications of the vowels, and his unwillingness merely to go along with Ladefoged in taking a definition of a Cardinal Vowel as one declared to be such by Jones, or one of his followers, is quite understandable (pp. 68–69). But he goes on to say (p. 69):

> Certainly from a purely phonetic point of view the precise and detailed notation of vowel (and for that matter consonant) sounds is nowadays largely redundant. It is no longer necessary as a device for transcribing the sounds of a language for subsequent reproduction. The days of the phonetician as human tape-recorder are over: magnetic tape does the job far more efficiently and does it for the dialectologist and for the speech pathologist as well as for the language teacher, for whom the Cardinal Vowels were originally intended.

This is true, but neglects two issues: the usefulness of the Cardinal Vowel system as a means of classifying raw data, and the fact that a large body of literature in all these disciplines, making use of the Cardinal Vowel system, already exists. Butcher, however, goes on to admit that reference vowels are needed "as a kind of shorthand" (p. 69)—though questions whether the categorisation need be as fine as in Jones's

[ʏ denotes a sound intermediate between RP u and ʌ. Long
aː is about cardinal No. 4. Short a is between this and the
present-day short a. In iu the i is more prominent than the u.
ɛi starts with a rather open variety of ɛ; the diphthong must
be carefully distinguished from əi.]

'antɒni. 'frɛndz, 'roːmənz, 'kʏntrimən, 'lɛnd mi iuɹ 'iːɹz;
əi 'kʏm tu 'bɛri 'siːzəɹ, 'nɒt tu 'prɛiz him.
ði: 'iːvil ðət mɛn 'duː 'livz 'aftəɹ ðɛm;
ðə 'guːd iz 'ɔft in'tɛrid wið ðɛiɹ 'boːnz;
'soː lɛt it 'biː wið 'siːzəɹ. ðə 'noːbl *'briutəs
haθ 'toʊld iu 'siːzəɹ waz am'bisiəs;
if it 'wɛːɹ soː, it waz ə 'griːvəs 'fɔːlt,
and 'griːvəsli haθ 'siːzəɹ 'ansəɹd it.
'hiːɹ, ʏndəɹ 'leːv ɔv 'briutəs ənd ðə 'rɛst—
fɔɹ 'briutəs iz ən 'ɒnərəbl man;
'soː aːɹ ðɛi 'ɔːl, 'ɔːl 'ɒnərəbl mɛn—
'kʏm 'əi tu 'spɛːk in 'siːzəɹz 'fiunərəl.
hiː waz məi 'frɛnd, 'fɛiθfʏl and 'dʒʏst tu miː;
bʏt 'briutəs 'sɛz hiː waz am'bisiəs,
and 'briutəs iz ən 'ɒnərəbl man.
hiː haθ brɔːt 'mɛni 'kaptivz 'hoːm tu *'ruːm,
huːz 'ransəmz did ðə 'dʒɛnərəl 'kɒfəɹz 'fil;
did 'ðis in 'siːzəɹ siːm am'bisiəs?

'antɒni. 'frɛndz, 'roːmənz, 'kʏntrimɛn, 'lɛnd miː juːɹ 'iːɹz;
əi 'kʏm tu 'bɛri 'sɛːzəɹ, 'nɒt tu 'prɛːz him.
ði: 'iːvil ðat mɛn 'duː 'livz 'aftəɹ ðɛm;
ðə 'guːd iz 'ɔft in'taːrid wið ðɛːɹ 'boːnz;
'soː lɛt it 'biː wið 'sɛːzəɹ. ðə 'noːbl *'brjuːtəs
haθ 'toːld juː 'sɛːzəɹ waz am'bisiəs;
if it 'wɛːɹ soː, it waz ə 'griːvəs 'fɔːlt,
and 'griːvəsli həθ 'sɛːzəɹ 'ansəɹd it.
'hiːɹ, ʏndəɹ 'leːv əv 'brjuːtəs and ðə 'rɛst—
fɔɹ 'brjuːtəs iz ən 'ɒnərəbl man;
'soː aːɹ ðɛː 'ɔːl, 'ɔːl 'ɒnərəbl mɛn—
'kʏm 'əi tu 'spɛːk in 'sɛːzəɹz 'fjuːnərəl.
hiː waz məi 'frɛnd, 'fɛːθfəl ənd 'dʒʏst tu miː;
bʏt 'brjuːtəs 'sɛz hiː waz am'bisiəs,
and 'brjuːtəs iz ən 'ɒnərəbl man.
hiː haθ brɔːt 'mɛni 'kaptivz 'hoːm tu *'ruːm,
huːz 'ransəmz did ðə 'dʒɛnərəl 'kɒfəɹz 'fil;
did 'ðis in 'sɛːzəɹ siːm am'bisiəs?

Figure 14.8. Extracts from Jones's two versions of Shakespearean pronunciation (*Pronunciation of English*[3] [1950],
p. 198, *Pronunciation of English*[4] [1956], p. 210).
Kökeritz's (1953: 362–363) reconstruction of the same passage, which appeared in the interim, is shown on p. 445.

Antony. 'frɛn(d)z, 'roːmənz, 'kʌntrɪmən, 'lɛnd mi ju(ː)ɹ 'iːɹz.
ɑɪ 'kʌm tʊ 'bɛrɪ 'sᶒːzɑɹ, 'nɒt-tʊ 'prᶒːz (h)ɪm.
ðɪ 'iːvɪl ðət 'mɛn 'duː 'lɪvz 'æːftəɹ ðᶒm,
ðə 'gʊd ɪz 'ɔːft m'tɜːrɪd wɪð-ðəɹ 'boːnz.
'soː lɛt ɪt 'biː wɪθ 'sᶒːzɑɹ. ðə 'noːbļ 'bruːtəs
(h)əθ 'toːld ju 'sᶒːzɑɹ wəz æm'bɪʃɹəs,
ɪf ɪt 'wɛːɹ 'soː, ɪt wɑz ə 'griːvəs 'fɔː(l)t,
ən(d) 'griːvəslɪ (h)əθ 'sᶒːzɑɹ 'æːnsəɹd ɪt.
'hiːɹ, ʌndəɹ 'lᶒːv əv 'bruːtəs ən(d) ðə 'rɛst—
fəɹ 'bruːtəs ɪz ən 'ɒnərəbļ 'mæn—
soː a(ː)ɹ ðᶒ 'ɔːl, 'ɔːl 'ɒnərəbļ 'mɛn—
'kʌm ɑɪ tʊ 'spᶒːk in 'sᶒːzɑɹz 'fjuːnərəl.
hiː wɑz mɑɪ 'frɛnd, 'fᶒːθfʊl ən(d)-'dʒʌst tʊ 'miː,
bət 'bruːtəs 'sᶒz hi wɑz æm'bɪʃɹəs,
ən(d) 'bruːtəs ɪz ən 'ɒnərəbļ 'mæn.
hi hæθ 'brɔːt 'mɛnɪ 'kæptɪvz 'hoːm tə 'ruːm,
huːz 'rænsəmz dɪd ðə 'dʒɛnrəl 'kɒfəɹz 'fɪl.
dɪd 'ðɪs ɪn 'sᶒːzɑɹ 'siːm æm'bɪʃɹəs?

Figure 14.8. (*cont.*)

system. He also accepts the need for something similar to the Cardinal Vowel system as a prelude to phonological analysis.

In fact, Butcher's case is somewhat overstated. The diagram represented in Figure 14.6 would show that suitably trained phoneticians seem in fact to be rather good at approximating to Cardinal Vowel values (the reverse of his claim). Furthermore, the very fact that so many scholars in the fields of phonetics and phonology call on the Cardinal Vowels (or modifications of the system) as an aid to linguistic description would seem to indicate that there is a need for a reference vowel model even in the era of cheap, efficient and reliable recording apparatus. This does not, of course, mean that the obvious errors and lacunae in Jones's thinking should be ignored, or regarded as above criticism. It would seem desirable, *pace* Abercrombie and Catford, to recognise the essentially perceptual nature of the model. Possibly a new standardised version of the vowels should be issued by the IPA, synthesised on the basis of formant values (cf. Bladon—Fant 1978, quoted by Butcher 1982: 70). This could replace the quavery last recording (made in Jones's old age, see Section 13.12) which is presently taken as a reference by those phoneticians who use the Cardinal Vowel system.

It is likely—notwithstanding the doubts of Butcher and others—that the Cardinal Vowels will survive, if only because of the huge corpus of work already extant which makes use of it. Whether, for the future, it will have to be modified to fit present-day knowledge, as has proved to be the case with the IPA transcription scheme, remains to be seen. Furthermore, Jones would probably be well satisfied if he knew that the latest (1993) version of the International Phonetic Alphabet chart still shows his vowel model virtually completely intact (see Figure 14.7).

14.15.   Chaucerian and Shakespearean reconstructions

One theoretical area in which Jones busied himself from the start of his career was the reconstruction of earlier forms of English, in particular the pronunciation of the Chaucerian and Shakespearean eras. As has been described in Section 3.2, he organised performances of play excerpts and poetry reading in reconstructed pronunciation as early as 1909, and included lectures on these topics in his courses at University College. He published a reconstruction of Elizabethan English at this point (Jones 1909c) and then played a major role in the production of Linguaphone gramophone records on the history of English pronunciation, writing a portion of an accompanying

'fleː frɔː ðə 'prɛːs, and 'dwɛl wiθ 'soːθfast'nɛsə;
su'fiːz θiːn 'ounə 'θiŋg, 'θoux hit beː 'smɑl.
fɔr 'houd haθ 'haːt, and 'kliːmbiŋg 'tikəl'nɛsə,
'prɛːs haθ ɛn'viː and 'wɛːl 'blɛnt ɔːvəɹ 'ɑl.
saː'vuːɹ 'nɔː 'moːɹ θan 'θeː bə'hoːvə 'ʃal;
'riul 'wɛl θiː'sɛlf θat 'oːðəɹ 'folk kanst 'rɛːdə;
and 'truːðə ʃal də'livɹ, it iz 'nɔː 'drɛːdə.

tɛm'pɛst θeː 'nouxt 'ɑl 'kroːkəd toː rə'drɛsə,
in 'trust ɔf 'hiɹ θat 'tuɹnəθ az a 'bɑl;
'grɛːt 'rɛstə 'stant in 'litl bɛzi'nɛsə.
beː 'waːr θɛːɹ'foːɹ toː 'spuɹn agɛin an 'ɑl;
'striːv 'nouxt az doːθ θə 'krɔkkə wiθ θə 'wɑl;
'daːntə ðiː'sɛlf θat 'daːntəst 'oːðɹəs 'deːdə;
and 'truːðə ʃal də'livɹ, it iz 'nɔː 'drɛːdə.

'θat θeː is 'sɛnt rə'sɛiv in 'buksum'nɛsə;
θə 'wrastliŋg fɔɹ ðis 'wuɹld 'aksɛθ a 'fɑl;
'heɹ niz 'nɔːn 'hɔːm, 'heɹ niz but 'wildəɹ'nɛsə.
'foːɹθ, ˌpilgrim, 'foːɹθ! 'foːɹθ, 'bɛːst, uɹt ɔf θiː 'stɑl!
'knou ðiː kun'treː! 'loːk 'up! 'θaŋk 'gɔd ɔv 'ɑl!
'hould ðə 'hiː 'wɛi, and 'lat θiː 'gɔːst θeː 'lɛːdə,
and 'truːðə ʃal də'livɹ, it iz 'nɔː 'drɛːdə.

CHAUCER

Figure 14.9. Extract from Chaucer (*Pronunciation of English*⁴, pp. 212–213).

pamphlet (Jones 1937i). In 1949, Jones produced his radio talks series for the BBC entitled "Our changing speech" (reissued, Jones 1985) and was the main force behind the interesting experiment of a radio programme of extracts from Shakespeare acted in Elizabethan English (see Figure 14.8).[9]

Although, oddly, he acknowledged no recent sources for his original (1909c) reconstruction of Shakespeare's pronunciation, Jones seems to have been greatly influenced by Viëtor's (1906a, 1906b) analysis. Jones undertook his own research in the area—perhaps also influenced by Passy's (1910) similar work on old French. His description in his radio talks (Jones 1985: 1–14) of the techniques of tracing sound values of previous eras make clear that he had consulted the works of the early orthoëpists (see Section A.2) and that he was familiar with the methods generally employed by philologists. Jones eventually moved away from the more archaic and stylised forms that Viëtor advocated, as can be seen from a comparison of the extracts from Viëtor (1906) and the *Pronunciation of English*[3] (p. 198); see Figures 3.1 and 14.8. Jones published two reconstructions as supplements to *Le Maître phonétique*—one of Chaucerian and one of Shakespearean pronunciation (Jones 1938c, 1944e).

In the *Pronunciation of English*[3], Jones included Chaucerian and Shakespearean English in the book for the first time; in the earlier editions, e.g. the *Pronunciation of English*[1] (p. 103), he had merely referred the reader to Viëtor (1906a, 1906b). However, any claims Jones might have had as a Shakespearean authority were soon considerably shaken when Kökeritz (1953) appeared, producing transcriptions which differed in many respects from Jones's work, and suggesting that Shakespeare's English was far closer to present-day language than Jones (and others) had implied. Kökeritz was also directly critical of Jones for being unduly influenced by Viëtor and adopting an unrealistically archaic pronunciation, with little vowel gradation in unstressed syllables and infrequent use of weak forms. These strictures seem somewhat harsh since Jones had in fact moved away from Viëtor's standpoint towards a position closer to that taken up by Kökeritz. Though Kökeritz grants that "Jones [1937i] is probably right in postulating the diphthongs [əɪ] and [əʊ] for ME ī and ū", he goes on to say that Jones had erred not only in his interpretation of much of the vowel system, but also in his treatment of the consonants, unstressed vowels and syncope. Kökeritz (1953: 50 n.) concludes that Jones's "reconstruction of Shakespeare's speech is at variance with the evidence of the text and with the testimony of contemporary orthoëpists".

Jones felt personally hurt by this criticism,[10] but he appears eventually to have recognised the validity of some of Kökeritz's views and changed his versions accordingly. The introduction to the *Pronunciation of English*[4] (p. viii) states that Jones had revised his texts "in the light of the latest researches", naming especially Kökeritz (1953) and Dobson (1957a [1968[2]]). He indicates that he was also strongly influenced in making changes by the views of his colleagues A.C. Gimson and Randolph Quirk. The Shakespeare text itself contained not only a change in the allocation of vowels, but also a different use of weak forms and more gradation in unstressed syllables. It confirms how far Jones had moved towards Kökeritz's view, which stressed the similarities of Shakespearean English and modern pronunciation. In comparison, the last Chaucer excerpt (Figure 14.9) shows fewer changes from the 1950 version, or the Jones (1938c) text, though Jones includes an introductory note stating that the pronunciation may possibly be "slightly archaic for the period" since the Great Vowel Shift might already have begun by Chaucer's time (*Pronunciation of English*[4]: 212).

Quite shortly after Kökeritz's book had appeared, a reaction against his more radical suggestions began to set in, see Dobson (1955), indicating that a substantial number of scholars felt that Shakespeare's English was in fact further removed from modern pronunciation than Kökeritz had proposed. This view is maintained in a more recent publication, Cercignani (1981); such reassessments suggest that Jones's later attempts at reconstruction of Elizabethan pronunciation will eventually come to be regarded more highly than once appeared to be the case.

14.16. The concept of the phoneme

The area where Jones's name is best known in present-day linguistics (outside articulatory phonetics) is phoneme theory, where he is frequently cited as a pioneer in the field.

However, as we have already seen, Jones never made any claims to having played any role in actually devising the phoneme concept. As he states explicitly (*HMTP*: 5–6), he had merely absorbed the work of the Kazan' School linguists, Baudouin de Courtenay and Kruszewski—firstly through reading the work of Baudouin's pupil Ščerba (1911), and later supplementing this with discussions with Benni. In addition, Jones had already been profoundly influenced by Sweet's notions with regard to broad and narrow forms of transcription, and the similar ideas of Passy. Though neither of these scholars used the word "phoneme", the essentials of the phonemic principle are clear from their writings and were absorbed by Jones so that he was ready to accept a more developed presentation of the concept once it was revealed to him.

The full import of the idea apparently took a little time to sink in, but as early as 1915, the phoneme concept was in everyday use in Jones's Department (*HMTP*: 6). The *Sechuana reader*, published in 1916, showed Jones working implicitly within the phoneme principle, though avoiding the use of the actual word. In this book, which is so full of innovative ideas (Section 6.8), Jones talks of "significant [sound] distinctions", and relates these explicitly to change of meaning (*Sechuana reader*: xi–xiv). He later included several explicit references to the phoneme in the Philological Society lecture on Sechuana (Jones 1917c). As stated in Section 7.5, examination of his actual lecture notes reveals that his claim (*HMTP*: 9-10) to have provided an explanation of the term phoneme in this talk is correct. The report of the lecture that appears in the *Transactions of the Philological Society*, incomplete though it may be, clearly shows that Jones has to be recognised as the first Western European linguist actually to employ the word "phoneme" in the present-day sense in a publication—many years before the American structural linguists began their long preoccupation with the concept in the thirties.

In the *Sinhalese reader* (1919a), Jones defined the phoneme in terms very similar to those he would adhere to for the rest of his career, namely a "group of related sounds of a given language which are so used in connected speech that no one of them ever occurs in positions which any other can occupy" (*Sinhalese reader*: 2). He had thus arrived at the dual criteria of phonetic similarity and complementary distribution—the latter term being a structuralist usage which Jones accepted for the first time in *HMTP* (p. 258)—whilst at the same time refusing to accept the validity of "free variation" within a phoneme definition (p. 258 n). These criteria were to be the cruces of Jones's form of phonemic theory. Yet, though meaning as such was excluded from his definition, Jones goes on immediately in the *Sinhalese reader* to specify the semantic function of the phoneme in distinguishing word meanings, as opposed to "speech sounds" belonging to the same phoneme (i.e. allophones), which cannot distinguish one word from another. He reiterated his views in similar terms in 1923 in the *Pronunciation of Russian* (p. 50), stating that the phonemes should be regarded as "distinctive" and such a distinction could be said to be "significant".

Jones made no further substantial changes in his view of the phoneme; the alterations that took place in his definition were from that point on largely a matter of tightening up the wording—"a progress towards precision", to quote the words of Twaddell (1935 [1966]: 64). In fact, to some extent, he even questioned the possibility—though not the value—of a formal definition in his article "Some thoughts on the phoneme" (Jones 1944d: 121):

Although I believe phonemes to be undefinable, like the fundamental units in other sciences, it is nevertheless needful for the purposes of linguistic study to examine in some detail the nature of these elements, and if possible to produce a so-called "definition" of the phoneme of a more precise kind...

In the same piece (p. 134), Jones goes on to arrive at the following often quoted definition of the phoneme: "A family of sounds in a given language which are related in character and are used in such a way that no one member ever occurs in a word in the same phonetic context as any other member". This statement was repeated word for word in the *Phoneme*[1] [1950], and also in the last revised edition which appeared in 1967, the year of Jones's death (*Phoneme*[3]: 10). One may therefore assume that it represents his definitive viewpoint.

Estimates of Jones's contribution to the development of phonemic theory usually centre around the criticism that his is essentially a practical view of the phoneme, tied closely to his phonetic experience, the demands of language teaching and the construction of transcriptional systems. It is claimed that he thereby misses the greater flexibility of more theoretical approaches; see for instance, Robins ([1979]: 215), Fischer-Jørgensen (1975: 50–58), and S. Anderson (1985: 175–176). Such criticisms are indeed to a large extent valid, but it should not be imagined that Jones was unaware of the limitations he was setting himself within this narrow definition. Both in his early definition of "significant" sounds in the *Sechuana reader* and also in his first public references to the phoneme in the Philological Society Lecture (Jones 1917c), he defines the concept with reference to word meaning (see above). In *HMTP* (p. 9) he states that he regards both views—which he terms the "physical" and the "psychological"—as equally tenable:

> In fact, when it became necessary for me to come to a decision between the two, I found it in the end impossible to escape the conclusion that the physical view of the phoneme is on the whole better suited to the needs of ordinary teaching of spoken languages and...for those who are called upon to reduce to writing languages hitherto unwritten or to improve upon existing unsatisfactory orthographies. I find the physical view more easily comprehensible to the ordinary student of languages than any other. At the same time I do not hesitate at times to resort to psychological criteria.

S. Anderson (1985: 176) points out that Jones did not eliminate meaning from his definition for the reason that the American structuralists later did, namely "from a general rejection of meaning as a valid linguistic category", but rather "from considerations of conceptual clarity". Jones himself admitted that he was in many ways attracted to a far more abstract psychological view of the phoneme as a "mental image", similar to that originally propagated by Baudouin (*Phoneme*: 213). This decision to exclude meaning from his primary definition of the phoneme (and yet to include it as an appended elaboration) has been explained by commentators, for instance Krámský (1974: 151), as being a result of his phonetic training and background:

> Daniel Jones was a phonetician and that explains why he regarded as the main object of grouping the sounds of a language together into phonemes the establishment of the simplest systems of phonetic transcription for every language.

There is undoubtedly much in the idea that Jones, schooled essentially as an articulatory phonetician, would regard the physical production of sounds, together with their auditory characteristics, as being decisive in the establishment of phonemic differences. Yet, his phonetic training, and his main aims of establishing transcription systems for language teaching, do not completely account for his decision to view the phoneme in the way that he did.

There was another possible influence at work, and Jones may have devised his definition of the phoneme, in part, to fit in with his wider view of the world. It is noteworthy that the period between 1916, when the *Sechuana reader* was published, and 1919, when the *Sinhalese reader* appeared, was also the time when Jones was beginning to be interested in the ideas of the theosophical movement (see Section 10.8)—something which was to be an increasingly dominating force in his life as he grew older. His obvious preoccupation with theosophical doctrine in "Concrete and abstract sounds" (Jones 1938a), see Section 11.4, gives extra weight to the notion that, especially in the latter years of his life, when considering the phoneme, Jones could often actually have had theosophy at the back of his mind. In considering how to define the phoneme, Jones may have decided to exclude semantic concepts and any type of mentalistic approach (such as that favoured by Baudouin and his followers) because reconciling such ideas with theosophical principles would lead to a statement which was too involved and controversial to function as a good working definition (see Collins—Mees 1997).

Jones was later to expand his view of the phoneme in several directions in order to cover a number of supra-segmental features excluded by his definition. The first of these extensions was the "toneme", according to Jones (*HMTP*: 12) "coined at my suggestion" and taken up by Beach and other members of the UCL Department; much of the *Phoneme* (pp. 152–192) is concerned with tonemic analysis. Later additions were "chroneme" and "stroneme" as units of linguistic structure determined by length and stress respectively (Jones 1944c). Because of the difficulties of categorisation, and the lack of precise phonetic correlates, Jones effectively abandoned the use of the latter term, but took up the chroneme with more enthusiasm (*Phoneme*: 124–134). The limitations of the chroneme, as applied to English, were recognised by Jones (*Phoneme*: 127–129), but the idea may have been one factor (together with considerations of typological simplicity) in his rejection of a transcription system for English based on vowel quality, such as he favoured in the 1920s. As a result, he returned to systems based on length distinctions, which fitted better into a chronemic approach (see Section 14.9).

The other aspect of Jones's theory which proved unduly restrictive was his insistence that the phoneme should be defined in terms of a single stylistically consistent idiolect (Jones 1929a: 44, *Phoneme*: 9). To cope with individual variation of style (covered by "free variation" in structuralist terminology), or dialect mixing, Jones invoked the concept of the "variphone" (*Phoneme*: 205–211). Dialect variation was covered by the "diaphone", a useful term which could be used to include all the dialectal realisational differences of, for example, a particular vowel sound (*Phoneme*: 193–205). With these extensions of the phoneme concept, and the elaboration of terminology involved, Jones and his UCL colleagues were able to construct a linguistic framework and metalanguage which, even if less rigorously defined, were more flexible and accommodating than those set up by the American structuralists, who took over several of Jones's ideas. Within this paradigm, the Jonesian phoneticians were able to conduct valuable pioneering work on a wide range of languages (see Section 10.13). Furthermore, Jones showed himself willing, even at a very late stage in his career, to accept structuralist terminology and conventions where these suited his purpose, e.g. slant/square bracketing, the term "allophone" (*HMTP*: 18–20) and even to coin neologisms on similar lines, e.g. "allochrone" (Jones 1956d: 99 n.). Nevertheless, he did not accept other structuralist phonological ideas, such as Trager—Smith's (1951) extension of the term "phoneme" to include intonation and juncture (*HMTP*: 19–20). (In this, Jones has been proved right, since the Trager—Smith treatment has proved to be largely a passing fashion.) Nor, of course, would he have any truck with Firthian prosodic phonology, even though many of his younger staff found it attractive and were prepared to follow Firth to SOAS for the extra theoretical scope it permitted them (see Section 12.3).

When Jones borrowed from the structuralists, he was in a sense reclaiming a debt, since there had been considerable borrowing by Bloomfield and the post-Bloomfieldians from him; for example, in their taking over Jones's physical view of the phoneme, with the notions of phonetic similarity and complementary distribution. The American linguists largely accepted Jones's ideas, although they cloaked them in new terminology (Fischer-Jørgensen 1975: 77). For instance, the basic concept of juncture is foreshadowed by Jones's work on word-boundary features (Jones 1931k). Indeed, Jones's role in providing the precursors to certain structuralist concepts was crucial for the history of linguistics—even though his significance increasingly went unrecognised. American linguistics in the 1940s and 1950s became more and more unwilling to acknowledge influences from outside the United States itself, as can be seen from the patronising and dogmatically structuralist reviews of the *Pronunciation of English*[3] (Smith 1952) and the *Phoneme* (McDavid 1952); see Sections 13.10 and 13.9, respectively.

14.17. Conclusion

In his contribution to the history of the phoneme concept, Jones can be seen to play the type of role which in a sense epitomises his importance to phonetics and linguistics. He was not a true innovator; he typically took over the ideas of others and put his own imprint on them. He was certainly not a great theoretician; he was happier working with practical realities than with elaborate theoretical edifices, though regularly managing to take existing theories and bring new insights to them. What he did best—superbly—was to recognise the worth of partially evolved ideas and concepts, develop these further, particularly in terms of practical phonetic description, and then disseminate them to a wider audience. In this way, he often inspired others to work using his methods, and in so doing to produce research of a thorough, well-ordered, practical type, often of a truly pioneering nature. For Jones, everything had to have a practical bias; he had little use for theories which could not easily be applied, and no regard at all for any form of academic pretentiousness.

In his difficulties with Firth, it is tempting to consider Jones as being at the wrong end of a Kuhnian-type scientific revolution; see Kuhn (1962) for the original exposition of this idea and Laudan (1977) for a critique of Kuhn's views.[11] Jones can be regarded as having established a cumulative paradigm, building on the efforts of the early nineteenth century British school and linking these with the work of Passy. To this amalgamation, Jones contributed a fully formulated model of vowel description and took over and developed his own variety of phoneme theory, borrowing the original concept from the Kazan' School of Baudouin. Within this paradigm, Jones established for two decades, during the 1920s and 1930s, a world primacy for London in descriptive phonetics, gathering a band of fellow-thinkers around him.

Yet even at this time, there were murmurs of dispute within his own ranks, as Abercrombie (1980) has nicely observed in his description of the theoretical division in the Department reflected in its "upstairs-downstairs" partitioning. The real challenge to the Jones paradigm was to come in the person of J.R. Firth, and the extent of Firth's inroads was only clear when Jones attempted to re-start his Department in 1943; he found that many of his best young scholars were now thinking along completely different lines from himself, and wanting to express themselves via the more complex and analytical path of Firthian prosodic phonology, rather than through a Jonesian approach. Whilst he would have been unable to analyse events in these terms, Jones was soon aware of the challenge to his position, and his hatred (not too strong a term) of Firth developed accordingly.

It is not at all curious that the threats to Jones originated in his own Department—"palace revolutions" are common in the academic world—but it is at first sight strange that reaction against Jones's views was delayed in the USA. Instead, the Structuralists first took over his ideas, incorporated them, developed them and then proclaimed them as their own. The explanation lies in the comparatively late arrival of the phoneme concept on the American scene (as compared with continental Europe, where Prague school linguists had worked with a variety of approaches and alternatives to phonemic analysis ever since the early 1930s). This late development allowed the American Structuralist school to have more than two decades of argument based around phonemic ideas before a reaction against the whole phoneme concept set in during the late 1950s. By then, Structuralism was established as the paradigm in the USA, and the destructive attacks (led in part by European Prague-influenced linguists such as Roman Jakobson and Morris Halle) were directed against the major scholars of the Structuralist school. Jones and his followers were largely forgotten about during the battles, and spared direct onslaught.

Now that a considerable interval has elapsed since Jones's death, it is possible to look back on his achievements and get some idea of his place in the history of phonetics and linguistics. Few would question that he must be considered as the leading figure in twentieth century British phonetics and he vies with Sweet, Ellis and Bell as the greatest of all British phoneticians. Bell was a remarkable innovator and his work can nowadays be appreciated for its originality and ingenuity, but nevertheless the passage of time has rendered it inaccessible and dated. Furthermore, it lacks the breadth of phonetic interest that characterises the contributions of Sweet and Jones. Ellis lives on mainly through his vast *Early English pronunciation* (Ellis 1869–89), but whilst this remains a fascinating work, and was a remarkable achievement in its time, it is fatally over-ambitious. This magnum opus is peppered with inaccuracies and it is also in large part a compilation of the efforts of others. Sweet's writings embraced wide areas of linguistics—phonetics was only one of his interests. His genius and scholarship are apparent on virtually every page he wrote and his phonetic descriptions are full of remarkable insights; his influence on his fellow phoneticians throughout Europe, not least on Daniel Jones himself, was immense and continues to this day. To find a rival to Sweet in these terms is impossible.

Nevertheless, it was largely Jones—not Sweet—who changed phonetics in Britain from an offshoot of philology into a linguistic science. In Jones's hands, phonetics became a proper academic discipline represented by numerous university departments, studied by a large body of dedicated scholars, and with a wide and varied collection of published work. This would undoubtedly have happened in due course without Jones; but it would have occurred later and would have followed a different course, probably lagging behind developments elsewhere. As it was, for much of the time that Jones was active in the field, the centre of gravity for phonetics was Britain; to be precise, Jones's own Department in University College, London, together with its sister foundation, staffed largely by his pupils, at the School of Oriental Studies. No such claim could ever have been made for Sweet—who was essentially a solitary worker, alienating his colleagues rather than gathering them around him to inspire them to greater efforts. In these respects, Jones achieved far more for phonetics than did Sweet.

Jones was a man of his time. He had the good fortune to arrive at a point when phonetics had not yet found its place among scientific disciplines and when linguistics was still dominated by the study of historical forms of languages, and the process of linguistic change was studied through writing rather than speech. On the other hand, he flourished when there was still insufficient instrumentation for experimental phonetics to assume the increasingly dominant role that it has held from the fifties onwards (see Sara 1990 for a summary of developments in articulatory, acoustic and auditory phonetics from the time of Jones's retirement onwards). Throughout the period of his university career, there was plenty of scope for a man with Jones's astonishing gifts as a practical "ear phonetician" to use them to the full. In this atmosphere, Jones was able to play a determining role in the establishment of phonetics as an essential component of linguistics, and took advantage of the opportunity to build on the work of the British phoneticians Pitman, Ellis, Bell and (above all) Sweet. Furthermore, Jones was able to incorporate the ideas of the great continental phoneticians of the previous generation, such as Sievers, Viëtor and, notably, his own teacher Paul Passy. But what Jones managed to achieve to a greater extent than any of these was the world-wide acceptance of phonetics not only by linguistic scholars, but also by a more general public of language teachers and students, and the recognition of the science as (to quote Sweet's own favourite phrase) "the indispensable foundation of all study of language".

Appendix

Historical Background

A.1. The roots of phonetic studies

Interest in the speech process and in the manners in which speech sounds are patterned in language can be traced back at least two and a half thousand years to the work of the ancient Indian phoneticians and phonologists, notably Pāṇini and Patañjali (Allen [1965]). Daniel Jones fully recognised the remarkable genius of these linguists, as is quite clear from this extract from notes for his 1916 Missionaries' Lecture:

> ...the Indians themselves discovered a good deal about the pronunciation of their languages. All the good features [in romanisation systems] are due to them, and all the bad features (particularly in the representation of vowels) are due to our inability to improve on what they discovered hundreds and thousands of years ago.[1]

The anonymous Semitic linguists who constructed the first alphabets on a syllabic consonantal phonemic basis are considered to have had remarkable insights for their time (Sampson 1985: 77–98). The early Greeks transformed these alphabets into one which was "broadly phonemic" in nature (Robins [1979]: 13). Later on, Greek scholars such as Dionysius Thrax (active c. 100 BC), although not as adept scientifically as their Indian forerunners, nonetheless showed great ingenuity in attempting to determine the nature of the speech process. The Greek linguists devised a descriptive model which, whilst inaccurate in many respects, continued to be used for nearly two thousand years; and they also produced a terminology for articulatory phonetics, much of which (filtered through Latin) is still employed today (Allen 1981, Robins [1979]: 9–44).

After the classical period, the development of phonetics stagnated although some original phonetic and phonological ideas emerged from a few individual linguists, such as the twelfth century Icelandic "First Grammarian", whose name is unknown (Haugen 1950 [1972²]), and the fifteenth century Korean king Se-Jong, discussed by Jones in his historical survey of the phoneme concept (*HMTP*: 1–2). See also Gim 1937). It was not until the sixteenth century that there was to be found in a single country a considerable number of scholars all working on aspects of speech.

A.2. The early development of the English School

England was the country where this flurry of linguistic activity took place and the output of work continued for about a hundred and fifty years. Wyld (1906: 300–301) has noted that these English linguistic pioneers came from a rich diversity of backgrounds:

> From the year 1530 onwards there exists a series of works by English writers in English, French, Welsh, and Latin which deal directly or incidentally with the pronunciation of English during the age in which the writers lived. These men belonged to several different classes of society; there were Divines, some of whom were Bishops and Court Chaplains, Oxford and Cambridge Professors and Heads of Houses, Schoolmasters of various ranks; there were Poets, Scholars, and Men of Science.

Firth (1946 [1957]: 92–93) regarded this group of linguists as the pioneers of what he termed (following Sweet 1913: 38) the "English School of Phonetics". Their worth has now been recognised and evaluated in such works as the surveys of Wyld (1906), Firth (1957) and Abercrombie (1948); later studies by Dobson (1957a [1968²]) and Salmon (1979) have provided extensive coverage of the sixteenth and seventeenth century British linguists.

The earliest known work in England included cross-linguistic phonetic descriptions—of English and French by John Palsgrave (1530) and of English and Welsh by William Salesbury (1547, 1550)—which were aimed mainly at language learners. Salesbury, writing in both Welsh and English, shows remarkable acuity in his description; the accuracy of his comments on the differences between the phonological systems of the Welsh of North and South Wales provides a fine demonstration of his observational powers. He is quoted by Jones (1909i: 122) as an early example of a contrastive phonetician, notable in particular for his transcriptions of English words using Welsh orthographic conventions.

Another early approach to the study of language is to be found in the work of the English spelling reformers, who extended their interest in orthography to take in phonetics and phonology. These included figures such as William Bullokar (1580), whose work is discussed by Danielsson—Alston in their [1966] reprint of Bullokar's work, and Richard Mulcaster (1582); see Howatt (1984: 89–93). These pioneers would not have referred to themselves as phoneticians, since the very word "phonetics" is not recorded until the very end of the eighteenth century, and are usually termed "orthoëpists" (Robins [1979]: 117); nevertheless, their interests lay clearly within what is now termed phonetics and phonology.[2]

The greatest of the sixteenth-century English phoneticians is considered by many to be John Hart, who provided in his publications (Hart 1551, 1569, 1570) not only a system for spelling reform, but also a competent description of the organs of speech. He managed to define vowels and consonants with considerable accuracy for his time (Jespersen 1907; Danielsson 1955; Howatt 1984: 83–88). Crystal (1969: 20) has pointed out that Hart can also be credited with "the earliest discussion of melody in spoken English" and for having devised a system of marking stress—aspects of phonetics to which relatively little attention was subsequently paid until the eighteenth century (see below). Dobson (1957a [1968²]: 62) asserts that: "John Hart deserves to rank with the greatest English phoneticians and authorities on pronunciation."

Although interest in such matters as language teaching and spelling reform continued undiminished into the seventeenth century, a group of scholars arose at this point who are, as Gimson (1962: 59) said, "interested in speech and language for their own sake". Gimson went on to claim:

> Because of their preoccupation with detailed analysis of speech activity, the comparative study of the sounds of various languages, the classification of sound types, and the establishment of systematic relationships between the English sounds, they can be said to be the true precursors of modern scientific phoneticians.

Early in the century, Robert Robinson in his *Art of pronuntiation* (1617) produced a relatively advanced form of consonant and vowel description. Robinson is also noteworthy for having devised a crude form of vowel diagram, dependent on "certaine eleuations and bendings of the tongue" (p. 23), thus foreshadowing, in some sense, the work of Bell, Sweet and Jones on vowel description. Shortly afterwards, Alexander Gil, the headmaster of St Paul's School, produced his *Logonomia anglica* (1619). Although this included a good system of reformed spelling, and also has interesting comments on the English of his time, together with examples of dialectal pronunciation, Gil has been criticised for his lack of objectivity and his conservatism. Wyld (1906: 304) accuses him of being "old-fashioned", with "a horror of modernisms". Furthermore, Gil's prescriptivism limits the value of his commentary.

John Wallis's (1653) *Grammatica linguae anglicanae*, which was aimed mainly at foreigners learning English, is preceded by a long treatise on speech, entitled "Tractatus de Loquela". This work is in fact largely devoted to a consideration of phonetics, pronunciation and spelling. He describes the speech mechanism in detail, and makes an attempt to set up a classification of speech sounds with potential universal linguistic application. Wallis provides a great deal of exemplification, not only from English, and classical Greek, Latin and Hebrew, but also from French, German, Welsh and other European languages, and also Arabic. His system of vowel and consonant classification, though showing deficiencies and confusion in his knowledge of the physiology of speech articulation, nevertheless "represents a serious attempt at the establishment of universal sound categories" (Gimson 1962: 60). Kemp (1972: 42–62) has written a detailed study of Wallis's vowel and consonant description and classification compared with those provided by other early phoneticians.

However, a more thorough phonetic description of consonant articulations is to be found in the ambitious work of Bishop John Wilkins, *Essay towards a real character and a philosophical language* (1668), which is discussed by, amongst others, Abercrombie (1948), Albright (1958: 6–17), Dobson (1957a [1968²]: 253–261), Shapiro (1969) and also by Jones (see below). Wilkins was largely concerned with the philosophy of linguistics—the problems of creating a universal language together with a system of universal phonetics. In order to cope with these concepts, Wilkins's interest in languages ranged further than Wallis's had done, and he quotes Japanese, Arabic and Chinese amongst his many examples. Wilkins's book is also of interest for the inclusion of a tableau of anatomical cross-sections of the speech organs (p. 378). Attempting to set up an organic system of transcription, in which the component parts of the symbols directly represented features of the articulation (Abercrombie 1967: 116), he anticipated alphabets such as Bell's "Visible Speech" (see Figure A.5), Sweet's "Organic Alphabet" (see Figure 2.12.) and Passy and Jones's "Alphabet Organique" (see Figures 2.13 and 2.14).

Wilkins is of interest as being a writer named by Jones in the 1949 radio series "Our Changing Speech" (republished as Jones 1985). He is quoted by Jones as an authority whom he had consulted for his research on the reconstruction of the pronunciation of Early Modern English. Jones (1985: 13) comments: "We can learn quite an amount from it [Wilkins's *Essay*] about the sounds used in English in the 17th century". He goes on to mention Wilkins's lists of long and short vowels, and shows how this provides evidence for the reconstruction of the Early Modern English vowel system. In the *Phoneme* (1950: 244 n.), Jones also makes reference to Wilkins, quoting his observations on an aspect of the English vowel system.

Yet, although the work of Wallis and Wilkins was impressive for its era, perhaps the best phonetic description of this period is contained in William Holder's (1669) *Elements of speech*. Robins ([1979]: 118) has described Holder as: "an observational phonetician...[who]...achieved remarkable succinctness and accuracy in describing the articulation of speech sounds". A striking aspect of Holder's work is the apparent freshness of his description; Firth (1946 [1957]: 108) called him "surprisingly modern" and Kemp (1972: 45) believes that his "classification comes nearest to modern schemes". Robins (1979: 118) points out the outstanding accuracy of the description of the phonation process, and the "excellence of his phonetic theory" in his description of vowel articulation. Fromkin—Ladefoged (1981: 3–6) have also noted that Holder's description of consonant articulation can be viewed as a primitive kind of distinctive feature system.

Another linguist of this period who was fascinated with the problems of universal phonetics and designing organic alphabets was Francis Lodwick, a Dutch merchant living in England. Lodwick was one of Abercrombie's (1948) "forgotten phoneticians", but he was later the subject of a full-scale study by Salmon (1972). The phonetic description in his *Essay towards an universal alphabet* (Lodwick 1686) is not considered as satisfactory as Holder's (see Salmon 1972, Fromkin—Ladefoged 1981), but Lodwick—like Wilkins—was interested in iconic symbolisation, and is known for having invented an alphabet (see Figure A.1), the ingenuity of which was not surpassed until Bell's (1867) "Visible Speech" nearly two centuries later (see Section A.3). Lodwick's other great interest was the application of principles of phonetics to systems of shorthand (an interest shared by Wilkins and others of his time, see Salmon 1972). In this respect, he can be viewed as a forerunner of nineteenth-century phoneticians such as Ellis, Pitman and Sweet.

A seventeenth-century linguist who was concerned essentially with other practical matters, namely elocution and language teaching, was Christopher Cooper, who in 1685 produced his *Grammatica linguae anglicanae*. This work, later translated as *The English teacher* (Cooper 1687), was a practical grammar which contained much perceptive observation on contemporary pronunciation. It is usually considered a particularly valuable source of information on the English speech of the period (Gimson

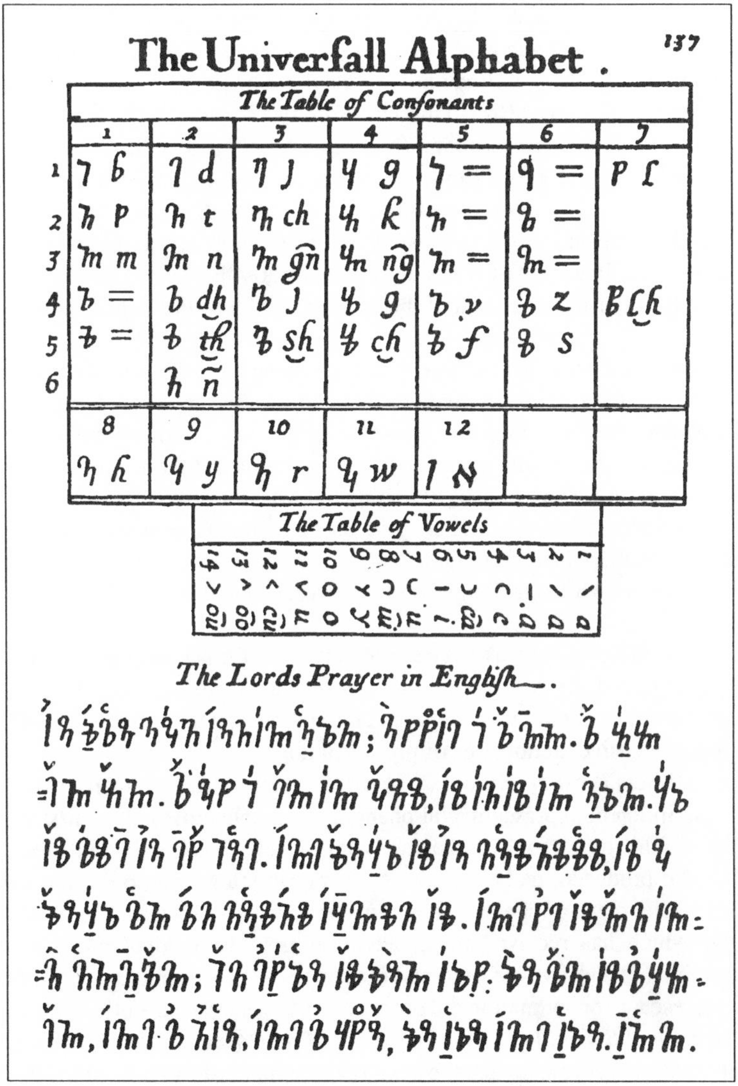

Figure A.1. Lodwick's "Universal Alphabet" (1686)

1962: 61). Cooper is regarded by Dobson (1957a [1968²]: 311) as "the best phonetician and one of the fullest recorders of pronunciation that England (and indeed modern Europe) produced before the nineteenth century".

Jones himself took a somewhat equivocal view of these early English scholars. Gimson (1977: 151–152) has said that Jones "was well versed in the writing of earlier phoneticians and had a special admiration for John Hart, John Wallis, Christopher Cooper, Alexander J. Ellis, and, particularly, Henry Sweet and Otto Jespersen". Though it is quite true that Jones used the early British phoneticians as evidence for his research on the reconstruction of Shakespearean English in his articles (Jones 1909c, 1937i: 38–41) and in his *Pronunciation of English* (Jones [1950³]: 171–172), it is actually difficult to find *direct* influences of the first three writers—or indeed of any pre-nineteenth century British linguist—on Jones's ideas. Nor does Jones appear to mention any early English scholar (except Salesbury and Wilkins) in his publications. Indeed, it would seem, from his comments, that although he considers their work interesting, and certainly a useful source of information, he felt that their statements should be treated with some suspicion. In the following passage taken from the 1949 radio talks, Jones (1985: 12) shows quite clearly that he recognises the limitations as well as the achievements of the 16th and 17th century British linguists:

> There were quite a number of these scholars—some thirty or more of them. Some of them gave descriptions of the speech sounds of their time (often rather crude descriptions which we have to interpret as best we can). Sometimes they compared English sounds with sounds of foreign languages; these comparisons are useful whenever we have means of finding out what the foreign sounds were like. And then some of these old writers gave lists of pairs of corresponding long and short vowels; these lists are quite useful as approximate indications of the stages of development which the long vowels had reached at that period.

The eighteenth century was to see relatively little further progress in the area of articulatory phonetic description, but was significant for two important developments: the systematic representation of stress and intonation, and the compilation of the first fairly comprehensive dictionaries of pronunciation.

Joshua Steele's *Prosodia rationalis* (1779) is an important landmark in the history of the description of suprasegmental phenomena. Steele provided the first sustained discussion of the stress and rhythm patterns of English, with considerable exemplification. He also produced the best analysis of English intonation up till that date, and included a brief piece of conversation transcribed with his own system of intonation marking, which has received much attention from later commentators such as Abercrombie ([1965]: 35–44), Crystal (1969: 22–25) and Sumera (1981). For over a century, research on intonation did not progress beyond Steele's efforts; not, in fact, until the work of Sweet. In terms of accuracy of representation of pitch and rhythm, Crystal (1969: 25) considers that the next true step forward was not until Jones's own youthful contribution in this field, which made use of the recently invented gramophone as an aid to transcription: "Daniel Jones's *Intonation curves* (1909a) in a sense takes up where Steele had left off, marking quality, quantity, loudness and pitch, using staves, though in a broader type of transcription" (see Section 3.3).

Another writer who contributed to the study of intonation and stress at this time was John Walker in his *Melody of speaking* (1787), but though this contains a number of passages marked for intonation, the analysis is coarse and confused, lacking the perceptiveness of Steele. However, Walker is the major figure in another area of linguistic activity, namely the production of pronunciation dictionaries. This can be viewed as a part of the general phenomenon of "fixing" of the English language at this time (Howatt 1984: 106–125), and a result of the interest in lexicography stimulated by the appearance of Samuel Johnson's (1755) dictionary.

Johnson gave very little information on pronunciation, apart from indicating primary word-stress, an innovation which had been made earlier in the century by less renowned lexicographers. Benzie (1972: 98 n.) cites Thomas Dyche's (1723) *Dictionary of words* as the very first to show stress. Dyche indicated primary stress by means of an acute accent following the stressed syllable—a system which was then employed by Nathan Bailey [1731] for the second edition of his *Universal etymological English dictionary*. In the fourth edition (1759), Bailey's dictionary introduced another important innovation in the history of the representation of pronunciation, namely the use of diacritics to indicate vowel quality. This scheme, actually the work of a Scotsman, James Buchanan, is incomplete for vowels, whilst no indication is given of consonants additional to that in the orthography. Furthermore, it is spattered with inconsistencies and errors. Nevertheless, Buchanan can be credited with introducing diacritical methods of indicating pronunciation—probably to this day still the most widely used system in non-specialist works. Benzie (1972: 100), in discussing the work of Buchanan and his followers, has said: "In spite of their shortcomings, these dictionaries represent the beginnings of modern lexicography. No longer was pronunciation treated as a mere appendage."

Thomas Spence's (1785) *Grand repository of the English language* can claim to be the first dictionary to make the indication of pronunciation its prime aim. Abercrombie (1981: 213) states that Spence "was the first to use a scientifically exact notation". Spence is also notable for having devised ten new symbols by means of ligatures (reproduced in Abercrombie 1981: 222). Beal (1995) provides the first thorough examination of Thomas Spence's work.

Thomas Sheridan (father of the playwright Richard Sheridan) was a writer who produced an influential series of lectures on elocution (Sheridan 1762, quoted in Benzie 1972: 35–54). Sheridan's (1780) *General dictionary* was, like Spence's, essentially a pronunciation dictionary; but it had much bigger sales and was the first to be regarded as any sort of authority on English pronunciation (Benzie 1972: 97–113; Sheldon 1967). However, Sheridan's work could not compete with Walker's *Critical pronouncing dictionary* (1791), which proved highly successful, continuing into numerous subsequent editions.

Amongst other features which Walker took over from Sheridan was the idea of marking vowel quality by means of superscript numbers. But, unlike Sheridan, Walker followed a "modern descriptive line" (Howatt 1984: 112), and was prepared to admit the many new pronunciations (often influenced by spelling) which were starting to arise at the end of the eighteenth century. Walker can also be regarded as making a contribution to English phonetics with his preface entitled "Principles of English Pronunciation". In most of his work, Walker appears to have made an honest attempt at recording educated current pronunciation accurately rather than imposing prescriptive views, thus coming close to Jones's (*EPD*[1] viii–ix) requirement that the phonetician should be "a kind of living phonograph". In Britain, Walker's dictionary remained unchallenged throughout the nineteenth century—as Viëtor (1882 [1984]: 349) noted with annoyance: "We make do with a pronunciation manual such as Walker's, originally published in 1791 (!) in order to study a language like English which has developed with all the energy of its native steam-engines" [Viëtor's punctuation]. In fact, no widely recognised successful authoritative rival was produced until 1917 when Jones brought out the *EPD* (see Section 7.2).

A.3. Britain and America in the nineteenth century

In the early nineteenth century, the work of the English pioneers of the previous three hundred years was largely forgotten and their publications ignored. In fact, Walker was the only writer on speech who, owing to the appeal of his pronouncing dictionary, continued to have any widespread influence. Apart from the noteworthy but isolated work of Batchelor (1809), the earlier orthoëpical tradition lay fallow. Yet, within the space of a few decades, Britain was to witness a remarkable revival in the study of speech, pioneered by three scholars: Alexander Ellis, Isaac Pitman and Alexander Melville Bell.

Alexander Ellis (1814–90) would appear to be the earliest writer whom Jones regarded as a phonetician who could provide him with ideas. There is direct evidence for the above claim, apart from Jones's borrowing of Ellis's phrase "received pronunciation" (see Section 7.2). It is known that in 1944, when Bernard Shaw was planning to leave money in his will for the development of a phonetic alphabet (see Section 12.8), Jones wrote to the playwright offering to lend him one of Ellis's works, in the hope of putting him right on phonetic matters:

> I venture to suggest that the Ellis-Pitman scheme of 40 sounds is an adequate and more definite list. It is to be found in Ellis' *Essentials of Phonetics*, 1848, p. 98. I could send you a copy of it if it would interest you. I think some of the symbols can be improved upon, but the list of sounds still holds good.[3]

Another of Ellis's publications, *Speech in song* (Ellis, n.d.), was also known to Jones, and he recommends its suggested rules for syllable division in the *Sounds of the French language* (Savory—Jones 1907c: 42 n.). Jones's personal copy of Ellis's book, heavily annotated, is still in existence.[4] Jones (1909c: 119) also mentions Ellis's *Early English pronunciation* (1869–89) as one of the works that he consulted in order to establish the pronunciation of Chaucerian and Shakespearean English.

Like Daniel Jones, Alexander Ellis began his academic life by reading mathematics at Cambridge. Something else which they had in common was an intense interest in music, perhaps connected in some way with their practical abilities as phoneticians. Ellis's talents were renowned and Jones (1912i: 98) considered—on what evidence is unknown—that "his ear was undoubtedly keener than Sweet's". On coming down from university, Ellis soon began to develop his interest in speech, spelling reform and systems of phonetic transcription. In 1843, Ellis met Pitman; from then on the two men worked closely together for several years.

Unlike Ellis, Isaac Pitman (1813–97) had enjoyed only a brief basic education, followed by a period of training as a schoolmaster. When he was only twenty-four, he published the first edition of his shorthand system on phonetic principles and to which he gave the name "phonography" (I. Pitman 1837). It was destined to become the most popular system of shorthand in the world and made him his fortune. From 1842 onwards, Pitman began producing his experimental phonetic alphabets, which appeared regularly in two publications, firstly *The Phonographic Journal* and subsequently *The Phonotypic Journal*.

The joint work of Ellis and Pitman culminated in 1847 with their "Phonotypic Alphabet" (I. Pitman 1847). The transcription had a vowel system closely related to conventional orthography—not surprisingly, since it was essentially a system of spelling reform. This alphabet (see Figure A.2) must be regarded as the greatest step forward up till that date in producing a widely acceptable phonetic notation system. J. Kelly (1981: 262–263) states:

> The labours of Pitman and Ellis during the ten years that preceded the 1847 alphabet can be said to have established phonetics as a modern science in Great Britain. Prior to 1837 phonetic work had been carried out in the main by isolated individuals as a scholarly pursuit, often one of many.... Pitman and Ellis have the right to be regarded as the founders of modern phonetic studies in Britain, and much that has been seen as an important part of the British tradition is a direct inheritance from their work. One thinks here of the insistence on observation and practical skills, the interest in transcription and its typology, the just balance of theoretical and pragmatic considerations in phonemic analysis and the regard for the practical applications of the subject in all its aspects.

Around the same time, Ellis completed his *Essentials of phonetics* (1848a), the book referred to by Jones in his letter to Shaw. Pitman continued with his work on spelling reform and the applications of his alphabetic systems to other languages (Abercrombie 1937: 106), but his main contribution had already been made; for further detail of his life and work, see J. Kelly (1981) and the biographies by Baker (1908) and Abercrombie (1937).

" Look on this Picture, and on This."   47

§ 18.

Hetéric and Phonetic Spelling compared.

After having thus seen how words *may be* distorted, it is worth while inquiring how they *are* distorted. Another version of this same letter in the received hetéric orthography, side by side with its phonetic representation, will enable the reader to judge, not only of the gulf that lies between hetéricism and phoneticism, but of the ease with which this gulf may be bridged over by means of the phonetic alphabet, which we propose to adopt.

"LOOK ON THIS PICTURE,   —AND ON ĐIS."

To the Editor of the *Phonotypic Journal.*

Sir,—I observe you propose to introduce a new system of writing, by which you express only the sounds, and not the orthography of the words; but I think you go too far in changing our time-honoured alphabet, and adding so many new letters. I make bold to say that it is quite easy to write according to sound, with the letters of the old alphabet, and, indeed, I have for many years been in the habit of doing so. I found, as most people do, that it was impossible to make any thing of the common spelling, from the total want of rules; so I made up my mind to discard orthography, and to spell by sound, but in a manner very different from yours, and, I flatter myself, very superior to it. It appears to me, that all the writers on this subject have altogether misunderstood the peculiar character of the English language, which I take to be this, that every word may be spelt in an infinite variety of ways, no one of which is more right than another. Any person will see that it must be so, if he considers that every "sound" in our language is expressed in a great number of ways; and consequently every "word" ought to be, for words are made up of single sounds. This infinitely diversified plan of spelling, as just observed, I take to be the peculiar characteristic and glory of our written language.

Tu đe Editer ov đe *Fonotipic Jurnal.*

Ser,—Ŧ obzérv u propoz tu introdús a nu sistem ov rįtiŋ, bį hwiç u ecsprés onli đe sundz, and not đe ertografi ov đe wurdz; but į tiŋc u go tú far in çanjiŋ ɘr tįmonurd alfabet, and adiŋ so meni nu leterz. Ŧ mac bold tu sa đat it iz cwįt ezi tu rįt acordiŋ tu sund, wiđ đe leterz ov đe old alfabet, and, inded, į hav fer meni yerz ben in đe habit ov duiŋ so. Ŧ fɘnd, az most pep'l du, đat it woz imposib'l tu mac eni tiŋ ov đe comun speliŋ, from đe total wont ov rulz; so į mad up mį mįnd tu discqrd ertografi, and tu spel bį sund, but in a maner veri diferent from uɹz, and, į flater misélf, veri superiur tu it. It aperz tu me, đat el đe rįterz on đis subject hav eltugéđer misunderstúd đe peculier caracter ov đe Ingliſ laŋgwej, hwiç į tac tu be đis, đat everi wurd ma be spelt in an infinit varįeti ov waz, no wun ov hwiç iz mɘr rįt đan anúđer. Eni persun wil se đat it must be so, if he considerz đat everi "sund" in ɘr laŋgwej iz ecsprést in a grat number ov waz; and consecwentli everi "wurd" et tu be, fer wurdz qr mad up ov siŋ'l sundz. Đis infinitli diversifįd plan ov speliŋ, az just obzérvd, į tac tu be đe peculier caracteristic and glori ov ɘr rit'n laŋgwej.

Ŧ of'n smįl hwen į red đe laborius efurts ov ertograferz tu fics đe speliŋ ov Ingliſ, hwiç woz never inténded tu be ficst, but,

Figure A.2.   Pitman and Ellis's "Phonotypic Alphabet" (Ellis 1848b: 47).

Ellis, however, went on to new achievements as a dialectologist and philologist. His monument is the vast—if over-ambitious—five-volume study *On Early English pronunciation* (1869–89). Jones used Ellis as an important source of information for his reconstructions of Chaucerian and Shakespearean English (see Section 3.2 and Section 14.15). The fifth part, entitled *The existing phonology of English dialects*, is the first plausible attempt at an overall survey of British dialects, and this alone would have ensured Ellis a permanent place in linguistic history. Though it has many obvious defects and was indeed greatly criticised by his successors (see Local 1983: 2 for discussion), the work is a landmark in British dialectology.

Ellis is also notable for devising new forms of phonetic transcriptions, such as his "Glossic" and the more elaborate and precise "Palaeotype" (see Figures A.3 and A.4). The latter, first produced in 1866, underwent further developments up to 1889 when it was used in *Early English pronunciation*, vol. 5. The Palaeotype achieved widespread fame by its appearance in the influential *Oxford English dictionary*, where it was employed in reprints and supplements until its replacement by an IPA type transcription in the completely revised [1989] second edition.

Sweet (1877: viii) claimed that:

One of Mr. Ellis's most important contributions to practical phonetics is his adaptation of the ordinary Roman alphabet for the accurate representation of minute shades of sound, which is effected without having recourse either to new types or...diacritics....

Though the Palaeotype has been much criticised, one scholar, Local (1983), has produced a modern exposition of the system with an account of its evolution and a defence of its qualities. The simpler alphabet, Glossic, was a major influence on Sweet's Broad Romic and through him on the IPA systems of transcription (see Section 4.8); Glossic can also be seen as a forerunner of spelling reforms of the type advocated by Jones and others in the Simplified Spelling Society (Rippmann—Archer 1910); see further Section 4.10.

Ellis's wider phonetic interests are evident from the fact that he translated Helmholtz's (1863) classic text on the acoustics of speech (see Section A.4), adding some new material of his own. The translation appeared under the title *Sensations of tone* (Helmholtz 1877).

The mid-nineteenth century can be seen as the period when British phonetics evolved from the isolated and—in some respects—dilettante efforts of a few enthusiasts to something which could be regarded as a recognised science. It was in large measure due to Ellis and Pitman that this evolution took place when it did. But the Scottish phonetician Alexander Melville Bell (1819–1905) must be considered a still greater figure—at least in terms of his powers of phonetic description and his understanding of the processes of speech.

Melville Bell's father, Alexander Bell, had been a famous elocutionist and stage reciter. All his offspring were steeped in speech analysis from infancy, and Melville

---

Spesimen ov Ingglish Glosik.

Nom·ix, (dhat iz, kustemeri Ingglish speling, soa kauld from dhi Greek *nom·os,* kustem,) konvai·z noa intimai·shen ov dhi risee·vd proanunsiai·shen ov eni werd.   It iz konsikwentli veri difikelt too lern too reed, and stil moar difikelt too lern too reit.

Ingglish Glosix (soa kauld from dhi Greek *gloas·sa,* tung) konvai·z whotev·er proanunsiai·shen iz inten·ded bei dhi reiter. Glosik buoks kan dhairfoar bee maid too impaar·t risee·vd aurthoa·ipi too aul reederz.

Ingglish Glosik iz veri eezi too reed.   Widh proper training, a cheild ov foar yeerz oald kan bee redili taut too giv dhi egzak·t sound ov eni glosik werd prizen·ted too him.   Aafter hee haz akwei·rd familiar·iti widh glosik reeding hee kan lern nomik reeding aulmoast widhou·t instruk·shen.   Dhi hoal teim rikwei·rd faur lerning *boath* glosik and nomik, iz not *haaf* dhat rikwei·rd faur lerning nomik aloa·n.   Dhis iz impoa·rtent, az nomik buoks and paiperz aar dhi oanli egzis·ting soarsez ov infermai·shen.

Figure A.3. Ellis's "Glossic"

Bell's brother, David Charles Bell, eventually became Professor of Elocution at Trinity College, Dublin. Melville Bell's son, Alexander Graham Bell, went on to become the most famous member of this extraordinary family (see below).

Melville Bell was one of the first persons to lecture on speech at a British university; from 1843 to 1865 he taught elocution at Edinburgh. In 1865, he moved to London and took up a post as lecturer in phonetics at University College, where he remained for five years, thus anticipating Daniel Jones's appointment to the same position in the same college by just over 40 years (see Section 2.5). During his Edinburgh period, Bell began to develop his theory of "Visible Speech", which was his name for an iconic organic alphabet which he devised to expound and illustrate his phonetic descriptive theory (see Figure A.5). As stated above, several types of organic alphabet had been developed before, notably by Lodwick (see Section A.2), but Bell's work broke new ground and was striking both for the general accuracy of phonetic description and for the ingenuity with which he allowed this to be displayed in each phonetic symbol.

Though generally considered to be difficult to read, the script appears to have succeeded in helping those for whom it was primarily designed, namely, the profoundly deaf. Bell's (1867) *Visible speech* gives a full explanation of the significance of each component of the organic alphabet symbols together with an exposition of his system of vowel and consonant classification. Sweet (1877: vii) enthused:

It is no exaggeration to say that Bell has in this work done more for phonetics than all his predecessors put together: it is at least certain that his system is the first which gives a really adequate and comprehensive view of the whole field of possible sounds. His analysis of the vowel-positions is almost entirely new and original. His system of notation, in which the mechanism of the sounds is most ingeniously symbolised, is not only founded on an adequate analysis, but is also thoroughly practical in character....

It was not merely the ingenuity of the system which was attractive in Visible Speech —great though this was. With Bell, the underlying phonetic analysis of articulatory processes took on a new level of sophistication which was a considerable advance on

T	t	E. *t*ea, (tii)
T	*t*	= (t*k), Newman's and usually received A. ♭
:T	ʀ	= (t↓), S. ⵣ
.T	.t	= (t⊦), tip of tongue on gums
Th	th	= E. *th*in, (thin), modern Greek *θ*
Th	*th*	= (th*kh), Newman's A. ﻉ
:Thh	ʀhh	Lepsius's Dravidian sound, nearly (ʀsh)
Tj	tj	= (t*ʒ) whisper of (dj), occ. E. vir*t*ue, (vɪ·tjiu)
Tsh	tsh	E. *ch*est, ma*tch*, ca*tch*ing, (tshest, mætsh, kætsh·iq)
T*w*	tw	= (t*w), F. *t*oi, (twa)
U	u	= (œw), F. p*ou*le, E. L*ou*isa, (pul, Lu,ii·za), see (*u*)
U	*u*	= (ʊw) = (u0), E. p*u*ll, c*oo*k, (p*u*l, k*u*k), generally confused with (u)
:U	ʊ	= (ʀw), Swedish *u* short·
*U*h	*u*h	= (yw) = (ʊ0), I. *o* chiuso, (o) verging into (*u*)
Ui	ui	F. *ou*i = (ui), F. *ou*ï = (u,i)
Uu	uu	long of (u), E. p*oo*l, (puul)
Uu	*uu*	long of (*u*)
:Uʊ	ʊʊ	long of (ʊ)
*U*uh	*u*uh	long of (*u*h)
V	v	E. *v*eal, (viil), F. *v*, North G. *w*, see (bh)
V	*v*	= (v⊦), buzz of (*f*), which see
.V	.v	buzz of (.f), which see
Vh	vh	= (v*gh), buzz of (fh), which see
V*w*	v*w*	= (v*w), F. *v*oix, (vwa)
W	w	E. *w*itch, (wɪtsh)
W	*w*	diacritic, labial modification of preceding letter
ʍ	ɯ	turned m, written *u*, defective lip trill, occ. E. ve*w*y *tw*ue, (veuɪ·i tuɯu)
Wh	wh	whisper of (w), E. *wh*ich, (whɪtsh)
X	x	Spanish *x*, *j*, Qui*x*ote, Me*x*ico, or Qui*j*ote, Me*j*ico, (Kiixoo·tee, Mee·xiikoo)
X	*x*	buzz of (x)
Y	y	= (i*w*) = (ɪ0), F. h*u*tte, G. l*ü*cke, (yt, lyk·e)
Y	*y*	= (ɪ0), Welsh *u*, and final *y*, p*y*mp, ewy*ll*ys, (pymp, ewɪlhh·ys), E. h*ou*ses, goodn*ess*, (ʀəuz·yz, gud·nys)
:Y	ʀ	Polish, Bohemian, Hungarian *y*, Russian (ʒerɪ)

Figure A.4. Ellis's "Palaeotype"

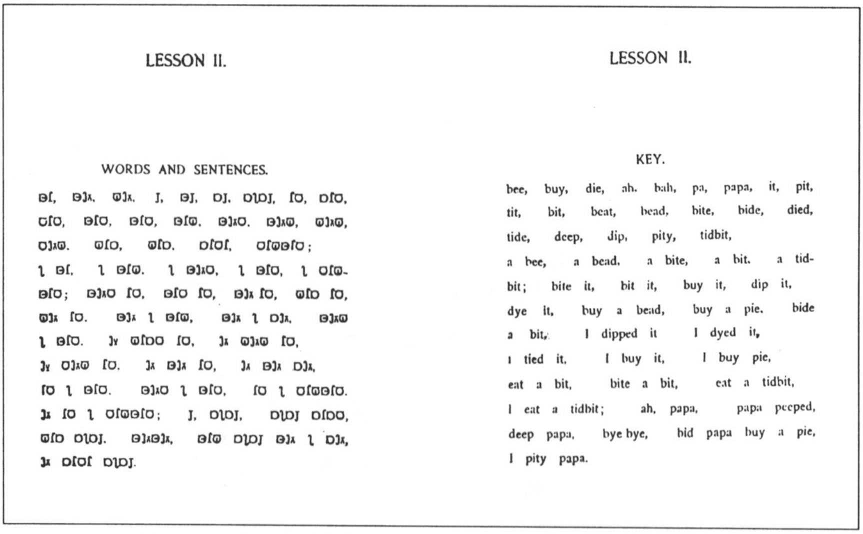

LESSON II.

LESSON II.

WORDS AND SENTENCES.

KEY.

bee, buy, die, ah, bah, pa, papa, it, pit,
tit, bit, beat, bead, bite, bide, died,
tide, deep, dip, pity, tidbit,
a bee, a bead, a bite, a bit, a tidbit; bite it, bit it, buy it, dip it,
dye it, buy a bead, buy a pie, bide
a bit, I dipped it I dyed it,
I tied it, I buy it, I buy pie,
eat a bit, bite a bit, eat a tidbit,
I eat a tidbit; ah, papa, papa peeped,
deep papa, bye bye, bid papa buy a pie,
I pity papa.

Figure A.5. Bell's "Visible Speech"

the work of Ellis and Pitman. Bell's alphabet was intrinsically phonetic and analytical and, because it abandoned Roman letter shapes in favour of signs which indicated the detail of articulatory movements, it also demanded a sustained level of awareness of the complication of the activity of speech from the reader. Bell also realised that its phonetic basis made Visible Speech a most flexible instrument, and he utilised its scope to include the description of sounds found in languages other than English—to represent clicks, for example. The system of vowel classification was also in advance of its time with a clear understanding of the significance of tongue height and the function of lip-rounding.

Both the concept of the organic alphabet and its underlying system of vowel and consonant classification were taken over by Henry Sweet (see Section 2.9), who re-fined and modified them further. Daniel Jones based his articulatory classification system largely on the same principles, which he derived in part from Sweet, but more directly from Paul Passy, who had himself taken adapted ideas from both Sweet and Bell. Melville Bell can be seen in this way as a crucial, though mainly indirect, influ-ence on Jones. In one important respect, Jones rejected Bell's approach. Although he collaborated with Passy on an "Alphabet phonétique organique" (Jones—Passy 1907d, see Section 2.11) he never used this system in any other publication; Jones indeed explicitly rejected the concept of non-Roman based letters for phonetic tran-scription, constantly restating that he believed that the IPA alphabet was the best for the purpose; see Section 2.9 for Jones's views on Sweet's organic alphabet.

Melville Bell emigrated to Canada in 1870, moving to the USA in 1881, where he spent the rest of his life. With him he took his son, Alexander Graham Bell (1845–1922), whom he helped to establish as a teacher of the deaf. Melville Bell continued

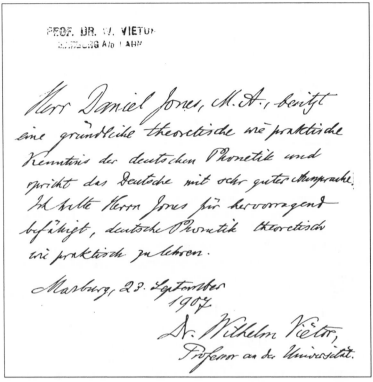

Figure A.6. Testimonial written for Jones by Viëtor.

to produce work himself in phonetics, publishing significant books on aspects of general phonetics, such as *Sounds and their relations* (A.M. Bell 1882) and *The science of speech* (A.M. Bell 1897).

Graham Bell developed an interest in phonetics and soon dramatically overtook his father's fame through the invention of the telephone. Nevertheless, he continued to use Melville Bell's methods, including Visible Speech, for his own teaching of the deaf, and for training teachers in this field. Bell, who married a deaf woman, became fascinated with the problems of deafness and established the Volta Bureau to encourage research into this area; in his lifetime, his most famous protégée was the deaf-blind prodigy Helen Keller. His interest in the physiology of speech (which he taught at Boston) is reflected in his *Mechanism of speech* (A.G. Bell 1906)—one of the first books ever to be reviewed by Jones (1907i) in his early days with *Le Maître phonétique*. See Bruce (1973) for a detailed biography of Graham Bell and the whole Bell family.

Another prominent American phonetician was E.W. Scripture (1864–1945), who began his academic career as a psychologist, being trained partly in Europe, and taking his doctorate at Leipzig. After publishing a number of books on psychology, Scripture produced his major work *Elements of experimental phonetics* (Scripture 1902)—a *tour de force* covering the development of experimental phonetics and the state of the science at the turn of the century. Much of the information is parallel to that in Rousselot (see Section A.5), but Scripture takes a less personal view, and not only included his own considerable work but ranged widely, bringing in the findings of the major contemporary researchers on speech. Scripture's massive book provides the most valuable overview available of the state of the hard science side of phonetics (both in the USA and Europe) as it stood in the period just before Jones embarked on his career.

Though no other publication of Scripture's has the same breadth as *Elements*, he went on to produce one more book in the same mould, *Researches in experimental phonetics* (Scripture 1906). His subsequent works reflect the interests which he concentrated on in his career and are concerned with speech pathology and the communication problems of the deaf.

The last great nineteenth century figure in the English-speaking world was Henry Sweet (1845–1912). In him we discover a phonetician who was not only an influence on Jones through his writing, but also known to Jones in person. With one exception—namely Passy (see 2.3.)—Sweet was the greatest single influence on Jones's evolution as a phonetician. Because of his significance to Jones, Sweet's life and work has been dealt with in greater detail in Sections 2.9, 2.10 and 4.8.

By the turn of the century, only Sweet could still be considered a major influence in the world of phonetics. Ellis had died in 1890; Pitman for some time had been—at least as far as phonetics was concerned—a spent force, and had died in 1897; Melville Bell was nearing the end of his life, although his son Graham was carrying on and extending his work. The remaining British phoneticians of the time are not of the same magnitude as these men, but nevertheless often have things of interest to say. Now that the contribution of the earliest pioneers has been rediscovered, the minor British scholars of the late nineteenth and the early twentieth centuries are truly today's "forgotten phoneticians"—to adapt Abercrombie's (1948) phrase. We shall consider here three who have left significant publications.

The importance of James Lecky (1855–90) has been pointed out by MacMahon (1979), who mentions the meticulous accuracy of his descriptions of Irish and Irish English. Lecky is also notable for his research on aspects of rhythm and its application to verse prosody. MacMahon (1979: 48) also quotes remarks made by Lecky, which indicate that he, like Henry Sweet, was conscious of the phoneme concept, discussing sound differences in terms of whether or not they were "used *independently* to distinguish the meanings of words". Lastly, Lecky will be remembered as the man who introduced Bernard Shaw to phonetics, and also to Ellis and Sweet, thus setting the playwright on the road to writing *Pygmalion* (Holroyd 1988: 102).

Laura Soames (1840–95), apart from her phonetic interests, was an educationist who devoted herself to religious causes. She was an early member of the IPA and a contributor to the *Le Maître phonétique*. Her most important work is her *Introduction to phonetics* (Soames 1891a), which is a survey of the elements of phonetics as applied to the sound systems of English, French and German. Though generally competent, given the state of knowledge at the time, it suffers from being somewhat over-prescriptive and excessively influenced by elocutionist precepts. It also draws heavily on the previous efforts of others, in particular Sweet, Passy and Viëtor. In fact, Viëtor took a sympathetic interest in Soames's work and produced a second [1899] edition of this book (*Introduction to English, French and German phonetics*), and also edited her *Teacher's manual*, which appeared posthumously in 1897.

Perhaps because she had the temerity to criticise his works in reviews (Soames 1891b, 1892a, 1892b), Henry Sweet could not stand her, or her writings, and attacked her both in print (Sweet 1892a) and privately in letters to his friend, the Norwegian linguist, Johan Storm (1836–1920). Her books (which until recently have been virtually ignored) are deserving of more attention if only for the evidence they provide of the way the ideas of Sweet, Passy and Viëtor were taken up and popularised amongst a wider circle of practising teachers. The Laura Soames Prize, set up in her memory, is awarded annually at University College London for a piece of work submitted by a student on a phonetic topic. MacMahon (1994) provides a detailed summary of what is known of her life, together with a perceptive assessment of the value of her published work.

Richard Lloyd (1846–1906) produced what is probably the earliest British doctorate on a phonetic topic; entitled *Vowel sounds*, it was submitted to London University in 1890. He was later appointed "Honorary Reader" in phonetics at Liverpool University, and taught there and at other institutions (E.D. Jones 1906). His book, *Northern English* (Lloyd 1899), presents a somewhat idealised and artificial view of the educated speech of the North of England, which Lloyd appeared to consider essentially as a conservative variant of southern Received Pronunciation, with the addition of post-vocalic r. An extract from the book, in what Jones claims to be a representation of Lloyd's idiolect, appears in the *Pronunciation of English*[1] (pp. 115–117). Lloyd was a long-standing member of the IPA and for a number of years a Vice-President. His books served to publicise the ideas and principles of the Association. On Lloyd's death in 1906, Daniel Jones succeeded to his place on the IPA Council (see Section 2.6).

Apart from Jones himself, a younger generation of phoneticians and language teachers, e.g. Walter Rippmann, D.L. Savory, E.R. Edwards and Benjamin Dumville were beginning to make themselves known around the turn of the century; all were to play a part in Jones's academic career, as we have seen in earlier chapters. However, to find linguists of this era with anything approaching the impact of Ellis, Pitman, Bell or Sweet, one has to look to the continent of Europe, where (particularly in Germany and France) phonetics was in many ways more advanced than in Britain, both in terms of its development as a scientific discipline, and its recognition by the academic world.

A.4. Germany and Scandinavia

Germany can be regarded as the centre of developments in linguistic research in nineteenth century Europe. It is striking that, compared with what occurred in Britain, the history of phonetics followed a quite different pattern in Germany.

Although he would not have regarded himself as primarily a phonetician, any survey of nineteenth century phonetics must give prominence to Herman von Helmholtz (1821–94). Helmholtz was virtually a polymath, showing interest in all aspects of science. Using simple apparatus, such as tuning forks and glass globes, he managed to establish some of the most basic concepts of speech acoustics, measuring the fundamental frequency and harmonics of the human voice, and also putting forward the formant theory of vowel resonances (though not himself using the word "formant"). In addition, he postulated the aerodynamic theory of laryngeal action. These findings were brought together in his major work on speech: *Die Lehre von den Tonempfindungen* (Helmholtz 1863). Daniel Jones appreciated the qualities of this book and refers his readers to Helmholtz at the beginning of the *Pronunciation of English*[1] (p. 6); see Section 3.4.

Whilst Helmholtz through his discoveries was establishing the acoustic basis of modern phonetics, at the same time, his fellow-countrymen were busily assembling information on the anatomy and physiology of the speech organs. Sweet (1877: vi) commented in his *Handbook*:

Until within the last few years phonetics was hardly recognised as a science in this country, and it is to Germany that we owe the first attempt to construct a general system of sounds on a physiological basis.

This research was, again, undertaken by scientists who were not primarily phoneticians. Ernst Brücke (1819–92), German-born, though based for most of his life in Vienna, was a physiologist whilst Carl Ludwig Merkel (1812–76) was a professor of medicine. Their books (Brücke 1856; Merkel 1857, 1866) on the physiology and anatomy of speech were to serve not only as a source of information for later writers but also as a model for attempting descriptive precision with an emphasis on scientific methods, and a close linking of the study of speech with the medical and biological sciences. See Kohler (1981) for further discussion and criticism of this period.

The most noteworthy writer to base his researches on the foundation laid by these scientists was Eduard Sievers (1850–1932); in his major work, *Grundzüge der Lautphysiologie* (1876[1]), the debt to all three (in particular Merkel) is acknowledged. Kohler (1981: 166) comments: "Sievers' familiarity with Helmholtz, Merkel and Brücke is well documented; they were his primary sources." But Kohler (1981: 161–165) has also pointed out the notable changes between the first and second editions of Sievers' book—the latter being, significantly, retitled *Grundzüge der Phonetik* [1881[2]]. In the revised version, Sievers emphasised the insights which he had gained from reading the work of the British phoneticians Ellis and Sweet. In its new form, the book moved away from the physiological emphasis of the first edition, and became much more linguistically orientated. This was a process which was continued in the third (and subsequent) editions (Sievers [1889[3]]).[5]

One of Sievers' most important contributions was to assemble the contemporary scientific work on speech, and place this in a linguistic setting; in so doing, Sievers provided source material for the bubbling activity in linguistics which took place in Germany in the last quarter of the nineteenth century. He eventually became the instigator of a reaction against what he saw as the dominance of phonetics by non-linguistic specialists with a hard-science bias. In this connection, Sievers' evolving awareness of the value of the linguistic orientation of the British approach to phonetics was crucial in the spread of the ideas of Ellis, Bell and, above all, Sweet in Germany and thence throughout continental Europe. Sievers also can be seen as clearing the way for the acceptance later of Jones's approach to phonetics, and the willingness of German publishers, such as Teubner, to accept his work. For biographical detail of Sievers, see Frings (1934).

Apart from its role in the development of phonetics, Germany was even more notable for the part it was playing in another branch of nineteenth-century linguistics, which was regarded then as having far more importance—namely, historical philology. Ever since the writings of Jacob Grimm and Franz Bopp (see Jespersen 1922 [1968]: 40–55, 60–62; Verburg 1950) in the early part of the nineteenth century, Germany had been the most important centre in the world for the study of the history of the Indo-European languages and the links between them (Pedersen 1931 [1962]: 254–277). This tradition was carried on throughout the nineteenth century, for instance in the work of August Schleicher (1821–68), who is notable for his concentration on sound change in language and the postulation of pseudo-Darwinian principles underlying them (Schleicher 1861–62, and 1863). However, in the seventies and eighties, the philological scene was transformed thanks to the activities of a group of young linguists working at the University of Leipzig. This was already a renowned centre for linguistic studies owing mainly to the presence there of the famous comparative linguist Georg Curtius (1820–85). Language scholars came to Leipzig from all over Europe at this time to study there and complete their doctoral theses.

The Leipzig linguists, who later came to be known as the "Junggrammatiker", or "Neogrammarians", were inspired in part by the contribution of Scherer (1868), but were spurred into action by the modifications to Grimm's Law produced by Verner (1875). The Neogrammarians were opposed to conventional contemporary linguistics as represented by Curtius and based their work largely on Leskien's (1876) principle (restated in Osthoff—Brugmann 1878) of "Ausnahmslosigkeit der Lautgesetze", namely that sound change laws should admit of no exceptions; see Robins (1978) and Koerner (1976b) for a detailed discussion. This linguistic movement dominated German philology in the last quarter of the nineteenth century, generating changes which not only revolutionised the philological tradition but also deeply affected the development of modern phonetics, phonology and linguistics—and also language teaching (Pedersen 1931 [1962]: 277–310; Howatt 1984: 176).

The Junggrammatiker brought new vigour to language studies and enhanced the already high esteem in which linguistics was held in Germany. Furthermore, their work was based largely on phonetic and phonological phenomena, namely the history of sound changes. This led to increased awareness of phonetics and in particular allowed the influence of Sweet to spread. Their statements on the regularity of sound patterns underpinned the early modern work in phonology such as Saussure, Baudouin de Courtenay and Kruszewski; see Sections A.5 and A.6. In addition, the discoveries relating to the continuity of sound change provided further encouragement for the study of phonetics. Robins (1967 [1979]: 186) states:

> Descriptive phonetics...received powerful reinforcement from the neogrammarian emphasis on living languages and on the inadequacy of the letters of dead languages in giving information on their actual pronunciations. Never again could there be an excuse for confusing written letter with spoken sound.

See also Kohler (1981: 169). Numerous writers have discussed the work and influence of the Junggrammatiker, for example, Hoenigswald (1978), Koerner (1976b), Kohler (1981: 168–169), Robins (1978; 1967 [1979]: 182–192), Pedersen (1931 [1962]: 277–310 *et passim*).

With Wilhelm Viëtor (1850–1918), one reaches the first German linguist who is known to have had personal contact with Jones, and to have directly influenced him. Viëtor held the chair of English Philology at the University of Marburg, and it was to Marburg that Jones had first gone to learn German at William Tilly's Language Institute, and where he had first been made aware of what phonetics had to offer (see Sections 1.7 and 1.8).

Viëtor was conscious of the need to change the classics-based tradition within which modern languages were being taught at this time in Germany. As a means of attacking the tradition of rote-learning, boring texts and the lack of any proper pronunciation training, he produced a passionately written pamphlet *Der Sprachunterricht muss umkehren!* (Viëtor 1882), which, in order for him to express his views without restraint, Viëtor published under the pen-name "Quousque Tandem".[6] It was to become, together with Sweet's *Practical study of languages* (1899) and a previous abstract which had appeared in article form as "The practical study of language" (Sweet 1885b), the principal expression of the Reform Movement in language teaching (Howatt 1984: 170).

His greatest work, *Elemente der Phonetik* (Viëtor 1884), provided the most successful comprehensive manual of articulatory phonetics yet produced; it sold well, going into numerous subsequent editions. Whilst much of the book was his own, Viëtor also drew heavily on the work of Sievers, Ellis, Bell and, above all, Sweet. Like Sweet, Viëtor's phonetic interests were primarily directed towards contrastive phonetics and its application to language teaching, and this is the theme that runs throughout the work.

In 1886, Viëtor joined Passy's "Phonetic Teachers' Association" and two years later became its President. In 1888, Viëtor also started a new journal devoted to phonetics, *Phonetische Studien*, which appeared for six years and then merged with the influential modern language teaching journal *Die neueren Sprachen*, which Viëtor began publishing in 1894.

Viëtor always had a strong affection for Britain, based largely on his experiences early in his career, when he had a temporary post in the newly founded college which was to become the University of Liverpool, and had gone holidaying in North Wales (Viëtor 1882 [1984]: 344). He became a friend of Sweet's, and took an interest in the work of Laura Soames, eventually editing reprints of her work, published after her death (see Section A.3). In 1905–07 he taught on Edinburgh University summer school courses with Sweet and Passy (forming what Jones, who also attended the 1907 summer school, later claimed was referred to as the "phonetic trinity", see Section 2.10). It is interesting to see that Viëtor was asked to write a testimonial for Daniel Jones when he applied for his post at University College, London. See Figure A.6.

Viëtor provides something of a counterbalance to the predominantly scientific and philological strains that characterised German phonetics and linguistics in the nineteenth century. Though German, Viëtor is closely allied with the practical British tradition, and his friendship with Sweet must have been built on a strong basis of mutual understanding of what was of urgency in language learning and teaching. His foremost efforts were in contrastive phonetics, but he was also interested in historical linguistics. A notable piece of work was his reconstruction of Early Modern English pronunciation in *A Shakespeare phonology* and *A Shakespeare reader* (Viëtor 1906a, 1906b). Although later criticised harshly by Kökeritz (1953: 48–50), the book was outstanding in its day; Jones initially leant heavily on Viëtor's research for his own work on Shakespearean English (Jones 1909c, 1909i). See Sections 3.2 and 14.15.

Late in his life, Viëtor produced a substantial contribution to German phonetics with the publication of his *Deutsches Aussprachewörterbuch* (Viëtor 1912). This provided German with a record of pronunciation based on an educated colloquial standard, using the IPA alphabet, and was without doubt the best pronouncing dictionary that had so far been published for any language. It is likely that Daniel Jones was considerably influenced by its orderly arrangement and businesslike appearance when he was editing the *EPD* (see further Section 7.2).

Viëtor's significance in the history of German language teaching is profound, and he is noteworthy for his constant support for the utility of phonetics for foreign language studies. He realised that it was necessary for phoneticians working in this field to adopt an articulatory approach, similar to that advocated by Henry Sweet and his British followers, rather than the more technical emphasis which had found favour in German universities. It was also necessary to make practising teachers aware of how to use phonetics in pronunciation training. His success in championing these views, based on a sound theoretical understanding of the subject combined with an essential practicality, leads to Kohler's (1981: 170) estimate that he was "certainly the most outstanding figure in the field of descriptive and practical phonetics of individual languages in Germany at the turn of the century". From the point of view of the present study, Viëtor was clearly a major influence on Jones, particularly in the first fifteen years of the latter's professional life.

Germany continued to play a major role in the development of phonetics up to the end of the century and beyond in the years leading up to the First World War. It is possible here to mention merely a few of the most noteworthy names.

Although he was born before Viëtor, Hermann Klinghardt (1847–1926) only began to play an appreciable part in the development of language teaching and phonetics relatively late in his life. In the 1880s, he began to be interested in new ideas in language teaching, and he arranged early trials with Sweet's (1885a) *Elementarbuch* to test the efficiency of "Reform Movement" methods (Howatt 1984: 170). Klinghardt's (1897) *Artikulations- und Hörübungen* provided a phonetics manual directed mainly at language teachers. However, Klinghardt's major contribution was to come when he was in his sixties, with innovative work on the intonation of French (Klinghardt—Fourmestraux 1911), English (Klinghardt—Klemm 1920) and German (Klinghardt 1927), together with a comparative study of intonation in the three languages (Klinghardt 1923). Klinghardt's dot-dash system of intonation marking appears to have been modified and adopted by Jones for classroom use during the 1920s, and first appeared in Armstrong—Ward (1926); Jones later used it in his revised third edition of the *Outline*); see Section 8.7.

The experimental side of German phonetics continued to be well represented. In Hamburg, the Italian-born Giulio Panconcelli-Calzia (1878–1966), a pupil of Abbé Rousselot (see Section A.5), began to investigate speech, employing an almost eccentrically non-linguistic hard-science biological approach. He regarded phonetics "as a part of physiology, a sub-section of the science of motion like walking, running, jumping" (Kohler 1981: 174). Panconcelli-Calzia managed, however, to build up a superbly equipped and well-staffed academic department. Jones visited the Hamburg Phonetics Department just before the First World War, and was deeply impressed— almost jealous—of its provision; see Section 5.10. It may have been one of the major spurs to his unsuccessful ambition to set up a huge Phonetics Institute in London; see Section 9.3. As has been stated, a crucial figure in Jones's contacts with German phonetics was William Tilly (see Section 1.7). For a more detailed survey of the history of German phonetics over this period and later, see Kohler (1981).

An area of Europe where interest in phonetics and linguistics was growing rapidly was Scandinavia. The Norwegian, Johan Storm, was not only a friend to Sweet but also a stimulus to his work (Howatt 1984: 181). His book, *Englische Philologie* (Storm 1881), is a notable compilation of linguistic work on English, much of which is concerned with phonetics and phonology.

A German-born phonetician, Ernst Meyer (1873–1953), was based in Sweden. His study of vowels and vowel duration, *Englische Lautdauer* (1903), influenced Jones's ideas on the classification of vowels. Meyer's work on the articulation of vowels, using the newly developed science of X-ray photography, was crucial in shaping Jones's theory of Cardinal Vowel description (see Section 7.6). Jones also drew on Meyer's researches for the concept of the "chroneme" (see the *Phoneme*: 125 n.).

In Denmark, linguistic studies had a distinguished history, including the fundamental work of the comparative linguist Rasmus Rask (1787–1832); see Hjelmslev (1950–51). As noted above, the brilliant, though eccentric, philologist Karl Verner (1846–

96), had published his famous eponymous law of consonant changes which was to be a pivot of the Junggrammatiker movement (see Jespersen 1933b).

However, perhaps the most distinguished of all the Danish linguists was Otto Jespersen (1860–1943). Jespersen, who had significant contacts with Jones, has been dealt with in greater detail in Section 10.10.

A.5. France and Switzerland

Phonetics developed somewhat later in France than in Germany. However, by the final decade of the nineteenth century, thanks especially to two phoneticians of genius, phonetics had developed strong roots in that country, and France could for a time be regarded as the world leader in two quite different branches of the subject. It was for good reason that, after his interest had been awakened in phonetics by Tilly's inspiring teaching, Daniel Jones was to make his way to Paris. It was here that Jones would be able to meet Paul Passy at the Ecole des Hautes Etudes of the Sorbonne, whom Jones knew to be the most influential articulatory phonetician of the time. Of all the scholars that Jones encountered during his career, none had greater impact on him than Passy, whose life and contribution has been described in detail in Section 2.3.

In Paris, another phonetician was at work and gathering a group of followers around him. Abbé Rousselot, an ordained priest and also a professor at the Institut Catholique de Paris, was making a crucial contribution to the study of speech in the development of what was now known as experimental phonetics. Despite eventually arriving at very different views of phonetics, both Passy and Rousselot had come through the same academic route. Both had begun in the area of language study which (partly under the impetus provided by the Junggrammatiker) attracted the most interest in late nineteenth century Europe—namely dialectology related to diachronic sound change.

Pierre-Jean Rousselot (1846–1924) has been regarded by many commentators as the founder of the experimental branch of phonetics. For example, Hardcastle (1981: 51) has said: "Experimental phonetics as a discipline in its own right probably began with Rousselot." Rousselot, although by training a philologist, rapidly became interested in dialectology. He collaborated with the famous Swiss pioneer dialectologist Gilliéron (see below) in founding a dialect research journal, *Revue des patois gallo-romans* (Roques 1966: 68). Rousselot's (1892) thesis was a study of his own dialect of Cellefrouin. However, Rousselot soon became fascinated by other aspects of phonetics and began to apply scientific analytical procedures to the investigation of speech. Whilst he was not a great innovator, Rousselot was notable for his application and development of experimental techniques. He was fortunate in living at a time when a number of methods employed in other scientific areas became available for phonetic research (Hardcastle 1981: 51).

The foremost among these was the kymograph, invented in 1847 by Carl Ludwig (1816–95) and designed as a means of recording changes in the human circulatory system. The instrument was improved by the development of the "Marey tambour", a drum-like device named after its inventor, Etienne Jules Marey (1830–1904), which was capable of detecting very slight physiological movements. The tambour was attached to a revolving cylinder covered with smoke-blackened paper, which permitted the registration of movements over a specific time interval.

Although not originally intended for the purpose, it was found that the kymograph could be utilised in the study of speech to strikingly good effect. Thanks largely to the efforts of Rousselot and his followers, the instrumentation soon became the most powerful and widely used device in the armamentarium of the early experimental phonetician, and provided the first relatively accurate means of measuring oral and nasal airflow and vocal fold vibration. The kymograph was of especial interest to Daniel Jones, particularly in his early career, and kymographic research formed the basis of many of his pronouncements on the English sound system; see Section 8.8.

Another technique applied by Rousselot was that of palatography, which provided useful information on linguo-palatal contact and tongue shape. Hardcastle (1981: 57) points out that the basic technique had been discovered by Coles (1872) and refined with the introduction of the artificial palate by Kingsley (1879). Thanks in large part to the efforts of Rousselot and his Paris colleagues, a great deal of (mainly contrastive) phonetic palatographic work was carried out around the turn of the century (Hardcastle 1981: 59). In addition, Rousselot made use of "manometric flames", a technique introduced by the German, Koenig, in 1872, but developed mainly in Paris, by which a tambour transmitted pressure changes to a specially designed gas-jet, thus producing a transform of the speech waveform, which was then susceptible to analysis (Scripture 1902: 26–31). Jones included "sensitive flames" in his lecture courses but (perhaps because of the unreliable nature of the information provided by the flames) says little about this type of research in his published work. On the other hand, palatography was an important early influence on Daniel Jones's phonetic ideas, and palatograms were used extensively as illustrations in the *Outline*; see Sections 8.2 and 8.4.

Rousselot, in his major work *Principes de phonétique expérimentale* (1897–1908), provided the first description of the use of these techniques and the results which he obtained using them. Together with his colleague Laclotte, Rousselot also wrote a short elementary textbook, *Précis de prononciation française* (Rousselot—Laclotte 1902). See Section 8.2 for Jones's use of significant portions of this work in the first edition of the *Outline*.

Switzerland was another country where linguistics flourished at this period, producing notable early research on dialects. Jules Gilliéron (1854–1926), who had contacts with Abbé Rousselot, is generally regarded as the greatest of the 19th century dialectologists. Another Swiss scholar, who is especially significant not only in the field of dialect research but in the total history of linguistics, is Jost Winteler (1846–1929). He produced a seminal work in his analysis of the Swiss German dialect of Kerenz (Winteler 1876), which is now recognised as being far ahead of its time in its phonological approach. In particular, Winteler developed in his thesis the concept of the phoneme—although the term itself is not employed, and can thus join Sweet (see Section 2.9) and Baudouin de Courtenay (see Section A.6) as being one of the earliest linguists to arrive at this crucial phonological idea; he is probably the very first to state the essentials in print (Koerner 1978b: 196–197, Kohler 1981: 163–164, S. Anderson 1985: 56).

However, the most notable Swiss linguist of this—or any other—period was without doubt Ferdinand de Saussure (1857–1913), widely acknowledged as the single greatest inspiration of modern approaches to linguistics and "the key figure in the change from nineteenth- to twentieth-century attitudes" (Robins [1979]: 199). Saussure studied sciences at Geneva before going on to take his doctorate at Leipzig, where he arrived in 1876, when the Neogrammarian linguistic revolution was in full swing. Before completing his doctoral thesis, he wrote his influential *Mémoire sur le système primitif des voyelles dans les langues indo-européennes* (Saussure 1879), a study which proved to be the only major work which ever came from his own pen. Apart from being notable for its emphasis on the significance of structure in sound systems, Saussure employed the word "phoneme" about forty times, albeit in the sense of "speech sound", for which the term had been coined by Dufriche-Desgenettes (Koerner 1976a). It is probably from this source that Baudouin de Courtenay derived the word. However, Saussure's tremendous impact on the development of linguistics was only to come much later, once his lectures had been collected by his students and published posthumously as his now renowned *Cours de linguistique générale* (Saussure 1916). Saussure went from Leipzig to Paris where he became a lecturer in Germanic languages at the Ecole des Hautes Etudes. He remained there for ten years and would have counted among his students at one time the young Paul Passy. In 1891, Saussure returned to take up a chair at Geneva, where he worked until his death.

Apart from being regarded as the "pioneer and founder of modern European structuralism" (Fischer-Jørgensen 1975: 11), Saussure is important in his approach to phonology for his emphasis on contrast and alternation within linguistic sound systems. The *Cours* employs the term "phoneme", though for the most part in its original sense rather than in its modern use; Jones (*HMTP*: 6 n.) states that in one portion of the book Saussure does appear to be "getting an inkling of the concept...as we know it". However, although Saussure is to be considered as the greatest early twentieth century force in linguistics, yet his direct influence on Jones was, in fact, minimal. Fischer-Jørgensen (1975: 51) has pointed out that Jones had already worked out his theory of the phoneme before Saussure's *Cours* was published and altered his views little thereafter. Indeed, as revealed in Section 14.10, Jones confessed privately that he had actually never even read Saussure's work.

A.6. Eastern Europe

Some of the most crucial developments in phonology in the late nineteenth century were to take place in Russia. In particular, a remarkable group of scholars were situated at Kazan', in a geographically remote area, hundreds of miles to the east of Moscow, and far removed from the mainstream of contemporary linguistic thought in

France, Germany and Britain. However, the University of Kazan' was not (as some-times thought) an intellectual backwater; it had a rich scholarly tradition numbering Tolstoy among its alumni and the brilliant mathematician Nikolaj Lobachevsky among its lecturing staff.

The leader of the Kazan' School, as it has come to be known (see Jakobson 1971 for an overall assessment), was the Polish-born aristocrat Jan Baudouin de Courtenay (1845–1929). After periods of study at Warsaw, Prague, and Berlin, Baudouin completed his doctorate at Leipzig in 1870. He worked at Kazan' from 1875 to 1883, and subsequently at Dorpat in Estonia and Cracow in Poland. He went back to Russia to take up a post at St Petersburg in 1901 and remained there until 1918, returning to his native Poland on his retirement.

S. Anderson (1985: 82) says of Baudouin:

> It is perhaps ironic that a linguist whose most important and best-developed work in general linguistics concerned the notion of [phonological] rules...should be best remembered for helping to form a particular notion of phonological representations.

Be that as it may, there can be no doubt that, as far as his influence on Jones is concerned, Baudouin's importance lies in his development of the concept of the phoneme, on which he worked together with his Polish colleague Mikołaj Kruszewski (1851–87). Kruszewski may have been crucial in realising the significance of the phoneme. He certainly appears to have been responsible for taking the actual word over from Saussure. Exactly how great a role he played is not clear (see discussion in Albrow 1981, and Koerner 1972 [1978a]: 114–120). In developing the "theory of alternations", which centred around the phoneme concept, Baudouin de Courtenay (1876–77 [1972b]: 150) clearly considers that Kruzsewski's contribution was essentially organisational rather than inspirational: "It cannot be denied, however, that Kruszewski merely gave another, finer form to what he had learned from someone else. (This was admitted by Kruszewski himself...)."

Baudouin appears to have used the phoneme idea first in the seventies, and it is clear from his lecture programmes of 1876–77 that he was devoting a considerable amount of time to the concept of the "smallest indivisible phonetic unit of language" (Baudouin de Courtenay 1876–77: 115). He was therefore using the concept around the same time as Sweet and Winteler. However, Baudouin's later writings take the idea much further, emphasising the importance of the principle of "alternation". By this terminology, Baudouin meant morphologically linked oppositions, and his views can be regarded as anticipating modern systems of rule-based phonology (Baudouin de Courtenay 1895). Furthermore, Baudouin's concept of the phoneme is clearly stated as essentially a psychological unit (1895: 152), and it is this aspect of phoneme theory which was later to form one facet of Jones's views. For general evaluations of Baudouin, see Koerner (1972) and Stankiewicz (1972a).

Another indication of Baudouin's stature is the large number of pupils and colleagues in Russia who followed up his ideas. Prominent among these was Lev Ščerba, (1880–1944), who, after having been a student at St Petersburg, went on to study under Rousselot and Passy in Paris, where he took his doctorate. He came back to work with Baudouin in St. Petersburg in 1909, taking charge of an experimental Phonetics Laboratory there, and attended Baudouin's lectures; he appears to have absorbed many of Baudouin's theories. Ščerba went on to become the leading personality of the "Leningrad School". Because of his connections with Passy, and his background as a pupil of Baudouin's, Ščerba must be regarded as the most obvious connecting strand between linguistic developments in Russia and the rest of Europe.

As far as Jones is concerned, Ščerba is of paramount importance; together with another of Baudouin's pupils—Tytus Benni—he provided the direct link with the theories of the Kazan' School. Jones acknowledged that it was in reading Ščerba's (1911) survey of the sound system of Russian (a paper which appeared as a supplement to *Le Maître phonétique*) that he first became aware of the phoneme concept and the word itself; and it was through discussion with Ščerba's colleague Benni that these ideas were clarified (*HMTP*: 5–6). In fact, Ščerba would appear to have been the first person to use the term "phoneme" in its present-day sense in a Western European publication. This earliest occurrence was not, as is often stated, in Ščerba (1911) but actually three years previously, in a review, also in *Le Maître phonétique*, of Baudouin's work on dialectology (Ščerba 1908).

Another linguist born and trained in Russian was Prince Nikolaj S. Trubetzkoy (1890–1938), termed by Koerner (1972 [1978a]: 111) "the acknowledged founder of modern structural phonology". Trubetzkoy was educated at Moscow University, where he specialised in the study of Caucasian languages, and later went on to Leipzig, when figures such as Brugmann and Leskien were still active. He taught briefly at Moscow, and became a leader of the Moscow linguistic circle, before being forced, because of his aristocratic background, to leave the country during the Revolution. After spending two years in Sofia, Bulgaria, Trubetzkoy accepted a post at Vienna.

Vienna was close enough to Czechoslovakia for him to take a conspicuous role (together with Mathesius, Jakobson and others) in setting up the Prague school of linguistics. By the late 1920s, Prague had become the world focus of developments in linguistics, particularly phonology, and the most significant source of opposition to the Jonesian view of the phoneme, which was increasingly despised as simplistic and inadequate. Under the influence of Baudouin and his followers, and of Saussure, the Prague linguists built up an imposing theoretical edifice, emphasising the cleft between the domains of phonetics and phonology, and introducing concepts such as neutralisation, the archiphoneme and morphophonemic analysis. By such means, they were able to find solutions (at least in part) for some problems which Jones had found intractable and had skated over or ignored. Trubetzkoy's contribution culminated in his posthumous *Grundzüge der Phonologie* (1939), which proved seminal in its influence on later developments in phonology, including Jakobson's distinctive feature analysis. For discussion of Trubetzkoy and his influence on the Prague school, see, for example, S. Anderson (1985: 83–115), Fischer-Jørgensen (1975: 19–49), Krámský (1974: 32–76).

A.7. Historical surveys of nineteenth and early twentieth century phonetics/phonology

In the above summary, the emphasis has been placed on those areas which are most significant for the life and work of Daniel Jones. At the time of writing, no comprehensive history of phonetics exists, but more detailed surveys of various aspects of the developments of phonetics and phonology can be found in numerous works, including the following (some of which have already been cited above): S. Anderson (1985), Fischer-Jørgensen (1975), Fry (1974), Jespersen (1922 [1968]: 32–89), Panconcelli-Calzia (1957), Pedersen (1931), Koerner (1978a), Kohler (1981), Robins (1967 [1979]: 164–206), Schmidt (1907), Trendelenburg (1957).[8] In addition, considerable biographical information is to be found in Sebeok (1966).

Examination Papers

The following is a selection of examination papers set by Jones for students taking various courses at University College London over a period of approximately twenty years.

UNIVERSITY OF LONDON, UNIVERSITY COLLEGE.

SESSION 1920–1921.

SPOKEN ENGLISH.

PHONETICS.

Monday, June 13th, 1921.—Afternoon, 5.30 to 7.30.

1. In what ways have you found phonetics of use to you in your study of Spoken English?

2. Describe fully the sounds represented by the italicised letters in the following sentence :—I saw him *going to* chur*ch.*

3. Indicate graphically the intonation of the sentence :—"What are we going to do now?" What other possible ways of saying it are there? Explain any difference in meaning that they indicate.

4. Write sentences to show that you know :—

    (*a*) when the English auxiliary verbs are stressed,

    (*b*) when the weak forms of the auxiliary verbs are used,

    (*c*) two compound words in which the first element is stressed,

    (*d*) two compound words in which the second element is stressed,

    (*e*) two compound words in which both elements are stressed.

5. Transcribe the following :—

"There!" she said with some pride. "If I had been reckless and imprudent I should have tried to get round that corner and had an upset. Didn't I show presence of mind, Jack?"
"Marvellous. And what are we to do now?"
Dodo looked round.
"We had better shout," she said. "And then somebody will come with a horse and pull us out backwards. It has happened before," she added candidly.
"But if nobody comes?" asked he.
"Somebody is sure to. It's unthinkable that we should remain till we die of exposure and hunger, and the crows pick our whitening bones. The only other thing to do is that you should jump out and fetch somebody. I wouldn't advise you to, as you would sink up to your knees in mud. But it's a lovely afternoon; let's sit here and talk till something happens. Haven't I learned to drive quickly?"
"Very quickly," said Jack. "We've covered the last three miles in four minutes."
"I didn't mean that sort of quickly," said Dodo, "though I dare say I said it."

D. JONES,
Examiner.

[227]

UNIVERSITY OF LONDON, UNIVERSITY COLLEGE.

SESSION 1927–1928.

SPOKEN ENGLISH.

(ENGLISH PHONETICS.)

Monday, June 11th, 1928.—Afternoon, 2 to 4.

1. Transcribe phonetically (with stress-marks) a *rapid* colloquial pronunciation of the following :—

—The traffic is pretty thick about here, isn't it ?
—Yes, but I do not think it is so bad as it is at the corner
of Tottenham Court Road.
—Which end do you mean ?
—Oh, the Oxford Street end, though of course they do have
pretty bad blocks at the other end as well.
—Yes. One day I was kept standing for more than five
minutes on the island in the middle of the road there.
—I wonder what will happen if the traffic increases still
more.
—It is very difficult to say what will be the end of it.
I suppose in the long run they will have to widen all
the principal streets.

2. Some foreigners make mispronunciations in the word *full*.
Who are they, and what is the nature of their mistakes ?

3. Give a method of teaching either the English vowel in
back, or the English vowel in *lock*, to a foreigner who has
difficulty with the pronunciation.

4. Which English vowels are generally longer than others ?
Mention the most important rules relating to the variability of
the length of these vowels, and give examples to illustrate
them.

DANIEL JONES,
Examiner.

[186]

UNIVERSITY OF LONDON, UNIVERSITY COLLEGE.

SESSION 1929–1930.

ENGLISH PHONETICS.

(FOR FOREIGN STUDENTS.)

Thursday, June 12th, 1930.—Afternoon, 5.30 to 7.30.

1. Which do you consider the two most difficult English vowel-sounds for people of your nationality? Describe the best ways of teaching them.

2. Write a short account of the " glottal stop" and its use in English.

3. Describe the chief members of the English *l*-phoneme, and contrast them with the *l*-sounds of some important foreign languages.

4. What are the principal relationships between stress and intonation in English? Illustrate them by examples. (Your examples should be written phonetically and with stress-marks, and the intonation should be shown by a graphic method.)

5. Give several examples to illustrate each of the following :— syllabic consonants, shortening of long vowels, assimilation.

DANIEL JONES,
Examiner.

[160]

University of London, University College

SESSION 1933–34

ENGLISH PHONETICS FOR FOREIGN STUDENTS

THURSDAY, 7TH JUNE, 1934.   AFTERNOON, 5.30–7.30

1. Describe the *two* most important mispronunciations of stressed vowels which people of your nationality are liable to make in saying the following sentence :—

He got up early in the morning, and wrote the three letters as fast as he could.

How would you correct a pupil who mispronounces in the way you mention ?

2. Draw rough diagrams showing the positions of the organs of speech in forming the English sounds *v*, *w*, *r*, *ŋ*. Indicate the chief variant values (if any) that these sounds have when they occur next to particular vowels.

3. How are compound words stressed in English ? Give numerous examples to illustrate the different methods of stressing them.

4. Describe the actions which the vocal cords perform in speech. Why is it useful for a teacher of English in a foreign country to know something of these actions ?

5. Give some examples (with intonation-marks) to show the difference between special intonation for intensity and special intonation for contrast.

DANIEL JONES (Examiner).

1695

UNIVERSITY OF LONDON

EXAMINATION FOR CERTIFICATE OF
PROFICIENCY IN ENGLISH (PART II) :
AUGUST, 1941

ELEMENTARY PHONETICS

FRIDAY, *August 8.*—11 *a.m. to* 1 *p.m.*

[N.B.—*Handwriting will be taken into consideration by
the Examiners in awarding marks. Carelessly
formed symbols will entail loss of marks.*]

1. Write the following in phonetic transcription,
marking the stress :—

(*a*) Holborn Viaduct; 2¾% ; 1,461 ; Lease and Lend
Act; Herbert Morrison; interment; casualties;
mercantile marine ; bomber squadron ; ration coupons.

(*b*) '' Please answer my questions, Major Warwick.
You saw your Colonel, instructed your solicitors imme-
diately on receipt of Mr. Cowbit's letter, yet you say it
wasn't the news in this letter that drove you to take
action, even at this late day, to try to defend your good
name? ''
'' I had wanted to do so before. I had already seen
my Colonel before I heard from Mr. Cowbit.''
'' How long before? ''
'' About a fortnight.''
'' You'd told your Colonel about the poker game
before you got this letter? ''
'' Yes, he'd heard the story and sent for me.''
'' What happened at this interview? ''

L.M. 2/539   3/70-255   17/6/41   [**Turn over**

2

" He asked for the facts, I gave them."

" You told your Colonel the truth? "

" I did."

" You confessed to him that you had been caught cheating? "

" No. I told him the truth, that Bradford and Grant had accused me of cheating, though I had done nothing of the kind."

" What did your Colonel say to this? "

" He said : ' That's that.' "

" Meaning? "

" That he believed me, that there was no more to be said."

" This was all that passed between you? "

" No. I said, since the story was out, that I must take proceedings. He asked me to wait. He said he didn't want the regiment involved in a scandal if it could be helped. He asked me to let him deal with Bradford."

2. EITHER—How would you describe and teach the " r " sounds in the following words :—*ride, cry, barren, three, shuddering?*

OR—

What are the differences between the " t " sounds of the following words :—*true, eighth, mutton, little, outpost?*

3. Using phonetic transcription, and a graphic method to show stress and intonation, give *five* different patterns for the following sentence :—

I thought he was.

4. " A large number of the commonest words in English are monosyllables, and many of them are distinguished from one another by differences of pronunciation which foreigners find it difficult to make." Discuss and illustrate the above statement.

International Phonetic Alphabet charts

	Bronch	Throat	Uvula	Back	Front	Tongue-point	Lip
Stopped		ʔ	q ɢ	k g	c ɟ	t d	p b
Nasal				ŋ	ɲ	n	m
Side				ʎ	ʎ	l	
Trilled			ʀ ʀ	ʀ		r	
Squeezed	H ʕ	h ɦ	ʁ ʀ	(ʍ w) x ɣ	(ɥ) ç j	ɹ, θð, ʃʒ, sz	fv ʍ w / q ɥ

CONSONANTS

Close	u ɯ ü	i ï y i
Half-close	ʊ	ʏ ɪ
Mid	o ʌ ö ë e ø e	ɘ
Half-open	ɔ ʌ ɔː æ ɑ ɐ ɒ ɜ œ	ɛ æ ɐ
Open	ɑ	ɑ

(ü ü y) (ʊ ʏ) (o ö ø) (œ ɔː ɒ)

VOWELS

The IPA chart current in 1904.

The IPA chart of 1912 (from *The Principles of the International Phonetic Association* 1912, p. 10).

	Labiales	Linguales	Palatales	Vélaires	Uvulaires	Laryngales
Plosives	p b	t d	c ɟ	k g	q ɢ	ʔ
Nasales	m	n	ɲ	ŋ	ɴ	
Latérales		l	ʎ			
Roulées		r			ʀ ʁ	
Fricatives	f v, ʍ w, ɸ β, ɥ (hɥ)	s z, θ ð, ʃ ʒ, ɹ	ç ʝ, j (hɥ)	x ɣ (ʍ w)	χ ʁ	h

CONSONNES

	Fermées	Mi-fermées	Mi-ouvertes	Ouvertes
Labiales	(u ʉ y)	(o ɵ ø)	(ɔ ɞ œ)	
	i y, ɨ ʉ, ɯ u	e ø, ə, ɤ o	ɛ œ, ɐ, ʌ ɔ	a ɑ

VOYELLES

A French version of the IPA chart published in 1921 (from *L'Écriture phonétique internationale* 1921, 2nd edition, p.6)

THE INTERNATIONAL PHONETIC ALPHABET.
(Revised to 1932.)

The IPA chart of 1932.

THE INTERNATIONAL PHONETIC ALPHABET.
(Revised to 1951.)

(Secondary articulations are shown by symbols in brackets.)

The IPA chart of 1951.

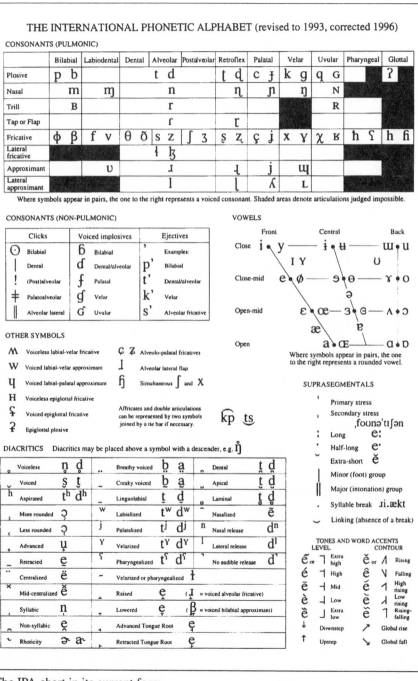

The IPA chart in its current form.

Notes

Chapter 1

1. Daniel Jones himself believed that there had been no Welsh connections in his paternal family for seven generations (Jones, letter to Caroline Monnington, 21 November 1954).
2. "Daniel Jones", obituary, *Lawn Tennis and Badminton* 9, 6 January 1916, p. 22. The issue features a full-page photograph of Daniel Jones Snr.
3. "Daniel Jones", obituary, *The Times*, 7 December 1915.
4. H.S. Scrivener, "Mr. Daniel Jones: A personal note", *Lawn Tennis and Badminton*, 6 January 1916, p. 22.
5. "Bridge", *Encyclopaedia Britannica*, 15th edn.
6. P.M. Platts, letter to author (BC), 29 September 1986.
7. Two years before his death, Dan Jones put down on record his own account of the stormy early history of lawn tennis, and an indication of the part played by himself and his brother Henry. *Lawn Tennis and Badminton*, 7 August 1913, pp. 689–690.
8. Obituary, *Lawn Tennis and Badminton*.
9. Note written in Jones's hand accompanying family records, 1 November 1947.
10. Programme of Jones's honorary degree ceremony, Edinburgh University, 1958.
11. M. Stanbury, interview.
12. Ludgrove School moved to Wixenford in 1937. Some of the old buildings were later used to house the former Trent Park College of Education.
13. D. Jones, letter to H.P. Hansell, 1 February 1921.
14. *Ludgrove School Notes*, 1895. Information on Ludgrove at this period and Jones's career in the school was supplied in a letter from D. Barber to author (BC), 18 October 1982.
15. A. Money (Hon. Sec. Radleian Society), letter to author (BC), 4 November 1981.
16. D. Monnington, interview.
17. M. Stanbury, interview.
18. Mentioned during several interviews with Jones's former colleagues; cf. Onishi (1981: 38–39).
19. G. Dannatt, interview.
20. Memo, D. Jones to UCL Secretary, 13 December 1948.
21. Memo, D. Jones to UCL Secretary, 13 December 1948.
22. O. Tooley, interview.
23. D. Jones, letter to J. B. Glass, 20 January 1962.
24. Details of Tilly's life have been obtained chiefly from the following sources: W. Tilley, letter to Dean of Marburg University, 14 March 1887; "William Tilly" (Jones 1935e); J.B. Glass (1963); "William Tilly", BDPS; "The spoken word", article in the *British Australian and New Zealander*, 19 March 1936 (p. 12).
25. "Londoner's Diary", London *Evening Standard*, 22 October 1935. The piece was possibly written by R. Bruce Lockhart.
26. E.W. Mammen, letter to author (BC), n.d., postmarked 2 June 1982.
27. "The spoken word". See note 24.
28. D. Jones, letter to J. B. Glass, 4 January 1962.
29. D. Jones, letter to J. B. Glass, 20 January 1962.

Chapter 2

1. M. Stanbury, interview.
2. M. Stanbury, interview.
3. G. Dannatt, interview.
4. G. Dannatt, interview; R. Upcott, interview.
5. These works are listed on both sides of the back cover of *MPh* (3) 19, July–September 1941. The bibliography was presumably drawn up by Jones, whose obituary of Passy appears in the same issue, but no compiler's name is appended.
6. D. Abercrombie, interview; M. Chapallaz, interview.
7. Additional biographical information on Passy is to be found in his autobiography (Passy 1930–32), in Jugnet (1929) and Simonsen (1939).
8. Daniel Jones Papers.
9. UCL Calendar, 1864–65, p. 29.
10. UCL Calendar, 1866–67, p. 50.
11. UCL Calendar, 1869–70, p. 59.
12. UCL Calendar, 1870, p. 51.
13. Jones (1948f [1973]: 180) states that Edwards worked for two sessions beginning in 1903. His name first appears in the UCL Calendar, 1904–05, p. 31.
14. UCL Calendar, 1906–07, p. 31.
15. M. Stanbury, interview; O. Tooley, interview.
16. *MPh* (2) 22 (1907), p. 73.
17. College Committee, 1906–07, min. 85d.
18. *MPh* (2) 22 (1907), pp. 97–98.
19. Lecture notes, "Phonetics for students of philology", n.d., Daniel Jones Papers.
20. Zürich Lecture (see Section 7.7): "At U.C. we also give attention to *historical phonetics* in relation to English & French. And we try as far as possible to treat this subject in a very practical way, as we do with the phonetics of living languages....We then try to make the language of different periods *alive* by transcribing *texts* phonetically according to our reconstruction."
21. *MPh* (2) 20 (1905), p. 133. Jones's membership number was 1052.
22. *MPh* (2) 20 (1905), p. 130. "En caisse au 30 septembre. 1 cot[isation] de membre actif à vie: Jones 90.—".
23. *MPh* (2) 21 (1906), p. 94.
24. *MPh* (2) 21 (1906), p. 94.
25. *MPh* (2) 21 (1906), pp. 122–123.
26. G. Dannatt, interview; R. Upcott, interview.
27. *Who's Who* entries.
28. *MPh* (2) 22 (1907), p. 34.
29. *MPh* (2) 23 (1908), pp. 64, 67 and 68.
30. The remark was originally made by C.T. Onions ("Henry Sweet", *Dictionary of national biography*), actually with reference to Sweet's (1885a) *Elementarbuch*.
31. For instance, Sweet (1877: 141) in claiming that Dutch [l, t, d, n] "seem to be the same as English, not being dental" ignores the differences in the portions of the tongue employed in the articulations, not to mention the obvious auditory dissimilarities. Furthermore, his Narrow Romic representation of the Dutch vowel in *lui* as [əi] shows that he appears to have missed the lip-rounding on the second element (p. 140).

32. Letter, Jones to L. van Buuren, 24 December 1964.
33. Letter, Jones to L. van Buuren, 24 December 1964.
34. Letter, Jones to L. van Buuren, 24 December 1964.
35. Letter, Jones to L. van Buuren, 24 December 1964.
36. "History of the College", an article which reappeared annually as part of the UCL Calendar. See also D. Taylor (1968: 29).
37. College Committee, 1907–08, min. 88c.
38. College Committee, 1908–09, min. 8of.

Chapter 3

1. UCL Calendar 1908–09, p. 32.
2. UCL Calendar 1906–07, p. 31.
3. UCL Calendar 1908–09, p. 32.
4. M. Phillips, interview. Jones gave a recitation at Mrs Phillips's wedding.
5. O. Tooley, interview.
6. Deutsche Grammophon-Gesellschaft, catalogue numbers 201392/3.
7. Although, apparently by a printer's error, the back vowels remained unaltered.
8. The discussion had originated in an article reporting on the pronunciation of classical languages in the Czech-speaking areas of the Austro-Hungarian Empire (Frinta 1907).
9. The Ndau prefix *chi* = "language".
10. *MPh* (2) 23 (1908), p. 30.
11. *MPh* (2) 23 (1908), p. 64.
12. *MPh* (2) 23 (1908), p. 67.
13. *MPh* (2) 24 (1909), p. 44.
14. UCL Calendar, 1909–10, p. 34.
15. UCL Calendar, 1910–11, p. 34.
16. Report of the College Committee 1910–11, p. 31.
17. J. Carnochan, interview.
18. UCL College Committee, 1909–10, min. 142b.
19. UCL Calendar 1910–11, p. 34.
20. *Pronunciation of English*[1] (p. 153 + 3) includes a brief note stating that the *Outline* is "in preparation".
21. UCL College Committee, 1910–11, report of meeting of Professorial Board, 25 October 1910.

Chapter 4

1. G. Dannatt, interview; R. Upcott, interview.
2. Passy considered his state of health sufficiently interesting to warrant two editorial notes under the headings "La santé" and "Encore la santé"; *MPh* (2) 1911, pp. 55, 179.
3. R. Upcott, interview.
4. G. Dannatt, interview.
5. R. Upcott, interview.
6. G. Dannatt, interview.

7. She was, in fact, responsible for all the French texts for students in the 1911 volume, *MPh* (2) 26.
8. The pronunciation used by all members of the Motte family is /pɔnarbryn/.
9. R. Upcott, interview; G. Dannatt, interview.
10. R. Upcott, interview.
11. R. Upcott, interview; G. Dannatt, interview.
12. For example, Passy (1913): "…je le tiens de mon neveu Daniel Jones, professeur à l'Université de Londres".
13. *MPh* (2) 26 (1911), p. 4.
14. G. Dannatt, interview.
15. *MPh* (2) 26 (1911), p. 78.
16. G. Dannatt, interview.
17. Though probably Dan Jones himself had some command of the language. His obituaries in *The Times* and the *Standard* (both dated 7 December 1915) mention his membership of the Alpine Club.
18. UCL Calendar, 1917–18, p. 37, states explicitly that her classes will be conducted in French.
19. D. Monnington, interview, and others. Daniel Jones eventually took on many household duties in an era when it was quite unusual for men to do so.
20. UCL Calendar, 1911–12, p. 36.
21. College Committee, 1911–12, min. 53c.
22. Report of College Committee on Budgets 1911–12 and 1912–13, section V.
23. Obituary of G. Noël-Armfield, source unknown.
24. College Committee, 1911–12, min. 165, II.
25. Dept Report, 1912–13.
26. Notes for "The Teaching of English Pronunciation to French Students", lecture delivered first at Guilde Internationale, Paris, 9 January 1912. In Daniel Jones Papers.
27. The sentences are mentioned earlier in *MPh* (2) 22 (1907), p. 58, in a discussion of a phrasebook, under the heading: "Transcription fantaisiste".
28. Dates written by Jones on title page of Paris Lecture.
29. *MPh* (2) 27 (1912), p. 86.
30. College Committee, 1911–12, min. 114d.
31. Dept Report, 1912–13.
32. Dept Report, 1912–13.
33. *MPh* (2) 28 (1913), p. 54.
34. M. Hunter, report from India, the *Pioneer* 2 (1913), p. 9.
35. *MPh* (2) 26 (1912), p. 81.
36. G. Dannatt, interview.
37. Letter, Jones to L. van Buuren, 24 December 1964.
38. Letter, Jones to L. van Buuren, 24 December 1964.
39. Letter, Jones to L. van Buuren, 24 December 1964.
40. Letter, Jones to L. van Buuren, 24 December 1964.
41. Letter, Jones to L. van Buuren, 24 December 1964. A photograph of Sweet still hangs in the Gordon Square building of the UCL Phonetics and Linguistics Dept (together with ones of Jones, A.C. Gimson and Dennis Fry).
42. Collins (1987) contains a fuller exposition of the material in this Section.
43. *Pygmalion* was begun on 7 March 1912 and finished in early June. It first appeared in

German translation in 1913, and was performed in German in Vienna in 1913. See definitive 7 vol. edition of Shaw's plays, D. Lawrence (1970–73) ed., New York: Dodd, Mead & Co.

44. The English law of this period, and indeed for many years after, was notoriously unfair to authors. Graham Greene has given some idea of the frequency of libel suits and the danger these posed to the successful author. See Graham Greene (1980), *Ways of Escape*, London: Bodley Head, pp. 27–29, 60–63.

45. A similar apparatus is illustrated in Rousselot ([1924]: vol. 1, p. 172).

46. J. Overton Fuller, letter, the *Observer*, 15 January 1978.

47. J. Overton Fuller, letter, the *Observer*, 15 January 1978.

48. This letter is reproduced in Tompkins's book as a photostat.

49. Jean Overton Fuller, letter, the *Observer*, 15 January 1978.

50. Notes for lecture "Applications of Phonetics", delivered at UCL, 29 October 1947.

51. "I joined about 1910, I think." In notes for speech delivered at Simplified Spelling Society, 18 November 1955. In Daniel Jones Papers.

52. In notes for speech delivered at Simplified Spelling Society, 18 November 1955. In Daniel Jones Papers.

53. SSS minutes, 10 October 1912. (We are grateful to Mr C. Jolly and Mr S. Gibbs of the SSS for allowing us access to the minutes of the Society.)

54. SSS minutes, 9 October 1913.

55. Lascelles Abercrombie, 1881–1938 writer, poet and critic; later Professor of Literature at Leeds and London, and Reader at Oxford.

56. See Phillips (1992) for a full biography of Bridges.

57. English Association Lecture (see note 59). The meetings were (1) Annual General Meeting, 28 January 1911, when Jones opened the debate on "Phonetic spelling"; (2) Annual General Meeting, 9 January 1915, when Jones chaired a meeting on "The teaching of English pronunciation" (reported in *English Association Bulletin* 12 and 13).

58. Notes for lecture delivered to the English Association, 25 January 1946. In Daniel Jones Papers.

59. Notes for lecture delivered to the English Association, 25 January 1946. In Daniel Jones Papers.

60. Letter, Bridges to H. Bradley, 30 June 1912. See Stanford (1983–84: 610).

61. Letter, Bridges to H. Bradley, 30 June 1912.

62. Letter, Bridges to L. Abercrombie, 4 February 1913. See Stanford (1983–84: 618).

63. Minor corrections have been made to Gimson's selections, and page numbers have been added.

Chapter 5

1. *Phonetic readings in English*, Deutsche Grammophon Gesellschaft (Collection Driesen) 201378–201391. These appear to have been made before 1914, since they are mentioned in *Outline*¹ (p. 193). Jones later produced further recordings for Odeon, Berlin, AA 53816–29.

2. The languages covered were: Cantonese (Jones—Kwing Tong Woo 1912a), Panjabi (Bailey 1914), French (Passy 1914), German (Egan 1914), Italian (Camilli 1921), English (Armstrong 1923a), Polish (Arend 1924), Burmese (Armstrong—Pe Maung Tin 1925), Czech (Frinta 1925), Welsh (S. Jones 1926), Bengali (Chatterji 1928), Dutch (Quick—

Schilthuis 1930), Danish (Uldall 1933), Tswana (Jones—Plaatje 1916), Serbo-Croat (Fry—Kostić 1939).

3. D.B. Fry, interview.

4. Letter, University of London Press to Jones, 29 February 1932.

5. Letter, University of London Press to D. Parkinson, 16 March 1936.

6. In the 1880s, the publishers Frederick Warne were advertising the following dictionaries featuring pronunciation: *Nuttall's standard pronouncing dictionary* (ed. P.A. Nuttall); *Walker's pronouncing dictionary* (ed. P.A. Nuttall); *Warne's bijou dictionary*; *Warne's popular edition of Walker's pronouncing dictionary*; *Nugent's improved pronouncing pocket dictionary of the French and English languages*; and *Williams's pocket dictionary of the English and German languages*. (See Nuttall 1883: inside front cover.)

7. *MPh* (2) 26 (1911), p. 90.

8. Note that in the collected version of *Le Maître phonétique*, published by Swets and Zeitlinger (Amsterdam, 1969), the *Exposé* has been incorrectly included in the 1905 volume.

9. These varieties, with the exception of Scots, were represented in the 1904 Principles; Northern English refers to the artificial invention of Lloyd (1899).

10. This piece was probably contributed by Johannes Smith, an IPA member living in London, who wrote a specimen of this type of Dutch for *Le Maître phonétique* (Smith 1911) and also began work on *An African Dutch phonetic reader* for the London Phonetic Reader series—though the book never reached fruition. It is noted in the 1912 *Principles* (p. 35) as being "in preparation".

11. *MPh* (2) 26 (1911), p. 89.

12. *MPh* (2) 27 (1912), p. 92.

13. *MPh* (2) 29 (1914), p. 82.

14. "Liste des membres de l'Association Phonétique Internationale", January-February 1914; supplement to *MPh* (2) 29, pp. 30–31.

15. *MPh* (2) 25 (1910), p. 141.

16. *MPh* (2) 26 (1911), p. 91.

17. *MPh* (2) 28 (1913), pp. 61, 84.

18. *MPh* (2) 27 (1912), p. 153. The British Museum joined as member no. 1629.

19. *MPh* (2) 27 (1912), p. 90.

20. *MPh* (2) 27 (1912), p. 126.

21. *MPh* (2) 28 (1913), p. 77.

22. Dept Report, 1912–13.

23. College Committee, 1912–13, min. 2 (ii) c.

24. Dept Report, 1912–13.

25. UCL Calendar 1912–13, p. 37.

26. UCL Calendar 1913–14, p. 41.

27. Curators, Taylor Institution, Oxford University, 5 May 1913, min. 4.

28. Curators, Taylor Institution, Oxford University, 15 June 1912, min. 4.

29. Oxford University Hebdomadal Council Report, 11 May 1913. (Letter, Curators of Taylor Institution to Oxford University Registrar, 7 June 1913.)

30. Oxford University Hebdomadal Council Report, 11 May 1913. (Letter, Curators of Taylor Institution to Oxford University Registrar, 7 June 1913, quoting Jones's words.)

31. Curators, Taylor Institution, 5 May 1913, min. 4.

32. Letter, Taylor Institution to Registrar, 7 June 1913.

33. Curators, Taylor Institution, 16 May 1913, min. 1.
34. College Committee, 1913–14, min. 76d.
35. Letter, Curators, Taylor Institution to Oxford University Registrar, 7 June 1913.
36. Jones (1926e: 398) later wrote "two years" but this must be a slip of the pen.
37. Dept Report, 1913–14.
38. Curators, Taylor Institution, 13 June 1914, min. 7.
39. Curators, Taylor Institution, 13 June 1914, min. 8.
40. UCL Calendar 1913–14, pp. 40–41.
41. Dept Report, 1913–14.
42. Notes, "History of the College: Department of Phonetics", n.d.; in Daniel Jones Papers.
43. Dept Report, 1913–14.
44. University of London, "Scheme for an Institute of Phonetics", 28 June 1919, p. 2. See also Section 8.2.
45. College Committee, 1913–14, min. 146b.
46. Dept Report, 1915–16, p. 2.
47. Dept Report, 1913–14.
48. Dept Report, 1913–14.
49. College Committee, 1913–14, min. 151 m.
50. *Punch*, 12 August 1914, p. 153.

Chapter 6

1. Dept Report, 1914–15.
2. Several phoneticians assisted in military and intelligence work in World War II. See Section 12.3.
3. M. Phillips, interview.
4. *Who's Who* entries for Arthur Daniel Derviche-Jones. (Jones's brother changed his name by deed poll.)
5. A.C. Gimson, interview.
6. UCL Calendar, 1914–15, pp. 40–43.
7. Dept Report, 1914–15.
8. Report on the French Phonetics Classes, 1913–14, Second Term.
9. Dept Report, 1914–15.
10. Dept Report, 1915–16.
11. UCL College Committee Report, 1915, p. 41.
12. College Committee, 1914–15, min. 5e.
13. College Committee, 1914–15, min. 83c.
14. College Committee, 1914–15, min. 99d.
15. UCL College Committee Report, 1915, p. 41.
16. UCL Calendar, 1915–16, pp. 40–43.
17. Dept Report, 1915–16.
18. Dept Report, 1915–16.
19. His enthusiasm for the IPA is shown by the fact that his daughter recalled: "When I was quite young, I could only read and write in phonetic notation" (D. Anderson 1969: 138).
20. For biographical detail of Palmer, see Jones (1950c) and D. Anderson (1969).
21. Dept Report, 1915–16.

22. "Mr. Daniel Jones" (obituary), *Lawn Tennis and Badminton* 9 (1916), p. 22.
23. "Mr. Daniel Jones" (obituary), *Lawn Tennis and Badminton* 9 (1916), p. 22.
24. M. Phillips, interview.
25. M. Stanbury, interview.
26. M. Phillips, interview.
27. M. Stanbury, M. Phillips and D. Monnington, interviews.
28. The name Sechuana includes the Tswana prefix *se*, meaning "language".
29. Missionaries' Lecture (see 32 below).
30. D.B. Fry, interview. It is noteworthy that Fry also quotes this proverb in his introduction to *Homo loquens* (Fry 1977: n.p.).
31. This symbol was replaced by ɸ after the 1925 Copenhagen Conference. See *MPh* (3) 42 (1927), p. 14.
32. The Missionaries' Lecture was first delivered at UCL, 30 October 1916.

Chapter 7

1. On Gimson's death, the work of editing the *EPD* passed to his UCL colleague Susan Ramsaran. It has now been taken over by Peter Roach and James Hartman.
2. Though Wells (1985: 3) observes that even in the *EPD*[14] "an embarrassingly large number of rather frequently used words" remained excluded. The 1988 edition of the EPD (revised 14th edn) remedies most of these omissions.
3. Notably, "General British" or GB (Windsor Lewis 1972) and "Southern British Standard" or SBS (Wells—Colson 1971). RP is a term rarely used by American linguists, who generally prefer the imprecise "British English".
4. A.C. Gimson, interview. The letter-doubling transcription is to be found in MacCarthy (1944). Jones, in his foreword to MacCarthy's book, indicates his approval of the system and mentions that the letter-doubling device was originally used by Sweet.
5. Jones's development of the Cardinal Vowel model has already been presented in the form of an article (Collins—Mees 1995).
6. This is the wording appearing on the title page. Many authors refer to the book as *Die Bell-Sweet'sche Schule*.
7. Several scholars, e.g. Ladefoged (1967: 70); Abercrombie (1967: 176); Butcher (1982: 50), err in stating, or implying, that the 1917 *English pronouncing dictionary* contains the very first mention of the Cardinal Vowels.
8. His Master's Voice (the Gramophone Company), catalogue no. B 804. Linguistic Record No. 1 "Speech Sounds Cardinal Vowels (Short and Long)"; No. 2 "Speech Sounds Cardinal Vowels (in pairs)". We are grateful to Professors J.C Wells and A. Fourcin of UCL for allowing us access to this recording.
9. "The Cardinal Vowels", Linguaphone Institute, DAJO 1D (20 January 1943) and DAJO 2G (10 May 1943).
10. "The Cardinal Vowels", Linguaphone Institute, ENG 252/253/254/255 (1956).
11. UCL Calendar, 1916–17, p. 36.
12. Dept report, 1916–17.
13. Palmer's report appears not to have survived.
14. College Committee Report, 1917, p. 36.
15. Dept Report, 1916–17.

16. College Committee, 1917–18, min. 45f.
17. College Committee, 1917–18, min. 45f.
18. College Committee, 1917–18, min. 45g.
19. College Committee, 1917–18, min. 45g.
20. College Committee, 1916–17, App. IV.
21. Dept Report, 1916–17.
22. Dept Report, 1916–17.
23. Dept Report, 1916–17.
24. Delivered at the Philological Society, 4 May 1917.
25. Jones did eventually produce a tonemic analysis of Tswana, which he used for the Tswana text in the IPA Principles (*IPA* 1949: 49). See *HMTP* (p. 16 n.).
26. Russell (1928: 48) reports that Meyer was using this experimental procedure as early as 1905.
27. The original prints of these X-rays are to be found in the Daniel Jones Papers in the library of University College London.
28. Dept report, 1917–18.
29. Preparatory notes for lecture "The London School of Phonetics", delivered Zürich, 11 October 1946, and at Copenhagen, 8 April 1948 (UCL Daniel Jones Papers). Later revised and published, see Jones (1948f).
30. In the lecture notes, Jones tellingly states that there was "not enough money to pay them [the staff] adequately", but this has been scored through.
31. UCL Calendar 1917–18, pp. 38–39.
32. UCL College Committee Report 1917–18, p. 40.
33. UCL College Committee Report 1919, p. 40.
34. Preparatory notes for lecture "The Sechuana Language", delivered to Philological Society, London, 4 May 1917 (Daniel Jones Papers). Later revised and published, see Jones (1917c).
35. Biographical details of Lilias Armstrong are partly derived from Jones's statement in support of her readership, June 1936. In Daniel Jones Papers.
36. College Committee, 3 July 1917, min. 181.
37. College Committee, 17 October 1917, min. 8.
38. College Committee, 17 November 1917, min. 25.
39. College Committee, 17 May 1918, min. 25.
40. Dept Report, 1918–19.
41. Mentioned by numerous ex-colleagues of Jones.
42. Dept Report, 1917–18.
43. M. Phillips, interview.
44. M. Phillips, interview.
45. Index cards, Daniel Jones Papers.
46. Index cards, Daniel Jones Papers.
47. Index cards, Daniel Jones Papers.
48. Index cards, Daniel Jones Papers.
49. Index cards, Daniel Jones Papers, 21 July 1918.
50. M. Phillips, interview.
51. Index card, Daniel Jones Papers.
52. Letter, W. Stanley Murrell (Manager, University of London Press) to Jones, 22 July 1918.
53. Index card, 14 August 1918.

54. College Committee, 4 July 1916, min. 160.
55. UCL College Committee Report 1916–17, p. 36.
56. UCL College Committee Report 1917–18, p. 36.
57. The School of Oriental Studies had been founded with this purpose partly in mind. But the School was heavily dependent in its early years on members of Jones's Department, who played a major part in its language teaching operations.

Chapter 8

1. The copy is in the UCL Library (Daniel Jones Papers).
2. This copy is in the possession of one of the authors (BC).
3. Jones did not get round to using bracketing conventions of this sort himself. But, late in his career, he was prepared to indicate his thorough approval of the idea (*HMTP*, p. 19).
4. Jones was most enthusiastic about "Atkinson's Mouth Measurer" and is quoted in an advertisement (n.d.) produced by Harold Atkinson to promote his product. See also Jones's brief article on the apparatus (Jones 1910h).
5. Jones (1924), *Phonetic readings in English*. Lloyd James, A. (1929), *Linguaphone conversational course: English*, London: Linguaphone Institute.
6. Jones suggested (in the *EPD*) that, as a phonetic term, *breathed* should be pronounced /breθt/.
7. The cinefilm sequence is stated by Scripture (1902: 353) to be originally the work of Demeny (1893), "Analyse des mouvements de la parole par la chromophotographie", *Journal de Physique*, p. 328.
8. Ball's (1984: 40–41) statement that Jones (1909b) had mentioned the use of monophthongal [ɛː] is misleading. As our reference shows, no such comment appeared until the *Pronunciation of English*[3]. Ball was presumably using the *Pronunciation of English*[4], where the quotation does appear on p. 64, as his reference would suggest.
9. Cf. Sweet (e.g. 1908: 52) for use of "diphthongic" rather than "diphthongal".

Chapter 9

1. UCL Prospectus, 1919–20, p. 42.
2. UCL Prospectus, 1919–20, p. 43; 1920–21, p. 43; 1921–22, p. 45.
3. UCL Prospectuses, 1919–20, p. 39; 1920–21, p. 40; 1921–22, p. 42.
4. See also BDPS and DNB.
5. See also BDPS.
6. Letter, H. Coustenoble to Provost Sir Ifor Evans, 8 July 1962.
7. A.C. Gimson, interview.
8. Letter, J.L. Paton to Jones, 18 September 1918.
9. Letter, Sir Henry Wood to Jones, 11 July 1918.
10. University of London, Scheme for an Institute of Phonetics, 7 January 1919, p. 7.
11. University of London, Scheme for an Institute of Phonetics, 7 January 1919.
12. UL Senate, min. 105, 4 March 1919.
13. Agenda for UL Committee on the Institute of Phonetics, 19 March 1919.

14. University of London, Scheme for an Institute of Phonetics, 28 June 1919. It is to this version that references have been made.
15. Letter, Jones to Foster, 4 March 1919.
16. The *Observer*, 23 November 1919.
17. Letter, Jones to Sir Rickman Godlee, 2 November 1919.
18. Letter, Jones to Stanley Leathes, 18 November 1919.
19. Letters, Jones to Sir Harry Johnston, 17 December 1919; B.G. Greig to Jones, 19 December 1919. The Committee met on 16 December 1919.
20. Letter, Jones to Foster, 21 November 1919. The project obviously had echoes of Jones's previous staging of Shakespeare in the original pronunciation (see Section 3.2) and of Arnold Jones's application of phonetic techniques for dramatic work with his pupils (see Section 6.6).
21. Report on "Post-War Needs of the Department of Phonetics, University College, London", Daniel Jones, 27 January 1944, p. 3.
22. Manchester University Press no longer possesses any correspondence on the *Sinhalese reader*. Letter, Juanita Griffiths (Manchester University Press) to author (BC), 7 February 1986.
23. The actual term "allophonic" is not used in the *Sinhalese reader*, not having been coined until many years later. See Section 14.16.
24. Jones's correspondence confirms his general dislike (typical of the British upper-middle class of his generation) of the use of first names outside the family circle.
25. See also BDPS and DNB.
26. The bound volumes are kept in the Department of Phonetics, University College, London. We are grateful to Professor J.C. Wells for being allowed access to them.
27. There is also evidence that Jones abandoned an earlier plan to write a French phonetic reader to appear in the London Phonetic Reader series. Paul Passy's *French phonetic reader* (1914) is announced for the first time with Jones—not Passy—named as the author (listing of the London Phonetic Readers in the *Cantonese reader* 1912a: ii).
28. Letter, D. Parkinson to Major S.G. Simpson, 1 January 1920.
29. In interviews, many of his former colleagues and relations mentioned Jones's preoccupation with avoiding nervous strain.
30. Jones's nephew recalled his former fondness for the game: "...[Jones] told me that he and my father played chess and that the games were most strenuous and exciting". Letter, P.M. Platts to author (BC), 29 September 1986.
31. College Committee, 6 January 1920, min. 88.
32. College Committee, 4 May 1920, min. 172 (c).
33. College Report, 1920, p. 44.
34. College Committee, 7 October 1920, min. 33: "...the Medical Adviser of Mr. Daniel Jones considers that he can now resume part of his College work, and that Mr. Jones hopes to do so shortly".
35. College Committee, 1 January 1920, min. 225.
36. College Committee, 7 October 1920, min. 33.
37. College Committee, 7 October 1920, min. 4h.
38. College Committee, 4 January 1921, min. 97d (Senate Report).
39. College Committee, 6 July 1921, min. 249g.
40. College Committee, 28 September 1921, min. 10b.
41. UL Senate, 30 July 1921, min. 7 iv.

Chapter 10

1. Mrs J. Talma-Schilthuis, interview.
2. Original in Dutch, translated by author (IMM).
3. Jones, letter to D. Ward, 21 May 1958.
4. Letter, Jones to D. Ward, 3 June 1958.
5. It is interesting to note that today a later trend to the *raising* of word-final /ɪ/ has resulted in several dictionaries, notably the *Longman Pronunciation Dictionary* (Wells 1990), differentiating the two vowels in *city*.
6. Stéphan refers to his ancestry in the course of an article written for the University College student magazine, *New Phineas*, when UCL was evacuated to Aberystwyth in 1939. He mentions (p. 6) being amongst "the Welsh, the blood brothers of the Bretons, my own people".
7. This passage in itself indicates the primacy of Stéphan since Jones elsewhere admits that he has never even read Saussure (see Section 14.10).
8. G. Dewey (n.d.), *Relativ* [sic] *frequency of English speech sounds*, is discussed at length, but deals with American English.
9. Publishing details of the first editions of these books are taken from Ransom (1938: 94, 254, 560).
10. M. Phillips, interview.
11. Letter, Jones to L. van Buuren, 24 December 1964.
12. *MPh* (3) 1 (1923), p. 16.
13. *MPh* (3) 5 (1927), p. 24.
14. *MPh* (3) 6 (1928), p. 51.
15. Jones appears as the sole author on the title-page of this publication, even though M. Heepe is mentioned as a co-author in the bibliography which appears in Abercrombie et al. (1964: viii). It is likely that Heepe's function was mainly that of a translator.
16. The recommendations of the Conference are reported in the *MPh* (3) 5 (1927), pp. 13–18. See also Jespersen (1938 [1995]: 214–216).
17. *MPh* (3) 4 (1926), p. 38.
18. *MPh* (3) 6 (1927), p. 14.
19. *MPh* (3) 6 (1927), pp. 14, 15, 18.
20. Several of these diacritics were changed in the 1989 Kiel Conference.
21. The click symbols were changed in the 1989 Kiel Conference.
22. These three symbols had been used by Jones in the *Sechuana reader* (see Section 6.9).
23. *MPh* (3) 6 (1928), pp. 51–52.
24. The contents of this section are based partly on information contained in files in the BBC Sound Archives, Caversham. We wish to acknowledge the help of the BBC in granting us access to these.
25. The other paid consultants were A. Lloyd James, H.C. Wyld and Harold Orton.
26. *MPh* (3) 8 (1924), p. 28.
27. *MPh* (3) 11 (1925), p. 21.
28. M. Phillips, interview.
29. *MPh* (3) 14, 1926, p. 38.
30. College Committee, 1926–27, min. 57.
31. H. Davies, interview.
32. *MPh* (3) 16 (1928), p. 53.

33. College Committee, 1926–27, min. 171 (ii).
34. UCL Calendar, 1928–29, p. 51.
35. J. Carnochan, interview.

Chapter 11

1. H.E. Butler, "Sir Thomas Gregory Foster", article in: *Dictionary of national biography (1931–1940)*.
2. M. Stanbury, interview.
3. A.C. Gimson, interview. Also mentioned by several other colleagues; cf. Onishi (1981: 38–39).
4. The quotations below are taken from the Preface to the 4th edition of the *EPD*, as reprinted in the *EPD*[10] [1949], pp. vi-vii.
5. These were published as 'companion volumes' under the heading of *Shakespeare's pronunciation*.
6. We have not been able to trace this work. The details appear in the *Outline*[4] [1934], p. 313.
7. H.J. Uldall, letter to Jones, 15 October 1938.
8. Jones, letter to H.J. Uldall, 11 December 1938.
9. Departmental Prospectus, 1933–34.
10. Departmental Prospectus, 1933–34.
11. Departmental Prospectus, 1933–34.
12. Departmental Prospectus, 1933–34.
13. Departmental Prospectus, 1933–34.
14. UCL Prospectus, 1930–31, p. 52.
15. E. Henderson, interview.
16. D. Fry, interview.
17. D. Fry, interview.
18. D. Fry, interview.
19. UCL College Committee, 1937, min. 5b.
20. Report "The Phonetics Laboratory", n.d.
21. The items shown in transcription on the menu (Figure 11.3) were as follows: crème de céleri; sole grillée au citron; tournedos de bœuf aux champignons; poulet rôti; pommes natures; petits pois; glace panachée; paille de parmesan; café.

    The alternative suggestions (Figure 11.4) were: crème de céleri mi-sonore; sole maître phonétique; tournedos de bœuf prépalatale; champignons synchroniques; poulet rôti entrebuccal; pommes neutres; chou-fleur agglutinant; glace panachée caduque; paille de parmesan allongé; café coup de glotte.
22. Information for this section is derived in part from the minutes of the Simplified Spelling Society. We are grateful to the officers of the Society for allowing us access to these. See also J. Pitman (1964) for an account of the history of the Simplified Spelling Society and Jones's role within it.
23. Full details of these signatories are contained in the appendix to *The case for the improvement of spelling* (Anon., n.d: 16–32).
24. Contrary to what is implied in J. Pitman (1964: 181–182), the title of the [1940] 5th edition of Rippmann—Archer (1910) was still *Simplified Spelling*.
25. *MPh* (3) 10 (1932), pp. 12–25.

26. Jones, letter to H.J. Uldall, 12 November 1935.
27. Jones, letter to H.J. Uldall, 12 November 1935.
28. Jones, letter to H.J. Uldall, 12 November 1935.
29. H.J. Uldall, letter to Jones, 14 November 1935.
30. Jones, letter to H.J. Uldall, 17 February 1932.
31. Jones, letter to H.J. Uldall, 17 February 1936.
32. Jones, letter to H.J. Uldall, 17 February 1936.

Chapter 12

1. Information within this section is derived largely from the contents of files held at the University College General Record Office. We are grateful to the College for permission to have access to these records.
2. Prof. Eugénie J.A. Henderson: see BDPS for biographical details.
3. Letter, Jones to A. Mawer, 19 September 1939.
4. Letter, A. Mawer to Jones, 23 September 1939.
5. Letter, A. Mawer to Prof. W.L. Renwick, King's College, Newcastle, 24 October 1939.
6. Letter, Charles Bridge (Head of British Council) to A. Mawer, 1 December 1939.
7. Letter, A. Mawer to Charles Bridge, 8 December 1939.
8. Letter, A. Mawer to Jones, 28 October 1940.
9. Letters, Jones to A. Mawer, 18 February 1940; A. Mawer to Jones, 20 February 1940.
10. M. Stanbury, E. Henderson and others, interviews. This is the most frequently repeated of the anecdotes told about Jones.
11. Letter, I. Ward to H. Coustenoble, 7 June 1940.
12. Photographs reproduced in Harte—North (1978: 175–179) give an idea of the appalling extent of the damage.
13. College Committee, 18 November 1940, App. I, "Damage to the College by enemy action"; also contains details of the re-evacuation.
14. Internal memo "Arrangements for students of University College, London, in the session 1940–41", n.d., but probably November 1940.
15. College Committee, 18 November 1940, App. II, "Air raid damage to the Library".
16. Letter, Jones to A. Mawer, 28 November 1940.
17. University of London Examination for Certificate of Proficiency in English (Part II): Elementary Phonetics, 8 August 1941, p. 1.
18. M. Phillips, interview.
19. J. Snagge, interview.
20. Letter, H. Coustenoble to D. Pye, 7 September 1943.
21. Letter, Jones to D. Pye 7 October 1943.
22. Lecturer UCL, 1937–43. Afterwards lecturer SOAS. Member IPA Council until 1972.
23. Letter, D. Pye to Jones, 11 October 1943.
24. Letters, Jones to D. Pye, 7 October 1943 and 16 October 1943.
25. Letter, Jones to D. Pye, 6 November 1943.
26. Eileen M. Whitley, née Evans, lecturer UCL 1932–43. Afterwards lecturer SOAS.
27. Letters, Jones to D. Pye, 3 July 1944; D. Pye's notes of telephone conversations with Jones and R.L. Turner (Director SOAS), 4 July 1944.

28. Letters, Jones to D. Pye, 3 July 1944; 11 July 1944; 19 July 1944; D. Pye to Jones, 31 July 1944; Jones to D. Pye, 4 August 1944.
29. Ivar Dahl was a temporary member of Jones's staff in 1944–45, returning afterwards to Argentina. Dahl was an IPA Council member until 1972.
30. O. Tooley, interview.
31. Letters, D. Pye to Air Ministry, 26 May 1944; Air Ministry to D. Pye, 25 June 1944; Jones to D. Pye, 2 July 1944. See BDPS for biographical details of Julian T. Pring.
32. O. Tooley, interview. See BDPS for biographical details of A(lfred) C. Gimson. J. D(esmond) O'Connor (1919–) was later Professor of Phonetics at UCL.
33. College Committee 1940, App. II.
34. Letter, Jones to D. Pye, 21 November 1944.
35. Letter, Jones to D. Pye, 13 September 1945.
36. Letter, D. Parkinson to D. Pye, 27 May 1946.
37. Letters, Jones to D. Pye, 13 May 1946; D. Pye to Jones, 20 May 1946.
38. Letter, D. Parkinson to D. Pye, 27 May 1946.
39. Dept Rep. 1946–47.
40. Dept Rep. 1946–47.
41. Letter, Jones to D. Pye, 15 October 1946.
42. By this point the school had acquired its present name.
43. After long drawn-out legal battles, a small portion of Shaw's legacy was used to organise a competition, which led to an alphabet being developed by Kingsley Read. An edition of *Androcles and the lion*, transcribed into the Shavian alphabet by Jones's former pupil Peter MacCarthy, was published by Penguin books in 1962 as *The Shaw Alphabet edition of Androcles and the lion*.
44. Another private member's bill, sponsored by Mont Follick and seconded by Pitman, was put through Parliament in 1953. This was withdrawn before a vote. In exchange, the government gave assurances that measures would be taken to tackle the problem of teaching reading in schools.
45. College Annual Report 1947 on the work of the Department of Phonetics for the year 1946.
46. Exercise books filled with Jones's comments on individual announcers can be found in the Daniel Jones Papers.
47. Letter, M. Hope Allen (BBC Talks Department) to Jones, 19 September 1949.
48. Extract from script of *The Elizabethan Tongue*, radio broadcast, BBC Third Programme, 28 December 1949.
49. *This English*, English by Radio; radio broadcast, 10 September 1961.
50. *MPh* (3) 20 (1942), p. 10.
51. *MPh* (3) 20 (1942), p. 27.
52. *MPh* (3) 16 (1938), pp. 30–40.
53. The "anonymous helpers" were Dorothy Parkinson, Hélène Coustenoble, Beatrice Honikman, N.C. Scott, B.D. Copland and A.C. Gimson (Jones 1947c).
54. *MPh* (3) 28 (1950), p. 40.
55. A.C. Gimson, interview.
56. A.C. Gimson, interview.
57. College Committee 1946–47, min. 108b.
58. Dept. Rep. 1947–48; College Committee 1947–48, mins 3n and 95g.
59. J. Overton Fuller, interview.

60. See BDPS for biographical details of Peter Denes.
61. Dept. Rep. 1947–48.
62. College Committee, 1947–48, min. 9z.
63. Christophersen, written communication to A. Juul. (It would appear from the College Committee minutes that Jones and O'Connor actually spent less than a term in Copenhagen.)
64. College Committee 1948–49, min. 110.
65. College Committee 1949–50, min. 3l.
66. Letter, D. Pye to D. Fry, 29 June 1949.
67. Written communication to author (BC), 2 November 1983.
68. College Committee 1948–49, min. 110.

Chapter 13

1. M. Phillips, interview.
2. J. Overton Fuller, interview.
3. J. Overton Fuller, interview.
4. Letter, Jones to G. Miller, 9 May 1952.
5. Letter, Jones to David Abercrombie, 12 October 1947.
6. Cf. letter, Jones to Ward, 23 March 1967 (quoted in Section 13.15), which reveals a similar concern about the dotted letters. Other former colleagues of Jones also stressed his remarkable preoccupation with aspects of typography and printing (A.C. Gimson and D.B. Fry, interviews).
7. In fact, the range is undoubtedly somewhat greater than Jones indicates in the full gamut of accents. The complete extent of the diaphone would include, for example, close variants in South African and New Zealand English, and very open types in Northern Irish (Wells 1982: *passim*).
8. Note that a misprint, surviving into the *Phoneme*[3], terms such a transcription system "allophonic", where Jones obviously intends "phonemic" (p. 203).
9. For more favourable assessments of the *Phoneme*, see Abercrombie (1950) and Martinet (1951).
10. The original extract, entitled "Insects in Lapland", had initially been used in the *Pronunciation of English*[1] as a vehicle to illustrate Lloyd's so-called "Northern English", see Section 3.4. Why Jones had neglected to find a more appropriate American English passage for the *Pronunciation of English*[3] is a mystery.
11. Letter to D. Ward, 25 July 1960.
12. Both have since been abandoned and are not used in the current *EPD*[14].
13. C.M. Wise, note to editor, *Southern Speech Journal* 18.2 (1952), p. 81.
14. C.M. Wise, note to editor, *Southern Speech Journal* 18.2 (1952), p. 81.
15. *The Cardinal Vowels* (1956a), Linguaphone Institute, ENG 252/253/254/255. This is the date supplied by Linguaphone Institute. (Note that the date of 1955, given in Abercrombie et al. 1964: xviii, is probably incorrect.)
16. Letter, Jones to D. Ward, 18 January 1958.
17. *This English*, English by Radio; radio broadcast, 10 September 1961.
18. *Phonetic readings in English*, Linguaphone Institute, ENG 401/406. Date announced on recording by Jones himself as 7 November 1963.
19. A.C. Gimson, interview.

20. Jones, letter to D. Ward, 20 March 1961.
21. D. Ward, interview.
22. Jones, letter to D. Ward, 10 June 1953.
23. Jones, letter to D. Ward, 13 May 1955.
24. Jones, letter to D. Ward, 10 June 1953.
25. Jones, letter to D. Ward, 15 June 1953.
26. Jones, letter to D. Ward, 11 July 1955.
27. Jones, letter to D. Ward, 26 April 1956.
28. Jones, letter to D. Ward, 19 April 1957.
29. Jones, letter to D. Ward, 27 November 1957.
30. M.H. Black (Education Secretary, Cambridge University Press), letter to D. Ward, 25 July 1962.
31. Jones, letter to D. Ward, 25 August 1962.
32. Black, letter to D. Ward, 3 August 1962, quoting Trim's comments.
33. Jones, letter to D. Ward, 3 November 1963.
34. Jones, letter to D. Ward, 8 April 1963.
35. Jones, letter to D. Ward, 1 August 1960.
36. D. Ward, interview.
37. Jones, letter to D. Ward, 25 July 1960.
38. Jones, letter to D. Ward, 21 January 1965.
39. Jones, letter to D. Ward, 27 March 1967.
40. Cyrille survived her husband by just over two years, dying on Boxing Day, 26 December 1969.
41. Many details of this period have been provided by M. Stanbury, interview.

Chapter 14

1. "At the 1989 Kiel convention it was decided that the Association should publish illustrations of the IPA consisting of short phonetic descriptions of a wide variety of languages. When enough of these descriptions have become available through publication in the *Journal*, they will be collected together and published in an *IPA Handbook*" (*JIPA* 20 (1990), p. 41).
2. Letter, Jones to A. Cohen, 4 October 1952.
3. No capitalisation of nouns in original text.
4. Letter, F.G. Blandford to H. Palmer, 23 August 1933.
5. Letter, F.G. Blandford to H. Palmer, 23 August 1933.
6. Letter, Jones to H. Palmer, n.d. (probably written towards the end of 1933).
7. The symbol now used in the International Phonetic Alphabet (IPA 1989) is ↓.
8. In an introduction, Ladefoged (1967: 50) states that his article is based on his 1959 doctoral thesis, and that similar work had already appeared in 1960 in the Coimbra University experimental phonetics laboratory report.
9. "The Elizabethan Tongue", radio transmission, BBC Third Programme, 28 December 1949.
10. J. Overton Fuller, interview.
11. We are indebted to Professor R.H. Robins for certain of the ideas in this section (R.H. Robins, interview).

Appendix A

1. Notes for the Missionaries' Lecture, 30 October 1916 (see Section 6.9). Jones was to return to problems of romanisation of Indian and other languages later in his life; see Sections 10.5 and 10.8.
2. According to the *OED*, the word "phonetics" is first attested in 1797.
3. Jones, letter to Bernard Shaw, 29 September 1944; in UCL Daniel Jones Papers.
4. In UCL Library.
5. Jones used the fifth edition [1901] (see the *Phoneme*: 274).
6. Taken from the opening words of Cicero's *In Catalinam*: "Quousque tandem [abutere, Catalina, patientia nostra]?" ("How much longer, pray [Catalina, are you going to abuse our patience]?"). It is interesting to note that Sweet chooses exactly the same passage for the sample of Latin in his *Primer of phonetics* (Sweet 1890a: 105–106).
7. Rousselot did not actually invent the kymograph, as is sometimes claimed (e.g. in the article "Rousselot" in BDPS, p. 180).
8. At the time of writing, an important new contribution to the historiography of nineteenth century linguistics has appeared, namely Anna Morpurgo Davies's (1998) *Nineteenth-century linguistics* (*History of Linguistics*, Vol. IV). Harlow: Longman.

List of interviews

Interviews have been held with the following persons; place and date of interview are stated below. We wish to thank them all for their help in our work.

All of those interviewed had been in personal contact with Daniel Jones (in all but one or two cases over a prolonged period). Most had known Jones as a teacher or a colleague; others are family relations or close friends. One or two were contacted because of their special knowledge of a particular area of Jones's life. The capacity in which the person concerned knew Jones is indicated briefly.

Two of the interviews listed below (Wells and McKee) were about 15 minutes in length, but most lasted over an hour—in some cases much longer. Those which were tape-recorded are marked *.

Professor David Abercrombie (student/lecturer UCL, head of Department of Phonetics, Edinburgh University); Edinburgh, 20 October 1983.*
Dr Audrey Baker (friend); Gerrards Cross, Bucks, 31 January 1984.
Professor J. Carnochan (student UCL/lecturer SOAS); London, 7 October 1983.*
Miss Marguerite Chapallaz (student/lecturer UCL); London, 6 March 1981.*
Mrs Gisèle Dannat [née Motte] (sister-in-law); Little Leighs, Essex, 8 November 1983.*
Mrs Hyacinth Davies (lecturer UCL); Puttenham, Surrey, 4 February 1980.*
Mrs J. de Mowbray (cousin); London, 14 October 1982.
S.S. Eustace (student UCL; formerly Secretary SSS); London, 31 January 1980.
Professor Eugénie Henderson (student/lecturer UCL, lecturer SOAS); London, 27 May 1981.*
Miss Beatrix Honikman (student/lecturer UCL, lecturer SOAS and Leeds University); London, 18 January 1984.*
Miss Jean Overton Fuller (student UCL, friend); Rushden, Northants, 31 October 1983.*
Professor D.B. Fry (student/lecturer and Head of Department UCL); London, 6 March 1981.*
Professor A.C. Gimson (student/lecturer UCL); London, 26 May 1981.*
Dr C. Maitland (neighbour); Gerrards Cross, Bucks, 31 January 1984.*
Miss Patricia McKee (Secretary UCL); London, 5 April 1981.
Miss D. Monnington (cousin, also formerly lecturer, Microbiology Dept, UCL); Salisbury, 15 October 1983.*
Mrs Meryl Phillips (niece); St Leonards on Sea, Sussex, 12 October 1983.*
Sir James Pitman (SSS); London, 4 February 1980.*
Dr J.T. Pring (student/lecturer UCL); London, 3 March 1981.*
Professor R.H. Robins (lecturer SOAS); London, 15 March 1982.*
Ms Barbara Smoker (Shaw Society); London, 30 October 1983.
John Snagge (head of BBC Announcing Dept); Dorney, Bucks, 25 January 1984.*
Michelle Stanbury [née Jones] (daughter); London, 2 February 1980, 19 April 1980*; 6 February 1982, 29 January 1984*; Gerrards Cross, Bucks, 31 January 1984.*
Mrs Johanna Talma-Schilthuis (student UCL); Bilthoven, the Netherlands, 29 October 1984.*
J.L.M. Trim (student UCL, Head of Department Cambridge University); London, 5 October 1983.*
Miss Olive Tooley (lecturer UCL); London, 25 October 1983, 7 November 1983.
Mrs Renée Upcott [née Motte] (sister-in-law); Reading, 3 December 1983.*
Mrs Elizabeth Uldall [née Anderson] (student/lecturer UCL, University of Edinburgh); Edinburgh, 21 October 1983.*

Professor D. Ward (Dept of Russian, Edinburgh University, co-author); Edinburgh, 21 October 1983.*

Mrs Eileen Whitley [née Evans] (student/lecturer UCL, lecturer SOAS); Woodbridge, Suffolk, 13 October 1983.*

Ms Joan Wilson [Mrs J. Snagge] (Pronunciation Unit, BBC); Dorney, Bucks, 25 January 1984.*

Jack Windsor Lewis (student UCL/lecturer University of Leeds); Leiden, the Netherlands, 16 June 1987.*

Professor J.C. Wells (lecturer UCL); London, 5 April 1981.*

A chronological bibliography of the publications of Daniel Jones

Jones's audio recordings have been listed separately in the discography at the end of this section.

A   Article.
B   Book.
O   Obituary.
P   Pamphlet or booklet.
R   Review of book.
S   Specimen of a dialect or language (usually with added descriptive notes).
T   Transcription.
M   Miscellaneous (i.e. letters and replies to correspondents, announcements, official decisions, etc.). These are for the most part to be found in *Le Maître phonétique* and have normally been included only if they are either signed by Jones or have obviously been written by him in an editorial capacity.

1906   a.   (M)   "En Angleterre", *MPh* (2) 21: 34–36.
       b.   (A)   "Development of the Danish stød", *MPh* (2) 21: 48–49.
       c.   (R)   Review of D.L. Savory's phonetic transcription of the first sixty lessons of Calvert—Hartog, *French oral teaching* 1. London: Rivington. Also of Savory's phonetic transcription of F.B. Kirkman 1906, *Première année de français*. London: Black. *MPh* (2) 21: 109.
       d.   (M)   "Here and there", *MPh* (2) 21: 114–115.
       e.   (S)   "Ecossais" [as read by Miss B. Robson], *MPh* (2) 21: 118–119.
       f.   (A)   "Notes on spelling", *MPh* (2) 21: 130–131.

1907   a.   (B)   *100 Poésies enfantines*. Leipzig: Teubner.
       b.   (B)   [Phonetic transcriptions] *Phonetic transcriptions of English prose*. Oxford: Clarendon.
       c.   (B)   D.L. Savory—Jones, *The sounds of the French language*. Oxford: Clarendon; trans. of P. Passy (1887 [1906⁶]); 2nd rev. edition [1913].
       d.   (A)   P. Passy—Jones, "Alphabet phonétique organique: avec les formes correspondantes de l'alphabet phonétique usuel". Supplement to *MPh* (2) 22.
       e.   (A)   "Simplified phonetic spelling", *MPh* (2) 22: 37–39.
       f.   (M)   "Here and there", *MPh* (2) 22: 43–44.
       g.   (M)   "Modern Language Association", *MPh* (2) 22: 58–60.
       h.   (M)   "Phonetics in Scotland", *MPh* (2) 22: 60–61.
       i.   (R)   Review of A. Graham Bell 1906, *The mechanism of speech*. New York—London: Funk and Wagnall. *MPh* (2) 22: 66–67.
       j.   (M)   "Diploma for Proficiency in Phonetics", *MPh* (2) 22: 92–93.
       k.   (A)   "French b, d, g", *MPh* (2) 22: 94–95.
       l.   (R)   Review of H.C. Wyld 1906, *The historical study of the mother tongue*. London: Murray. *MPh* (2) 22: 98–100.
       m.   (A)   "Implosive sounds and clicks", *MPh* (2) 22: 111–114.
       n.   (R)   Review of G.E. Fuhrken, *Phonetic transcription* of Jespersen-Rodhe 1907, *Engelsk läsebok för realskolan*. Stockholm. *MPh* (2) 22: 117–118.

1908   a.   (R)   Review of G. Camerlynck, *The girls' own book*. Paris: Didier. *MPh* (2) 23: 35.
       b.   (R)   Review of S.A. Richards, *French speech and spelling*. London: Dent. *MPh* (2) 23: 35–36.
       c.   (M)   "The Modern Language Association", *MPh* (2) 23: 44.
       d.   (R)   Review of H.C. Wyld, *The growth of English*. London: Murray. *MPh* (2) 23: 73–74.
       e.   (M)   J. Ewert—E. Phipson—Jones, "Enquête, 'English' pronunciation of Latin and Greek", *MPh* (2) 23: 98–101 (unsigned, but probably by Jones).
       f.   (R)   Review of W. Rippmann 1908, *Specimens of English*. London: Dent. *MPh* (2) 23: 115–116.
       g.   (A)   "The m.f. alphabet and spelling reform", *MPh* (2) 23: 125–128.
       h.   (M)   A chart of English speech sounds. Oxford: Clarendon.

1909   a.   (B)   *Intonation curves*. Leipzig: Teubner.
       b.   (B)   *The pronunciation of English*. Cambridge: Cambridge University Press; 2nd edition [1914]; 3rd (rewritten) edition [1950]; 4th enlarged edition [1956].
       c.   (P)   *Scenes from Shakespeare in the original pronunciation*. Supplement to *MPh* (2) 24: 1–7.
       d.   (R)   Review of H.R. Beasley, *Sure steps to intelligent French*. Sonnenschein. *MPh* (2) 24: 35–36.
       e.   (A)   "International language", *MPh* (2) 24: 49–51.
       f.   (M)   O. Jespersen—A.R.G. Vianna—P. Passy—S. Lund—Jones, "Adresse à W. Viëtor", *MPh* (2) 24: 73–74.
       g.   (M)   "The Simplified Spelling Society", *MPh* (2) 24: 80–82.
       h.   (T)   "The musicians", *MPh* (2) 24: 110–112, 133–135.
       i.   (A)   "The pronunciation of early English", *MPh* (2) 24: 119–123.
       j.   (M)   "Phonetics at Grenoble", *MPh* (2) 24: 143–146. See also 1910a.
       k.   (T)   "The hedgehog and the hare", *MPh* (2) 24: 155–157. See also 1910c.
       l.   (M)   "Notes on the reconstruction of Shakespeare's pronunciation", preface to "Programme of scenes from Shakespeare to be performed in the original pronunciation", University College London, July 3.

1910   a.   (M)   "Phonetics at Grenoble" (cont.), *MPh* (2) 25: 41–44.
       b.   (R)   Reviews of W. Rippmann, Phonetic section of *Dent's first French book*; B. Dumville, *The science of speech*; S. Smith, *Phonetic French syllabaire for schools*; I. Williams, *Phonetics for Scottish students*. *MPh* (2) 25: 49–50.
       c.   (T)   "The hedgehog and the hare", *MPh* (2) 25: 60–61; cont. of 1909k.
       d.   (R)   Review of G. Noël-Armfield 1909. *100 Poems for children*. Leipzig: Teubner. *MPh* (2) 25: 82.
       e.   (T)   "The sensible wild boar"; "The traveller and his dog", *MPh* (2) 25: 86–87 (no authorship indicated, but the passages also appear in the *Pronunciation of English*).
       f.   (R)   Review of P. Verrier 1909, *Principes de la métrique anglaise*. Paris: Welter. *MPh* (2) 25: 111–112.
       g.   (A)   "The transcription of English vowels", *MPh* (2) 25: 128–129.

h. (M) "Mr. Atkinson's 'Mouth Measurer'", *MPh* (2) 25: 134.
i. (S) E. Paegle—Jones, "Lettish", *MPh* (2) 25: 138–139.
j. (S) "Albanian (Gheg dialect)" [from dictation of M.E. Durham], *MPh* (2) 25: 139–141.
k. (A) "Uniform spelling for the African languages (with a short analysis of the Chindau language)", *MPh* (2) 25: 148–152.
l. (R) Reviews of H.C. Wyld, *Elementary lessons in English grammar*. Oxford; J.A. Afzelius, *A pronouncing dictionary of modern English*. Stockholm: Norstedt. *MPh* (2) 25: 156–157.
m. (A) "Notes on English pronunciation", *NS* 17: 571–573.

1911 a. (P) [Chindau] *The pronunciation and orthography of the Chindau language*. London: University of London Press [revised version of 1910k].
b. (M) "Phonetics in English schools; Eagle House School, Sandhurst", *MPh* (2) 26: 3.
c. (A) "The transcription of English vowels", *MPh* (2) 26: 46–48.
d. (M) Additional note to R. Grant Brown, "Suggestions for typewriters". *MPh* (2) 26: 49.
e. (M) "Pronunciation of English interjections and Dutch *ui*", *MPh* (2) 26: 78.
f. (S) Jones—Ernö Stern, "Magyar (Hungarian)", *MPh* (2) 26: 79–80.
g. (S) "Chinese (Standard Cantonese dialect)" [from dictation of Kwing Tong Woo], *MPh* (2) 26: 80–84.
h. (T) "Christmas Eve", *MPh* (2) 26: 86.
i. (R) Review of F. Rausch, *Lauttafeln* (a set of 26 charts). Marburg: Elwert. *MPh* (2) 26: 111–112.
j. (M) De Saram—Jones, "English pronunciation", *MPh* (2) 26: 116.
k. (T) "The woodman and his axe", *MPh* (2) 26: 122.
l. (R) Review of W. Rippmann, *English sounds*. London: Dent. *MPh* (2) 26: 144.
m. (R) Review of F. Jones, *A first English course*. London: Blackie. *MPh* (2) 26: 144.
n. (T) "Making himself at home", *MPh* (2) 26: 153–154.
o. (S) "Tyneside dialect (Northumberland)" [from dictation of S.G. Horsley], *MPh* (2) 26: 184.
p. (T) Extract from Scott, *MPh* (2) 26: 186.
q. (A) "Phonetics and ear training", *NS* 19: 318–319; also publ. in *Der Vereinsbote*, February, 1911.
r. (R) Review of Klinghardt—de Fourmestraux, *Französische Intonationsübungen*. *NS* 19: 377–379.
s. (R) Review of Raudnitzky, *Die Bell-Sweetsche Schule*. *NS* 19: 445.
t. (A) "L'enseignement de la prononciation des langues vivantes", *Revue de l'Enseignement des Langues Vivantes* 2.
u. (A) "The pronunciation of English, past, present and future", *Revue de l'Enseignement des Langues Vivantes* 3.
v. (M) F. Rausch—Jones, *Sound charts*. London: Dent.

1912 a. (B) Jones—Kwing Tong Woo, *A Cantonese phonetic reader*. London: University of London Press.

b. (B) [Phonetic readings] *Phonetic readings in English*. Heidelberg: Winter; rev. 31st edition [1956].

c. (S) "Mono (Western Solomon Islands Melanesian)" [from dictation of G.C. Wheeler], *MPh* (2) 27: 12–14.

d. (T) "Paving stones", *MPh* (2) 27: 15.

e. (R) Review of Camerlynck-Guernier—Camerlynck, *Miss Rod*. Paris: Didier. *MPh* (2) 27: 62.

f. (R) Review of Thiergen—Hamann, *English anthology*. Teubner. *MPh* (2) 27: 62.

g. (S) "Chinese (Standard Cantonese dialect, colloquial style)" [from dictation of Kwing Tong Woo], *MPh* (2) 27: 67–68.

h. (T) "The daisy", *MPh* (2) 27: 71–72.

i. (O) Henry Sweet (obituary), *MPh* (2) 27: 97–99.

j. (T) "Early rising", *MPh* (2) 27: 112.

k. (S) "London dialect (Cockney)", *MPh* (2) 27: 144.

l. (M) "Articles in ordinary spelling"; "French [ʒ]", in: "Partie administrative", *MPh* (2) 27: 150–151.

m. (P) P. Passy—Jones, *The principles of the International Phonetic Association*. London: IPA. Supplement to *MPh* (2) 27.

n. (A) "How to teach English pronunciation to Germans", *Der Vereinsbote*.

1913 a. (B) [Phonetic dictionary] H. Michaelis—Jones, *A phonetic dictionary of the English language*. Hanover—Berlin: Carl Meyer (Gustav Prior).

b. (A) "Chinese tones" [pronounced by W. Pettus], *MPh* (2) 28: 95–96.

c. (A) "English short [e]", *MPh* (2) 28: 96.

d. (M) "Representation of t, d, etc.", *MPh* (2) 28: 101.

e. (S) "Dialect of north west Lancashire" [pronounced by R.D. Ellwood], *MPh* (2) 28: 104.

f. (T) "Some unintentionally amusing advertisements", *MPh* (2) 28: 106.

g. (A) "Phonetic spelling of English", *MPh* (2) 28: 113–116.

h. (R) Review of C.M. Rice 1912, *Voice production with the aid of phonetics*. Cambridge: Heffer. *MPh* (2) 28: 118–119; also published in *Cambridge Review*, 11 June 1913.

i. (T) Extract from F.M. Crawford, *MPh* (2) 28: 122.

j. (M) Reply to T. Grahame Bailey on [tʃ] and [dʒ], *MPh* (2) 28: 136.

k. (M) Reply to P. Passy (*MPh* (2) 28: 120) on Syriac, *MPh* (2) 28: 136–137.

l. (S) Dialect of north west Lancashire, "North wind and the sun" [pronounced by R.D. Ellwood], *MPh* (2) 28: 141–142.

m. (T) "The name on the portmanteau", *MPh* (2) 28: 144–145.

n. (A) "Phonetics and its applications", *Educational Review* 19: 201–206.

o. (M) "Standard English pronunciation", reply to letters from F.E. Corley, *Madras Christian College Magazine*, December 1913.

p. (M) Chapter on phonetic publications in: Oliphant—Anderson—Ferrier, *A bibliography for missionary students*. London: Board of Study for Preparation of Missionaries.

q. (M) Report on lecture tour of India, *Pioneer* 2: 43.

1914 a. (P) P. Passy—Jones (eds.), *Miscellanea Phonetica* I. London: IPA.

b. (M) "What is a syllable?", *MPh* (2) 29: 12.

c. (T) "The boy and the button", *MPh* (2) 29: 18.

d. (R) Review of G. Marseille—O.F. Schmidt 1914, *Englisches Elementarbuch.* Marburg: Elwert. *MPh* (2) 29: 29–31.

e. (R) Review of H. Johnston, *Phonetic spelling.* Cambridge University Press. *MPh* (2) 29: 32.

f. (T) "An important distinction", *MPh* (2) 29: 36.

g. (M) Footnote in reply to W.L. Thompson on representation of [tʃ] and [dʒ], *MPh* (2) 29: 50.

h. (M) "The Congress of Experimental Phonetics", *MPh* (2) 29: 50–51.

i. (M) "Variant pronunciations", note in reply to J. Erhardt, *MPh* (2) 29: 71.

j. (S) "Manx" [pronounced by W. Radcliffe], *MPh* (2) 29: 74–75.

k. (T) Extract from Charles Kingsley, *MPh* (2) 29: 76.

l. (A) "Phonetics and its applications", *Hindustan Review*, February 1914.

m. (M) Preface to Bailey's *A Panjabi phonetic reader* (pp. v–vii).

1915 a. (R) Review of N.W. Thomas, *Anthropological report on the Ibo-speaking peoples of Nigeria*, Pts. 4, 5 and 6, and *Specimens of language from Southern Nigeria.* London: Harrison Thomas. *Journal of the Society of Comparative Legislation*, January 1915.

b. (A) "Introductory note on phonetics in relation to African languages", in: A. Werner, *The language families of Africa.* London: Kegan Paul, Trench, Trubner, v–vii.

1916 a. (B) Jones—S.T. Plaatje, *A Sechuana reader.* London: London University Press.

b. (B) Jones—Kwing Tong Woo, *Supplement to the Cantonese phonetic reader.* London: University of London Press.

1917 a. (B) [EPD] *An English pronouncing dictionary.* London: Dent; 2nd edition [1924]; 3rd edition [1926]; 4th edition [1937]; 7th edition [1945]; 10th edition [1949]; 11th edition [1956]; 12th edition [1963]; 13th edition [1967]; 14th edition [1977]; 15th edition [1997].

b. (A) "Analysis of the mechanism of speech", *Nature* 99: 285–287.

c. (A) "The phonetic structure of the Sechuana language", *Transactions of the Philological Society* 1917–1920: 99–106.

d. (A) "The value of phonetics to the language student", *International Review of Missions* 1917: 196.

e. (A) "Experimental phonetics and its utility to the linguist", *Nature* 100: 96–98.

1918 a. (B) [Outline] *An outline of English phonetics.* Leipzig: Teubner, n.d. (see Section 8.2 for discussion of doubt over date of publication); 2nd edition [1922]; 3rd edition [1932]; 4th edition [1934]; 5th edition [1936]; 6th edition [1939]; 7th edition [1949]; 8th edition [1956], Cambridge: Heffer; 9th edition [1960]; 9th edition, rpt. [1964].

b. (A) "Use of experimental phonetics to the linguist", *Modern Language Teaching* 14: 125–132.

1919   a.   (B)   H.S. Perera—Jones, *A colloquial Sinhalese reader*. Manchester: Manchester University Press.
       b.   (B)   *Examination papers in phonetics*. Oxford: Clarendon.
       c.   (A)   "The use of experimental phonetics and its utility to the linguist", *Proceedings of the Royal Institution* 22: 8–21.
       d.   (R)   Review of E. Kruisinga, *A handbook of present-day English* (3rd edition). Utrecht: Kemink. *English Studies* 1: 157–158.

1920   No known publications.

1921   No known publications.

1922   (A)   "Why we are bad linguists", (London) *Evening News*, 13 December 1922.

1923   a.   (B)   M. Trofimov—Jones, *The pronunciation of Russian*. Cambridge: Cambridge University Press.
       b.   (S)   "Cornish dialect", *MPh* (3) 1: 7.
       c.   (S)   "Chinese" (Hwa Miao), *MPh* (3) 1: 4–5.

1924   (S)   K. Minn—Jones, "Korean", *MPh* (3) 2: 14–15.

1925   (S)   Gã [pronounced by K.K. Lokko], *MPh* (3) 3: 6–9.

1926   a.   (A)   "Unstressed English 1 ", *MPh* (3) 4: 3–4.
       b.   (S)   Jones—J. Kabraji, "Gujarati", *MPh* (3) 4: 18–19.
       c.   (M)   "New signs", reply to P. Passy 1926 (*MPh* (3) 4: 13–15), *MPh* (3) 4: 26–27.
       d.   (R)   Review of C.M. Doke 1926, *The phonetics of the Zulu language*. Johannesburg: University of the Witwatersrand Press. *MPh* (3) 4: 36–37.
       e.   (M)   "In the days of my youth", *T.P.'s and Cassell's Weekly*, 2 January 1926, p. 394, p. 398.

1927   a.   (B)   E.M. Stéphan—Jones, *Colloquial French*. London: The Gramophone Company; rpt. (5th imp.) [1940].
       b.   (M)   Note, in reply to J.S. Kenyon, on ɛ and æ in American English, *MPh* (3) 5: 5.
       c.   (R)   Review of H.E. Palmer—J.V. Martin—F.G. Blandford, *A dictionary of English pronunciation with American variants*. Cambridge: Heffer. *MPh* (3) 5: 8–9.
       d.   (M)   Comments on Copenhagen Conference 1926, *MPh* (3) 5: 14.
       e.   (M)   University of Marburg 400th anniversary, *MPh* (3) 5: 39.
       f.   (A)   "Words distinguished by tone in Sechuana", in: *Festschrift Meinhof*. Hamburg: Friederichsen, 88–98.

1928   a.   (P)   *The tones of Sechuana nouns*. London: International Institute of African Languages and Cultures. (No date specified on the actual booklet.)
       b.   (P)   "Das System der Association Phonétique Internationale (Weltlautschriftverein)", in: *Lautzeichen und ihre Anwendung in verschiedenen Sprach-*

gebieten. Berlin: Reichsdruckerei, 18–27; rpt. as supplement to *MPh* (3) 6.

c. (A) "The transcription of Pekinese", *MPh* (3) 6: 2–4.

d. (S) "Greek" [pronounced by Skipis], *MPh* (3) 6: 38–39.

e. (O) W.H.T. Gairdner (obituary), *MPh* (3) 6: 49–51.

f. (M) "The First International Congress of Linguists", *MPh* (3) 6: 53.

g. (T) Extract from Max Beerbohm's *Seven men*, *MPh* (3) 6: 58–59.

h. (A) "Priniciples of practical orthography for African languages.--II", *Africa* 1: 237–239.

1929 a. (M) "Homage to Paul Passy", *MPh* (3) 7: 15.

b. (T) "A view from a hill" (simplified transcription), *MPh* (3) 7: 35.

c. (A) "Definition of a phoneme", *MPh* (3) 7: 43–44.

d. (T) Extract from *Adam Bede* (simplified transcription), *MPh* (3) 7: 50–51.

1930 a. (R) Review of C.M. Doke 1929, *The problem of word-division in Bantu* (Dept of Native Development, S. Rhodesia, Occ. Paper 2, 1929). *MPh* (3) 8: 2–3.

b. (T) Extracts from Thomas Huxley and John Masefield (precise and simplified transcription), *MPh* (3) 8: 6–7.

c. (T) "Theodore Hook" and "The passing of the middle age" (narrow and broad transcription), *MPh* (3) 8: 42–43.

d. (M) Reply to B. Dumville, "Middle e", *MPh* (3) 8: 49.

e. (M) Reply to P. Passy, "Représentation des tons", *MPh* (3) 8: 50-51.

f. (T) "On living to oneself" and "Sir Toby Butler" (narrow and broad transcription), *MPh* (3) 8: 54–55.

g. (T) "Sheridan Knowles" and extract from *Dombey and Son* (extra broad transcription and narrow transcription), *MPh* (3) 8: 67–68.

1931 a. (A) "On phonemes", *Travaux du Cercle Linguistique de Prague* 4: 74–79.

b. (T) "The man who didn't like tripe" and extract from Hazlitt (narrow and extra broad transcription), *MPh* (3) 9: 11–13.

c. (A) "The phonetic representation of the Swedish close vowels", *MPh* (3) 9: 21–23.

d. (R) Review of *The practical orthography of African languages* (rev. edition, 1930). London: International Institute of African Languages and Cultures. *MPh* (3) 9: 24.

e. (R) Review of G. Laziczius 1930, *Egy Magyar Mássalhangzóváltozás Phonologiája*. Budapest. *MPh* (3) 9: 24–25.

f. (M) Reply to H. Palmer, "Extra broad transcription", *MPh* (3) 9: 27–28.

g. (T) Extract from Hume and "Marie Antoinette" (narrow and extra broad transcription), *MPh* (3) 9: 29–30.

h. (M) P. Passy—Jones, circular to IPA Council, *MPh* (3) 9: 34–36.

i. (M) Report of replies to Passy—Jones 1931h, *MPh* (3) 9: 40–44.

j. (T) Extract from *Miss Eden's letter* and *The story of Dr Dolittle* (narrow and broad transcription), *MPh* (3) 9: 53–54.

k. (A) "The word as a phonetic entity", *MPh* (3) 9: 60–65.

l. (M) "The Second International Congress of Linguists", *MPh* (3) 9: 67–68.

m. (M) Reply to R. Butlin, "Double affricates", *MPh* (3) 9: 69.

1932 a. (A) "The theory of phonemes, and its importance in practical linguistics", *Proceedings of [1st] International Congress of Phonetic Sciences*, Amsterdam, 23–24.
    b. (M) Reply to H. Peterson, "The symbol æ", *MPh* (3) 10: 4.
    c. (R) Review of H.J. Melzian 1931, *Die Frage der Mitteltöne im Duala*. Glückstadt—Hamburg: Augustin. *MPh* (3) 10: 38–39.
    d. (R) Review of G.E. Fuhrken, *Standard English speech*. Cambridge: Cambridge University Press. *MPh* (3) 10: 39.
    e. (T) "The crow and the pitcher of water" and "The philosopher and the jewels" (extra broad transcription and narrow transcription), *MPh* (3) 10: 44–45.
    f. (M) Reply to A. Lloyd James, "Extra broad transcription", *MPh* (3) 10: 61.

1933 a. (P) Jones—A. Camilli, *Fondamenti di Grafia Fonetica*. London: IPA.
    b. (A) "Some tendencies of modern English pronunciation", *Commemorative Volume, 10th Annual Conference of English Teachers*, Tokyo: Institute for Research in English Teaching, 98–101.
    c. (R) Review of H.E. Palmer 1930, *The principles of romanization*. Tokyo: Maruzen. *MPh* (3) 11: 28–30.
    d. (R) Review of W. Ripman 1932, *A pocket dictionary of English rhymes*. London: Dent. *MPh* (3) 11: 31.
    e. (R) Review of W.A. Amiet 1932, *Literature by languages*. Sydney: Angus & Robertson. *MPh* (3) 11: 32.
    f. (R) Review of W. Kuhlmann 1933, *Deutsche Aussprache: Lehr- und Lesebuch für Ausländer*. Heidelberg: Winter. *MPh* (3) 11: 32–33.
    g. (R) Review of A. Barbeau—E. Rodhe 1930, *Dictionnaire phonétique de la langue française*. Stockholm: Norstedt. *MPh* (3) 11: 33–34.
    h. (M) P. Passy—Jones, circular to IPA Council, *MPh* (3) 11: 44–46.
    i. (R) Review of I.C. Ward 1933, *The phonetic and tonal structure of Efik*. Cambridge: Heffer. *MPh* (3) 11: 52.
    j. (M) Addition to C.F. Voegelin's review of L. Bloomfield 1933, *Language*. New York: Holt. *MPh* (3) 11: 53.
    k. (S) "Sindhi", *MPh* (3) 11: 75–77.
    l. (S) "Assamese", *MPh* (3) 11: 78.
    m. (M) Reply to A. Camilli, "Diaphoni e variphoni", *MPh* (3) 11: 81–82.

1934 a. (M) Reply to B. Bloch, "The American vowel in *bird*", *MPh* (3) 12: 11.
    b. (M) "American pronunciation", *MPh* (3) 12: 19.
    c. (M) Addition to M. Joos's review of R.E. Zachrisson 1932, *Anglic* (rev. 2nd edition); and R. Zachrisson 1933, *An English pronouncing dictionary and spelling-list in Anglic*. Uppsala. *MPh* (3) 12: 52–53.
    d. (M) Reply to L. Bloomfield, "A note on transcription", *MPh* (3) 12: 54.
    e. (R) Review of H. Pernot 1934, *Introduction à l'étude du dialecte tsakonien*. Paris: Raspail. *MPh* (3) 12: 75.
    f. (R) Review of O. Jespersen 1933, *Linguistica*. London: Allen & Unwin. *MPh* (3) 12: 98–100.
    g. (S) "Marathi (literary)" [pronounced by B.R. Kolatkar], *MPh* (3) 12: 102–105.
    h. Jones—T. Lauphit—D.K. Chu, *English-Chinese phonetic dictionary* (Chung

Hwa Book Co, Shanghai). (Mentioned in *Outline*⁴ in 1934 but with no date stated.)

1935   a. (O) Max Walter (obituary), *MPh* (3) 13: 2.
        b. (M) Reply to E.B. Davis, "English l", *MPh* (3) 13: 30.
        c. (S) "Marathi (colloquial)" [pronounced by B.R. Kolatkar], *MPh* (3) 13: 30–32.
        d. (M) "Notre assemblée générale" (report to 50th anniversary meeting of the International Phonetic Association, University College, London, 27 July 1935), *MPh* (3) 13: 41–53.
        e. (O) William Tilly (obituary), *MPh* (3) 13: 61–63.
        f. (A) "Speech training: the phonetic aspect", *British Journal of Educational Psychology* 5: 27–30.
        g. (O) Jones—R. Weiss, Professor [Karl] Luick (obituary), *The Times*, 1 October 1935.

1936   a. (B) Jones—D.B. Fry (eds.), *Proceedings of the Second International Congress of Phonetic Sciences 22–26 July 1935*. London: Cambridge University Press.
        b. (M) P. Passy—Jones—Arend, "A propos de ɡ et g" (advice on symbols), *MPh* (3) 14: 24–25.
        c. (M) "Un nouveau rédacteur pour m.f." (letter proposing H.J. Uldall as deputy editor), *MPh* (3) 14: 32–33.

1937   a. (A) "On 'Received Pronunciation'". Supplement to *MPh*, (3) 15.
        b. (M) "Where are the complete sets of m.f?", *MPh* (3) 15: 71–72.
        c. (M) Reply to B. Dumville, "Broad Transcription", *MPh* (3) 15: 73–74.
        d. (M) Circular to IPA Council, *MPh* (3) 15: 29–31.
        e. (M) Advice from IPA Council on symbols (comments from Jones interspersed between members' replies), *MPh* (3) 15: 38–44.
        f. (S) Jones—I. Moskowska, "Bulgarian", *MPh* (3) 15: 44–45.
        g. (S) "Greek" [pronounced by K. Yannakis], *MPh* (3) 15: 71.
        h. (M) Reply to J. Kenyon's letter on retroflex vowels, *MPh* (3) 15: 72.
        i. (A) "Some notes on the pronunciation of English at the time of Shakespeare", in: *English pronunciation through the centuries*. London—New York: Linguaphone, 38–41.
        j. (A) "The aims of phonetics", *Archiv für Sprach- und Stimmheilkunde und angewandte Phonetik* 1, pt. 1. Berlin: Metten, 4–10.
        k. (A) H.S. Perera—Jones, "The application of World Orthography to Sinhalese", *Bulletin of the School of Oriental Studies* 9: 705–707.

1938   a. (A) "Concrete and abstract sounds", *Proceedings of the Third International Congress of Phonetic Sciences*, Ghent, 1–7.
        b. (P) *The aims of phonetics*, London: IPA. Supplement to *MPh* (rpt of 1937j with minor revisions).
        c. (P) "Chaucer" (passage from Prologue to *Canterbury tales* in pronunciation of the period). Supplement to *MPh*.
        d. (O) Lilias Armstrong (obituary), *MPh* (3) 16: 2.
        e. (A) "Orthophonics in London", *MPh* (3) 16: 5–6.

1939   No known publications.

1940   a. (M) Reply to M. Hicklin, "The representation of English ʌ and æ", *MPh* (3) 18: 35.
        b. (M) Addition to L. Sprague de Camp, "Two unsymbolised American vowels", *MPh* (3) 18: 44.
        c. (A) "r-coloured vowels", *MPh* (3) 18: 56–65.
        d. (M) Preface to Armstrong's *Phonetic and tonal structure of Kikuyu* (pp. v–vi).

1941   a. (M) Additions to A. Classe, "Broad Transcription", *MPh* (3) 19: 14–15.
        b. (M) Additions to B. Dumville, "r-coloured vowels, ɛ, ɛ̧, ɹ", *MPh* (3) 19: 15–16.
        c. (O) Paul Passy (obituary), *MPh* (3) 19: 30–39.

1942   a. (P) *The problem of a national script for India*. Lucknow: Pioneer Press; Hertford: Stephen Austin.
        b. (M) Additions to L. Sprague de Camp, "Symbols of marginal utility", *MPh* (3) 20: 2–3.
        c. (S) "Shan" [pronounced by Sao On Kya], *MPh* (3) 20: 6–7.
        d. (O) Christian Cloos (obituary), *MPh* (3) 20: 13–14.
        e. (A) "The letters ɪ and ʊ", *MPh* (3) 20: 14–15.
        f. (M) Additions to R. Grant Brown, "Broad Transcription", *MPh* (3) 20: 21–22.

1943   a. (O) Otto Jespersen, George Thudichum (2 obituaries contained within one article), *MPh* (3) 21: 17–20.
        b. (M) Letter to council, *MPh* (3) 21: 27–28.

1944   a. (P) *Dhe fonetik aspekt ov speling reform*. London: Simplified Spelling Society.
        b. (P) Jones—I. Dahl, *Fundamentos de escritura fonética: Según el sistema de la Asociación Fonética Internacional*. London: IPA. Supplement to *MPh* (3) 22.
        c. (A) "Chronemes and tonemes", *Acta Linguistica* 4: 1–10 (publication dated 1944, but in fact delayed until 1946).
        d. (A) "Some thoughts on the phoneme", *Transactions of the Philological Society*, 119–135; rpt. in: W.E. Jones—Laver (1973), 168–179.
        e. (P) "A specimen of Shakespeare in the original pronunciation". London: IPA. Supplement to *MPh* (3) 22.
        f. (S) A. Gugushvili—Jones, "Georgian", *MPh* (3) 22: 5–6.
        g. (R) Review of J.S. Kenyon—T.A. Knott 1944, *A pronouncing dictionary of American English*. Springfield, Mass.: Merriam. *MPh* (3) 22: 7.

1945   a. (M) Letter to members on council decisions, *MPh* (3) 23: 11–17.
        b. (S) P.C.B. Deo—Jones, "Oriya", *MPh* (3) 23: 26–27.
        c. (R) Review of R. Curry 1940, *The mechanism of the human voice*. London: Churchill. *MPh* (3) 23: 30–31.

1946   a. (A) "G.B.S. and phonetics", in: S. Wisten (ed.), *G.B.S. 90: Aspects of Bernard Shaw's life and work*. London: Hutchinson, 158–160.

b. (A) "ʌ and ə in British English", *MPh* (3) 24: 2.
c. (S) I.C. Grøndahl—Jones, "Norwegian", *MPh* (3) 24: 2–3.
d. (R) Review of P.A.D. MacCarthy 1944, *An English pronouncing vocabulary*. Cambridge: Heffer. *MPh* (3) 24: 4.
e. (M) Addition to L. Sprague de Camp, "What is narrowness?", *MPh* (3) 24: 20–21.
f. (S) E. Mesterton—Jones, "Swedish", *MPh* (3) 24: 25–26.
g. (M) Circular letter discussing IPA symbolisation, *MPh* (3) 24: 32–40.

1947 a. (M) Jones—C.L. Wrenn, Chart illustrating the Great Vowel Shift. London: Department of Phonetics.
b. (O) Walter Ripman (obituary), *MPh* (3) 25: 2–3.
c. (M) "Acknowledgements", *MPh* (3) 25: 3–4.
d. (M) Note, in reply to J.T. Pring, on transcription, *MPh* (3) 25: 27.
e. (M) Note, in reply to P. Delattre, on typing phonetic transcription, *MPh* (3) 25: 28.
f. (A) "Phonetic representation of the vowels in 'cut' and 'cat'", *English Language Teaching* 1, 185–187.

1948 a. (R) Review of E.L. Tibbitts, *A phonetic reader for foreign learners of English*. Cambridge: Heffer. *MPh* (3) 26: 10–11.
b. (O) Sophie Lund (obituary), *MPh* (3) 26: 18–20.
c. (O) E. R. Edwards, L. Ščerba (obituaries), *MPh* (3) 26: 20.
d. (M) Letter concerning shape of letter g, in: "Partie administrative", *MPh* (3) 26: 28–30.
e. (P) *Differences between spoken and written language*. London: IPA. Supplement to *MPh* (3) 26.
f. (A) "The London school of phonetics", *ZPh* 2, 3/4: 127–135; rpt. in: Jones—Laver (1973), 180–186.
g. (A) "Difficulties of English pronunciation" 1–4, *London Calling Europe*, nos. 19–22, n.p.

1949 a. (A) "The romanization of Japanese", *ZPh* 3: 68–74.
b. (A) "A Romanic orthography for the Oriya language", *ZPh* 3: 74–76; also published in *Siddha-Bharati*, Hoshiarpur: Vishveshvaranand Vedic Research Institute, 1950.
c. (A) "The tongue that Shakespeare spake…", *Radio Times*, December 16.

1950 a. (B) [*The phoneme*] *The phoneme: its nature and use*. Cambridge: Heffer; 2nd edition [1962]; 3rd edition (with appendix containing *History and meaning of the term "phoneme"* [1967]).
b. (O) Ida Ward (obituary), *MPh* (3) 28: 2–3.
c. (O) Harold Palmer (obituary), *MPh* (3) 28: 4–7.
d. (M) Letter in: "Partie administrative" announcing retirement as Secretary and Treasurer of IPA, *MPh* (3) 28: 21–22.
e. (O) L. Sorzano-Jorrin (obituary), *MPh* (3) 28: 29.

1951 (M) "Pronunciation of foreign words", in: L.H. Dawson (ed.), *Nuttall's standard dictionary of the English language*. London: Warne.

1952   a.   (O)   Simon Boyanus (obituary), *MPh* (3) 30: 20–22.
        b.   (M)   Report of speech at reunion meeting of IPA members, 3 September 1952, *MPh* (3) 30: 23–24, 30.
        c.   (M)   "A letter from Daniel Jones", *Southern Speech Journal* 28.2: 81–86.

1953   a.   (R)   Review of A.S. Hornby—E.C. Parnwell 1952, *An English-reader's dictionary*. Oxford University Press. *MPh* (3) 31: 15.
        b.   (M)   Reply to R. Grant Brown on "Broad transcription", *MPh* (3) 31: 18–19.

1954   (A)   "Falling and rising diphthongs in Southern English", *Miscellanea Phonetica 2*, 1–12.

1955   a.   (T)   Extract from Mazo de la Roche (broad transcription), *MPh* (3) 33: 21–22.
        b.   (A)   "Phonetics", in: *Chambers' Encyclopaedia*, vol. 10, 670–675.

1956   a.   (P)   *Cardinal vowels*. London: Linguaphone; booklet to accompany disc recordings ENG 252–255.
        b.   (R)   Review of A.N. Tucker—J. Tompo Ole Mpaayei 1955, *A Maasai grammar*. *MPh* (3) 34: 48–50.
        c.   (A)   "The use of syllabic and non-syllabic *l* and *n* in derivatives of English words ending in syllabic *l* and *n*", in: *Festschrift Panconcelli-Calzia*, supplement to *ZPh* 1956; rpt. in *ZPh* 12: 136–144 [1959].
        d.   (A)   "The hyphen as a phonetic sign", *ZPh* 9: 99–107.

1957   a.   (P)   *The history and meaning of the term "phoneme"*. London: IPA. Supplement to *MPh* (3) 35; rpt. with corrections 1964.
        b.   (O)   H.-J. Uldall (obituary), *MPh* (3) 35: 30–31.
        c.   (A)   "Trends in English pronunciation", *Ici Londres* 503: 6–7; rpt. in: *London Calling Europe* 1957, nos. 500–501; texts of broadcasts in "English by Radio" series.
        d.   (A)   Jones—W.E. Skillend, "Report on the Koreanisation of foreign words", paper presented to the Korean Language Society, Seoul.

1958   (M)   "Arthur Lloyd James", in: *Dictionary of national biography 1941–50*, 430.

1959   No known publications.

1960   (O)   Jones—M. Chapallaz, Amerindo Camilli (obituary), *MPh* (3) 38: 22.

1961   (M)   "A message from Daniel Jones", *London Calling Europe*, 717 (October); text of "English by Radio" broadcast series "This English", 10 September.

1962   No known publications.

1963   (O)   Hélène Coustenoble (obituary), *MPh* (3) 41: 24–25.

1964   No known publications.

1965   No known publications.

1966   No known publications.

1967   No known publications.

1969   (B)   Jones—D. Ward, *The phonetics of Russian*. Cambridge: Cambridge University Press.

1985   (M)   A. Juul—H.F. Nielsen (eds.), *Our changing speech: Two BBC talks by Daniel Jones*. Copenhagen: National Institute for Educational Media; originally broadcast on February 8 and 16, 1949, BBC Third Programme. With accompanying tapes.

Discography

The following discography has been taken from Abercrombie et al. (1964) with minor additions and adaptations.

Pronunciation of English[2]. Texts 8 and 9. Deutsche Grammophon-Gesellschaft. 201392/3.

The eight cardinal vowels (1917). The Gramophone Company (His Master's Voice). B 804.

The cardinal vowels (1943). Linguaphone Institute. DAJO 1/2

The cardinal vowels (1956). Linguaphone Institute.
    Primary Vowels. ENG 252/253
    Secondary vowels and cardinal vowels compared with each other. ENG 254/255.

The English vowels and diphthongs; voiced and voiceless consonants (1921). Odeon, Berlin. A 66084/5

Kulturkundliche Lautbücherei (Wilhelm Doegen-Lautverlag) (1921).
Extracts from *Phonetic readings in English* and other English passages. Odeon, Berlin.

A 66004	A 66008/9	A 66010/1	A 66014
A 66050/1	A 66053	A 66080/1	A 66082

Extracts from *Metodisk Nybörjarbok i Engelska* (Björkelund-Danielsson) (1925). The Gramophone Company (His Master's Voice). X 1977–82.

English conversational course (1929). Linguaphone Institute.

The English vowels and diphthongs (1932). Otto Sperling, Stuttgart. 3636

English spoken here (1932). Otto Sperling, Stuttgart. 3651–56.

Phonetic readings in English (1932). Otto Sperling, Stuttgart. 3637–43.

Pronunciation of early XVIIth century English—Shakespeare. (1939). Linguaphone Institute. EE 47/48.

The Linguaphone English course (1949). Linguaphone Institute. ENG 146/147.

The new method records (1959). Bokförlaget Niloe, Stockholm. HEP 1/2–9/10.

Our changing speech: Two BBC talks by Daniel Jones (1985). National Institute for Educational Media, Copenhagen. Audio cassettes. 840098.

Published 1920–1930 (precise dates unknown)

Phonetic readings in English and extracts from *The pronunciation of English.* Deutsche Grammophon-Aktiengesellschaft (Sammlung Dr Driesen). 1678–85.

Extracts from *Phonetic readings in English.* Odeon, Berlin. AA 53816–29.

Readings from *Hausknecht's Lehrbücher.* Odeon, Berlin. A 66086–123.

Extracts from *Lehrbuch Lincke* (M. Diesterweg, Frankfurt-am-Main). Odeon, Berlin. AA 53802/3.

References

Abercrombie, D.
1937   *Isaac Pitman: A pioneer in the scientific study of language.* London: Pitman.
[1965]   [Rev. rpt. as "Isaac Pitman", in: D. Abercrombie 1965, 92–107.]
1948   "Forgotten phoneticians", *TPhS*, 1–34.
[1965]   [Reprinted in: D. Abercombie 1965, 45–75.]
1950   Review of Jones 1950a, *The Phoneme: Its nature and use. MPh* (3) 28: 31–33.
1951   "How Garrick spoke Shakespeare", radio broadcast, BBC Third Programme, 9 March 1951.
[1965]   [Rev. rpt. as "Steele, Monboddo and Garrick", in: D. Abercrombie 1965, 35–44].
1964   "Syllable quantity and enclitics in English", in: D. Abercrombie et al. (eds.), 216–222.
1965   *Studies in phonetics and linguistics.* London: Oxford University Press.
1967   *Elements of general phonetics.* Edinburgh: Edinburgh University Press.
1980   "Fifty years of phonetics", *Work in Progress* 13, 1–9. Edinburgh: Department of Linguistics.
1981   "Extending the Roman alphabet: Some orthographic experiments of the past four centuries", in: R.E. Asher—E.J.A.Henderson (eds.), 207–224.
1983   "Daniel Jones's teaching", *Work in Progress* 16, 1–8. Edinburgh: Department of Linguistics.
Abercrombie, D.—D. Fry—P.A.D. MacCarthy—N.C. Scott—J.L.M. Trim (eds.)
1964   *In honour of Daniel Jones.* London: Longmans.
Abercrombie, L.
1913   "Phonetics and poetry", *English Review* 13: 418–429.
Afzelius, J.A.
1909   *A pronouncing dictionary of modern English.* Stockholm: Norstedt.
Aitken, A.
1962   Vowel length in modern Scots. [Unpublished paper, Department of English Language, University of Edinburgh.]
Akhmanova, O.
1971   Review of Jones 1912b, *Phonetic readings in English. Journal of Linguistics* 7: 298–301.
Albright, R.W.
1953   The International Phonetic Alphabet: Its backgrounds and development. [Unpublished Ph.D. dissertation, Stanford University.]
1958   *The International Phonetic Alphabet: Its backgrounds and development.* Bloomington, Indiana: The Indiana University Research Centre in Anthropology, Folklore and Linguistics.
[1958]   [Reprinted in: *International Journal of Linguistics*, 1958, 24.1 (Part 3).]
Albrow, K.H.
1981   "The Kazan' School and the London School", in: R.E. Asher—E.J.A. Henderson (eds.), 9–17.
Allen, W.S.
1953[1965²]   *Phonetics in ancient India.* (2nd edition 1965.) London: Oxford University Press. First published 1953.
1965[1970²]   *Vox Latina.* (2nd edition 1970.) Cambridge: Cambridge University Press. First published 1965.

530   *References*

1968[1987³]   *Vox Graeca.* (3rd edition 1987.) Cambridge: Cambridge University Press. First published 1968.

1981   "The Greek contribution to the history of phonetics", in: R.E. Asher—E.J.A. Henderson (eds.), 115–122.

Althaus, L.H.

1911   "The means of training in phonetics available for modern language teachers", supplement to *MPh* (2) 26.

Amos, W.

1985   *The originals: An A-Z of fiction's real-life characters.* Boston—Toronto: Little, Brown.

Anderson, D.

1969   "Harold E. Palmer: A biographical essay", in: H.E. Palmer—H.V. Redman [1969²], 133–166.

Anderson, S.

1985   *Phonology in the twentieth century.* Chicago: University of Chicago Press.

Andrésen, B.S.

1968   *Pre-glottalization in English standard pronunciation.* Oslo: Norwegian Universities Press; New York: Humanities Press.

Anon.

1913   "Poëts, fonetics, and unstrest silablz", *Pioneer* 2: 35–38.

Anon.

1917   "The black man's burden: Interview with Mr. Solomon T. Plaatje", *Christian Commonwealth* (3 January), 169–170.

Anon.

1927   *Practical orthography of African languages.* London: International Institute of African Languages and Cultures.

Annakin, M.L.

1922   *Notes on the dialect of Nidderdale Yorkshire.* London: IPA.

Arend, Z.-M.

1924   *A Polish phonetic reader.* London: University of London Press.

Armstrong, L.E.

1923a   *An English phonetic reader.* London: University of London Press.

1923b   "A narrower transcription for English", *MPh* (3) 1: 17–19.

1926   "The B.B.C. Committee on Pronunciation", *MPh* (3) 4: 34–35.

1932   *The phonetics of French.* London: Bell.

1934   *The phonetic structure of Somali.* Berlin: Mitteilungen des Seminars für orientalische Sprachen.

[1964]   [Reprinted Farnborough: Gregg.]

1940   *The phonetic and tonal structure of Kikuyu.* London: International African Institute.

Armstrong, L.E.—Pe Maung Tin

1925   *A Burmese phonetic reader.* London: University of London Press.

Armstrong, L.E.—I.C. Ward

1926   *Handbook of English intonation.* Leipzig—Berlin: Teubner; Cambridge: Heffer.

Ashby, M.

1989   "A note on the vowel quadrilateral", *JIPA* 19: 83–88.

Asher, R.E.—E.J.A. Henderson (eds.)

1981   *Towards a history of phonetics.* Edinburgh: Edinburgh University Press.

Bailey, N.
[1731²]   *A universal etymological English dictionary*. (2nd edition.) London: T. Cox, quoted in: Benzie 1972.
Bailey, T.G.
1914   *A Panjabi phonetic reader*. London: University of London Press.
Baker, A.
1908   *The life of Sir Isaac Pitman: Inventor of phonography*. London: Pitman.
Ball, M.J.
1984   "The centring of diphthongs in southern English—a sound change in progress", *JIPA* 14: 38–44.
Barker, A.T. (ed.)
1923   *The Mahatma letters: To A.P. Sinnett*. Pasadena: Theosophical University Press.
Barnard, H.C.
1970   *Were those the days? A Victorian education*. Oxford: Pergamon Press.
Batchelor, T.
1809   *An orthoëpical analysis of the English language*. London: Didier and Tebbett.
[1973]   [Reprinted in: A. Zettersten 1973, *A critical facsimile of the works of Thomas Batchelor*. Lund: Gleerup.]
Baudouin de Courtenay, J.
1876–77   "A detailed programme of lectures for the academic year 1876–77", in: E. Stankiewicz (ed.) 1972b, 92–113.
1895   "An attempt at a theory of phonetic alternations", in: E. Stankiewicz (ed.) 1972b, 144–212.
Beach, D.
1923   The phonetics of Pekingese. [Unpublished Ph.D. dissertation, University of London.]
1938   *The phonetics of the Hottentot language*. Cambridge: Heffer.
Beal, J.C.
1995   The first pronouncing dictionaries of English: Thomas Spence's *Grand repository of the English language* (1775) and its contemporaries. [Unpublished Ph.D. dissertation, University of Newcastle.]
Bell, A. Graham
1906   *The mechanism of speech*. New York: Funk and Wagnall.
Bell, A. Melville
1867   *Visible Speech: The science of universal alphabetics*. London: Simpkin Marshall.
1882   *Sounds and their relations: A complete manual of universal alphabetics*. London: Trubner.
1895   *English Visible Speech in twelve lessons*. Washington DC: Volta Bureau.
1897   *The science of speech*. Washington DC: Volta Bureau.
Bennot, H. Hale,
1929   *University College London 1826–1926*. London: University of London Press.
Benzie, W.
1972   *The Dublin orator: Thomas Sheridan's influence on eighteenth-century rhetoric and Belles Lettres*. Leeds: University of Leeds School of English.
Besant, A.
1897[1924²]   *The ancient wisdom*. (2nd edition 1924.) London: Theosophical Publishing House. First published 1897.

Bladon, R.A.W.—G. Fant

1978   "Two-formant models of vowel perception and the cardinal vowels". [Paper given at Colloquium of British Academic Phoneticians, Reading, 1978.]; quoted in: Butcher 1982.

Blavatsky, H.P.

1877   *Isis unveiled.* New York: Bouton.

1888   *The secret doctrine.* London: Theosophical Publishing Society.

Bloomfield, L.

1942   *Outline guide for the practical study of foreign languages.* Baltimore: Linguistic Society of America.

Boyanus, S.C.

1947   "The Russian ɨ phoneme", supplement to *MPh* (3) 25.

Boyd, A.K.

1948   *The history of Radley College 1847–1947.* Oxford: Blackwell.

Brazil, D.—M. Coulthard—C. Johns

1980   *Discourse intonation and language teaching.* London: Longman.

Bridges, R.

1910   "On the present state of English pronunciation", *Essays and Studies* 1: 42–69.

1913   *English pronunciation.* Oxford: Clarendon Press; rev. and expanded version of Bridges 1910.

1919   *On English homophones.* (Tracts of the Society for Pure English, No. II.) Oxford: Clarendon Press.

Bronstein, A.J.—L.R. Raphael—C.-J. Stephens (eds.)

1977   *A biographical dictionary of the phonetic sciences.* New York: Lehmann College Press.

Bronstein, A.J.

1986   "The history of pronunciation in English language dictionaries", in: R.R.K Hartmann (ed.), *The history of lexicography. (Papers from the Dictionary Research Centre Seminar at Exeter, March 1986.)* Amsterdam: Benjamins.

Brown, G.

1977   *Listening to spoken English.* London: Longman.

1981   "Consonant rounding in British English: the status of phonetic descriptions as historical data", in: R.E. Asher—E.J.A. Henderson (eds.), 67–76.

Bruce, R.V.

1973   *Bell: Alexander Graham Bell and the concept of solitude.* Boston: Little Brown.

Brücke, E.

1856[1876²]   *Grundzüge der Physiologie und Systematik der Sprachlaute.* (2nd edition 1876.) Vienna: Gerold. First published 1856.

Brynildsen, J.

1902–07 *Engelsk—Dansk—Norsk Ordbog.* 2 vols. Copenhagen: Gyldendal.

Bullokar, W.

1580   *A short introduction or guiding to print, write, and reade Inglish speech.* London: Denham.

[1966]   [Reprinted in: B. Danielsson—R.C. Alston eds. 1966.]

Burchfield, R.

1986   *The English language.* Oxford—New York: Oxford University Press.

Butcher, A.
1976   The influence of the native language on the perception of vowel quality. [M Phil thesis, University of London.]
1982   "Cardinal vowels and other problems", in: Crystal (ed.), 50–72.
Camerlynck, G.
1913   "Pour la liberté des articles en orthographe ordinaire", *MPh* (2) 28: 45–47.
Camilli, A.
1921   *An Italian phonetic reader*. London: University of London Press.
Catford, J.C.
1939   "On the classification of stop consonants", *MPh* (3) 17: 2–5.
1947   "Consonants pronounced with closed glottis", *MPh* (3) 25: 4–6.
1964   "Phonation types: The classification of some laryngeal components of speech production", in: D. Abercrombie et al. (eds.), 26–37.
1968   "The articulatory possibilities of man", in: B. Malmberg (ed.), 309–333.
1977   *Fundamental problems in phonetics*. Edinburgh: Edinburgh University Press.
1981   "Observations on the recent history of vowel classification", in: R.E. Asher— E.J.A. Henderson (eds.), 19–32.
Cercignani, F.
1981   *Shakespeare's works and Elizabethan pronunciation*. Oxford: Oxford University Press.
Chao, Y.-R
1934   "The non-uniqueness of phonemic solutions of phonetic systems", *Bulletin of the Institute of History and Philology Academia Sinica*, Vol. IV, Part 4, 363–397.
[1966⁴]   [Reprinted in: M. Joos 1966⁴, 38–54.]
Chatterji, S.K.
1928   *A Bengali phonetic reader*. London: University of London Press.
1968   "A personal tribute to Professor Daniel Jones". [No indication of publisher.]
[1981]   [Reprinted in: M. Onishi 1981, 19–25.]
Chomsky, N.—M. Halle
1968   *The sound pattern of English*. New York: Harper and Row.
Christaller, J.G.
1875   *A grammar of the Asante and Fante language called Tshi [Chwee Twi]*. Basle.
[1964]   [Reprinted Ridgeway NJ: Gregg.]
Christophersen, P.
1956   *An English phonetics course*. London: Longman Green.
Clark, J.—C. Yallop
1990   *An introduction to phonetics and phonology*. Oxford—Cambridge, Mass.: Blackwell.
Cohen, A.
1952   *The phonemes of English*. The Hague: Uleman.
1956–57 Review of Jones [1956⁸], *An outline of English phonetics*. *Lingua* 6: 321–325.
Cole, D.T.
1955   *An introduction to Tswana grammar*. London: Longmans Green.
Coleman, H.O.
1914   "Intonation and emphasis", *Miscellanea Phonetica* 1: 6–26.

Coles, J.O.

1872   "A plan for ascertaining more accurately the physiology of speech", *Transactions of the Odontological Society of Great Britain* 4: 110–123.

Collins, B.S.

1986   "Alias Sweet or Jones", in: C.C. Barfoot—E.M. Knottenbelt (eds.), *A plain sense of things*. Leiden: Department of English, Rijksuniversiteit Leiden, 77–90.

1987   "Sweet, Jones and Bernard Shaw", *Henry Sweet Society Newsletter* 9: 2–7.

Collins, B.S.—I.M. Mees

1995   "Daniel Jones, Paul Passy and the development of the Cardinal Vowel system", *Historiographia Linguistica* 22: 197–216.

1996   "Spreading everywhere? How recent a phenomenon is glottalisation in Received Pronunciation?", *English World-Wide* 17.2: 175–187.

1997   "Daniel Jones, the phoneme and the 'Joneme'", *RASK*: 161–176.

Comaroff, J. (ed.)

1973   *The Boer War diary of Sol. T. Plaatje*. London: Macmillan.

Comrie, B.—G. Stone

1978   *The Russian language since the revolution*. Oxford: Clarendon Press.

Cook, V.

1968   *Active intonation*. London: Longman.

Cooper, C.

1685   *Grammatica linguae anglicanae*. London: Benjamin Tooke.

[1968]   [Reprinted Scolar Press.]

1687   *The English teacher, or the discovery of the art of teaching and learning the English tongue*. London: John Richardson.

[1953]   [Reprinted with commentary in: B. Sundby (ed.) 1953.]

Coustenoble, H.

1945   *La Phonétique du provençal moderne en terre d'Arles*. Hertford: Austin.

1964   "Daniel Jones: a personal tribute", in: D. Abercrombie et al. (eds.), p. xxi.

Coustenoble, H.N.—L.E. Armstrong

1934   *Studies in French intonation*. Cambridge: Heffer.

Crowley, T.

1989   *Standard English and the politics of language*. Urbana and Chicago: University of Illinois Press.

Cruttenden, A.

1981   The intonation of English sentences with special reference to sentence adverbials. [Unpublished Ph.D. dissertation, University of Manchester.]

1986   *Intonation*. Cambridge: Cambridge University Press.

Crystal, D.

1969   *Prosodic systems and intonation in English*. Cambridge: Cambridge University Press.

1982   (ed.) *Linguistic controversies*. London: Arnold.

Danielsson, B. (ed.)

1955   *John Hart's works on English orthography and pronunciation*. Stockholm: Almqvist and Wiksell.

Danielsson, B.—R.C. Alston (eds.)

1966   *The works of William Bullokar I: A short introduction or guiding, 1580–1*. Leeds: Scolar Press.

Danielsson, B.—A. Gabrielson (eds.)

1972   *Alexander Gill's Logonomia anglica* (1619). Stockholm: Almqvist and Wiksell.

Davies, H.M.

1930   Review of E.H.A. Robson 1929, *How shall we train the teacher of modern languages?* Cambridge: Heffer. *MPh* (3) 8: 32–34.

De Silva, M.W.S.

1969   "Sinhalese", in: T. Sebeok (ed.), 235–248.

Dietrich, G.

1969   "A suggestion for an improvement on the vowel diagram", *MPh* (3) 47: 8–9.

Dobson, E.J.

1955   Review of Kökeritz 1953. *The review of English Studies* 6: 404–414.

1957a[1968²]   *English pronunciation 1500–1700.* 2 vols. (2nd edition 1968.) London: Oxford University Press. First published 1957.

1957b   (ed.)

        The phonetic writings of Robert Robinson. London—New York—Toronto: Early English Text Society/Oxford University Press.

Doke, C.M.

1926   *The phonetics of the Zulu language. Bantu Studies* 2.

[1969]   [Reprinted Johannesburg: University of Witwatersrand Press.]

Drage, C.L.

1972   Review of Jones—Ward 1969, *The phonetics of Russian. Modern Language Review* 67: 475–478.

Dumville, B.

1904   *Elements of French pronunciation and diction.* London: Dent.

Dyche, T.

1723   *A dictionary of all words commonly used in the English tongue.* London: Samuel Butler and Thomas Butler.

Edwards, E.R.

1903   *Etude phonétique de la langue japonaise.* [University of Paris doctoral thesis, Leipzig: Teubner.]

Egan, A.

1914   *A German phonetic reader.* London: University of London Press.

Ekwall, E.

1942   "Sir Allen Mawer: in memoriam", *English Studies* 24: 169–171.

Ellis, A.J.

1844   *Phonetics: A familiar exposition of that science.* Bath: Pitman; London: Bagster.

1848a   *The essentials of phonetics.* London: Pitman.

1848b   *A plea for phonetic spelling: Or the necessity of orthographic reform.* London: Pitman.

1869–89   *On early English pronunciation.* Parts 1–5. London: Philological Society.

n.d.   *Speech in song.* London: Novello.

Endemann, K.

1876   *Versuch einer Grammatik des Sotho.* Berlin.

[1964]   [Reprinted Ridgeway NJ: Gregg.]

Essner, C.

1947   "Recherches sur la structure des voyelles orales", *Archive Néerlandaise de phonétique expérimentale* 20: 40–77.

Eustace, S.S.
1967   "Present changes in English pronunciation", *Proceedings of the 6th International Congress of Phonetic Sciences*. Prague: Academia/Hueber, 303–306.

Firth, C.H.
1929   *Modern languages at Oxford 1724–1929*. London: Oxford University Press.

Firth, J.R.
1930   *Speech*. London: Benn.
[1964]   [Reprinted in: J.R. Firth 1964.]
1937   *The tongues of men*. London: Watts.
[1964]   [Reprinted in: J.R. Firth 1964.]
1946   "The English School of Phonetics", *TPhS* 1946: 92–132.
[1957]   [Reprinted in: J.R. Firth 1957, 92–120.]
1957   *Papers in linguistics 1934–1951*. London: Oxford University Press.
1964   *The tongues of men* and *Speech*, rpt. of Firth 1930 and 1937. London: Oxford University Press.

Fischer-Jørgensen, E.
1975   *Trends in phonological theory: A historical introduction*. Copenhagen: Akademisk Forlag.
1981   "Fifty years with phonetics and phoneticians", *Annual Report of the Institute of Phonetics University of Copenhagen* 15: 61–75.

Fowler, H.W.—F.G. Fowler (eds.)
1911   *Concise Oxford Dictionary of Current English*. Oxford: Clarendon Press.

Frings, T.
1934   "Eduard Sievers", *Berichte über die Verhandlungen der sächsischen Akademie der Wissenschaften zu Leipzig* 85: 1–56.
[1966]   [Reprinted in: T. Sebeok (ed.) 1966, vol. 2, 1–52.]

Frinta, A.
1907   "Enquête" on pronunciation of Greek and Latin in schools, *MPh* (2) 22: 118–122.
1925   *A Czech phonetic reader*. London: University of London Press.

Fromkin, V.
1985a   (ed.) *Phonetic linguistics*. Orlando, Fla: Academic Press.
1985b   "Interview with Peter Ladefoged", in: V. Fromkin 1985a (ed.), 3–13.

Fromkin, V.—P. Ladefoged
1981   "Early views of distinctive features", in: R.E. Asher—E.J.A. Henderson (eds.), 3–8.

Fry, D.B.
1961   "Daniel Jones", *English Language Teaching* 15: 151–156.
1968   "Daniel Jones" (obituary), *English Language Teaching* 22: 198–199.
1974   "Phonetics in the twentieth century", in: T. Sebeok (ed.), 2202–2239.
1977   *Homo loquens*. Cambridge: Cambridge University Press.

Fry, D.B.—Đ. Kostić
1939   *A Serbo-Croat phonetic reader*. London: University of London Press.

Fudge, E.C.
1977   "Long and short [æ] in one Southern British speaker's English", *JIPA* 7: 55–65.
1984   *English word stress*. London: Allen and Unwin.

Fuhrken, G.E.
1907   *Phonetic transcription of Jespersen—Rodhe Engelsk Läsebok*. Stockholm: Fritze.

Gil, Alexander
  1619   *Logonomia anglica*. London: John Beale.
  [1972]   [Reprinted in: B. Danielsson—A. Gabrielson 1972.]
Gilliéron, J.—E. Edmont
  1902–10 *Atlas linguistique de la France*. Paris: Champion.
Gim, Sun-Gi
  1937   The phonetics of Korean. [MA thesis, University of London.]
Gimson, A.C.
  1949   "The retirement of Daniel Jones", *MPh* (3) 27: 18–22.
  1962   *An introduction to the pronunciation of English*. London: Arnold.
  1968   "Daniel Jones" (obituary), *MPh* (3) 46: 2–6.
  1973   "The Association's alphabet", *JIPA* 3: 2–3.
  1977   "Daniel Jones and standards of English pronunciation", *English Studies* 58: 151–158.
Gimson, A.C.—A. Cruttenden
  1994   *Gimson's Pronunciation of English*. (5th revised edition of Gimson 1962.) London: Arnold.
Glass, J. Blidner
  1963   William Tilly. [MA thesis, Queens College, New York.]
Gouin, F.
  1892   *The art of teaching and studying languages*. London: George Philip, trans. by H. Swan and V. Bétis of Gouin 1880, *L'Art d'enseigner et d'étudier les langues*. Paris: G. Fischbacher.
Grant, W.
  1913   *The pronunciation of English in Scotland*. Cambridge: Cambridge University Press.
Halle, M.—J. Keyser
  1971   *English stress: Its form, its growth and its role in verse*. New York: Harper and Row.
Halliday, M.A.K.
  1963   "The tones of English", *Archivum Linguisticum* 15, Fasc. 1, 1–28.
  [1973]   [Reprinted in: W.E. Jones—J. Laver (eds.), 103–127.]
  1964   *Intonation in English grammar*, *TPhS*: 143–169.
  1966   *Intonation systems in English*, in: A. McIntosh—M.A.K. Halliday (eds.), *Patterns of language*. London: Longmans, 111–113.
  1967   *Intonation and grammar in British English*. The Hague: Mouton.
Hammarström, G.
  1973   "Revision of cardinal vowels, and some other problems", *JIPA* 3: 22–28.
Hardcastle, W.
  1981   "Studies in lingual coarticulation", in: R.E. Asher—E.J.A. Henderson (eds.), 50–66.
Hart, J.
  1551   The opening of the unreasonable writing of our inglish toung, ms.
  [1955]   [Reprinted in: B. Danielsson 1955.]
  1569   *An orthographie*, London.
  [1955]   [Reprinted in: B. Danielsson 1955.]
  1570   *A methode*, London: Henry Denham.
  [1955]   [Reprinted in: B. Danielsson 1955.]

Harte, N.—J. North
1978   *The world of University College London 1828–1978*. London: University College.
Haugen, E. (ed.)
1950[1972²]   *First grammatical treatise*. (2nd edition 1972.) London: Longman. First published 1950.
Hellwag, C.F.
1781   Dissertatio inauguralis physiologico medica de formatione loquelae. [Dissertation, University of Tübingen.]
[1967]   [Facs. repr., with Dutch translation, Amsterdam: Instituut voor Fonetische Wetenschappen, University of Amsterdam.]
Helmholtz, H.L.F. von
1863   *Die Lehre von den Tonempfindungen als physiologische Grundlage für die Theorie der Musik*. Braunschweig: Vieweg & John; trans. by A.J. Ellis 1877, *On the sensations of tone as a physiological basis for the theory of music*.
[1954]   [Reprinted New York: Dover.]
Henton, C.G.
1987   "The IPA consonant chart: mugwumps, holes and therapeutic suggestions", *JIPA* 17: 15–25.
Heward, G.A.L.
1910   "A Chaucerian entertainment", *MPh* (2) 25: 101–102.
Hjelmslev, L.
1950–51   "Commentaires sur la vie et l'œuvre de Rasmus Rask", *Conférences de l'Institut de Linguistique de l'Université de Paris* 10: 143–157.
[1966]   [Reprinted in: T. Sebeok (ed.), vol. 1, 179–195.]
Hoenigswald, H.
1978   "The annus mirabilis 1876 and posterity", *TPhS*: 17–35.
Holder, W.
1669   *The elements of speech*. London: J. Martyn.
[1967]   [Reprinted Scolar Press 1967.]
Holroyd, M.
1988   *Bernard Shaw*, vol. 1, *1856–1898: The search for love*. New York: Random House.
Howatt, A.P.R.
1984   *A history of English language teaching*. Oxford: Oxford University Press.
Humphreys, C.
1966   *The field of theosophy*. London: Theosophical Publishing House.
Hyman, L.M.
1975   *Phonology: Theory and analysis*. New York: Holt, Rinehart and Winston.
International Phonetic Association
1904   *Aim and principles of the International Phonetic association*. Bourg-la-Reine: International Phonetic Association.
1908   *Exposé des principes de l'Association Phonétique Internationale*, supplement to *MPh* (2) 23.
1949   *The principles of the International Phonetic Association*. London: International Phonetic Association.
International Phonetic Association
1954   *Miscellanea Phonetica* 2. London: IPA.

Jakobson, R.
1971   "The Kazan' School of Polish linguistics and its place in the international develop-
        ment of pholology", in: R. Jakobsen, *Selected writings*. The Hague: Mouton, 394–
        438; trans. from original Polish.
Jespersen, O.
1889   *The articulation of speech sounds represented by analphabetic symbols*. Marburg:
        Elwert.
1897–99 *Fonetik, en systematisk fremstilling af læren om sproglyd*. Copenhagen:
        Gyldendal.
1904a   *Phonetische Grundfragen*. Leipzig—Berlin: Teubner.
1904b[1920³] *Lehrbuch der Phonetik*. (Third edition 1920.) Leipzig—Berlin: Teubner.
        First published 1904.
1907   *John Hart's pronunciation of English. Anglistische Forschungen* 22, Heidelberg:
        Winter.
1909   *A modern English grammar on historical principles*, Part I, Sounds and spellings.
        Heidelberg: Winter.
1912   *Engelsk fonetik*. Copenhagen: Gyldendal.
1922[1968¹³] *Language: Its nature, development and origin*. (13th edition 1968.) London:
        Allen and Unwin. First published 1922.
1932   *Tanker og studier*. Copenhagen: Gyldendal.
1933a   "Farewell Lecture at the University given on 25th May 1925", in: O. Jespersen
        1933c; reprinted in O. Jespersen n.d., 835–845. Originally published in Danish
        under the title "Slutningsforelæsning" in O. Jespersen 1932.
1933b   "Karl Verner", in: O. Jespersen 1933c; reprinted with minor alterations in: O. Jes-
        persen n.d., 805–816. Originally published in Danish in *Tilskueren* 1897: 3–17.
1933c   *Linguistica: Selected Papers in English, French and German*. Copenhagen: Levin
        & Munksgaard.
1938   *En sprogmands levned*. Copenhagen: Gyldendal.
1995   Juul, A.—H.F. Nielsen—J.E. Nielsen (eds.), *A linguist's life*; transl. by D. Stoner
        of Jespersen 1938. Odense: Odense University Press.
[n.d.] *Selected writings*. London: Allen and Unwin.
Jespersen, O.—H. Pedersen
1926   *Phonetic transcription and transliteration: Proposals of the Copenhagen Confer-
        ence April 1925*. Oxford: Clarendon Press.
Johnson, S.
1755   *A dictionary of the English language*. London: W. Strahan.
Jones, A.
1909   Review of W. Rippmann 1908, *English, French and German sound charts*. Lon-
        don: Dent. *MPh* (2) 24: 104–105.
Jones, E.D.
1906   "Richard John Lloyd" (obituary), *MPh* (2) 21: 106–107.
Jones, S.
1914   "Welsh" (spécimen), *MPh* (2) 29: 54–55.
1923   Review of R.O. Walker n.d., *Introduction to Spanish*. London: Harrap, *MPh* (3) 1:
        27–28.
1926   *A Welsh phonetic reader*. London: University of London Press.

Jones, S.
1929   "Radiography and pronunciation", *British Journal of Radiology* 2: 149–150.
Jones, W.E.—J. Laver (eds.)
1973   *Phonetics in linguistics.* London: Longman.
Joos, M.
1948   *Acoustic phonetics*, supplement to *Language* 24.
1957[1966⁴]   (ed.)
        Readings in linguistics I: The development of descriptive linguistics in America 1925–56. (4th edition 1966.) Chicago: University of Chicago Press. First published 1957.
Jugnet, L.
1929   *Paul Passy: un apôtre.* Laon: Imprimerie des Tablettes de l'Aisne.
Juul, A.—H.F. Nielsen (eds.)
1989   *Otto Jespersen: Facets of his life and work.* Amsterdam—Philadelphia: Benjamins.
Kaiser, L. (ed.)
1957   *Manual of phonetics.* Amsterdam: North Holland. (See also Malmberg 1968.)
Kelly, J.
1981   "The 1847 alphabet: an episode of phonotypy", in: R.E. Asher—E.J.A. Henderson (eds.), 248–264.
Kelly, J.—J.K. Local
1984   "The modernity of Henry Sweet", *Henry Sweet Society Newsletter* 2: 3–9.
Kelly, L.G.
1969[1976²]   *25 Centuries of language teaching.* (2nd edition 1976.) Rowley, Mass.: Newbury House. First published 1969.
Kemp, J.A. (ed.)
1972   *John Wallis's grammar of the English language.* London: Longman.
Kingdon, R.
1958a   *Groundwork of English intonation.* London: Longman.
1958b   *Groundwork of English stress.* London: Longman.
1964   "The representation of vowels", in: D. Abercrombie et al. (eds.), 112–115.
Kingsley, N.W.
1879   "Surgery or mechanism in the treatment of congenital cleft palate", *New York Medical Journal* 29: 484–492.
Klinghardt, H.
1897   *Artikulations- und Hörübungen.* Cöthen: Schulze.
1923   "Sprechmelodie und Sprechtakt", *NS* 31: 1–29.
1927   *Übungen in deutschem Tonfall.* Leipzig: Quelle und Meyer.
Klinghardt, H.—M. de Fourmestraux
1911   *Französische Intonationsübungen.* Cöthen: Schulze.
Klinghardt, H.—G. Klemm
1920   *Übungen im englischen Tonfall.* Cöthen: Schulze.
Koerner, E.F.K.
1972   "Jan Baudouin de Courtenay: His place in the history of linguistic science", *Canadian Slavonic Papers* 14, 663–682.
[1978]   [Reprinted in: E.F.K. Koerner 1978a, 107–126.]
1976a   "A minor figure in 19th-century French linguistics: A. Dufriche-Desgenettes", *Phonetica* 33: 222–231.

[1978]   [Reprinted in: E.F.K. Koerner 1978a, 127–136.]
1976b   "1876 as a turning point in the history of linguistics", *Journal of European Studies*
4: 333–353.
[1978]   [Reprinted in: E.F.K. Koerner 1978a, 189–209.]
1978a   *Toward a historiography of linguistics*. Amsterdam: Benjamins.
1978b   "Zu Ursprung und Entwicklung des Phonem-Begriffs: eine historische Notiz", in:
D. Hartmann—H. Linke—Ludwig (eds.), *Sprache in Gegenwart und Geschichte:*
Festschrift für Heinrich Matthias Heinrichs. Vienna: Böhlau, 82–93.
[1978]   [Reprinted in: E.F.K. Koerner 1978a, 177–188.]
Kohler, K.
1981   "Three trends in phonetics: The development of the discipline in Germany since
the nineteenth century", in: R.E. Asher—E.J.A. Henderson (eds.), 161–178.
Kökeritz, H.
1953   *Shakespeare's pronunciation*. New Haven: Yale University Press.
Krámský, J.
1974   *The phoneme: Introduction to the history and theories of a concept*. Munich:
Wilhelm Fink.
Kuhn, T.S.
1962   *The structure of scientific revolutions*. Chicago: Chicago University Press.
Ladefoged, P.
1967   *Three areas of experimental phonetics*. London: Oxford University Press.
1975   *A course in phonetics*. New York: Harcourt Brace and Jovanovich.
1987a   "Updating the theory", *JIPA* 17: 10–14.
1987b   "Proposed revision of the International Phonetic Alphabet: A conference", *JIPA*
17: 34.
Langendoen, D.T.
1968   *The London School of Linguistics*. Cambridge, Mass.: MIT.
Large, A.
1985   *The artificial language movement*. Oxford: Blackwell.
Laudan, L.
1977   *Progress and its problems: Towards a theory of scientific growth*. London:
Routledge Kegan Paul.
Laver, J.
1965   "Variability in vowel perception", *Language and Speech* 8: 95–121.
Leadbeater, C.W.
[1907²]   *Man visible and invisible*. (2nd edition.) London: Theosophical Publishing Society.
Lee, H.B.
1968   "A remark on the IPA cardinal back vowels", *MPh* (3) 68: 26–29.
Lee, W.R.
1960   *An English intonation reader*. London: Macmillan.
Leitner, G.
1982   "The consolidation of 'Educated Southern English' as a model in the early 20th
century", *IRAL* 20: 91–107.
Lepsius, R.
1863   *Standard alphabet for reducing unwritten languages and foreign graphic systems*
to a uniform orthography in European letters. (2nd rev. edition.)
[1981]   [Reprinted in: J.A. Kemp 1981 (ed.), Amsterdam: Benjamins.]

Leskien, A.
1876   *Die Deklination im Slavisch-Litauischen und Germanischen.* Leipzig: Hirzel.
Lloyd, R.J.
1899   *Northern English.* Leipzig—Berlin: Teubner; rev. W. Viëtor 1908.
Lloyd James, A. (ed.)
1928–39   *Broadcast English.* London: BBC.
1935   *The broadcast word.* London: Kegan Paul, Trench and Trubner.
Local, J.K.
1983   "Making a transcription: The evolution of A.J. Ellis's Palaeotype", *JIPA* 13: 2–12.
Lockhart, R. Bruce
1957   *Friends, foes and foreigners.* London: Putnam.
Lodwick, F.
1686   *An essay towards an universal alphabet.* London. (See also Salmon 1972.)
MacCarthy, P.A.D.
1944   *English pronunciation.* Cambridge: Heffer.
MacMahon, M.K.C.
1979   "British phonetics in the 1880s: The work of James Lecky", *Historiographia Linguistica* 6.1: 47–56.
1981   *Henry Sweet's system of shorthand,* in: R.E. Asher—E.J.A. Henderson (eds.), 265–281.
1985   "Henry Sweet as a novelist", *Henry Sweet Society Newsletter* 2: 10–14.
1986   "The International Phonetic Association: The first 100 years", *JIPA* 16: 30–38.
1991   "Sweet, Europe and phonetics", *Henry Sweet Society Newsletter* 17: 12–18. (Text of a paper read to the Inaugural Meeting of the European Society of the Study of English, 7 September 1991.)
1994   "Laura Soames' contributions to phonetics", *Historiographia Linguistica* 21.1: 103–121.
Maddieson, I.
1987   "Revision of the IPA: Linguo-labials as a test case", *JIPA* 17: 26–32.
Malmberg, B. (ed.)
1968   *Manual of phonetics.* (2nd completely rev. edition.) Amsterdam—London: North Holland. (See also Kaiser 1957.)
Martinet, A.
1951   Review of Jones 1950a, *The Phoneme: Its nature and use. Word* 7: 253–254.
McClure, J.D.
1972   "A suggested revision for the Cardinal Vowel system". *JIPA* 2: 20–25.
McDavid, R.I.
1952   Review of Jones 1950a, *The Phoneme: Its nature and use. Language* 28: 377–386.
Meinhof, C.
1928   "Principles of practical orthography for African languages.—I", *Africa,* Vol. 1: 228–236.
Merkel, C.L.
1857   *Anatomie und Physiologie des menschlichen Stimm- und Sprach-Organs (Anthropophonik).* Leipzig: Abel.
1866   *Physiologie der menschlichen Sprache (physiologische Laletik).* Leipzig: Wigand.
Meyer, E.A.
1903   *Englische Lautdauer.* Leipzig: Harrassowitz; Uppsala: Lundström.

1910   "Untersuchung über Lautbildung", in: *Festschrift Wilhelm Viëtor*. Marburg: Elwert, 166–248.

Michaelis, H.—P. Passy

1897[1914²]   *Dictionnaire phonétique de la langue française*. (2nd edition 1914.) Hanover and Berlin: Carl Meyer/Gustav Prior. First published 1897.

Miller, G.M. (ed.)

1971   *BBC Pronouncing dictionary of British names*. London: Oxford University Press.

Motte, C.

1912   *Lectures phonétiques*. Paris: Didier.

Mugglestone, L.

1995   *"Talking proper": The rise of accent as a social symbol*. Oxford: Clarendon Press.

Mulcaster, R.

1582   *The first part of the elementarie*. London: T. Vautrollier.

[1970]   [Reprinted London: Scolar Press.]

Murray, J.A.H. (ed.)

1933[1989²]   *Oxford English dictionary*. Oxford: Oxford University Press. [Previously published in separate volumes between 1884 and 1928 as *A new English dictionary on historical principles*.]; 2nd edition 1989, J.A. Simpson—E.S.C. Winer (eds.).

Murray, K.M.E.

1977   *Caught in the web of words: James A.H. Murray and the Oxford English dictionary*. New Haven: Yale University Press.

Nearey, T.M.

1977   Phonetic feature systems for vowels. [Ph.D. dissertation, University of Connecticut.]

Noël-Armfield, G.

1909a   *100 Poems for children*. Leipzig: Teubner.

1909b   "Scenes from Shakespeare in the original pronunciation", *MPh* (2) 24: 117–119.

1916[1919²]   *General phonetics: For missionaries and students of languages*. (2nd edition 1919.) Cambridge: Heffer. First published 1916.

Nuttall, P.A. (ed.)

1883   *The standard pronouncing dictionary*. London: Warne.

O'Connor, J.D.

1965   The perception of time intervals. *Progress Report*. London: University College London Phonetics Laboratory.

1967   *Better English pronunciation*. Cambridge: Cambridge University Press.

1973   *Phonetics*. Harmondsworth: Penguin.

O'Connor, J.D.—G.F. Arnold

1961[1973²]   *Intonation of colloquial English*. (2nd edition 1973.) London: Longman. First published 1961.

Oliphant—Anderson—Ferrier (eds.)

1913   *Bibliography for missionary students*. London: Board of Study for Preparation of Missionaries.

Omananda Puri

1959   *The Boy and the Brothers*. London: Gollancz.

Onishi, M.
    1981   *D. Jones, H.E. Palmer and phonetics in Japan: In commemoration of their 100th birthday.* Tokyo: Phonetic Society of Japan.
Osthoff, H.—K. Brugmann
    1878   *Morphologische Untersuchungen auf dem Gebiete der indogermanischen Sprachen*, vol. 1. Leipzig: Hirzel.
Palmer, H.E.
    1910   "The transcription of English vowels", *MPh* (2) 25: 102–107.
    1917a[1920²]   *A first course of English phonetics.* (2nd edition 1920.) Cambridge: Heffer. First published 1917.
    1917b[1969²]   *The scientific study and teaching of languages.* (2nd edition 1969.) London: Oxford University Press. First published 1917, London: Harrap.
    1922   *English intonation: With systematic exercises.* Cambridge: Heffer.
    1930   *The principles of romanization.* Tokyo: Maruzen.
    1933   *A new classification of English tones.* Tokyo: Institute for Research in English Teaching.
Palmer, H.E.—C. Motte
    1916   *Colloquial French.* Cambridge: Heffer.
Palmer, H.E.—H.V. Redman
    1932[1969²]   *This language learning business.* (2nd edition 1969.) London: Oxford University Press. First published 1932, London: Harrap.
Palsgrave, J.
    1530   *Lesclarcissement de la langue francoyse.* London.
    [1969]   [Reprinted London: Scolar Press.]
Panconcelli-Calzia, G.
    1957   "Earlier history of phonetics", in: L. Kaiser (ed.), 3–17.
Passy, J.
    1894a   "La dictée phonétique", *MPh* (2) 9: 34–38.
    1894b   "La dictée phonétique", *MPh* (2) 9: 50–52.
Passy, P.
    1887[1899⁵]   *Les Sons du français.* (Fifth edition 1899; sixth edition 1906.) Paris: Firmin
    [1906⁶]   Didot. First published 1887.
    1888   "Kurze Darstellung des französischen Lautsystems", *Phonetische Studien* 1: 18–40; 115–130; 245–256.
    1891   *Etude sur les changements phonétiques et leurs caractères généraux.* Paris: Firmin-Didier.
    1905   "Cours de vacances", *MPh* (2) 20: 109–110.
    1906[1912²]   *Petite phonétique comparée.* (2nd edition 1912.) Leipzig: Teubner. First published 1906.
    1907a   *The sounds of the French language.* (See Savory—Jones 1907c.)
    1907b   "Ecriture phonétique simplifié", *MPh* (2) 22: 35–37.
    1907c   "Alphabet organique", *MPh* (2) 22: 55–57.
    1907d   "Examen de phonétique", *MPh* (2) 22: 79–80.
    1908   Review of Sweet 1908, *The sounds of English.* Oxford: Clarendon. *MPh* (2) 23: 68–71.
    1909   Review of Jones 1909b, *The pronunciation of English.* *MPh* (2) 24: 126–128.
    1910   "Vieux français" (spécimen). *MPh* (2) 25: 88–89, 118–119.

1913   Review of Jones—Kwing Tong Woo 1912a, *A Cantonese phonetic reader. MPh* (2) 28: 71–72.

1914   *A French phonetic reader.* London: University of London Press.

1920   *Conversations françaises.* London: University of London Press.

1923   "Vie nouvelle", *MPh* (3) 1: 1–3.

1930–32 *Souvenirs d'un socialiste chrétien.* 2 vols. Issy-les-Moulineaux: Editions "Je sers".

Pedersen, H.

1931[1962²]   *The discovery of language: Linguistic science in the nineteenth century.* (2nd edition 1962) Bloomington: Indiana University Press, trans. with revisions by J.W. Spargo of Pedersen 1924. *Sprogvidenskaben i det nittende aarhundrede: Metoder og resultater.* Copenhagen: Gyldendal. Translation first published 1931 under the title *Linguistic science in the nineteenth century.* Cambridge, Mass.: Harvard University Press.

Phillips, C.

1992   *Robert Bridges: A biography.* Oxford—New York: Oxford University Press.

Phipson, E.A.

1908   "Teutonised Latin and Greek", *MPh* (2) 23: 53–54.

Pike, K.L.

1943[1966¹⁰]   *Phonetics.* (10th edition 1966.) Ann Arbor: University of Michigan Press. First published 1943.

1981   "An autobiographical note on phonetics", in: R.E. Asher—E.J.A. Henderson (ed.), 181–185.

Pitman, I.

1837   *Stenographic shorthand.* London: Samuel Bagster.

[1908]   [Reprinted in: A. Baker 1908, App. 1, 333–348.]

1847   "The English phonotypic alphabet", *Phonotypic Journal* 6: 2; quoted in: J. Kelly 1981.

Pitman, J.

1964   "The Simplified Spelling Society", in: D. Abercrombie et al. (eds.), 177–184.

Plaatje, S.T.

1930[1978²]   *Mhudi.* (2nd edition 1978.) London: Heinemann. First published 1930, Lovedale Press.

Pring, J.T.

1959   *Colloquial English pronunciation.* London: Longman.

Prins, J.P.

1921   "Vacantie-cursus te Londen", in: *De School met den Bijbel,* 139–140.

Pullum, G.K.—W.A. Ladusaw

1986   *Phonetic symbol guide.* Chicago: University of Chicago Press.

Quick, E.E. and J.G. Schilthuis

1930   *A Dutch phonetic reader.* London: University of London Press.

Ransom, Josephine

1938   *A short history of the Theosophical Society, 1875–1937.* Adyar, Madras: Theosophical Publishing House.

Raudnitzky, H.

1911   *Die Bell-Sweetsche Schule: Ein Beitrag zur Geschichte der englischen Phonetik.* Marburg: Elwert. [Marburger Studien zur englischen Philologie. Vol. 13.]

Rip(p)man(n), W.
1903   *Elements of phonetics.* London: Dent; trans. and adapted from Viëtor 1897.
1906   *The sounds of spoken English: A manual of ear-training for English students.* London: Dent.
1908[1911²]   *Specimens of English: Spoken, read, recited.* (2nd edition 1911.) London: Dent. First published 1908.
1922   *Good speech.* London: Dent.
Rip(p)man(n), W.—W. Archer
1910[1940⁵]   *Simplified spelling.* (rev. 5th edition 1940.) London: Pitman. First published 1910, London: Simplified Spelling Society.
[1948⁶]   *New spelling* (6th edition of Rippmann—Archer 1910.) Revised by D. Jones and H. Orton, London: Pitman.
Roach, P.
1983   *English phonetics and phonology: A practical course.* Cambridge: Cambridge University Press.
Robins, R.H.
1961   "John Rupert Firth", *Language* 37: 191–199.
[1966]   [Reprinted in: T. Sebeok 1966, vol. 2, 543–554.]
1967[1979²]   *A short history of linguistics.* (2nd edition 1979.) London: Longman. First published 1967.
1970   *Diversions of Bloomsbury.* Amsterdam—London: North Holland.
1978   "The Neogrammarians and their nineteenth-century predecessors", *TPhS*, 1–16.
Robinson, Robert
1617   *The art of pronuntiation.* London: Nicholas Okes.
[1957]   [Reprinted in: E.J. Dobson 1957b, 1–28.]
Roques, M.
1930   "Jules Gilliéron", *Bibliographie des travaux de Jules Gilliéron.* Paris, 3–13.
[1966]   [Reprinted in: T. Sebeok 1966, vol. 2, 65–73.]
Rousselot, P.-J.
1892   *Les modifications phonétiques du langage, étudiées dans le patois d'une famille de Cellefrouin Charente.* Paris: Welter.
1897–1908
[1924²]   *Principes de phonétique expérimentale.* 2 vols. Paris: Welter; rev. 2nd edition 1924, Paris: Didier.
Rousselot, P.-J.—F. Laclotte
1902   *Précis de prononciation française.* Paris—Leipzig: Welter.
Russell, G.O.
1928   *The vowel: Its physiological mechanism as shown by X-Ray.* Columbus: Ohio State University Press.
Salesbury, W.
1547   *A dictionary in Englyshe and Welshe.*
[1871]   [Reprinted in: A.J. Ellis 1871, vol. 2, 743–794.]
1550   *A playne and familiar introduction.*
[1871]   [Reprinted in: A.J. Ellis 1871, vol. 2, 743–794.]
Salmon, V. (ed.)
1972   *The works of Francis Lodwick.* London: Longman.
1979   *The study of language in seventeenth century England.* Amsterdam: Benjamins.

Sampson, G.
1980   *Schools of linguistics*. London: Hutchinson.
1985   *Writing systems*. London: Hutchinson.
Sara, S.I.
1990   "Phonetics and phonology 1949–1989", *Historiographia Linguistica* 17.1: 211–229.
Saussure, F. de
1879   *Mémoire sur le système primitif des voyelles dans les langues indo-européennes*. Leipzig: Teubner.
1916   *Cours de linguistique générale*. Paris: Payot.
Savory, D.L.
1908   Review of Jones 1907b, *Phonetic transcriptions of English prose*. *MPh* (2), 23: 47–49.
1912   "Henry Sweet" (obituary), *NS* 20: 191–199.
Ščerba, L.
1908   Review of J. Baudouin de Courtenay 1904, *Materialy dlja južnoslavjanskoj dialektologii i etnografii* II. St Petersburg: Imperial Scientific Academy (published simultaneously in German translation), *MPh* (2) 23: 71–73.
1911   "Court exposé de la prononciation russe", supplement to *MPh* (2) 26.
Schleicher, A.
1861–62 *Compendium der vergleichenden Grammatik der indo-germanischen Sprachen*. Weimar: Böhlau.
1863   *Die darwinsche Theorie und die Sprachwissenschaft*. Weimar: Böhlau.
Scherer, W.
1868   *Zur Geschichte der deutschen Sprache*. Berlin: Weidmann.
Schmidt, P.G.
1907   Trans. by P.J. Hermes of *Les Sons du langage et leur représentation dans un alphabet linguistique général*. Salzburg: Zaunrith'sche Buch-, Kunst- und Steindruckerei.
Schubiger, M.
1952   Review of Jones 1950a, *The Phoneme: Its nature and use*. *English Studies* 33: 39–43.
1958   *English intonation: Its form and function*. Tübingen: Max Niemeyer.
Scripture, E.
1902   *Elements of experimental phonetics*. New York: Scribner.
1906   *Researches in experimental phonetics*. Washington DC: Carnegie Foundation.
Scrivener, H.S.
1916   "Mr Daniel Jones: A personal note" (obituary), *Lawn tennis and badminton*, 6 January 1916, pp. 22–23.
Sebeok, T.
1966   (ed.), *Portraits of linguists*. 2 vols. Bloomington—London: Indiana University Press.
1969   (ed.), *Current trends in linguistics* 5. The Hague: Mouton.
1971   (ed.), *Current trends in linguistics* 7. The Hague: Mouton.
1974   (ed.), *Current trends in linguistics* 12. The Hague: Mouton.
Seers, O.
1908   "Chinese Phonetics", *MPh* (2) 23: 30–34.

Shapiro, B.J.
1969   *John Wilkins, 1614–1672: An intellectual biography.* Berkeley: University of California Press.
Shaw, G.B.
1916   *Pygmalion.* (1st book edition, with preface.) London: Constable. [English play edition, 1914; performed previously in German translation.]
1965   (ed.) A. Tauber, *Bernard Shaw on language.* London: Peter Owen.
Sheldon, E.K.
1967   *Thomas Sheridan of Smock Alley.* Princeton: Princeton University Press.
Sheridan, T.
1762   *A course of lectures on elocution together with two dissertations on language and some other tracts relative to those subjects.* London.
1780   *A general dictionary of the English language.*
[1968]   [Reprinted London: Scolar Press.]
Sievers, E.
1876[1881²]
[1889³]   *Grundzüge der Lautphysiologie.* Leipzig: Breitkopf und Härtel; 2nd and subsequent editions retitled *Grundzüge der Phonetik.* First published 1876.
Simonsen, E.
1939   "Paul Passy", *MPh* (3) 17: 20–21.
Sivertsen, E.
1968   "Daniel Jones" (obituary), *Phonetica* 18: 193–197.
Smith, J.J.
1911   "South African Dutch", *MPh* (2) 26: 79.
Smith, H.L.
1952   Review of Jones [1950³], *The pronunciation of English. Language* 28: 144–149.
Soames, L.
1891a   *An introduction to phonetics (English, French and German).* London: Swan Sonnenschein; New York: MacMillan.
[1899²]   *Introduction to English, French and German phonetics.* (2nd edition of Soames 1891a, rev. W. Viëtor.) London: Swan Sonnenschein; New York: Macmillan.
1891b   Review of Sweet 1890a, *Phonetische Studien* 4: 369–379.
1892a   Review of Sweet 1890a, 1890b. *Englische Studien* 16: 107–113.
1892b   "Answer to Dr. Sweet". *Phonetische Studien* 5: 119–120.
1894   *The teacher's manual.* London: Macmillan; 2nd edition 1913, rev. W. Viëtor.
Sommerstein, A.
1977   *Modern phonology.* London: Arnold.
Spence, T.
1775   *The grand repository of the English language.* Newcastle: T. Saint.
[1974]   [Reprinted London: Scolar Press.]
Stanford, D.E. (ed.)
1983–84 *The selected letters of Robert Bridges*, Vol. 2. Newark: University of Delaware Press; London—Toronto: Associated University Presses.
Stankiewicz, E.
1972a   "Baudouin de Courtenay: His life and work", in: E. Stankiewicz (ed.) 1972b, 3–48.
1972b   E. Stankiewicz, (ed.)
        A Baudouin de Courtenay anthology. Bloomington: Indiana University Press.

Stannard Allen, W.
   1954   *Living English speech*. London: Longmans.

Steele, J.
   1779   *Prosodia rationalis*. London: Nichols; rev. and enlarged version of Steele 1775.

Stewart, J.
   1971   "Niger-Congo Kwa", in: T. Sebeok (ed.), 179–212.

Stirling, W.F.
   1935   *The pronunciation of Spanish*. Cambridge: Cambridge University Press.

Storm, J.
   1881[1892²]   *Englische Philologie*. (2nd edition 1892.) Leipzig: Reisland. First published
           1881. Heilbronn: Henninger.

Sundby, B. (ed.)
   1953   *Christopher Cooper's English teacher*. Lund: Gleerup; rpt. of Cooper 1687 with
         commentary.

Sumera, M.
   1981   "The keen prosodic ear: A comparison of the notations of rhythm of Joshua Steele,
         William Thomson and Morris Croll", in: R.E. Asher—E.J.A. Henderson (eds.),
         100–112.

Swadesh, M.
   1947   "On the analysis of English syllabics", *Language* 23: 137–150.

Sweet, H.
   1869   "The history of the TH in English", *TPhS* 1868–69: 272–288.
   [1913]   [Reprinted in: H. Sweet 1913, 169–184.]
   1874   *A history of English sounds from the earliest period*. Oxford: Clarendon Press.
   [1888]   [Reprinted 1888.]
   1877   *A handbook of phonetics*. Oxford: Clarendon Press.
   1879   "Sounds and forms of spoken Swedish", *TPhS* 1877–79: 457–543.
   [1913]   [Reprinted in: H. Sweet 1913, 362–445.]
   1884   "Spoken North Welsh", *TPhS* 1882–84: 409–484.
   [1913]   [Reprinted in: H. Sweet 1913, 499–574.]
   1885a[1904³]   *Elementarbuch des gesprochenen Englisch*. (3rd edition 1904.) Oxford:
         Clarendon Press. First published 1885.
   1885b   "The practical study of language", *TPhS* 1882–84: 577–599.
   [1913]   [Reprinted in: H. Sweet 1913, 34–55.]
   1890a   *A primer of phonetics*. Oxford: Clarendon Press.
   1890b   *A primer of spoken English*. Oxford: Clarendon Press.
   1892a   "Answer to Miss Soames". *Phonetische Studien* 5: 117–119.
   1892b   *New English grammar*, Part 1, Introduction, phonology and accidence. Oxford:
         Clarendon Press.
   1898   *New English grammar*, Part 2, Syntax. Oxford: Clarendon Press.
   1899   *The practical study of languages: A guide for teachers and learners*. London: Dent.
         [rev. and enlarged version of Sweet 1885b.]
   [1964]   [Reprinted London: Oxford University Press, 1964.]
   1906a   "Normalised phonetic spelling", *MPh* (2) 21: 71–73.
   1906b   "Simplified phonetic spelling", *MPh* (2) 21: 125–127.
   1908[1929²]   *The sounds of English: An introduction to phonetics*. Oxford: Clarendon
         Press.

Sweet, H.

1911   "Phonetics", *Encyclopaedia Britannica* (11th edition), 465–466.

1913   (ed.) H.C. Wyld, *Collected papers of Henry Sweet*. Oxford: Clarendon Press.

1971   (ed.) E.J.A. Henderson, *The indispensable foundation: A selection from the writings of Henry Sweet*. London: Oxford University Press.

Taylor, A.J.P.

1966   *From Sarajevo to Potsdam*. London: Thames and Hudson.

Taylor, D.

1968   *The godless students of Gower Street*. London: University College London Union.

Thomas, N.W.

1914   "Some notes on the tones of the Ibo language of Nigeria", in: Passy—Jones 1914a (eds.), *Miscellanea Phonetica* 1, 38–43.

Thompson, W.L.

1909   "Roman orthography for the dialects of Rhodesia", *MPh* (2) 24: 56–57.

Titone, R.

1968   *Teaching foreign languages: An historical sketch*. Washington DC: Georgetown University Press.

Tompkins, P. (ed.)

1960   *To a young actress: The letters of Bernard Shaw and Molly Tompkins*. London: Constable.

1961   *Shaw and Molly Tompkins: In their own words*. London: Anthony Blond.

Trager, G.L.—B. Bloch

1941   "The syllabic phonemes of English", *Language* 17: 223–246.

Trager, G.L.—H.L. Smith

1951   *An outline of English structure*. Washington DC: American Council of Learned Societies.

Trask, R.L.

1996   *A dictionary of phonetics and phonology*. London—New York: Routledge.

Trendelenburg, F.

1957   "Technical developments of phonetics", in: L. Kaiser (ed.), 18–28.

Trofimov, M.V.—J.P. Scott

1918   *Handbook of Russian* vol 1: Introduction, Phonology, and Elementary Morphology. London: Constable.

Trubetzkoy, N.S.

1969   *Principles of phonology*. Berkeley: University of California Press, trans. by C.A.M. Baltaxe of Trubetzkoy 1939. *Grundzüge der Phonologie*. Prague: Cercle Linguistique de Prague.

Tucker, A.N.

1929   *The comparative phonetics of the Suto-Chuana group of Bantu languages*. London: Longmans.

1964   "Systems of tone-marking African languages", *Bulletin of SOAS* 27: 594–611.

1971   "Orthographic systems and conventions in sub-Saharan Africa", in: T. Sebeok (ed.), 618–653.

Twaddell, W. Freeman

1935   *On defining the phoneme. Language* monograph 16.

[1966]   [Reprinted in: M. Joos 1966⁴, 55–79.]

Uldall, H.J.
1933   *A Danish phonetic reader.* London: University of London Press.
Usher, H.J.K.—C.D. Black-Hawkins—G.J. Carrick
1981   *An angel without wings: A history of University College School 1830–1980.* London: University College School.
Verburg, P.A.
1950   "The background to the linguistic conceptions of Franz Bopp", *Lingua* 2: 438–468.
[1966]   [Reprinted in: T. Sebeok 1966, vol. 1, 221–250.]
Verner, K.
1875   "Eine Ausnahme der ersten Lautverschiebung", *Zeitschrift für vergleichende Sprachforschung* 23: 97–130.
Viëtor, W. [pseud. Quousque Tandem]
1882[1886²]   *Der Sprachunterricht muss umkehren! Ein Beitrag zur Ueberbürdungsfrage.* (2nd edition 1886.) Heilbronn: Henninger. First published 1882.
1984   trans. by A.P.R. Howatt and D. Abercrombie as "Language teaching must start afresh", in: A.P.R. Howatt 1984, 340–363.
Viëtor, W.
1884[1898⁴]   *Elemente der Phonetik des Deutschen, Englischen und Französischen.* (4th edition 1898.) Leipzig: Reisland. First published 1884. Heilbronn: Henninger.
1897   *Kleine Phonetik.* Leipzig: Reisland.
1906a   *A Shakespeare phonology.* Marburg: Elwert. (Published as a companion volume to Viëtor 1906b, under the heading of *Shakespeare's pronunciation.*)
1906b   *A Shakespeare reader.* Marburg: Elwert. (Published as a companion volume to Viëtor 1906a, under the heading of *Shakespeare's pronunciation.*)
1912   *Deutsches Aussprachewörterbuch.* Leipzig: Reisland.
Walker, J.
1787   *The melody of speaking.* London: J. Walker.
[1974]   [Reprinted London: Scolar Press.]
1791   *A critical pronouncing dictionary and expositor of the English language.* London: G. and J. Robinson.
[1968]   [Reprinted London: Scolar Press.]
Wallis, J.
1653   *Grammatica linguae anglicanae.* Oxford: Leon. Lichfield.
[1969]   [Reprinted: Scolar Press. See also Kemp 1972.]
Ward, I.C.
1923   *Speech defects, their nature and cure.* London: Dent.
1929   *The phonetics of English.* Cambridge: Heffer.
1933   *The phonetic and tonal structure of Efik.* Cambridge: Heffer.
1936a   *An introduction to the Ibo language.* Cambridge: Heffer.
1936b   "Professor Daniel Jones, Dr. Phil.", *MPh* (3) 14: 53.
1952   *An introduction to the Yoruba language.* Cambridge: Heffer.
Wardle, I.
1979   "The plays", in: M. Holroyd 1979 (ed.), *The genius of Shaw.* New York: Holt Rinehart Wilson.
Welmers, W.E.
1973   *African language structures.* Berkeley: University of California Press.

Wells, J.C.
1970   "Local accents in England and Wales", *Journal of Linguistics* 6: 231–252.
1971   *Practical Phonetics*. Bath: Pitman.
1982   *Accents of English*, vol. 1, An Introduction; vol. 2, The British Isles; vol. 3, Beyond the British Isles. Cambridge: Cambridge University Press.
1985   "Professor A.C. Gimson 1917–1985" (obituary), *JIPA* 15: 2–3.
1990   *Longman pronunciation dictionary*. London: Harlow.
Wells, J.C.—G. Bodinetz
1992   "Higgins and Jones", programme notes for *Pygmalion* (National Theatre production first performed at the Olivier Theatre, 9 April 1992).
Westermann, D.—I. Ward
1933   *Practical phonetics for students of African languages*. London: Oxford University Press.
Wilberforce, H.W.W.
1890   *Lawn tennis*. London: George Bell.
Wilkins, J.
1668   *An essay towards a real character and a philosophical language*. London: Gellibrand and John Martin.
[1968]   [Reprinted Scolar Press.]
Willan, B.
1984   *Sol Plaatje: South African nationalist 1876–1932*. London—Ibadan—Nairobi: Heinemann.
Windsor Lewis, J.
1966   "The symbolisation of vowels by diagram", *Språk og Språkundervisning* 2.1: 2–11.
1969   *A guide to English pronunciation*. Oslo: Universitetsforlaget.
1972   *A concise pronouncing dictionary of British and American English*. London: Oxford University Press.
1974   Symbols for the General British English vowel sounds. [Unpublished MS.]
1975   "Linking /r/ in the General British pronunciation of English", *JIPA* 5: 37–42.
1976   "The official IPA vowel diagram", *JIPA* 6: 29–31.
n.d.   Received Pronunciation. [Unpublished MS.]
Winteler, J.
1876   *Die Kerenzer Mundart des Kantons Glarus in ihren Grundzügen dargestellt*. Leipzig—Heidelberg: C. Winter.
Wise, C.M.
1952   Review of Jones [1950³], *The pronunciation of English*. *Southern Speech Journal*.
Wood, S.
1982   "X-ray and model studies of vowel articulation", *Working Paper* 23. Lund: Department of Linguistics.
Wrenn, C.L.
1946   "Henry Sweet", *TPhS* 46: 177–201.
[1966]   [Reprinted in: T. Sebeok (ed.), vol. 1, 512–532.]
Wyld, H.C.
1906   *The historical study of the mother tongue: An introduction to philological method*. London: Murray.
1909   *The teaching of reading*. London: Murray.
1914   *A short history of English*. London: Murray.

1920[1936³] *A history of colloquial English*. (3rd edition 1936.) Oxford: Blackwell. First
published 1920.
1932 *Universal dictionary of the English language*. London: Amalgamated Press.
Zachrisson, R.E.
1913 *The pronunciation of English vowels, 1400–1700*. Gothenburg: Göteborgs Kung-
liga Vetenskaps-och Vitterhets-Samhälles Handlingar.

Index